FEE

THE PAUL CARUS LECTURES

TWELFTH SERIES

REASON AND ANALYSIS

REASON AND ANALYSIS

BY

BRAND BLANSHARD

Published on the Foundation
Established in Memory of
PAUL CARUS
1852-1919
Editor of the Open Court and the Monist
from 1888 to 1919

OPEN COURT PUBLISHING COMPANY
LA SALLE, ILLINOIS

PRINTED IN GREAT BRITAIN

To My Colleagues
in the
Yale Department of Philosophy
in Admiration and Friendship

PREFACE

This book stands first in a sequence of three volumes whose titles are *Reason and Analysis*, *Reason and Goodness*, and *Reason and Belief*. The second of these volumes has reached print already; the third is still to be completed. The first represents the Carus Lectures given in New York in December 1959, the other two the Gifford Lectures given in 1952-53 at St Andrews.

The auditors of these Carus Lectures were members of the Eastern Division of the American Philosophical Association. They were a most generous audience. But even they could hardly be expected to sit patiently through five hundred pages of a colleague's meditations. What was actually delivered was a token offering of three lectures, based on Chapters V, VIII, and IX.

The book is, in the main, a critical study of the analytic philosophy of the last forty years. During that period philosophy has changed with unexampled speed. Indeed the change has been so rapid that even devoted readers of the philosophical journals have had difficulty in keeping up with it; any critic who selects some position for scrutiny is likely to be met with the comment that this position was abandoned months ago, and that he is doing battle with ghosts. This comment will no doubt be repeated about the present work. In one sense it will be quite correct. Some of the theories examined have had their day and ceased to be; others are as certainly on their way out; and I make no pretence of giving the reader the last word from the Magdalen or New College common room. Nor is the book a history of the analytic movement; I am far from knowing enough to write such a history. Why, then, should the book be written or read at all?

There are several reasons. First, any attempt at philosophical revolution by first-rate minds is interesting; the analytic revolt is such an attempt, made by some of the ablest philosophers of the century. Secondly, though this philosophy is a disorderly and sprawling development, I believe that its main theses can be singled out and effectively dealt with by themselves, without considering all their entangling historical alliances. A number of these theses received their best formulation and defence from the logical empiricists or positivists, a school that accordingly bulks large in the text. Thirdly, these theories, particularly those central to positivism, remain very much alive, despite their depreciation and disavowal by many *avant garde* analysts. Finally, they are important. They are important philosophically because they concern the nature and range

of knowledge. They are important practically because their acceptance would affect profoundly the place of philosophy among academic
disciplines, and its public interest and influence. I think they are
false, though not wholly false. That is the main issue the book
attempts to adjudicate.

None of the following pages has been published before, though I
have read some of them to philosophical groups. I recall in particular
exhilarating evenings with the Moral Science Club at Cambridge and
the Dons' Philosophy Club at Oxford, where my heresies were given
a characteristically generous hearing. The manuscript has been read
as a whole only by the editor of the Library of Philosophy, Professor
H. D. Lewis, from whose practised criticisms it has emerged a better
book. Apart from a monumental debt to my wife for moral support,
my chief indebtedness is to institutions. I am very grateful to the
Carus Foundation, to the American Philosophical Association, and
to its committee of selection, for the great honour of being appointed
Carus Lecturer. The American Council of Learned Societies,
through one of its munificent senior awards, enabled me to spend a
year of continuous work abroad, far from telephones, classes and
committee meetings. Yale more than once let me go without murmur,
and my department chairman of many years, Charles Hendel, was
always more than co-operative.

Finally, I have been happy in my publishers. Ordinarily this book
would have been an exclusively American publication, produced,
like all other Carus Lectures, by the Open Court Co. But the book
deals very largely with developments in British philosophy; I was
most eager that it should be available to British readers; and I was
aware that, at the current rate of exchange, few British colleagues
would or could invest in a fat American book. I took the problem
both to my distinguished English publisher, Sir Stanley Unwin, and
to my prospective American publisher, Dr Eugene Freeman, editor
of the Open Court and a philosopher himself. With full sympathy
for my wishes, they worked out a plan between them by which the
book would be printed in England under the auspices of Allen and
Unwin, and published simultaneously in this country with the
imprint of the Open Court. I could only think how different our
plight would be if other international problems were handled with
a like understanding and good will.

B.B.

ANALYTICAL TABLE OF CONTENTS

CHAPTER I

THE REVOLT AGAINST REASON

1. Reason in its nuclear sense is the grasp of necessity, p. 25.
2. It has lost respect through a cultural revolution, p. 26
3. Which has had many causes, p. 27
4. The decline has continued over several decades, p. 27.
5. Philosophy at the turn of the century was dominated by idealistic rationalism, p. 28.
6. Which has now almost wholly vanished, p. 29.
7. The attack on it was opened by realists, p. 30.
8. And continued by naturalists, p. 30.
9. Instrumentalism sought to replace contemplative reason by practical intelligence, p. 31.
10. Logical empiricism discountenanced the rational knowledge of nature, p. 32.
11. Linguistic philosophy has shifted interest away from speculative thought, p. 33.
12. Existentialism is deeply sceptical of reason, p. 34.
13. In theology the current emphasis is on the inadequacy of reason, p. 36.
14. In psychology, Freud reduced the work of reason largely to rationalization, p. 37.
15. Making reason the veneer of powerful non-rational impulses, p. 38.
16. In sociology belief in an objective reason gave way to cultural relativity, p. 39.
17. Which was applied by Mannheim to reason itself, p. 40.
18. In politics, the trust in reasonableness was a casualty of two wars, p. 42.
19. And of three anti-rational dictatorships, p. 43.
20. Irrational nationalism remains a major peril, p. 44.
21. In literary criticism the appeal to sanity appears outmoded, p. 45.
22. And there is a wide acquiescence in meaninglessness, p. 47.
23. The most popular revivals from the past are those of anti-rationalists, p. 48.
24. The subject of this book is the revolt against reason in philosophy, p. 49.

CHAPTER II

THE IDEA OF REASON IN WESTERN THOUGHT

1. Reason is taken to differentiate man from the animals, p. 50.
2. When so taken, reason has four distinguishable components, p. 50.
3. Its chief early application is in the connection of means with ends, p. 52.
4. The free use of theoretic reason seems to have been achieved first by the Greeks, p. 54.
5. And depended on their notion of form, p. 55.
6. (1) Form as *essence* meant logical definition, p. 56.
7. (2) Form as *end* involved implicit purpose, p. 58.
8. (3) Form as *law* made possible a knowledge of the connection of concepts, which was, p. 60.
9.   (i) Certain, p. 60.
10.   (ii) Novel, p. 60.
11.   (iii) Independent of sense, p. 61.
12.   (iv) Universal, p. 61.
13.   (v) Objective, p. 62.

14.   (vi) Independent of time, p. 64.
15. (4) Form as *system* implied a world of interlinked concepts, p. 65.
16. The exercise of reason was, for the Greeks, a condition of the good life, p. 67.
17. The Greek conception of reason has been dominant in western thought, p. 68.
18. Descartes held certainty to be the product of reason alone, p. 69.
19. He analysed the method of reason as pursued in mathematics, p. 70.
20. This method could be applied universally, in spite of inner obstacles, p. 72.
21. And even more formidable ones in nature, p. 72.
22. Spinoza's rationalism had richer motives than that of Descartes, p. 73.
23. Progress in reason was for him the end of life, p. 74.
24. The advance was from the contingent knowledge of common sense, p. 75.
25. Through the abstract necessities of science, p. 76.
26. To the comprehensive vision of *scientia intuitiva*, p. 76.
27. Advance in reason was advance also in goodness and freedom, p. 77.
28. The 'eternal truths' of Leibniz were analytic, p. 78.
29. As were also truths about individuals, p. 79.
30. These latter were warranted only by the law of sufficient reason, p. 80.
31. Which itself was warranted teleologically, p. 81.
32. For Kant reason was the artificer of nature as well as its contemplator, p. 82.
33. It operated on three levels, p. 83.
34. In 'pure intuition' of spatial and temporal relations, p. 83.
35. In 'understanding' through the categories, p. 84.
36. And in the 'ideas' of reason, p. 85.
37. His attempted escape from scepticism was not successful, p. 85.
38. Hegel accepted much from Kant, p. 86.
39. But his conception of reason was original, p. 87.
40. Requiring a movement from the abstract to the concrete, p. 87.
41. By means of a dialectic process, p. 88.
42. Governed at all its levels by an idea of the whole, p. 89.
43. The British idealists' 'nisus toward wholeness' was an adaptation of Hegel, p. 90.
44. As was their principle that the real is the rational, p. 91.
45. The empiricist criticism of reason is best studied through contemporary analysis, p. 91.

CHAPTER III

THE RISE OF POSITIVISM

1. Philosophers of analysis do not form a single school of thought, p. 93.
2. But are united by tendencies, tastes, and aversions, p. 93.
3. They have changed the conception of philosophy, p. 95.
4. In a manner which limits its programme and influence, p. 97.
5. Logical positivism, maintaining four principal theses, has formed the core of the analytic movement, p. 99.
6. All these theses were anticipated by Hume, p. 100.
7. Though they are now differently phrased, p. 103.
8. Logical positivism owes its modern origin to the Vienna Circle, p. 105.
9. Which reacted vigorously against German speculative philosophy, p. 106.
10. But did not physics itself contain speculative elements?, p. 108.
11. A method of eliminating these had been proposed by Mach, p. 109.

CONTENTS

12. Whom the Circle defended against his scientific and philosophic critics, p. 110.
13. In his philosophy the Circle found a method for the unification of the sciences, p. 111.
14. And a criterion for the meaningfulness of statements of fact, p. 112.
15. The positivists rejected rationalist views of *a priori* knowledge, p. 113.
16. Particularly as held by Kant, p. 114.
17. Whose views were refuted by new developments in geometry and physics, p. 115.
18. Following Poincaré they adopted conventionalism in mathematics, p. 117.
19. And, as a result of Russell's work, adopted the same theory in logic, p. 119.
20. The new theories of a priori and empirical knowledge were united in the logical atomism of Wittgenstein, p. 120.
21. Which conceived philosophy as the logic of science, p. 122.
22. The positivist theory of knowledge implied emotivism in ethics, p. 124.
23. We shall examine the main contentions of positivism, p. 125.

CHAPTER IV

LOGICAL ATOMISM

1. The logical and empiricist strands in logical empiricism require separate examination, p. 127.
2. According to the empiricist strand, the reference of empirical statements must be to particular facts, p. 127.
3. Which are neither sense data, p. 129.
4. Nor things, which are conceived by positivists as families of sense data, p. 129.
5. An apparently simple statement may be resolved into many atomic statements, p. 131.
6. These refer to atomic facts with a definite structure, p. 131.
7. Their predicate denotes a quality or relation, p. 132.
8. And their subject a particular, p. 132.
9. The 'unpacking' of implicit atomic statements is one goal of analysis, p. 133.
10. *Principia Mathematica* was taken to supply an ideal language both for simple statements, p. 134.
11. And for the relations between statements, p. 135.
12. Which it most ingeniously simplified, p. 137.
13. This logic, which was 'truth-functional' and 'extensional', p. 138.
14. Was an important factor in logical atomism, p. 139.
15. Through pre-determining its metaphysics, p. 140.
16. In Wittgenstein's view, the atomic proposition pictured the fact, p. 141.
17. The form of the fact could be shown but not represented, p. 142.
18. Hence philosophy is confined to the clarification of science, p. 143.
19. Logical atomism is the antithesis of the monism that preceded it, p. 144.
20. Its statement by Wittgenstein is extremely obscure, p. 145.
21. He discusses with abandon what he says is undiscussable, p. 146.
22. Nor is his defence that he is talking 'important nonsense' plausible, p. 147.
23. The reference by words to formal relations is clearly possible, p. 148.
24. His theory that propositions picture facts is fantastic, p. 149.
25. This may be shown in many ways, p. 151.
26. He tended to confound thought with the apparatus of its expression, p. 153.
27. The philosophic value of mathematical logic has disappointed earlier hopes for it, p. 154.

28. It ignores many necessities found in actual thought, p. 156.
29. Both within 'atomic facts', p. 157.
30. And between them, since in material implication there is no necessity, p. 158.
31. This logic, again, abstracts from the content of its terms and propositions, p. 160.
32. And reduces necessity to tautology, p. 161.
33. Which may be read off from truth-tables, p. 162.
34. But actual inference involves the linkage of meanings, p. 164.
35. So also does inconsistency, which is misconstrued in mathematical logic, p. 165.
36. As are necessity, possibility, and impossibility, p. 166.
37. The support given to atomism by such logic is valueless, p. 167.
38. Logic neither should, nor wholly can, ignore the requirements of inference, p. 168.
39. For the atomist, the world is a congeries of contingent atomic facts, p. 169.
40. There was difficulty, however, in producing examples of such facts, p. 170.
41. About the nature of particulars there was a sharp debate, p. 171.
42. Which plunged the analysts into metaphysics, p. 171.
43. And led to the notion of a characterless subject of predicates, p. 172.
44. This involves both scepticism, p. 174.
45. And an abandonment of the picture theory, p. 174.
46. Here we are more empirical than the empiricists, p. 175.
47. Necessity was reluctantly admitted into atomic facts by the atomists, p. 175.
48. Including Wittgenstein, p. 176.
49. Who held, like Kant, that characters were necessarily linked through serial orders, p. 178.
50. But insisted that no fact was necessarily related to any other, p. 179.
51. This view is untenable, p. 180.
52. It rests in part on a misapplication of the logician's use of 'necessary', p. 181.
53. Examples of facts necessarily connected are plentiful, p. 181.
54. Extensional logic fails over intensional necessities, p. 183.

CHAPTER V

THE THEORY OF MEANING

1. Meaning is not a bodily response, p. 189.
2. Nor merely a psychical event, p. 190.
3. But, for our purposes, what a mind intends or refers to, p. 190.
4. In the empiricist tradition this is a sensible object, p. 191.
5. The American forerunner of positivism was C. S. Peirce, p. 192.
6. Whose theory of meaning is confused and inadequate, p. 194.
7. Stage I in the development of a criterion of significance: Wittgenstein, p. 197.
8. His account of factual meaning entailed solipsism, p. 198.
9. It is not in essentials new, p. 200.
10. Its acceptance would not only render science impossible, p. 200.
11. But would cut off communication with other minds, p. 201.
12. And make the mention of them meaningless, p. 202.
13. Indeed, on its own terms, it must itself be meaningless, p. 202.
14. The limits of its 'self' or 'world' are left in obscurity, p. 203.
15. Positivists generally rejected solipsism, p. 204.
16. Stage II. Verifiability by me, p. 205.
17. This theory broke down over (1) references to the remote past, p. 206.

CONTENTS

18. Which were unplausibly construed as references to the future, p. 206.
19. And (2) the ambiguity of the theory, p. 208.
20. Stage III. Verifiability by me in principle, p. 208.
21. This involved reducing others' experiences to my own experiences of their bodies, p. 209.
22. Which is incredible, p. 211.
23. Positivists thought physicalism necessary to the unification of science, p. 212.
24. Physicalism may be taken either as (1) old-fashioned behaviourism, or, p. 214.
25. (2) More plausibly, as the study of mind through physical terms alone, p. 215.
26. Such physicalism is, on many grounds, absurd, p. 216.
27. Stage IV. Verifiability in principle by anyone, p. 221.
28. This would exclude the logically impossible, which Schlick misconstrued, p. 221.
29. If 'verifiable' means perceptible, it would admit more than the positivists desired, p. 222.
30. Taken literally, it would exclude much that is obviously meaningful, p. 223.
31. Such as, in philosophy, the assertion of an external world, p. 224.
32. In common sense, the assertion of material objects, p. 226.
33. And in science, the assertion of general laws, p. 226.
34. Stage V. Falsifiability in principle, p. 228.
35. This entailed impossible logical consequences, p. 228.
36. Stage VI. Weak verifiability, p. 229.
37. This would readmit much of metaphysics and theology, p. 230.
38. Positivists were stimulated to try again by curious difficulties in logic, p. 232.
39. Stage VII. Translatability into an empiricist language, p. 233.
40. The old difficulties arise again in constructing such a language, p. 234.
41. The essential demand throughout has been for (a) the empirical, (b) the verifiable, p. 235.
42. This has made for self-criticism and clarity, p. 235.
43. But the two demands conflict with each other, p. 236.
44. Producing an ambiguous attitude toward science, p. 238.
45. The verifiability criterion is self-destructive since (a) it can be neither empirical nor a priori, p. 239.
46. Nor can it be merely a recommended rule, p. 240.
47. (b) The act of meaning is not empirically discernible, p. 241.
48. 'Sentences' are no substitute for it, p. 242.
49. Nor can it be adequately studied by introspection, p. 244.
50. (c) In terms of the criterion, verification itself is meaningless, p. 245.
51. Contrary-to-fact conditionals may be significant, but are unverifiable, p. 246.
52. The value of a criterion is questionable both logically and practically, p. 247.
53. Our criticism, if valid, reopens the road to speculative philosophy, p. 248.

CHAPTER VI

ANALYSIS AND A PRIORI KNOWLEDGE

1. Philosophy has traditionally relied on insight into necessities, p. 249.
2. Aristotle recognized three types of such insight, p. 249.
3. And later philosophers many more, p. 250.
4. But how we come by such insight is mysterious, p. 251.
5. (a) Rationalism holds it to apprehend necessities in nature, p. 252.

6. (b) Kant held necessities to be mind-imposed, p. 252.
7. (c) Traditional empiricism holds these to be the product of fixed habits, p. 253.
8. (d) Logical positivism would confine them to discourse, p. 254.
9. It contends (I) that necessary statements report linguistic usages, p. 255.
10. (II) That they are conventions, p. 256.
11. (III) That they are tautologies, p. 257.
12. (IV) That they assert nothing about fact, p. 258.
13. This position would destroy rationalism, p. 259.
14. But I. Necessary statements are not reports of actual usage, p. 260.
15. As is evident from many facts about language, p. 261.
16. And as universal syntax is impracticable in positivist terms, p. 262.
17. Still less are necessary statements *prescriptions* regarding usage, p. 264.
18. II. To make necessary propositions conventions confuses symbol with symbolized, p. 266.
19. And real with verbal definition, p. 268.
20. We cannot justify our choice of 'conventions' without going beyond positivism, p. 269.
21. Are logical laws conventions?, p. 271.
22. Alternative geometries have suggested this, but mistakenly, p. 271.
23. 'Alternative logics' themselves employ a necessity that is not conventional, p. 273.
24. Indeed, the thesis that logic is conventional is self-refuting, p. 275.
25. 'Logic without ontology' does not really exclude ontology, p. 276.
26. Nor can it be defended on pragmatic grounds, p. 278.
27. It ends in a tangle of inconsistencies, p. 280.
28. Conventionalism in logic has not discredited reason, p. 281.
29. III. Are all necessary statements analytic?, p. 283.
30. Kant denied this, p. 284.
31. His criterion for the analytic is commonly rejected, p. 285.
32. But a validity depending on definitions also gives an unsound criterion, p. 286.
33. As does the self-contradictoriness of the contradictory, p. 287.
34. The issue is one of insight versus stipulation, p. 288.
35. 'Entails' does not mean 'is contained by', p. 289.
36. As may be seen in examples from various fields, p. 291.
37. No satisfactory notion of containment has been offered, p. 293.
38. Is 'all a priori propositions are analytic' analytic or synthetic?, p. 295.
39. Logic distorts meaning when it makes all necessary reasoning tautologous, p. 296.
40. IV. May necessary statements assert about fact?, p. 298.
41. Yes; the grounds on which this is denied are confused, p. 299.
42. As is the logic based on this denial, p. 301.
43. Universal and necessary statements may hold of given fact, p. 302.
44. The failure of the positivist view of the a priori leaves the way open for rational construction, p. 304.

CHAPTER VII
LINGUISTIC PHILOSOPHY—SOME EARLIER FORMS

1. Positivist analysis soon proved inadequate, p. 308.
2. 'Look for the meaning' was replaced by 'look for the use', p. 309.

CONTENTS

3. The pioneer of linguistic analysis was G. E. Moore, p. 310.
4. Though his avowed interest was not in language, but in concepts, p. 311.
5. He elevated common sense into a touchstone for philosophy, p. 311.
6. Holding that knowledge of the truth of a proposition might precede that of its analysis, p. 312.
7. And that adherence to common usage would prevent many violations of common sense, p. 313.
8. But common usage is (1) ambiguous, p. 314.
9. (2) Vague, p. 314.
10. And (3) inconsistent, p. 315.
11. And (4) common sense meanings are quite inadequate to philosophy, p. 315.
12. Mr. Malcolm has held philosophers to be proposing new linguistic usages, p. 316.
13. But (1) this misreports the philosophers' intention, p. 318.
14. (2) Which is at times to make empirical assertions, p. 319.
15. And (3) it imposes on philosophy a needless conservatism, p. 319.
16. Is common usage trustworthy when descriptive and underivative? p. 319.
17. No; for this confuses truth with propriety, p. 320.
18. And even such winnowed usage is a false guide, p. 321.
19. Mr Ayer has conceived philosophy to offer 'definitions in use', p. 322.
20. Which are necessitated by illicit suggestions of language, p. 323.
21. Some of these were exposed in Russell's theory of descriptions, p. 325.
22. And in his theory of logical constructions, p. 326.
23. This latter was a potent instrument for eliminating metaphysics, p. 327.
24. The rigor of this linguistic programme is admirable, p. 327.
25. But is it really linguistic?, p. 328.
26. The theory of descriptions is metaphysical in both motive and application, p. 328.
27. The theory of logical constructions must go beyond language to interpret 'translatability', p. 329.
28. Philosophic analysis must analyse objects meant, p. 331.
29. The theory of descriptions rests on a theory of proper names, p. 332.
30. Which rests in turn on several mistaken assumptions about meaning, p. 333.
31. The theory of logical constructions rids science of some needless inferences, p. 334.
32. But its application in philosophy entails a mass of paradoxes, p. 336.
33. This type of linguism provides a basis for neither philosophy nor science, p. 337.

CHAPTER VIII

LINGUISTIC PHILOSOPHY—SOME LATER FORMS

1. 'Ordinary language philosophy' is elusive and amorphous, p. 339.
2. But its exponents are united in certain philosophic tastes and distastes, p. 340.
3. They have carefully defined the meaning of 'ordinary use', p. 341.
4. Such use is said to mislead philosophers, though not plain men, p. 343.
5. Through leading to the confusion of categories, p. 344.
6. Which are reconceived by Ryle as 'proposition factors', p. 345.
7. To clear up such confusion is taken as the function of philosophy, p. 347.
8. But the main problems of philosophy do not spring from category mistakes, p. 347.

9. Nor have philosophers been as uncritical of language as is alleged, p. 351.
10. To judge the propriety of use, philosophy must go beyond words to facts, p. 353.
11. The stress on language is due (1) to the reluctance to admit this, p. 355.
12. (2) To the illusion that the 'logic of use' escapes reference to fact, p. 355.
13. And (3) to the belief that expressions provide the locus of absurdities, p. 357.
14. But (i) the aim of philosophy is not primarily at avoiding absurdities, p. 358.
15. (ii) To deny absurdities in nature is to engage in metaphysics, p. 359.
16. (iii) To deny absurdities in propositions implies that philosophers cannot argue, p. 359.
17. Which belies their history and present practice, p. 361.
18. (iv) Words or expressions cannot in themselves be true, false, or absurd, p. 361.
19. Nor can statements, if these are words as interpreted, p. 362.
20. Reflections on use may indeed be variously helpful, p. 363.
21. And in a trivial sense, all inquiries are about what words mean, p. 364.
22. (v) It is only ideas or beliefs that can be true, false, and absurd, p. 365.
23. Nothing is commoner than confused thought, p. 366.
24. Testing linguistic propriety by fact leads to metaphysics, p. 367.
25. Hence the linguistic philosophers sought an alternative test, p. 368.
26. Which they found in ordinary use, p. 369.
27. Analysis of the meaning of words may have philosophic utility, p. 371.
28. But (1) our capital of meaning is inadequate for philosophic purposes, p. 372.
29. (2) Ordinary use limits its refinements by the requirements of practice, p. 373.
30. (3) Such use cannot at once be ordinary and super-sophisticated, p. 375.
31. (4) Standard meanings may vary greatly in nature and importance, p. 376.
32. (5) The appeal to ordinary use commonly confuses correctness with truth, p. 377.
33. (6) Such use often commits us to untruth, p. 377.
34. Even when approved by linguistic philosophy, p. 379.
35. Which lacks a criterion for distinguishing the important from the trivial, p. 380.

CHAPTER IX

UNIVERSALS

1. How far does reason apply to nature?, p. 382.
2. One's cosmology and theory of reason are likely to correspond, p. 382.
3. The rationality of the world may be accepted as a postulate, p. 383.
4. Thinking is a teleological, not a mechanical, process, p. 383.
5. And expresses an ancient human drive, p. 384.
6. Which is directed toward the grasp of necessity, p. 385.
7. And satisfied only by a necessary system, p. 386.
8. Rational explanation is only one of various types, p. 388.
9. Such explanation moves through the connecting of universals, p. 389.
10. A process implicitly active at very low levels, p. 390.
11. Since the use of universals antedates that of words, p. 391.
12. Universals are not banished by an appeal to verifiability, p. 392.
13. The problem of universals is unavoidable, p. 392.
14. Generic, qualitative and specific universals have been alleged, p. 393.
15. Of which the specific universal alone is here accepted, p. 393.
16. Its acceptance commits us to the identity of indiscernibles, p. 395.

17. Otherness is based on dissimilarity, not dissimilarity on otherness, p. 396.
18. Two spheres cannot differ only numerically, p. 396.
19. And a purely formal difference is unthinkable, p. 398.
20. Specific universals are of very common occurrence, p. 399.
21. They compose the field of immediate experience, p. 399.
22. The common arguments for particulars are confused, p. 400.
23. The universe alone is individual, p. 401.
24. Qualitative and generic universals also seem of common occurrence, p. 401.
25. But qualitative universals do not exist in nature, p. 402.
26. Nor do generic universals, p. 403.
27. Such conclusions may seem stultifying to reason, p. 403.
28. The Platonic view of generic universals is unconvincing, p. 404.
29. The Aristotelian universal has no clear place in thought, p. 404.
30. Or lodgement in nature, p. 406.
31. Locke's conceptualism seems more promising, p. 406.
32. But his theory was both inconsistent and undeveloped, p. 407.
33. Pure nominalism seems never to have been held, p. 408.
34. Our own theory is eclectic, p. 409.
35. James defended similarity against identity with three arguments, p. 409.
36. Bradley's reply to the first is arbitrary, p. 411.
37. His reply to the second misconceives the issue, p. 411.
38. His reply to the third involves an infinite series of identities, p. 412.
39. His own account of identity is not clear, p. 413.
40. Not all resemblance is based on identity, p. 414.
41. Resemblance need not itself be taken as a universal, p. 414.
42. Nor the 'respect' in which things are similar, p. 415.
43. Science can work with classes based on resemblance, p. 416.
44. Mathematical logic is uncommitted on universals, p. 417.
45. Our thoughts of universals are neither images nor words, p. 418.
46. And differ with the character of their objects, p. 419.
47. The kinds of concept may be shown in an illustration, p. 420.
48. Reason finds its chief work in tracing the linkage of universals, p. 420.

CHAPTER X

NECESSITIES IN NATURE

1. Analysis has not disproved the presence of necessities in nature, p. 422.
2. (1) Logical laws hold of existent things, p. 423.
3. They are not laws of our own thought merely, p. 424.
4. Nor are they linguistic rules, p. 425.
5. But they report the actual structure of things, p. 426.
6. (2) Arithmetical statements also are true of nature, p. 427.
7. The belief that they are not springs from confusions, p. 428.
8. The applicability of arithmetic is an embarrassment to positivists, p. 429.
9. Its application is a joint function of reason and sense, p. 430.
10. (3) How geometry applies to nature is a puzzle, p. 431.
11. Which is solved by Broad through a theory of limits, p. 432.
12. And by Whitehead through a theory of extensive abstractions, p. 433.
13. Science justly postulates a mathematical framework for nature, p. 434.
14. (4) There are various types of necessary serial order, p. 436.

15. Including internal and external infinities, p. 437.
16. (5) Necessity may link categories and types of quality, p. 438.
17. (6) It may link determinates of the same determinable, p. 439.
18. (7) It may be truly asserted in judgments of intrinsic good, p. 440.
19. And in ethical judgments of other types, p. 441.
20. These necessities present a massive demurrer to empiricism, p. 442.

CHAPTER XI

NECESSITY IN CAUSATION

1. Causal relations are of extreme importance theoretically as well as practically, p. 444.
2. Recent reflection on causality has returned to Hume, p. 445.
3. Who denied that causality involved power, p. 446.
4. And, by a more complex argument, that it involved necessity, p. 447.
5. But (1) his exclusion of necessity as not sensed was question-begging, p. 449.
6. (2) He must disjoin cause and effect not in imagination only, p. 450.
7. But also in conception, which is difficult, p. 451.
8. Since the cause cannot be clearly marked off in time, p. 452.
9. And is inexhaustibly complex, p. 452.
10. (3) Hume was mistaken in denying necessity among ideas, p. 453.
11. For it may, in part, determine the course of inference, p. 454.
12. To this it has been objected (1) that necessity is not a sufficient condition of inference, p. 456.
13. (2) That a timeless relation cannot determine events, p. 456.
14. (3) That what functions is not necessity but our apprehension of it, p. 457.
15. (4) That what functions is dispositions, p. 457.
16. (5) That invalid thinking cannot be necessitated, p. 459.
17. (6) That our theory confuses implication with inference, p. 461.
18. (7) That the movement of inference is contingent, p. 462.
19. Is necessity at work in causality generally?, p. 465.
20. Yes, for (1) the alternative is 'an outrageous run of luck', p. 465.
21. (2) We know some necessary propositions about causation, p. 466.
22. (3) Causal necessities are more than 'contingent necessities', p. 467.
23. For they imply a connection between characters as such, p. 469.
24. The necessity in causation may be reasonably accepted even if not demonstrable, p. 471.

CHAPTER XII

SOME INTIMATIONS OF COSMIC NECESSITY

1. Is the world a system of necessarily connected parts?, p. 472.
2. Yes, if that means a single causal system, p. 473.
3. Hence it is in our view also a necessary system, p. 473.
4. This raises the problem of internal relations, p. 475.
5. Are the relations of a thing to be included in its 'nature'?, p. 475.
6. Delimiting what is essential to a thing is harder in some cases than in others, p. 476.
7. Its relations may be necessary without being analytically so, p. 477.
8. What is to be included in a term's nature has been held to be arbitrary, p. 478.
9. But this is an extreme position, 478.

CONTENTS

10. What is associated with any such 'nature' has been held contingent, p. 479.
11. But this is not true if the nature is made fully specific, p. 480.
12. The characters of a thing are not all equally essential, p. 482.
13. An individual is a set of characters, p. 482.
14. This does not imply that these are unorganized, p. 483.
15. Nor that statements about individuals are analytic, p. 483.
16. Nor that understanding their nature is a false goal, p. 484.
17. Things have manifold necessary relations to other things, p. 485.
18. Indeed all things are connected necessarily through the relation of difference, p. 486.
19. This has been alleged to confuse a thing with its nature, p. 486.
20. And to fail through the contingency of the thing-property relation, p. 487.
21. But this relation does not seem on analysis to be contingent, p. 489.
22. Nor is the destruction of one relation logically indifferent to another, p. 489.
23. To equate 'rational', as necessary, with good is a confusion, p. 490.
24. Which ends in confounding all values, p. 491.
25. An order at least causally determined is essential to ethics, p. 492.
26. And determination by reason is freedom, p. 492.

Books mentioned in the text, p. 494.
Index, p. 500.

CHAPTER I

THE REVOLT AGAINST REASON

1. Since this is a book in defence of reason, we may well begin by saying, at least provisionally, what 'reason' means.

Unfortunately it means many things. For the philosopher it commonly denotes the faculty and function of grasping necessary connections. The function is seen in its most obvious form in reasoning, in the deductions, for example, of the logician and the mathematician. This may be taken as the narrowest and nuclear meaning of the term. But there radiate out from it a large number of subsidiary meanings. Reason for many writers shows itself not only in the linkage of propositions, but also in the grasp of single truths, provided these are necessary truths; the insight that two straight lines cannot enclose a space would be as truly an insight of reason as any demonstration in Euclid. Sometimes the meaning of reason and cognate terms is further extended to include reasonings that are less than necessary, such as inferences from past to future. Mr Ayer writes: 'for us, "being rational" entails being guided in a particular way by past experience';[1] and Mr. Feigl goes as far as to say: 'the procedure of induction, therefore, far from being irrational, defines the very essence of rationality.'[2] Sometimes reason is broadened again to describe the sceptical and reflective turn of mind generally. For Hobhouse it is 'that which requires proofs for assertions, causes for effects, purposes for action, principles for conduct, or, to put it generally, thinks in terms of grounds and consequences.'[3] Reason in the widest sense of all, says Thomas Whittaker, is 'the relational element in intelligence, in distinction from the element of content, sensational or emotional,' and he points out that both the Greek term λογος and the Latin *ratio*, from which 'reason' has largely drawn its meaning, were sometimes used to denote simply 'relation' or 'order'.[4]

[1] A. J. Ayer, *Logic, Truth and Language*, 2nd ed., 50.
[2] H. Feigl, in *Twentieth Century Philosophy*, 389–90.
[3] L. T. Hobhouse, in *Contemporary British Philosophy*, I, 154.
[4] *Reason*, 12.

What is present through all these expanding meanings is the grasp of law or principle.[1] Such a grasp is intellectual; it is not a matter of sensing or perceiving, but of understanding. The principles thus understood are assumed to be valid independently of our grasping them, and therefore to be valid for all men alike. Hence it belongs to the idea of the rational man to be objective or impartial. So far as one is governed by reason, one's conclusions will follow the evidence without being coloured by feeling or deflected by desire, and one's conduct as well as one's thinking will be ordered by principle. If, in addition to being rational, one is also a rationalist, one will hold that the truths apprehended through intellect are the most important and certain that we possess, and probably also that they reveal, at least in fragmentary fashion, an intelligible structure in the world.

We shall see in the next chapter that the belief in reason in its wider senses has been a cardinal component of western culture since the time of the Greeks. It has determined the main tradition of western philosophy. In great measure, though less exclusively, it has fixed the pattern of Christian theology. And though it formed no part of the original Christian idea of goodness, it contributed powerfully, through the influence of such men as Socrates and Marcus Aurelius, to the ideal of the good life as the rational life.

2. Both reason as a source of knowledge and rationality as a practical ideal are today under attack. Indeed there has been no period in the past two thousand years when they have undergone a bombardment so varied, so competent, so massive and sustained, as in the last half-century. The purpose of this volume and the two that follow it is to examine the most important of these criticisms as they apply to the theory of knowledge, theology, and ethics. This book will be concerned with the theory of knowledge only, and we shall therefore be concerned with reason in its narrower senses alone. The criticism here has been more technical than in the other two fields; and though the path of the argument will be made as clear as possible, it will take us over parched sands and through some rather dense thickets. Plainly the journey is not one to take unless it is necessary.

How necessary it is we shall know only if we have some idea of the range and power of the revolt against reason in all its aspects. This revolt is not merely a technical attack by specialists. It is that, to be sure, but it is very much more. The suspicion of rational standards is

[1] Cf. G. P. Adams: 'I shall take the common denominator of reason to be the existence, the awareness and, it may be, the employment of organizing principles.' 'Reason and Purpose', *California Publications in Philosophy*, Vol. 21 (1939), 209.

part of the attitude of our day, which enters in subtle and manifold ways into our artistic criticism, our religious belief, our psychology, our sociology, and our politics, as well as our philosophy. It is part of the revolution of our time. 'Since the Renaissance,' as MacNeille Dixon says, 'there has been no such upheaval of thought, no such revolution of values as in the century upon which we have entered. Now as then, within about fifty years, within the span of a single lifetime, all the old conceptions, the previous beliefs in science, in religion, in politics, have been wholly transformed; a change has taken place, one might almost say, in the inclination of the earth's orbit.'[1]

3. What has produced this revolution? Most conspicuously, of course, two world wars. To one who, like the present writer, can look back to student days in the American middle west, in England, and in Germany, just before the first of these wars, the old order has the distance and unreality of a dream, and August, 1914, marks the breaking of a dam and the submergence of a civilization. Secondly, three powerful dictatorships have appeared, two of them destroyed in war, one of them still remaining, which undertook to conscript reason in the service of their own ends. Thirdly, there has been the advance of science, which according to Whitehead, has covered a greater distance in fifty years than in the whole preceding history of man. Fourthly, there is the resulting advance in technology— lengthening life, multiplying populations, raising standards of living, spreading literacy, bringing New York and the south seas, Paris and the Congo, within easy range of each other. Fifthly, and as a co-ordinate result, there is the secularization of life, the withering away of divinities above and demons below, the disintegration, in the new and sharp scientific atmosphere, of the great cloud-castles of dogma in which men once lived so securely. Sixthly, there is the continuing cold war of east and west, with its menace of incalculable destruction.

4. There was nothing in these events, cataclysmic as they were, that led necessarily to an eclipse of reason; and the advance of science, which has had so conspicuous a part in the revolution, might even be expected to raise its prestige. But this is not what happened. Along with the advance of science went an increasing insistence that the reason employed in this advance had nothing to say about values, and a readiness to surrender the whole field of value to the non-rational side of human nature. Our interest for the moment, however, is less in the causes for the depreciation of reason than in the fact. That it is a

[1] *The Human Situation*, 26.

fact few will doubt, but some testimonies may be in order. The English philosopher L. T. Hobhouse in the twenties, lamenting irrationalism, wrote: 'philosophy itself, once the appointed guardian and advocate of reason, shares in the irrationalist tendency. We shall end by defining man as the irrational animal, and the modern philosopher as his prophet.'[1] The American philosopher Morris Cohen noted in the thirties that 'the decline in the avowed faith in reason is . . . one of the central facts of recent intellectual history.'[2] Addressing the British Academy in the forties, Dr A. C. Ewing remarked that 'if there is one thing more characteristic of the intellectual climate of the world as a whole during the last ten years than any other, it is the widespread distrust of reason.'[3] A few years later the German philosopher Max Horkheimer complains of 'a state of affairs in which even the word reason is suspected of connoting some mythological entity. Reason has liquidated itself as an agency of ethical, moral, and religious insight.'[4] And the Cambridge critic, F. L. Lucas, wrote, as he looked back from the middle fifties: 'the irrational, now in politics, now in poetics, has been the sinister opium of our tormented and demented century.'[5]

This reaction against reason has taken very different forms in different provinces. It will be well to see first what has happened in the field with which we shall be chiefly engaged, philosophy.

5. At the turn of the century rationalism was in a complacent ascendancy in Britain, Germany, and America, though it was being sharply challenged in France. The form it most commonly took was absolute idealism. For Bradley, Bosanquet, and Edward Caird in Britain, for Windelband, Wundt, and Eucken in Germany, for Josiah Royce and John Watson in North America, reason was the yardstick of reality. That the world was rational was a philosophic postulate, for philosophy was the attempt to understand, and why set out on the enterprise of finding intelligibility in the world unless one believed it was there to be found? For the present, to be sure, the world has a recalcitrant way of rebuffing our attempts to find in it a rational order: we do not know why roses are red or the sky is blue; we do not know, as Hume showed so conclusively, why one billiard ball rolls away when another strikes it. Of course the idealists were familiar with Hume's arguments. They held that in this matter he was right about

1 *The Rational Good*, 20.
2 *Reason and Nature*, 6.
3 *Op. cit.*, 1.
4 *Eclipse of Reason*, 18.
5 *Style*, 68.

what we did know, and wrong about what we might know. Granting that we could not now answer these questions, there must be some reason for the colour of rose and sky; and if billiard balls, rivers and planets follow an invariable course, we cannot suppose this to happen by chance or miracle. Within the unvarying sequence there must be some thread of necessity, and with time reason may isolate it. Indeed, 'nothing in this world is single'; every thing, event, and quality stands in relation to others, and is what it is because of those others. Hence we shall not fully understand it unless we see it in the context of the relations that determine it, and ultimately in the context of the universe as a whole. Whether any bit of alleged knowledge is true will depend in the first instance on whether it coheres with our system of knowledge as a whole, and the degree of truth possessed by this system will depend in turn on its coherence with that all-inclusive system which is at once the goal of our knowledge and the constitution of the real.

The idealists carried their rationalism still farther. They held that reason supplied the measure for beauty and religion as well as for truth. Each mind was a little world, struggling to widen and set in order its own experience, and the good life lay in harmonious self-realization. They hastened to add, however, that the powers to be realized were not those of one's own mind only, but those of humanity, conceived somewhat metaphorically as one great organism in which our various minds were cells. So again of beauty and values generally. Bosanquet in his Gifford Lectures of 1911[1] argued that the test of truth appointed by logic, namely coherence within a system, provided also an objective standard of taste. And it was the thesis of Watson, Royce, and the Cairds, of Ward and Haldane and Sorley, in an impressive shelf-full of further Gifford Lectures, that religion itself could become adequate to its object only as this object was conceived, and continually reconceived, by an advancing reason.

6. To mention these philosophers is to evoke an era that seems already more remote than that of Hume, though they are all within easy memory of persons still living. There are very few philosophic chairs in Britain or America now occupied by persons of their outlook; their philosophy is gone like Prospero's pageant, leaving hardly a wrack behind. Their main conclusions are either rejected or set down as merely meaningless. Their logic is pronounced naive. The reason of which that logic was the organ, and which supplied at once the main instrument of their philosophizing and the main test

[1] *The Principle of Individuality and Value.*

of its validity, is widely held to give no knowledge of the world at all. Even their style, which, in Bradley and the Cairds at least, was thought to have distinction, is dismissed as painfully loose and over-charged with 'emotive meaning'. Their earnest and laborious books gather dust on library shelves.

The structure they built was not destroyed quite abruptly. What happened was rather that its foundations were sapped by a rapid succession of waves. They threw up such breakwaters as they could, but the blows followed each other so fast and with such mounting force that resistance had little effect. These waves call for separate mention. They bear the not very inviting names of realism, natural-ism, pragmatism, existentialism, and the philosophy of analysis.

7. The realistic attack was led, in England, by Moore and Russell, and in America by the six 'neo-realists' and seven 'critical realists' who produced joint manifestoes. What they all disliked in the idealists was the taint of subjectivism, the suggestion that what exists is dependent for its existence on some experiencing mind. The marches and counter-marches of the realists would make an engross-ing tale; it is significant that one of their leaders, Lord Russell, came round in his later years to a position close to Berkeley's about the status of what we immediately perceive.[1] But the realist attack, effective as it was in undermining idealism, was not directed in the first instance against the rationalistic side of that doctrine, and is not to be included among the movements hostile to rationalism.

8. Naturalism, at least in its extremer form, must be so included, and we are noting it as the first of five schools in philosophy that have done most to undermine the older ambitions of reason. The naturalist is a philosopher who reduces consciousness either to identity with bodily behaviour or to the status of a by-product of it. The first of these positions was taken by the behaviourists, of whom that sturdy gladiator John B. Watson was the best-known representative. Strangely enough, the theory has been revived in a more sophisticated form by Professor Ryle of Oxford, who thinks that to talk of a private non-physical consciousness is to put a 'ghost in the machine'.[2] The other form of naturalism, in which consciousness is a by-product of the brain, had its most persuasive exponent in Santayana. For the rationalist, the difficulty with both views is the same: they destroy the autonomy of reason. According to Santayana, for example, we never

[1] *Human Knowledge: its Scope and Limits,* 217 ff.
[2] See his *The Concept of Mind.*

reach any conclusion because we see that the evidence requires it, but always because our thought happens to be carried along to it by 'the dark engine of nature' which is churning away in our body. In the working of this engine there is no necessity whatever. There is only the blind movement of atoms, governed by physical laws that are ultimate surd facts. Not even the logician or the geometer is inclined in the slightest towards his conclusion by the requirements of his premisses. Rationality in the rationalist's sense is an illusion.

9. The second attack was, if possible, more radical still, since it concerned itself directly with the traditional conception of reason, and in the most damaging way. For the Greeks and their philosophic successors, reason was a contemplative faculty. Thought was like a beam of light playing upon the world and illuminating its structure; its business was not to act but to see; and its highest achievement was to see things *sub specie aeternitatis*. This contemplative role of thought was sharply challenged by John Dewey. For him, thinking was not opposed to action; it was itself an instrument of action; that is why he called his theory instrumentalism. Like walking, running, and swimming, thought is an instrument slowly fashioned by trial and error to help a precariously struggling organism to survive. It was originally a product of practical necessity and a tool of adjustment; and in essence it has remained so. It is a means of solving conflicts— conflicts between man and nature, which force us to use our wits to get food and shelter; conflicts between man and man, which force us to devise laws and courts in order to keep the peace; conflicts between our own impulses, which compel us to put a reflective brake upon our passions. Dewey's call to philosophers was to bring reflection back from sweeping the skies to what he conceived as its more pressing and natural business of bettering the human lot.

This new conception of thought required a 'reconstruction in philosophy'. Dewey held that in the momentous debate between Plato and Protagoras, philosophy had taken the wrong turning, committing itself to an age-long sterile pursuit of essences and abstract relations. It was remarked by Santayana that a fanatic was one who redoubled his effort when he had forgotten his aim. For Dewey, this would apply to the rationalist in his stubborn pursuit of a timeless truth. For the appropriate end of thought is not truth as such, truth pure, fixed, and eternal; there is no such thing; the end is rather the solving of particular problems of behaviour as they arise. To think *is* to form a 'plan of action' for dealing with such a problem; the truth of the thought is the success of this plan in attaining its particular goal. Thought that is aimed at eternal fixities has missed its calling and is at least mildly pathological. Metaphysics, as Michelet said, is the art of losing oneself methodically; so is theology; and the self-critical mind will abandon them both as profitless. Logic it will retain, but in a new form. Instead of searching for timeless patterns of reasoning, logic will become 'the theory of inquiry', a study of the techniques of forming and testing hypotheses. Ethics too will be reconstructed. It has traditionally concerned itself with goodness and rightness as such. Dewey was sceptical of these and all other 'as suches'. Ethics was the study of the techniques by which communal desires could be most richly satisfied.

Dewey's statement of instrumentalism, though lacking both the persuasiveness of James and the rhetorical skill of Schiller, was the most carefully elaborated statement of the pragmatist case. It has had but little attention in Europe, largely no doubt because of its uncouth and fumbling form. But it is a highly original philosophy, and it is characteristically American in spirit. Americans have had their Emersons and other eloquent exponents of the contemplative life, but their main drive has been in another direction; and of this practical drive, Dewey was the major prophet. He was sceptical of 'the life of reason' if that meant the pursuit of theory for its own sake; sceptical of the world's being intelligible, or being a system of any kind; sceptical about self-evident truths and unchanging principles; suspicious of intellect as opposed to practical intelligence. His influence, once enormous, and in many ways beneficial, is now on the wane in philosophy as in education. But it will be long before the reverberations of his assault on reason, as conceived in philosophic tradition, die wholly away.

10. One strand of Dewey's thought was taken up and developed by a third group of anti-rationalist writers, the logical positivists. This was the thesis that thinking, to be meaningful, must concern itself with what may be given in experience. But this support for Deweyan empiricism was an uncovenanted blessing, for logical positivism had nothing to do in its origin with pragmatism or with America. It came directly from Vienna, indirectly through selection and combination from Hume, Mach, Poincaré and Russell. Its best known theses are: the first a doctrine about meaning, the second about a priori know-ledge, the third about values. Its doctrine about meaning was that whenever we say anything about things or words, what we really mean or refer to is the experience (usually taken as sense experience) that would verify the statement as true. Its doctrine of a priori knowledge is that when we make necessary statements, such as those of mathematics and logic, we are saying nothing about the actual world at all, but only reporting the meanings with which we propose to use words. According to the positivists, all the knowledge we possess is reducible to one or other of these two kinds of statement. But that seems to leave our knowledge of values, our insights into good and evil, right and wrong, beauty and ugliness, with no place in the scheme. Here the positivists offer their third doctrine. Value statements are not expressions of knowledge or insight at all, and hence are neither true nor false; they are expressions not of cognitive meaning, but of emotive meaning, that is, of our feeling or attitude toward the object valued.

At first sight, these doctrines may seem too technical to be of general interest. But I am inclined to think that if one takes positivism together with the school of linguistic analysis that grows out of it as forming a single analytic development, it is the most important philosophical movement of this century. It has captured British philosophy; it has penetrated to all the British dominions; and to say the least it has achieved a very wide influence in the United States.

Why is it important to consider positivism in a study of the function of reason? First, because if it is true that we can speak significantly only of what may be given in sense experience, the range of objects that reason can deal with must be sharply cut down; such veteran terms as 'God', 'freedom', and 'immortality', for example, will either lose their meaning or survive only in radically altered form, and most of the stock in trade of traditional metaphysics and theology will be jettisoned. Secondly, if positivism is right about a priori knowledge, rationalism has obviously been on the wrong track. From Plato to McTaggart, it has been attempting to arrive at truth about the world by self-evident insights, or by self-evident deductions from these insights; and this method is now seen to be futile. Thirdly, if positivism is correct about judgments of value, right and wrong are beyond the scope of reason; the search for a standard of conduct that is objective because rational—an ancient dream of moralists—is revealed as a mirage. It is important not to prejudge the issue here by suggesting unfortunate practical consequences, both because these consequences have been denied and because they would not disprove the theory even if they occurred. Suffice it to say for the present that the analytic philosophers have made the most formidable and competent criticism yet made of the traditional idea of reason.

11. The linguistic philosophy that has held the stage in Britain since

B

the end of the second war should be kept distinct from positivism, though in one of its forms it is rooted in the second positivist thesis. Starting with the idea that a priori statements were proposals about how to use certain words ('2+2=4' is a proposal to use the second expression as meaning the same as the first), it went on to the view that philosophic propositions generally were really disguised definitions ('no material thing can be in two places at once' tells how we use the word 'matter'). Other forms of linguistic philosophy take their starting point in the later thought of G. E. Moore. Moore held that on many important issues, philosophy must be guided by common sense, rather than common sense by philosophy. There was nothing essentially linguistic in this view. But it was developed by some of Moore's followers into the view that the expressions as well as the beliefs of common sense were entitled to a special regard, and that the problems of philosophy arose through disrespect for ordinary language. At Oxford, linguistic philosophy turned in a different direction. Neither ordinary usage nor ordinary thought was sacrosanct; indeed ordinary usage was full of the sort of syntactic constructions which, taken at face value, led to theoretic disaster; the philosophers of the past had generally been victims of this disaster; and the true task of philosophy was to enable critical minds to avoid it by being self-conscious about the maladjustments of syntax to meaning. Is there anything here that bears importantly on the office of reason? On the face of it, No. When we look below the surface, however, and ask by what test the linguistic philosophers determine correctness of syntax, we get strange and diverse replies. At times the 'logic' they appeal to is held explicitly to have nothing to do with the structure of things, so that their scepticism of reason in its speculative use is as deep as that of the positivists. Linguistic philosophy deserves study as a distinct and fourth form of reaction against rationalism.

12. Though positivism took its rise on the continent, neither it nor its analytic progeny had much influence there; it had to be transplanted across the channel or the Atlantic in order to take root. As late as the world congresses at Brussels in 1953 and at Venice in 1958, European philosophers listened with ill-concealed boredom to what they regarded as the trivialities of positivist and linguistic wordcatching. It would be a mistake, however, to suppose that this was because the traditional rationalism of continental thought still reigned unchallenged among them. To be sure, the Catholic philosophers, constituting a large bloc in any such congress, kept the even tenor of their way; on the most important points they had the advantage of knowing the truth without having to win it by argument. But among those who lacked this insight, the most conspicuous school was existentialism; and in its scepticism of reason, this school left positivism far behind. Positivism believed, indeed, that the great systems of rational theology and metaphysics were one and all illusions, but it worshipped science, both in its mathematical and empirical forms; and many positivists have had strong convictions, or as they would prefer to say, strong feelings, of a liberal kind about moral and political issues. Existentialists agreed with them as to the futility of rationalist constructions. But why, they asked, should scepticism end there? Was there anything men once believed that had survived the holocaust of the last half century? In the most advanced nations on the continent the political creeds of liberalism, fascism, and communism seemed all to have worked out into disaster. Religious belief had been rendered untenable by knowledge of how myths are formed; the thought of Sartre and Heidegger was atheistic in its tendency. There were no common moral principles, and each man must make his own. The exaltation of love after Freud had spoken, of business success after Marx had spoken, of art in view of the current inanities and insanities, of courage in view of the windrows of French and German dead, of mechanical civilization in view of the bomb and the rocket, was merely fatuous. Even science, competent to discredit much of what we believed, could tell us nothing with confidence about what lay behind the veil of perception. The power that did lie there, whatever it might be, had produced a world of cruelty and unreason, in which man was lost and an alien. As the existentialist contemplated this world, his feeling was one of nausea.

Was there anything in this nightmare that he could tie to? One thing only—his own existence. Certain of nothing else, he could be certain at least that he existed, and that he was somehow fashioning his own fate. And in doing so, his safety lay in the depth of his disillusionment. He was weak; he was a pilgrim and stranger in a world not of his own making; he would be defeated shortly by death; there were no principles that he could adhere to; his life therefore was bound to be one of *Angst* and *Sorge*, of anxiety and care. But, for Heidegger, 'deliverance from illusion is to be achieved by the man who, opening himself to anguish, resolutely faces Nothingness in anticipation of his own extinction.'[1]

Existentialism of the secular kind gains a meagre response from the Anglo-Saxon soul. It was viewed with embarrassed incomprehension

[1] H. Kuhn, *Encounter with Nothingness*, 34.

in Britain, where no philosophy can afford to forget common sense, and in America, where high spirits, regardless of whether there is any obvious ground for them, are part of the national mores. Its strength has lain in those countries where the ravages of two world wars destroyed the landmarks by which people once guided their lives, and above all in France and Germany.

The five movements last mentioned—naturalism, instrumentalism, positivism, linguistic analysis, existentialism—are perhaps the most influential philosophic movements of recent years, and they are all derogatory of reason in its traditional use. This is particularly striking because philosophy *is*, supposedly, an attempt on the nature of things by reason, and if that attempt is futile, philosophy would appear to be futile too. But the rebellion of the last half century has gone far beyond philosophy; indeed it has broken out in every department of culture, and in most of them with marked virulence. We now turn to these other developments.

13. What of theology? Has anything notable happened there in recent decades? It has; nor is there any doubt about what it is. It is the rise of 'the theology of crisis'. And what is the main thesis of that theology? This—that the entire attempt by searching to find out God has ended in failure, that God stands over against us as the absolutely Other, with whom human thought has nothing in common, who can and does on occasion come to us, though by no effort of rational reflection or even of mystical discipline can we ever penetrate to him.

It is in this antipathy to reason, this conviction that what man needs is not more cerebration, however sophisticated and clever, but something that will engage his whole being in decision and action, a commitment of his life as opposed to a new set of ideas, that brings Barth and Brunner into one camp with Heidegger and Sartre. They are all in this sense existentialists. The word existentialism, this school tells us, comes from the words 'ex' and 'sistere', to step forth into action. The common point is that on both sides the act of stepping forth is taken as irrational, though otherwise it is conceived very differently indeed. With the secularists, the act is a desperate self-assertion by way of escape from the nauseating rottenness of the human scene. With the theists, it is not an act of our own at all; it is an act on the part of God in a divine-human encounter through which our being is transformed by a descent of grace. This gift of grace is unprocurable by anything we can do, unpredictable from even the completest knowledge of our past, and discontinuous with all our thoughts, feelings, and impulses. The insight it gives is the

most certain we can have; yet it cannot be put into words; it cannot
be grasped by human faculties; it is so different from the knowledge
acquired by science and philosophy that not only can they provide
no support for it, they cannot even contradict it; they are merely
irrelevant to it. God's ways are not as our ways.

If we consider the row of Gifford Lectures, the reversal of emphasis
in recent decades is especially striking. Many of the most impressive
of the earlier lectures, as we have noted, were expositions of the thesis
that human reason is the window by which all light enters the mind,
that the knowledge of God must be arrived at, if at all, by the extension and refinement of human faculty, and that how much of Deity
we can come to know depends on our capacity to receive, on the
dimensions of our own spirit. This precisely is what a number of
equally eminent but more recent lecturers, such as Barth, Brunner,
and Niebuhr, have been concerned to deny. To take this line, they
hold, is essentially to make man the measure of all things; it is to
surrender to naturalism and humanism; it is to substitute man in
his pride of knowledge for God, transcendent and absolute. To this
God as the absolutely Other, no human reason can approach. There
is no way up, there is only a way down, which God in his inscrutable
grace has sometimes deigned to take, and which, with no claim
whatever on his justice or mercy, we may venture to hope he will
take for us. Luther's rejection of 'the harlot reason' must be re-
affirmed for our day. When the gauntlet is thrown down as uncompromisingly as this, a believer in reason can hardly fail to take
it up.

14. Let us turn next to psychology. The most significant name
among psychologists of the last half century is undoubtedly that of
Freud; indeed if we are to believe a competent critic, William
McDougall, Freud has contributed more to psychology than any
other man since Aristotle. His most important discovery was the
extent to which conscious processes were influenced by the unconscious. Now reason, as far as it is a search for grounds and
consequences is of course a notable example of a conscious process.
Did Freud have anything to say about its governance or control?

He had a great deal to say, most of it highly disparaging to reason.
That he was not a total sceptic of the power of reason, at least as
embodied in scientific method, to arrive at truth is plain from his
vehement insistence that on many points he had actually arrived at it.
But the general effect of his teaching in this matter was negative. It
was to render suspect any attempt at the rational justification of

belief. One of his favourite doctrines was that of 'rationalization', which may be put as follows. We pride ourselves on being reasonable in our beliefs and actions; when we accept a belief, we like to think that we have adopted it on good grounds; when we decide on an action, we like to think that we have done so because it is right; and if challenged, we readily produce reasons. But these reasons turn out, when examined, to be 'rationalizations' merely, that is, attempts to dress up in rational guise beliefs or actions that sprang, not from reasons at all, but from non-rational causes. Bradley, in an often quoted remark, said that metaphysics was 'the finding of bad reasons for what we believe on instinct'. Freud would so describe almost all attempts to find grounds for belief or conduct. It is to be noted, however, that Bradley, having made the disparaging remark, immediately added, 'but the finding of these reasons is no less an instinct'; for him the most significant thing about man was this drive towards rationality, with its consequence that he sometimes goes right. What fastened the attention of Freud was that man continually goes wrong. His religious beliefs record an attempt, 'patently infantile', to find a father-substitute; his philosophical systems are projections upon nature of his half hidden desires; his scientific and artistic pursuits mark the sublimation of frustrated instincts; his political convictions are apologies for, or protests against his position in society; even his ethics is an uneasy compromise between selfish desire and group pressures. 'I am sure only of one thing,' Freud wrote, 'that the judgments of value made by mankind are immediately determined by their desire for happiness; in other words, that those judgments are attempts to prop up their illusions with arguments.'[1]

15. Freud's pessimistic theory of man seemed to many to be tragically confirmed in two world wars. It was in a sense an evolutionist theory which stressed that man was imperfectly released from his animal status. The biologist E. G. Conklin remarked that 'feelings and emotions are immensely older than reason, and they are accordingly much more potent in shaping behaviour';[2] this was a main point of Freud. Man was a creature of instinct with only a veneer of reason. When this veneer broke, as it always did in times of stress, the imprisoned cave-man burst out with all his selfishness, lust, and cruelty. This seemed to be just what happened in the two great wars, when apparently civilized people went berserk and reverted to savagery.

[1] *Civilization, War and Death*, ed. by J. Rickman, 2nd ed., 80.
[2] *What is Man?*, 248.

Many of Freud's theories were confirmed more quietly, but more exactly, through their success in therapeutic practice.

Philosophers and historians soon began to draw upon these theories for keys to the development of culture. Dewey's *Reconstruction in Philosophy* accounted for the respect paid to the contemplative life in the west by making it a rationalization of leisure-class activity, first adopted by Greek aristocrats; and James Harvey Robinson, in his widely read book *The Mind in the Making*, frankly took the line that traditional philosophy and theology were not worth refuting; they could be dealt with more decisively by showing those roots in frustrated desire from which they had sprung. Other philosophers of culture suggested that the pursuit of reason for its own sake, which seemed to the Greeks an ideal occupation for the free man, was not only abnormal but a biological liability. ' "Thought for thought's sake",' wrote Joseph Wood Krutch, 'is a kind of perversion whose essential character is not changed because it happens to illustrate the fact that human virtues may be biologic vices . . . Civilizations die from philosophical calm, irony, and the sense of fair play quite as surely as they die of debauchery.'[1]

Freud did not quite hold that all theories are puppets controlled from below by irrational strings. To hold that would have been self-stultifying. For then the theory that they are so controlled must itself be so controlled, and would have as little rational foundation as any other theory. Furthermore, he held that we could do much towards defeating irrational forces by understanding them. But he never made clear the extent to which, if at all, he thought reason had free play. His constant emphasis was on its control and distortion by the non-rational unconscious. Thus the most powerful voice of the century in psychology pronounced upon human reason a jeremiad that was almost an elegy.

16. In the province of sociology, if we may now turn to that, there is no figure that stands out as does that of Freud in psychology. But there can be little doubt as to what is the greatest achievement in this field. It is the amassing of a mountain of ordered comparative evidence regarding the beliefs and customs of mankind. The period opened with the two massive volumes of 1906 by Westermarck on *The Origin and Development of the Moral Ideas*, followed quickly by Sumner's *Folkways* in 1907. The twelve volumes of *The Golden Bough* first appeared as a single set in 1915, though Frazer had been at work on them for more than twenty-five years.

[1] *The Modern Temper*, 44–45.

Then in rapid succession appeared works of original research on the ways of primitive peoples by Lowie and Linton, by Hrdlicka and Malinowski, by Ruth Benedict, Margaret Mead, Clyde Kluckholn, and many others. No colony of cliff-dwelling Pueblos or islet among the Trobriands was quite safe against the anthropologist, with his notebook and calipers. From the Torres Straits to Alaska, primitive people had their heads measured, their superstitions recorded, and their marriage customs described in remorseless detail.

What was the upshot of all this indefatigable field work? It was to show with the fullest documentation the diversity not only in men's outward behaviour but also in their moral standards and ideals. The natural conclusion was uncompromisingly drawn by the two men we have named as pioneers; the mores, said Sumner, can make anything right, and the explanation, said Westermarck, is that there is no such thing as objective rightness at all; moral judgments are not an expression of reason, still less of a universal reason, but of an infinitely variable human feeling. One distinguished sociologist, indeed, who significantly enough was also a distinguished philosopher, L. T. Hobhouse, took a different view, and in his *Morals in Evolution* attempted to show a convergence toward a common morality under the pressure of a common reason. But his was not the approach of the empirical sociologists. They were more interested in observable differences than in underlying identities. The result was that where, as in the United States, sociology was a favourite subject of college and university study, the relativity of morals to local habit and feeling became part of the creed of sophisticated youth. The notion of an objective and rational standard for right and wrong came to be thought antiquated, provincial and, if truth be told, pharisaical.

17. Most of the sociologists who busied themselves with bringing to light the apparent anarchy of human standards had no clear awareness, perhaps, of where their researches were leading them. As civilized scientists observing 'primitive' cultures they had no doubt of the superiority of science over magic, or of fair play over head-hunting. Westermarck in his opening pages clearly implies that civilization is better than savagery. But it is difficult on his theory to see why. For on that theory, if the aborigine has a favourable feeling toward head-hunting and Westermarck an unfavourable one, to call either practice superior to the other is merely the expression of a third feeling or else sheer dogmatism. There was something large and tolerant about the relativist view that won it many youthful converts between the two wars. In practice the most effective

argument against it was provided by Hitler. Sociologists who were
committed to the view that the Nazis' approval of their own action
made it right found themselves vehemently denouncing that action,
not merely as jarring to their feelings, but as irrational, inhuman, and
intolerable. It was plain that they could not stay where they were.
They must either return to some kind of objectivity or adopt a more
whole-hearted irrationalism.

The latter step was courageously taken by Karl Mannheim. He saw
that implicit in the relativism of the sociologists was the suggestion
that not only were art, religion and morals relative to the various
cultures of the world, but also the very forms of thought and standards of valid reasoning. He therefore went on to develop what he
called a sociology of knowledge. All theories are 'ideologies' and
'merely a function of the generally prevailing social situation'.[1] There
is no such thing as genuinely objective thinking. 'The view which
holds that all cultural life is an orientation towards objective values
is just one more illustration of a typically modern rationalistic disregard for the basic irrational mechanisms which govern man's
relation to his world. . . . There is, then, no norm which can lay
claim to formal validity. . . .'[2] Ultimately, said Mannheim, one must
make one's choice between two views: on the one hand that there is
a reason working in and through men's minds which can lay hold of
a timeless structure of things; on the other, that thinking is a series
of temporal events determined, like all other events, non-rationally.
He elected the latter view. Of course the objection was promptly
made, as it was to the Freudian theory, that such relativism is self-
refuting, that if knowledge itself is relative to a particular culture,
then the theory that it is thus relative is also relative, and any claim
on Mannheim's part that his theory was entitled to general belief
must be abandoned. He saw the difficulty and tried to meet it by
arguing that, though each man's thought is inevitably governed by
biases, these biases might be ironed out and mutually cancelled when
one man's thought is compared with others.[3] But this surely
involves a standard that is not itself just a product of bias, but is
capable of sitting in judgment on bias and dismissing it. The truth
is that Mannheim was attempting an impossible task. There is some
plausibility in a relativist ethic. There is little or none in a relativist
theory of knowledge. One may intelligibly say that the line of argument Mannheim presented for his thesis may *seem* valid to him and

[1] *Ideology and Utopia*, 62
[2] *Ibid.*, 73.
[3] *Ibid.*, 269 ff.

seem invalid to the people of another culture; but to say that his reasoning really *is* both valid and invalid at the same time, his conclusion both true and false, is to break the mainspring of thought.

18. From sociology it is natural to turn to politics and political theory. At the turn of the century the type of thought that held the field was derived from idealism. T. H. Green's great book on *The Principles of Political Obligation* was essentially a re-writing of Rousseau to make the general will a drive toward rationality, seeking the same end in all men, and providing a basis for rights and duties, both within states and between them; and this theory, as developed in a more Hegelian manner by Bosanquet,[1] achieved a kind of orthodoxy.

Its hold was destroyed by the first war. Hobhouse, in a book dedicated to a son he had lost in that war, poured hot wrath upon it as a glorification of arbitrary state power;[2] and though this was unjust to the idealist theory and his own view was surprisingly near to it, the theory suffered much from 'guilt by association'. And it was harder after the war than before to believe that there was any effective drive towards reasonableness in men's minds. 'I used to be an idealist,' said Clemenceau to John Morley, 'but the older I grow, the more I am convinced that it is force that counts.'[3] Even the cultivated and reflective Morley himself, when asked what he thought of the covenant of the new League of Nations, answered, 'I have not read it, and don't intend to read it. It's not worth the paper it's written on. To the end of time it will always be a question of "thy head or my head." I've no faith in these schemes.'[4] In 1925 Austen Chamberlain was cheered by his party when he said in Parliament, 'I profoundly distrust logic when applied to politics, and all English history justifies me'.[5] Bosanquet was not unnaturally almost in despair. He wrote:

'with a significantly proud self-depreciation we say of ourselves . . . that we are not a logical nation, that we do not love logic; that England—was it not Disraeli who told us so . . . ?—is not governed by logic but by rhetoric. So that it seemed to me "like a sober man among drunkards" when Dr McTaggart with his indomitable courage declared that "no man ever went about to break logic, but in

[1] In *The Philosophical Theory of the State*, 1899.
[2] In *The Metaphysical Theory of the State*, 1918.
[3] J. H. Morgan, *John, Viscount Morley*, 91.
[4] *Ibid.*
[5] Quoted in Graham Wallas, *The Art of Thought*, 174–5.

the end logic broke him" ... We feel the full nauseousness of
modern superficial sentiment on this point when we read in a clever
article that "men are busied today in lifting the jewel of human vision
out of the mire of logic".[1]

19. The gloom deepened as the years between the wars went on and
the postulates of democracy were more and more widely questioned.
'Anyone who now reflects upon the beginnings of democratic social
philosophy . . . will see that at its root lay a fundamental act of faith.
This was the belief in the essential reasonableness of human nature
and of human action.'[2] The belief that such reasonableness was a fact
or even desirable as an ideal was now denied by three systems of
political thought that commanded not only the belief but the militant
support of many millions. There is happily no need to recall either
the cynical irrationalism of the nazi and fascist creeds, or the incalculable ruin and misery they brought with them. They are dead,
one hopes beyond resurrection.

The third dictatorship is very much alive. And while it is more
internationalist and perhaps humanitarian in its sympathies than the
other two, it shares their distrust of a reason that follows its own
line. A former Marxist who had been in a position to meet men in
power in the communist hierarchy wrote: 'What struck me most
about the Russian communists, even in such exceptional personalities as Lenin and Trotsky, was their utter incapacity to be fair in
discussing opinions that conflicted with their own. . . . An adversary
in good faith is inconceivable to the Russian communists. . . . To
find a comparable infatuation one has to go back to the Inquisition.'[3]
If this were true only of the personalities in power at a given time,
one would expect it to pass as new times brought new men. Unhappily the communist leaders generally have shown a distrust of the
free play of thought; indeed they must, for the system to which they
are committed regards it as idle and misdirected. A principal doctrine
of Marxism is that one's social, religious, and speculative views are
functions of the class to which one belongs, and hence that reason
and moral suasion will never cure the ills of a sick society; the ultimate resort must be to force. This makes the rational discussion of
differences between communist and non-communist peoples very
difficult. 'It may, in fact, be argued,' wrote a critic friendly to
Marxism, 'that the root error of the Communist International is a

---

[1] *Contemporary British Philosophy*, 1924, I, 61.
[2] G. H. Sabine, *Democracy and Preconceived Ideas*, 4–5.
[3] Ignazio Silone, as quoted in *Time*, January 9, 1950.

psychological one. It assumes that any diversity of view from its own
is the proof of cowardice or crime in those who venture to differ.'[1]
Such 'cowardice or crime' it cannot root out in other countries
unless, as in the case of Hungary, they lie too close to gain effective
help from outside. But that it can inhibit 'dangerous thoughts'
among its own people and harness their intelligence to its partisan
ends has been shown with alarming cogency. A disillusioned social
philosopher hardly overstates the case when he writes of
Marxism:

'It promises a Paradise on earth, a Land of Heart's Desire full of
happiness and enjoyment, and—sweeter still to the losers in life's
game—humiliation of all who are stronger and better than the multitude. Logic and reasoning, which might show the absurdity of such
dreams of bliss and revenge, are to be thrust aside. Marxism is thus
the most radical of all reactions against the reign of scientific thought
over life and action, established by Rationalism. It is against Logic,
against Science, and against the activity of thought itself—its outstanding principle is the prohibition of thought and inquiry, especially
as applied to the institutions and workings of a socialist economy.'[2]

20. One who believes, as does the present writer, that there is a drive
towards reasonableness in human nature, gentle, perhaps, but
persistent and universal, will be slow to believe that in either the
Russian people or those many other peoples who are beginning to
stir with the knowledge and envy of larger ways of life, this drive can
be permanently thwarted or twisted. But that it should happen
temporarily is the greatest political danger of our time. To many who
place high hopes in the United Nations as a forum for rational discussion, a little incident arising out of the Franco-British invasion of
Suez is suggestive. It was reported that Gilbert Murray, the great
scholar who had so largely given his life to two interests, Greek
culture and the United Nations, was asked by a group of fellow
Oxford dons to join in a letter of protest against this invasion. To
their astonishment, he declined. The ground, apparently, was his
mounting and discouraged conviction that the judgments of the
United Nations itself were being given in accord with national bias,
that with the entrance of many small powers, smarting with real or
fancied wrongs, there was developing a widespread animus against
the more advanced and fortunate peoples, which was in danger of

[1] H. J. Laski, *Communism*, 194.
[2] Ludwig von Mises, *Socialism*, 17.

shouting down the voice of civilization itself. One may recognize the danger without condoning this method of dealing with it. 'The love of truth,' said another great scholar, Housman, 'is the faintest of human passions', and when hurt pride and envy are at work, its whisper is too easily drowned out. Democracy, whether within a nation or between nations, calls for more than counting heads. It requires the pocketing of small egotisms in the attempt to find a common good and an objective better and worse.

Oddly enough, in the powerful nations what is to be feared is, rather, fear itself, the fear of being overtaken in amassing the means to security; and boredom, the boredom of doing nothing with them, once they are amassed. In reviewing the outbreaks of violence that preceded the first war, Dean Inge remarked, 'The main cause of these outbreaks was probably one which has not received sufficient attention, namely boredom. No nation can stand being rationally and pacifically governed more than a few years. Rational politics are dull. . . .'[1] Probably at no time has there been more good will in the world than now, or a clearer perception that reason has no racial or national boundaries. Even more certainly, there never was a time when unreason, once out of hand, had at its disposal such unimaginable powers of destruction.

21. We shall glance at but one more field, that of art. Literary criticism in both Britain and America was still much influenced, at the turn of the century, by Arnold and Pater; and both stood for the appraisal of literature against the background of an extended past, a background in which the Greek and Latin classics held the place of honour. Arnold's plea for these classics was that 'They can help to cure us of what is . . . the great vice of our intellect . . . namely that it is *fantastic* and wants *sanity*. Sanity—that is the great virtue of the ancient literature: the want of that is the great defect of the modern, in spite of all its variety and power.'[2] Pater insisted on 'severe intellectual meditation, that salt of poetry, without which all the more serious charm is lacking to the imaginative world.'[3] Such academic critics as A. C. Bradley and such aestheticians as Bosanquet would certainly have said the same; indeed Bosanquet wrote, 'we adhere to Plato's conclusion that objects of our liking possess as much satisfactoriness—which we identify with value—as they possess of reality and trueness. And that is a logical standard, and a standard

[1] *The Fall of the Idols*, 232.
[2] *The Poems of Matthew Arnold*, 1840–1867, Preface, 17.
[3] *Marius the Epicurean*, 103.

involving the whole';[1] he even said, 'bad taste is bad logic, and bad logic is bad taste'. In America, W. C. Brownell, Irving Babbitt, Paul Elmer More, and Stuart Sherman were also developing a broadly philosophical criticism, and insisting that if poetry was not the criticism of life, at least criticism could ask of poetry some significance for life. The wayward, the primitive, the merely impulsive, the unintelligible, the assorted outpourings of 'the lunatic fringe', were put aside because they came out badly in the test of sanity. Aspiring writers, whether they conformed to such criticism or not, were keenly aware of its presence.

Probably no one would say that sanity has been a conspicuous feature of the literature or art of recent years, even if one declined to go so far as Lowes Dickinson and say that 'modern literature is one vast hospital'. 'We can assert with some confidence,' writes T. S. Eliot, 'that our own period is one of decline; that the standards of culture are lower than they were fifty years ago; and that the evidences of this decline are visible in every department of human activity.'[2] Mr Eliot himself is a very thoughtful writer, and if, in his poetry, he is at times needlessly obscure, one is always confident that something significant is being said. But much recent verse seems to pride itself on saying what is trivial in a form that makes it unintelligible. 'You may find that the author is disclaiming, almost anxiously, the idea of tarnishing the minute mirror of his sensibility with any breath of thought. "Nothing in my brain I bring"—he seems to hymn with a pious complacent humility his freedom from intellectual baggage.'[3] A reviewer's comment on the work of a young American poet could no doubt be made on that of many another: 'His longish poem, "The Worm in the Whirling Cross", is as interesting as a cross-word puzzle, though not much more so; yet the reader cannot help admiring the author's virtuosity and the brilliance with which he delivers volley after volley of pun and paronomasia, as if his mind were playing tennis with the sound it utters and the sound were winning a love set.'[4] In such writing there can be no great nutriment for the spirit. The head of one of the largest British publishing houses told me that he was ready to consider any kind of manuscript except poetry, in which he thought the interest had largely died away. If true, this is a pity, since poetry has meant much even to

---

[1] *Principle of Individuality and Value*, 317.

[2] *Notes Toward a Definition of Culture*, 19; 'the arts without intellectual content are vanity.' 23.

[3] C. E. Montague, *A Writer's Notes on His Trade*, 74–75.

[4] Raymond Holden, *Saturday Review of Literature*, December 29, 1951.

THE REVOLT AGAINST REASON

plain men in the past. 'The arts,' said Santayana, 'may die of triviality, as they were born of enthusiasm.'[1]

Sometimes intellectual aversion in the artist passes over into a conscious creed. It was so with D. H. Lawrence. 'My great religion is a belief in the blood, the flesh, as being wiser than the intellect. We can go wrong in our minds. But what our blood feels and believes and says, is always true. The intellect is only a bit and a bridle. What do I care about knowledge? All I want is to answer to my blood, direct, without fribbling intervention of mind or moral, or what not.'[2] Does this sound exhilarating? Many in our time seem to have found it so. The trouble with it is simple: once the anchor of reason has been cut, one's craft may go anywhere. One may become a St Francis or equally a Hitler, who was notoriously adept at 'thinking with his blood'. It is more likely that one will become neither, but merely a tiresome freak. As Morris Cohen remarked, 'not all who rave are divinely inspired'.[3]

22. Scepticism of rational standards has been most marked, perhaps, in the plastic and pictorial arts. Our age is one of uninhibited artistic experimentation, which may of course lead to achievements of great value. But its most conspicuous achievement so far is a state of aesthetic anarchy in which the critic may be genuinely uncertain whether he is standing before the groping experiment of a child, or a Fauvist, Dadaist, or Daliist 'masterpiece'. 'We once had an art which was enjoyed and admired by ordinary intelligent people,' said Gilbert Murray; 'now we have school upon school, system upon system, of art—all transient, and each in its time enthusiastically admired by cliques of artists and up-to-date reviewers, while the ordinary intelligent man mostly remains sceptical or repelled.'[4] 'There is something that sounds old-fashioned about beauty,' says Bertrand Russell, 'though it is hard to say why. A modern painter would be indignant if he were accused of seeking beauty. Most artists nowadays appear to be inspired by some sort of rage against the world, so that they wish rather to give significant pain than to afford serene satisfaction.'[5]

There is, to be sure, a kind of philosophy behind the development of abstract art. It is felt that the sentimentalism of the nineteenth

---

[1] *The Philosophy of Santayana* (ed. by Schilpp), 21.
[2] In a letter quoted by Herbert Asquith, *Moments of Memory*, 187.
[3] *Reason and Nature*, 9.
[4] *Then and Now* (Romanes Lecture, Oxford, 1935), 17–18.
[5] *Let the People Think*, 96.

century, the attempt through painting or sculpture to tell a story or paint a moral, was artistically impure because it introduced so much that was not properly aesthetic, and that the right way to get rid of this embarrassing freight is to confine oneself to arrangements of line and colour; 'you revert to what the spinal column might feel if it had a separate consciousness, or what the retina might see if it could be painlessly cut off from the brain.'[1] If this is the only way in which art can achieve integrity, we must wish it well. But is there any reason to believe this? I cannot think so. The painter or poet who prefers the fall of man to a pinhead as his subject is choosing what gives him larger scope *as an artist*; and he has not felt in the past that he was immolating his art when he used it for the expression of significant ideas and feelings. And an art so pure as to be meaningless can hardly complain if a busy and burdened humanity passes it by.

23. We have peered into a variety of fields, and in all of them we have found similar movements in progress. These movements have little in common except the object of their dislike. Their replacements for reason vary widely. In philosophy, the appeal is commonly from reason to convention, perception or practical consequences; in theology it is to revelation; in psychology to the requirements of our instinctive nature; in sociology to men's diverse feelings and desires; in politics to the demands of class or nation; in art to a taste disburdened of principle. But on this they are united, that they must reject the pretensions of any reason which would hand down canons of necessary and universal validity.

This is not the whole story, of course. Every one of these fields has had its defenders of rational standards. But we are talking about the general trend, and certainly these defenders, when they have appeared, have felt relatively isolated. One of them, George Plimpton Adams, reports of the philosophic field that 'like the *deus absconditus* of Calvinistic theology, reason has retreated, leaving the world of nature, experience, and life to be the scene of relations, patterns, and organizing principles which are wholly factual, contingent, and non-rational'.[2] And Russell, who, though not a rationalist in philosophy, is a rationalist everywhere else, remarks that 'we have almost reached the point where praise of rationality is held to mark a man as an old fogey regrettably surviving from a bygone age'.[3] Where philosophy has turned to the past and revived great names, these

[1] Santayana, 'Penitent Art', *Works*, Triton ed., VII, 224.
[2] *California Publications in Philosophy*, Vol. 21, 206.
[3] *Unpopular Essays*, 95.

have been drawn from anti-rationalist camps. In Britain and America the chief revival has been that of Hume. On the continent, the reaction has been toward philosophers who were both anti-rationalist in temper, as Hume was not, and in their technical conclusions. 'The present philosophical situation,' Karl Jaspers has written, 'is characterized by the fact that two philosophers, Kierkegaard and Nietzsche, who in their lifetime were ignored and for a long time after were made no account of in the history of philosophy, are now steadily increasing in importance. All the other post-Hegelian philosophers are receding more and more into the background, while today these two men already stand out undeniably as the really great thinkers of their age.'[1]

24. The purpose of this book is to inquire whether the revolt against reason has made out its case. If the inquiry is to be effective, it must plainly limit itself. I shall not venture outside the fields of philosophy and theology, nor in the present volume outside the theory of knowledge. It will be evident that I do not take existentialism very seriously; what I have to say about it will be said in two chapters of the third volume. On the other hand, I take the philosophy of analysis very seriously indeed; it is this sort of logically competent criticism of older ideas of reason that will discredit them if anything can. The larger part of this book, therefore, will be devoted to analytic philosophy, principally logical positivism and the linguistic philosophies that have succeeded it.

We have said something about what 'reason' means. But its meaning in western history has been at once variable, rich, and nebulous; and it would be idle to study the revolts against it unless we know more exactly what it is. Our first business, then, must be to set out its main components.

---

[1] Quoted by W. Lowrie, *Kierkegaard*, 13.

CHAPTER II

THE IDEA OF REASON IN WESTERN THOUGHT

1. Man, Aristotle said, is a rational animal; and the possession of 'reason' is commonly thought to be what makes him distinctively a man. The term 'reason' is being used here in a large and loose sense, but reflection on it is a helpful way to begin. What does it mean? Not consciousness, of course; for no one can sensibly doubt that animals feel fear, hunger, pleasure, and pain. They even make mistakes, as when the dog drops his bone for the more inviting one in the water; and since only judgment can be mistaken, they must in some sense judge. And since judgment is thought, they think. Yet they do not think as we do. Our thought is somehow a different kind of affair; it is the thought of a rational being. And what may that mean? It means, I suggest, four things, which we commonly take together without distinguishing them or making them explicit.

2. (1) Animal thought is tied to perception; human thought is not. Hence while our own thoughts can 'wander through eternity', the animal can think of the absent only when his idea remains tethered to sense. To be sure, the dog will wait at the door where his master went in; he will go to meet him at the habitual place and time; and in order to do these things, he must in some way think of the absent. But if there is no sensible cue on hand that has been associated with his master and can serve to carry the reference, he is helpless. He cannot sit on his haunches and meditate on the missing paragon; he can never contemplate what is 'far away and long ago'; his thought is tied, not free. When we say that man is rational, we imply that his thought is *not* so tied, that he is master of it in the sense that he can direct it where he will. Dr McTaggart was reproached for allowing his cat, Pushkin, to occupy his own chair. 'But I,' replied the philosopher, 'can think of the Absolute, and poor Pushkin cannot.'

(2) The cleverest of animal minds is brought to a stop by the hurdle of an abstraction; man takes the hurdle in his stride whenever he uses language. There can be no doubt that animals see shapes,

feel pains, and smell odours. But apparently no animal ever thinks of shape or pain or odour. If it did, it would coin a word for it, for words would be enormously helpful, and most higher animals have plenty of sounds at their disposal. If they never speak, we can only conclude that they have no ideas to express of the sort that words are used for. Most words—'red', 'run', 'roof'—are tags for abstractions. If animals fail to invent them, it is not because they lack usable tags, but because they lack the baggage to tag with them. A man who does not have such baggage in abundance is less than normal. 'I see a horse,' said Antisthenes to Plato, 'but not horseness.' 'That,' said Plato with more candour than tact, 'is because you have eyes but no intelligence.'[1]

(3) The animal mind cannot infer explicitly; human minds can. I say explicitly because there is no doubt that animals do reason after their fashion. Even Lloyd Morgan's chick, which after a bitter experience with a piece of orange peel, looked askance at the next piece offered, was in a sense inferring; it was passing from a similar appearance to the anticipation of a similar result. But *what* in the appearance was connected with what in the result? Here the chick would be dumb, and unfortunately in both senses of the word. It can infer, but not explicitly, for it cannot abstract.

(4) Finally, human reason has added an extra dimension to the animal consciousness in the form of self-consciousness. An animal lacks the power which is the source, in ourselves, of so much achievement and so much woe, of standing off from itself and contemplating what it is doing. It eats, sleeps, and cavorts, but never pauses in the midst of a meal to take note that it is eating greedily, never asks whether it is not unseemly to sleep the hours away, apparently never reflects, as it leaps and runs, that it is a little off form today. It makes mistakes, but having made one, it cannot sit down and consider what principle of right thinking it violated. Because it cannot contemplate its own behaviour it cannot criticize itself; being below the level of self-criticism, it has no norms; and having no norms, it lacks one great obvious essential of the life of reason, the power to be guided by principle.

When we say that man is a rational animal, then, we seem to imply that he can command ideas independently of sense, that he can abstract, that he can infer explicitly, and that he can sit in judgment on himself. The highest of animals can do none of these things. The stupidest man, if not a pathological case, can in some measure do them all.

[1] *Parmenides*, 131.

Now the best thinking that can be achieved by the most rigorous and systematic of philosophers is an exercise of the same reason that belongs to man generally. Yet the difference of level is wide. Where does it lie? Chiefly in the higher development of each of the characteristics we have mentioned, but partly also in the greater definiteness given to the ideal of reason. The first of these advances may occur independently of the second. A man may be at once highly reasonable and an admirable reasoner who has never paid any attention to what either of these consists in, and would have great trouble in formulating it. Indeed men seem to have been exercising the reason we have just described for at least five hundred thousand years before they had anything like an adequate idea of what being reasonable meant. Aristotle, who struggled long to achieve such an idea, pointed out that what was first in order of nature may be last in order of recognition; and he would certainly have agreed with Locke's remark that 'God has not been so sparing to men, to make them barely two-legged animals, and left it to Aristotle to make them rational'. But while rational practice may be developed independently of theory, the theory of reason does depend on a developed practice; it is only with instances of an accomplished use of reason before them that philosophers have ever succeeded in giving an account of that use. The great advances in understanding what reason means have accompanied or shortly followed bursts of reflective activity. Let us consider a stage or two of the advance.

3. When man escaped from the animal mind, his use of reason seems to have been concentrated for some hundreds of millenniums on the connection of means and end. Pragmatism, which is the logic of the primitive mind, is no doubt right that thought arose as the instrument of practical need; hence Dewey's name for his philosophy, instrumentalism. After all, we are animals still; the impulses of action within us are as deep as our racial roots, while the impulse to think for its own sake is so weak and recent that some philosophers deny its existence. As a result of this overpowering animal heritage we remain, as James put it, hair-trigger mechanisms made to act. In the long infancy of mankind, the man who could fight best, hunt best, make canoes and huts and spears best, was the best fellow, and likely to end as 'king', which means 'he who can'. His knowledge—to use Professor Ryle's distinction—was probably a 'knowing how' rather than a 'knowing that'. Such 'know-how' is partly that combined 'wisdom of the body' and mysterious shrewdness of instinct which makes superb football players or forest guides of men who are helpless in explaining how they perform their feats. But behind every feat and contrivance there is causal law. If that law can be seen and set out, lesser men may to some extent learn the secret and command for themselves a knowledge that is power. And though lesser men cannot invent a new process, they may refine and improve a borrowed one. The civilization of Babylonia, Carthage and the Aztecs consisted chiefly of a set of crafts smoothed into effectiveness by long adjustment in practice.

Such reason may achieve high development while other forms of reason remain in their infancy. Unhappily, when it does, the men and peoples who embody it are more dangerous to their fellows than a horde of wild beasts. Whitehead has distinguished two figures as symbolic of types of reason, Plato and Ulysses: 'the one shares reason with the gods, the other shares it with the foxes'.[1] We all know men of the Ulysses type, though no one embodies it in its purity, not even Ulysses himself; nor would such men be tolerated if they did. Crafty, cunning, adroit, always able to fall on their feet, equal to any emergency, their eyes fixed on the main chance, these men are competent, formidable, and hateful. Ulysses has produced an enormous progeny of Iagos, Machiavellis, and Mussolinis, big and little, whose common characteristic is that with a scheming sagacity in tracing out the means to their ends, they do not, cannot, or will not, apply any rational criticism to these ends themselves. To be sure, many persons are now telling us that ends are incapable of such criticism, and that reason has no function in practice except this of calculating means. An eminent economist writes: 'The spheres of rational action and economic action are . . . coincident. All rational action is economic. All economic activity is rational action.' And what is the end of economic activity? One's own pleasure. 'Action based on reason,' goes on Professor von Mises, 'action therefore which is only to be understood by reason, knows only *one* end, the greatest pleasure of the acting individual.'[2] In such a view the function of reason is to devise more and more efficient means to one's own pleasure, this being a goal that is unvarying and beyond rational criticism. Here is Ulysses exalted into the sole type of rational man. But even if reason as craft goes on improving its means while retaining unchanged

[1] *The Functions of Reason*, 7.
[2] *Socialism*, 113, 112. Von Mises adds, to be sure, that 'pleasure' covers all human ends, 'noble or ignoble, altruistic or egotistical'. But he presumably means that it is the pleasure involved in beauty, knowledge, and the rest, that is actually sought; to *identify* pleasure with knowledge, e.g., would hardly be possible. And how the aim at 'the greatest pleasure of the acting individual' could be described as 'altruistic' I do not understand.

its foxlike end, it will not be getting nearer the life of reason as conceived in the main western tradition.

4. In that tradition reason means more than the best skill or knowledge of the mechanic, technician, or inventor. This larger reason is a discovery of the Greeks. It sprang into full flower in the great century between 450 and 350 B.C. Western culture is often said to be the confluence of three streams—the reason and art of Greece, the religion of Judaea, and the law of Rome. But it is worth pointing out that only the Greek contribution comes to us pure, that Christian theology and Roman jurisprudence are deeply impregnated with Greek ideas. So extraordinary was the development of reason, both in conception and in exercise, in that family of Greek geniuses, Socrates, Plato, and Aristotle—grandfather, father, and son—that later thinkers have been content for the most part to embroider their pattern; 'the word "philosophy"', says Burnet, 'is Greek, and so is the thing it denotes'.[1] Reason, as we shall see, is a very complex affair. But its most obvious association is with reasoning; and more perhaps than any other people, the Greeks took delight in reasoning. Georg Brandes has said of the modern French that there is 'a hard algebraic base' to their minds; the rationalist tradition is strong in France, and educated Frenchmen take obvious pleasure in the logical play of ideas. The Athenians were the Parisians of the ancient world. They liked to meet in market-place or temple portico and, for the mere exhilaration of the give and take, argue tirelessly about politics and morals, philosophy and religion and taste. Young Athenians followed the game of argument as many of us would play chess. William Minto thought that the Platonic dialogues themselves were an extension of a popular game of question and answer played by Athenian gentry, and that the formidable logic of Aristotle was a kind of glorified Hoyle on whist, which laid down the rules and strategy of that game.[2] These are probably overstatements, but in their stress on the Athenian delight in the free play of intelligence, they suggest the truth. 'What in the last resort gave its peculiar note to Hellenism as against all that existed outside it? Surely just the singular development of those mental faculties which we associate with rationalism, the critical intellect, the bent to submit traditions and beliefs to examination. . . . All the development of knowledge, of command over the forces of Nature, of purposeful order, what is meant by the term "Western Civilization" today, has had for its

[1] *The Legacy of Greece*, 58.
[2] *Logic*, 3–4.

moving principle a rationalism whose origin is to be found in the Greek city-states.'[1]

5. Behind all this in the Greek mind lay the conception of form. Form is identity of structure, a one in many, a pattern or framework that maintains itself through diversity and change. It has already been pointed out that among the senses of the Greek and Latin terms for reason, λογος and *ratio*, a common one was *relation* or *order*. Now the order and relations of things are not seen or heard, as sound and colour are. They are not sensed at all, but apprehended in a different way by what is called intelligence. In our common thought reason is rather like an X-ray that penetrates through the fleshy outside of things to the skeleton underneath, that sees the abstract in the concrete, the universal in the particular—an insight, furthermore, that has so freed itself from the inner forces of liking and disliking as to be influenced only by the logic of the case. Its objects may seem remote to us because they are not visible to the eye of sense; its temper seems austere and perhaps a little inhuman because it calls for that severe impartiality which discounts feeling and desire. Now the Greeks were the first to conceive of this sort of reason. They were able to conceive of it because they had the idea of form.

No doubt this idea did not burst on the world as suddenly as appears; if one looks attentively, one can see it making its way in Greek reflection from Thales on. Perhaps its first unequivocal appearance is in the thought of that dim genius Pythagoras. Pythagoras was a devotee of music. He used to experiment with a simple instrument called a monochord, which was like a violin with one string; and he noticed not only what everyone else would notice, that if one moves the bridge, the tone deepens as the string gets longer, but also, what is very much harder to see, that pitch and length can be precisely correlated, so that, given a certain note, you can calculate exactly how much longer the string must be to produce one a fourth, or a fifth, or an octave lower. To Pythagoras this seems to have been an intoxicating discovery, not so much for itself as for a 'wild surmise' it led to about the nature of the world. If it were true that the scale of sounds was hung upon a trellis of numerical relations, might not this also be true of colours and shapes and odours? Where indeed was one to stop? Might not the whole sensible world be woven on a frame of impalpable relations? 'All things are numbers,' said Pythagoras; it is one of the few things that at this distance of time one can be fairly sure he said. It has a curious sound, suggesting

[1] Edwyn Bevan, *Hellenism and Christianity*, 15.

the esoteric pronouncement of some extreme modern rationalist—Sir James Jeans, perhaps, reporting God to be the great mathematician—or, if one is less charitable, the oracle of a mystic or even drunken babbling. It may well have been all these things. Pythagoras seems to have seen a vision, the rationalist vision of the world as an intelligible structure, and since, so far as we can tell, he was the first man to have seen it, it may not improbably have gone to his head. He tried to introduce a new religion in which science was to be the means of purifying the soul, and there is nothing surprising, perhaps, in the fact that his fellow townsmen rose and drove him out. It would be interesting, nevertheless, to speculate what the western world would have been like if it had accepted the religion as well as the rationalism of its first martyr of science.

But form as it presented itself to Pythagoras was still a primitive notion compared to what it became for his Greek successors. In order to grasp what reason meant either to them, or in turn to their own successors, we must see more fully what this notion involved. The first vague idea of form as common structure seems to have broken up, as they contemplated it, into four sub-ideas, those of (1) essence, (2) end, (3) law, and (4) system. Let us consider these.

6. (1) *Form as essence.* Reason deals with the general, not the particular; or if it deals with the particular at all, it does so by means of the general. When a physician tries to diagnose someone's disease, he is treating a particular case, but he will make no headway until he can find in it symptoms which convert it into a type. An eruption of this *kind* means measles; a bacillus of this *kind* means typhoid. Causal laws are statements connecting occurrences of sort A with those of sort B. Understanding moves through *as suches*. If reason is to have material to work on, therefore, the mind must already have taken a long stride beyond sensation or perception. Of course perception itself involves the use, in a sense, of general ideas; to perceive a triangle as a triangle is already to have got beyond *this* triangle, and to have found in it an embodiment of what makes anything a triangle. But between recognizing the figure and achieving a *conception*, which one can manipulate with closed eyes, of what makes anything a triangle, of what triangles have in common, in a word of triangularity, there is an interval that marks very different levels in the emergence of mind.

The Greeks, so far as we know, were the first to reach a point where they could move with ease on this second level. They were beginning to be interested not merely in the geometry which brought the term into being, which was primarily a set of rules for marking out land, but in geometry as a science, in which one inquired into what was true of triangles and circles as such. To do this, one must isolate what is essential to a certain figure, what belongs to it through all its kinds and instances; it would be inept to make statements about *the* triangle which held only of the right-angled species of it. The Greeks were confident that if one searched assiduously for this essence of a figure, one could find it and fix it in a definition. And what is more important, they believed that what could be thus done with geometrical figures could be done with everything else. The brilliant intellectual displays to be found in Plato's dialogues are devoted very largely to the attempt at definitions, that is at statements of the essence, of many principal objects of human concern, of justice in the *Republic*, of the soul in the *Phaedo*, of courage in the *Laches*, of the sophist in the dialogue of that name. Whenever we say anything about man or pebbles or the state, Socrates suggested, we are using universals; we are ascribing a character to a class in virtue of its belonging to, or following from, a core of qualities essential to that class; and he went about continually making the point that it was absurd to talk as confidently as we do when we literally do not know what we are talking about. The first step, he insisted, if we are to talk sensibly about courage was to get clear what we mean by courage. He proposed and effectively practised a method for achieving such clearness. His chief contribution, says Aristotle, was 'induction and general definitions',[1] or to put it more briefly still, inductive definition. You want to know what you mean by courage; how should you set about it? You have a vague notion of it to begin with, or you could not recognize cases of it when you met them. Now the right strategy is to use the two elements that you do know—the foggy outline and the particular cases—to close like the jaws of a vice upon what you do not know. Formulate your vague notion as best you can and then clip or expand it to suit the examples at your command. 'Courage,' you say at a hazard, 'is readiness to carry on the fight, no matter what the odds.' No, this will not do, for it covers too much; it would include suicidal foolhardiness, which you do not want to recognize as true courage. You must try again to find a concept that will close the gap, that will extend to all your instances, but not beyond them. Only when you succeed will you be prepared to talk about courage with clear knowledge of what you mean.

This search after the essence had dangers which even Plato hardly realized. By 'courage', for example, we may mean various things so

[1] *Metaphysics*, i, 6; xiii, 4.

different as to have no common core worth finding. Many logicians would go farther; 'this activity of searching for essence is bad,' one of them writes, 'because there is no such thing as essence in the sense intended';[1] the distinction between essence and property is regarded as belonging to an outmoded logic. Whether we accept this view or not, we may still say that the Greek discovery that we think in universals and that reason, to work effectively, must make these definite, marked a great advance in the technique of understanding.

7. (2) *Form as end.* Suppose we are asked to think the concept of 'oak tree'. If we follow Socrates's method, we shall compare a variety of oaks in thought or perception, and isolate as sharply as we can what they have in common. Unfortunately when we have done this, we are likely to find nothing left in our hands but a dissolving wraith. We shall have to include in our review everything between tall oaks and little acorns, for a sapling and a blade just peeping from the ground are in a sense as truly oaks as some mighty veteran. Yet what have all these in common? To meet such cases, the Greeks had another idea of form. What bound together the blade, the sapling, and the tree, was their common *end*. The blade and sapling were stages on the way to the tree; and they were one because they were degrees in the realization of one pattern, ideal, or goal. The blade was not much like the tree, but it was an oak nevertheless, for the dominant pattern was in some sense at work in it, determining what it should become. At the same time it was an imperfect oak because the pattern was so faintly and meagrely realized. Here we have a very different notion of form. It is still what may be called essential, but the essence is not now the common attributes of a class, but a common end realized in varying degrees by the individuals that have it.

As applied to living things, this method of finding what they essentially were might be defended, but can it be applied to other things too? Rightly or not, the Greeks did so apply it, and in whole-sale fashion. Plato carried it all the way up and down the scale from philosophers to articles of furniture. An ordinary bed was called a 'bed' in virtue of what it had in common with other beds; but was that the whole story? No, for this which it had in common was not present in equal measure in all beds. Could one say that the pile of straw in the corner and the bed of Ware realized equally what beds were for? Surely not, Plato would answer gravely. Hence bedness is a matter of degree; any particular bed was a bed only so far as it

---

[1] R. Robinson, *Definition*, 154. Cf. 'it seems to me a muddle-headed notion, incapable of precision', B. Russell, *History of Western Philosophy*, 187.

embodied what beds were supposed to be. For the Greeks, as for William James, 'the meaning of essence is teleological'.

The case is more plausible when one comes to human nature. This notion of form as end is the fundamental idea of Aristotle's ethics. Man himself is a half-grown being, trying to become what as yet he is not, and if we are to find what he is essentially, we must project ourselves forward along the line of his growth and catch the form, in the sense of goal or ideal, which he is trying to realize. It would be absurd, in Aristotle's view, to surrender after the modern fashion to a cleft between naturalism and ethics, between fact and value, since you can determine what man is only through what he is striving to become, which is what we mean by 'the goal'. Reason works alike in biology and in ethics. If scientific men disregarded values as they are now expected to do, Aristotle would have said that they were second-rate scientists without vision; and if moralists disregarded the facts of human nature, he would have put them down as incompetent in their own field. Nor was there any conflict for the Greek between the scientist or moralist on the one hand and the metaphysician on the other. How were you to determine what the world as a whole was like? Simply by carrying through to the end the process that revealed to you the nature of a bed or the nature of man. Having discovered the essential natures or purposes of these and other things, we must try to put these purposes together, to discover the joint design, the over-arching purpose, of the whole. This is still the work of reason operating with forms as ends, though what is now being felt after is that form of all forms which Plato described as 'the form of the good'.

Form as end is clearly different, as we have intimated, from form as essence. To think of the pattern of trunk, bark, branches, and leaves in a perfect oak is clearly different from grasping what logicians call the intention of the class oak, the character that all oaks have in common. It is important to keep the two distinct, since they lead on to different views of the world. If essence is conceived as end, one will naturally be carried on, as Plato was, to a purposive world-view, in which the business of reason is to reveal the place of everything in that comprehensive plan or purpose that orders 'the scheme of things entire'. If form is conceived as essence, it is rationalism of a different kind toward which we are headed—the mathematical rationalism that uses concepts as the starting points for lines of implication. It must be admitted that the two notions are not kept sharply enough distinct in Greek thought, even by the masters, and that in consequence the philosophy of Plato remains an uneasy blend of different rationalist strains, that of the teleologist and that of the logician, or—to leap far forward—of Paley and Descartes.

8. (3) *Form as law.* Suppose one does conceive form as essence; the reflective mind will not stop there. If one were to supply a mind like Euclid's with the concept of triangle or quadrilateral, it would start burgeoning there, for he would want to know all that is implied in it in the way of species, properties, and relations. Now geometry was Plato's ideal of scientific knowledge; it was the most advanced science of his time; and the importance he attached to it is attested by the legend of that inscription over the Academy door, 'Let no one who is not a geometrician enter here'. The modern doubts whether there is anything in mathematics but convention and tautology seem never to have troubled him. He was so thorough-going a rationalist as to believe that all scientific knowledge would prove in the end to be of this necessary type. Why this exaltation of a specifically rationalist insight? The reasons that would be given by later rationalists are already implicit in Plato's discussions, and it will be well to set them out in order.

9. (i) Such knowledge was *certain.* Where the senses are concerned, as in the colour of a dress or the speed of a runner or the beauty of a picture, we are easily and often mistaken. But if we genuinely understand what we are saying in arithmetic or geometry, we can be confident that we are not mistaken; indeed in mathematics we really see that a conclusion is true only when we also see that it *must* be true, and therefore *why* it is true. 'This knowledge,' says Plato, 'may be truly called necessary, necessitating as it clearly does the use of pure intelligence in the attainment of pure truth.'[1] For centuries in the Middle Ages mathematicians were suspect, because, by manipulating strange symbols, they brought out results with which it was impossible to argue; there was felt to be something magical about it, suggestive of the black arts. Something of this same mystery and fascination hung about the subject for Plato, and he makes Socrates in the *Meno* fall back on pre-existence to explain how the slave-boy could pass to fresh geometric theorems without having learned the way to them. However we may have stumbled on it, here was a marvellous inner path, which could apparently be travelled by anyone, and which conducted to absolute certainties.

10. (ii) Such thinking gave *new* truth. Plato would have scouted as

[1] *Republic*, VII, 526.

vigorously as Kant the view so widely held today that in such reasoning one was merely unpacking in the conclusion what was already there in the premises. What the slave boy discovered about the square, namely that you get a square double the size by drawing another on its diagonal, was not contained, in any relevant sense of 'contained', either in his premises or in his consciousness. Whether Plato was right or wrong in holding this view we cannot here argue, though the issue is of first importance and will concern us later.[1] But hold it he did. Purely a priori reasoning gave us fresh knowledge about the world.

11. (iii) Such knowledge was *independent of sense*. This did not mean, of course, that sensible things were of no aid in reaching it. Even the best of reasoners was helped by fixing his eye upon a triangle drawn before him. But it was of course not *that* triangle he was thinking about. It was rather the triangle of the geometer, an altogether more gossamer affair, with lines that had length without breadth, and with no particular size or shape, a figure that would never be observed by anyone because it was not the sort of thing that bodily eyes could see. Sensible figures on the board were useful symbols of it, approximations to it, vehicles of it, partial embodiments of it, aids to it, anything you like except *it*. That could never be caught or confined in any of its sensible disguises. We saw it not with sense but with intelligence, which 'is more precious far than ten thousand bodily eyes, for by it alone is truth seen'.[2]

12. (iv) Such knowledge, again, was *universal*; that is, there were no exceptions to it, and for all men it was the same. As for there being no exceptions to it, that follows from its necessity; if you once see that the Pythagorean theorem about triangles *must* be true, you need not worry about a triangle turning up tomorrow that proves to be a maverick. Nor need you worry about others disagreeing with you in regard to the theorem. They never will. They may, to be sure, have no interest in the matter; they may fail to understand you when you talk about it; they may use other words for the same things; all this is beside the point. You know that if they start with the same concept as you do, and develop it by genuine thinking, not by imagination or association, they will not, because they cannot, arrive at results at odds with yours. It is really absurd to speak of Euclid's geometry or the logic of the Greeks, as if these things admitted of proprietorship,

[1] See Chapter VI.
[2] *Republic*, VII, 527; cf. *Theaetetus*, 185.

and someone could stake out a claim to the multiplication table. 'East is east, and west is west,' it is said; Plato had no doubt heard this; and no doubt too, as regards issues such as this, he considered it absurd. That men prefer fezzes and turbans east of Suez is no reason why they should also take 7 + 5 to equal 11, or have a taste for illicit majors. Plato would have said, as Bosanquet did, that the solidarity of mankind lies in the intellectual life.

In moral matters too, all men, if you went deep enough, would be found to think alike. Of course they were often confused as to what they meant, and they misunderstood each other wildly and wilfully. But let Thrasymachus or Callicles or any other sophist suggest that justice was an arbitrary convention about which anyone could think as he pleased, and Plato always had Socrates standing ready in the wings with the dialectical apparatus needed for trussing the miscreant, and putting him in his place. If any definition but one, of justice or courage or temperance were adduced, Socrates was prepared to show to all comers that they could not adhere to it consistently. It was admitted to be far harder to think clearly about right and wrong than about triangles, for no man was likely to be outraged at what one said about a triangle, though he might be furious at a view of virtue that would make him out to be cowardly or treacherous; in our thinking about morals, our passions and prejudices are dangerously involved. But the fact that it is harder to think clearly about morals does not imply that when we do think clearly we think differently; indeed the truth is just the opposite. Plato would say that so far as we succeed in defining our moral ideas clearly and exactly, we find that they are everywhere the same. Reason is one, in ethics as in mathematics.

13. (v) How account for this fact that reason gives the same answers everywhere? The simplest way, Plato thought, was to say that such knowledge is *objective*; which means that if, when men think, they lay hold of the same laws, it is because the laws are there to grasp. It is an odd fact that the term 'idea', which for us names the most subjective of all things, a flitting shadowy something in our own private history, should be used by Plato for the unchanging and permanent framework on which the world is constructed. He was sure that concepts or universals were found, not manufactured. We did not make the numbers of the multiplication table; if we did, we could destroy them, a grotesque suggestion. Neither did we invent the relations between them. We could no more make three apples and four add up to eight than we could push the pyramids about. Kant had a reason for this that was different from Plato's; but Plato's remains the answer of the main rationalist tradition. That answer is that you cannot change at will the laws discovered by reason because they belong to the nature of things; they belong, as it were, to the bony structure of the world. Many modern logicians, as we shall see, regard the laws of logic as conventions. Plato would have replied that a convention is something you can change, and that the law of contradiction is, of all the structures in the universe, the least plastic to thought or will.

When Plato referred to science, what he really had in mind was his ideal science, mathematics. But granting that the laws of this science were rational, that is, necessary and intelligible, what were we to say about the laws of the other sciences, such as astronomy, physics, biology? Were they too necessary and intelligible? They certainly did not seem so. Nevertheless, the major Greek succession, following Pythagoras, was convinced that they were. Plato was no natural scientist and said little about the matter. But Aristotle, who founded biology as well as logic, did have something very pertinent to say about how the two types of science were related. Start with the premises that all men are mortal, and that Socrates—who has died a million deaths in this syllogism—is a man, and his mortality follows; that is, the conclusion is linked to the premises by necessity. But what about the major premise, all men are mortal; is there any necessity in that? Is the biological law that man is mortal also a rational law, such that, given a man, you can see from his nature that he must die? Modern science would officially jeer at such an idea. Aristotle nevertheless held it, and one is by no means sure he would retreat if he were living now. He held that there is such a thing as intuitive induction, by which, in particular instances, you could see that such and such a character implied or necessitated another, very much as you see this in the case of a triangle. The causal laws of science are commonly assumed to be mere fixed conjunctions in which we link A and B together for no better reason than that we have never found them apart. Regarding many of these laws, Aristotle would have conceded that we do not see their necessity; we have no idea, for example, why horned animals should all be ruminants. Regarding many others he would have insisted that we are not wholly in the dark about them; flesh and blood as put together in the human body form the sort of thing that *would* disintegrate. But he would have said that where we had a genuine law before us, we could always, if we looked sharply enough, see the bright thread of necessity running through the causal link. This conviction, like so much else in

Aristotle, comes from Plato, of whom it may be said that 'wherever he finds law, and he finds it everywhere, he finds rationality and the Good'.[1] 'In the childlike confidence inspired by the still fresh perception of the nature of mathematical and geometrical truth, he leaps the barrier which modern thought has erected between deductive and experimental science, and boldly surmises a state of human knowledge in which the whole web of cosmic conditions should be as rigorously intelligible as the simplest relations of number and figure.'[2]

14. (vi) It will now be apparent that the laws so apprehended are *eternal*, in the sense that they never come to be, never change, and never cease to be. Spring comes and the orchard branches burst out into countless blossoms, which wither and give place to apples, which fall in their turn and decay. These apples and blossoms have numbers, and between these numbers there hold the relations of the prosaic multiplication table. Do those numbers or their relations ever begin or flourish or die, like the things of which they hold? To Plato the question seemed strange and somewhat absurd. That which changes must be either sensible, like a blossom, or if not sensible at least existent, like a memory or a desire. But universals and their relations are neither existent nor sensible, and hence are beyond the reach of change. 'The knowledge at which geometry aims,' says Plato, 'is knowledge of the eternal, not of anything perishing and transient';[3] and if the mind succeeds in penetrating through the curtain of sense, 'it passes into another world, the region of that which is pure and everlasting, immortal and unchangeable; and feeling itself akin to this, it dwells there under its own control and has rest from its wandering, and being in communion with the unchanging, is itself unchanging.'[4] Plato's world is a little like that of modern physics, in which the sensible appearances of things are all ephemeral, while the enduring realities are those elements and laws behind the scenes which can only be described in equations. How exactly are the things we are and feel related to the invisible structures behind them? To that question Plato never succeeded in giving a satisfactory answer; nor, it is to be feared, has the physicist either.

We have now seen what form as law meant to the Greek thinkers. In laying hold of it, one apprehended a connection of concepts that

[1] W. G. DeBurgh in *The Legacy of Greece*, 154.
[2] R. L. Nettleship in *Hellenica*, 147.
[3] *Republic*, VII, 527.
[4] *Phaedo*, 79; cf. *Philebus*, 59.

was certain, fresh, non-sensible, universal, objective, unalterable. Yet from time to time the possibility of a still more desirable knowledge presented itself to the Greek mind.

15. (4) *Form as system.* Plato felt compelled to admit that the mathematical sort of reason was not enough in itself to give us the highest kind of insight. It raised questions that it could not answer. First, if you are to carry on a chain of mathematical reasoning, you must start somewhere; your chain must be attached to some sort of peg. For geometry the peg consists of its axioms and postulates. But why are these to be accepted? Plato would not be satisfied with the account of the many present-day mathematicians who hold them to be conventions merely, nor would he trust an account of them as self-evident; if this was the best that mathematics could do with them, he would say that it was less than an ideal science after all. In a fully rational system, there would be nothing arbitrary, nothing isolated. Everything would not only entail other things, but be entailed by them, so that all the parts, as in a perfect organism, would give each other support. Secondly, geometers, as we have seen, are curiously dependent on sensible things, such as figures drawn on boards, to keep their thoughts under control. Perhaps these are not strictly necessary. In any case, in a really ideal science, no such crutches would be required. Thought would move exclusively among concepts and their relations. Finally, each of the sciences, as now practised, tends to be pursued in independence of the others. Each arrives at principles of great importance and stops there. But these principles, at least on the surface, may conflict with each other. Physics as taught by Democritus, concludes that all things are controlled mechanically; ethics as taught by Socrates, insists that human beings behave responsibly and purposefully. How are these views to be reconciled? There must be, so to speak, a science of the sciences, more resolute and more rational than any of them, to carry through to unity the work they do severally. Plato never developed in any detail the character of this science, and probably felt unable to do so. But he thought it both possible and necessary. For in discussing the famous divided line in the sixth book of the *Republic*, instead of halting at the third segment with διάνοια, the mathematical kind of insight, he went on to a fourth segment in which he placed νοῦς, conceived as a still higher kind of insight.

What was this like? As so often when he did not see quite clearly, Plato fell back on myth, and this myth we shall not try to interpret. But we may gain some clue to his meaning if we ask how he

c

conceived the stuff of which the impalpable frame of things is made. It was made, he tells us, of 'ideas' and their relations, which are apprehended only by intelligence. Now these are not material things. Two material balls may be equal in size, but roundness and equality are not material; they are neither sensible nor confined to any position in space or time. What sort of being do they have? Plato seems to have thought they had, apart from us, the same sort of being they have when we think them, namely experienced being, which must mean being in another mind. An 'idea' or concept was an object, to be sure; when you thought of justice, you were not thinking of your own thought of justice. At the same time, this abstract justice must itself be such stuff as thought is made of. The framework of the world was not a dead system of logic or geometry. It was alive. 'O heavens,' exclaims the wise Stranger in the *Sophist*, 'can we ever be made to believe that motion and life and soul and mind are not present with perfect being? Can we imagine that being is devoid of life and mind, and exists in awful unmeaningness an everlasting fixture?'[1] 'Wherefore, using the language of probability, we may say that the world became a living creature truly endowed with soul and intelligence by the providence of God.'[2] In following the conceptual framework of things, intelligence was answering to intelligence, the reason of the creature greeted the immanent reason of the creator.

Now reason in its highest sense was that which must be exercised by the architect of nature; or if the inference to such a mind were thought an unwarranted leap, it was the reason which *would* be exercised by such a mind if it existed, and which in any case marks the end toward which our own minds are striving. Such an understanding would see all things as connected necessarily. Indeed our present reason could do that if only it had energy enough; Socrates makes the astonishing suggestion that, 'as all nature is akin, and the soul has learned all things, there is no difficulty in her eliciting, or as men say learning, out of a single recollection all the rest, if a man is strenuous and does not faint'.[3] We are condemned, through feebleness of attention to see things fragmentarily, plodding along step by step from premise to conclusion. But sometimes within a fragment, when we are quite familiar with it, we have a glimpse of a better way of thinking. The man who knows his subject never thinks in syllogisms. The minor, with the help of the middle, is seen at once in

[1] *Sophist* (Jowett), 249.
[2] *Timaeus* (Jowett), 30.
[3] *Meno* (Jowett), 81.

the light of the major, as when a friend is recognized. Such recognition is very different from first seeing an unknown man and then concluding, on the ground of some identifying mark, that your friend he must be. When recognition is instant, the figure before you looks different from what it would otherwise because seen *as* your friend. Similarly a mind that saw things whole would see them differently because, instead of moving its attention slowly from part to isolated part, it would see each in the light of its relations to the other. And since its relations connect it with everything else in the world, one would then be apprehending its place in the inclusive system of things. What Plato was reaching for in his ultimate idea of reason as νοῦς or νόησις was an understanding that grasped things as a timelessly complete and necessary system in which everything was made intelligible through the part it played in the whole.

16. Such knowledge seems to be purely theoretical, with no bearing on practical life. But that was not how the Greeks conceived it. To be sure, Plato and Aristotle were intellectualists in the sense that they thought the best and happiest life, for anyone endowed for it, was the life of contemplation. This was the life that Plato's philosopher kings would lead when they were released from the tasks of office. It was the life that Aristotle held as the ideal for those happy few who were able to live in the rarefied air of theoretical reason; and in one of the few passages in which that sober mind ever lets itself go, he argues that this is the only activity that we can appropriately ascribe to God. In the activity of reflection, and there alone, the lumbering awkwardness of the body is left behind, satisfaction may follow at once upon desire, and thought can move at will into the remote past, the far future, or the space between the stars, indeed can become 'the spectator of all time and all existence'. No doubt there was a touch of autobiography in these encomiums on the life of thought by two of its greatest exponents.

But there was certainly more than that. Both believed that philosophical discipline was essential to the best character. Just as the study of logic, for all the criticisms of it, does make a difference in the practice of reasoning through clarifying one's ideas of what precise and cogent reasoning is, and thus making one more ready to detect defections into fallacy, so a clear vision of what rightness in conduct means sharpens one's vision also for what would violate it. Plato and Aristotle would have scoffed at the self-depreciation of some recent teachers of moral philosophy who have held that their study could not be expected to make any difference in practical life.

They would have held emphatically that it does make a difference, and indeed that any other sort of philosophy, responsibly pursued, does so too. Scrupulousness about truth does not easily go with unscrupulousness about people's rights, or the suppression of prejudice in thinking with its indulgence in behaviour, or the habit of looking to implications in thought with that of unreflective impulsiveness in conduct. Reason, even if taken as no more than a disciplined power of reasoning, may lift the whole level of moral life.

But besides theoretic reason, which thus influenced conduct indirectly, Plato and Aristotle recognized a practical reason whose influence was more direct and permeating. It appears in the list of virtues under the name of wisdom. In Plato's familiar image, it is the charioteer, keeping a firm and equal rein upon the black horse and the white, the appetites and the passions. How exactly the practical reason was to judge when passion was getting out of hand or appetite becoming gross, we are never told. But the two philosophers agree as to the court of appeal. Form as end is to prescribe form as law or rule. On the active side, man is a bundle of impulses which may be dealt with in various ways. They may be given their head, as they were by Plato's democratic man, and life will then dissipate itself in schizophrenia and anarchy; or one impulse may be given its head at the expense of the others, as it is by the glutton and the alcoholic; or they may be developed in harmony in the interest of the man as a whole. Wisdom would choose the last of these. Its course will allow for differing emphases with differing needs and talents; Milo the wrestler will indulge more in exercise than in dialectics; Aristotle will do the reverse. But what gives the rule is the same in both. It is the appropriate form of life for the individual human being.

How was this form to be discovered? By studying one's powers experimentally? Partly, yes. That was needed to tell us what capital we have. But it would never tell us what to do with it. That was the business of wisdom or practical reason. How did it proceed? Plato in the *Republic* and Aristotle in the *Ethics* both tried to suggest an answer. It amounted to this, that just as a sculptor at work on a statue knows, though perhaps dimly, the ideal figure he wants to embody, and knows that in the light of it a larger nose or an extended arm would be unfitting, so men generally, who are the sculptors of their fate, know dimly the form of life that in the end will satisfy them, and see that cowardice, untruthfulness, unfaithfulness, do not fit into the pattern. The perception of the form of life most appropriate to one's powers and the perception of what that form requires and rejects in the way of action are thus both matters for practical reason. 'To Plato the laws of proportion, which are the condition of beauty in art, seemed to betoken the presence of the same mind as is revealed in the immutable order of the universe, and more imperfectly in the moral order of human life.'[1] Aristotle put it most simply—'nothing in excess'. In the mind of the Greek, the three values traditionally recognized in the west, truth, beauty and goodness, were far less sharply separated than among ourselves. Aristotle's ethics has often been described as aestheticism, since the beauty of a life was the test of its goodness; indeed, to describe the good man he had a single compound word, καλοκαγαθος, fair *and* good. And Plato held the somewhat mystical view that if we were ever to achieve the final truth about things, we should have to see them under the form of the good. Thus reason for him was far more than a power of framing or following an argument. It was that in us upon which we must call if we would form an adequate notion of the ends of our life, or plan that life competently. Whether we know it or not, every life was lived on a scale at whose top lay perfect knowledge, goodness, and beauty, and which would record full achievement in any of these things only if it could record it simultaneously in all.

17. We have now before us fairly fully the idea of reason developed by Greek thought. It has been stated at some length not only because it is one of the dominant ideas in western culture, but also because it contains all the major elements that later philosophers have found in reason. Whitehead has remarked that western thought is a series of footnotes to Plato. To be sure, none of the great rationalists have accepted the Greek idea of reason entirely. Yet, directly or indirectly, their rationalism has in every case stemmed from it. The philosophy of the Stoics, which urged that the good life lay in conformity to the reason immanent in nature, came almost straight from Plato, as did the neo-Platonism of Plotinus. It is Greek rationalism again, this time in its Aristotelian form, that was taken over by Thomas Aquinas and used as the instrument for systematizing Christian belief. Aristotle's account of reasoning was almost as canonical as Scripture in the Middle Ages, and remained so till the sixteenth century. Even in such notably original thinkers as Descartes, Spinoza, and Leibniz, it is surprising to find how much is an expansion or refinement of what Plato had suggested some two thousand years earlier.

18. With Descartes, however, we come to another major interpreter of reason. Jacques Maritain writes of him: 'The figure of Descartes

[1] R. L. Nettleship in *Hellenica*, 110.

dominates all philosophy of the past three centuries; his historical significance is inexhaustible', but it is easy to understand why M. Maritain should add that 'Descartes has been the great French sin in modern history'.[1] For Descartes occupied in the intellectual reformation a place similar to Luther's and Calvin's in the religious reformation, and though he remained a loyal Catholic all his life, the Church did not fail to see the actual tendency of his thinking and to place his works on the Index. For a thousand years reason had been the handmaiden of faith. Descartes made it autonomous.

Reason, he held, was a 'natural light' with which all normal men were born. It was our one source of clear and distinct, and therefore certain, knowledge. We often suppose that our most certain knowledge of the world is gained from the senses. Descartes admitted that sense knowledge could be clear, if that meant immediate and vivid, but denied that it was distinct. We may clearly perceive grass to be green and a pain to be in one of our fingers, but there is no good reason to think the grass is really green, or that the pain is actually in our hand; Descartes cited the case of a girl in hospital whose hand had been amputated without her knowledge, and who continued to complain of the pain 'in her hand'. Such appearances depend on conditions of which we are largely ignorant, and they change or vanish when these conditions change. But knowledge that is distinct is absolute. By means of it we grasp what things are in themselves with no distorting conditions; and such knowledge is timelessly true. The best examples of it Descartes found in mathematics, of which he was a master. Our sense knowledge of a ball of wax is deceptive, and even if true, may cease to be true at the next instant, whereas what the geometer has to say about the properties of a ball is certainly and changelessly true.

Descartes did not believe that such knowledge was confined to mathematics; he was convinced that the mathematician's great advantage lay in his method, and that if this method were analysed and clearly understood, it could be applied in every province of thought. He therefore set himself to find why it was that mathematical method was so superior. Its superiority lay in (1) the terms it dealt with, (2) the relations between those terms, (3) the order in which its assertions were set out.

19. (1) Mathematical thought deals ultimately with 'simple natures', or, as we should now say, with abstractions of such great simplicity that there is no vagueness or ambiguity about them. 'Three', 'a line',

---

[1] *The Dream of Descartes*, vii, 150.

'extension', 'triangularity' give us definite ideas which it would be impossible to confuse with any others, even though we found it hard or impossible to analyse them. The simplicity of an idea did not mean that it was obvious and easy to grasp; complex ideas like 'animal' or 'plant' may be much more familiar; and it requires determined self-training, Descartes pointed out, to enable us to tell when we have really reached the simple. And he insisted that what he meant was the conceptually simple, not the easily imaginable. When we think of triangles we may help ourselves by imagining one, but this image is not our concept, for the image must have some particular shape, while the concept is of *any* plane figure with three straight sides. The ultimate elements of understanding are always concepts, never sensations or images. And if they are simple concepts, vision goes clear through them and possesses them wholly; nothing is left in them that is obscure and unilluminated.

(2) How are they related? Seemingly in the most hit-or-miss fashion, but really, Descartes said, by logical necessity. In ordinary experience the properties of things are lumped together because of repeated association or mere convenience; we think of snow as cold and white, not because it *must* have these qualities, but because it always has had them; and we think of table-top and legs as going together because, so grouped, they serve our purposes. But such mere togetherness does not give *understanding*. If we ask *why* snow should be cold, we see at once that we do not understand in the slightest. On the other hand, if we ask why two parallel lines do not enclose a space, we can see the reason why with all possible clearness. Being parallel makes the enclosure of space impossible; the one character *necessarily* excludes the other; if we do not see this, we have merely not understood, and if we do, we see it with a plainness of vision that makes any further 'why?' superfluous.

Now the relations of mathematics are of this latter sort. They are grasped, Descartes said, either by intuition or by deduction, though these turn out to be essentially the same kind of process. Intuition is the insight that two properties are necessarily connected. Deduction is the insight that two or more propositions are necessarily connected. If the geometer is asked why the angles of a triangle sum up to a straight line, he starts a little farther back, with a line drawn through the apex parallel to the base, and shows by a series of steps that the proposition to be explained follows necessarily. This is what understanding it means. Deduction is merely intuition serially applied.

(3) Such a chain of propositions must obviously have a start. Ordinarily we start from any proposition that we are willing to

accept as true; if this proposition itself is questioned, we shall have to begin still farther back. Where is the ultimate starting-point? Here we see the third advantage of the mathematical method: it distinguishes between those propositions that can be proved and those genuinely ultimate ones that must be accepted in their own right; and starting with these ultimates, it deduces the others in orderly sequence. Descartes had no doubt that the first principles of geometry, its axioms and postulates, could be established by sheer self-evidence.

Now if reason is to achieve the success in other fields that it had achieved in this favoured one, it must proceed in the same way. It must build with the same sort of bricks, namely distinct and simple concepts; it must put them together with the same mortar, and refuse to be satisfied with any connection that is less than necessary and self-evidencing; and it must build from foundations in the same order, going from the logically prior to the logically posterior. Could this be done? Descartes anticipated two kinds of difficulty, one coming from the refractoriness of our own minds, the other from the recalcitrance to reason of nature itself.

20. The difficulties of holding our mind to the path of reason were difficulties of character rather than ability, and could be overcome, Descartes thought, by discipline. He held the curiously democratic doctrine that all men were endowed with an equal measure of the 'natural light of reason'. But they differed greatly in their impulsiveness, their emotionality, the vividness of their imagination, the strength of their will, and, above all perhaps, in their education. In Descartes's own nature there was a good deal of iron, and before he began the application of his method of philosophy, he imposed on himself a long and rigorous discipline in which, for the freshest hours of each day, he devoted himself to intense reflection. Reason, he thought, never errs. If it seems to, this is because non-rational influences break in upon it and divert its course. The strategy of the rational man is to anticipate these and inhibit them. Most men are too restless and impatient to give their intellects a fair chance. In their impulsiveness they would rather act on a belief that is obscure and uncertain than wait for a clear one; this precipitancy, which is really weakness of will, is the major source of error. Its cure is intellectual, and lies in that firm control of the attention which insists on winning through to clarity before surrendering to the impulse to act.

21. The other and outward source of difficulty was even more formidable. Was nature really reducible to that rational system in terms of which Descartes hoped to construe it? At two of the three points we have mentioned he encountered obstacles that, with all his patience and acuteness, he never succeeded in surmounting. For one thing, he could not wholly resolve particular things into concepts. In an apple, for example, the sense-datum of red did not seem to be a concept, and he did not know what to do with it; like Plato, he had no satisfactory place in his system for sensible things. Again, the roundness that he talked of was not the actual shape of the apple; he admitted that we probably never see anything perfectly round in the geometer's sense; and he had to fall back on the view that round-ness was an innate idea, supplied from the resources of our own mind. Secondly, try as he would, he could find no necessary con-nection between some of his 'simple natures' and others. The mass of a physical thing seemed to have nothing to do with its size, and its size could vary indefinitely while its shape remained the same. Only in respect to its third feature was he sure that he had applied his system successfully. At least he had found an absolutely firm capstan to which he could attach his chain of deductions. His own thought existed. That was a statement about the existent which was guaran-teed completely, both by its self-evidence and by the incoherence of doubting it; you cannot doubt that you doubt without doing the doubting you are doubting about. From this base he moved cautiously on to the existence of other things and other selves. Unhappily every step of that cautious advance has now been questioned, and even the famous *cogito* with which he started is no longer accepted as he interpreted it. Descartes never realized his dream.

He failed, but it was one of the most splendid failures of intellectual history. His dream, like that of Pythagoras, mankind has been unwilling to let die. His central conviction remains that of every rationalist still. Reason is a natural light by whose aid we can discern lines of structure running, like the veins in a leaf, through the frag-ment of nature which is open to us. These lines run out and away into the world beyond, and are continuous with that web of relations on which that world appears to be woven. And because these lines are necessary, they are intelligible. The end of reason would be reached only when they were so extended as to include all things in their meshes.

22. Within a few years of Descartes's death his enterprise was renewed by Spinoza, who began by steeping himself in the works of the master. Like Descartes, he was an enthusiast for mathematics, and two of his books were modelled on Euclid's *Elements*, with the definitions and axioms set out at the beginning and the theorems deduced with an appearance of rigour. But the enterprise of reason, as conceived and conducted by Spinoza, was in some respects new. He was governed by different motives. His chief work was on ethics, on which Descartes never wrote at all; and in the famous opening sentence of his treatise on the improvement of the understanding, he says that the purpose of his philosophizing was to find some unchangeable good which would make enduring happiness possible. Again, no one can read the fifth book of the *Ethics* without feeling in it a groundswell of mystical exaltation; like Sir Thomas Browne, Spinoza loved to pursue his reason to an *O Altitudo*! His motives were mixed, as those of Descartes were not, for reason with him was an instrument of moral and religious promptings. But one of the things that have made him so compelling a figure is that in spite of this complexity of motive, he seems never to have allowed his thought to be diverted from its own course by a hair's breadth under the pressure of desire or feeling. To reach his ethical end he had to go a long way round. For in order to know what was good for man, he had to know what man was like, and what his true place was in the order of nature; in order to know this he had to elaborate, at least in outline, a system of philosophy. But 'the only instrument which he allowed himself, or thought necessary to his purpose, was his own power of logical reasoning; at no point does he appeal to authority or revelation or common consent; nor does he anywhere rely on literary artifice or try to reinforce rational argument by indirect appeals to emotion'.[1] Here he had a courage that Descartes lacked. When Descartes's thinking brought him to a point where a challenge to religious or moral authority seemed inevitable, as it did on revelation and the freedom of the will, he drew timorously back. Spinoza went straight on, abandoning both traditional theism and traditional freedom because his logic required it. The result was that for a century after his death, he was almost unknown, and mentioned only to be reviled. He now holds an assured eminence not only as a metaphysician but also as a 'saint of rationalism'.

23. He is the most thoroughgoing rationalist in the history of ethics. For his reflection on the end of human endeavour led him to the conclusion that this was knowledge itself, in the form of rational understanding. This conclusion he regarded as forced on him by a consideration of man's nature. A human being was an organism with

[1] S. Hampshire, *Spinoza*, 11.

a bodily and mental side, animated by a drive or *conatus* to maintain and expand itself. Contemplating this on its mental side only, we may ask *what* it is that this drive is seeking to maintain and expand. Spinoza assumes that the mind at any moment is a set of awarenesses or ideas. These ideas, as they actually appear, are a miscellaneous and ill-organized lot, in which perceptions stimulated by our surroundings are mixed with memories, images, casual associations, and idle conjectures. The *conatus* is this mass in motion, so to speak; it is our mind of the moment considered as in process of evolving toward its natural end. Now the natural end of imperfect ideas is to become more adequate ideas, and ultimately to become ideas that are adequate wholly; and such perfect adequacy would be reached only with perfect understanding. Reason, for Spinoza, was thus the very essence of mind; a mind was a mind in the degree to which this immanent end was realized. For Descartes, reason tended to be an all-or-nothing process, in which you saw something with mathematical distinctness or simply failed to see. For Spinoza thought was continually rising or falling in the rational scale, and there were infinite possible degrees of success and failure.

24. He made several attempts to describe the chief levels of advance. In his *Tractatus* on improving the understanding he mentioned four; in the later and more mature *Ethics* he named the following three. All were ways of grasping connections, for knowledge is an apprehension of what is true or false, and only such assertions as that A is B are capable of truth or falsity. In the first or lowest kind of knowledge, the connections we grasp are merely contingent, in the sense that, for all we can see, they might have been otherwise. The connections of words with the things they mean are of this kind. The Romans, on seeing a certain thing, would say *pomum* where we should say 'apple'; and the one name is no more right than the other, since both are arbitrary. The soldier, looking at a horse, thinks of warfare; the farmer, looking at the same horse, thinks of his plough; neither in the true sense is thinking at all, but following lines of association.[1] Most of our ordinary thought is of this loose kind. As we go about our house or about the streets, we are engaged constantly in recognizing persons and things; but between the persons and their names, between the sense-data and the concepts we attach to them, there seems to be nothing but an association so fixed that we take it for granted and do not realize that thinking, even of the lowest grade, is involved. It is, to be sure, a kind of thinking, though

[1] *Ethics*, Pt. II, Prop. 18, Scholium.

mere conjunction, however inveterate, is not necessity. So far, we are creatures of habit without true understanding, and hence with no dependable means of avoiding error. We think in terms of the unanalysed wholes that present themselves to our senses; we vaguely associate night air with malaria, broken mirrors with bad luck, Frenchmen with frivolity. We are a little like Polonius, to whom Hamlet suggested that yonder cloud was very like a camel. 'By the mass, and 'tis like a camel, indeed.' 'Methinks it is like a weasel.' 'It *is* backed like a weasel.' 'Or like a whale?' 'Very like a whale.' Nature finds us gullible, and has her own sport with us.

25. The man of scientific mind makes a partial escape from this level into a second kind of knowledge. He does so by dissecting out the threads of necessity that connect the unanalysed wholes of common sense. It is not the night air that causes the malaria, but something often associated with that, the virus carried by a kind of mosquito which is hard to guard against at night; and between broken mirrors and bad luck, Frenchmen and frivolity, there is no fixed link at all. Spinoza is obviously right that this scientific insight is on a higher level than that of common sense. But the name he gave it, 'ratio', suggests a very deep difference between him and present-day philosophers of science. He thought that when he grasped a causal law, he was grasping a connection that was necessary and therefore intelligible, that a physician who isolated the cause of malaria was understanding the disease in the sense in which the mathematician understands why the angles of a triangle have 180 degrees. Ground and consequent, cause and effect—two relations that for the modern scientist differ in kind—were for Spinoza merely differing aspects of the same relation. The most general laws of physics seemed to him as truly self-evident as the axioms of geometry.

26. Suppose one reached the level of insight of the geometer or the philosophical physicist; was this the end of the road, or was there a still higher plateau of insight? For Descartes such a suggestion would have been meaningless, since in mathematics we had the perfect embodiment of reason. It was not meaningless for Spinoza, great as his admiration was for mathematical reasoning. There seem to have been two grounds for his desire to go beyond such reasoning. In the first place, it always proceeded step by step; it could not, at the beginning, see where it was going to come out, and when it reached the end, the beginning had usually dropped out of mind. A knowledge in which the whole succession was grasped as immediately as its various steps would obviously be better than this inch-worm progression. Secondly, mathematical thinking is too abstract. It purchases its sharp clearness by isolating certain characters and studying them alone, without reference to the mass of other characters that go to the making of a concrete thing. An understanding that was complete would disregard none of these characters. It would place each of them in its own context of necessary relations. What we call a concrete thing would then be seen as a focal point for innumerable lines of necessity converging upon it from the universe as a whole. Such a knowledge, still scientific in the sense that it grasped the connections between abstract characters, would be intuitive in the sense that all the characters of the concrete world and their relations would be seen in one vast vision. This vision, which is to be gained only at the summit of the intellectual ascent, Spinoza called *scientia intuitiva*. We cannot know fully what it would be like until we have it. But in some moments of present experience we have a vague adumbration of it. We know what it means for knowledge acquired analytically, step by step, to pass over into immediacy; for we know how the study in detail of a work of art can bring us back to the whole with a richer response, in which the details keep their subordinate place and yet each contributes to the appreciation of the whole.

27. Spinoza believed that when reason attained this consummation, human knowledge would have fused itself with God's, and man have risen into unity with the divine. He spoke of *Deus sive Natura*, as if the terms were interchangeable; God *was* the universe considered as a single system, at once fully comprehensive and fully comprehensible; and from one point of view the *conatus* was the divine element in man seeking to throw off its fragmentariness and identify itself with what alone was wholly true and real. 'Philosophy in fact, in its highest form, is to Spinoza at the same time and essentially the noblest form of human life: the life of religion.'[1]

It was not possible, in his view, to live religiously in this sense without also living morally. Morals too were a matter of intelligence. To live well was to live reasonably. When people go wrong, it is because, usually under the influence of emotion, they misconceive their own good and that of others. Distorting emotion must therefore be brought under control. The best way to conquer such emotions as malice, hatred, and envy is to understand them—to see how they arise and to realize that the people against whom they are directed are only doing what, given their natures, they could not have avoided

[1] H. H. Joachim, *A Study of the Ethics of Spinoza*, 181.

doing. Spinoza sees that in a fully necessitated world there can be no undetermined choices. But on this matter he finds much confusion in the popular mind. There is no conflict between freedom and necessity if the necessitation is by reason. It is true that people commonly feel free when they follow their impulses. But that is what animals do, who have no freedom at all; if impulses are completely determined, as in fact they are, so is the person who is a prey to them. To be free is to be self determined, that is, determined by one's real self. And one's self is real just so far as it is rational. This rational self, to be sure, is governed in its thought and choice by rational law, but there is no bondage in that; for so to be determined is the very meaning of freedom. The geometer whose mind is carried by logical necessity along the line of his deductions is determined to think in this fashion, but it would be absurd to complain that he is not free, for to think in this way is precisely what he wants. Growth in rationality means being increasingly laid under constraint by rational law. But surrender to such necessity is the open secret of freedom. Spinoza adds that it is also the secret of happiness. For happiness is bound up with the 'awareness of heightened vitality', and this in turn is the by-product of the ordering and widening of the mind.

28. Reason was thus central in the philosophy of Spinoza, central in his psychology and ethics, his theory of knowledge and metaphysics. In the thought of his great successor in the rationalist tradition, Leibniz, it had a less conspicuous place. For Spinoza the world was a single intelligible substance; for Leibniz it was an infinite assembly of different substances between which, unless God were counted as one of them, no influences were exchanged. Each of these substances, or monads, had a career of its own, in which the striving to rise from confused to clear thought was similar to the *conatus* of Spinoza. But what interests the student of reason is not so much Leibniz's metaphysic, which is one of the most bizarre of philosophical systems, as his idea of rational or necessary insight. He focused upon this idea the powers of a logician of the first order. His conclusion was that rational or necessary insights were of two very different kinds. On the one hand were necessities proper, 'eternal truths' which are valid for all possible worlds; on the other, contingent necessities, of which we may be certain while still seeing that they might have been other than they are.

Of eternal truths we have examples in the propositions of logic and mathematics. We can see that these *could* not be other than true, and hence must hold everywhere and always. Now the most striking thing about these truths, apart from their necessity, is that they are analytic. In a sense, Leibniz remarks, they say nothing, but only 'repeat the same thing'; the predicate merely sets out what has already been thought in the subject.[1] '4 = 3 + 1' is really nothing but a definition of '4'. 'The foundation of mathematics is the principle of contradiction or identity . . . and this principle suffices alone for the demonstration of the whole of arithmetic and geometry.'[2] Since the predicate is part of what is meant by the subject, to deny it of that subject would be self-contradiction. But how is the principle itself guaranteed that we ought not to contradict ourselves? Hardly by the contradiction involved in denying it, since the question is why that should be avoided. This principle is not itself to be established by a further appeal to identity or contradiction (Leibniz takes these two principles as one) but by an ultimate intuition; and if such an intuition is possible in one case, it may be in others. The fact is that Leibniz's attempt to show that all his eternal truths were statements of identity broke down.[3] We shall have to return to the matter later when we consider the attitude towards necessary statements of the logical positivists, of whom on this point Leibniz was the precursor. What made him a rationalist, whereas his positivist successors were not, was just that he held the statements of logic and mathematics to be statements about the real world, and secondly, that he held that all true statements about the real world would, if we saw far enough, also turn out to be necessary.

29. This last is, on the face of it, an astonishing view. Could Leibniz really say that 'grass is green' states a necessary truth, or that 'Caesar was stabbed by Brutus' asserts something that followed inevitably from Caesar's nature? However astonishing, Leibniz did hold just that. In a famous passage that scandalized his friend Arnauld, he wrote that 'every true predication has its foundation in the nature of things', and that necessity underlay the most seemingly casual of linkages.

'The subject term always includes the predicate term in such manner that anyone who grasped fully the idea of the subject would judge also that the predicate belonged to it. . . . God, seeing the individual notion or haecceity of Alexander, sees in it at the same

---

[1] *Nouveaux Essais*, iv, ii, 1; *Philosophische Schriften* (Gerhardt), V, 343, where assorted examples are given.

[2] Second letter to Clarke, Gerhardt, *ibid.*, VII, 355.

[3] For the argument, see Arthur Pap, *Semantics and Necessary Truth*, Ch. 1.

time the foundation and reason of all the predicates that can be truly asserted of him, as for example that he would conquer Darius and Porus, even to seeing there a priori (and not by experience) whether his death would be natural or by poison, which we could know only by history.'[1]

Here was a rationalism so extreme as to deny that there were in the end any true statements at all that were merely empirical, except assertions that something existed. Did this mean that if we know enough, we should see that everything that was true at all was an eternal and mathematically necessary truth? At first reading, the passage just cited seems to be saying this. But it was apparently not quite what Leibniz intended.

30. Here we come to his second kind of necessary truth. What guaranteed truths of this kind was not the law of contradiction, but 'a great principle, not much employed', the law of sufficient reason. This is roughly the principle that nothing happens for which a person who saw deeply enough could not also see *why* it happens. The principle can be interpreted in more than one way. Bertrand Russell has pointed out that Leibniz had two philosophies, one that he really believed, the other a sugar-coated version of the first that he offered for public consumption.[2] One suspects that in his private thought the law of sufficient reason was an expression of a genuine speculative faith, the statement of a postulate on which his thinking actually proceeded. He was trying to understand the structure of the world, and this law supplied his working assumption, namely that the world was understandable. But in the popular version of his philosophy, the account was very different. To say that the necessity of Alexander's dying a natural death was based on the law of sufficient reason was to say that this death was a necessary means to a divine end. How did he come by this notion?

One source of the notion is to be found in an insight in which Leibniz differed sharply from Spinoza. We have seen that to Spinoza the main principles of physics—the laws of motion, for example— seemed self-evident truths. Leibniz realized that they were not. There was nothing inconceivable in a ball's not continuing to roll in a straight line, but indulging in capricious hops, skips and jumps. We may well be grateful that it does not, for conformity to the laws of motion makes its behaviour in that degree predictable. Both

---

[1] *Discours de Metaphysique*, Sec. 8 (Gerhardt, iv, 433).
[2] *History of Western Philosophy*, 604, 613.

REASON IN WESTERN THOUGHT

nature and human nature seem to be governed throughout by laws that render their course inevitable and in theory calculable. But it is idle to argue that because, if these laws do hold, the course of nature is inevitable, the laws themselves are inevitable, in the sense that they could not be otherwise. And if they could be otherwise, how is one to explain their being what they are? One cannot explain a law, as one can an event, by tracing it back to a prior event, and that again to a still earlier event; for a law is not an event in a series, but the principle governing the series. If this principle was neither self-evident nor deducible from what was self-evident, Leibniz could conceive no explanation for it but divine creation. He said, accordingly, that the laws of nature were decreed by Deity.

But this led, as it always does, to the ancient and intractable problem of evil. For the laws of nature make inevitable a prodigious amount of suffering, privation, and frustrated desire; and was all this evil to be laid to the account of God himself? Was there any way of saving belief in his goodness while retaining the necessity of evil? Only, replied Leibniz, if creation were regarded as a choice between alternative possible worlds. And such alternatives were really possible if natural law had no logical necessity. Why, then, did God choose the set of laws that actually prevail? If he is good, the reason must be that, foreseeing the series of events entailed respectively by the alternative sets of laws, he chose that which entailed least evil. Having decreed the laws, God himself was bound to what logically followed from them, for even Deity cannot do what is logically impossible. God thus by implication created evil, but only such evil as was unavoidably incident to the best of *possible* worlds.

31. We can now see what Leibniz meant by his second kind of 'truths of reason', his contingently necessary truths. They were truths that followed logically from laws adopted teleologically. The ultimate laws of nature were decreed by God as means to his end; they could have been otherwise, but they were decreed for the sufficient reason that without them the world would have been worse than it was. But once they are in force, the course of things is logically necessary. Given the collocation of qualities and relations that forms the nature of Alexander, and the laws that govern these, all that he does and even suffers will, to a Divine intelligence, be not only foreseeable but deducible. Thus the rationalism of Leibniz, though far-reaching, was more qualified than that of his predecessor. Spinoza held in straight-forward fashion that everything in the universe was logically necessary and intelligible. Leibniz held that logic and mathematics were thus intelligible, but little or nothing else. The rest of the world was intelligible as necessitated by laws which were not themselves thus intelligible, but chosen on the non-logical ground of being means to the greatest good. Rationalism had begun to beat a retreat.

32. The retreat went much farther in the philosophy of Kant. What is remarkable about the great *Critique* is the combination of minute and elaborate analysis of reason with ultimate scepticism as to what it can tell us of the world. Let us take the latter point first.

Kant was as firmly convinced as either Leibniz or Spinoza that reason gives universal and necessary knowledge. He had no doubt that when man reaches the moon, or goes further afield, he will find that seven and five make twelve exactly as they did at home. And this certainty as to what will hold everywhere and always cannot have been derived from sense experience, no matter how long continued, for such experience can yield probability only. How then account for the extraordinary fact that we can anticipate at least the pattern of what nature will offer us, and do so with complete certainty? Kant thought there was only one satisfactory answer: we can be certain of this pattern because we supply it ourselves. We know that we should find seven and five making twelve in Arcturus and the Pleiades because we know that if we went there, we should take our reason with us; and our reason is an ordering faculty that imposes its own structure or design upon any material of sense that may be given to it. This was Kant's 'Copernican revolution'. Assume that knowledge is an adjustment of our ideas to the world, and our possession of universal truth is an inexplicable anomaly. Assume that nature adjusts itself to our reason, and the explanation is plain. Man creates nature.

Still, to put it in this unqualified way will hardly do. It is true that our reason fashions the framework of nature; and Kant held, following Berkeley, that even the qualities of things, the reds and sweets and hots, were contributions of our own. But it is not our own doing that the sensations of these qualities should arise in us. That is the work of some independent agency. Can we know what this is like? Here Kant held that reason was helpless. This something, this thing in itself, was utterly beyond our grasp. All we could know of it was that it pressed the button, so to speak, that set the machinery of our mind in motion. It so acted upon us as to arouse sensations; these sensations were arranged by our reason in its own manifold patterns; but behind the curtain of patterned qualities we could not hope to penetrate.

Thus reason for Kant was both more and less than it had been for his rationalist predecessors. It was more, because it was now the artificer of nature as well as its contemplator. It was less, because it paid for its creative power the price of total ignorance of things as they were in themselves.

33. Granting, however, that reason is confined in its operations to the sphere of appearances or 'phenomena', it is still all-important for the world we actually live in, and philosophers should know what its operations are. Kant used reason (*Vernunft*) in different senses, depending on the faculty with which he wanted to contrast it. When he opposed it to sense knowledge or intuition (*Anschauung*), he meant by it 'the faculty which supplies the principles of a priori knowledge'.[1] Reason was what apprehended form as distinct from matter; it covered the whole hierarchy of functions considered in the first *Critique*. When he wished to contrast it, within that hierarchy, to the understanding (*Verstand*) he meant this same ordering faculty working at its highest level and seeking to bring the products of the lower levels into the most comprehensive wholes. It is the first and wider of these senses that is important for us. Kant recognized three levels on which reason in this sense may supply us a priori knowledge. We shall recall only the main points.

34. The lowest level of such knowledge, that which is closest to sense, he called 'pure intuition' (*reine Anschauung*). The forms that it deals with are space and time. Neither of these is really sensed; we do not see or hear or feel such relations as above and below, before and after; they are not sense data, but orders in which sense data are arranged. Neither are they concepts or general ideas like whiteness or weight, which denote a range of particular instances; for space and time are continuous wholes. We never experience sensations except in their context, and we can see that it would be impossible to do so, since they supply the structures in which alone sense data could appear. It is because we can know these structures independently of their content that we can anticipate what our future spatial and temporal experience will be like. Kant was convinced that Euclidean geometry supplied us knowledge that was not only necessary, in the sense that it could not be otherwise, but also factual, in the sense that it informed us about the actual space of nature. Both these contentions, as we shall see in the next chapter, have been severely treated in recent times. Kant did not fail to see the

[1] *Critique of Pure Reason*, Introduction, Sec. 7.

distinction between pure and applied geometry, but he thought that at any rate pure geometry did apply, in the sense that our actual figures would be found to obey Euclid's reasonings in the degree to which they approached the ideal figures he described. Geometry gave us a rational grasp of the actual spatial structure of the world.

35. The space and time of pure intuition are not the only matrices in which things are presented to us. If we study our apprehension of any ordinary thing, such as a tree or a table, we shall see that the thing is embedded in a further matrix of necessary relations, this time imposed by the 'understanding'. Understanding is reason operating at the second level through concepts and judgments. Kant held that owing to the activity of understanding there were four different kinds of statement that we could make a priori about any *thing* that we shall ever experience. These he thought he could derive from the four heads, or categories, under which logic had traditionally classified the types of judgment—quantity, quality, relation, and modality.

As respects quanity, we could say in advance that every such thing would be a whole of parts. Since it would be extended in space, it would be divisible—indeed infinitely divisible—into smaller parts; and since it would also be in time, it would again be infinitely divisible into shorter moments. We know a priori not only that this whole-part relation will apply, but also that the relation can be dealt with through numbers, which themselves are wholes of parts, and whose relations are apprehended a priori.

Secondly, as respects quality, we can say that everything will have this, and have it in some definite degree. We cannot say with certainty that tomorrow at nine we shall be experiencing colour or sound or pain, but we know that if we do experience one of these qualities, it will have some degree of intensity, which could in theory be placed on a scale running indefinitely up and down.

Thirdly, as regards 'relation', we have several secure assurances. Every thing will present itself to us as a substance with attributes. Kant took this as meaning that certain features of it will be relatively permanent and others in process of change; the former gave the meaning of 'substance'; the latter were incidents or attributes of this; 'only the permanent changes'. Again, we know that every event we experience will have a cause in some preceding event and an effect in some succeeding one. *What* the cause may have been and what the effect will be, we have to gather from experience. But if a physician who did not know the cause of a disease were to venture the guess that there was no cause for it at all, we should regard him as talking absurdly. We are certain that it has a cause, whether that cause ever comes to light or not. Once more, Kant thought we could be assured that all objects in space constituted a single far-flung order, every object being in interaction, direct or indirect, with every other.

Fourthly, there are relations of modality. These are not quite on a par with the others, for they hold, not of things, as the others do, but of our attempts to know things by inference. Given our premises, some of our conclusions are necessary, some possible, some merely actual. Of two parallel lines, we say that they are producible indefinitely and that they cannot enclose a space; both these conclusions are necessary, one telling us what must be, the other what cannot be; to see that something is impossible is itself to see a kind of necessity. So also of the possible. To see that something is possible is to see that certain conditions we know to hold, for example that there are parallel lines, are compatible with certain others that we do not know to hold, for example, their having the same length. Necessary and possible insights are thus both a priori. Assertions of the merely actual are not; they seem to have wandered into the ranks of the a priori as a result of Kant's passion for rounded symmetry.

36. There remains a third and highest level on which reason operates. Kant's account of this is disappointing, since the 'ideas' which reason here uses have none of the necessity that marks the lower levels and, instead of constituting the very framework of nature, as space-time and the categories do, are merely ideals which 'regulate' our attempts to order our knowledge. As such, they serve a useful purpose. Kant thought that, as we surveyed the world of experience, it broke into two distinct divisions, the system of outward nature and the system of inward feelings, thoughts, and volitions. Reason would seek to organize these as wholes and deal with them by distinct disciplines—nature by rational cosmology, consciousness by rational psychology. But the two must be somehow related in a more inclusive whole in which the phenomena of the inward life, with its purposiveness and moral effort, were shown in their relation to the order of nature; and this was the work of rational theology.

37. Kant's appeal to reason in theology was strange and not wholly consistent. In his first Critique, he argued that reason was impotent in this field, and that the arguments for the existence of God were all fallacious. In the second Critique he return to theology, as it were, by a back door. He convinced himself that moral duty was itself a prescription of reason, that this prescription applied, not to the self that psychology could study, since this was wholly determined, but to an underlying or real self, which must be free. Reason could thus tell us something of reality in morals, even if it could not in metaphysics. And if the prescription to perfect ourselves was legitimate, its fulfilment must be possible. If this were to be possible, we must have a longer span to achieve it than the fragmentary life now vouchsafed to us. We may therefore reasonably hope for a life beyond the present one. And if this hope is realized, it must be through a power that orders both nature and human nature, namely God, who must, therefore, be presumed to exist. Unfortunately the positive arguments of the second Critique have not been found as cogent as the negative ones of the first.

Reason for Kant was plainly a complex affair. It included an extraordinary variety of insights, formal and material, drawn from logic, mathematics, physics, ethics, and other disciplines, and differing widely in generality. In one respect only they were all alike: they were a priori, that is, universal and necessary. How informative were these insights? Were they analytic, as Leibniz thought, in the sense that they merely made explicit a meaning already in mind? Kant recognized that there were such propositions, but what raised the main problem of the great Critique was precisely his conviction that some a priori propositions are not analytic, that simply by the exercise of reason and with no resort to experience, we can arrive at fresh knowledge of nature. Even arithmetic, he thought, was made up of synthetic propositions: 12 was not identical with the concepts of 7, 5, and addition. The fact that our insight carried us on occasion to what was new as well as universal and necessary was a very strange fact, but an undeniable one, and nothing less than his Copernican revolution would, in his opinion, explain it.

38. The step from Kant's conception of reason to that of Hegel is not so much a step as a long leap. Hegel's originality here was profound. His new conception of reason required a reconstitution of logic itself, and even this he undertook to supply. He accepted, indeed, a substantial part of Kant's account. (1) He conceived reason, as indeed all rationalists have done, as apprehension a priori, as a grasp of truth which, as necessary, could not be derived from perception alone. (2) He recognized that rational insight is of no one type, but has many forms and subject-matters. Kant had distinguished seventeen categories,[1] or types of a priori relation. Hegel distinguished about eighty. (3) He recognized that these forms of knowledge were not all on a level, and that if their function in knowing was to be understood, they must be arranged, as Kant had suggested, in hierarchical order. (4) He agreed that rational insights are, or may be, synthetic, though the flights of which he considered reason to be capable would have made Kant gasp.

39. He differed from Kant in the following respects. (1) He declined to confine reason to the sphere of phenomena, holding that an unknowable thing in itself was gratuitous and inconsistent, and that rational apprehension grasped directly the structure of the real. (2) He held that the difference between form and matter was not, as Kant thought, absolute but a difference of degree. For Kant there was a sharp distinction between even the forms of space and time and their content or filling. For Hegel every concept, however abstract, had content; and every content, however concrete, was in some measure moulded by concepts. (3) This gave him a new ground for the hierarchical ordering of categories. His logic replaced the three levels of the *Critique* with a long flight or ladder of categories, the steps of which marked an ascending order of concreteness. Instead of the hard distinctions between the three Kantian levels, we find each of the Hegelian categories passing over into its successor by almost indiscriminable degrees. (4) In consequence, Hegel regarded necessity, truth, and reality themselves as matters of degree. The necessity became firmer, and one's understanding more complete, as one rose in the scale. The truth of one's thought was measured by its approximation to the comprehensive and ordered vision that would lie before us at the top of the ladder. To achieve that consummation would be to know the world as it is.

40. Hegel's theory of reason is often regarded as eccentric and artificial. In some of its details it undoubtedly is, but in its main outlines it gives an illuminating account of the actual advance of thought. He held that we must conceive of thought from first to last as an attempt to understand. To judge or think even at the lowest level is to embark on such an attempt. And to understand something, as the earlier rationalists had maintained, is to see it in a context that renders it necessary and therefore intelligible. Though

[1] If we may include under this heading the two forms of pure intuition, the twelve sub-divisions of the categories of the understanding, and the three ideas of reason.

Hegel accepted this, he did so with a large amendment. That there was need for such amendment had already been acknowledged by Plato and Spinoza in describing their highest levels of reason, but the need had never been adequately filled by them. The proper procedure of reason, according to the earlier rationalists, was to isolate certain characters and trace their lines of connection with other characters similarly isolated; this was the function of science as conceived by Descartes, Spinoza, and Leibniz, and as described by Kant under the name of 'understanding'. It made a large assumption: it assumed that the characters isolated by such abstract thinking would 'stay put', so to speak, would remain firm and unaffected by the widening contexts in which an enlarged understanding placed them. To Hegel this seemed at odds with the actual facts of thinking. To be sure, we must abstract if we are to think at all, for both common sense and science proceed, and must proceed, by the linkage of abstractions. Their mistake is to petrify these abstractions into permanent mosaic components of the real. In actual thought, on the contrary, they are tentative, plastic, and self-modifying. The concepts used at the lower levels are continuously transformed as one rises to the higher levels. How is this done?

41. It is done by the process called 'dialectic', which Hegel developed in detail in the longer and shorter *Logics*. In these subtle and difficult books he works his way upward from the most abstract concepts he can find to the most concrete, showing how the lower ones, by reason of their very abstractness, become unstable as one contemplates them and pass over into their complements. The process has a rhythmic movement, in which the abstraction with which one starts swings over into its opposite, and then fuses with this in a unity that includes them both at a higher level. This zig-zag advance from thesis across to the antithesis and then up to the synthesis takes place over and over again till the original abstraction has expanded into a concrete system and disappeared in it. To take the famous first triad as an example: one makes some generalization about being, supposed to be the character possessed by all that is. If one tries to make that character distinct in thought, one finds that one can say nothing definite about it; it is not this rather than that, not anything rather than anything else. The thought of mere and pure being thus turns out to be indistinguishable from the thought of nothing. Yet they are not wholly identical; for otherwise there could be no recognizable passage from one to the other, whereas in fact there is; the one concept has passed over into the other before our eyes. Hence we now have a third concept in which the first two are united—the concept of becoming. This serves as a new platform or thesis, which starts another triadic movement, and so on up the scale. If one wants an image of the process, one may imagine a pendulum attached to a lofty point and shortening its swing slightly with each arc it describes, until in time it reaches the still point at the top.

42. For Hegel, then, reason is a continuous process operating at many levels. A word should be said (1) about the immediate experience from which in practice it starts and (2) the kind of vision in which it ends. (1) Thinking for most of us is occasioned by sense experience: is that the postman at the door? it is 12.30, had I better go to lunch? it is a fine day, shall I walk home from the office? This is the sort of simple question that commonly engages us. Such examples have often been thought to throw Hegel's grandiose account of thought out of court, and that in two ways. They involve brute given facts, which he never properly accounted for; and they do not seem in the least to be attempts at explaining the world. To the first objection Hegel would reply that he made no pretence of deducing all particular facts; indeed it is doubtful whether he thought he could deduce any.[1] We must accept much simply because it is given to us and be content with partial explanations. What Hegel did hold was that neither the sensory content given to us nor the judgment made about it stood as an isolated term. Each was so related to what lay beyond it that neither could have been different without logical repercussions that extended out from it like ripples in a lake and did not come to a stop short of the universe as a whole. As for the objection that ordinary thought is more often practical than speculative, Hegel would not have been troubled by it. When one concludes that it is the postman at the door, one may, to be sure, be more interested in letters than in the ascertainment of truth. But even to attain practical ends, some ascertainment of truth is necessary, and what Hegel was trying to do was to trace the career of the theoretical interest by itself.

(2) In order to understand that career, we must recall that, for Hegel, the end or aim was immanent in it at every level. A mind that is in possession of a concept or judgment is not like the wind that blows where it lists; it cannot develop this in any direction it pleases. What is before it is a fragment of the real world; and 'the opposition between the real, in the fragmentary character in which the mind

[1] On this, see J. M. E. McTaggart, *Studies in Hegelian Dialectic*, Sec. 15, 16, 31–45, 99.

possesses it, and the true reality felt within the mind, is the moving cause of that unrest which sets up the dialectical process'.[1] When we think, particularly when we think at our best and develop our thought along the lines of implication, we recognize that we are under constraint from without by a system of which our thought of the moment reveals a fragment only. We assume that if we could follow its threads of connection to the end, we should have before us a whole that would at once satisfy our impulse to understand and in so doing supply us the truth about the world. Hegel knew that the attempt to show in detail the rationality of the world was an impossibly ambitious one, for to succeed in such an attempt would require that one should have arrived already at the end of the dialectic process. But there was no presumption in postulating such rationality. Indeed why philosophize at all if you begin by assuming that your attempt to render the world intelligible is bound to fail? Such failure as has occurred is amply accounted for by our own limitations. The impressive thing is how far the postulate will take us toward understanding both the course of individual thought and the course of world history.

43. Hegel's conception of reason has had a large influence in every department of philosophy. Except for the triadic movement of the dialectic, which has not weathered criticism well, it was taken over in all its essentials by the British idealists. For Bradley and Bosanquet, reason was the presence in experience of something described variously as a 'nisus towards wholeness', 'the spirit of totality', and 'logical stability'. The terms were somewhat forbidding, but there was nothing mysterious in their meaning. 'Wholeness' meant two things: completeness and interdependence of parts. In all human human experience we find a pressure towards such wholeness. Each life begins with an experience that is below the level of distinctly apprehended qualities or relations, a 'blooming, buzzing confusion', as James called it, in which feelings and sensations are indiscriminably blended. Out of this mass, qualities gradually emerge for explicit attention, and with the appearance of the first rudimentary judgment, reason has begun its work. The earliest recognition that water wets is a connection of universals. From there on the business of reason remains the same, namely an attempt to refine these connections and extend them. The child does not know why water wets, nor do we. But reason is that in us which refuses to accept this conjunction as an accident or a mere conjunction, and continues to look for necessity.

[1] F. H. Bradley, *Principles of Logic*, Book III, Pt. I, Ch. 2, Sec. 20.

And while it insists on purifying the connection as far as may be, it insists also on extending the lines of connection outward. If it works in a pure science like mathematics, it develops its theorems logically; if it works in natural science, it develops them causally. But a causal law is itself the statement of a connection between characters or universals, and such connections were always believed by these idealists to contain a filament of necessity, whether it has yet been detected or not.

44. Their principle, like Hegel's, was that the real is the rational. The office of reason as it works in each of us is thus to construct, or reconstruct, the rational whole. The world of common sense is the result of a long attempt at such construction. The world of the sciences is the result of the same attempt, carried out more critically and resolutely. The reason at work in philosophical speculation is not something different from that of these disciplines; it is the same, but operating now under a more urgent feeling for what integrated knowledge demands. The most obvious of its demands is consistency, and Bradley developed an almost morbid sense for inconsistencies not only between the results of the various sciences, but within the firmest structures of experience, such as space, time, and causality. Not all idealists followed him here. But they did in general follow him in holding that the real was coherent in a double sense, first in being consistent throughout; in spite of apparent incongruities, secondly in being interdependent throughout, that is, so ordered that every fact was connected necessarily with others and ultimately with all. The degree of satisfaction of the logical impulse was also the measure of truth. The more systematic our knowledge could become, the greater was its 'logical stability', that is, the less modification it would have to undergo in entering into the ideal knowledge which would bring reason to rest.

45. In sketching the development of the idea of reason, we have said nothing about the empiricists. There are two reasons for this. In the first place empiricism is committed by definition to scepticism of the claims of reason as an independent source of knowledge; its interest is not in supporting these claims, but in invalidating them. There is one great figure, indeed, commonly included among the empiricists, who was not, as respects reason, an empiricist at all. It would not be difficult to show that John Locke's 'perception of agreement between ideas' was really an apprehension by reason of entailment or compatibility between universals. 'Truths belonging to essences of things (that is, to abstract ideas) are eternal, and are to be found out by the contemplation only of those essences. . . .'[1] Locke's conception of such truth is strikingly similar to Descartes's. But his empiricist successors did not follow his lead; indeed their attack on this part of his position became increasingly unsparing. Berkeley began it by denying that we could even achieve those 'essences' that provided the terms of Locke's 'eternal truths'.[2] Hume continued it by insisting that these eternal truths held only among our own ideas, and that we could not make good our claim to them even in geometry.[3] Mill took the last step possible when he held that even the necessities which Hume allowed among our own ideas were not necessities in the strict sense, but only associations or habits made firm by repetition.[4] For such empiricism, the reason that had been accepted by all rationalists from Plato forward had been explained away.

These criticisms are not to be ignored, nor do we propose to ignore them. But everything that is plausible in them has been stated with more force and discernment by contemporary empiricists than it was even by these eminent forerunners. That is the second ground for our confining ourselves to the rationalists in this historical sketch. The most formidable attack ever made on reason as an independent source of knowledge has come from those positivists and analysts who are the present-day successors of Hume. The next six chapters, which form the central part of this book, will be devoted to a survey of the rise of this philosophy and its principal contentions. In the last four chapters we shall ask what office, if any, remains for reason, when the criticisms have been appraised.

[1] *Essay Concerning Human Understanding*, IV, iii, 31.
[2] *Principles of Human Knowledge*, Introduction.
[3] *Treatise of Human Nature*, Pt. III, Sec. 1; Pt. II, Sec. 4.
[4] *System of Logic*, Bk. II, Ch. 6.

CHAPTER III

THE RISE OF POSITIVISM

1. By far the most important challenge offered in this century to the older conceptions of reason has come from the philosophy of analysis. Every reader of philosophy has heard of this school and of the revolution it has effected, but the popular impression of it is in some respects wide of the mark. It is not a school, and its philosophy is not in essence new.

It is not a school because there is no distinctive thesis that the analysts hold in common. Some students have thought to find such a thesis in the verifiability theory of meaning, the theory that only those statements are meaningful which might be verified in sense perception. But this theory itself means so many different things as to be not a bond of unity but a bone of contention and division. Again, most analysts would agree on the analytic character of a priori statements; they hold that such statements merely explicate ideas already in mind and hence supply no new knowledge. But there are competent analytic philosophers, such as Arthur Pap, Wilfrid Sellars and C. H. Langford, who have argued with force against this thesis. If one's interest lies in ethics, the most challenging doctrine of the 'school' will be the emotivist theory, to the effect that 'judgments' of right and wrong are not judgments at all, but expressions of feeling. Yet the most effective case against such subjectivism in ethics was offered by one of the founding fathers of the new philosophy, G. E. Moore. There appears to be no doctrine whatever that is at once common and peculiar to the analysts.

2. What unites them is a set of tendencies, tastes and aversions. They are all admirers of science, and tend to give it a place in the order of knowledge above that of philosophy. As a critic has written, 'whereas philosophy in the middle ages was to become the handmaid of theology, it is now to become the handmaid of science'.[1] It is a very useful handmaid, to be sure, so long as it keeps to its proper work of clarifying scientific ideas and methods, but it cannot go out by itself

[1] W. H. F. Barnes, *The Philosophical Predicament*, 24.

and conquer new knowledge; it must be contented to serve as the camp-follower of science. A further common bond among analysts is an aversion to metaphysics. Metaphysics is by tradition the queen of philosophic disciplines. But it is notorious that while science has been going from strength to strength, metaphysics has been revolving essentially the same questions that were being canvassed by the Greeks two thousand years ago, and that the metaphysicians are as divided about them now as they were then. This, say the analysts, is no accident. If the questions remain unanswered, it is because they are unanswerable, because those who asked them had never got clear as to what they were asking, or what sort of answer would really satisfy them. So far as clarity on these points is achieved, metaphysics fades away and is revealed as the by-product of mental obscurity.

Closely connected with this exaltation of science and aversion to metaphysics is the dislike for anything pompous or high-flown in language, speculation, or moral claim, an aversion to what C. D. Broad once described as 'the sort of philosophy that emanates from the west of Scotland', and to the sort of philosophers, described by McTaggart, 'who wanted to believe that they ate a good dinner only in order to strengthen themselves to appreciate Dante'. For the august pronunciamentos of a Hegel or a Heidegger about being, nothing, and the Absolute, they have as little respect as for the claims of some theologians to be privy to the desires and designs of Deity. They belong to the no-nonsense party among philosophers; they are tough-minded, at times self-consciously so; they prefer to take their facts bare of unction or spleen, and are suspicious particularly of any view that answers to the heart's desire. It is part of this general down-to-earthness that they should all stress sense experience as the terminus *a quo* and *ad quem* of our thinking, and—outside logic and mathematics, which they hold to be a field apart—should regard with suspicion any talk of universals or necessary connections; no such dubious entities are to be found among the data of sense. Once more, they are precisionists. Some of them, like Russell and Ramsey, Carnap and Wittgenstein, are original mathematicians; all of them count mathematical logic as an important philosophical achievement; and they are all eager to give to the language of philosophy something of the clearness and exactitude of this logic. Finally, they are agreed on the importance of language, though their views differ widely as to what this importance is. Some of them insist that common usage should serve as a touch-stone of meaning and truth; some of them, on the contrary, find the roots of philosophic confusion in taking common usage too seriously; some of them exercise their patience and ingenuity in trying to construct an ideal language.

3. Thus, when the general reader thinks of the analysts as forming a school, as pragmatists or Thomists form a school, he is mistaken. Is he equally mistaken when he thinks of them as having made a revolution? Undoubtedly they have done so in more than one sense. Though they have had curiously little influence on the continent of Europe, they have unseated the philosophies that were in the ascendant throughout the Anglo-Saxon countries before the first world war. If memory serves me rightly, there was a time shortly before that war when every philosophical chair in the universities of Oxford, Cambridge and London was held by an idealist of some stripe. At the present time there is not an idealist left in any of them, and their places have nearly all been taken by analysts. The provincial and colonial universities are following suit. In the United States the picture is less clear, for while the idealism, the realism—both 'new' and 'critical'—and the pragmatism of the first two decades of the century are little talked about, no single school has arisen to take their place. But the analytic philosophy is probably the nearest approach to such a successor. If it is a revolutionary achievement to have captured the position of chief academic influence throughout the Anglo-Saxon world, then the analysts have indeed carried through a revolution.

They are effecting an attendant revolution of a subtler kind. They are changing the temper and atmosphere in which philosophy is pursued. Students of philosophy are usually attracted to it by one or other of two motives, which may be called the humanistic and the scientific. The humanistic interest is brooding, vague, groping and personal. It wants to know what are the pole-stars by which a life may be most profitably steered, where one stands in the larger scheme of things, what sort of creature man is—whether an animal whose destiny it is to occupy six feet of ground, or an immortal soul, what sort of place the world is—whether a vast, mindless mechanism or a universe in whose structure and history an inquiring intelligence meets an answering intelligence, and perhaps even values and affections more or less like its own. This motive, in which poetic, mystical, and religious impulses are blended with the speculative, seems to have been the moving force in most of the great philosophers of the past. The temper of it is apparent in Plato's feeling about philosophy, 'than which no greater good ever was or will be given by the gods to mortal man', in the *Confessions* of St Augustine, in the opening sentences of Spinoza's *De Intellectus Emendatione*, in Bradley's introduction to *Appearance and Reality*.

'All of us, I presume, more or less, are led beyond the region of ordinary facts,' says Bradley. 'Some of us in one way and some in others, we seem to touch and have communion with what is beyond the visible world. In various manners we find something higher, which both supports and humbles, both chastens and transforms us. And, with certain persons, the intellectual effort to understand the universe is a principal way of thus experiencing the Deity. No one, probably, who has not felt this, however differently he might describe it, has ever cared much for metaphysics. And wherever it has been felt strongly, it has been its own justification.'

These words of Bradley, so clearly autobiographical, are surely true of many minds. To such minds the appeal of philosophy is complex. Yet the motive at work is dangerous. It is largely compounded of longings, apprehensions, religious aspirations, the need of solace and support, the delights of the free play of speculative imagination. But these are emotions, and to the philosopher emotion is dangerous because it solicits his assent on irrelevant grounds. And the higher the emotion, the greater the peril. A mind like Augustine's or Spinoza's is in small danger of warping its conclusions to suit mere spite or petty egotism. But in issues where the dignity or destiny of mankind is at stake, it is only too likely to be the victim of its own generous passions; it is most open to deception where its impulses are noblest. Thus the very power that turns the drive wheels of the speculative mind has often forced it off the track into conclusions that would have been avoided with ease by harder and colder heads.

The analysts have seen this. They are clearly aware of the difference between thinking on the one hand and the indulgence, on the other, of poetic or mystical or religious or ethical feeling. They insist that they have nothing against such feeling—in its place. But its place is not in philosophy or science, which are strictly cognitive enterprises. Toward the philosophy that sought to satisfy such feeling their attitude is something like disdain, and since a very large part of the philosophy of the past has been pursued from such motives, their interest in the history of philosophy is notoriously feeble. The 'great names' in philosophy leave them cold.

What moves them to the pursuit of the subject is the second kind of motive, the scientific. The scientist who is self-critical often becomes self-conscious about his methods or the terms he is using. He generalizes from a few cases; what, if anything, justifies that sort of inference? He says his conclusions are more or less probable; but does probability mean the same thing as applied to the thousandth decimal of π, the toss of a coin, and tomorrow's weather? Physics is the leading science of the day, and mathematics is the chief tool of physics; but does mathematics by itself give us any information about the nature of things? And does talk about the nature of things have any meaning unless it refers to the colours and sounds, the shapes and sizes, that we actually sense? These are not cloudy wonderings, welling up out of frustrated emotions, but definite questions that arise inevitably out of scientific inquiry. The scientific worker himself does not commonly stop to deal with them. But they have to be dealt with by someone, and here the philosopher steps in as an assistant to the scientist, with the assignment of clearing up his theoretical puzzles about methods and meanings. This is a comparatively humble service. It is not philosophy in the grand style; it has none of the glamour belonging to adventure among 'the eternities and immensities'. It is essentially an inspection of the theoretical tools of science.

4. This conception of the philosopher's business, if it prevails, is bound to be followed by large changes in the position and influence of his discipline. The level of intellectual acuteness of those engaged in it may well rise. It will become a specialist's province, inviting to those with exceptional powers in logic, conceptual analysis and theory of knowledge, but unattractive and even repellent to most others. Its appeal will be ascetically intellectual. Many of those who would under other circumstances have thought of themselves as philosophic specialists will be excluded from this inner circle of specialism. Those who thought of philosophy less as the analysis of scientific terms than as the synthesis of scientific results, those who looked to it for illumination of the *summum bonum* or of 'man's place in the cosmos', still more those philosophers who, like Sir Thomas Browne, conceive it as the ascent of a mount of vision, will go elsewhere for their food, to literature perhaps, or to religion. Will this be a loss? I can only think it will. For the ancient questions about life and death and the world which are asked by the plain man are not meaningless questions nor unimportant, and it is far better that his guidance on them should come from those who are committed to reason than from the slogan-mongers of the day. If the truth on these

D

matters is ever brought to light at all, it will be by sustained and critical thought.

Does someone reply that, by our own admission, philosophy too has been motivated by much else than the love of truth? So it has. But it is committed to truth none the less. We may admit its gross defects. That it is often muddled is shown by the continuing conflicts among philosophers, and by the incoherencies within their individual minds; further, it is to be doubted whether any philosopher has ever emancipated himself wholly from prejudice for the space of a single day. But what does all this prove? Merely what we knew before, that it is exceedingly hard to be reasonable. It does not show that some men are not more reasonable than others, and therefore better guides, or that we cannot be more reasonable than we are, or that by being more reasonable we cannot approach the truth more nearly. In any genuine philosophic mind the love of truth is a steady gravitational pull which operates to correct all defections from it, even when the sun that exerts the pull is clouded over. The true philosopher is a man with an intellectual conscience, and though no doubt he is a miserable sinner, the point is that he carries the remedy in the Socratic monitor that is always at work inside him. And philosophy as Plato, Spinoza, Hegel, McTaggart and Royce conceived it, not as the sharpening of scientific tools, but as the determined application of reason to all the ultimate problems of thought and practice, is of quite inestimable value.

The fact that some of the mainsprings of that philosophy lie outside intelligence proper only gives it, if rightly practised, an added potency. For then the answers given by reason are not alien impositions on feeling and impulse; they come by invitation; their authority is acknowledged; and reason has its best opportunity to permeate and civilize a life. It will chasten whim and arbitrariness in the criticism of the arts; it will be the antidote to superstition in religion; it will give justice to one's judgments of others and sanity to one's own outlook on the ends of living; even in science it will lend perspective by revealing the bearing of some inquiries on larger issues and the triviality of others. To philosophy in this generous sense the philosophy of analysis is by temper and habit alien. Most of these old problems, it thinks, can be done away with by a little expert verbal analysis, which would reveal them to be unanswerable because meaningless. For my own part, I do not so regard them. I suspect that the dominance of the analytic philosophy would shrink the horizons of both theory and conduct, and make life a bleaker and drearier business. But I cannot, like some of my colleagues, take this philosophy lightly. It seems to me significant, formidably advocated, and in some respects highly plausible. The only proper way to deal with it is to approach it with the respect due to its extremely able proponents, and with the assumption that they may be right. That is what I shall try to do.

5. We have seen that analysis has gone some way towards producing a revolution in philosophy, both in its content and in the conception of its office. Is the movement revolutionary in the further sense that its teaching is a new thing in the world? We might avoid this question by repeating what the analysts themselves have sometimes protested, that they have no distinctive common teaching, either old or new. But this would be an evasion. They would admit that there have been central trends in the movement as opposed to peripheral ones. The historical trunk of the widely spreading tree was logical positivism or empiricism. This clearly formulated position served as the rallying point in the twenties and the thirties and the point of departure for new developments in the forties and fifties. Of course there is much more to the philosophy of analysis than logical positivism, and positivism itself has shown tendencies to splinter into factions. This makes the task of the expositor a baffling one. He has no sooner, with some effort, mastered a particular position and matured his estimate of it than he is told that this position was abandoned some years or some weeks ago, and that he is therefore flogging dead horses. The philosophy of analysis is not only an amorphous movement; it has been kaleidoscopic in the quickness of its changes, which have followed each other at such a pace that the writing and printing of books could not keep up with it and it has had to register its changes in a bewildering profusion of notes and articles.

But this makes it all the more necessary for the reviewer of the movement to find relatively fixed points in the flux, not in the sense of dogmas generally accepted, for there are none, but in the sense of theses propounded by acknowledged leaders, and widely admitted as true and momentous. If, then, we recognize logical positivism as having been the stem of the later movements and ask what, in the above sense, have been its main theses, I think we can distinguish four. These have to do with the four principal types of statement that it is possible to make: statements of how facts are related, statements of fact themselves, statements of necessary truth, and statements of value. The four theses in these respective fields are: (1) logical atomism, the doctrine that all complex statements of fact depend for their truth on simple statements about what may be sensed, and that none of these simple statements entail any others; (2) the verifiability theory of meaning, which holds that a statement means what would verify it in sense; (3) the analytic character of a priori knowledge, i.e., that all necessary statements unfold the contents of our ideas rather than report truths about nature; (4) the emotive theory of values, i.e., that statements of value are neither true nor false, but expressions of attitude.

If now we ask whether the philosophy of analysis is essentially a new philosophy, the most helpful answer will be one that makes clear the extent to which these positions are themselves new. That answer is a surprising one, and particularly so in view of what we have said about the analyst's depreciation of philosophies of the past. But to this downgrading of great names, there is one outstanding exception. This exception is David Hume. Hume anticipated all the positions that we have just named as central to logical positivism. He lacked, to be sure, the elaborate logical apparatus that analysts now have at their command, and he had nothing like their acquaintance with physics and mathematics. But perhaps for that very reason he put the positions so simply that his account of them is a good introduction to the more sophisticated formulations of his philosophic grandchildren; and the shock and bafflement he aroused among his contemporaries was a curious dress rehearsal of what is happening today. We will therefore begin our study of the Humean revolution of the present by a glance at the Humean revolution of the past.

6. Most philosophers before Hume had no doubt that one could reach by reasoning important truths about the nature of things. Not only such devotees of mathematical method as Descartes and Leibniz, but also such empirically minded thinkers as Locke and Berkeley were ready to offer arguments, for example, that demonstrated the existence of God. Nearly all of them believed in a substantial self and accepted its immortality; they all believed that reason entered in an important way into moral judgment; and if they did not all think that Christian theology was wholly a matter of reason, most of them thought that at the least it contained nothing unconsonant with reason.

Hume's scepticism was devastating not because it offered particular refutations for these doctrines, but because it purported to show that such conclusions were ruled out by the very nature of the knowing process. These beliefs were arrived at by thinking. Now thinking was a mental activity that required certain materials and worked with them in certain ways. It might be perfectly competent to do all the desirable things that these great men thought it could; but then again it might not, and Hume undertook to find out. Suppose you believe, as all Catholics and perhaps most Protestants do, that the existence of God can be established by thinking. What is needed if such reflection is to be carried through? You must in the first place be able to reason from nature as effect to God as cause, and hence there must be a connection between these that would qualify your saying: given such an effect, it *must* have had such-and-such a cause. Secondly, you must be able to form the idea of God as a spiritual being who is presumably all-wise, all-powerful, and all-good. Thirdly, you must be sure that your logic holds good in the nature of things; otherwise you might only be getting farther and farther away from the truth the more logical you were. Fourthly, if reason is to show of God not only that he is wise and powerful but also good, you must be sure that goodness and badness are the sort of attributes that can be proved to exist by argument.

Now the reason why Hume's scepticism was so shattering was that by astonishingly simple considerations he apparently showed that none of these four requisites for such thinking was at our command. Take the argument from effect to cause, from the world to its creator. Every student of philosophy knows what Hume did to this argument; indeed philosophy has never been quite the same since he did it. So little do we understand what goes on when one thing causes another, he held, that for all we can see, anything could cause anything else; something might come from nothing, and in turn give rise to nothing. Worlds and billiard-balls wear nothing on their faces that enables us to *deduce* what causes them or their changes. If anyone supposes that they do, this only shows his confusion. He is confusing logical necessity with the wholly different relation that links colliding billiard-balls. In this latter there is no necessity whatever. What seemed to be necessity was merely force of habit, linking A with B in expectation because we have repeatedly found them linked. Now we have never experienced God being followed by the world. We have never found any creation, not even a movement of our own hand, following necessarily from anything that went before. Even the analogies, therefore, on which we might base an argument from world to creator are vitiated at the outset, since none of them have a trace of necessity, and necessity we must have if we are to offer proof.

We must obviously have, secondly, the power to form an idea of God. Hume points out that since our ideas of things and persons are in no sense innate, we must draw them, if we have them at all, from experience, and in the end that means sense experience. Very well, have we ever experienced in sense an infinite being? In particular, have we ever experienced a being who, as all-powerful, could make a weight so heavy that he could not lift it, or who, as all-intelligent, could contrive a puzzle so difficult that he could not solve it? Or if this is thought to misinterpret these characters, have we ever experienced a being that is spaceless, timeless and disembodied, as God is supposed to be? No. Then how can we form the notion of such a being? Since only sense-experience can provide us with the material for the notion, and it obviously does not, the idea must be a pseudo-idea. If we examine our thought more closely, Hume would say, we shall see that we are using confused anthropomorphic images, and that the thought we supposed we had is really beyond our powers.

Is all knowledge, then, a knowledge of what is given in sense? No, Hume would not go so far as that. We know that a thing cannot both exist and not exist; we know that two and two make four; these are not cases of sense knowledge, but they are certainties none the less; such insight is different in kind from knowing that we now have a headache. What sort of knowledge is it? Hume answered that it was knowledge of the relations among our ideas. 'Propositions of this kind are discoverable by the mere operation of thought, without any dependence on what is anywhere existent in the universe.'[1] We know that two and two make four because we see immediately that what we mean by 'four' is the same as what we mean by 'two and two': this knowledge is certain. But it buys certainty at the cost of triviality. Not being drawn from our experience of the world, it can tell us nothing about that world. So of the propositions of logic and mathematics generally. They are not, as rationalists suppose they are, universal and certain insights into the structure of the external world. We do not know whether that world is an order or an inconceivable chaos, for we do not know for certain whether there is such a world at all. Not that Hume doubted this in practice. His scepticism lay in holding that if anyone questioned it, we were unable to assure ourselves of it. Our belief was a matter of animal faith.

Finally, what could reason tell us about values—about the goodness or badness of the universe, or of conduct, or of a toothache? Hume's answer was, nothing whatever. Reason deals with either facts or relations; beauty and goodness are neither. They lie altogether in our feelings. The most that reason can do is to prepare the way for feelings by giving one a fuller view of the objects that may arouse

[1] *Enquiry Concerning Human Understanding*, Sec. 4, Pt. 1.

them. An accomplished architect may show us a Greek temple and point out cornices and friezes and entablatures and shafts; but he cannot point out to us the beauty, for it is not 'out there' among the facts, but 'results from the whole, when that complicated figure is presented to an intelligent mind, susceptible to those finer sensations'.[1] So of right and wrong. Reason can enlarge the context of an act; it can bring home to us what the consequences will probably be; but on the crucial question whether those consequences are worth having, it has nothing whatever to say. That question is settled by feeling, and it must be decided by each man for himself. But so far as mere reason is concerned ' 'tis not contrary to prefer the destruction of the whole world to the scratching of my finger', or 'to prefer even my own acknowledged lesser good to my greater', or 'to choose my total ruin'.[2] Hume's main contention in morals is that all preference is non-rational, because it is entirely a matter of feeling. 'The hypothesis we embrace is plain. It maintains that morality is determined by sentiment.'[3]

7. There has been no question in the minds of philosophers that if these conclusions of Hume were made out, the sovereignty held by reason in metaphysics, theology and morals must be abdicated. There is no doubt about it still. That is why I propose to devote this and the next three chapters to the neo-Humism of the present day. The new empiricists have revived all four of these contentions of Hume. It may be asked why we should not discuss them, then, in the clear and simple forms he gave to them. I only wish we might. But it would be very unfair to his successors, since they have at command so many techniques and arguments unknown to him. It is worth recalling that the Hume who wrote the *Treatise* was a philosophic amateur and scarcely more than a boy; he wrote his great book in his early twenties almost entirely out of his own amazing head. Whether the empiricists of the present day have his genius or not, they have his shoulders to stand on, and many of them have a range of scientific and logical mastery that makes him seem almost naïve. But when they have brought this mastery to bear on the place of reason in philosophy, theology, and morals, they report that on all the major issues Hume was right. Let us see a little more clearly what this means.

First, he was right about the contingency of the things and events in nature. What do we mean by a thing? In the end, a group of

---

[1] *Enquiry Concerning the Principles of Morals*, App. I.
[2] *Treatise of Human Nature*, II, iii, 3.
[3] *Enquiry Concerning the Principles of Morals*, App. I.

sensible qualities arranged in a certain way. Does any of these qualities entail any of the others? Does the redness of a rose, for example, entail its shape, or its shape its redness? Clearly not. Does an event entail any event that went before it or will come after it? No again. 'Every distinct perception is a distinct existence,' said Hume, 'and is independent of every other.' 'Any one (fact),' said Wittgenstein, 'can either be the case or not be the case, and everything else remain the same.'[1] Hume is right that the actual world is an immense unintelligible plurality.

Secondly, he was right about what made thought meaningful. His way of putting it was that if ideas were to mean anything, they must be copies of impressions. The new way of putting it is that the meaning of ideas is the mode of their verification, that this verification must lie in sense experience, and that any idea which is unverifiable in sense must therefore be meaningless. The ground of Hume's theory of meaning was psychology; that of the newer empiricists is the requirements of science; but the doctrine itself and its implications for philosophy and theology are in essence the same.

Thirdly, Hume was right about *a priori* knowledge. Such knowledge, he said, was certain but barren, in the sense that it revealed to us only the relations of our own ideas. This is the central contention of positivism regarding the *a priori*. It holds that necessary propositions report only conventions of our own thinking, or more properly of our language, and rules of usage are in no position to throw light on the ultimate nature of things. Indeed they are not ultimate even for ourselves, since, as rules or conventions, they are arbitrary and may be changed if we see fit. Here Hume's followers have outstripped him. He never held, so far as I know, that alternatives to the laws of logic were open to us. But on the all-important point that *a priori* knowledge is only knowledge of the relations of our meanings and is therefore not a disclosure of factual truth, he and the positivists are at one.

Finally, they hold that he was essentially right about values. Here again the agreement is not complete. Hume held that when we call an act right, what we really mean to say is that in the light of its anticipated consequences most people have an approving feeling about it. Our statement is therefore a statement of fact, though the fact it asserts is not that the act has a certain character but that people feel about it in a certain way. The positivists are more extreme. When we call an act right, they say, we are not asserting about anything, even the feelings of ourselves or others; we are

[1] *Tractatus*, I, 21.

expressing a feeling or attitude, and since such an expression is essentially an exclamation, it is not a statement at all, and so neither true nor false. This is a difference of theoretical moment. Still in the great debate over objectivism in morals, the debate whether actions are right or wrong independently of man's attitudes towards them, the positivists are on Hume's side.

Here are the main theses of the most widely influential movement in philosophy of the half century just past. They are essentially reaffirmations of what was urged long ago. But they would hardly have created such a stir if they had been expressly offered as the views of an eighteenth century thinker; and in fact Hume seems to have been little in mind among those who inaugurated the new movement. Their interests, their proficiencies, their linguistic and cultural backgrounds, their prevailing habits of thought, even the considerations they offered for very similar conclusions, were widely different from his. The fact that lines of thought so different converged to such similar conclusions is a point in favour of these conclusions. Still, when like conclusions are reached on widely differing grounds, it is probable that the conclusions themselves are less coincident than they seem. One cannot understand the thinking of modern empiricists merely by reading and digesting Hume; for even when they repeat him, their words are charged with manifold echoes, scientific, philosophic, and logical, which even his ears could hardly have heard.

8. One reason for the neglect of Hume by the founders of the modern movement was that they owned neither his country nor his language. The philosophy of analysis has two geographical roots, one that runs through logical positivism to Schlick in Vienna and another that runs through the analysis of common usage to Moore in Cambridge; and the latter root will have to be followed in due time. But our present concern is with the former. Logical positivism, which has formed the main stem of the philosophy of analysis, owes its origin to a group of students and teachers at the University of Vienna, which was later to become famous as the Vienna Circle. Its meetings were at first entirely informal. As early as 1907 a few pioneer members of the group were meeting on Thursday nights in local cafes for coffee, beer, and discussion, but it was not till Moritz Schlick came to Vienna as professor of philosophy that the group had clear leadership and something like an organization. Most of its members were then younger men. There was one conspicuous bond among them which turned out to have much significance. They were all scientists by profession or avocation. Schlick himself had written his doctoral dissertation in physics under the direction of Max Planck. Rudolph Carnap and Philipp Frank, like Schlick, were theoretical physicists. Hahn, Mengers, and Gödel were mathematicians; Otto Neurath was an economist and sociologist; Ludwig Wittgenstein, who never attended the Circle meetings even when living in Vienna, though his views were actively discussed in it, was an engineer.

Throw together a group of lively young minds with such interests as these, and it is not difficult to conjecture where the talk is likely to drift. Though anything may be fair game, a pull will be felt by all towards their scientific research, to the questions how important it is, how hard it is to get results, whether they can borrow with profit the new techniques which their friends are applying. And if their minds are reflective and self-appraising, as these minds emphatically were, they may find, as the smoke thickens and the steins empty, that they are telling each other with a modest flush of pride, companionship and beer, how valuable a thing, how incomparably valuable a thing, the life of science is.

9. To the science which was their deep and common concern there was only one serious rival. That was philosophy. Whether philosophy had anything to offer that was really comparable to science was a question canvassed eagerly and often. The question was a serious one, even for devoted scientists, for philosophy in those days held a position of supreme prestige throughout the German learned world. Scholars and scientists were of course respected, but it was in philosophy that the German mind seemed to come into its own, and if one wanted to see it in full flower, one must go to the successors of Kant and Hegel. These philosophers spoke with oracular authority. Dilthey, Paulsen, and Riehl at Berlin, Wundt at Leipzig, Windelband and Kuno Fischer at Heidelberg, Husserl at Göttingen, Eucken at Jena, Külpe at Bonn, Natorp and Cohen at Marburg, Deussen at Kiel, Cassirer at Hamburg—these men were the pride of German university life. It was my own privilege as a young and curious traveller to hear Wundt at Leipzig and Windelband at Heidelberg, and I carried away a vivid impression of the reverence with which they were regarded by their student audiences. For the most part these philosophers were men of monumental erudition. A few of them, notably Wundt, Külpe, and Cassirer, could speak with firsthand knowledge about science. Yet with all their learning and prestige, these priests and prophets of German *Kultur* had little to say that the group in Vienna cared to hear.

Why? Because in nearly every case their thought was what the young critics called 'school-philosophy'; it was anchored in what seemed to them the stagnant backwaters of the Kant-Hegel tradition. According to this tradition the path to secure and important knowledge made a circuit round the evil-smelling laboratories and wound up in some dim arbour where nothing broke the meditations of the philosophers but the decorous hootings of the owl of Minerva. The ministers of this tradition wore a semi-religious aura, and if anyone were inclined to be profane, the vast yardage of their *Werke*, reposing massively on the library shelves, induced a certain numbness.

But there were circumstances that raised doubt. While German mathematicians and German physicists generally agreed with each other, and one of their students could traverse without incident the few miles from Jena to Göttingen, he would find that the philosophers held little courts of their own, and that he could make this same journey philosophically only by renouncing allegiance to Eucken and swearing a new fealty to Husserl. Now bickerings on Olympus carry a painful suggestion that the gods are not infallible. When, as on occasion happens, they speak in testable terms, it is important that the tests come out right. And it was notorious that they had not always done so when these particular oracles spoke. The tremendous Hegel himself had undertaken in the longer *Logic* to give an account of mathematics, but mathematicians who knew their Cantor and Frege had ventured the opinion that he had only darkened counsel. The same great authority had deduced by logical processes that there must be just seven planets, but a week after the deduction was given to the world, unco-operative astronomers discovered an eighth planet. Was it merely an error in deduction that had been made? Or was it something more serious and culpable, an attempt on the part of philosophy to do what it could not possibly do?

Most philosophers said the latter, in this returning to Kant. Kant had laid it down that the determination of facts and laws should be left to science, and that the business of the philosopher was to deal with the transcendental, that is, either with the concepts that made experience possible, such as space, time, substance and causality, or else with that which lay beyond all experience, such as God. This seemed to be a satisfactory division of labour. But what it meant in practice, the Vienna group observed, was that for a century and a half, the philosophers and scientists had gone their respective ways, retreating farther and farther into their own provinces, until they had moved so far apart as to be barely aware of each other's existence. This was surely not as it should be. To the young scientists it appeared that such new discoveries in physics as those of Planck and Einstein were not only relevant but vital to the philosophic concepts themselves of space, time, causality and substance, though the philosophers whose special concern they were seemed to be now out of sight and sound of what was happening. On the other hand the scientists, lost among their test-tubes and Bunsen burners, found themselves nodding after a page or two of any book on metaphysics. It became a main concern of the Vienna group to reopen the road between philosophy and science. It might be that for a meeting of minds, one party or the other would have to go more than half way. As scientists the group were disposed from the beginning to say that this must be done by the philosophers. For after all, the scientists were getting results that were precise, confirmed, and agreed upon, and they were winning new territory every year. Such results as the philosophers could show were anything but precise; they were not confirmed in any manner that brought agreement; and on many traditional problems, they seemed scarcely to have advanced since Plato.

10. Then why not leave philosophy to its own dubious devices and get on? One awkward fact made this impracticable. This was that the science in which the Circle was most interested, the one among the natural sciences that was clearly fundamental, was itself deeply tainted with philosophy. This science, of course, was physics. When the group began its discussions, the physics of the nineteenth century was disintegrating. It had been built on the theory of mechanism, namely that everything in the universe was composed of minute bits of matter which behaved in the same way as the aggregates that we see and feel. For Lord Kelvin, to explain something in physics meant to be able to construct in his laboratory or his mind's eye a model in which he could see how the result was brought about, and with extraordinary ingenuity he produced working models even of such things as atoms and ether waves.

But as physics pressed its researches in the realm of the sub-microscopic, the value of such models became more and more questionable. Maxwell had shown in 1861 that the energy supposed to be 'in' a magnetic circuit did not really reside there, but was diffused through a 'field'. Planck showed about 1900 that light rays behaved like both particles and waves, though of course a model that behaved in both ways at once could be neither made nor imagined. In 1911 and 1913 Rutherford and Bohr proposed models for the atom that revived the hopes of those who were Kelvin-minded; but the evidence, which was not long in coming, that electrons somehow leaped timelessly from orbit to orbit, again dashed these hopes. In 1927 when Heisenberg pointed out that it was impossible to assign to an electron, for any given instant, both a place and a momentum, the mechanical physics of the nineteenth century was in ruins. Physicists were now talking confidently about entities of which it was argued not only that no one had ever perceived them, but that no one ever would or could perceive them, or even imagine them. Now if the young enthusiasts of the Circle were to admit such speculation in physics, how could they denounce it in metaphysics?

11. The answer was given them by Mach, in whose honour they organized themselves in 1928 into the 'Verein Ernst Mach', with Schlick as chairman. Mach, of whom William James reported that no one had ever given him 'so strong an impression of pure intellectual genius', had been at the turn of the century a professor of physics at Vienna. He lived to see only the beginnings of the scientific revolution. But he would have agreed entirely that the new physics was wandering off into metaphysics, for he believed that even the classical physics had allowed itself to be seduced into irresponsible speculation. If no one had ever seen an electron, neither had anyone ever seen the ether or an atom or a light ray. Mach had taken his courage in his hands and said that, in introducing these things, the physicist was as truly falling back on mythology as the savage who found spirits in twisted trees. It was commonly said, to be sure, that if you admitted these entities, your predictions would come out right, and that this confirmed their existence; but this was a mere fallacy of the consequent unless you happened to know that your predictions would come out right on no other hypothesis, and that was just what you did not know. If the physicist was to mock at the mote in the philosopher's eye, he must first attend to the metaphysical beam in his own.

How was he to do this? Mach's answer was radical but simple. The scientist must do it by confining his talk and restricting his laws to what he could observe. He must conceive the laws of physics as statements linking percepts. This was only carrying a little further a well-established tendency of all civilized thought. Such thought has got rid of the gods of winds and waves; it has exorcised the spirit of the twisted tree; it does not take ghosts very seriously. But it does still play with the archaic notion that there is a substantial table in the room which somehow *has* the brownness, squareness, and coldness that we perceive, though when we strip it in thought of these

and its other qualities, we find to our astonishment that nothing is
left. Hume showed long ago that this substantial table is a ghost, and
it is time we exorcised it along with the other ghosts. Conceive your
table as the set of qualities you can perceive, and you are dealing with
a table you know. Go on to describe what you generally experience
when you push it, upset it, or bang it, and you are in effect describing
the laws that govern it. Refine these laws by the exact measurements
of science, and you have all that science can justifiably claim as
knowledge. To these laws you add nothing whatever but unverifiable
conjecture if you start talking about a material substance, unseen and
invisible. Now, in the final reckoning, are you doing anything better
when you talk about atoms? No, Mach answered. They constitute a
mass of superfluous baggage that merely clutters the scientific
workshop. There is not a single physical law that cannot be stated
with all its former precision, objectivity, and verifiable meaning,
without reference to such entities. All that is needed is to formulate
the law as the statement of a connection between percepts, between
elements of actual or possible experience. One notes in the laboratory, for example, that as one increases the pressure on a gas, its
volume decreases proportionately. Take that as a statement of what
anyone will find if he tries a similar experiment, and you have a law
that is both exact and publicly verifiable. Take it as a statement about
masses of impalpable bullets, shooting about in the space that the
gas is occupying, and you have mythology or metaphysics. After all,
said Mach, they amount to the same thing.

12. Planck and other microphysicists fell on Mach with a sense of
outrage. But the Vienna Circle felt that their master had been
unfairly dealt with; he was taken to say more than he had meant,
particularly on two vital points. Did he mean to say of atoms and
molecules that there were no such things? To be sure, he seemed to
be saying just that when he protested against the trend to 'resolve
ourselves into a nebulous and mystical mass of molecules, or make
nature a haunt of hobgoblins'. But to deny that such things existed
would be as dogmatic as to affirm them, and he was concerned to
avoid dogmatism of either type. Nor would he outlaw all use in
science of these imperceptibles. He was willing to admit the notions
of atoms, light waves, and so on, if they were used as 'auxiliary
concepts', concepts, that is, which do not pretend to refer to actual
existents, but which serve as bridges from percept to percept. They
may be used as the mathematician uses the square root of two, not
with the idea that there is anything in nature corresponding to them,

but as a means of simplifying equations. The only data of science are phenomena and their connections, and if it holds this firmly in mind, fashions among the auxiliary concepts may move from molecules through atoms to electrons or in any other direction as fast and as far as fashions in hats without affecting physical laws in the very least.

The second score on which Mach was attacked was that of idealism. Was he not ridding his subject of metaphysics merely by adopting the metaphysics of Berkeley? If he expelled from his system the notion of matter and admitted nothing, even in physics, besides percepts, was not that equivalent to saying that there was nothing in the world but consciousness? And what was this but idealism? Mach replied in a way that will help us shortly to understand how positivism could leap so swiftly from the solipsism of Wittgenstein to the physicalism of Neurath and Carnap. He insisted that the mental was as truly fiction as the material. There was no 'I' distinct from a series of percepts, and there was nothing in these percepts themselves to mark them as either mental or physical. They were regarded, as James also came to regard them, as in this respect neutral. The 'cash value', as he would have said, of the terms 'mental' and 'physical', lay in the differing contexts in which the same set of data may be taken. Is an apple mental or physical? In itself, said Mach, it is neither, for the data of sense, the red, round, and sweet, are just what they are 'experienced as', and resist being placed in metaphysical pigeon-holes. To be sure, if you consider them in a context independent of your body, as produced by trees in an orchard, as ripening and decaying, they are physical. But if you consider them as dependent on your retina and brain, then precisely the same data are being taken as mental.[1] Mach thus anticipated both the neutral monism of James and Russell and the radical empiricism of the Vienna Circle in holding that if the words 'mental' and 'physical' were used with a proper regard for their 'cash value' in experience, the old metaphysical problem of how two utterly different substances were related would simply vanish.

13. These reflections, suggested by Mach, opened up another inviting prospect. This was the unity of science. It was later to become a prime concern of the Vienna Circle, leading on to a series of monographs and to several international congresses. When the group began its discussions, natural science was marked off into areas, like a map of Europe with coloured countries. Each science

[1] Mach, *Die Analyse der Empfindungen*, 14.

had its own subject-matter; physics dealt with 'material' bodies, biology with bodies that had 'life', psychology with bodies that had 'consciousness' or 'selves' or 'souls', sociology with what was called 'the group mind'. According to the young empiricists, these distinguishing entities were fictions. No one had ever perceived matter, or life, or consciousness, or selves, or souls, or minds, to say nothing of such monstrosities as the group mind. They were sheer myths, all of them, and yet they were the traditional ground of division between the sciences. Get rid of them and the barriers fell; science would be dealing with the same sort of thing throughout. That did not mean that stones, plants, animals, and men would now exhibit no differences at all. It did mean that the subject-matter of science would be identical throughout, namely observed behaviour. What was admitted and rejected as evidence would now be everywhere the same. A single scientific method would be valid for all sciences alike. The biologist could talk with the chemist without introducing 'entelechies' that could be expected to tamper with chemical reactions, and the psychologist could talk with the biologist without invoking undetermined selves that might rush causelessly out of their lairs to ensnarl the traffic of the physical universe. The Circle members began to think of themselves as the prophets of a new age, in which the materials and methods of the various sciences would at last have become homogeneous.

14. Did this mean that there was nothing in the universe except sense contents? Mach did not say quite that, and neither did his disciples; such a denial would be metaphysics. Still they said something very like it. They said that if you anywhere ventured upon a remark about what was not sensible, your remark, though not false, was meaningless. The argument was this: to assert something is to say that something is the case or is a fact; if we understand what we are saying, we must know what facts would make the assertion true; to know that, we must know what experiences would be necessary to assure us of these facts, or verify their existence; these experiences, then, are what we really refer to when we make the assertion; and these experiences are sense experiences. This is the now famous verification theory of meaning: the meaning of an assertion *is* the mode of its verification. In what sense, if any, it is true, we must soon inquire. Meanwhile we may point out that it is anything but the innocuous formula that it may seem. Its implications are many and devastating. If it is true, in any of its more obvious senses, the spreading vine of metaphysical and theological speculation must be severely pruned if not cut off at the root. Everything non-sensible is ruled out as non-thinkable. God and the absolute, the soul, other selves, ideas, substance, causal necessity, truth, beauty, and goodness, protons and electrons, all sense qualities that are beyond our own powers of perceiving, all the objects of present sensation in their unperceived status, are *prima facie* ruled out as meaningless. The new theory thus cleared the board at a stroke of most traditional philosophy.

15. But in logical empiricism, besides empiricism there is a great deal of logic. The school has a clearly marked logical theory of its own. On this side it is not less sceptical than on the empirical side. But it is notably more original; for whereas in its empiricism it is essentially a return to Hume, it employs in its logic a theory and a technique beyond anything at Hume's command.

The western tradition in philosophy and theology has, in the main, been rationalist. It has held that by mere speculation one can arrive at important truth about the ultimate nature of things; it has exalted, and sought to refine, its logic; it has regarded mathematics as the ideal science, and affirmed, with Descartes, that if a belief could be conceived with the clear and distinct necessity of a mathematical axiom, its truth was guaranteed. So if Spinoza wished by searching to find out God, he need only take care that as he moved up the ideal ladder stretching from his room to the infinite, every rung should be securely fastened in its place by self-evident necessity. The ascent was long, and dizzying at times; it took patience and a level head; but it called for no range of experience beyond the ordinary. And the result was nothing less than ultimate truth about the world, securely and finally demonstrated.

To rationalism of this type the logical empiricists believe that they have dealt the deathblow. How did they come to deal it? We must note, to begin with, that the members of the Vienna Circle were all mathematicians of some proficiency. It was natural that as the prospect receded of knowing anything beyond phenomena by empirical methods, they should raise the question how much could be known by means of a priori construction. How, for example, was mathematical knowledge related to perceptible things? The Platonizing rationalists believed that the mathematician's numbers and figures were themselves realities, independent and eternal, which sensible things imperfectly copied. If this view was ever mentioned in the Circle, it must have received short shrift; non-sensible circles and triangles would have been dismissed as nonsense. Yet the problem that had troubled Plato and all his successors remained a challenging one: how is it that by purely mathematical thinking we are able, as we apparently are, to gain knowledge of the natural world? And not only probable knowledge, but certain knowledge, which we can seldom if ever get from sense experience itself. For example, we may have seen thousands of robins, all red-breasted, but it is perfectly possible, for all we know, that there should be robins without red breasts, and we can never be sure till we have seen it that the next robin we meet will not be one of these. On the other hand, even the geometer may have seen far fewer triangles inscribed in semi-circles than he has robins, but he has no doubt that a triangle so inscribed is a right angle, and if anyone were to suggest to him that the next triangle of the kind that he met with might be a rebel against the rule, he would scoff at the idea. For knowledge about the robin, someone needs to see it. For knowledge about the figure, no one needs to see it. When a man enters an unexplored area in Africa or the Antarctic, he never believes that he should keep an open mind as to whether three fives will make fifteen in this new territory, or whether they may present the amusing novelty of equalling seventeen. He is sure of what he will find in advance. Here seems to be certain knowledge gained about empirical fact through the exercise of abstract reason. How is it possible?

16. The man who had made the most sustained effort to solve this puzzle was Kant, and to Kant the Circle now turned in inquiring though suspicious mood. Kant believed as firmly as his rationalist predecessors in the power of reason to forecast the structure of experience; he knew, or thought he knew, that no event would ever occur uncaused, and that if men were ever in a position to make pilgrimages to remote galaxies, they would find that, though creatures with different senses might live there, they would deal with their sums and their geometrical puzzles in the same way that we do. This power to anticipate what experience would bring was for Kant the most astonishing fact about human knowledge, and he devoted his first *Critique* to the endeavour to explain it. There was only one possible way to explain it, he concluded, and that was to assume that the framework of our world, the systems of space, time, and number, for example, was not *found* in nature by our minds—if that were true, we might at any moment hit on exceptions to them—but were *brought* by our minds to nature, unwittingly imposed by our-selves on the material of sense experience. They were coloured spectacles on our own noses, so regularly worn that we did not know they were there. This being true, of course, we could anticipate experience, for we had ourselves prearranged it. We knew that every future event would have a cause for the excellent reason that we had 'cooked' the result; causality was a category by which experience must be governed if it was to be experience at all. In like manner we knew about the triangle and semi-circle; Euclidean geometry gave the rules in accordance with which we constructed the spatial world.

Now it was this last contention of Kant that proved his undoing for the Vienna inquirers. As students of the newer mathematics, they knew he had blundered. He had taken it for granted that in physics Newton was right, and at this point Newton had nodded. In his calculations about the physical universe Newton had always used the traditional geometry; it seemed never to have led him astray; on the contrary, with the help of it he had been able to chart the solar system and predict its changes with unprecedented accuracy. Everything had confirmed his belief that the geometry of Euclid was the frame-work on which the physical universe was constructed, and naturally Kant followed suit. His own addition, as we have seen, was to say that this framework was mind-imposed. That explained why abstract speculations in the study could predetermine what would be found among the stars. The mind-dependence of space was required by the double insight that Euclidean geometry was self-evidently necessary and that it actually applied to the physical world.

17. On both these points the Vienna group was satisfied that he was in error. What revealed his error on the first point was the develop-ment of geometries differing from Euclid's. It is clear that if you can substitute for any of Euclid's propositions another and intelligible one that contradicts it, and go on to develop by means of this a perfectly consistent geometry, Euclid's system cannot be considered logically necessary. Was there any weak link in Euclid's apparently self-evident chain? A number of mathematicians believed they had found one in his fifth postulate, commonly called the axiom of parallels. This says in effect that through a point outside a line you can draw only one other line that is parallel to it. This did not seem quite self-evident, and suspicions deepened when efforts to prove it from the other postulates failed. Early in the nineteenth century two mathematicians working independently, the Hungarian Bolyai and the Russian Lobachevski, convinced themselves that there was an alternative to it. Let us see how such a conclusion might be suggested. Suppose you draw a straight line and place a dot above it. Mark off a number of points on the line and draw connecting lines with the dot above.

It is clear that the farther out you go along the line in its two directions, the nearer will the bent line at the top approach a straight line as a limit. Now suppose the basic line continued to infinity in each direction. Then you seem to have a line which, while meeting the basic line is still parallel with it, since it has reached the limit at which it coincides with the independently drawn parallel. But if this is true, how can you say it is self-evident that through the dot there can be drawn only one line parallel to the given line? Bolyai and Lobachevski held it to be conceivable that many such lines should be drawn. They found, furthermore, that by combining this denial of Euclid's fifth postulate with his remaining postulates, they could achieve a perfectly consistent system of geometry which, while differing widely from Euclid's, was just as rigorously derived. Riemann a little later reached the same result by substituting still another postulate, namely that *no* parallels could be drawn. Thus the a priori necessity of the old geometry, which Newton and Kant had accepted so unquestioningly, had to be abandoned.

Newton and Kant were apparently wrong also in their second contention, namely that Euclidean geometry was that of the physical world. Here it was Einstein who was the agent of disillusion. His theories of relativity did not, indeed, attempt to show that Euclidean geometry *could* not be applied to physical space, but rather that when astronomical distances were taken into account, the non-Euclidean calculations both applied and were simpler. The relation between his own view and Newton's was a little like that between Newton's and Ptolemy's; in the light of the new facts, Ptolemy's theory became unmanageably complicated, while Newton's covered both the old facts and the new with a single simple formula. Even now Newton's is accurate for all practical purposes, and requires supplementation only when enormous distances are dealt with. But in such cases the assumption that physical objects are in a non-Euclidean space has repeatedly proved to yield the more accurate prediction, its great triumphs coming in its explanation of the slow changes in the perihelion of Mercury and in the precession of the equinoxes. Today it is, I believe, generally accepted among astronomers that in dealing with the sort of triangles and polygons whose apices are scattered among the galaxies, non-Euclidean calculations are more useful because more simple than Euclidean.

18. Where did these reflections leave the Vienna inquirers? If classical geometry was neither necessary in itself nor descriptive of the actual frame of things, what sort of knowledge, if any, did mathematics give us? It was at this juncture that the French mathematician Poincaré came to their aid. To suppose that geometry was somehow at fault because there was more than one system of it, or because one system was less useful in application than another, was in his view to misunderstand what mathematics was trying to do. Mathematical axioms and the systems derived from them were *conventions*. The interest of the pure mathematician was to take a set of definitions and postulates and play with them, so to speak, to develop them into a system as far-reaching and consistent as he could. To him the question whether his system would ever be applied was irrelevant. The geometries of Lobachevski and Riemann were, merely as geometries, as sound and respectable as Euclid's. It was true that they had not, when Poincaré wrote, proved as useful as Euclid's in physics and astronomy, but usefulness had nothing to do with validity, or even with truth. Indeed we have on our hands four ideas that must be clearly distinguished from each other: convention, validity, usefulness, truth. A *convention* is a proposition or system of propositions adopted more or less arbitrarily from among a set of alternatives. A system is *valid* when it is derived in accordance with the laws of logic from the conventional propositions with which it starts. It is *useful* when it enables us to order our experience in a simple and convenient way. It is *true* when its propositions correspond to fact. Poincaré's position was that mathematics was a system of propositions, or rather a set of such systems, derived from starting points that were mere conventions. If we were to choose between the systems, we must do so on the basis of usefulness only. To choose on the basis of truth or falsity was impossible, for none of them was more true or false than any other.

This last may appear strange, and yet for both Poincaré and the positivists it was the essence of the matter. If a mathematical statement is designed to report some fact about the actual world, the principle of verification tells us that we must be able to specify not only the sort of experience that would confirm it but also the sort that would disconfirm it. If we say that $2+2=4$, we have no trouble in finding examples among matches and pencils that accord with it, but if it is meant as a report of fact rather than necessity, it must be theoretically possible that the fact should not be as stated, and that experience could show this. But just what experience could raise a question in our mind about two and two making four? One would have to do better than produce the well-worn case of the two lambs added to two lions, which works out so quickly at two and two making two, or the case of the drops of quicksilver in which two and two make one. No one supposes that such cases shake the multiplication table, for it is obvious that the pure mathematician is not talking about solids or liquids, still less about units with wool or hide on them. $2 + 2 = 4$, said Poincaré, is not an assertion about things at all; there is no imaginable experience that you would accept as belying it; it is a statement that if 4 and the numbers below it are defined in a certain way—which we almost never think of because there is no need for it—then the symbols flanking the $=$ sign have the same meaning. Similarly of geometry. Poincaré did not believe that Euclid could be refuted by any sort of observation, and those who supposed he could were making the same sort of confusion as those who identified the number two with two lions or two lambs; they were not talking about pure geometry, but geometry as interpreted; not about a geometrical straight line, but about a taut cord or the path of a light ray or the edge of a ruler. A discovery that these did not behave in Euclidean fashion would leave the validity of Euclid's reasoning precisely where it was; at best it could only show that Euclid's system was less convenient than some other. Poincaré personally did not believe that even this would ever be shown, but he died before Einstein had presented his main evidence to the contrary.

Now in Poincaré the Vienna group were convinced that they had found the answer to Kant's problem. That problem was how to explain our strange possession of certain knowledge which could not have come from experience. Poincaré's answer was that the problem was an unreal one, because the knowledge that gave rise to it did not exist. Mathematical knowledge is not another road to the objects revealed to us by empirical knowledge; it is not knowledge in the same sense at all. When we think mathematically, we are either adopting certain conventions in the way of definitions and postulates, or else we are spinning out the implications of these. We are not attempting, as Kant supposed, to characterize the world of existing things. We are playing a game with our own ideas. Our interest, when we play it, is not to say 'x is in fact y', 'this cord, stretched taut, is the shortest line between its ends', but 'if I assume that x is y, what follows?', 'if I assume that a straight line is the shortest one, what theoretical consequence does that lead to?'. People have known for thousands of years that if they took the cord to be the straight line the geometer was talking about, they could generally apply his inferences to it, greatly to their advantage. Because this was true, they took it for granted that he was talking about such cords. He was in fact doing nothing of the sort. He was talking about concepts fabricated by himself. That was why he could be so certain about them. Obviously if he went to Mars or Neptune carrying his counters with him and playing his game with them by the old accepted rules, he would always get the same results. Kant's astonishment at our power to anticipate nature was thus based on misunderstanding. But *could* we be certain that actual strings or chalk lines would behave in Mars or Neptune as they do here? No, we could not. The laws governing such things were empirical laws; these laws, as Mach pointed out, were descriptive only; there was no whit of necessity or certainty about them. What Poincaré did for the Vienna circle was thus to convince them that Kant was right in holding mathematical knowledge to be a creation of our own, but wrong in holding it to be a knowledge of anything that exists. Of Poincaré a member of the group writes: 'for us, he was a kind of Kant freed of the remnants of medieval scholasticism and anointed with the oil of modern science.'[1]

19. The picture of the later logical empiricism was now beginning to emerge. At this stage it was a combination of the phenomenalism of Mach with the mathematical conventionalism of Poincaré. But soon the school was advancing well beyond either of these, particularly on the logical side. Poincaré was of course primarily a mathematician, not a logician or a philosopher. Logic and mathematics were for him distinct disciplines. A proof, then, that geometry or arithmetic was based on axioms that were conventional only did not carry with it the corollary that logic too was conventional. Of course if it could be shown that logic and mathematics were really the same discipline, then what Poincaré had shown to hold of the one could also be said of the other; but was this premise true? It was at this point that another figure destined to be important in the thought of the group, Bertrand Russell, appeared on the horizon. In the early chapters of *Principia Mathematica*, 1910, he and Whitehead showed to the satisfaction of the circle that logic and mathematics were one, by proving that the whole of pure mathematics was the development of a few simple

---

[1] Philipp Frank, *Modern Science and Its Philosophy*, 8. The introduction to this book supplies a helpful historical sketch of the Vienna movement.

logical ideas. They showed that everything in mathematics, even irrational numbers, could be brought within the theory of natural numbers or positive integers, and that these natural numbers themselves could be defined in terms of a few logical notions. It had commonly been supposed that such a statement as 'snow is white' was the ascription of a predicate to a subject and was to be analysed not by mathematics but by logic, while the equation $2+2=4$ belonged specially to mathematics. Russell argued that 'snow is white' could be read as a statement of class inclusion, 'snow is a member of the class of white things', and if you wanted to convey what 'white' meant, you must in the end point, your statement then becoming 'snow is a member of the class of things similar to this'. All other statements could be dealt with in the same way, including statements about number. A number is a class. If you want to say what you mean by 'three', the way to do it is to indicate what you take to be three chairs or tables and say that 'three' means the class of all classes that are similar to this class. Now if all statements alike can be interpreted thus extensionally, that is as asserting membership in classes, the business of logic, which deals with the structure of valid thought, is to analyse what is involved in constructing and relating such classes. The achievement of *Principia Mathematica* is to show in detail how from a few basic ideas like 'and', 'not', 'or', 'similar', 'successor', one can develop in orderly fashion not only an entire system of logic, but also everything essential in pure mathematics. Logic, said Russell, is the earlier, more fundamental segments in the chain of mathematical theorems. Mathematics is logic carried out into its implications.

Russell thus opened the way for the application to logic of that theory of conventions which Poincaré had applied to mathematics. This step was not taken by Russell himself. He accepted, at least in his early days, the view of the Platonic rationalists that logic reveals the structure of the actual world. The view that logic tells us nothing about the nature of things and is itself a set of conventions is due to his pupil Wittgenstein, who has the strange distinction of having produced a work on logic beside which the *Logic* of Hegel is luminously intelligible.[1]

20. In this curious work, it is as if a set of Sibylline oracles, scattered

---

[1] The *Tractatus Logico-Philosophicus*, of 1922. Wittgenstein himself did not agree that mathematics could be derived from logic if one defined number as Russell did. If '3' is the class of all classes similar to a given class, it is required that one member of the class should be given; and pure logic cannot guarantee this.

on flying leaves, had been gathered together, some of them extremely astute, some of them absurd, and many of them too dark to be confidently classified as either. It is full of dogmatic pronouncements, introduced abruptly and left without explanation or defence; the reader is puzzled whether its 'take-it-or-leave-it' manner is due to wilfulness or to expository ineptitude, and is only too likely to throw the book impatiently aside. I share the reader's impatience with this way of writing philosophy. But the book remains an important one, not only because of its historical influence, but also because it sums up the results, as of 1922, of both the logical and empirical trends within the movement. What, in the main, it attempted to do was to reduce philosophy to the logic of science by analysing the nature of assertion. It maintained that there were only two kinds of significant assertion and that these two were poles apart. On the one hand there were statements of fact—the statements of common sense and the natural sciences. The reference of these statements was to the facts that would verify them, and such verification must be through sense. But most of the statements we ordinarily make are omnibus statements which, if they are to be made quite clear, must be broken down into a set of component statements, each asserting a single and simple fact. To run down the ultimate reference of some innocent-sounding statement, such as 'There is a flock of grey-and-white pigeons flying about in the yard', may be a matter of great complexity, for many distinguishable statements of fact are involved in it. What does Wittgenstein mean by a fact? It is not a mere sense-impression; it is a state of affairs that cannot be reported short of a proposition 'that x is white', 'that x is larger than y'; and an atomic fact is the simplest kind of such fact—e.g., this spot's being white—which cannot be broken up into any component facts.

The truth or falsity of our statement will depend on the correspondence between the elementary propositions it contains and the atomic facts they refer to. In Wittgenstein's view, the world is an aggregate or collection of such facts. Are they inter-connected in any intelligible system? No. So far is rationalism from being true that no fact necessitates any other; logical necessity is to be looked for not in the nature of things but only in the relations that connect certain of our meanings. This is the position known as logical atomism. The world is a collection of atoms in the form of logically unrelated facts.

We noted that according to Wittgenstein there is a second kind of significant assertion. This is exemplified in the statements of logic and mathematics. These are so different from the first kind that it is

doubtful whether they should be called assertions at all; 'all propositions of logic say the same things,' says Wittgenstein, 'that is,
nothing.'[1] They do not refer to the sensible world; they are not,
strictly speaking, true or false; yet they undoubtedly express something; what is this? It is the formal element in our thinking; more
particularly the pattern in which our meanings must be put together
to make sense, and the rules by which a statement can be transformed
into another of equivalent meaning. Every process of deduction, and
therefore the whole of logic and mathematics, other than their
arbitrary initial definitions and postulates, consists of such trans-
formations. 'I thought of mathematics with reverence,' Russell wrote,
'and suffered when Wittgenstein led me to regard it as nothing but
tautologies.'[2] This, however, it now became. Every mathematical
inference is a statement that something implies something else, and
to say this is merely to make explicit what is already contained in the
premises. This need not mean, of course, that you are thinking of
the conclusion already; you may be surprised when it comes; but any
novelty it may have is psychological, not logical. If we were clever
enough, we should have no need of logic or mathematics, for 'proof
in logic is only a mechanical expedient to facilitate the recognition
of tautology, where the reasoning is complicated.'[3] With intelligence
enough we should see the whole of logic and mathematics in a flash.

21. If these things are true, philosophy must content itself with
being the logic of science. There is nothing else for it to be. For
philosophy to compete with science as a means of discovering facts
would of course be absurd. It would be equally absurd for it to try to
deduce the nature of things by reasoning, for such reasoning would
be merely a spinning out of the implicit contents of our meanings.
These two fields are amply covered already, the field of fact by
natural science, the field of deduction by logic and mathematics.
What work is left for philosophers to do? What they have done in the
past is to indulge in pseudo-assertions which both they and their
readers have been too uncritical to see through. They have either
made non-empirical statements about the actual world, supposing
that these really meant something, as when they have discussed
material or mental substance, the self, or God; or they have attempted
to spin genuinely new conclusions from what they already knew, not
realizing, in their ignorance of sound logic, that this was quite

[1] *Tractatus*, 5.43.
[2] *The Philosophy of Bertrand Russell*, ed. by P. A. Schilpp, 19.
[3] *Tractatus*, 6.1262.

impossible. Once it is seen that both attempts are illegitimate in their very nature, philosophy has a clear alternative. It may either bow itself off the stage as the anachronism it has now become, or it may content itself with the elucidation of what is said by science. If it elects to take the latter course, it will have a useful though humble office. Elucidating the scientist's meanings will not, of course, include telling the chemist what he means by CCl_4 or the biologist what he means by a phagocyte. But these scientists do very commonly use, without analysis, ideas of great generality and importance, such as 'cause', 'force', 'necessity', 'teleology', 'life'; somebody must undertake to separate within these ideas what has cash value in experience and what must be dismissed as irredeemable paper. This is the philosopher's proper office. 'Philosophy is not a theory, but an activity. A philosophical work consists essentially of elucidations. The result of philosophy is not a number of "philosophical propositions", but to make propositions clear.'[1] Thus the former queen of the sciences is conducted to the servants' quarters, with the suggestion that servants with so dubious a past would do well not to render themselves conspicuous. And if the servant rebels against her assignment, her work can readily be transferred; it is merely an extension of science anyhow. Patents of nobility are no safeguards against liquidation.

Wittgenstein had a touch of genius which, combined with personal eccentricity and the commanding platform he inherited as successor to Moore at Cambridge, gave a wide hearing to his doctrine. This doctrine could have been put before the philosophic public in more persuasive form by Schlick, who seems to have been the only member of the circle with any considerable acquaintance with the history of philosophy or understanding of what it had meant to the philosophers of the past. Schlick's death in 1936 at the hands of a demented student was a cruel waste of fine endowments and a heavy blow to the movement. The blow was the heavier because the movement was lacking from the beginning on the humanistic and literary sides, in the sense for the human bearings and importance of what it was saying, and the power to communicate this without pedantic jargon and a parade of esoteric symbols.[2] It was more fortunate then for the movement than first appeared when, owing to Nazi oppression, its capital was transferred to Britain, where a more humane tradition

[1] *Tractatus*, 4.112.

[2] Santayana's remark about Russell might be applied to many members of the positivist school: 'I should be inclined to say of his philosophy what he himself has said of that of Leibniz, that it is at its best in those subjects which are most remote from human life.' *Winds of Doctrine*, 113–14.

of philosophic writing prevails. In Professor A. J. Ayer's *Language, Truth and Logic*, of which the first edition appeared in 1936 and a second ten years later, the position of the school was stated with so much force and clarity as to make it for the first time generally intelligible.

22. We have seen that the chief interest of the continental founders of the school was in science. The ethical implications of their doctrine were reserved for development in Britain and America. It soon became apparent that the position of judgments of right or good under this doctrine was a very curious one. Only two types of statement were recognized as meaningful, as we have seen, statements of sensible fact on the one hand and statements of analytic necessity on the other. Into which class did statements of value fit? They seem clearly not to be statements of empirical fact; when we say, for example, that lying is wrong, the word 'wrong' does not seem to point to any attribute that can be seen or heard, or otherwise sensed. Nor is the statement a necessary truth, for if it were, there could be no exceptions to it, and most of us do not mean this. But if the statement is neither empirical nor necessary, what is to be done with it? The alternative before the positivists was either to revise their theory of knowledge or to deny that statements of value were in the ordinary sense statements at all.

They took the latter course. Statements of value were held to assert nothing whatever; they were neither true nor false; they were pseudo-assertions, which had no cognitive meaning. Does it follow that because they asserted nothing, they expressed nothing? No, for there are other sentences than indicatives and other meanings than cognitive; words may be used by a speaker to express his attitudes; exclamations express his feelings; imperatives express his commands. This opens various possibilities for the interpretations of value statements. The simplest interpretation, which was put forward by Russell and Ayer in the thirties, was called 'emotivism' because such statements were read as exclamations expressing feeling. This view was worked out in detail, with slight modifications, by the American, Charles Stevenson, in his book on *Ethics and Language* of 1944. Since then it has undergone many further modifications, not so much by way of abandoning its central contention that statements of value are not assertions, as by way of developing the many types and shades of attitude that these statements may express. It is clear that to all objectivists in morals, i.e., those who believe that the rightness or wrongness of an action does not depend on our attitudes toward it, this theory is a sharp challenge. For it implies, *prima facie* at least, that there is and can be no objective standard of morals, that if, for example, the communist and non-communist worlds differ ultimately in their attitude toward an action or way of life, it is meaningless to say that either is really right, or more nearly right than the other, or that there is any course, distinct from the actual one, that they ought to follow. This has shocked many moralists. But one cannot refute an ethical analysis by pointing to the unfortunate practical consequences of adopting it. The arguments for emotivist and imperativist views are surprisingly plausible and merit closer examination. Such examination is offered in another book by the present writer.[1]

23. We began by showing that the philosophy of analysis in its main positions was a return to Hume. We have seen that these positions, as repeated by the analysts, were given a fresh significance by the many changes in philosophy, natural science, logic, and mathematics, which had taken place since Hume wrote; indeed, it was these intervening developments far more than any influence from Hume himself that produced the new philosophy.

A study of positivism in all its aspects would take us beyond our restricted purpose, which is to inquire how far, if at all, the philosophy of analysis has invalidated the conception of reason as a means to philosophical knowledge. Fixing our attention for the time on the positivists as the pioneers and for long the moving spirits of the philosophy of analysis, we have seen that their main achievement was to refurbish and restore to credibility four contentions of Hume. These are—to give them their modern names—logical atomism, the verifiability theory of meaning, the conventional and analytic character of the *a priori*, and the emotivist theory of value. All of these theories bear in the most intimate way upon the range and function of reason. If the first theory is true, such monistic philosophies as those of Spinoza, Hegel, and Bradley will be ruled out, together with the notion of the concrete universal, the coherence theory of truth, and internal relations among facts. If the second theory is true, the ideas of self, substance, matter, universals, God, reality—ideas that rightly or wrongly have formed part of the stock in trade of philosophy in the past—must be either radically revised or else discarded as meaningless. If the third theory is true, rationalism in every form from Plato to McTaggart must be admitted to be based on a radical misunderstanding of the nature and office of reason. If the fourth theory is true, moral values and indeed values

[1] *Reason and Goodness*, Ch. 8, 9.

generally must be moved out of the sphere of knowledge and rational criticism. Any one of these theories, and still more the four of them jointly, would, if true, reduce very sharply the range within which reason has been accustomed to move. In the face of so varied an attack, some restriction of its old empire would appear to be inevitable. What sort of shrinkage is necessary, and how great must it be? These are the questions we must try to answer. Leaving the theory of value for later consideration, we shall deal successively in the three chapters that follow with the three other main contentions of positivism.

CHAPTER IV

LOGICAL ATOMISM

1. Logical atomism is the view that the world consists of simple facts, each of them independent of all the rest. It is a view to which logical positivism, and indeed the philosophy of analysis generally, has tended from the first. To be sure, it is a metaphysical theory, and logical empiricists, who eschew metaphysics, might be expected to reject it. Many of them have done so. Others, like Wittgenstein, have admitted that on their assumptions it is nonsense, but have held it to be 'important nonsense'. Others still, like Russell, have thought that while most metaphysics is nonsense, this is not. Why is it that this type of philosophy, which is not particularly plausible on the surface, has held so strong an attraction for the analysts? The reason, I think, is that it is the philosophy upon which the two strongest trends in logical empiricism converge. These, intelligibly enough, are logic and empiricism. We said that, according to atomism, the facts of which the world is composed are at once simple and independent. Their simplicity is demanded by empiricism, for which analysis has always involved the breaking up of wholes into the simplest sensible parts. Their independence is the demand of the particular kind of logic to which analysts generally have been inclined, the logic of *Principia Mathematica*. It will repay us to examine these two demands separately. We shall begin from the empiricist side.

2. Suppose that a person given to analysis remarks 'we have had an unusually fine summer', and then pauses to ask himself what exactly he means by this. The remark is perfectly commonplace; no one but an analyst would raise such a question about it, since to the plain man it says nothing that is in the least ambiguous or obscure. But is the plain man right about this? By a fine summer he means, no doubt, a summer of fine weather. By fine weather he means sunny weather, but not so sunny as to be excessively hot, nor so continuously sunny as to be excessively dry, though he is not clear how much of either excess is excluded by his statement. Again, he is not saying that today

is a fine day, or that the last week has been fine, for both may have
been miserable; yet he must mean that many days have been fine.
How many? All of them? No; for that would be desert weather. Most
of them? Probably, since he said that the summer had been 'unusually'
fine, and this means, presumably, that the ratio of sunny days to
those that were rainy, cold, and cloudy, has been higher than usual.
But just what does *this* mean? In order to be quite clear, we should
have to know what the usual ratio is and how far beyond this the
present summer has gone. And in order to know that, we should have
to know something about every day in the whole summer.

The plain man, if asked whether he had meant anything as complicated and definite as this, might well be puzzled. He had certainly
not considered the precise meaning of sunniness or the ratio of
sunny to rainy days in his notion of fine weather; on these points his
thought was lax and unformed. It has sometimes been said that the
main task of the philosophy of analysis is to analyse ordinary usage.
If this means examining the actual content of the ordinary mind
when it uses ordinary terms, it would be as unprofitable a business
as the sort of fiction that describes unselectively the 'stream of
consciousness' of any housewife or bricklayer taken at random. When
most of us talk about the weather or the cause of the headache we
had this morning or the shingle that just fell off the roof, it would be
idle to explore our meaning for something profound and precise
about meteorology, causality, or matter; if our thought is definite
enough for practical purposes, that is all we are interested in at the
moment. If an analyst hectors us with questions we never thought of
raising, he is bound to get dusty answers; our thought is too blundering to yield anything else; and if he succeeds in extracting from it
something significant and definite, the probability is that the rabbit
he has pulled out of the hat was put there by himself. 'Everything,'
says Russell, 'is vague to a degree you do not realize till you have
tried to make it precise, and everything precise is so remote from
anything we normally think, that you cannot for a moment suppose
that is what we really mean when we say what we think.'[1]

The interesting question therefore is not what is actually in mind
when we engage in ordinary talk, but what would be in mind if,
saying the same things, we were thinking exactly. It is this sort of
analysis rather than exercises in psychology or the running down of
dictionary meanings that most interested the positivists from the
beginning. We offer our remark about the weather as true. If so, we
presumably have some idea of what will render it true; indeed to

[1] *The Monist*, 1918, 498.

assert anything responsibly, the positivists said, just *is* to assert what will render it true. Very well, what is it that would render true our remark about the weather? Plainly not the existence of some vague state of 'fineness' persisting throughout the summer, for there has been no such state; and equally plainly not some average of heat or moisture or cloudiness, for when such an average is worked out, it may be found not to have been realized on any single day. So even if we assert that a certain average did hold, which is likely enough, what we mean by it, that is, what we must mean if we were thinking of what would make our statement true, was a *great number of particular facts about the weather on particular days*.

3. The next question is what sort of facts these are. The positivists answered that they were empirical facts, and by empirical facts they meant facts given in sense perception. This seems straightforward enough. As I sit in my study at this moment I hear a car passing; looking through the window I see a rhododendron bush; my dog runs in and I pause for a moment and pat his head. These statements record sensible facts. But do they? Analysts have a commendable passion for precision, and they would stop us here to point out that none of these cases, as we commonly take them, is an example of merely sensible fact. We 'hear' the passing car. But surely what we hear is a kind of noise. This kind of noise has so often been linked with experiences of cars that we have no hesitation in taking it as the sound of a car, but the car itself is not given; we reach the thought of it by some process that is clearly not sensation. Strictly speaking, no one ever hears a motor-car. Again, I say that I 'see' the rhododendron bush. But do I? I see certain colours and perhaps certain shapes; but is my recognition that these are the colours and shapes of rhododendron leaves a matter of sensation merely? Obviously something more is at work, for my grasp that this is a rhododendron involves an interpretation of the given qualities that goes far beyond mere seeing. So with the other example. I pat the dog, and say without hesitation that I feel his head. But what I have actually felt is a certain roughness and hardness. However silly it might be to doubt that these belong to my dog's head, the fact that they do is not something I can feel, as I can the roughness and hardness themselves. It is arrived at by another and further process. Thus statements about things heard or seen or felt turn out to go beyond what is given in sense almost as obviously as do statements about the summer's weather.

4. Does it follow that if we are to think clearly, we should never refer

E

to things at all? If clarity requires confining ourselves to what may be given in sense, that does seem to follow, for in strictness we never do sense a *thing*; we see colours and hear sounds and smell odours, and so on, but such direct and simple awareness will not carry us to tables and chairs. Whether these things can still be talked about consistently with clear thinking depends, the positivist tells us, on how we construe them. If we construe them as many or most philosophers of the past have done, we shall have forfeited the right to talk about them at all, for we shall have made them into ghosts. These philosophers have said that, in addition to all the qualities of a thing, there must be something for them to belong to; the table *is* not its shape plus its colour plus its hardness, and so on; it is that which *has* them, the substance in which they inhere; and to identify the table with its qualities would leave this *it* without a meaning. Quite so, replies the positivist; it really is meaningless, and we are very well rid of it; the substance of the table, if this is opposed to its sensible qualities, is a metaphysical myth. Other philosophers have insisted that the real table is that which endures, and since our sense impressions of it do not endure, we must go behind and beyond them if we would reach the reality. The real table is a timeless, universal essence, an abstract 'tableness' which may be apprehended readily enough by intelligence, but is certainly not visible to any bodily eye. Nonsense again, says the positivist; no such invisible, inaudible, intangible, untasteable, and unsmellable entity ever was on sea or land. It too is a myth. The thought of a thing can be made definite on one condition only, namely that the thing be construed in sensible terms altogether.

Is this practicable? Yes. To be sure, the table is not exhausted by the set of qualities we see. We never perceive a table without implicitly admitting more in it than meets the eye. But this 'more' means more of the same. When we perceive the table as having a leg and an underside that we do not see, our reference is still to sense data, not to substances or universals. We assume that if we looked at it from other angles, we should see a leg and an underside, and that is all we mean when we ascribe these things to it. Similarly, when we speak of its having been here yesterday, we are saying that if an observer had cared to look, he would have seen it here. The table *is* the family of sense data through which it does or might present itself to us, the sum total of its appearances, the ordered aggregate of data that it would present to observers at all angles and distances. Granting that it would be a somewhat complicated business to work out the rules of membership in this family, the difficulty does not seem insuperable; indeed such rules have already been formulated by Russell and Price.

5. Thus to think with ultimate clearness, even about the most commonplace matters, may require us to break up our statements into many component statements. We may believe we have arrived at simplicity long before we have actually done so. 'There is a black ink-spot.' That seems to be simple enough. But it is not really a simple statement; it is at least four different statements rolled into one: first, 'that is a spot', second, 'that is caused by ink', third, 'that is black', the fourth, 'that is at a certain place'. The proof is that the denial of any of these statements would be felt at once as a denial of our original statement. And so long as we suppose ourselves to be making simple statements when we are not, we are confused. Even when we say, 'that spot is black', we are still making a compound statement. Being a spot and being black are different facts; something could be a spot without being black, and black without being a spot; clearness requires two separate assertions. In general, then, clearness is achieved only when we have brought to light, in distinctness from each other, all the simple statements of fact that would have to be true if our original statement is to be true.

6. What do we find when we reach the end of this quest? What is an atomic fact like? Does its simplicity mean that it is itself without parts or elements? No. The simplest fact is not the simplest entity. For a fact is the sort of thing that is reported in a proposition or statement, and the simplest such thing must have at least two elements, corresponding to the S and P of a proposition. What sort of entities are these? According to Russell, they are of two kinds, particulars on the one hand and characters or relations on the other. Particulars are what are referred to by the subjects of atomic statements, and were called by Russell constituents of these; characters and relations are what are named by the predicates, and were called components. An atomic fact may have more than one constituent. In terms of the symbols commonly used, it may be of the form φa, e.g., 'this is red', or of the form $R(a, b)$, e.g., 'this is equal to that', in which the two constituent particulars are connected by a relation; it may have an even more complex form when a connection is asserted between three or more constituents. All compound or molecular facts are composed of atomic facts; every atomic fact in turn is composed of these logical protons and electrons.[1]

[1] Wittgenstein ineptly called these 'objects'—ineptly because the name suggests the relation, not here in question, of object to subject.

7. Here, said Russell and the atomists, we reach the ultimate elements of nature. What are they like? As is suggested by calling them ultimate, they cannot be divided or dissected further. If we say 'this is red', the red we mean to assert is a simple unanalysable quality. To be sure, doubts arose even here. Professor Wisdom pointed out that 'red' may be ambiguous and stand for a variety of shades. So if our meaning is to be quite clear, it must stand for one shade only, which is absolutely specific. And this shade is a universal. If this seems odd in view of its specific character, we may recall that by definition a universal is what may occur in diverse contexts, and since precisely this shade may be given elsewhere, it falls under the definition. Relations also are universals; for example, the relation of equality that unites 2 and 2 with 4 is identical with the equality that unites 4 and 4 with 8. It is the early Russell that is speaking here, the Russell of *The Problems of Philosophy* (1912) and the lectures on *Logical Atomism* (1918-19). Such views could hardly be congenial to empiricism, since in accepting universals it was accepting much that admittedly could not be sensed. The later and more empiricist Russell convinced himself that he could do without universals. Whether this was an advance we shall not stop here to enquire.

8. The predicate of an atomic proposition denotes, then, a universal character or relation. What about the subject? This denotes a particular. And what is that? Curiously enough, one cannot say. One can of course give the general meaning of 'particular'; we can say it is that which can serve only as subject, never as predicate, of an assertion, or, as Russell does, that it is a term related or characterized in an atomic fact. But that does not put a particular before us; it only tells us what sort of thing a particular is. Every descriptive word we may use fails in the same way. Suppose we say 'This spot is red'. Does 'this spot' denote our subject? Not without intruding an unwanted description again. For the word 'spot' means a universal which might have many instances; it is really a predicate and, as we have seen, calls for expression in a separate statement. The particular we are in search of must not be confused with its characteristics of being a spot and being red, for it is that to which we ascribe them. Hence any word that is to refer to it unambiguously must denote without connoting, must point without characterizing.

Is there any kind of word that does this? John Stuart Mill thought that it was done by proper names, that whereas if one mentioned Socrates by a descriptive phrase like 'the teacher of Plato', both types of reference were present, the proper name 'Socrates' merely pointed to the individual without carrying any description. All particulars might in theory be designated by proper names, Russell suggested; if I am thinking of a particular dot on a blackboard, might I not save trouble by calling it 'John'? But he saw that this would not do. When the dot is first christened thus, the name does denote a particular; but when it is used, as it chiefly is, to communicate my meaning or serve as a later reminder to myself, it has lapsed into a description; it now means 'the dot that was pointed at under certain conditions yesterday'. It clearly connotes as well as denotes. And if truth must be told, so do all ordinary proper names. We think of Socrates through one or more characteristics of Socrates. Mill was therefore wrong about proper names. In their ordinary use they characterize. Are there any that do not, any names that can be called *logically* proper names? Only such terms, Russell answered, as 'this' and 'that', which serve solely as pointers to something given at the moment. The particular *is* this unique and fleeting something that is immediately given in sensation, characterizable but not itself a character. And since it is given in *my* sensation, it is incommunicable. What is thus given to me cannot be given to you. To be sure, my toothache may have a character that can appear in yours also, but that does not make my toothache yours. The particular in each case is that which makes the experience non-transferable.

The empiricist here runs into difficulties. He wanted no part in the substance which Aristotle, Locke, and even common sense find in ordinary things as that to which their qualities belong; but the particular he now offers us, contentless, incommunicable, and apparently non-sensible, is uncomfortably like this notorious will-o'-the-wisp, and we shall soon have to look at it more narrowly. Again, each of us is supposed to bring all things to the test of experience, but of the myriad of facts in the world, the only ones that he can bring to this test are the few that appear in his own little field of awareness. Does he then talk irresponsibly if he refers to anything outside it? Wittgenstein, not over-inhibited by common sense, gave a strange and uncompromising answer, as we shall see.

9. Meanwhile the empiricist line of analysis had apparently reached some firm conclusions. It we are to think clearly, we must unpack our omnibus statements so that we may see distinctly all their component statements. These component statements must refer to empirical facts, and ultimately to atomic facts. Each atomic fact is a particular qualified by a character, or else a set of particulars united by a relation. The ultimate cash value, then, of the statement 'we have had an unusually fine summer' would be an immense range of facts, presented through manifold experiences of many persons, facts of temperature, humidity, sunniness, breeziness, and so on, at particular times and places. Each of these atomic facts could be expressed in an atomic statement such as 'this is hot' or 'this is hotter than that'. To reach these ultimates is the goal of philosophic analysis.

We remarked in beginning this chapter that atomism is the joint result of two factors in logical empiricism, its empiricism and its logic. We have been examining the empirical factor, the endeavour, that is, to analyse all factual statements into a set of simple sensory references, and we have seen how this runs out into atomism of fact and statement. It is time we turned to the other or logical factor and saw how this contributes to the same result.

10. When Russell and Whitehead were at work on *Principia Mathematica*, they did not think that what they were doing was merely playing an elaborate game. Mathematics for them was a study of the most fundamental, in the sense of the most general, relations that held things together, the structure or framework of the actual world. Identity and difference, the various kinds of series and relations, continuity and infinity, the linkages described by axioms and their implications, were not conventions or linguistic rules, but an integral part of the fabric of things, and to study them was a philosophical pursuit. This does not mean, of course, that mathematics is concerned with any existent thing rather than any other; it never mentions this table or Socrates, never makes a factual statement, never refers to any one of the million empirical characters that give content to experience. Its statements concern *any* particular, *any* character, *any* proposition, *any* class. They are as basic as they are bleak. In telling us virtually nothing about anything, they tell us something about everything; and that something, though little, is important.

What was important about it in Russell's mind was that it provided the syntax of an ideal language. The most obvious use of a language is to help us communicate with each other. No possible language, to be sure, will enable us to communicate the particular thises and thats of our experience, our sense data of toothaches, burns, and flashes. These are confined to the little island on which each of us lives alone. We can communicate only generalities. And the wider those generalities, the more certain it will be that the language expressing them will be a universal language. Now mathematics is precisely the language of these widest generalities. If we look behind the endlessly varying ways in which we express ourselves in common speech, we shall find a comparatively few patterns that form its stock in trade, patterns that recur so constantly that we take them for granted and seldom notice or speak of them. Mathematical logic singles these out and provides us symbols for them. We have seen that, according to the analysts, whenever we make a simple judgment, we ascribe or deny a character to some particular, or state a relation between particulars. By giving us simple symbolic schemes for these forms of statement, mathematical logic supplies outlines for everything we could possibly say. Particulars or individuals it usually denotes by letters of the alphabet, such as a, b, c. Characters it denotes by Greek letters such as φ or ψ. When we say 'this is red', we think we are saying something very different from 'Socrates is mortal', and so we are. But not in form: in both cases we are affirming a character of a particular, and hence mathematical logic would express them both by symbols of the same form, for example, φa and ψb. Relations it denotes, not by isolated letters, since relations never occur in isolation, but in such manner as to indicate in the symbol itself that they occur as links between terms; a relation that links two terms, for example, is referred to as aRb, or R(a,b). This pattern remains the same for all two-term relations. 'Darby loves Joan' is a very different statement from 'this is to the left of that', but since each asserts a relation between two terms, the symbol of aRb gives us the scheme of both. If now we recall the atomists' analysis of simple statements, as asserting either a character or a relation, it will be evident that whenever we open our mouths and make such a statement, we are saying φa or aRb. The concrete filling of these blank forms will be as various as the infinitely diverse experiences that life brings to us. But the syntax, the pattern of pigeon-holes in which we place them, is everywhere and always the same.

11. So far of single statements. But if our talk consisted only of a series of single and simple statements, it would be an intolerable succession of disconnected, staccato pronouncements. We neither think nor talk in this fashion. Ordinary language, as we have seen, is a kind of shorthand in which a great many statements may be telescoped into one, with their meanings and relations left vague. But often we need to make the relations between our statements explicit, to make statements in which the terms related are themselves statements. It would seem at first glance as if our statements could be connected in so many different ways as to be beyond all classification. The things they say may in all degrees resemble each other or tend to support each other. But we must remember that mathematical logic has no interest in *what* we think; it leaves this out entirely in order to fix attention on the form. Hence when it studies the relations between p and q, it disregards what they say, and takes them as just *any* two propositions, stating anything whatever. But how can you relate assertions except through what they assert? Mathematical logic has its own way—a somewhat curious way—of dealing with this problem. Even if you do not know what p and q say, it points out, you know at least that they must be either true or false, and you can classify their relations on that basis alone. It substantiates its claim with another astonishing example of simplification. *Principia Mathematica* gets along with just four compound statements, or statements of relation between other statements, namely, contradiction, disjunction, conjunction, and implication, and even of these it derives the last three by combining the first with one of the others. If we are to see why this work was accepted by many analysts as providing an ideal language, we must look a little more closely at its way of arriving at these relations.

You have any two statements, p and q, and you know beforehand that each is either true or false, though you do not know which. What relations are possible between them?

(1) One obvious possibility is that they should contradict each other, that the truth of either should exclude the truth of the other. If p contradicts q, it may be regarded simply as the denial of q and may be written '$\sim q$', the wave being the sign of denial; and q may be written '$\sim p$'. (2) But suppose they are not contradictories; there are various further possibilities which are best brought out by considering how their 'truth-values' may be combined, the truth-value of a statement being its truth or falsity. The combinations may be shown in a simple table:

p	q
T	T
F	F
T	F
F	T

This indicates on the successive lines that p and q may both be true, or that they may both be false, or that the first may be true and the second false, or the first false and the second true. (3) Regarding any two or more of these values we might wish to assert them as alternatives; for example, we might say that p or q is true, i.e. one of them at least; and we should then write our statement symbolically p v q. (4) Or again, we might wish to state that p and q were true together; and then we should write their conjoint statement as $p.q$. (5) Or, finally, we might want to state both a disjunction and a conjunction— a disjunction, for example, between various combinations of truth-values. There are clearly many possibilities here, but even in the elaborate deductions of *Principia Mathematica* only one was found necessary, the one described as 'implication' and denoted by the sign ⊃. Implication is a disjunction between lines 1, 2, and 4 in our truth-table; that is, p will imply q whenever they are both true, or both false, or p is false while q is true. In short, it always implies q except where the third combination holds, i.e. where p is true while q is false.

12. In this scheme the relations most commonly asserted between statements are reduced to four. But our simplification is not yet at an end. For the relations are not really independent of each other; we can start with either disjunction or conjunction and by combining it with negation get all of the last three, and hence can freely translate one form of statement into another. Suppose we start with disjunction, p v q; we can see that this is equivalent to its not being true that both statements are false; to state an alternative is to deny a conjunction; in symbols, p v $q. =.{\sim}({\sim}p.{\sim}q)$ Df.; i.e. p v q may be defined as meaning that p and q are not false together. If we start with conjunction, $p.q$, we can by combining it with negation, get disjunction, for we can see that this is equivalent to its not being true that p or q is false; in symbols, $p.q. =.{\sim}({\sim}p$ v ${\sim}q)$ Df. And finally, starting again with conjunction we can combine it with negation in a slightly different way to get implication. We saw that p was taken to imply q in all cases other than the one in which p was true and q false. Putting this in symbols, $p{\supset}q. =.{\sim}(p.{\sim}q)$ Df. By the aid of these equivalences, all assertions of types (2), (3), or (4) of how statements are connected can be translated without difficulty into each other. Shortly after *Principia Mathematica* was written, Professor H. M. Sheffer pointed out that these derivations could be reduced still further, for, if he were given the single relation 'p and q both false', which he denoted by p/q, he could derive all the others.[1] But the scheme and symbols of *Principia* are those that are most generally followed.

[1] *Trans. Amer. Math. Soc.*, Vol. 14, 481–8. P. F. Strawson has shown that the same result can be achieved if 'p/q' is taken to mean that *either* p or q is false. See his *Introduction to Logical Theory*, 96.

13. To this logical scheme the technical terms 'truth-functional' and 'extensional' have often been applied. It is now easy to see what these terms mean. To say that the scheme is 'truth-functional' means that when a statement is made within it whose terms are themselves statements, its truth depends exclusively upon the truth of the constituent statements. In many cases this stands for mere common sense. If we say 'Mr X is old and wise', we are conjoining two statements about Mr X, and it is plain that our statement as a whole will not be true unless each of its constituent statements is true. It is not very likely that we should say 'Mr X is *either* old or wise', but if we did, it would be clear again that the truth of the statement would depend entirely on the truth-values of the subordinate statements; if either of these is true, the major statement is true; if both are false, it too is false. But suppose someone says 'If Mr X is old, it follows that he is wise'; we should obviously protest, 'Not at all; it does not in the least follow that a man must be wise just because he is old'. Here the truth-functional logic sharply diverges from common sense. Declining to consider *what* statements affirm, or how their contents are connected, insisting on making its statements as abstract and formal as may be, and therefore confining itself to the sort of properties that all statements have in common, it decides even the question whether one statement implies another by looking solely to their truth or falsity. If Mr X happens in fact to be both old and wise, it would say that his age implied his wisdom.

This will make clear what is meant by calling mathematical logic 'extensional'. The term does not mean what it does in traditional logic, though the uses are analogous. In the older logic a general term was read in intension when used to refer to the properties in virtue of which anything was recognized as the member of a class; it was read in extension when it referred to the various members themselves. Similarly, logic is called extensional when, abstracting from all that is asserted by propositions, it deals with those propositions merely as units of truth or falsity. Common sense, before it could say whether p implied q, would have to know what p and q said; if p was 'this is a triangle' and q was 'this has angles which sum up to a straight line', it would say that p did imply q; if the predicates were age and wisdom, it would deny that implication was present. Not so with extensional logic. It is concerned solely with whether truth-values in fact accompany each other. If p and q are called incompatible, that means that they are never in fact both true; if p implies q, that means that p is never in fact true while q is false. The only necessity it recognizes belongs to the rules of the game, and this necessity itself, as we shall later note, it regards as more or less arbitrary.

14. We are now in a position to see why *Principia Mathematica* contributed so powerfully not only to the advance of analytic philosophy, but also to the logical atomism which was the implicit metaphysic of the movement. The analysts wanted above all things a philosophy that was clear and precise. *Principia* supplied a language which, if its requirements were met, would guarantee that clarity and precision. 'It aims at being that sort of a language,' said Russell, 'that, if you add a vocabulary, would be a logically perfect language.'[1] Every truth about the world would be ultimately analysable into a statement, or set of statements, asserting a character of a particular or a relation between particulars, and expressible in such forms as φa and aRb. The proper filling for these forms must be left to experience to supply, and of course we might fill them wrongly by using a particular that was not simple or a character that was not single. But that would be our fault, not that of the language, which in matters of form would always take us right. And it supplied not only the forms of the ultimate or atomic statements, but also the system in which these statements were to be related. Assuming that, as philosophers, we wanted a systematic account of the world, it showed us how such an account must proceed. It will proceed by the four methods of compounding statements given above, and it will move by deductive steps from comparatively simple sets of atomic statements to statements of such complexity that our minds would break down under them unless we could handle them through symbols. The chain of implications is rigorous and unbroken. Here was a language in which everything true could be said, a language in which, if its forms were properly filled, nothing false could be said, a language in which the relation of every possible statement to every other could be made clear by its place in one completely articulated system.

It was a splendid vision. No wonder that empiricists, little given as a rule to mathematical speculation and somewhat wanting on the side of system, should have welcomed with enthusiasm this uncovenanted support. Logic has commonly been the weak point with empiricists, and they were naturally both pleased and surprised to find the most formidable logic of modern times, elaborated with an unexampled virtuosity, thrown into the balance in their favour. It was as if a little band of campaigners against the main tradition of philosophy, armed with somewhat primitive weapons and fighting

[1] *The Monist*, Vol. 28 (1918), 520.

against large odds, suddenly found the legions of Napoleon marching in order at their side.

15. But, after all, mathematics is not philosophy. Mathematics or logic (*Principia* showed that they were continuous) can tell us that *if p* is false or *q* is true, *p* implies *q*; it cannot tell us whether *p* or *q* is true in fact. It does not even undertake to tell us whether the laws and structures that it uses, the 'laws of thought', for example, or the structures of Euclidean geometry, are figments of our own creation or reflections of the nature of the things. When mathematicians have philosophized, they have held both views, but these views were no part of their mathematics. One of course does not prove that the world is made of atomic facts, related to each other only externally, by showing that a wonderfully convenient system of statements would be applicable to them if only there were such things. An ideal language is surely to be devised by first noting what things exist and then adjusting the language to their nature and relations.

Now in the intercourse of mathematics with atomism the curious fact is that this process was reversed. The language was not accepted because the facts required it; the facts were construed to be thus rather than so because the conditions of what was conceived as an ideal language required it. 'It is important,' as Professor Urmson has said, 'to see that in accordance with the derivation of the metaphysics from logic the atomists did not say that some particular things appeared to be the basic ingredients of the world from which they would try to build it, but decided a priori what the basic ingredients would be like, and then looked round for things to fill the bill. . . .'[1] In beginning his lectures on logical atomism, Russell said: 'The kind of philosophy that I wish to advocate, which I call Logical Atomism, is one which has forced itself upon me in the course of thinking about the philosophy of mathematics . . . I shall try to set forth . . . a kind of logical doctrine which seems to me to result from the philosophy of mathematics—not exactly logically, but as what emerges as one reflects: a certain kind of logical doctrine, and on the basis of this a certain kind of metaphysic.'[2] Wittgenstein, like Russell, came into philosophy through mathematics, as the reader is constantly reminded by the language and arrangement of his *Tractatus*; and one gains the

---

[1] *Philosophical Analysis*, 17.

[2] *The Monist*, Vol. 28 (1918), 495–6. In his essay on 'Logical Atomism' in *Contemporary British Philosophy*, Vol. I, he returns to the discussion of 'an ideal logical language' in order 'to suggest, by enquiring what logic requires of a language which is to avoid contradiction, what sort of structure we may reasonably suppose the world to have'. 377.

impression even more strongly in his case than in that of his teacher that his intellectual cosmos is the by-product of his logic. In this logic statements that are not tautologies are connected only by conjunction and disjunction; none ever necessitates another. If these statements and their connections are to reflect facts, the facts too must be hard atoms unrelated by necessities—that seems to be the drift of the argument. So far as that is the argument, it is of course invalid. But the conclusion may be true without being validly drawn, and whether it is or not depends on whether our statements do actually reflect the nature of things. On this point the atomists, and particularly Wittgenstein, had interesting things to say.

16. All compound propositions, they said, are truth-functions of the propositions which are their terms. On what does the truth of these component propositions depend? On the truth of the atomic propositions into which they can be analysed. On what, then, does the truth of atomic propositions depend? It depends, Wittgenstein answered, on the faithful *picturing* by the proposition of the atomic fact it asserted; 'the proposition is a picture of reality'; 'it *shows* how things stand *if* it is true.'[1] And what does this picture reveal the atomic fact to be? We have seen the answer to this. An atomic fact is a particular characterized by some sensible quality, or a pair or more of particulars connected by a relation. The proposition that reports it correctly will do so through likeness of structure. In the typical case its subject will name the particular, its predicate will name the quality, and its arrangement of terms will reflect the arrangement existing in nature.

At first glance this seems clear. But on a point that is so vital in the conception of both meaning and truth, the utmost precision is wanted, and unfortunately Wittgenstein's own account of his doctrine is so obscure and incoherent that one cannot make out with certainty what he meant, if indeed he had any precise meaning in mind. He often speaks as if by a proposition he meant a sentence; the term he uses for statement or proposition is the German word for sentence, *Satz*; and he insists that when he refers to a picture, he is referring to a fact, that is, a sensible fact. This leads one to suppose that the picture consists of the ordered words, either heard or seen, that compose a sentence. But he can hardly have meant this, since then if one spoke in French or German, what was true, and asserted as true, would be quite different from what it would be if one spoke in English, which is absurd. Recognizing this perhaps,

[1] *Tractatus*, 4.01, 4.022.

Wittgenstein seems to fall back on a different doctrine, that what pictures the fact is not the sentence, but the 'propositional sign' (*das Satzzeichen*). What is this? We are told that the elements of this sign are words, which would seem to bring us back to the sentence, but then we are assured that 'the essential nature of the propositional sign becomes very clear when we imagine it made up of spatial objects (such as tables, chairs, books) instead of written signs'.[1] (To be sure, the uninstructed reader might have supposed that the written signs were themselves spatial objects.) Wittgenstein goes on: 'The mutual spatial position of these things then expresses the sense of the proposition.'[2] What he seems to mean is this: One cannot say that that which means, and is true or false, is merely this set of marks on paper, for the same assertion may be made with a quite different set of marks; indeed it can be made through gestures, flags, or sounds. Very well; suppose you make the same assertion through a variety of these physical means. Consider the arrangement of parts that is common to them. This will be 'the propositional sign'. 'The gramophone record, the musical thought, the score, the waves of sound, all stand to one another in that pictorial internal relation, which holds between language and the world.'[3] All of these have in common an arrangement of physical parts, and it is this, rather than a string of words merely, that constitutes the propositional sign; it is this that is essential, this that is true or false, and this that reveals, through community of pattern, the architecture of the fact. The gramophone record, the score, and the sound waves, since 'to all of them the logical structure is common',[4] carry the same propositional sign and are thus vehicles of the same assertion.

17. If a propositional sign, then, is to mean a fact or be true of it, it must have a similar structure. This requires that between the elements of sign and fact there must be a one-to-one relation. So far we have been speaking chiefly of the *terms* of the fact and the sign; the names in the sign correspond to the particulars and qualities of the fact. But what of the *relations* in the fact? How are they indicated in the sign? Here appears one of Wittgenstein's most characteristic theses. He says that when it comes to indicating these relations, language breaks down; they cannot be indicated, denoted, or spoken of; they can only be shown. He would deny that when we say 'this is

[1] *Tractatus*, 3.1431.
[2] *Ibid.*, 3.1431.
[3] *Ibid.*, 4.014.
[4] *Ibid.*

red', the '*is*' stands for a distinct element in the fact, as 'this' and 'red' do; it serves rather as a mere intimation that something is being asserted. Hence the relation holding between the terms of the fact must be conveyed, if at all, not by words or signs, but by the patterns of their arrangement. 'The picture consists in the fact that its elements are combined with one another in a definite way.'[1] 'Propositions cannot represent the logical form; this mirrors itself in the propositions. That which mirrors itself in language, language cannot represent. . . . The propositions *show* the logical form of reality. They exhibit it. . . . What *can* be shown *cannot* be said.'[2]

18. This doctrine is one of the two main grounds for Wittgenstein's rejection of metaphysics. One of these grounds is the verifiability theory of meaning, which would put down as meaningless any statement about fact that could not be verified in sense. The other was this doctrine that it was impossible to denote through words the structure of things. Of course if philosophy cannot do this, neither can science. The forms of scientific facts it can express only through statements—ultimately atomic statements—whose structures mirror the structures of nature. But though the form of a fact cannot be denoted, its terms can. The terms of a true scientific statement will correspond to a particular and a quality that can be verified in sense. But all statements of this kind will fall somewhere or other within the domain of science, and there will be none left over for philosophy. 'The totality of true propositions is the total natural science (or the totality of the natural sciences)' and 'philosophy is not one of the natural sciences'.[3] Of course philosophy has often made pronouncements about fact. It has often rushed incontinently into the field of science and pontificated about the theory of evolution (which belongs to biology) or the self (which belongs to psychology) or the relation of matter and mind (which belongs to psycho-physics). But this is brash and naïve. If it leaves such matters to science, as it should, what will be its true office? Can it retreat to the narrower plot that metaphysics has tilled traditionally, the field of the categories? These would certainly give it importance, for they are the fundamental types of structure exhibited in the world, for example, substance and attribute, cause and effect, identity and difference, falsity and truth. But no; philosophy is excluded from this area too. If it is to deal with these categories, it can do so only through language, and since they

[1] *Tractatus*, 2.14.
[2] *Ibid.*, 4.121, 4.1212.
[3] *Ibid.*, 4.11, 4.111.

are inexpressible, they are beyond discussion. 'Whereof one cannot speak, thereof one must be silent.'[1] So far as they can be dealt with at all, they are mirrored in the statements of science, and any attempt to go beyond this and to describe or even denote them directly can only be self-defeating. What then is philosophy to do? Wittgenstein answers:

'The right method of philosophy would be this: to say nothing except what can be said, i.e. the propositions of natural science, i.e. something that has nothing to do with philosophy; and then always, when someone else wished to say something metaphysical, to demonstrate to him that he had given no meaning to certain signs in his propositions. This method would be unsatisfying to the other—he would not have the feeling that we were teaching him philosophy—but it would be the only strictly correct method.'[2]

So the philosopher's occupation is not wholly gone. Knowing what clarity requires, he can criticize scientific statements, not on the ground of their falsity, which would be impertinence, but on the ground of their lack of clarity, of their using forms of language that are likely to distort the facts, or their contentment with partial analyses, or their introducing of unverifiables. 'Philosophy is not a theory but an activity', and its object is 'the logical clarification of thoughts'; 'the result of philosophy is not a number of "philosophical propositions", but to make propositions clear'.[3] To call philosophy 'the queen of the sciences' is to talk absurdly. It is rather the servant of science, or, if one is to use metaphor at all, one of the more useful implements in the tool-bag of science.

19. Here in outline is logical atomism. We have seen that it was the outcome of two independent lines of thought which converged toward the same view of the world. The analysis of factual statements led to the conclusion that they could be broken up into atomic statements reporting atomic facts. On the other hand, mathematical logic supplied a language which, if the world did consist of such facts, would order them with ideal clarity and precision. And what these two lines of thought so strongly suggested seemed to be confirmed by the enquiry into meaning and truth that was made by Wittgenstein. This indicated that a statement could mean a fact or be true

---

[1] *Tractatus*, 7.
[2] *Ibid.*, 6.54.
[3] *Ibid.*, 4.112.

of it only through embodying the structure of the external fact in its own form. So far, then, as our ultimate factual statements did thus reflect the nature of things, what sort of world did we live in? The conclusion was irresistible; it was a vast congeries of atomic facts.

With the appearance of the *Tractatus* in 1922, British philosophy had completed a full circle in ten years. In 1912 had appeared Bosanquet's *Principle of Individuality and Value*, whose thesis was that the world is a single individual whose parts are connected with each other by a necessity so intimate and so organic that the nature of the part depended on its place in the Absolute. A decade later found Wittgenstein maintaining that the very opposite was the truth, that a full knowledge of the world, instead of revealing it as a complete unity, would pulverize it into atoms. These atoms could be dealt with, to be sure, by logic. But one must not misinterpret that. The logic was radically different from the philosophical logic which served the purposes of the older philosophy. It was a logic which to Bradley and Bosanquet, who viewed its beginnings with incomprehension and dismay, seemed like a self-contradiction, for it was a logic without necessity. (It did admit necessities in the form of tautologies, but in Wittgenstein's version held these to be conventions of our own which had no application to atomic statements or atomic facts.) The role of reason in philosophy was thus also fundamentally altered. It had been conceived as the tracing of necessities in the structure of the world. No necessities between facts were now admitted; on the first page of his book Wittgenstein reverted to Hume and maintained that 'the world divides into facts' of which 'any one can either be the case or not be the case, and everything else remain the same'.[1] The function of reason was not to understand the world, for the world was not in the traditional sense intelligible at all. Reason was a highly specialized function which could be properly performed only by experts, the function of identifying the logical or linguistic equivalences that appeared in mathematical systems.

20. The appraisal of logical atomism, to which we must now turn, is both important and difficult. It is important because, though most analysts, including Wittgenstein himself, later abandoned some of its theses, it underlies much analytic writing and is by far the most impressive philosophy that the movement has produced. Hence an appraisal of it will help us to evaluate more justly the analytic methods that led to it. But such appraisal is also difficult, largely because of the style and the type of mind of its most authoritative exponent. The

---

[1] *Tractatus*, 1.2, 1.21.

strange figure of Wittgenstein has been in some ways a liability to the analytic movement. It is not only that his *Tractatus*, devoted to expounding the text that 'everything that can be said can be said clearly',[1] is so obscure that its exegesis has baffled and divided even those who were closest to him; it is also that the attitudes he displayed toward his own work, toward co-workers in the field, and toward philosophers of the past, were such as to alienate rather than to ingratiate. He gave his *Tractatus* to the world with the announcement that 'the truth of the thoughts communicated here seems to me unassailable and definitive. I am, therefore, of the opinion that the problems have in essentials been finally solved'.[2] The book displays no knowledge of previous philosophies, nor any interest in them; 'It is indifferent to me,' he writes, 'whether what I have thought has already been thought by another.'[3] Apart from this oracular manifesto, he published practically nothing in his lifetime. His teaching he confined to a small coterie, severely reprimanding some of its own members who tried to interpret him to a wider public. Such attitudes could be ill afforded by anyone but a genius. Was Wittgenstein a genius? I can only think that he was, since philosophers whom I much respect and who understand him better than I, like Moore and Wisdom, Braithwaite, Ryle, and Urmson, do plainly so regard him. Mr Urmson thinks that the metaphysics of the *Tractatus* is comparable to 'the great metaphysical systems of the past' and that 'for breadth of sweep, clarity, detailed working-out, and consistency, it can have few rivals'.[4] My own judgment, I am sorry to say, must be very different indeed.

21. Let us begin with the doctrine of picturing. Language, Wittgenstein says, cannot express the structure of fact; it can only show or exhibit it through the structure of its own statements. We must agree that this brings to light a curious awkwardness about language which perhaps few of us have noticed. The relations we take to hold between things must often be gathered, not from any mention of them in what we say, but by reading between the lines, or rather, between the words. Suppose we say successively, 'this surface is blue', 'blue is a colour', ' "blau" is "blue" '. In each of these cases the relation holding between the terms is an essential part of what we mean, but in none of them have we named or described it. The word 'is' serves

[1] *Tractatus*, 4.116.
[2] *Ibid.*, Preface, p. 29.
[3] *Ibid.*, p. 27.
[4] *Philosophical Analysis*, 4.

as a mark of predication in all three, but it does not denote any one relation, for the relations meant are different in each case. The relation involved in 'this surface is blue' is the attributive relation; in 'blue is a colour', it is the relation of genus and species; in ' "blau" is "blue" ', it is identity of reference. But these are nowhere specified. We have to gather them from the characters of the terms. Thus it is true that there are some very common and important relations that we do not attempt to single out through ordinary language. We are content that they should be suggested by the context.

Does this hold generally? Wittgenstein would say yes; he tells us that the 'fundamental thought' of his book is that the logic of facts, their abstract and formal structure, cannot be represented by anything we say; that is why philosophical statements are nonsense, and why philosophers are reminded in the last sentence of the book that 'whereof one cannot speak, thereof one must be silent'. Yet he violates both theory and injunction on every page. He mentions the unmentionable and discusses the undiscussable with singular abandon, for he scarcely refers to particular facts anywhere in his work, and instead talks constantly about their structure, about the structure of propositions and signs, about identity, negation, necessity, contingency, implication. All of this is what we are at the same time assured to be quite impossible. As Russell says, 'the things that have to be said in leading the reader to understand Mr Wittgenstein's theory are all of them things which that theory itself condemns as meaningless.'[1] Now I should not wish to say that Wittgenstein talks *no* nonsense in his book. But surely it is not all nonsense. Many of its statements, however ineptly put, are really intelligible. According to his theory they could not be. The theory, therefore, is wrong.

22. This objection is of course an obvious one, and he foresees it. But he meets it in a surprising way—by frankly admitting it. He agrees that if his theory is true, it must be inexpressible, and hence that his own expression of it is not an expression, but nonsense. Ordinarily this sort of admission would be thought fatal to a theory, but neither the author nor his followers considered it so in this case. Why? Wittgenstein's own explanation was that his theory, though nonsense, was 'important nonsense'. Just what does this mean? It might mean either that the theory was practically important or that it was theoretically important. To say that it was practically important would be to say something about the value of adopting it. But according to Wittgenstein and other positivists, statements of value

[1] *Tractatus*, 11. Cf. E. E. Harris, *Nature, Mind and Modern Science*, 322 ff.

were not statements at all, but interjections; hence, to say that the theory was in this sense important was again to say nothing. At the end of his book, the importance is declared to be intellectual, in the sense that it is a propaedeutic to true insight. 'My propositions are elucidatory in this way; he who understands me finally recognizes them as senseless when he has climbed out through them, on them, over them. (He must, so to speak, throw away the ladder after he has climbed up on it.)'[1] But if the rungs of the ladder make no sense, how can he climb up on them? Wittgenstein is in a dilemma from which he can hardly escape by a metaphor. If the structures he is talking about cannot be talked about, and all such attempted talk is nonsense, then the book is nonsense, and we should close it and turn to something more profitable. On the other hand, if the book is profitable—and Wittgenstein considered it 'unassailable and definitive'—this can only be because it does succeed in saying something about its subject, namely the structure of language and fact. And if it does thus succeed, what better evidence could be offered that the theory is mistaken?

23. Indeed the theory is so plainly at variance not only with Wittgenstein's own practice but with the inveterate habit of thoughtful minds that it is hard to see why it was taken so seriously. We can denote things and attributes by words, Wittgenstein holds, but not the connectives that tie them together. To what, then, am I referring when I use the word 'difference' by way of distinguishing it from likeness or implication? Am I not referring to a fundamental relation, and doing so by a word? It may be replied that difference as such is a myth, that there are only particular differences, and that to say anything about these, we must make reference to their terms. We shall then find that this is our only verbal reference, since the relation we also mean will be embodied or shown forth by the difference in our words. But, in the first place, we clearly *can* talk about difference without talking or thinking about any particular difference. We can refer to difference as a kind of relation distinct from, say, likeness or implication; and we can denote it by its own special name. We all talk this way when we turn to analysis, and expect others to understand us, which they normally do. Of course, Wittgenstein constantly uses words in this way himself with the same evident expectation. But, secondly, suppose we were to grant that we could think only of particular differences, the difference between Damon and Pythias, let us say, or between Gandhi and Hitler. Here it is true that we can

[1] *Tractatus*, 6.54.

think of the difference only when we think of the terms. But to say that we cannot name or denote or refer to this difference, and can only exemplify it through the combination of names, seems contrary to fact. Having called up the difference by means of the names, we can go on to fix attention on the relation as distinct from its terms, and say, for example, that the difference between Gandhi and Hitler was greater than that between Damon and Pythias. Here we are not merely *showing* the two relations. We are explicitly doing what Wittgenstein tells us we cannot do; we are talking about them by name.

24. We have admitted, however, that we do not always refer by word to the relations we mean, but sometimes leave them to be suggested by the character of the terms. Such cases are less intractable for Wittgenstein's theory. Are they cases of picturing? If we say 'this is red', is the sentence a picture of the fact it refers to? It is fantastic to say so. Of course everything in the world has something in common with everything else and so is in some degree like it. But Wittgenstein was not trying to say that everything means everything else. He seems to have meant what he said. 'At first glance the proposition— say as it stands printed on paper—does not seem to be a picture of the reality of which it treats. . . . And yet these symbolisms prove to be pictures—even in the ordinary sense of the word—of what they represent.'[1] It would appear to follow that when we truly say 'this is red', the word 'red' is like the quality red, the word 'this' is like the point or spot that is red, and the relation between the two words on paper is like the relation of inherence that links the 'objects' in the fact. There is no plausibility in any of these statements. The natural way for a word to resemble the colour red is to be red, which the word in this case is not. The natural way for a word to resemble a place or spot would be to be like it in colour, shape, or size; no such likeness is here present. As for the relations, that which appears between the words is the relation of spatial proximity, one word being to the right of the other. Is this *like* the relation in the fact? Is the red of the fact to the left or right, or in any way spatially outside of, the place that it characterizes? Plainly not. And if not, the question presses how one relation can 'mirror' another that is totally different from it. I cannot guess.[2]

[1] *Tractatus*, 4.011.

[2] Professor Wisdom introduced a variation in the picture theory. He suggested that what a sentence may picture is not the fact, but the 'first derivative' of that fact, which is roughly the form in which the fact would present itself at the next logical level, i.e. the next level of reflection. ' "This red" is identical in form not

Perhaps, however, we are taking too seriously Wittgenstein's doctrine that what pictures things is sentences. He says this, to be sure, but he also says that we can use tables and chairs as our sentences, and that 'the mutual spatial position of these things then expresses the sense of the sentence'.[1] Mr Wisdom and Mr Urmson both illustrate this wider use of 'sentence' by an odd example. Suppose you want to say that Mr Wisdom has killed Al Capone; you can do this by letting a glass stand for Wisdom, a knife for killing, and a dish for Capone; you can put the glass on the knife and the knife on the dish, and so express your meaning. But this is not, apparently, the most delicate mode of expression, partly because the three things are too much like a mere collection instead of an ordered whole, and partly because killing, which is a relation, should not be expressed by a thing, but rather by a relation which would itself show or exhibit it. Hence, if we now put the glass (Wisdom) straight on the dish (Al Capone), and symbolize the relation of killing by the spatial relation (on) in which the things stand, the matter becomes much clearer; the special difficulties of the coarser expression are now removed. 'It is this superior type of symbolization that Wittgenstein recommends in 3.1431, though it must be admitted that through the greater part of his work he speaks as if he were contenting himself with more ordinary methods.'[2] Do we find that 'the matter becomes much clearer' through this kind of example? I fear not. For the question is whether in such a case there is anything that could more plausibly be called picturing than in the case of a sentence, and it is hard to see that there is. The glass is not like Wisdom, nor the dish like Capone, nor the spatial relation of being *on* like the activity of killing, nor the combination as a whole in any relevant degree like the supposed fact.

Sometimes Wittgenstein suggests that the relation of symbol to symbolized is that of projection. The pictures in a cathedral window can project themselves on the floor in elongated and distorted forms, but rules can be given for relating the two by which either could be derived from the other. This may still hold when the resemblance is so remote that without the aid of the rules we should be wholly

with the fact expressed by "This red" but with the fact expressed by "This characterized (by) red".' (*Mind*, 1931, 205.) But the *words* 'this red' seem no more like the latter fact than the former. The word 'red' does not *characterize* the word 'this', and if not, the relation between them no more pictures the relation in the fact than its words picture the terms of the fact.

[1] *Ibid.*, 3.143.

[2] J. O. Urmson, *Philosophical Analysis*, 79. I have gained much help from this lucid little book.

unable to detect it. One can go farther. If we were clever enough, we could, as Mr Urmson has pointed out,[1] discover laws of projection by which practically anything could be regarded as the projection of anything else; the crudest child's sketch could be regarded as a perfect likeness of the face of Napoleon. But if this is all that Wittgenstein meant, the insistence that the proposition must picture the fact becomes virtually pointless. And it is hard to believe that anything so far from obvious was meant by one who said 'It is obvious that we perceive a sentence of the form *aRb* as a picture. Here the sign is obviously a likeness of the signified.'

25. Let us try again. We suggested that the least implausible interpretation of the picture theory was one that took neither sentences nor gross physical things as the symbols, but rather the form possessed in common by all those arrangements of things that might be used in expressing our meaning. In the only illustration Wittgenstein deigns to give, he says that 'the gramophone record, the musical thought, the score, the waves of sound', may all be regarded as propositions, representing in their various languages the same fact. The propositional sign, or purified picture, will then be that form of arrangement which they have in common. (It will be noted that he includes here, among arrangements of physical things, 'the musical thought'. What he meant by this, or by its inclusion in such a company, I shall not try to say.) Will the theory, so interpreted, pass?

No. (1) The picture is supposed to be a fact, whose parts are sensible things. But the abstraction reached by omitting all that is different in the gramophone record, the score, and the sound waves, is neither a fact nor anything sensible. The picture in the required sense has vanished.

(2) The propositional sign, which is the picture, is supposed to *evince* the form of the fact. This is ambiguous. Does it mean that the sign—what signifies—is the form of the fact? At times it seems so. When we leave out all that differentiates the various arrangements of symbols that might mean the fact, and arrive at that which is identical in form with it, what remains would seem to *be* simply this form, the common pattern of fact and symbol. But if the propositional sign is thus to be identified with the form, then in perceptual judgment at least it is not needed at all. If we can apprehend the form directly when we find it in the various symbols, why should we not apprehend it directly when we think of it in the fact? And if we cannot do this, if we can think of a form only through a propositional sign that is

[1] *Philosophical Analysis*, 88–90.

distinct from it, how do we manage to think of the propositional sign itself? We could only do so through another sign, and that through still another, and so on without end.

(3) But is not the very notion inept that we can arrive at the relations asserted of things by abstracting from the symbols we use in referring to them? Take the gramophone record, the score, the sound waves. These are all wholes of spatial parts. Suppose you work out some spatial pattern that all of them have in common. Would this 'show' or 'exhibit' the relation of the heard sounds? Far from it. The sounds in music are not spatially related to each other; a high note is not an inch, or a mile, above a low one. 'Very well,' says the proponent of pictures, 'drop the spatial pattern and make it one of mere isomorphism; then you will have on the one side an abstract scheme of points and on the other a second scheme, and surely the first will picture the second point by point.' But apart from the impropriety of calling this 'a picture in the ordinary sense', the first would not 'show' or 'exhibit' the sort of relations we wish to refer to in the second. When we talk of music as heard, we refer to relations that only sounds can have to each other, and an abstract scheme of soundless points would lose everything characteristic of those relations. The notion that propositional signs or sentences are pictures would seem to be untenable whichever way one turns it.

(4) Again, in an isomorphic picture there must be point-for-point correlation with what it stands for. Suppose that Wisdom did slay Capone, and we make this assertion through words or through glasses and dishes. Let us recall that if the proposition is true, it must correspond, not with what a first glance reveals, but with what on analysis the fact would prove to be. Very well; how many ultimate distinguishable facts are there in Wisdom and Capone? I should suppose an inexhaustible number. Is it to be presumed that analysis would reveal an exactly similar number in the words, or the dishes, by which we referred to these? The presumption seems quite wild.

(5) We may well remind ourselves that whether it is so or not is an issue that on Wittgenstein's theory cannot be discussed. The relation of sign to thing signified is one of those relations that can only be exemplified in the form of the proposition, not denoted by words. Of course Wittgenstein does discuss it, but we need not return to that. Our point here is this, that though the relation of sign and signified is said to be one of showing, it cannot in this case even be shown. For the relation of the subject to the predicate words in a sentence is never that of sign to thing signified, or anything resembling

this; in the statement 'the proposition shows the structure of the fact', the word 'proposition' is not a symbol of the words that follow. How, then, can the relation between the words 'mirror' the structure of the fact? As we have seen, a relation cannot 'show' another that is utterly different from itself. Thus the picture theory is not merely inexpressible; it is incapable even of that queer adumbration that Wittgenstein would allow it.[1]

26. There is curiously little interest displayed in his book as to what thinking is actually like. One wonders what James or Ward, who were practised in the introspection of thought processes, would have made of his account. It is as if a mathematician, or perhaps a technician in photography, unacquainted with philosophy or psychology, had formed a preconceived notion, drawn from projective geometry, of what thought must be like, and had read this view into the facts. Wittgenstein often talks as if one set of things could mean another simply and solely by repeating its structure, and as if living thought had nothing to do with the matter. 'That "a" stands in a certain relation to "b" says *that aRb.*'[2] But facts do not 'say' things about each other. If the mere fact that the terms are arranged in a certain way can *say* things about similar arrangements, very odd results follow. Czar Nicholas looked like George V, so he must have said him or meant him. St Peter's presumably means St Paul's, and St Paul's St Peter's. This, of course, is nonsense. But why? Because to mean is a process of a conscious mind. Arrangements in nature do not mean. Sentences by themselves never mean. Nothing actively means but minds, and though minds may make use of sentences or kings or churches as aids in their thinking, their thoughts are certainly not reducible to the machinery that they use.

Wittgenstein can hardly have been unaware of this, and occasionally indeed the fog lifts and there appear 'islets of the blest and the intelligible'. He then seems to recognize that what is asserted, and is true, is neither the sentence nor the proposition nor the propositional sign, but the *sense* of these things. 'What the picture represents is its sense. In the agreement or disagreement of its sense with reality, the

---

[1] Cf., the following from Professor J. L. Austin: 'There is no need whatsoever for the words used in making a true statement to "mirror" in any way, however indirect, any feature whatsoever of the situation or event; a statement no more needs, in order to be true, to reproduce the "multiplicity", say, or the "structure" or "form" of the reality, than a word needs to be echoic or writing pictographic. To suppose that it does is to fall once again into the error of reading back into the world the features of language.' *Arist. Soc. Proceedings*, Sup. Vol. 24 (1950), 119.

[2] *Tractatus*, 3.1432.

truth or falsehood consists.'[1] No explanation of this term is vouch-safed. But the fact that it appears at all is significant, and if that significance were dwelt upon, it would reveal, we suspect, that the whole paraphernalia of sentences, propositions, and propositional signs was of comparatively small importance. Similarly of the word 'thought'. 'The thought is the significant proposition.'[2] 'The applied, thought, propositional sign[3] is the thought.' 'In the proposition the thought is expressed perceptibly through the senses.'[4] What is this 'thought' that arrives mysteriously to give significance to the pro-position, to apply it, and to get expressed through it? It is evidently not the picture, but something that uses the picture. Wittgenstein never adequately explains it. Indeed he could not have explained it without disrupting the cramped framework of forms and sensed particulars within which he chose to move. The sense of a sentence is not the sentence. The thought of something is not the words on paper, or the uttered sounds, or the flags or gestures, or even the inner images, which may be used to fix and carry the reference. Regarding the connection of thought with these its vehicles, much interesting research has been carried on, which has revealed that, in their use of words and images in thinking, people differ enormously. There have been psychologists like Titchener, and at one time Russell, who were content to identify thought with images; there have been behaviourists who were ready to identify it with spoken words,[5] and Wittgenstein himself was a behaviourist as regards the thought of others. But he seems to have recognized haltingly that thought in a non-behaviourist sense must be present to use the proposition or sentence if the sign is to signify. For it is really this that refers, this that corresponds, this—not a sentence or the form of a sentence—that is true or false, and this that must play the central role in any account of the relation of ideas to things. Unfortunately it is precisely this that is an alien in Wittgenstein's world, presenting itself without any sort of valid passport.

27. The reader will by now have had enough, and more than enough, of the picture theory. It is time we turned to the more important influences that led to logical atomism. These we said were two: the timely provision of an ideal language for such a philosophy in the

[1] *Tractatus*, 2.221, 2.222.
[2] *Ibid.*, 4.
[3] 'Das angewandte, gedachte, Satzzeichen', 3.5.
[4] *Ibid.*, 3.1.
[5] These and other views have been examined in my *The Nature of Thought*, Vol. I.

form of mathematical logic, and the apparent success of empiricist analysis in resolving all assertions about fact into atomic propositions. Let us look at the first of these.

It would perhaps now be generally agreed that symbolic or mathematical logic has less revolutionary consequences than were at first expected of it. In an early article, Russell held that its philosophical importance was threefold: first, it resolved the ancient problems of infinity and continuity; secondly, it demonstrated the purely formal character of mathematics; and thirdly, it refuted empiricism and idealism by showing that we had a priori knowledge of an independent non-sensible world. Both the first achievement and the second would seem to belong rather to the philosophy of mathematics than to mathematics or logic itself, and it is further to be remarked about the first that the solutions offered by Russell of the paradoxes of Zeno, based on his theories of continuity and infinity, have not commanded general assent. As for the third claim, it has long ago been withdrawn. The Russell of *Principia Mathematica* thought that mathematics required the existence of independent Platonic essences, that in a priori knowledge we laid hold of their necessary linkage, and that this linkage was sometimes synthetic. These are important philosophical positions. But Russell and his analytic followers have long abandoned the view that their logic requires any of them. In 1914 Russell was writing, 'mathematical logic, even in its most modern form, is not *directly* of philosophical importance except in its beginnings'.[1] Neither he nor Whitehead seems to have made much use of the apparatus developed in *Principia* in the course of their distinctively philosophical writing. Indeed Whitehead, with his later doctrine that everything is internally related to everything else and his rejection of the deductive procedure in metaphysics, repudiated both the philosophy and the method which mathematical logic suggested; 'Philosophy,' he wrote, 'has been misled by the example of mathematics.'[2] This does not mean, of course, that as a tool in the handbag of thought, mathematical logic is of no value, though Russell and Whitehead have both insisted that its utility here is as a means of *not* thinking, of making the manipulation of symbols a substitute for the work of thinking; so little is it necessary for the worker in this field to think of what his symbols refer to that Russell has suggested that a half-minute or so in six months would be enough.[3] Mr Braithwaite has summed up the value of the discipline judiciously. 'It is

---

[1] *Our Knowledge of the External World*, 50.
[2] *Process and Reality*, 10.
[3] *Monist*, Vol. 25 (1935), 147.

therefore a great assistance to be a master of symbolic logic in studying philosophy and to be a master of the infinitesimal calculus in studying economics. But in neither case is it an essential qualification. And if the symbolic logic or the mathematics is not subordinated to the subject-matter—if it is master and not servant—errors may be produced more serious than any which would have arisen had these methods of symbolizing not been used at all.'[1]

28. Now we saw that in the development of logical atomism this type of logic did figure at times as master rather than as servant. It suggested a pattern for the real world, and because this pattern was so neat and connected and comprehensive, its devotees went on to argue that the world must be like this. If the world did consist of logical atoms, the language of *Principia* would supply a superlative instrument for dealing with it; hence let us assume that it really is so constituted. Rationalists have usually venerated mathematics, and being rationalistically inclined, I may be expected to greet this assumption with a cheer. I cannot do so. I do not believe that the degree of rationality in the world can be determined by a priori methods, nor do I think that the expectations aroused by mathematical logic regarding the structure of the world have been confirmed by further experience and reflection. What are these expectations? For our present purpose, the most important of them are two: (1) that facts will be found to be connected with each other by external relations only, never by necessity; (2) that when necessity does appear, it will appear only in formal relations. Mathematical logic strongly suggests both these things, and they are clearly of great philosophic importance. Both, I think, are false.

It may seem odd to say that a logic which insists so strongly that it never mentions a particular fact should be charged with imposing upon us a theory about the relations of such facts. Let us be clear, therefore, how the suggestion is conveyed. It is conveyed negatively rather than positively, that is, by providing an 'ideal' language in which the necessary connection of facts, even of classes or kinds of fact, cannot be reported. Take such statements as 'red is a colour', or 'whatever is coloured is extended'. We may obviously mean by these statements that something is necessarily connected with something else, that red not only is, but must by its nature be, a colour, or that what is coloured could not fail to be extended. Yet, strangely enough, in the ideal language that the *Principia* was supposed to provide, even such simple statements as these cannot be made. And

[1] *Cambridge University Studies*, ed. by H. Wright, 10.

it was naturally assumed that if they could not be made in such a language, they should not be made at all. We must see a little more fully what this means.

29. It is true that symbolic logic never mentions any particular thing or fact or proposition. What it offers us is a system composed of symbols for which individuals, characteristics, relations, or propositions, may be substituted according to rule. Thus the symbol 'a' is commonly used to indicate that some individual is being referred to, without indicating which; 'x' is used when the reference is to any individual; 'φ' 'ψ', etc., are used to indicate 'functions', among which all characteristics are included. If we use these symbols, the form for saying 'this is red' or 'Socrates is a man' will be φa. If we want to say 'all shades of red are colours' or 'all men are mortal', the form will be $(x).\ \varphi\ x$, 'for all values of x, x is φ'. Sometimes formulae are used which bring out more explicitly that these are statements of class inclusion. Greek letters, α, β, γ, etc., are commonly used to indicate classes and the particular letter 'ε' to indicate inclusion within a class. The formula, then, for 'this is red' or 'Socrates is a man' would be a ε α, and for 'all men are mortal', $(x).\ x\ \varepsilon\ \alpha$. Such expressions in the 'functional' language as φa and $(x).\ \varphi\ x$ are taken as the equivalent of the expressions in the class language, a ε α and $(x).\ x\ \varepsilon\ \alpha$ respectively. What is the importance of these details? It is this: they make it clear that, in this logic, to ascribe a character to a subject is equivalent to including the subject in a class. No doubt that is sometimes what we intend. When we say 'that man is a policeman' or 'policemen wear blue uniforms', our interest may be in recognizing that something does fall within a class. But it is equally plain that we sometimes mean more than that. When we say 'this shade is red', we do not mean that this shade happens to fall in the class of reds as this man happens to be a policeman, for we can see that this shade could not be other than red and still be the shade it is, while we certainly do not want to say that this man could not be other than a policeman and still be the man he is. When we say that whatever is red is coloured, we are saying that what is red is *necessarily* coloured, that it could not be, or be conceived to be, otherwise; when we say that policemen wear blue uniforms, we are not saying that they could not be policemen unless they did. The relations asserted in the two cases are obviously and fundamentally different. Yet the logic of *Principia* has no means of recognizing this difference. If we want to say 'this shade is red', we must do so by φa, which means that an individual *has in fact* the character φ, or by a ε α, which means that it *falls in fact* within the class α. If we want to say that all red things are coloured, we must do it by (x). φ x or (x). x ε α, both of which are again merely statements that x always does in fact possess a certain character. We are forced by the limitations of the language to assimilate such statements to the radically different type found in 'all policemen wear blue uniforms'. In short, in the language provided we cannot say what we mean.

30. Thus, if there existed a necessary connection between the objects of an atomic fact, *Principia* could not express it. But what about the relations between facts themselves? Here again the same curious situation holds. Facts are expressed by propositions, which are symbolized by such letters as p, q, r. Suppose we wish to say that one fact necessitates another, for example that this figure's being a triangle necessitates its having angles equal to 180 degrees. The nearest we can come to saying that in the language of *Principia* is φ a ⊃ ψ a, i.e., a's having φ *implies* its having ψ, or, if we wish to say this about *any* such triangle, as we should no doubt be ready to do, (x). φx ⊃ ψ x, i.e., for all x's, the fact that x is φ *implies* its being ψ. It may be said that this recognition of implication is a quite sufficient answer to the criticism just made that in this logic necessity goes unrecognized. For wherever in a statement of classification necessity is involved, it can always be expressed by a statement of implication between propositions. If one wants to insist on the *must* in 'whatever is red is coloured', one will say, not (x). φ x or (x). x ε α, which do express mere class inclusions, but rather (x). φ x ⊃ ψ x, i.e., for all values of x, being φ *implies* being ψ. Hence the language, after all, is equal to reporting any necessities we may find.

This defence is most misleading. If there is one thing about the logic of *Principia* that later discussion has made clear, it is that the 'material implication' there used, and represented by the familiar horseshoe symbol, does not mean entailment and involves no necessity.[1] Strictly speaking, 'p⊃q' does not assert any relation at all. What it asserts is simply that p is never in fact true while q is false. Now if p really does entail q, this latter statement will of course hold, for p's truth will always carry along with it the truth of q; 'p entails q' entails 'p⊃q'. But one cannot convert this statement. No ingenuity can extract entailment from material implication. It may be well to insist briefly on the depth of difference between them.

When a responsible person says that one proposition entails

---

[1] The point has been a commonplace since G. E. Moore made it in 1920. See his *Philosophical Studies*, 303 ff.

another, it is because he sees that if the first is true, the second *must* be true; for example, if 3 is added to 3, the result *must* be equal to 4 added to 2. Unless such a 'must' is seen or presumed, he would not talk about entailment. But consider the conditions under which, in the logic in question, one proposition implies another. According to the truth-table given above,[1] p implies q when any of the three following conditions holds—(a) when both are true, (b) when both are false, or (c) when, p being false, q is true. Let us take examples. (a) Byron had a deformed foot. Scott also had a deformed foot. Since these are both true, Byron's having had a deformed foot *implies* that Scott had one. (b) Lead is lighter than aluminium; Mark Twain wrote *Paradise Lost*. These are both false. The first therefore implies the second. (c) Wellington defeated Caesar at Waterloo; $7+5=12$. Of these, the first is false while the second is true. The first therefore again implies the second. These are all cases of implication without any seen or asserted necessity. And material implication has still odder consequences. Since, of any two propositions, if the first is false it will always imply the other, a false proposition will imply any proposition at all; the proposition that Wellington defeated Caesar implies that Caesar defeated Wellington. Since, again, of any two propositions, if the second is true, it will always be implied by the first, a true proposition is implied by any proposition whatever; 'it is raining' is implied by 'Cromwell had a wart on his face'. It is needless to prolong this parade of eccentricities. We should think it absurd in any of these cases to say that the implying statement required or necessitated the other, or that the second followed from the first. Two propositions may materially imply each other when there is not the faintest intimation of a necessary link between them. Hence if there really is a necessary connection between any fact and any other, the language of material implication does not and cannot report it.

We said that the logic of *Principia* contributed to logical atomism by raising at least two expectations. The first was that the facts of which the world was composed would be found externally related to each other. This sprang from the realization that an apparently complete system of logic, supplying a kind of syntax for all possible statements, could be constructed—indeed had actually been constructed—without any reference to necessity either within facts or between them. Now the possibility of such a construction without reference to such necessities did not of course prove their non-existence. But it did strongly suggest it and made the corresponding metaphysic seem natural and desirable. For Russell the supposition

[1] p. 136.

of necessary connections between empirical facts was like that of the Deity for Laplace; *Sire, je n'avais besoin de cette hypothèse*; and the inferences actually drawn in the two cases were alike. If the logic were the adequate language that the atomists took it to be, the necessities reported by Hegelians and by others whose hearts were better than their heads were presumably fictions which would be dispelled by further analysis. Whether further analysis bore out this expectation we shall presently inquire.

31. The other prepossession that their logic imposed on the atomists was that necessity between propositions is exclusively a matter of form. By a purely formal relation we mean one that links its terms without regard to their nature, i.e., would still link them however their nature were changed. It may be a surprise to learn that there are necessary relations of this kind, at least among propositions. Certainly as a rule it is in virtue of their content, of what they say, that one proposition is seen to entail or follow from another. We say that John is older than James, and James is older than William, so John is older than William; and we do not seem to be moving here upon the level of mere abstraction. It may be said, however, that the necessity does really lie in the form, since we can see that it holds without regard to the persons named; it would hold equally of Tom, Dick, and Harry, or indeed of three elephants, or three trees. This is correct—in part. It is not in virtue of being these individuals that they are thus related, but in virtue of being each an individual having an age. But then having an age is a matter of content, not of form; so the conclusion follows, after all, in virtue of *what* the propositions say. To which the formalist replies that if we narrow our gaze, we shall see that within this abstract content there is an even more abstract skeleton in virtue of which the conclusion really follows. 'Older' is just one kind of 'transitive relation', of which there are other kinds, such as 'taller', 'hotter', and 'larger', and it is because our terms are linked, not by 'older than', but by a purely formal link, a transitive relation as such, that the conclusion follows. Correct again—in part. We say 'in part' only, because 'transitive' after all is not purely formal; it does not belong to relations generally; some are transitive and some are not; substitute 'father of' for 'older than' and the conclusion would not follow. The formalist then seems to be in a dilemma. If he admits that the conclusion follows because of something special to the subject-matter, he is a formalist no longer. On the other hand, if he makes his form so thin and general as to leave out all special content, say aRb, bRc, therefore aRc, it becomes simply invalid. It would prove that if Erasmus Darwin was the father of Charles, and Charles of Francis, Erasmus was the father of Francis.

This presents the formal logician with a difficult problem. To him logic is and must be a science of complete generality, and he has committed himself to working among purely formal relations, relations that hold among propositions regardless of their content. Is he now to give up this vocation? According to the mathematical logician, there is one condition on which formal logic—and in his view there is no other—can be saved. We have seen what that condition is. It lies in abstracting from everything in propositions except their truth and falsity, and dealing with them as true or false counters, nothing more. Does this abolition of content from his science involve the abolition of necessity too? Not quite, he would say. A kind of necessity remains, though a rather curious kind. It will be pure tautology, consisting in conformity to the requirements of an arbitrary definition. We must try to be clear about this.

32. Suppose we say that p implies q. This does not mean that q follows in virtue of anything asserted by p. It means, as we have seen, simply that one of a certain set of combinations of truth and falsity which we have arbitrarily assigned as the meaning of implication happens to be found in the present case. 'Arbitrarily' because, so far as logic is concerned, there is no reason why any one of a number of other combinations should not equally have been chosen. The only necessity in the case lies not in the relation of p and q, for none is there, but in the requirement of sticking to our definition when its conditions are fulfilled. We begin by constructing a little table of the possible combinations of truth and falsity in p and q; we find that there are four of these; and we then define implication as meaning the occurrence of either No. 1, No. 2, or No. 4. With this in mind, we are supplied with an example of alleged necessity linking two propositions. What do we need to know in order to decide whether it is present or not? Is it what the propositions say? No, that is needless if only we know whether or not they are true. Once supplied with this information, e.g. that they are both false, we merely look at our table and see whether p—false $+q$—false is included among the possibilities we decided to describe as implications. We see that it is, and therefore pronounce that p implies q. But, as we have seen, that points to no necessity either among the facts or among the statements that report them. The only necessity involved falls in our own mind. The necessity is that of conforming to our own convention. And that is

F

not necessity at all in the could-not-be-otherwise sense, since we are supposed to be free to break the convention if we wish.

In strictness, then, no necessary reasoning says anything about the world. It merely reports that a certain connection among p's and q's is part of an agreement we have made with ourselves to use the word 'implies' in a certain way. 'Hence there can *never* be surprises in logic,' says Wittgenstein; 'proof in logic is only a mechanical expedient to facilitate the recognition of tautology, where it is complicated.'[1] Russell at first resisted this interpretation of what he had done in *Principia*, and he has never been able to persuade himself that logic shows nothing about the structure of the world. But he did come to accept the view that mathematics is entirely tautology. To repeat: 'I thought of mathematics with reverence, and suffered when Wittgenstein led me to regard it as nothing but tautologies.'[2] The view that statements of necessity merely report that counters of truth and falsity are combined in an agreed-upon way is easy to understand in a simple case like that of p's implying q if both are false. It is harder to see, and is sometimes denied, when the pattern of inference becomes more complex. We shall do well, therefore, to take a slightly more complicated case and show how, in terms of mathematical logic, the only necessity involved is that of tautology.

33. If we were called upon without warning to give an example of reasoning, probably most of us would think first of the syllogism. If Socrates is a man, and all men are mortal, then Socrates must be mortal. The conclusion seems to carry us one step beyond the premises. But many logicians have denied that it really does, and mathematical logic agrees. The principle of syllogism it offers is $p \supset q. q \supset r : \supset . p \supset r$, i.e., if p implies q, and q implies r, then p implies r. It is not difficult to see that the conclusion here is a mere summary of what has been said already. Let us make a row of columns. The first will give a set of truth-values of p, the second of q, and the third the resulting truth-values of $p \supset q$, assuming that it is defined in the usual way. The fourth, fifth, and sixth will repeat this performance for q and r, and the eighth, ninth and tenth for p and r. The seventh column will report, on the basis of the items on the same line in 3 and 6, whether the conjunction of $p \supset q$ and $q \supset r$ is or is not the case. The last column will report whether the conjunction really does imply that $p \supset r$, that is, whether the conclusion is valid. How is this decided? In a purely mechanical way. According to definition, what

[1] *Tractatus*, 6.1251, 6.1262.

[2] *The Philosophy of Bertrand Russell*, ed. by P. H. Schilpp, 19. Cf. above, 122.

we mean by saying that the conjunction of $p\supset q$ and $q\supset r$ implies $p\supset r$, is simply that this conjunction is never in fact true while $p\supset r$ is false. And we can see by looking at the table that it never is. If we put together the T's and F's in columns 7 and 10, we shall see that in each of the four cases the combination is one of the alternatives included in the meaning of implication. Our conclusion, then, that the conjunction of $p\supset q$ with $q\supset r$ gives us $p\supset r$ is not a case of

1	2	3	4	5	6	7	8	9	10	11
p	q	$p\supset q$	q	r	$q\supset r$	$p\supset q.q\supset r$	p	r	$p\supset r$	$p\supset q.q\supset r:\supset.p\supset r$
T	T	T	T	T	T	T	T	T	T	T
F	T	T	F	T	T	T	F	T	T	T
T	F	F	T	F	F	F	T	F	F	T
F	F	T	F	F	T	T	F	F	T	T

arriving by reasoning at something new; it is simply a spelling out in detail of what the formula of implication means when, instead of taking simple propositions we take implicatory propositions as our units. What is said by the propositions enters nowhere into consideration in the smallest degree. Thus the relations are purely formal. Deriving the conclusion is a process of manipulating the counters according to rule, a process that could be performed more swiftly and unerringly by a well-constructed machine than by a mind.

Here again we can feel the pressure exerted by mathematical logic in the direction of logical atomism. Its first kind of pressure was exerted through presenting a language with no provision for reporting necessities either within facts or among them. Its second pressure was exercised through analysing away the necessities previously recognized by logic. By insisting that necessity held, not between the contents or meanings of propositions but solely among their 'truth-values', and then reducing every statement of such necessity to a tautology, to the effect that here was one of the cases envisaged by definition, it abolished necessity altogether except as conformity to convention.

The newer logic thus set the stage for atomism. Did it also provide effective evidence for the theory? That depends on how one appraises the two lines of suggestion through which the influence moved. When this logic contends—to look first at the line just followed—that necessity is only the tautology that binds a thinker to his conventions, is its case a sound one? If so, the argument against a rationalist metaphysic would be a powerful one, since a necessity among facts would then be unthinkable. Whether necessity can be so analysed will have to be considered in Chapter VI, when we examine the positivist theory of the a priori, and hence it will be better if we defer its consideration for a time. What about the other line? It was there shown that a logic can be constructed without appeal to necessity in the ordinary sense, and suggested that if necessities can be dispensed with in the ideal language, they may be presumed to be similarly dispensable among facts. How important this contention is depends on the answer to two further questions: first, is a logic without necessity discharging its proper office? second, do necessities in fact exist? Let us consider these questions.

34. Logic, according to an old tradition, is chiefly concerned with the conditions of valid inference. Words, to be sure, are helpless against us if we decide to take them from wonted tasks and assign them new ones, but where a tradition of usage is ancient and well established, it is simpler to adhere to it, and in this case we shall do so. That valid inference is also, at least in part, the concern of mathematical logic seems clear from Russell's words in *Principia*: 'in order that one proposition may be inferred from another, it is necessary that the two should have that relation which makes the one a consequence of the other. When a proposition q is a consequence of a proposition p, we say that p implies q. Thus deduction depends upon the relation of implication. . . .'[1] The question, then, whether logic should concern itself with necessity, and if so, with what kind of necessity, depends upon the sort of linkage that valid reasoning actually employs. What sort of linkage is this?

It is normally a linkage between meanings. Let us see this in a few random examples. (*a*) If New York is east of St Louis and Montreal is north of New York, then Montreal is north-east of St Louis. (*b*) If it is now 7.45, and the lecture begins at 8, and my quickest way of getting there is by bus, which takes twenty-five minutes, then I am bound to be late for the lecture if I go. (*c*) Other things equal, I ought to help Jones rather than Smith, for he needs my help far more. (*d*) It is silly to say that thought is sub-vocal speech, for thought can go on when the organs of speech have all been removed. (*e*) John was the apple of his father's eye; his death will be a grief to the old man. This is a very heterogeneous collection. But the cases would certainly all be taken as inferences from something to something else. And it will be noted that in all alike the conclusion is not a bare abstraction following by an abstract thread from other bare abstractions; it is a conclusion with a definite content arrived at

[1] I, 90.

through a connection of that content with what was offered before; it has a character determined by what was said in the premises and growing inevitably out of that. No doubt something like forms of inference can be dissected out of these reasonings. The first, for example, depends on spatial relations that could appear in other instances, and the second on relations in space and time. But in neither case is the conclusion confined to what the abstract form would give. And even if it were, it would not be abstract enough to be formal in the logical sense; we have seen that spatial and temporal relations do not apply to everything that logic deals with, and hence that from its austere point of view they are elements of content, not of pure form. Perhaps the best case for saying that the inference is purely formal would be found in (d). There we begin, it may be said, by conceiving thought in a certain way, i.e., non-material, and confirm this by pointing out that the removal of what is material does not mean the removal of thought. Of course not, since if it did, we should be contradicting ourselves; we should be saying that what is non-material is material. The argument therefore turns on the abstract relation of inconsistency. And this is purely formal in the sense that it turns on nothing special to the content, but on a relation that all propositions have to at least some others.

35. This is a very instructive case, for the notion of inconsistency is central to that of valid reasoning. If the assertion of a proposition were not inconsistent with its denial, no one could assert anything, for *what* would he be saying? It is essential, then, that this relation be rightly conceived. In the actual work of thinking it is taken to be a relation of mutual exclusion between meanings. In mathematical logic it is conceived as holding between propositions not in virtue of their meanings but solely in virtue of their truth or falsity. Russell defines 'p and q are incompatible' as 'either p or q is false'. Reflect on this for a moment. It means that if we were to start with a proposition known to be false, and consider its relation with other propositions, we should find it incompatible with every one we could think of; for all that any pair of propositions needs for inconsistency is that one of them should be false, and we have that false one in our hands. The assertion that Macaulay was born in 1801 (which is false) will then be inconsistent equally with every other false proposition, such as that spiders have six legs, and with every true proposition, such as $2+3=5$. Inconsistency in this sense has little or nothing to do with the inconsistency appealed to in actual reasoning.

This is worth showing a little more fully. (*a*) Many propositions which the theory would call inconsistent are, so far as we can see, entirely consistent, for example that Macaulay was born in 1801 and that he had grey eyes. (*b*) If we were given a false proposition and asked whether it was inconsistent with another, we should of course want to know what the other was, and think it absurd to give an answer without knowing this. On the theory before us we never need to know. (*c*) What we should have to know, on this theory, is that one of our propositions was false. But in fact we are continually perceiving inconsistencies when all we know is that one proposition is *true*. Indeed it is usually *because* we perceive that a suggestion is inconsistent with what we know to be true that we take it as false. The procedure of this logic is thus the reverse of that of actual reasoning, which somehow manages the impossible by moving from inconsistency to falsity rather than from falsity to inconsistency. For that matter, we often see two propositions to be inconsistent before we know *either* of them to be true. Starting from their seen inconsistency, we can conclude that at least one of them must be false, whereas starting from the mere knowledge that one or both are false, we can conclude nothing whatever about their consistency. It follows from all this that inconsistency is not, as this logic takes it to be, a truth-function at all. A truth-function is something that depends on the truth or falsity of its component propositions. Inconsistency does not.[1]

36. The same holds of other essential ideas of logic, such as necessary, possible, and impossible. These too are defined as truth-functions. Russell says that φx 'will be *necessary* if the function is always true, *possible* if it is sometimes true, and *impossible* if it is never true'.[2] Consider this in the concrete. Let φ stand for 'past President of the United States' and ψ for 'Caucasian'. Then $(x) . \varphi x \supset \psi x$ will mean that all past Presidents of the United States are Caucasians, and since the function holds for all cases of its 'argument', the proposition is necessary. But the statement is clearly one that is in the ordinary sense contingent, since there is no necessity, logical, legal, or other, that the Presidents should all have been Caucasians. Again, suppose we say 'some Presidents have been Caucasians', symbolized by $(\exists x) . (\varphi x . \psi x)$, 'there is an x such that x is φ and also ψ'. On the theory before us, this is a statement of possibility, and its form gives us all that possibility means. Hence if we want to say, 'it is possible that the President should have been a Negro', we should say it in the form

---

[1] Cf. E. J. Nelson on 'Intensional Relations', *Mind*, Vol. 39 (1930), 441.
[2] *Introduction to Mathematical Philosophy*, 165.

'some President has been a Negro'. This is obviously not what we mean, for we know that there has been no such case; we mean that there is nothing in our law (and perhaps in our society) that is incompatible with its being the case. The reply may be made that this merely means 'it is not impossible', and that the logic in question provides us the means of saying that. So let us turn to the definition of 'impossible'. It means, Russell tells us, that in no case is the function φx true. The statement 'it is impossible that a President should have been a Negro' will take the form $(x). (\varphi x \supset \sim \psi x)$, 'no past Presidents have been Negroes', and its denial will be $\sim[(x).(\varphi x \supset \sim \psi x)]$ 'it is not true that no past Presidents have been Negroes', which can only mean that there has been a Negro President. Both the assertion and its denial distort our meaning. To say it is impossible that the President should be a Negro is to say, not that no President has been or will be such, but that he *could not* be such, that there is something in our constitution or society that is incompatible with his being so.

37. These are not mere cavilings. If they are correct, they indicate a radical defect at a crucial point in the newer logic; and they serve to protect us against a misconception of reason which that logic has fostered. Speculative philosophers of the past have sought to arrive by reasoning at general truths about the world. They assumed that so far as this reasoning was valid, it somehow reflected necessities in the nature of things. Now logic is the connoisseur of valid reasoning. If its final verdict is that in such reasoning there is no necessity linking differing contents together, then the rationalist argument cannot so much has get under way. The logic of the *Principia* seemed to give that verdict, if only by its silence, and the atomists accordingly dismissed the rationalist case as logically incompetent. We were therefore moved to ask whether this logic had in any way nullified the rationalist view of reason. Our answer is, not at all. For the strange fact is that this logic hardly concerns itself with the conditions of valid reasoning. Actual reasoning appeals to *musts* and *cannots* that belong to the content of what is asserted; without these, the nerve of the inference would be gone and validity would be meaningless. It is therefore the business of logic to analyse these connections. *Principia* does not analyse them; it ignores them. At the crucial points it turns its face away from the necessities of actual thought, and substitutes for them ideas which it regards as more convenient in the elaboration of its system. For entailment it substitutes implication, material and formal, in neither of which is there anything beyond general accompaniment. For inconsistency it substitutes 'not both true', from which necessity has evaporated. Possibility and impossibility are cut down to assertions of 'some' and 'none'. Now if a logic by explicit profession abjures necessity, the fact that it gets on without it is not philosophically significant. If it had so analysed valid reasoning as to have found the claim to necessity fictitious, the verdict would have been important and indeed catastrophic. But no verdict in fact has been rendered. The defendant never appears.

38. If such criticism of mathematical logic is disputed, it will probably be on one of two grounds. The first is that in defining such terms as 'implies' and 'consistent', a logician is free to follow convenience. If he finds the ordinary meanings less to his purpose than new ones of his own, there is no reason why he should not give his preference the right of way. In one obvious sense this is true. We can make anything mean anything if we want to. What is not true is that we shall gain an equally significant port if we abandon the compass of actual meaning for that of convenience, or for any preference of our own. When men in business, science, or philosophy, use the term 'follows', they mean something by it with which preference has nothing to do, something that makes their thought compelling, and the absence of which renders it of little account. Most persons study logic because they regard such thinking as essential if they are to know their world as it is, and consider that so valuable a tool should be understood and used. It is possible to construct logics—many of them have been constructed—in which entailment is ignored. These systems have their interest. So do the alternative strategies opened to chess-players by re-defining the function of queen or knight. They are innocent enough as amusements. But they are not means of enlightenment about the nature of things, or the nature of thought, or even the nature of logic, responsibly conceived. *Principia Mathematica* is an almost incredible technical achievement; the whole logic of Aristotle, on its formal side, makes only a small enclosure within it; and the logics of Lotze and Hegel, of Sigwart, Johnson, and Bradley, have nothing of its virtuosity in the weaving of symbolic chains. But because these logicians fixed their eyes less on the requirements of a system than on the ways of thinking men have in fact found most convincing, the value of their work for philosophy is high. Owing to the influence of such works as *Principia*, the time may now have come to transfer the name of logic to the mathematical discipline, and to say of these earlier writers that they do not know what logic means. But it would be a serious philosophic loss if, because of the transfer of a name, the illuminating older discipline were to be abandoned for one which, despite its ingenuity, completeness, and order, is in comparison mechanical and external. Russell argued in his earlier days that mathematical logic was 'the essence of philosophy'. If it is, one can only deplore, with Marx, '*la misère de la philosophie*'.

Secondly, it may be said that though *Principia* does not adopt and baptize entailment under that name, it uses it throughout, that every successive deduction exemplifies not only material or formal implication but also necessary connection. This in a sense is true. $[(p \supset q) \equiv (\sim p \vee q)] \supset (\sim q \supset \sim p)$; if p's implying q is equivalent to 'either not-p or q', then not-q implies not-p. Is that a case of formal implication, or a case of following in the ordinary sense? Surely it is both. *If* one conceives implication in that way, then to say that p implies q does entail a great many interesting things. We must agree, then, that far from failing to show entailment, *Principia* shows it constantly. It remains true, however, (*a*) that implication, as there defined, is very different from entailment, (*b*) that if it were identified with entailment, a different set of deductions would follow, and (*c*) that while the deductions offered do follow from the offered premises, this logic cannot recognize that they do without exceeding any notion of 'follow' that is provided by its own terms. Its practice is better than its profession.

39. We said long ago that the two chief influences in producing logical atomism were two, the new mathematical logic and the empiricist analysis of meaning. We must turn now to the second. According to the early Russell and Wittgenstein, every statement about things or events, such as 'the summer has been unusually fine', reduces to a statement, or more probably a set of statements, of atomic facts, empirically perceivable. Each of these facts, in turn, consists of a particular qualified by a character, or a pair or more of particulars linked by a relation. Between these facts the linkage is not necessary but contingent; any one of them might be otherwise; any one or group of them could indeed be banished from the world, without affecting the rest. This cosmology is not, of course, an a priori deduction, though it is the sort of theory for which *Principia* had prepared a language. It is the view to which we seem driven when we take any statement of fact and invite ourselves to make our meaning wholly clear. Wherever we start, analysis seems to run out into the same sort of ultimate data. If we take these data as typical of the further data that we might come upon, a certain kind of metaphysic is virtually forced upon us. Our world will not be an intelligible whole or system. It will be an enormous catalogue or congeries of contingent facts.

40. In examining this view, it will be convenient to deal first with the structure of an individual fact, and then with the relations between facts.

Regarding atomic facts and the atomic statements that correspond to them, we are faced by a curious difficulty at the outset. There is some doubt whether anyone has ever met with a specimen of either, and there is hence a reluctance to give examples. 'This table is brown' will not do, because the table is not simple; it is a construction involving many qualities and many relations. 'This spot is black' will not do, because two different things are asserted, namely that this is a spot and that it is black. 'This is black' is better, but it is still unsatisfactory because it suggests that the relation between the objects in the fact forms a separate element in the whole in the same way as the word 'is' in the sentence. The nearest practicable approach to an atomic proposition appears to be 'this black', where there is a word for each 'object' in the fact and where their relation is symbolized—or, as Wittgenstein would say, mirrored—by the juxtaposition of words. Wittgenstein and Ramsey both thought that 'we are not acquainted with any genuine objects or atomic propositions, but merely infer them as presupposed by other propositions'.[1] Wisdom thought that even in 'this-black', 'this' might carry an element of description, just as 'this spot' did, and that 'black' was ambiguous, since there could be various shades of black;[2] hence the statement was not quite atomic. Russell, however, accepted this form as a statement of genuine atomic fact.

The acceptance of a world of atomic facts which our statements might approach at least asymptotically supplied a purpose of some importance to the early analysts. It gave their preoccupation with language a philosophical justification. They were not lost, as Carnap was later to become, in a wilderness of words with no apparent path by which to escape to the real world. They were interested in linguistic forms because these forms were more or less distant reflections of things as they were, and if we could correct their distorting influences, our philosophic puzzles would, for the most part, solve themselves. A perfect language would virtually consist of 'yea, yea' and 'nay, nay', pronounced of indubitable atomic facts.

[1] F. P. Ramsey, *Foundations of Mathematics*, 123.
[2] *Mind*, 1931, 203.

41. The analysts agreed that the subjects in atomic statements always stood for particulars. What did they mean by a particular? The windings of their thought on this question would make an instructive study, but we can only point out that opinion about it varied and vacillated widely. Russell in 1911 thought that the difference between universals and particulars was radical and self-evident.[1] Ramsey thought the distinction essentially one of convenience rather than of logic or ontology.[2] Those who were most empirically minded among the analysts were for doing away with universals altogether and reading the world as an aggregate of particulars. Russell, after many years of reflection, reached the opposite conclusion, namely that the particular is strictly unthinkable, and that both terms in atomic judgments stand for universals.[3]

The grounds for such vacillation are not difficult to see. Take the statement 'this is black', and ask yourself what you mean by 'this'. A natural answer would be, 'this black spot', or, if one were a philosopher, perhaps 'this black sense datum'. But that would make the atomic judgment analytic and necessary. G. E. Moore would so regard it. That was not the view, however, that commended itself to the atomists; they were not saying merely 'this black spot is black'. 'The predicate,' Russell said, '. . . is never part of the subject, and thus no true subject-predicate proposition is analytic.'[4] Furthermore, if by 'this spot' one meant something having a certain extent, shape, and colour, one had obviously not reached the pure particular, for these were all characters that might appear elsewhere, and were therefore universals. Suppose that one pared down the subject further and reduced it to this surface or that extent. But there are innumerable surfaces and extents in the world, and the use of such words shows that one is still roaming about among universals instead of getting down to the sheer particular. The particular must be a bare this, which may have character, to be sure, but is not itself characterizable, which owns them without *being* any of them, which supplies the 'it' of which they are attributes or hangers-on.

42. Now for persons who had renounced all statements about the world that were not empirically verifiable, this conclusion was very odd. Indeed it was an abrupt plunge into mystical metaphysics. The particular could not be identified with any colour one ever saw, or

[1] 'On the Relations of Universals and Particulars'. Arist. Soc. Proc., Vol. 12 (1911–12).

[2] *Op. cit.*, and Arist. Soc. Proc., Supplementary Vol. 6 (1926), 17 ff.

[3] *Inquiry into Meaning and Truth*, chap. 6, and pp. 127–130.

[4] *Arist. Soc. Proc.*, 12 (1911–12), 23.

any extent or hardness one ever felt, because these were *whats*, and a what or character was, by its very nature, universal. The particular that owns these characters must then, by *its* very nature, or lack of nature, be invisible, intangible, and generally non-sensible. But if non-sensible, must it not to empiricists be meaningless? If the analysts had been more interested in the history of speculation, they could hardly have failed to see that they were proposing here a theory dogged by all the venerable difficulties that had hounded the conception of substance from Aristotle to Locke. When Aristotle had peeled off the successive forms concealing the matter of the material thing—the house from the bricks, the bricks from the clay, etc.—he arrived at something of which he could only say, not that it was this or that, but that it was the mere potency of this or that. When Locke stripped the material thing of its secondary and then of its primary qualities, he too was left with only a 'something I know not what'. The atomists would have given short shrift to these metaphysicians. They would have held that if Locke or Aristotle found it so hard to say what he meant, it was because the benighted soul had really meant nothing. They insisted, however, that when they themselves spoke of particulars they did mean something, though it was unfortunately impossible to say what. Wittgenstein's *Tractatus* was based upon the identification of the particular with a kind of substance which metaphysicians had long discussed and which many or most of them had dismissed as untenable. It was only gradually that the analysts realized this. The first clear awareness of it seems to have been Russell's, who abandoned his earlier view in the late 1930's. In his *Inquiry into Meaning and Truth* (1940), he wrote: 'One is tempted to regard "this is red" as a subject-predicate proposition; but if one does so, one finds that "this" becomes a substance, an unknowable something in which predicates inhere, but which, nevertheless, is not identical with the sum of its predicates. Such a view is open to all the familiar objections to the notion of substance. . . . I wish to suggest that "this is red" is not a subject-predicate proposition, but is of the form "redness is here" . . . and that what would commonly be called a "thing" is nothing but a bundle of co-existing qualities such as redness, hardness, etc.'[1] The particular here has vanished into a set of qualities which, as capable of appearing elsewhere, are all of them universals.[2]

43. What lay behind this incursion into a not very plausible meta-

[1] p. 97.
[2] It is argued in my *The Nature of Thought* (1939) that this view is inescapable.

physic? Partly considerations of common sense. Two black spots on a sheet of white paper may be indistinguishable in respect to colour, shape and size, but they will still be two; and in that case there must be something about them that differs, other than their qualities. What can that be? It might be taken as the surface or volume of space where they are. But to call these unique carried dubious suggestions of absolute space; besides, they were themselves 'whats', and very complex ones at that. It was natural, therefore, to look elsewhere on behalf of the somewhat forlorn qualities that were in search of an owner. A second pressure towards pure particulars came from the functional language of the analysts' logic. In the function φx, φ stood for some kind of character, but what did x stand for? Not another character or group of characters, nor for an individual so far as that was itself a group of characters. Of course one could write 'φ Socrates', if one wished, but that would always be because the subject was imperfectly analysed; Socrates was really a complex 'logical construction'. If the thing were to answer to the intention of the symbol, it must be a mere and pure subject, an *it* taken as distinct from all its qualities and relations. A third influence making toward the same end came from a curious doctrine of proper names, derived perhaps from Mill. Mill thought that a proper name had denotation without connotation, that is, that it merely indicated or pointed at something without in any way characterizing it. This was obviously untrue of names referring to the absent; if 'Socrates' conveys to another the same reference as to ourselves, it is because the name conveys the thought of a Greek philosopher, characterized thus and so. Russell recognized this and conceded that 'the names that we commonly use, like "Socrates", are really abbreviations for descriptions'.[1] But he held that when we speak of something we are actually sensing, and use the word 'this' or 'that', we are using a 'logically proper name' in the sense of a symbol that refers without characterizing. Unless from time to time we were in a position to use such words, our thought would be left for ever hanging in the air and playing about among universals. The only particulars that appeared in person, the only ones we could ever verify, were those given in sensation. Hence if an assertion could be correctly analysed into statements whose subjects fell outside the experience of our here and now, we literally did not know whereof we spoke. It was only a step from this position to Wittgenstein's solipsism. If one adds to Russell's doctrine the point that what is unverifiable is meaningless, one has crossed the narrow bridge between them. No two persons can then ever refer to the same

[1] *The Monist*, Vol. 28 (1918), 524.

matter of fact, nor can the I of today mention anything that happened to the I of yesterday.

44. We shall review in our next chapter the analysts' reflections about meaning. For the present, it must suffice to remark on some of the difficulties in which this view of particulars involved them. It implied, for one thing, that every empirical analysis must end in impenetrable mystery. Suppose one says that this is red or that is hard, and stops to ask why it should be so. There can be no answer. If one asked why red stirred the emotions or why the square on a hypotenuse equalled the sum of the other two squares, an answer might be forthcoming, because we have a character to start with which may entail certain properties or even—though the atomists would deny this—certain effects. But what is characterless can entail nothing, can explain nothing, can in any intelligible sense be associated with nothing. Something supposed to be luminously clear to the speaker, though unknowable to everyone else, is red or hard or sour; that ends the matter; *why* it should have such a quality, how it acquired this, and why it should not be otherwise, are questions beyond answering even in theory, for they all presuppose a character in the characterless. Now a philosophy may be none the less true because it implies a large measure of scepticism. 'All things end in bafflement', as George Saintsbury said, but then, as he added, 'it is well not to be baffled too soon'. This implanting of a mystical agnosticism in the heart of the simplest statement runs counter to the whole spirit and tenor of empiricism, and Russell himself, as we have seen, was unable to accept it in the end. When an empiricist theory of analysis finds itself marching arm in arm with what it would call existentialist obscurantism, it is time for it to review its notion of analysis.

45. Again, what becomes of the idea of *picturing* on this theory of the particular? In Wittgenstein's view, the meaning and truth of every atomic proposition lay in its mirroring of atomic fact. It now turns out that the subject in any such fact is incapable of being mirrored, since there is no content there to mirror. We have seen already how hard it is to make sense of a resemblance between the arrangements of words in a sentence—to say nothing of glasses and dishes—and the arrangement of elements in a fact. This becomes harder still when the subject element in the fact is conceived to be something which, as characterless, could not in principle resemble anything. The disintegration of the picture theory is here all but complete. The first stage of collapse comes when one realizes that any likeness between the relation of words on the one side and the relation of 'objects' on the other must be purely coincidental. The second stage comes with the awareness that any likeness between the subject in the sentence and the subject in the fact is ruled out by the metaphysics of the particular. The third stage comes with the perception that between the predicate in the sentence and the universal in the fact, between 'red' and red, there is again no resemblance whatever. It might be maintained that we can still picture an arrangement of two objects, even when one of them is nothing at all; can we not photograph the doughnut with its hole? But this, of course, will not do. The hole in the doughnut, as seen or photographed, *is* distinguishable in sense; the particular is not. Indeed it has far to go before it reaches the humble dignity of a hole.

46. Enough now of this phantom particular. We suggest that there is no such thing. We shall find ourselves more than once insisting to the empiricists that they rid themselves of their baggage of dogmatic metaphysics and become more genuinely empirical. We hold that in 'this is red', the logical subject is always a content, for example a surface, and that the two contents—subject and predicate—are asserted jointly of a reality that falls beyond either. This reality is not to be known by burrowing under the qualities and relations of things in search of some mysterious 'existence'. So far as it is know-able at all, it must be known by studying the threads of connection within the content asserted, and then between this and the world outside it. These connections may or may not be necessary. So far as they are not, and empiricists believe that most or all of them are not, the world falls short, in our sense, of intelligibility. We believe that many of them *are* necessary, perhaps in the end all of them, and that it is the business of the philosopher, without prejudging the outcome, to carry rational understanding as far as he can. There is nothing starry-eyed or even new in this approach. It seems to us only a statement, a little bald and bleak perhaps, of what all who are engaged in the quest for understanding are trying to do.

47. This view of the philosopher's task would be vetoed by the atomists. We must now try to see why, and how decisive the veto is. It is imposed because the necessity in which the rationalist believes is considered not to hold in the actual world. If one did believe it to hold there, one would have to find it in one or other of two places, either within the atomic fact or between one such fact and another. Is there any necessity, first, *within* the fact?

On this point it is hard to get a clear answer from the atomists. One would expect from them a flat denial of such connections, and indeed we are told emphatically that no existent is connected necessarily with any other. What is meant by an existent? Presumably a particular. And if a particular is the mere characterless x that the atomists so often assumed it to be, there will naturally be no necessity either in φa or in aRb. For the 'a' and 'b' will then stand for zeros which could entail nothing and be entailed by nothing. But the atomists did not steadily hold to this view. The 'this' which is black becomes for Russell first a dot, and then a dot with a surprising hold on life; 'you can keep "this" going for about a minute or two. I made that dot and talked about it for some little time. . . . If you argue quickly, you can get some little way before it is finished.'[1] Clearly, if this sort of thing were to be included among Russell's 'particulars' and Wittgenstein's 'objects', the notion of the particular as a contentless x had been abandoned and the question whether existents necessitated each other was still wide open.

Indeed we find strong intimations that even here within the atomic fact necessity must be admitted. Ramsey reminds us that in the very symbolism Russell offered for atomic facts, the predicate could not stand alone, but required a subject. 'He says that about an adjective there is something incomplete . . . so that the adjective-symbol can never stand alone or be the subject of a proposition, but must be completed into a proposition in which it is the predicate. Thus, he says, the appropriate symbol for redness is not the word "red" but the function "x is red". . . .'[2] That is, we can see that in whatever atomic fact red appears, it is the sort of thing that *cannot* stand alone; its nature is such as to demand, if it is to exist at all, a completion in something else. Necessity thus finds a place in the heart of the atomic fact.

48. Where did Wittgenstein stand on this matter? We may describe him as semi-necessarian. That is, he held that in the atomic fact each object determines the general, but not the specific, character of the other object. 'If I can think of an object in the context of an atomic fact,' he writes, 'I cannot think of it at all apart from the *possibility* of this context.' 'If a thing *can* occur in an atomic fact the possibility of that atomic fact must already be prejudged in the thing.' 'Incidentally, objects are colourless.'[3] These Delphic utterances may perhaps

---

[1] *The Monist*, Vol. 28 (1918), 527.
[2] *The Foundations of Mathematics*, 114.
[3] *Tractatus*, 2.0121, 2.012, 2.03, 2.0232.

be construed as follows: if we know that an object occupies space, we know that it has a colour, though we do not know whether that colour is green, brown, or red. Similarly, if we know that an object is coloured, we know that it must belong to something extended, though nothing follows as to shape or size. 'Objects are colourless' means that only as a particular enters into a fact and achieves a character can it be coloured. Again, if we know that a sense datum is one of taste, we know that it must be bitter or sweet or something else of the kind, though we do not know which; and we know that if it is bitter or sweet, it must be a taste. And so on of other qualities. Wittgenstein indeed thinks we can see necessity in the constitution of fact as such. To say 'it is essential to a thing that it can be a constituent part of an atomic fact' is in effect to say 'we can see that it is a universal and necessary truth about particulars that they have attributes or relations.'[1]

All this makes sense if Wittgenstein construes the 'it' or subject of which we are asserting as a presented character. We can see that if something is coloured, it must be extended, and that if it is extended, it is, or may be, coloured. His statements make no sense if the particular is taken as the neo-Aristotlelian pseudo-substance that he sought to make it. A mere complexionless x cannot necessitate anything. If we are to discuss the matter profitably, therefore, we must assume that in speaking of the particular, he is referring to what possesses, or rather *is*, a content already.

In relating these contents within the fact, did he ever go beyond the very general necessity just noted? He clearly did. He went so far as to say, 'this blue colour and that stand in the internal relation of brighter and darker *eo ipso*. It is unthinkable that *these* two objects should not stand in this relation'.[2] (He adds, having said this, that it is really impossible to say it, since the internal relation in the fact cannot be referred to in words, but must be reproduced by such a relation among the words themselves. We shall spend no more time over this.) He clearly means that if object No. 1 is brighter than object No. 2, they are so related that if this relation were altered, one or other or both would have to be different from what it is. He then goes on to develop from this insight a generalization which, coming from an atomist and an empiricist, awakes surprised attention. He points out that the character of a particular may be related internally to other characters in a series, that these series are of various kinds, and hence that the given character may be connected necessarily

[1] *Tractatus*, 2.011.
[2] *Ibid.*, 4.123.

with an inexhaustible set of further characters. We must pause over this.

49. Kant pointed out—it was the chief meaning of his category of quality—that every sense quality that presents itself to us does so as a member in an order of intensities. If it is a sound, it has a certain pitch and loudness; if it is a colour it has a certain brightness and saturation; if it is a pain, it has some degree or other of painfulness. Now the being related in this way to other intensities is not merely an empirical discovery about the character of this sensum. The relation is a necessary one because essential to the sensum's being what it is. It is constitutive of its character in the sense of being part of what is meant by having that character; relation and character are so bound up with each other that if the first were to vanish, the second would go too. Middle C, without the other notes on the scale, would not be middle C. This does not mean that whenever we hear middle C, we think explicitly of the notes above and below it. Nor does it mean that the notion is inconceivable of a man born deaf to all sounds but this, though in such an experience the sound would certainly differ from what it is for us. What the statement does mean is that whether we apprehend them or not, this note has relations of higher and lower to other pitches, without which it would not be what it is, and by grasping which we understand what it is more fully.

The fact that a quality given in sense thus belongs to a series or system all members of which are internally related has been stressed again and again in recent philosophy. W. E. Johnson, using the word 'determinable' for such concepts as colour, and 'determinate' for the more specific kinds that fall under it, such as red, points out that a determinate may be connected necessarily, and in more than one way, with others under its own determinable. In the order of colour, for example, if we see that a surface at a certain place is red, we can see that it *cannot* also be blue, though it may have various qualities that fall under other determinables, such as round and hard. This relation of mutal exclusion is clearly necessary. Again, the determinates may often be arranged in a series such that 'the whole series has its order directly determined by the nature of the adjectives themselves', and one can see, for example, that 'the difference between red and yellow is greater than that between red and orange.'[1] Substantially the same view was taken by Moritz Schlick, suspicious as he was of all claims of necessary connection. 'These relations which hold between the elements of the system of colours are

[1] *Logic,* I. 181–2.

obviously *internal* relations, for it is customary to call a relation internal if it relates two (or more) terms in such a way that the terms cannot possibly exist without the relation existing between them—in other words, if the relation is necessarily implied by the very nature of the terms.'[1] And recently Nelson Goodman has made a more elaborate analysis of such series with what appears to be the same result. He constructs series through the 'matching' of items. Two qualities match when they appear to be the same. A quality *b* is 'between' two others, *a* and *c*, when, though *b* matches both, they do not match each other. Using this notion of betweenness, we may construct series whose ordering obviously depends upon the natures of the terms.[2]

The character of every sense datum seems to be caught up in one or more of these flights of qualities. How many such there are it would be hard to say. Three very important ones not yet mentioned are those of number, space, and time. We can see that if the number of objects before us is three, that number must relate them internally to every other number of objects; it is so interwoven with the infinite web-work of arithmetical relations that all the connections possessed by it with other numbers of the system will necessarily apply to this group. Suppose the sensum is located in space. The very meaning of 'located' is that it bears certain relations to other things in space, and if this were specified completely, *all* other things in space would be involved. If any of these relations were different, all of them would have to be different. Again, suppose the sensum is regarded as an event, as it always can be. Then we can say that it is connected necessarily with all events that precede it, accompany it, or follow it, in the sense that if A were to come a second before B rather than after it, an infinity of other temporal relations would have to be altered too.

50. Respecting the characters of the world, logical atomism is thus far from being atomic. These characters are conceived as woven into systems which, whether connected or not with each other, are each closely knit internally. Where, then, does the atomism enter? It enters not in the order of characters, but in the order of facts. 'The world divides into facts,' says Wittgenstein, of which 'any one can either be the case or not be the case, and everything else remain the

---

[1] *Gesammelte Aufsätze*, 162.

[2] *The Structure of Appearance*, Ch. 9, 10. The possibility of constructing such orders has been acutely questioned by Mr W. C. Clement (*Mind*, April 1956, 184 ff). He bases his case on a study of hues. These offer special difficulties, however, and it is not clear that if his case were conceded with regard to hues, it would hold of loudness, brightness, and pitch.

same'; 'outside logic all is accident'.[1] Granted that if the objects before me are three, their number is related necessarily to all other numbers, the fact that they are three rather than four is itself contingent. Granted that if a note I hear has a certain pitch, it must be higher or lower than certain other pitches, it is still an accident, in the sense of being non-necessary, that I should have heard a note at all, or, if I did hear one, that it should have been of one pitch rather than another. The *fact* that a is φ rather than ψ, or is related to b by R rather than S, the fact that anything whatever has occurred, the fact that anything existent exists rather than a million other things which might equally well have existed—all these are 'brute' facts. We have not the least idea *why* they should be as they are. Each one sits so loose to the others that any or all of them might change or disappear without the smallest influence on what remained. This is essentially what Hume meant by his doctrine that 'every distinct perception is a distinct existence'. The world is dissolved away into atoms with as little cohesion as a sand pile, and the necessary connections alleged between them are ropes of sand. However, Wittgenstein made an attempt—an obscure and clumsy one, to be sure—to make his atoms more definite than Hume's. They are not 'impressions', or simples, or characters; they are complexes in which there are two or more related 'objects'. These are facts. Characters have internal relations to at least some others. Facts do not.

51. We are convinced that this conclusion will not stand. Our conviction is essentially that of the plain man. Intuitions may be of small weight in philosophy, but we cannot think that the 'invincible surmise' of most thoughtful minds that the world is not in the final account a rag-bag of loose ends, is wholly without significance. When chemists announced that the universe was composed of just 92 elements, there were many who presumed to 'feel in their bones' that there was something absurd about this. They had little enough ground for their divination, but they did, of course, turn out to be right. We confess that we approach this contention that the world is an unintelligible miscellany in which no event occurs for any reason and no fact requires any other, with a confidence, perhaps equally ill grounded, that it cannot be the last word. It looks like the sort of theory that would be offered by some very clever person like Leibniz who, from the security offered by a belief, with one half of his brain, that the world possessed some intelligible unity, could 'take off' from the other half into speculations about a world of windowless monads.

[1] *Tractatus*, 1.2, 1.21, 6.3.

But we cannot, after all, depend on 'hunches'. Are there *reasons* for thinking the theory misguided? Yes, and strong ones.

52. We may note, to begin with, that the theory, as often held, turns on the ambiguity of a word. It has become common in recent years to confine 'necessity' to logical necessity, and to mean by logical necessity what it means in extensionalist logic. And then, as we have seen, it becomes tautology, and deduction is reduced to a setting out more explicitly of what has been said before. One can so use the terms if one wishes, and one can throw any inference regarding fact (thought not without distortion) into the form of such a deduction. But to go on and say that because what the logician means is present, and because this does not include what the plain man means, therefore what the plain man means is not there, looks like mere confusion and is certainly unwarranted. Indeed it is time a protest was made against the appropriation of so old and useful a term as necessity to this special and technical application. For the mathematical logician, necessity links propositions irrespective of contents; for the ordinary man, it is a link that is based on content. We are constantly assuming its presence in cases with which the logician's tautology has nothing to do. We say that if we *ought* to do something, we *can* do it; that all right angles are equal; that every line must be straight or curved, and every integer odd or even; that two straight lines can intersect only once; that orange resembles yellow more than it does green; even that a composer, if he is to conform to aesthetic requirements, *must* write a note as natural, not as flat. These are not logical tautologies. Yet for most minds they are far more typical cases of necessity than p.⊃.p v p, or even than p⊃q. q⊃r: ⊃. p⊃r, interpreted extensionally. The real issue about the linkage of facts is whether necessity of the former type, not of the latter, exists among them. And to settle this issue in one way, on the ground that 'necessity' can be so defined as to exclude the meanings of real interest, is pedantry.

53. The question before us, then, is whether, in the ordinary and important sense, one fact ever necessitates another. Wittgenstein said it never does. We think it often does. Suppose that, looking at a patch and enumerating its characters, we begin by noting that it is red and that it is extended. Have we noted one fact here or two? Ordinary usage would be content to lump several possible statements into one, and say simply, 'this red patch is extended'. The analysts have insisted, with reason, that this will not do, that 'this is red', 'this is a patch', and 'this is extended', are distinct assertions, reporting distinguishable facts. We have seen that if we then ask them what is meant by 'this', they shuffle from one foot to the other. Let us look at both postures. 'This' may mean some presented content or character, as in 'this surface is extended' or 'this shade is extended'. In that case necessity is clearly present, though it is regarded as linking, not different facts, but different 'objects' in the same fact. Wittgenstein admitted such necessities, though we have seen that he was committed at the same time to a view that rendered them meaningless. This view, which he held while on the other foot, was that 'this' named a pure particular, denoting without connoting. In that case 'this is red' and 'this is extended' would be two statements expressing different facts. Would they then be more independent of each other than they were on the first view? Surely not. Of course in a sense the question is meaningless, since a statement with a vacuum for its subject is not a statement at all and can neither entail nor be entailed. But we can say to the analyst: 'Make your own choice as to what "this" shall mean. So long as it means the same thing in "this is red" and "this is extended", the first statement will entail the second. And it will do so because the facts reported by the statements are themselves not independent. The *fact* of x's being red requires, entails, necessitates its also being extended.' Thus, whether an original statement is taken as reporting one fact or two, necessity is equally present. 'From an elementary proposition no other than be inferred,' says Wittgenstein.[1] Here we are caught red-handed in doing the impossible.

If Wittgenstein thinks otherwise, it appears to be owing to a curious assumption. This is that though qualities that are components of facts may have necessary connections, these connections never suffice to establish similar connections among the facts themselves. Suppose we say, 'John is ten years old, James is twenty, and George is thirty.' Here are statements of three facts. Wittgenstein would say that the three numbers named are members of a series whose parts are connected necessarily, but would insist that the facts of which these members are components are connected only contingently. Can this really be defended? Where we reason that because George is ten years older than James, and James ten years older than John, George must be twenty years older than John, our thought is surely not confined to a row of disembodied characters. We are linking facts *through* their characters; granted; but it is facts we are linking never-theless, and our conclusion asserts that a certain fact must be what it is because of the relations sustained through its character to those

[1] *Tractatus*, 5.134.

of other facts. And this 'must' is an internal relation. It relates internally the facts themselves, since if the fact reported in the conclusion were not what it is, the facts reported in the premises could not be what they are.

54. Here facts are necessarily related through their predicates, or rather, through the characters named in the predicates of our statements about them. They may also be related through the subjects that bear these characters. What Wittgenstein meant by the particulars that supplied him his subjects is a baffling question, as we have seen; but the preference of some of his interpreters for such statements as 'here-hard' and 'there-blue' as the purest examples of atomic statements is significant.[1] They suggest that the subject is, or includes, position in space. But if this is true, atomic facts must be admitted once more to be connected with each other necessarily. For 'here' would have no meaning without 'there', nor 'there' without 'here'; and the same holds of 'now' and 'then'. If spatial and temporal positions are determined by relations within their own orders—or within the two orders combined—then every fact that can be correctly reported by a 'here-hard' or a 'now-pain' is internally related to others.

Take, again, the relation of genus and species, and consider how atomists must deal with it. 'This is red' and 'this is coloured' clearly report different facts, since the second may hold without the first. We should ordinarily say, of course, that the first entailed the second, because we can see that being red is, and can only be, a way of being coloured. Our thought moves from one character or meaning to another by an internal track laid down by the characters themselves. But according to the atomist we have before us two distinct facts, and since all facts are independent of each other, the fact that this is coloured must be independent of the fact that this is red. And plainly it is not. What we have here is another distortion of actual thought, the result of a logic that persistently ignores content.

This logic, like atomism itself, discountenances the attempt to think in as-suches. For traditional thought a class was a group of things or characters united by a common nature, and a general proposition, as opposed to an enumerative one, stated not merely that all A's were in fact B's, but that all A's *as such* were B. Neither of these views is accepted by extensional logic or by logical atomism.

---

[1] 'The particular portion of reality is the particular, because this has a definite position in space and time. . . .' R. B. Braithwaite, *Arist. Soc. Proc.*, Sup. Vol. 6 (1926), 30.

Russell introduced a budget of empiricist economy, called the theory of descriptions, to eliminate unverifiable entities like hippogryphs and the present king of France, and since classes in the older sense seemed to involve universals and other empirically dubious features, he attempted to show that logic could get on without them. We can replace the class of men by something very like it, but less objectionable, as follows: first, we note a certain particular which we call human. We then see that this particular is replaceable by other particulars of which the statement that they are human will also be true. This gives us the 'propositional function' 'x is human'; and the class of men is now to be understood as the range of particulars of which this propositional function may be truly asserted. Why the function 'x is human' should be supposed less open to difficulties about universals than the term 'man' is not as clear as one could wish. The function is applied to other particulars because they are found to resemble in some respect the particular one taken as the starting point. But the man whom one took as the starting point resembled other things in many ways. In order to give to the function 'x is human' a definite meaning, one would have to single out among the properties of this starting point a set that could appear elsewhere; otherwise one could not select the other particulars to which the function applied. Thus the function 'x is human' involves all the difficulties about universals or common properties that it was designed to avoid. Mr Joseph somewhere remarked that if you define the number three by pointing at a group and saying that 'three' means the class of all classes similar to this group, you have still to say in what respect these other classes are to resemble the group before you. If you do not specify this, you have no ground on which to constitute your other classes. If you do specify it, then you have fallen back on intensional thinking, and the resort to the class of all classes is otiose.

It is instructive to see how atomists used this replacement of classes by functions in their dealing with general propositions. Every general proposition regarding fact (all others being tautologies) became what would formerly have been called a statement of class inclusion, but was now regarded as a statement of implication between propositional functions. If φ stands for 'human' and ψ for 'mortal', then the statement that all men are mortal becomes $(x).\varphi x \supset \psi x$, 'for all x's, φx implies ψx'. This statement will be true if any one of these conditions holds: first, that all cases in which x is human are also cases of its being mortal; second, that all cases where 'x is human' is false are also cases of the falsity of 'x is mortal'; and third, that all cases of its not being human are cases of its being mortal. As a statement of what we mean by 'all men are mortal', this is of course absurd. If, when we made the remark, some eager logistical beaver were to reply, 'Quite so, since stones are neither human nor mortal' or 'Yes indeed, for elm trees, which are not human, still die', we should be mystified. These statements which, on the extensional interpretation, would help to confirm our statement, would seem to us wholly irrelevant to what we were trying to say.

What *were* we trying to say? Surely something like this: 'All men do die, and die in virtue of being men.' Analysts of the atomist school would say that there are two distinguishable assertions here, one an allegation of fact and the other of necessity; we agree. Unfortunately the atomist account of both assertions is unsatisfactory.

Look first at the statement of fact. This is supposed to be given in the formula, when interpreted, $(x).\varphi x \supset \psi x$. Now this is not a statement of fact at all. It says that for all xs, the *proposition* that x is human implies the *proposition* that it is mortal. What it asserts of is propositions, not facts. The sign '$\supset$' does not mark a linkage between existents in the natural world. But we are clearly talking about such existents, and if the formula will not allow us to refer to them, then so much the worse for the formula. Language should be moulded on thought, not thought on the demands of a Procrustean language.

There is a further and more serious difficulty. Having insisted on interpreting the general proposition as essentially a statement of the inclusion of one class in another, the atomist logicians found this interpretation colliding with their empiricism. They were committed, as we have seen, to the view that every factual statement must refer to something given in sense-experience—Wittgenstein even said in one's *own* sense experience. Leaving this last wild suggestion aside, and interpreting the demand as only that the facts referred to should be given in *someone's* experience, the atomists were still in difficulty, which they met in various ways. Wittgenstein held that a general statement was simply a summary of particular statements, and for a time Ramsey agreed. But this theory shortly collapsed over the obvious objection that when a scientist proposed a general law, he was not suggesting that it held only for a set of instances that he might enumerate, or even for a set that might fall within human experience generally; what proportion of instances of the law of gravitation could human beings hope to observe? Russell tried another way out, by holding to the existence of 'general facts'. Even if you knew of every individual man that he was mortal, you would not have exhausted what the proposition means, said Russell, for it means also the further fact that these which you have inspected are *all* the men. And that is not a particular but a general fact. It turned out, however, to be an exceedingly awkward fact. For of course it was not verifiable in sense experience; you may show by this experience that there are such things as men, but not, when you have observed a certain number of them, that there are no more. So this view too failed to commend itself. Ramsey now came up with a third theory, which Mr Urmson has described as a 'superb specimen of a priori metaphysics'.[1] This was to the effect that since Wittgenstein was in error, general propositions not being reducible to summaries of particulars, and since Russell also was in error, all facts being particular facts, the 'general proposition' must be set down as no proposition at all. What was it then? It was a rule proposed to direct our belief. To say that all men are mortal was to adopt a certain practice, the practice of regarding as mortal each man of whom the question might arise.[2] This was no doubt ingenious. But to take it as exhausting what the scientist means when he lays down a general law is wide of the mark. Far from merely stating a rule for his own or others' practice, he is stating what he believes would still hold even if there were no people at all to make rules or to follow them.

The leading atomists, then, while insisting that general statements were summaries of particulars, were unable to explain satisfactorily what these summaries meant. They recognized, however, that a quite different interpretation had been suggested for the general proposition, one that would regard it not as a statement of fact, but as a hypothetical and necessary statement, 'if human, then mortal'. They admitted that we sometimes do mean this. But when we do, what we are really saying is that being mortal is *part of what we mean* by being a man. For the atomists were committed to holding that the only necessary statements were analytic statements, whose truth was involved in the very definition of their terms. We are saying nothing, then, about whether men or mortals exist, or about the relation in fact of being human and being mortal; we are merely saying that in our adopted usage, the term 'man' contains being mortal as one component of its meaning.

Now this again is not what we mean. It is not what we mean even when we are thinking in as-suches. For we are then still talking about relations in nature, not about our own linguistic habits; and even if we were talking about those habits, it would never occur to us to offer the fact of man's dying as part of the *meaning* of 'man'. We are

---

[1] *Philosophical Analysis*, 66.
[2] *Foundations of Mathematics*, 237 ff.

trying to say that man's actual nature (not our thought of him merely) carries with it, involves, necessitates (not accompanies merely) the fact (not the conclusion merely) of his dying. If anyone then asks us whether we claim to *see* that men must die as we see that a triangle must have certain properties, candor requires us to say no. If anyone tells us we must therefore be talking about the *de facto* deaths of Tom, Dick, Harry, and the rest, we say no again—not, certainly, about them only. If any pursuing positivist then argues that we must mean one or the other, since there is nothing else for us to mean, we have a frivolous impulse to answer, Fiddlesticks. Our very point here is that this doctrinaire either-or does not apply to our actual thinking. We do mean to say something about all men; granted. We also mean to say something about their nature, namely that if, being human, they die, that is no mere accident, that they are *such as* to be mortal. Between these characters we see no self-evident connection; granted again. But we do mean to affirm a connection, whether seen or not. To put it with laboured explicitness, we are saying that there is something in human nature, as now constituted, though we do not at present quite know what, which is such as to make death inevitable.

If this is indeed our meaning, then it cannot be right unless atomism is wrong. For in this and numberless other judgments we are asserting necessary links among the facts themselves; we are saying that a certain fact, in virtue of being what it is, *requires* that another fact should be what it is.

We say that love and hate will behave, or tend to behave, differently, that men who think little of their own deserts will tend by nature to be more grateful than those who think highly of them, that if water wets and fire burns, the difference in the result is due to something in the nature of the agents, whether we can see the precise connection or not. The unsophisticated reader who picks up Hume or one of his recent followers and finds that if lovers sigh or fires burn, that is as much in the end an accident as one's drawing an ace from a pack, can only say that he has never meant or believed that. Of course he may be wrong; his 'invincible surmises' have sometimes proved so. His belief, indeed, involves three assumptions that recent analysts have all but universally denied. One is that necessity links characters in nature, and not merely in our own minds. The second is that the characters linked may genuinely differ, that the connection may be synthetic, not analytic. The third is that necessity is present in causation, that when one fact exists or occurs because of another, something more than accompaniment, even than uniform accompaniment, is at work.

Regarding the first point we have already made clear where we stand, but both on it and on the second we shall have more to say in our sixth chapter, on the analytic treatment of necessity. The third point is a most important one, on which we have as yet said nothing. We reserve it for discussion in Chapter XI on 'Necessity in Causation'.

CHAPTER V

THE THEORY OF MEANING

1. The volume of writing on meaning since the appearance of Ogden and Richards' *The Meaning of Meaning* in 1923 has been enormous. Unhappily much of it is dreary beyond description. The reason, in part at least, is that meaning has been conceived as the use of signs, and that such use has been conceived in terms of physical response. On this basis an entire science of 'semiotic' has been constructed with three grand divisions: 'pragmatics', which deals with the relation of signs to the user's history, 'semantics', which deals with the relations of signs and what they signify, and 'syntactics', which deals with the way signs are put together in statements and expressions. In the attempt to make the study 'scientific', the discussions have often been conducted carefully in such a way as to avoid any suggestion that in meaning something we ever think of it, since to think is to be conscious, and consciousness is not 'publicly verifiable'; a sign A is said to mean B if its influence on behaviour is in certain ways similar to B's. The paradigm of meaning is found in Pavlov's dog, which, being exposed simultaneously to a buzzer and to food, came to salivate when the buzzer was sounded alone; the buzzer then meant food since it produced a like reaction. We feel pretty sure that this is an oversimplified account even of the meanings of buzzers to dogs; and when we learn that all that distinguishes such meanings from those employed by Mr Eliot and Mr Whitehead, to say nothing of our sophisticated selves, reduces to differences in behaviour, we feel even more strongly that the new science is not all it might be.

We would not deny, of course, that useful evidence as to what goes on in consciousness can be gained from bodily responses. But we should have thought that the identification of meaning, or any other conscious process, with bodily change had been so often refuted, and the inadequacy of such change even as a tool in the understanding of mental process so often exposed, that these errors could now be filed away in a historical cabinet. In any case, the fact that they have been dealt with over and over again exempts us from any need to traverse the dreary acreage of 'scientific' semiotic. Our concern will be exclusively with meaning as a conscious process.

2. Such meaning may be studied from two very different points of view, those of the psychologist and of the epistemologist. Both types of study run quickly upon extremely puzzling problems where at first glance all seems to be plain sailing. The problem of the psychologist is that of describing meaning, of noting and sketching the traits that distinguish an act of thought or conscious reference from other mental states. If anyone supposes this an easy matter, let him try the experiment of thinking of some familiar object, say the house he lives in, and then introspecting to see what the thought of the house consists in. He will be tempted to say at first that it is an image; but that this is not a sufficient answer is shown by the fact that different persons may mean the same house with equal definiteness while their imagery varies from somewhere near zero to photographic fullness. But if the meaning is not the image, what is it? How difficult it is to give any satisfactory answer is shown by the long and tortured history of the inquiry—by the controversy between Locke and Berkeley as to how we think the general idea of man, by Galton's and Huxley's revival of the notion of a 'compound photograph', by the laborious explorations of the Würzburg school in the field of 'image-less thinking', by James's 'psychic fringe', by Titchener's revival of the image theory, by Watson's frank and philistine denial of any such thing as conscious meaning, and by the recent and more sophisticated behaviourism of Gilbert Ryle. The problem remains. There is no approximation to a consensus of opinion about it among either philosophers or psychologists.

3. Fortunately our problem is the still more interesting and important one raised by the theory of knowledge. The question here is not what meaning is like as a state of mind, but how to determine the object meant. This too at first looks easy. No doubt at times it is difficult to make out what *other* people mean; they may use words loosely, or in ways not our own, but they presumably know themselves what they mean; and whether they do or not, we surely know our own intentions. But do we? There are two modern schools of thought which have shown from different points of view how small is our title to such complacency. One is the Freudian school of psychologists which has made clear how hard it is to know our own motives. The other is the analytic school in philosophy, which has made it equally clear how hard it is to know what we are thinking of when we think. This school

has not abandoned philosophy for verbalism, as some critics have charged; indeed in its emphasis on the dissection of meanings it is harking back to an ancient tradition of Western thought. The first fully competent representative of that tradition was Socrates, whose avowed and main purpose was to develop a 'maieutic', a method of bringing to the light of explicit definition the meanings of common speech. We talk daily of justice and courage and piety; we know that they are important, because our lives are in many ways regulated by our regard for them; and we assume when we use their names that we know what these stand for. The Socratic dialogues are one long exposure of this pleasing assumption. Their standard plot is that someone should mention one of these fundamental terms, that Socrates should ask him what he means by it, that he should offer a glib and confident definition, that Socrates should then show him that he could not possibly mean this consistently with his other ideas, and that the company should then join in an arduous and sinuous pursuit of what they all seem to mean in common, but none of them can firmly lay hold of. There is many a reader who would say that after pursuing the meaning of justice in this unwearied company through the ten books of the *Republic*, he has still not quite managed to salt the tail of this elusive bird. It is, of course, not philosophers alone who feel the challenge of these puzzles. Such analysts as Schlick and Wittgenstein have held that it is precisely because scientists themselves become confused when they try to define their fundamental terms—cause, material thing, number, continuity, etc.—that the philosophers must be called in. Even when they suppose themselves to have achieved the clarity of complete self-evidence, they may still be confused. What could be more straightforward than saying that two events are simultaneous with each other? Yet Einstein showed the scientists that they were very far from clear even about that.

4. Thus both scientists and philosophers need a technique for determining whether their words have meaning, and if so, what that meaning is. This the logical positivists sought to supply. Their now familiar formula was that the meaning of a factual statement is its mode of verification. Deferring for the moment the question of the precise sense, or senses, of this formula, let us note, to begin with, that the test is designed as an empirical one. It derives from the same conviction about the source of our knowledge that was held by Locke, Berkeley, Hume and Mill. These philosophers were convinced, some inconsistencies apart, that all we knew about the actual world came from experience, either introspective (which they preferred not to talk about) or sensory. It was from the experience of the senses that we drew all we knew about the world outside ourselves. Name any existent thing, they would say, and you will find on examination that it presents itself to us exclusively through characters that appeal to one or more of the senses. A rose reveals itself through a certain shape, size, colour, odour and texture. Some philosophers have held that these qualities of the rose were merely vehicles through which was revealed to us a trans-empirical rose, an essence of roseness, as for Plato, a substantial rose, as for Locke, who sometimes forgot his empiricism, or a rose-*an-selbst*, as for Kant. But the empiricists have all insisted that the rose we know is the rose we experience, and that when we talk about transcendental roses, we are talking meaninglessly, because no such things have ever put in an appearance, and hence we have no material out of which we could frame an idea of them. To experience a rose is to experience a set of sensible qualities; to think of it is to think of these qualities; to check the suggestion that there is a rose on the mantelpiece is to find whether, with the appropriate steps, we can get sensations of these qualities. This is the heart of the empiricist theory of meaning as it has been held from Locke to Carnap.

It is, of course, an attractively simple theory. Indeed, in this general form, it has proved too simple. In order to cover the facts, it has had to specify, modify, and extend itself in ways that were bound to provoke disagreements, and if we go beyond this very general sketch, we find that there is no single empiricist theory of meaning, even among the positivists. Rather, there has been a succession of theories, each profiting by the criticisms upon its predecessors. Our best course would appear to be to consider the main stages in recent empiricist history and to examine each briefly as we proceed.

5. We say 'recent', but it would be well to interpret this rather widely, in order to include a distinguished American figure who anticipated the later theory in significant ways. It is not unnatural that the work of Charles Sanders Peirce should lately have attracted fresh attention. His essay of 1878, with the promising title 'How to Make our Ideas Clear', was essentially a statement of the positivist theory of meaning with a pragmatic twist, and with the anti-metaphysical bearings of both these types of philosophy already realized.

Peirce was persuaded that many hours, years, and even lives had been frittered away in attempting to solve philosophic problems that were insoluble because meaningless, and in defending theses that, strictly speaking, were unthinkable.

'Many a man,' he wrote, 'has cherished for years as his hobby some vague shadow of an idea, too meaningless to be positively false; he has, nevertheless, passionately loved it, has made it his companion by day and by night, and has given to it his strength and life, leaving all other occupations for its sake, and in short has lived with it and for it, until it has become, as it were, flesh of his flesh and bone of his bone; and then he has waked up some bright morning to find it gone, clean vanished away like the beautiful Melusina of the fable, and the essence of his life goes with it. I myself have known such a man; and who can tell how many histories of circle-squarers, metaphysicians, astrologers, and what not, may not be told in the old German story?'[1]

This disillusionment might be prevented if we had some sort of test which would tell us when we were thinking clearly and when foggily or not at all. Such a test Peirce announced he had found. In order to grasp it properly, one must distinguish two strands within it which we may call the pragmatic and the positivist theses.

The pragmatic thesis concerns the nature of belief. All thinking, said Peirce, seeks the achievement of belief, and belief is what? Contrary to common opinion, 'belief is a rule for action'; 'the final upshot of thinking is the exercise of volition'; 'the whole function of thought is to produce habits of action'. 'To develop its meaning, we have, therefore, simply to determine what habits it produces, for what a thing means is simply what habits it involves'; 'there is no distinction of meaning so fine as to consist in anything but a possible difference in practice'. And if we are in doubt as to how two beliefs differ, we have only to recollect that 'different beliefs are distinguished by the different modes of action to which they give rise. If beliefs do not differ in this respect . . . then no mere differences in the manner of consciousness of them can make them different beliefs. . . .'[2] A belief, then, that makes no difference in practice is meaningless, and when a belief is meaningful, the meaning reduces to effects in practice.

What is the nature of these effects in practice? Here enters the positivist thesis. 'Our idea of anything *is* our idea of its sensible effects; and if we fancy that we have any other we deceive ourselves. . . .' 'I only desire to point out how impossible it is that we should have an idea in our minds which relates to anything but conceived sensible effects of things.'[3] What do we mean, for example,

[1] *Chance, Love and Logic*, ed. by M. R. Cohen, 37.
[2] *Ibid.*, 41, 43.
[3] *Ibid.*, 45.

G

by calling anything hard? We mean that if we touched it we should feel certain sensations of resistance and pressure, and that if we saw it collide with another body, we should find that it was not readily dented or scratched.

Summing up his instructions for making our ideas clear, Peirce writes: 'Consider what effects, which might conceivably have practical bearings, we conceive the object of our conception to have. Then our conception of these effects is the whole of our conception of the object.'[1]

6. I do not know whether we should be cheered or depressed by the contemplation of this theory. It is, I can only think, a mass of confusion. What is depressing is to consider that it was offered by a logician of distinction with the specific purpose of furthering clarity; what is cheering is to think that in the course of seventy-five years philosophy has gone so far in self-criticism that a logician of equal distinction would hardly be capable of writing so loosely today. Peirce's pragmatic thesis has been a Pandora's box of misconceptions, largely because William James seized upon it so gratefully and emptied its contents broadcast with such shouts of delight. Consider what it says. It says that a belief is always concerned with action, that it is indeed a 'rule for action'. Is this true? Let us try it out in an instance. I have the belief that Mars is not quite a globe, but has flattened poles, as the earth has. I do not suppose that Peirce would doubt that this is a meaningful and definite belief. If it is, there must be some equally definite course of action to which its acceptance commits me. What is this course? I can think of none. To be sure, if I were an astronomer, the belief might affect in some degree what I did; I might go about my observation slightly differently and make slightly different entries in my record. I am not an astronomer, however, but a plain man, and even so I find myself able to entertain the belief with a high degree of clearness and with no visible practical effect. It may be insisted that what the belief means for me is that *if* I were to see Mars from a favourable point, I *should* have the sensation of a certain shape. But this will not do. For one thing, having a sensation is not an action in Peirce's sense of the word or any other plausible sense; for another, it plainly falls short of what I intend. I am not saying merely that *if* I were to see Mars from a certain point, I should sense a certain shape, but that, whether I see it or not, it has the shape now. Surely I can believe that with great clearness without any reference to action whatever. Is it replied that this is merely

[1] *Chance, Love and Logic*, ed. by M. R. Cohen, 45.

another case of self-deception? I can only reply that I am far more sure that I am now thinking of Mars as a somewhat flattened globe than that Peirce's theory is either sound or clear.

Again, Peirce says that we can determine the differences of beliefs by looking to the differences in the actions to which they lead. Now the beliefs that Mars does and that it does not have a certain shape are contradictories of each other and therefore assert extremely different things. Hence the actions they prompt should likewise be sharply different. But for the ordinary man who makes the judgment, there is no discernible change in action when he first reads and believes one authority and then reads and believes an opposing one. Difference in belief is clearly not reducible to difference in action.

Once more, belief is said to reduce to a 'rule' or 'habit' of action. We have commented on 'action'; let us now remark upon 'habit'. History books record that when Latimer stood with Ridley at the stake, he made a remark that has long reverberated: 'Brother Ridley, we shall this day light such a candle by God's grace in England as, I trust, shall never be put out.' So far as we know, this is the last thing Latimer said. Let us suppose that it really was the last belief he expressed or entertained. It was, of course, a belief about the future. But is there any intelligible sense in which it could be said to refer to future action of his own, or to be the adopting of a 'habit of action'? He knew that his action was at an end. But there is surely no reason, merely on this ground, for saying that his belief was less meaningful than any other; a belief does not cease to be significant because it is one's last. If so, a belief is neither a *habit* of action nor the adoption of such a habit.

Let us turn to Peirce's positivist thesis. 'Our idea of anything,' he says, '*is* our idea of its sensible effects.' How this is to be reconciled with the pragmatic thesis is not clear. Peirce plainly implies that ideas and beliefs are to be clarified in the same way; yet whereas we are told that to clarify a belief we are to look to the consequences of the belief itself, we are told that to clarify the idea of something we are to look, not to the consequences of the idea, but to the consequences of the thing thought of. But these two sets of consequences may, of course, be extremely different. I have the belief that Alexander died at thirty-three. The consequences of that fact would involve much of the history of the world since it happened. The consequences of my belief in it are negligible. We have seen that the meaning of the belief cannot be identified with the second of these. Can it be identified with the first? Surely it is mere self-contradiction to say so. For to say that the thought of a fact or event *is* the thought of its effect is at once to distinguish the fact, as the cause, from its effects, and also to identify it with them. One cannot intelligibly do both. If there is really no difference between cause and effect, it is idle to use either term, since each implies their distinctness. If there is a difference, to think of the one is admittedly not the same as to think of the other. No doubt Peirce did not mean what he said, though when a logician issues a prescription for clarity, one is perhaps justified in asking that he should. What he said when attempting to state his theory formally was this: 'Consider what effects, which might conceivably have practical bearings, we conceive the object of our conception to have. Then our conception of those effects is the whole of our conception of the object.' What this tells us is that to make clear our thought of Alexander's death, we are to concentrate exclusively on what happened after that event was over. It says that to think clearly about something, the best way is to think about something else. Such a doctrine hardly calls for further discussion.

One can only believe that Peirce would agree with such criticism and would protest that it was not conceptions of this sort that he had in mind; that he was thinking rather of our conceptions of physical things. This is confirmed by his illustrations. He contends that it is idle for the Roman Catholic to maintain that bread and wine are really flesh and blood when they have none of the sensible qualities of flesh and blood and all the sensible qualities of bread and wine. He asks what we mean by 'force' in physics, and says that, once we know the descriptive laws according to which bodies gain acceleration, our idea of force is as clear and complete as it can be. What he is objecting to is the thought of a material substance underlying and distinct from all of 'its' qualities, and a non-sensible 'force' which somehow causes the accelerations we see. And in saying that we must think of the cause in terms of the effects, he is really saying that there is and can be nothing in our thought that answers to these non-sensible causes, and hence that it is idle to say they exist. The rule he is seeking to lay down could perhaps be formulated as follows: When thinking about physical things or events, try to think definitely of the experienceable qualities and changes in which, for our knowledge, these consist; if you find you cannot do this, your thought of the object is less than fully clear; if you find yourself going beyond this and talking of the unexperienceable, you are using words rather than ideas. This is, of course, a far more restricted rule than Peirce proposed, and it does not commit one to either pragmatism or positivism; but it seems to me genuinely helpful. The literate public would be saved a deal of unprofitable effort if young philosophers could accept as a rule of thought and style: 'Stick to the specific. Bring every generalization to the test of instances. If you must read thinkers like Hegel and Heidegger, do it with the appropriate aversion to their ways of thinking and speaking, and with the readiness to do the continual translating into the specific which they were too discourteous, too indolent, or too cloudy, to do for you.'

Stage I: Solipsism Without a Subject.

7. The positivist test of meaningfulness has a history. Between Peirce's essay and Wittgenstein's *Tractatus* of 1922 there was an interval of more than forty years. The later essay, however, has substantially the same theme as the earlier one, namely, 'how to make our ideas clear'; it was an attempt to show that philosophy consists in the clarification of ideas and to indicate how philosophers should go about it to achieve this end. Unfortunately, though devoted to expounding the texts 'everything that can be thought at all can be thought clearly' and 'everything that can be said can be said clearly'[1] the book is a masterpiece of obscurity. Furthermore, the reader will look in it in vain for any systematic statement or defence of a criterion of meaning. But there is no doubt that such a criterion is there, if only between the lines, and the *Tractatus* has been so central and influential a document in the analytic movement that it will be well to begin our review of later theories of meaning by considering its teaching.

For Wittgenstein, as for positivists generally, there were only two kinds of statement that were significant, in the sense of saying anything true or false. One was the a priori or necessary statement, which would always be found to set forth our own meanings merely, to explain how we were using words. The analysts' various accounts of such statements we shall review in the next chapter. The other type of statement had to do with matters of fact; it offered itself as true of the actual world. In this class fell the whole vast mass of statements about what we perceive, expect or remember, and (apart from valuations, which are not regarded as statements at all) the whole of history and natural science. When in this chapter we speak of the criterion of meaningful statements, the reference will always be to statements of this factual kind.

Wittgenstein was a logical atomist, and the atomists held, as we have seen, that all such statements resolved themselves on analysis into statements about atomic facts. And these facts were of a type that could be presented through sense perception; they were all

[1] *Tractatus*, 4.116.

particulars characterized by an attribute or connected through a relation; our nearest approach to them in expression was something like 'here—red' or 'this brighter than that'. When we indulge in sweeping statements like 'all men die' or 'the summer has been unusually fine', we may suppose ourselves to have escaped confinement to such particulars into a freer conceptual air. This would be a mistake. It may be difficult to bring to light the full range of perceptual data to which we are referring, but we shall find that, so far as we have any meaning at all, it is exhausted in such data, and that every hair's breadth of departure from them is a slipping away into meaninglessness.

8. Regarding so much of Wittgenstein's theory we are clear already, but here a question arises to which we have not yet had the answer. How large is the range of given facts of which we can meaningfully speak? We ordinarily assume that no limits can be set to this; we read with no feeling of protest of 'thoughts that wander through eternity', and if the 'eternity' does give us pause, we at least have no difficulty over minds that 'look before and after and pine for what is not'. But *is* it so obvious that our thoughts can make these leaps into the 'before and after'? Can we even say precisely where we want to leap? We say we shall have cornflakes at breakfast tomorrow, but of course that event, if it occurs, will be something absolutely specific, and if we try to think of it now, we are bound to miss that specificity which makes it what it is; we are confined to generalities; we are saying: 'something will happen that is more or less like this image that I now have'; but what exactly its character will be we do not know. And there is a more serious difficulty. My thought of this moment, or rather my sentence—for positivists dislike talk of thoughts—is itself a particular confined to a particular time. The future event is another particular, which, since it does not exist, is nothing. It is obvious, therefore, that when I now think of this event, I cannot be apprehending it, for there is nothing to apprehend. If one says that meaning is a relation that links the first event to the second, that is absurd, since if at the time when the first appears there is no second, there would not be two terms to relate. To say in such a case that A *means* B is to say that A is a particular that is somehow not a particular; it sets up a strange non-empirical relation to something else that does not exist; and it owes its very character to something else, which no good particular would think of doing. The same holds about statements of the past. I say that Caesar had a furrowed face. But what I mean by that precisely I do not know, for I have never seen Caesar, and the particulars of the past, like those of the future, are not kept in cold storage for our convenience; they would appear to be nothing at all. Regarding the character of events that fall within our own memory we are more confident, but even here the difficulty about particulars remains. The present act of recollection is a particular, no doubt; but the particulars to which it refers are lost among *les neiges d'antan*. The recalled events of my own life, for all the vividness of the remembrance, are as dead and buried as anything in Gibbon.

We do not know whether it was reflections of this kind that led to the theory of meaning in the *Tractatus*; Wittgenstein was more disposed to announce conclusions than to vouchsafe arguments for them. What is clear is that the singular conclusion to which they tend was in fact embraced by him. He announced himself a solipsist. 'The limits of my language mean the limits of my world.' 'I am my world.'[1] If a statement is to be meaningful, it must refer to particular facts, and the only such facts I am acquainted with are those of my own experience; to talk of others is to talk vacuously, for it is an attempt to leap out of 'my world'. What did Wittgenstein mean by '*my* world'? Did he mean what fell within the experience of a single ordinary self? No, since for him there was no ground for believing in any such self. If we are to speak of a self significantly, it must consist of particular sense-given facts, and is there any such fact, or set of facts, which I can identify with myself? None. Hence the self is a metaphysical notion, that is, a notion putting itself forward as a notion of fact, but to which nothing sensible corresponds—a mere pseudo-idea. The suggestion, then, of an ego that owns my present field of consciousness and also yesterday's, and somehow holds them together, has no meaning. Nor is there any identity of content that persists from one field to the other. Hence, Wittgenstein's solipsism was apparently not only the solipsism of a single self, but the extremer solipsism of a single moment. It was even more extreme still. It was a 'solipsism without a subject'. When he said 'I am my world', there was nothing in either me or my world beyond an assortment of sensibly and instantaneously given facts—only sensed by no one and given to no one. To call this a 'field of consciousness' or an 'immediate experience' would thus strictly be incorrect, because it would again suggest an experiencing agent, which means nothing. The given facts of which I and my world consist must be described as neither experienced nor independent of experience. They merely *are*. Wittgenstein explained that for him, 'solipsism strictly carried

[1] *Tractatus*, 5.6, 5.63.

out coincides with pure realism'.[1] But he did not mean by realism what realists generally mean. What they mean is that experienced fact would still be what it is even if not experienced. To say this would, for him, be senseless. His realism is like the 'neutral monism' of James and Russell, in which facts simply *are*, without reference to any further status as mental or physical.

The upshot of all this as regards meaning would appear to be as follows: a factual proposition has meaning when, and only when, it refers to what is given within the set of sensible facts comprising 'one self'.

9. What are we to say of this theory? Our first remark must be one of astonishment, as much at the reception of the view as at the view itself. It is obviously a theory that rides rough-shod over common sense, but then common sense is not for us a philosophic court of appeal. What is odd is that Wittgenstein should have been taken with a seriousness almost reverential by those who did accept common sense as the test and touchstone for philosophy. Among these latter were some of the acutest thinkers of the century, and one can only believe that if they had turned upon this theory the critical attention which they devoted, say, to the refutation of idealism, they would have torn it into small pieces. There must have been some-thing hypnotic about Wittgenstein which made listeners accept as oracles what in other mouths they would have dismissed as absurdities. Fortunately or not, the present writer never fell under the basilisk eye. He has therefore no inhibitions in calling absurd, even in Wittgenstein, what plainly seems so. He is also free to express astonishment at the unoriginality of this view. For in essentials it is Hume over again—his solipsism without any vestige of his humour, clarity, or grace. Of course the difficulties of Hume have been discussed almost *ad nauseam*. They were discussed, for example, with monumental thoroughness by Green in the great 'introduction', now so seldom opened. If Wittgenstein had ever read a page of this or any other criticism of Hume, there is no indication of it. The theory cannot receive much of our space or time. But we should perhaps list the more obvious difficulties with it.

10. First, it would make science impossible. Science has as its chief concern the discovery of laws, and laws as conceived by the scientist apply to *all* cases of a certain kind. Our own experience, no matter how far extended, could never cover all cases; what proportion of the

[1] *Tractatus*, 5.64.

instances of gravitation, for example, could any single mind engage? To be sure, Wittgenstein did, like Ramsey, attempt for a time to maintain that a law of science could apply with meaning only to experienceable cases, but both later abandoned this view. It may be protested that the theory of knowledge need not bow to science, and that science may be an impossible enterprise after all. We shall not argue this thesis. Suffice it to say that it was not Wittgenstein's. He believed in science thoroughly, and indeed reduced philosophy to the position of a minister to it. Whatever, therefore, may have been open to other philosophers in the way of a dismissal of science, it was not consistently open to him.

11. Secondly, the theory would render impossible all communication with other minds. It holds that the facts to which statements must refer are atomic facts, and that the objects composing these, because simple, are incapable of definition or description. When I say 'this is red', the 'this' of which I speak is indescribable because it is not a character, and only characters can be described; it is a unique datum which is mine and no one else's. The 'red' does denote a character, to be sure, but since this is simple, it cannot be analysed nor therefore defined, but only named, and the object that I so name is no one else's object. As for the relation that links the two objects in the fact, it cannot be expressed at all, on Wittgenstein's theory; it can only be 'mirrored' in the relation between the words of my proposition. But this proposition is itself a particular fact occurring among the other particular facts that compose me and my world, and hence cannot belong to anyone else's world. It might seem as if a relation that was mirrored in my own mind might be similarly mirrored in other minds, and thus some identity of content be achieved between my own mind and another's; positivists have often maintained that this, and this alone, is the communicable element in meaning. But on Wittgenstein's theory, to say that there is any such identity of meaning would be to make a statement that was itself meaningless since obviously unverifiable. In sum, we can assert meaningfully only of facts, and facts are compounded of particulars, characters, and relations. No particulars or characters mentioned by me can be the same as those mentioned by another; no relation mirrored in my experience can be intelligibly said to appear in any other. It is therefore senseless to hold that I can ever communicate anything that I mean. Here again we shall not argue that this is false. It is enough to say that nobody can believe it for two minutes together, and that any theory entailing it involves itself in a like incredibility.

12. Thirdly, the theory would not only cut off all communication, it would cut off the possibility of even mentioning another mind. Suppose I say 'John believes himself to be clever'. We should ordinarily take this as an intelligible remark about John's state of mind. But of course that state of mind is not among the data that are, or might be, presented to me; I am never (telepathy apart) acquainted with his thoughts or desires. Hence Wittgenstein tells us —itself a strange achievement on his theory—that they are unmentionables. His curiously doctrinaire approach to such issues is revealed by one of the considerations that apparently led him to this conclusion. In accordance with his extensionalist logic, he held that all compound propositions were truth functions of the propositions they contained, that is, their truth depended on the truth of these components. But if I interpret 'John believes that he is clever' in the common way, this doctrine must be given up, since the proposition contains a subordinate proposition on whose truth the major proposition does not in the least depend; obviously the statement, 'John *believes* that he is clever' may be true whether the minor proposition that he *is* clever is true or not. How was the philosopher to escape from the dreadful abyss that thus opened at his feet? He saw that he could save himself and this precious jewel of the extensionalist logic if he could deny that in referring to the proposition believed by John he was referring to a proposition at all. This he did. What he was really asserting, he suggested, was not that John believed the proposition P, but that he *said* P; that is, he uttered the words of the sentence.[1] The inexorable demands of logic were thus triumphantly met. The assertion made no claim beyond the strictly empirical one that John's body was issuing certain noises, and these could be directly verified. The relief to the philosopher's mind may be imagined when this solution came in sight. He had saved the doctrine about compound propositions, and he had achieved it at no greater cost than that of the archaic and indefensible dogma that other people have desires and beliefs.

13. Fourthly, this theory of meaning, if the theory itself is to be accepted, is inexpressible, and therefore any attempted statement of it must be meaningless. We are assured that the relation holding between a proposition and the fact it refers to, like those within the fact and the proposition themselves, cannot be significantly mentioned. Even 'fact' and 'proposition' are properly meaningless, the first because it refers to an entity with a non-sensible structure, the

[1] *Tractatus*, 5.54–5.542.

second because it too, when taken as something true or false, cannot be sensibly given. We say that the names in propositions refer to objects, but not only are 'refer' and 'propositions' meaningless, but also 'objects', which Wittgenstein sets down as a pseudo-concept. So also with 'truth' and 'falsity'. So with 'solipsism' itself: 'what solipsism *means* is quite correct,' he writes, 'only it cannot be *said*, but it shows itself.'[1] It is hard to see, however, how it could show itself except by leading one to entertain and then deny the possibility that there are other minds than one's own, a suggestion also ruled out as meaningless. Indeed the very theory that the meaning of factual statements exhausts itself in atomic facts must on that theory be nonsense, since it refers to no fact which could be given in my experience. Thus virtually everything that the theory says is marked as nonsense by its own decree. Wittgenstein tried to salvage something by distinguishing kinds of nonsense, for example, important and unimportant nonsense. But, as Mr Weinberg points out, this distinction too must, on the theory, be nonsense.[2] So far as the theory is really meaningless, our discussion of it is not a discussion of fact, and hence we must be talking about nothing. So far as the theory does succeed in saying something, its very success is proof that it is mistaken, for then it *is* possible to do what it denies, namely to talk intelligibly about what is other than sensible fact.

14. We shall make but one more remark about this extraordinary view. While it insists that 'I am my world' and that any statement I make about what falls beyond its boundaries must be meaningless, it leaves these boundaries in darkness. How large is my self? Granting for the moment that a 'pure ego' is meaningless, how much is to be included in the phenomenal self that is left? When Wittgenstein talks about scientific laws, one gathers that there may be included in one's legitimate reference all the instances in one's 'own' past experience that tend to confirm the law; and in that case 'I' include within my scope a considerable segment of the past. But since I can refer meaningfully only to 'thises', i.e. to particular given facts, and these past instances have irrevocably lost that status, to extend the self in this manner seems impossible, and I must be content to shrink back within the compass of present immediacy. The self on Wittgenstein's theory is thus an affair of spasmodic expansions and contractions, like those of the hair spring of a watch, and one never quite knows what area of experience he is at the moment taking as his base.

[1] *Tractatus*, 5.62.
[2] *An Examination of Logical Positivism*, 198.

His writing, and presumably his thought, were so obscure that here, as often elsewhere, one can only make alternative conjectures as to what he may have meant, and look hopefully among them for one that makes sense. We have paid our respects already to the solipsism of the moment. If Wittgenstein goes beyond this, on what principle is he to annex the outlying territories for the self? Will he say that all experiences are to count as mine that might be recalled by a perfect memory? But an incalculable number of them have vanished utterly, and if I am allowed to refer to them, why should I not also be allowed to refer to the experiences of others? If this is going too far, and my past is to include only the experiences I can remember, it becomes meaningless to say that I was ever born, or had a first sensation. Again, if the present self is linked to the past, as Hume believed, merely by continuity and resemblance of content, how much of either or both is needed if a past experience is to be claimed as mine? Hume at any rate raises such questions, however unsatisfactorily he dealt with them. Wittgenstein seems to think it unnecessary to raise them at all. He may have thought that to raise them was merely to wake metaphysical ghosts in the form of pseudo-concepts. If he did, he was wrong. The question how far, and in what sense, my experience of five minutes ago is the same as my experience now is a hard but significant question, over which thinkers of all levels have exercised themselves. Even Hume, who was not in logic entitled to raise it, had to admit its point and do his best with it. Wittgenstein would have been clearer, whether more convincing or not, if he had done the same.

15. We have dealt at some length with this strange theory because it was put forward by the most influential treatise and the most original mind of the analytic movement. Few analysts actually accepted it, however. For a time Carnap was very close to it. Of his earlier position Reichenbach has said, ' "I now see a red square with a white point on it" is the generic type of statement to which every possible proposition reduces.' ' "I see a sparkling spot on a black line and some numbers on a brass instrument" is all that astronomy aims to say; and it cannot wish to say more because that would be impossible.'[1]

But positivists soon saw that they could not stay in this position, and sought a more liberal criterion of meaningfulness. They tried many expedients, the more important of which we are to review. It is well to remember, however, that from first to last they conceived themselves to be merely refining Schlick's original manifesto: 'the

---

[1] *Journal of Philosophy*, Vol. 33, 149. See also the criticism by E. E. Harris, *Nature, Mind and Modern Science*, Ch. 16.

meaning of a proposition is the method of its verification. The question "What does the sentence mean?" is identified with (has the same answer as) the question "How is this proposition verified?" [1] Through all their later variations, positivists adhered unwaveringly to at least two theses of this position: first, that a factual proposition refers to empirical fact alone, and second, that this fact was always what its assertor would regard as the best warrant for the truth of his assertion. To Schlick and his early colleagues these statements seemed, when considered attentively, to be all but self-evident. The three decades that followed were disillusioning years. First there was the shock of Wittgenstein's solipsistic reading of the common creed. Then there was the slow retreat from one qualification to another as the creed had to be accommodated to cases not at first thought of.

Stage II: Verifiable by Self in Widened Sense.

16. For empiricists discontented with Wittgenstein's solipsism, what was the natural next step? It was to loosen up this solipsism by making it less alien to common sense. However hard it may be to demonstrate that we have a past or a future, a standard that would forbid us even to speculate about it is too cramping to be borne. Let us retain the important insight that what is referred to by me must in some sense be verifiable by me. But let us not be sticklers about the range of what is thus verifiable. We may begin by extending this range from my present experiences to such past experiences as I can remember. We may surely extend it a little further to experiences that I once had but have now forgotten, for these too I could once have mentioned meaningfully, and still know what this would be like. May we not stretch the net an inch further still, and include all those experiences that I *might* have had if circumstances had been propitious? I never saw Mr Churchill or Mr Roosevelt. But I might quite well have seen them if I had taken a little trouble, and I know well enough what I mean when I have occasion to speak of them. But if anyone asks me what it would be like, not only to see one of these gentlemen, but to *be* one, or—to carry speculation further—to be Queen Elizabeth I, I must answer that I cannot say because I do not know, because that sort of experience is impossible. Such things fall outside any range of experience that I might have had. This kind of empiricism, non-solipsistic but self-oriented, seems to have been accepted by some early positivists as supplying a quite sufficient criterion of meaningfulness. 'Originally,' writes a well-informed member of the school, 'the permissible evidence was meant to be

[1] *Gesammelte Aufsätze,* 181.

restricted to what is observable by the speaker and perhaps his fellow-beings during their lifetimes.'[1]

17. This theory broke down almost as soon as proposed. It ran aground on an obvious difficulty mentioned by Professor Hempel, that 'thus construed, the criterion rules out, as cognitively meaningless, all statements about the distant future or the remote past'.[2] Although Churchill and Roosevelt are possible experiences of mine because I could with small pains have seen either of them, the existence of a dinosaur 30 million years ago, or a total eclipse 30 million years in the future is not a possible experience of mine in the same sense. I could not be the person I am, that is a person of normal powers, living in the twentieth century and for a short span of years, and still have experienced these facts. Strictly, therefore, to refer to them must be meaningless. But in the name of both science and common sense, is it not silly to say that? What would become of the sciences that deal with the past if it were accepted? No archaeologist could talk about dinosaurs. No geologist would be permitted to discuss the formation of the earth. No higher critic could inquire into the formation of the canon. History, 'that vast Mississippi of falsehood', would, for the most part, not even be falsehood, but a farrago of meaningless verbiage. The criterion is far too narrow. Obviously all these matters can be, and are, talked about with perfect intelligibility.

18. The verifiability theory seemed to have met with ignominious defeat by these judgments of the past. Where there was so plain a conflict, one party or the other had to give way, and in the minds of most critics, what had to give way was the verifiability theory. But to one brilliant young member of the school, it occurred that perhaps the tables could be turned and the troublesome judgment of the past itself be compelled to give ground. What made that judgment so formidable was that, if taken at face value, it found clear meaning in statements that were beyond any verification. Now it is a familiar but important fact that, while records of the past are not verifiable by me, this is not invariably true about predictions of the future; if I predict that a few minutes from now I shall hear the clock strike twelve, I can shortly verify this in perception. If therefore the statement about the past could be reconstrued into a prediction about the

---

[1] C. G. Hempel, 'Problems and Changes in the Empiricist Theory of Meaning', *Revue Internationale de Philosophie*, January 1950, 44.
[2] *Ibid.*

future, the dependence of meaning on verifiability by me might be saved. This course was proposed by Professor Ayer. In the first edition of his *Language, Truth and Logic* (1936) he suggested that a statement about the past, like other synthetic statements, should be read as 'a rule for the anticipation of future experience'. 'For my own part, I do not find anything excessively paradoxical in the view that propositions about the past are rules for the prediction of those "historical" experiences which are commonly said to verify them, and I do not see how else "our knowledge of the past" is to be analysed.'[1] How does this work out in particular cases? Suppose I say that Queen Elizabeth on a certain occasion swore a loud oath. This statement is now taken to mean the experienced facts by which, if challenged, I should seek to verify it. And what are these? They are certain sentences in, say, Green, Froude, and Lingard, which I should fall back on as my authority. To assert that Elizabeth swore is thus to assert that, if I looked, I should see certain sentences in certain books.

This plainly will not do. For (1) I can see by direct inspection that I mean nothing of the sort. I mean to say something about what happened in the England of the sixteenth century, not about what may happen in the twentieth century in the Sterling library at New Haven. No theory as to what I ought to mean can set aside so unequivocal a testimony as to what I do mean. (2) The account is implicitly self-contradictory. It implies that when I see the words on the page, I shall recognize (*a*) that they express statements about Queen Elizabeth, and (*b*) that these statements support a former statement of my own. But in both cases I should plainly be referring to the past in a sense which the theory is supposed to exclude.

It may be replied that, though future experiences cannot verify directly my statements of the past, they may still do so indirectly. These statements were held by Professor Ayer to be really empirical hypotheses, and empirical hypotheses are often said to be verified by what they entail. Unfortunately this will not do either. For (1) on positivist principles, no fact or factual statement entails any other. (2) It follows that the verifying statement cannot form any part of what was meant by the original statement, for the only way, on these principles, in which it could form such a part is to be entailed by the original, and this is ruled out by (1). (3) Even if entailment were interpreted more liberally, how could one make out a case for it in the present instance? That Elizabeth's act *necessitated* the writing of certain sentences by persons who came after her is something that

[1] *Language, Truth and Logic*, 1st ed., 146, 147.

Hegel himself would not have averred that he could see.[1] Indeed Professor Ayer found it impossible to adhere to this interpretation of the judgment of the past, and in the second edition of *Language, Truth and Logic* (1946), he frankly abandoned it.[2] If the verifiability theory came into conflict with this judgment, it was clearly the theory and not the judgment that had to suffer revision.

19. The phrase 'what might be verified by me' was proving a treacherous one. A further pitfall in it soon became apparent. When it was said that I could meaningfully refer only to 'what I might verify', did this phrase signify what I might perceive by my normal powers and with the means at my disposal? Many readers so interpreted it and made complaints, which long reverberated, on behalf of the mountains on the moon. There is no prospect, they pointed out, that in my present life I shall ever be able to perceive the mountains on the other side of the moon, since the moon presents to us the same face always, and there is no way of getting round her and having a look from the other side. Yet I can surely think of those mountains with all necessary clearness. Again, it is entirely possible that ten miles beneath my feet there is a block of stone whose shape is exactly like the head of Sir Walter Scott. Could one ask for a more definite idea? But there is no possible present way of testing it. Hence, if 'verifiable by me' means *practically* verifiable by me, the criterion must be thrown out. Clearly, this argument was unanswerable. In fairness to the positivists, however, it should be added that its target was a straw man. There seems to be no good evidence that any responsible positivist, the original solipsists apart, ever limited the meaningful to what was *technically* or *practically* verifiable by me.

Stage III: Verifiable by Me in Principle.
20. Still, verifiability by me, in any ordinary sense, must evidently now be abandoned. What next? The range of the verifiable must again be extended. It must no longer be limited to what I do experience, to what I have experienced or will experience, or even to what I might have experienced if my life had been longer or my lot cast in other places. It must include nothing less than the whole of what I might *in principle* verify. In spite of the technical difficulties of viewing the lunar mountains or the stone in the interior of the earth, I know quite well what perceiving them would be like; and though I

---

[1] Cf. W. H. F. Barnes, *The Philosophical Predicament*, 109.
[2] P. 19. And cf. G. Ryle, 'Unverifiability by Me', *Analysis*, October 1936.

could not, consistently with my actual span of life, have heard Elizabeth's words, it makes clear sense to say that, *if* I had been present at a certain time, I *should* have heard them. Thus the conceivability of my verifying an assertion is all that is needed to make it meaningful. On the other hand, nothing less will serve. To say that a hippogriff exists is to say that under some circumstances we might have certain perceptions. We may not know exactly what those circumstances would be, and do not need to, but unless we know what sort of perceptions would enable us to point and say 'there is a hippogriff', we are deceiving ourselves if we talk about hippogriffs at all. This view of the criterion of meaning had escaped from solipsism, and also from the narrower bounds of 'verifiability by me'. But it still held to the latter 'in principle'. If a statement was to be meaningful, I must be able to verify it, not necessarily in practice, nor even in my lifetime, nor even in the race's lifetime, but at least conceivably in theory. This was substantially the view reached by Schlick in 1932 and described by him as 'consistent empiricism'.[1] It was the first of our formulations of the verifiability principle to have strong *prima facie* plausibility. We must therefore look at it closely.

Note first that, though it is content with verifiability in principle, it demands that this verifiability be conclusive. As Schlick said a few years later, 'there is no way of understanding any meaning without ultimate reference to ostensive definitions';[2] that is, what we mean must be capable of appearing in our experience in person or at first hand; no consequence of it can serve as a substitute, and any reference that goes beyond the directly presentable must be set down as a pseudo-meaning. This seemed fair enough. But as reflection on it developed, it was quickly seen by outside critics, and rather more tardily by positivists themselves, to involve incredible consequences.

21. We shall confine ourselves, by way of criticism, to only one of these, though it is one of the first importance. It was already foreshadowed in Schlick's article of 1932. He took the seemingly trivial case of my looking at two pieces of paper and saying 'this has the same green colour as that'. Is this statement meaningful? Yes, of course, since I could verify it by looking. But now complicate the statement a little. Another person is looking at the pieces, and he too calls them green. Does he see the same colour as I do? That, says

[1] 'Positivismus und Realismus', *Gesammelte Aufsätze*, 84 ff, reprinted from *Erkenntnis*, 1932.
[2] *Phil. Review*, 1936, reprinted in Feigl and Sellars' *Readings in Philosophical Analysis*, 148.

Schlick, is a question I cannot hope to answer. I can offer him a series of shades, and note whether he reports that the shade he has been seeing falls in the same place in the series as I do, but beyond that I cannot go. Why is this psychological curiosity worth our attention? Because it presents a crucial case to the present theory of meaning. If it is true that I cannot, even in principle, verify the statement that you are seeing the same colour as I do, must not the very suggestion be meaningless? Schlick saw that this was involved, and drew the inference unflinchingly. 'The statement that two experiences of different subjects not only occupy corresponding places in a systematic order, but also resemble each other qualitatively, has for us no sense. Note that it is not false, but senseless (sinnlos); we have no idea what it means.'[1]

Now this is not very convincing. That I cannot *verify* your having the same kind of sensation as I have seems clear enough, but that such a suggestion conveys nothing to me at all seems merely absurd, for the meaning is surely as definite and intelligible as its verification is difficult. Here is a case in which meaning and verifiability fall apart, and hence to identify them must be wrong. The positivists did not fail to perceive the danger for their theory. It would not do simply to rule out talk of other minds as meaningless, for such a proscription would spread havoc through literature, history, and social intercourse. Such discussion must plainly be permitted. But how could it be permitted if I could in fact refer to nothing but what I might directly perceive? If the verifiability view was to be saved, the judgment about other minds must somehow be reinterpreted, just as on the previous theory it had been found necessary to reinterpret the judgment of the past.

This was done. Statements about other minds were declared to be, despite appearances, statements about what I might directly perceive. This involved the heroic step of eliminating all suggestion that other persons were conscious, since 'to ascribe to our fellow men consciousness *in addition* to overt behaviour with discoverable physiological processes implies a transcendence, an introduction of empirically unverifiable elements'.[2] On this as on other points, Professor Ayer was gratefully forthright. He held that 'each of us must define the experiences of others in terms of what he can at least in principle observe', and hence that 'I must define other people in terms of their empirical manifestations—that is, in terms of the behaviour of their bodies, and ultimately in terms of sense contents.' He thus effected

[1] *Gesammelte Aufsätze*, 98.
[2] H. Feigl, in *Philosophy of Science*, I, 4 (1936).

what he frankly called 'a reduction of other people's experiences to one's own'.[1]

22. With many of the positivists' suggestions, directed as they were to bringing more clarity into philosophic discussion, outsiders could only sympathize, whether they agreed or not. But this outcropping of a dogmatic behaviourism strained this sympathy to the breaking point. A. E. Taylor somewhere remarks that philosophers of the first rank have always been distinguished by something beyond acuteness of analysis and rigour of logic, namely a 'massive common sense'. This was certainly not in evidence in such writing as the above. Perhaps we should pause and consider for a moment what we are being told. We are being told that to ascribe the sort of conscious life with which we are familiar in ourselves to any other being is impossible; our words are meaningless when they seem to refer to it. It is meaningless to say that the dog that has caught his foot in the door is suffering pain. It is meaningless for me, as I write this, to suppose that it will arouse any sort of consciousness in you who read it, or for you to suppose that, as I write, I have any idea to convey. It is meaningless for the husband or wife to suppose that the other body which sits there by the fire is anything but an elaborate physiological mechanism, devoid of thoughts, sensations, and sympathies. We cannot take this theory very seriously. When we ask which is more likely, that a group of enthusiasts for a new formula of meaningfulness should somewhere have made an error, or that the judgments about other men made by every philosopher and historian, every biographer and poet on record should be nonsense, we cannot hesitate long.

One knows the replies that are offered. The theory, it is sometimes protested, is methodological merely. It does not deny that there are other minds, for that itself would be a meaningless metaphysical statement of the kind which the theory excludes; it merely says that one cannot meaningfully refer to them. We are unmoved. Between saying that in referring to other minds one is not referring to anything, and saying that there are no such things, the difference for present ends is negligible. We are told, again, that it is perfectly possible, in terms of the theory, to refer to 'other people'; it is merely that the term 'other people' is redefined; 'I must define other people in terms of the behaviour of their bodies, and ultimately in terms of sense contents', i.e. my own. Does this make the theory more plausible? Not in the least. It repeats the absurdity in another form.

---

[1] *Language, Truth and Logic* (1st ed.), 203, 202.

Instead of saying that when we 'refer' to others' experience we mean nothing at all, it admits that we do refer to something, only this something is totally different from what we always thought it was. The reply may come that in 'what we always thought it was' we are begging the question. And we must admit that if, after honest self-examination, anyone insists that what he is thinking of when he refers to another's toothache is a set of sub-microscopic motions in a nerve fibre, which a sufficiently keen-eyed dentist could see, there is nothing more to be said; one person cannot dictate to another—assuming that there is another—what his words are to mean. But let us recall that people were talking about pleasures, aches, and emotions, for many centuries before they knew anything about the physiological changes underlying them. On empirical grounds it seems hardly likely that such persons were talking, not about the sort of aches and pains that were familiar to them, but about hidden bodily changes that had never entered into their experience at all.

This may be accepted. We may then be told that the reference to another's toothache is not to changes in a dental nerve, but to the grimaces, contortions, and lamentations by which the 'sufferer' expresses his 'feelings'. These are observable by all. What is not observable, and therefore not assertible, is that the other person has any 'feelings' distinct from these. We must confess to a strong indisposition to argue about this solemnly. Happily, we have observed no tendency on the part of positivists to live up to it. They give every sign of being sensitive and sympathetic persons, who not only believe, for example, that their children on occasion suffer pain, but actively concern themselves to relieve it. It does not seem to occur to them how odd a performance this is in terms of their theory. If there is no ground to believe that anything is going on in their child except physiological events, why should his tears and grimaces give them concern? If in fact they do, the reason is plain enough. Some bodily events are the causes or signals of pain—pain in the ancient familiar sense which this theory would ignore. The positivist would ordinarily care nothing about a process in his dental nerve, or anyone else's, except for its effects in consciousness. He cannot justify one hour of his social life without references which would be vetoed by his theory.

23. Nevertheless we must pause over this curious theory a little longer. If positivists adopted a criterion of meaningfulness which outraged common sense, it was not from mere wantonness or caprice.

One of the motives that animated them was an interest, commendable surely, in the unity of science. The representatives of the various sciences seem at present to talk different languages, in the sense that terms fundamental in one field may seem meaningless in another. Physicists and chemists, indeed, understand each other fairly well. But when they pass over into biology, they frequently find themselves baffled. Many biologists speak of 'life', of an *'élan vital'* or 'vital principle', even of 'entelechies', as if these things, though not observable by sense, were as unquestionable as if they were. And when the physical scientist goes a step further down the hall and catches scraps of phrase from his colleagues in sociology and psychology, the plurality of worlds becomes even more apparent. 'Instincts', 'personalities', 'general wills', 'group minds', 'unconscious minds', and the like crop up in profusion. What is anyone who is intent on using verifiable concepts only, to make of these strange wraiths? The physicist has his pointer-readings; the chemist can not only see, but smell and taste if necessary, the liquids in his test-tubes; but how is anyone to put to the test a pronouncement about the 'general will' or a psychical 'id'? It would seem to be impossible. From which the conclusion may be drawn that science can only be a set of anarchic raids upon the darkness, with no general staff and with no common standards of clearness, significance, or verification. To the positivists this seemed to be the actual state of affairs, and some of them—Otto Neurath in particular—gallantly set themselves to reverse the tendencies towards chaos.

This reversal could be achieved, Neurath argued, only by agreeing on a common language, a language whose terms were used and tested in the same way. He maintained that such a language must be that of physical science, not that of the social or psychological sciences. Why? Because, though the characteristic terms of the physical sciences, such as solids and liquids, pointers and test-tubes, could not be translated into 'mental' terms, mental terms could always be translated into physical. Thus if someone is 'perceiving blue', there is always taking place an impact upon his retina of light vibrations of a certain frequency, or at least a certain change among the neurones of his cortex. And if two statements are so related that they are always true together, and always false together, they are 'equipollent'; each is the logical equivalent of the other and may at will be translated into it. If such equipollence is recognized, the road to the unity of science is clear. Every factual statement in every science will have an identical test of meaning and of truth. All laws will be interconnected as parts of a single system. As Carnap put it, science will become intersensible, intersubjective, and universal. It will be inter-sensible because we need no longer regard taste, sound and colour as incommensurable data; they can now all be read as physical changes, differing only in measurable ways. Again, science will be inter-subjective because, when we say for example, 'the room is hot', we shall not mean that we have a private feeling inaccessible to everyone else, but that the room has physically a certain temperature, which can be tested by a thermometer open to the observation of all. And the language of science will be universal because 'every sentence of any branch of scientific language is equipollent to some sentence of the physical language, and can therefore be translated into the physical language without changing its content'.[1] Thus the new criterion of meaning, interpreted as requiring 'physicalism', becomes the most powerful of engines for the unification of science.

24. That scientists should be intelligible to each other everyone will agree to be desirable. But if the understanding is to be genuine, each must understand what the other actually means, not some substitute for it that may suit his own convenience. Does 'physicalism' provide such understanding? Unfortunately not. Let us see why in a simple case. John says he has a toothache, and we accept his statement as true. The physicalist tells us that what we thus accept is really that John's body is performing certain grimaces and verbalizations, or—since John may admittedly be deceitful—that certain changes are going on in his neurones. But there are no two things in the world more completely different than John's sensation of pain and the changes of position of material particles in his neurones. Yet the assertions of these two things are said to be 'equipollent'. What exactly does that mean? It sounds as if two statements of differing content were being regarded, for certain purposes, as equivalent. But that is not what the physicalists meant to say. They meant that the 'mental' and 'physical' statements really said the same thing, differing only verbally; this was why they held that one could be translated into the other 'without changing its content'.

Now this is simply behaviourism again, of the old discredited kind. What can have led logically acute minds to such a result? Probably in part their very devotion to logic, that is, to the extensional brand of logic

---

[1] Carnap, *Philosophy and Logical Syntax*, 89. For Neurath's statement of the case, see his 'Soziologie im Physikalismus', *Erkenntnis*, Vol. II (1931), 393–431; for Carnap's, besides the above, 'Die physikalische Sprache als Universalsprache der Wissenschaft', in *ibid.*, 432–465.

which we saw in the last chapter to provide so crude an instrument
for the handling of actual meanings. According to that logic, when
the truth conditions of two statements are the same, that is, when
they are always true or false together, the two are taken as equivalent;
this logic is indifferent to *what* they assert, so long as it is informed
of their truth or falsity. And it may be that, by some process difficult
to divine, the physicalists passed from this coarse 'logical equivalence'
to identity of content. However they reached this conclusion, two
things are clear: first, that logical equivalence in this case is consistent
with the widest difference in content asserted, and second, that the
physicalists did actually resolve the one content into the other. As to
the first point, we may grant that a certain conscious process may
occur when, and only when, a certain process occurs in the brain, so
that the truth or falsity of the assertion of either is always accompanied by that of the other. But this would not have the least tendency
to show that the two are the same. Uniform accompaniment is not
identity. As for the second point, namely that physicalists resolved
the one assertion into the other, we need only consult Professor
Hempel's article, 'Analyse Logique der Psychologie', of 1935. He
there holds roundly that 'psychology is an integral part of physics'
and points out that if the physicalists are not behaviourists, it is
because the behaviourists denied the existence of such processes as
feelings and voluntary acts, whereas the physicalists consider even
this denial meaningless; the non-physical cannot be meaningfully
mentioned.[1] Psychological assertions thus reduce without remainder
to assertions of physical states or movements.

25. Physicalism, like solipsism, soon showed signs of disintegration.
As early as 1938 Carnap was writing: 'A person sometimes knows he
is angry without applying any of those procedures which another
person would have to apply. . . .' 'Anger is not the same as the
movements by which an angry organism reacts to his environ-
ment. . . .'[2] When a person is angry, then, he is experiencing
something that is neither the knitting of his brows nor the clenching
of his fists on the one hand, nor, on the other, the movements in his
cortex, since, as Carnap admits, nobody knows just what these are.
Anger is thus an experience, not a bodily reaction. On this I am
content to echo a comment of Martha Kneale's: 'This seems to me
the bankruptcy of the policy of translation. The stories are

---

[1] *Revue de Synthèse*, X, 35, 38.
[2] From an article reprinted in Feigl and Sellars, *Readings in Philosophical
Analysis*, 419, 420.

acknowledged to be different stories and not different versions of one story.'[1]

Physicalism might quite well have decided at this point to close its books and quietly adjourn. It did not in fact do that. It took the line that while the mental and physical assertions were not really identical in content, the first was still *reducible* to the second. This was the course taken by both Carnap and Hempel. Since we have already seen what Hempel's earlier view was, it will be instructive to study his later doubt about it. Regarding his earlier essay he wrote in 1947:

'I now consider the type of physicalism outlined in this paper as too restrictive; the thesis that all statements of empirical science are *translatable*, without loss of theoretical content, into the language of physics, should be replaced by the weaker assertion that all statements of empirical science are reducible to sentences in the language of physics, in the sense that for every empirical hypothesis, including, of course, those of psychology, it is possible to formulate certain test conditions in terms of physical concepts which refer to more or less directly observable physical attributes. *But those test conditions are not asserted to exhaust the theoretical content of the given hypothesis in all cases.*'[2]

What exactly does this mean? It means, I take it, this; that when we talk about someone else's toothache, we are not referring exclusively to bodily reactions, since these reactions are not now taken as identical with his pain, which itself is unobservable, but as the outward signs of that pain. But there is so firm a connection between the pain and these outward signs that we may safely take them as 'symptoms' (Carnap) or 'test conditions' (Hempel) of the pain, and verify our judgment by them alone.

26. Regarding this we may comment as follows: It is not a revision of physicalism; it is an abandonment of it in principle, and along with it of the present version of the verifiability principle itself. Professor Hempel is offered the statement: 'John is in pain', and asked for a Yes or No as to whether the meaning of this statement is exhausted by 'observable physical attributes'. With courage and candour he answers No, John's pain is not to be identified with any 'test conditions' of a physical kind that it is possible to formulate.

---

[1] *Arist. Soc. Proceedings*, Vol. 50 (1949–50), 114.
[2] Feigl and Sellars, *op. cit.*, 373; the last italics mine.

(Of course if Mr Hempel means only that we have not yet brought to light the right physical conditions, but that when we have, they will prove identical with the pain, he is still clinging to the behaviourism that has been discredited; but it seems clear that he has gone beyond this.) Now to recognize that a concept may be significant without referring to any observable states or movements is to break with physicalism altogether, and there is no reason in principle why introspective psychology in general and the free reference to others' experiences should not be restored. Once we admit that by 'John is in pain' we mean more than that 'certain motions are taking place in John's body', we cannot reasonably deny this of our further statements about John's hopes and fears, volitions and desires. In short, 'reducibility' is an attempt at compromise which amounts either to nothing or to total surrender. If it means what the word suggests, that the mental assertion is reducible to the physical in meaning or content asserted, it falls short even of compromise; it is simple physicalism, naked though a little ashamed. If it means that the mental assertion may now be taken in its ordinary sense, namely that John is genuinely conscious and not an intricately constructed robot, then again it has offered no compromise; it has gone over to the enemy, lock, stock and barrel. And since it admits the meaningfulness of what is even in principle unverifiable by me, it must look for a new criterion of meaning.

The later Carnap and Hempel are agreed, as we have seen, that though the concept of another's pain is not exhausted by observable states of his body, these states are at least a universally present and reliable index of what is beyond. As held by some philosophers this is a natural and intelligible view. But as urged by positivists we are bound to say that it is a mass of confusions and contradictions. We shall point out a half dozen or so.

(1) On this view, the physical change P can be taken as the 'symptom' of the conscious change C only if P and C have been observed to accompany each other uniformly. But it is admitted that C cannot be observed at all. Hence the uniform connection by which, if P is to be the 'symptom' of C, the two must be linked together, could never be made out.

(2) One would gather, from the hesitation with which conscious events are admitted, and the firmness with which psychology is restricted to bodily behaviour, that the bodily aspects of anger or pain were good plain measurable things which psychologists could look at and argue about, while the conscious events were fugitive and dubious will-o'-the-wisps which it was hardly good form to mention.

This is approximately the reverse of the truth. It is these unmentionables that to plain men are of all things the most pointedly vivid and real, and it is chiefly to get some means of producing and mitigating them that their elusive physical bases are sought out. What is more real than an excruciating pain? Yet not even a Penfield or an Adrian could give more than an extremely schematic sketch of the neuronic changes that 'condition' it. So of other types of experience. Of course one cannot identify men's hopes and fears with the gross play of their arms and legs, or even with their facial contortions, since all these are sometimes present (as on the stage) when the emotions are absent, and absent (as under strong self-control) when the emotions are present. The 'symptoms' or observable expressions through which the feelings are to be studied must therefore be the hidden changes of brain and nerve. And of these we know almost nothing. A psychology of the kind here demanded, which confined itself to them with due austerity, would be barren past belief.

(3) It may have been noted that on the present theory *every* conscious event is assumed to have its bodily correlate; that is why observable 'test conditions' can always be formulated. This assumption may be true. But no reason is offered for it, and if a reason were asked, what could the positivist say? He cannot at this stage reply that it is a tautology, since the identity of conscious with nervous process is no longer maintained. The generalization must therefore be synthetic. But if so, it can at best be only probably true. In that case, to say it is *always* true is to beg the question. In the light of certain results of psychical research, it is even questionable to say that the inductive evidence we have points invariably in that direction, and in any case to rule out such research a priori is dogmatism.

(4) The positivist's assumption here is not only unestablished; on his present reading of the verifiability theory, it must be meaningless. How could you show by empirical evidence that no conscious event ever exists without a physical correlate? Suppose you were to observe all the conscious events that ever occurred (which, by the way, could not be done, since they are unobservable) and found that every one of them had its correlate, would that entitle you to say that no such event would lack a correlate? Plainly not. This statement is beyond empirical verification. The new psychology, therefore, is to be based on a meaningless principle.

(5) What the positivist is here appealing for is the replacement of data supposed to be private and inaccessible by 'physical' data

supposed to be public. I cannot see John's pain, but we can all see his grimaces, and if only we had instruments of the proper delicacy, we could presumably see the nervous changes correlated with his pain. But note the quietly made assumption that what I see when I look at John's body is really public. This may again be true, though many philosophers and scientists think it improbable. 'Ultimately,' as Eddington says, 'visual, tactual, and other sensations are provoked in the mind. It is from these remote and indirect effects that we have to argue back to the properties of the physical objects at the far end of the chain of transmission. . . . To confuse the mental object with the physical object is to confuse the clue with the criminal.'[1] None of the arguments offered by realists to show that the primary or secondary qualities exist as I perceive them, in a public and independent realm, seems, to me at any rate, convincing, and at this time of philosophic day to assume without question that they do, that what I see when I look at John's body is public property which may also be observed by you, is surely dogmatism again. And what makes it so odd in the present case is that it is not only an undefended dogma, it is a mean-ingless dogma. When Carnap suggests that we translate our expression of feeling hot into a statement about the temperature, and look at a thermometer to verify it, he assumes that the thermometer will give us a public instead of a private check, that what presents itself to you will be the same as what presents itself to me. But obviously the statement that the object of your awareness is the same as that of mine is not perceptually verifiable by me, and hence to me must be unmeaning. The positivist may reply that 'is aware of the same object' means only 'physically reacts to the same object'. But that would be a retreat to the behaviourism from which at the present stage he is trying to escape.

(6) Let it be remembered that throughout this long discussion the positivist is seeking to make us understand what is passing in his mind and adopt beliefs like his own. It is scarcely credible that all he means by 'understanding what is passing in his mind' is accepting the fact that his body is making certain noises or marks on paper, or even that his cortex is in a certain state of agitation. He has gone through a course of thought, and it seems plain that he wants us to do the same with a similar clearness and strength of conviction. Nor is his attempt to make us adopt certain beliefs merely an attempt to induce in us a line of behaviour; if so, exactly what line? He wants us to have certain insights, to apprehend certain distinctions, to infer certain conclusions, and to find satisfaction in them. How much of

---

[1] *Proceedings of Arist. Soc.*, Sup. Vol. 10 (1931), 167.

all this would be intelligible if translated into his own terms, namely those obscure intra-bodily changes which are now to provide the cash value of his consciousness and ours? The assumptions, aims, and interests with which in fact he conducts his discussion burst the bounds of his theory continually.

It is hard to resist the conclusion that physicalism, and the criterion of meaning behind it, are forms of unconscious obscurantism. Put forward in the avowed interest of clearness of thought, they compel their exponents—otherwise very clear heads—to veil and muffle their meaning in round-about talk of the translatability of sentences. Offered as more precise and coherent than philosophical discussion of these problems, their theory not only leads, as we have seen, to confusion and incoherence, but persistently moves on a level where the real problems of philosophical thought are hardly allowed to emerge. But though the new interpretation of science does seem to put back the clock, it is less clear whether in the long run it will prove a liability or an asset. Science has reached an apogee of prestige. Mr Russell has said that what is knowable can be known by science, and what is not science is not knowledge. The physicalists would agree, and would add that therefore the consciousness of men, in its rich proliferations, is not, as distinct from its physical manifestations, a true object of knowledge at all. And of course they are right if science *is* a study of physical states and changes only. But the acceptance of that view would mean an immense restriction of the field of science and a corresponding diminution of its importance. Would this be an unfortunate result? That depends. If the advocates of the unity of science were to convince their humanistic colleagues that sociology and psychology should be 'reduced' to the new terms, the result would surely be disaster. To see this, one need only imagine an account of the French Revolution written in terms of Neurath's extraordinary physicalist sociology, and compare it for illumination with the account of Carlyle, who knew no science, but did have some insight into the human mind. On the other hand, if the new conception of science is pressed, it may produce an unanticipated renaissance of humanistic study. This conception of science is so cramping and illiberal that it might well incite a revolt against the whole scientific enterprise on behalf of a more enlightened study of the human spirit. Such study is sure in the end to assert its rights. Whether that assertion is made within the bounds of science more generously conceived, or is made in the name of philosophy, is a point of minor importance. In either case it will have left physicalism, in all its forms, behind.

Stage IV : Verifiability in Principle by Anyone.

27. We have been discussing the curious consequences of the third interpretation of the verifiability principle, according to which a statement is meaningful if it is, at least in principle, conclusively verifiable by me. We now come to the fourth interpretation, made necessary by the untenable consequences of the third. According to this new interpretation, a statement is meaningful if it might conceivably be verified *by anyone at all.* Here is a further extension of the range of the meaningful. The third formula cut me off from talking about your experience because I could not even in principle verify such experience myself, nor could I significantly say that you on your part had ever verified anything. I can now say both these things. I can admit, as significant, statements verifiable by you, and indeed only by you. Any statement will be meaningful that *might* be conclusively verified by *any* observing being. I can speak of the remote past before the earth was inhabited, and of the remote future when it will be uninhabited again, because, though no observers did or will exist at these times, it is conceivable that they should, and that they should have such and such perceptions. There are whistles with a note higher than human ears can catch, but still audible to dogs, and though I cannot clearly imagine what their sound is like, I can speak of it meaningfully because it *is* heard by some perceiving beings and *might* be heard by others. Indeed there are only two kinds of statement that this comparatively liberal criterion would rule out. One is the statement of a logical impossibility, which defies 'the rules of grammar we have stipulated for our language'; examples would be, 'My friend died the day after tomorrow' and 'The lady wore a dark red dress which was bright green.'[1] The other is a statement which, though not logically impossible, asserts a state of affairs which, in the nature of the case, is not perceivable or verifiable by anyone. This view, or something very like it, was held by Schlick in his final period. Does it give us the criterion of meaningfulness of which we are in search? Let us look at the two kinds of statement that it would exclude.

28. There would appear to be no objection to ruling out the logically impossible. But when we inquire what Schlick means by the logically impossible, we get an answer that gives us pause. He means by it the combining of words in a certain way when 'the rules of our language have not provided any use for such combinations'. 'We could change these rules, of course, and thereby arrange a meaning for the terms "both red and green" . . . but if we decide to stick to the ordinary

[1] Schlick, 'Meaning and Verification'. Feigl and Sellars' *Readings,* 154.

definitions (which reveal themselves in the way we actually use our words) we have decided to regard those combined terms as meaningless. . . .'[1] We have *decided* to regard them as meaningless? We could, then, if we chose, regard them as meaningful? This linguistic theory of necessary knowledge will demand our attention later. Suffice it to say for the present that it seems merely eccentric. If we cannot meaningfully say that our friend died the day after tomorrow or that the lady wore a dress that was at once red and green all over, it is surely more than 'rules of grammar' that stand in our way; it is the intractable nature of things. To be sure, we may use the words 'red' and 'green' in any way we want, and if we use them in their ordinary sense, the rules of usage do forbid their combination; but these rules do not come out of the air, or out of our choice; it is only in some Lewis Carroll world that we could, by manipulating our grammar, make the same surface red and green. The rule has got itself adopted because it conforms to a seen truth about surfaces; surfaces do not rally round and adjust themselves to whatever rules of grammar we decree. If Schlick's criterion involved this queer doctrine as an essential part, we could only reject it out of hand. But we prefer to regard the doctrine for the present as tangential and a caprice. If the logically impossible is taken in its more ordinary sense of that which can neither be nor be conceived because of the incoherence of its characters, we may agree to the first exclusion that this theory formula requires. The logically impossible is surely meaningless.

29. What of the other exclusion? According to it, all terms are excluded as meaningless that refer to what is not perceivable or verifiable by anyone. Unfortunately this leaves room for doubt. 'Perceivable' and 'verifiable' were supposed to cover the same ground, but the criterion turned out to have different ranges of application as the one or the other was stressed. Stress the first, and the test of meaningfulness will be whether the object referred to is by nature sensible; stress the second, and the test will be whether it is so related to an observer as to make verification possible. These give different grounds of selection. The first test is so wide as to admit much that the positivists would at the beginning have rejected as 'metaphysical' and meaningless. The second is so narrow as to exclude much that any sensible person could see to be meaningful. Let us look at them more closely.

According to the first, anything could be significantly referred to

[1] Schlick, 'Meaning and Verification'. Feigl and Sellars' *Readings*, 155.

whose nature was such as to render it theoretically perceptible. This would admit the reference to sounds audible to dogs but not to men; and since it is conceivable that, even if no one can now see colours corresponding to infra-red and ultra-violet rays, still there *might* be such beings, the reference to their possible perceptions must be called meaningful. Thus we can refer to what may never in fact be verifiable and what is even unimaginable. Read as widely as this, the criterion aroused misgivings in many positivists. Would it not leave the door sufficiently ajar for metaphysics to insert a cloven hoof? For example, it admitted as meaningful the problem of immortality, if this were taken as the problem of surviving death. Schlick made the shocking remark: 'I can easily imagine witnessing the funeral of my own body and continuing to exist without a body . . .'[1] To be sure, what he meant by the self that might imaginably survive was not a non-sensible pure ego, but that part of his field of consciousness which would remain after the subtraction of its somatic sensation and its perceptions of trunk, arms, and legs. But if this survival of mere consciousness were imaginable in his own case, it was no doubt imaginable also in others', and then we should have the idea of a society of disembodied consciousnesses, no one of whom was perceptible to any other. This was travelling a very long way beyond the behaviourism of Wittgenstein and the physicalism of Neurath and Carnap, so far indeed that some other positivists reacted sharply. Ayer thought that 'it is self-contradictory to speak of a man as surviving the annihilation of his body'.[2] Even if one meant by the self nothing more than a single sense-history, this sense-history, if it was to belong to the same self, must 'contain organic sense-contents which are elements of the same body'.[3] I am not clear what this means. Indeed I think Schlick right that the problem of survival is a significant one, which can be investigated by scientific methods. But in admitting into the circle of the meaningful such entities as dis-embodied selves and unimaginable sounds and colours, he was bound to impose a strain on the credence of his fellow positivists. They had developed a keen scent for the noisome traces of metaphysics.

30. But what the formula gave with one hand it took away with the

---

[1] Schlick, 'Meaning and Verification'. Feigl and Sellars' *Readings*, 159. In the same essay, however, he says that perception is to be defined 'only by reference to living *bodies*, to physical organs' (169). This, I think, is inconsistent with what he says above. If perceiving, or witnessing, *is* the activity of a living body, how can it be imagined to go on in the absence of that body?

[2] *Language, Truth and Logic*, 2nd ed., 127.

[3] *Ibid.*, 125.

other. If one side of the theory emphasized that what is referred to must be sensible in nature, the other side emphasized that it must be verifiable; 'the meaning of a statement can be given only by indicating the way in which the truth of the statement is to be *tested*'.[1] This emphasis on the connection between meaning and mode of verification is too often repeated by positivists to be regarded as anything but central in their thinking. But if taken seriously, it limits the range of reference in an almost intolerable way. Suppose—to continue the line of thought of a moment ago—one thinks of death as involving the extinction of consciousness. This is surely an intelligible notion, whether true or not. But how could it be so if its intelligibility depends on its being verifiable? I can never verify my own death, for obviously I cannot be conscious of my own lack of consciousness. Other people cannot verify it, for they can never even perceive my consciousness, let alone my lack of it. My loss of consciousness at death is thus in principle unverifiable by anyone. It ought, therefore, to be meaningless. But it is not. So there must be something wrong with the criterion.

Such difficulties multiply as one reflects, and we may mention a few more of them. Professor C. I. Lewis has asked the question: 'is the phrase "too small to be directly perceived" meaningful or is it not?'[2] He thinks it is, and he is surely right; we know that we mean something by it, and something fairly definite; no theory of what we ought, and ought not, to be able to mean can affect our confidence on that point. But the reference is to the unverifiable—not merely the practically unverifiable, for positivists admit that we can think of that—but the unverifiable even in theory. Professor Lewis supplies further examples. 'It is entirely meaningful, for example, to think of those inventions which nobody has ever thought of, or those numbers which no one will ever count; we can even frame the concept of those concepts which no one will ever frame.'[3] Indeed concepts of constant use not only in philosophy but also in common sense and science would be ruled out by this criterion. We shall take an example or two from each field.

31. A time-honoured philosophical issue is that between subjectivists and realists. The American and British 'new realists' had held, as against subjective idealists, that the qualities of perceived objects existed independently of, and were unaffected by, being perceived.

[1] *Gesammelte Aufsätze*, 179.
[2] Feigl and Sellars' *Readings*, 139.
[3] *Ibid.*, 143.

Most philosophers thought that whether this position was true or not, it was perfectly intelligible. Positivists, too, wanted to believe this; they shrank from subjective idealism as a metaphysical theory. But then was not realism an equally metaphysical theory? It held that qualities existed at times when they were unobserved. That was not a proposition that could be directly verified, and if not, it was a pseudo-proposition only, and realism became meaningless. It might be thought that the idealists at least would welcome this conclusion, but they showed little disposition to do so, since they had no taste for this method of disposing of an ancient and honourable foe. So the positivists found themselves in the middle of a pitched battle, and accounted enemies by both sides. Their response was to tone down the charge that realism was meaningless. But they did so in different ways. Schlick maintained that the criterion admitted all that the realists needed to say. They were quite justified in saying, for example, that the stars will go on in their courses when there are no beings to observe them, for the inability to verify is in this case empirical, not logical; the stars are in their nature observable, and there might have been observers.[1] But this surely is a confusion. It is true that a star that is not observed may be observable, because an observer might have been there. It is not true that the star is observable under conditions that expressly specify the absence of observers. The unobservability of the star is then not empirical but stipulated. Hence, to say that it exists under such conditions should be meaningless. But obviously it is not. In accepting the assertion as meaningful, Schlick is really abandoning the part of his criterion that demanded verifiability and falling back on the more liberal clause that was satisfied with perceivability by nature. Ayer took a different though hardly more satisfactory line. He held that in asserting the existence of the unperceived we were asserting what is essentially a hypothetical, not a categorical, proposition. 'For what we are asserting when we say of a thing that it exists although no one is perceiving it is . . . that certain sense-contents would occur if certain conditions relating mainly to the faculties and position of an observer were fulfilled, but that in fact the conditions are not being fulfilled.'[2] But this will not do either. For (1) it conflicts with what direct inspection reveals as our meaning. To say that a star exists is not to say merely that *if* someone looked he would see it; it is to say that the star is there, whether anyone looks or not. And (2) on the present version of the verifiability theory, the hypothetical proposition is as meaningless

[1] Feigl and Sellars' *Readings*, 168–9.
[2] *Language, Truth and Logic*, 2nd ed., 145.

H

as the categorical, since it is equally unverifiable. There is no way of verifying in direct perception that something would have happened if that which actually happened had failed to happen. Hence the positivists were still committed to calling realism nonsense.[1]

32. The present criterion, then, rejected as meaningless some eminently respectable philosophical theses. But as regards philosophy the positivists were iconoclasts who rather enjoyed the clatter of falling idols. It was more distressing to find their theory in conflict with common sense. The plain man looks at the mantelpiece and has no doubt whatever that a clock is standing there. Now it is a curious fact, but a fact nevertheless, that he can never conclusively verify this assertion, or any other assertion that a material object exists. The trouble is not merely that he may be deceived by a paper appearance, or suffer from hypnotism or illusion; it also 'arises from the fact that material objects are, by their nature, extended in time and public to different observers. Moreover, these propositions cannot be strongly verified by any finite number of experiences; it is possible that there should not, in fact, be a clock on the mantelpiece now even if there appears to be one whenever I (or indeed other people) look.'[2] To be sure, this is not a difficulty that is likely to keep anyone awake at night; perception gives us all the answers we ordinarily need. Still, if a material object is conceived as it commonly is, there is no finite number of observations that would give us absolute evidence that it exists. And—this is the point—if the statement that it exists cannot be conclusively verified, that statement is supposed by the test to be meaningless. But there is something very queer indeed about telling us that we are talking meaninglessly if we so much as venture to remark that there is a clock on the mantelpiece.

33. Embarrassing as these conflicts were with philosophy and common sense, they were less worrying than another wrangle in which their theory involved the positivists. This was with science itself. The main business of science is the discovery of laws. Laws are general statements to the effect that something of the kind X is always associated with something of the kind Y. This association may have been observed in very few instances; that does not matter

---

[1] It should be added that the last criticism would not apply to Professor Ayer's own formulation of the criterion. He did not contend, as Schlick did, that the meaningful must be conclusively verifiable.

[2] R. B. Braithwaite. 'Propositions About Material Objects', *Proc. of Arist. Soc.*, Vol. 38 (1937–38), 273–4.

if the conditions of observation are right; the law is not a summary of instances observed but a generalization, a statement covering *all* instances, observed and unobserved, past, present, and future. The question now arose for the positivists, is any such statement verifiable? It is obviously not in practice, but is it verifiable even in theory? There are laws regarding the motion of liquids that, if valid at all, are exemplified in every movement of every drop of water in every ocean of the earth or any other celestial body through all past and future time. To exhaust what such a statement intends would require nothing short of the completion of an infinite series. But this is impossible even in principle. The law, therefore, is not conclusively verifiable. Hence it must be meaningless. And since natural laws generally are unrestricted in their scope, it follows that the most important statements of science are meaningless. But this is intolerable. As Karl Popper, himself very close to the positivists, said, 'the radical positivist would destroy not only metaphysics, but also natural science'.[1]

The verifiability principle was taken so seriously that the positivists set about it to reconstrue the enterprise of science itself in order to make it square with their principle. Carnap held for a time that laws were simply records of present and remembered experiences. In spite of the difficulty about an infinite series, Wittgenstein argued that a universal proposition must be read as an infinite conjunction of singulars, though he soon abandoned this. Russell, who did not number himself among the positivists, but who always carried weight with them, held that we must assume the existence of general as well as particular facts. Ramsey and Schlick both experimented with the view that scientific laws were not statements at all, but 'directions for possible acts', practical rules that help us in classifying what we observe and in finding our way about. None of these views was able to win general assent. For the most part they broke at once upon the testimony of the direct inspection of meaning. It was idle to tell us that when we said all *X*'s were *Y*'s we could not possibly mean *all*. We could because we did.

By now it was evident that the criterion so hopefully urged by Schlick of conclusive verifiability in principle was doomed. Professor Ayer summed up against it forcibly. He held at this time that *no* statement of fact was conclusively verifiable, and maintained that 'if this is correct, the principle that a sentence is factually significant only if it expresses what is conclusively verifiable is self-stultifying as a criterion of significance. For it leads to the conclusion that it is

[1] *Logik der Forschung*, 9.

impossible to make a significant statement of fact at all.'[1]

Stage V: Falsifiability.

34. The positivists were compelled to try again. The suggestions that most naturally came next was offered by Professor Popper. We can only admit, he held, that universal statements are meaningful, whether we can verify them or not, and hence their meaningfulness cannot be based on their verifiability. What then is the ground? It is not the possibility of verifying the proposition, but that of *falsifying* it. 'Our theory rests,' he wrote, 'on an asymmetry between verifiability and falsifiability which follows from the logical form of generalizations; for although these are never derivable from particular statements, they can stand in contradiction with them.'[2] We cannot show conclusively that all swans are white by counting them, but we can show conclusively that this is false by pointing to a single swan that is not white. If we take falsifiability in principle as our criterion, we can thus continue to hold that scientific laws are significant; and Popper suggested that we had here a reliable touchstone for statements of fact generally.

35. But, alas, this hope also faded. It faded for a reason inherent in the very distinction of status between universal and particular propositions that Popper took as his starting-point. You can falsify, but not verify, the proposition that all swans are white; true. But unhappily, though you can verify, you cannot falsify, the proposition that *some* swans are white. Why not? Because, since it is a logically particular proposition, you can contradict it only by establishing a universal proposition, and this we have just seen to be impossible through empirical means. To falsify 'some swans are white' you must verify that no swans are white. Now you may have observed any number of swans and found no white swan among them, but that will never entitle you to say there are no white swans. A white one may turn up tomorrow. It follows that if the criterion of significance for an assertion is to be its falsifiability, we must set down as meaningless so innocent a proposition as that some swans are white. And this clearly will not do.

As positivists meditated on this criterion and its predecessor, they came to see that both of them involved a very odd consequence. Both committed one to saying that while a certain proposition, P, could be meaningful and true, its contradictory, P, was meaningless and

[1] *Language, Truth and Logic*, 2nd ed., 38.
[2] *Logik der Forschung*, 13.

therefore neither true nor false. On theory No. IV (conclusive verifiability), one could say that 'some swans are white' was meaningful and true, but one could not deny it, because a universal negative, as unverifiable, was meaningless. Similarly, on theory No. V (conclusive falsifiability), one could say that all swans are white, but found oneself baffled if one tried to assert its contradictory, since that contradictory, 'some swans are not white', was itself not falsifiable. Plainly there was something wrong here. It was absurd to hold that if you affirmed P you were talking sense, while if you denied the very same proposition, your statement was neither true nor false, but nonsense. Our logic itself is constructed on the assumption that if P is true, its contradictory must be false, and that if its contradictory is true, P must be false. To give up logic itself for the sake of a controversial theory of meaning would be irresponsible.[1] And since both theories alike imposed this grim demand, both must be abandoned.

Stage VI: Weak Verifiability.
36. Positivists had, therefore, to gird up their loins for a sixth attempt. Since propositions must be admitted as meaningful that were not *conclusively* verifiable nor falsifiable, could the criterion be saved by sacrificing conclusiveness and accepting propositions that were less than completely verifiable? This was proposed by Professor Ayer in 1936. He distinguished between strong, or conclusive, and weak verification. 'A proposition is said to be verifiable in the strong sense of the term if, and only if, its truth could be conclusively established in experience. But it is verifiable in the weak sense if it is possible for experience to render it probable.' 'We say that the question that must be asked about any putative statement of fact is not, Would any observations make its truth or falsehood logically certain? but simply, Would any observations be relevant to the determination of its truth or falsehood. And it is only if a negative answer is given to this second question that we conclude that the statement under consideration is nonsensical.'[2] This theory marked a clear advance. It admitted as meaningful universal affirmatives and negatives. It admitted propositions about the past in their ordinary sense, and propositions about other people's minds, though regarding these Professor Ayer continued to hold, with some loss of confidence indeed, his behaviouristic view.[3]

[1] Cf. C. G. Hempel, *Revue Internationale de Philosophie*, January 1950, 46–7.
[2] *Language, Truth and Logic*, 2nd ed., 37, 38.
[3] *Ibid.*, 19, 20.

37. But the ghost of trouble would not down. The trouble that now arose was not with what the criterion excluded but with what it included. If every statement were to be called meaningful about which some item of empirical evidence could be found, was there any statement, however wild, that could not put in a legitimate claim? Dr Ewing pointed out, for example, that this criterion would open the door wide to the metaphysics it had been designed to exclude.[1] Professor Ayer had taken as a peculiarly clear example of meta-physical pseudo-proposition the statement that the world of sense experience is unreal, but our sense experience is at least relevant to this issue, since without it there would be no issue at all; hence the pseudo-proposition is restored to its former place. He had also instanced as an example of metaphysical futility Bradley's question whether the Absolute transcended the process of evolution; but since scientific observations were clearly relevant to whether there was such a process as evolution, Bradley's question must be called significant after all. Theologians could discuss God's omnipotence, at least in terms of the schoolboy's query whether he could make a stone so big that he could not lift it; they could discuss his goodness, since the distribution of pain supplied evidence that was both clearly empirical and clearly relevant; they could discuss immortality, for if God's goodness was now meaningful, it had an obvious bearing on whether his creatures would be blotted out; they could even discuss such distinctively theological dogmas as the incarnation, since the evidence for this lay partly in historical fact. But if such matters as these could be significantly canvassed, what speculative issue could be ruled out? The gate-keeper assigned to guard the precincts was suddenly found dispensing tickets right and left to deplorably seedy specimens of the metaphysical and theological underworld.

As if to guard his criterion against such democracy, however, Mr Ayer went on to formulate it in more technical terms. 'Let us call a proposition which records an actual or possible observation an experiential proposition. Then we may say that it is the mark of a genuine factual proposition . . . that some experiential propositions can be deduced from it in conjunction with certain other premises without being deducible from those other premises alone.'[2] Why this sort of formulation? Apparently to make clear the conditions under which a statement that was not strongly verifiable could still be admitted as meaningful. 'Arsenic is poisonous.' That is not con-clusively verifiable, because it would require more observations than

[1] 'Meaninglessness', *Mind*, Vol. 46 (1937).
[2] *Ibid.*, 38–9.

could ever be completed; but it is clearly significant. How could this significance be recognized consistently with the requirement of verifiability? Only by admitting that a partial verifiability was enough. By this was meant that though the assertion was not verifiable in its whole extent, it still enabled us, when we took it in conjunction with other statements, to make confirmable inferences which we could not make from these statements alone. Merely from 'John has taken arsenic' we cannot conclude that John will be poisoned. But from this in conjunction with 'arsenic poisons', we can conclude that John will be poisoned, and this conclusion can be confirmed by observation. The general proposition is thus at least partially verified by experience, and may be admitted as significant, on this ground.

This new formulation enabled positivists to deal successfully with those statements, such as general laws and propositions about material objects, which could be established only by an infinite series of observations. But what about statements of other kinds? The theologian would certainly claim that from an assertion of the existence of God, in conjunction with statements about mystic experience or historic fact, he could derive many confirmable conclusions not derivable from these latter alone. The metaphysician would say the same about the hypotheses of an external world and an enduring self. Indeed Isaiah Berlin pointed out that, according to the new criterion, one could meaningfully say 'This logical problem is bright green', since with the help of another premise, 'I dislike all shades of green', one can deduce a verifiable conclusion not deducible from either premise alone, namely, 'I dislike this problem'.[1] Professor Ayer himself, ten years later, agreed that the formula would not do. One could apparently prove by it that any indicative statement at all was meaningful. Take, for example, 'the Absolute is lazy'. Attach to this any empirical consequent you wish, such as 'if the Absolute is lazy, this is white'. The statement, 'this is white', is then a verifiable one which does not follow from either premise taken alone, but does follow from the two together. Both of them thus fulfil the requirement for meaningfulness, and the statement 'the Absolute is lazy' must be admitted to all the rights and privileges pertaining thereto.[2] It may be complained that nothing can be deduced from a statement that is meaningless, and since 'the Absolute is lazy' is such a statement,

---

[1] 'Verification', *Proc. Arist. Soc.*, Vol. 39 (1938–39), 234.

[2] *Language, Truth and Logic*, 2nd ed., 11–12. A further refinement of the formula is suggested on p. 13. But this too fails to exclude such propositions as the above. Cf. *Hempel, op. cit.*, 50, and A. Church, *Journal of Symbolic Logic*, Vol. 14 (1949), 52–3.

nothing can be derived from it. But this implies that there is some antecedent criterion that can be applied to a statement by way of testing whether it is fit for use by the present criterion, whereas the present one was supposed to suffice by itself.

38. It was evident that the weary burden must be taken up again. In what direction were the positivists now to move? To an outsider it would seem as if the time had come for questioning whether the enterprise was wisely conceived. Consider what had been going on. One criterion after another had been proposed, only to be rejected on the ground that it would include some statements that were meaningless, or exclude some that were not. But does this not plainly imply that we already have a criterion more reliable than the technical formulations? What is the point of a test if that test itself must be brought to the test of an inspection of actual meaning, which is thereby conceded to be the court of last appeal? To us this appears a sensible question, and many analysts seem to have thought so too. The drift of the British analytic movement in recent years has been away from the discussion of a general criterion and toward a consideration of types and shades of meaning as exemplified in actual usage. But in the United States, under the stimulus of many transplanted members of the continental school, the pursuit of a general criterion has gone on. The character of the advance, which combines, as it seems to us, logical virtuosity with a curious philosophic naiveté, is suggested by some of the grounds on which these thinkers rejected the earlier criteria of Schlick, Popper, and Ayer, and felt compelled to take up the quest anew.

Suppose you say 'this is white'. This is regarded as clearly verifiable and hence a good empirical statement. But according to the logical scriptures handed down in *Principia*, we are told that $p \supset p \text{ v } q$. Let p be 'this is white'. And since p and q may stand for any propositions, let q be 'the Absolute is moonstruck'. We then find ourselves committed with all the rigour of this sort of logic to saying that 'this is white' implies 'either this is white or the Absolute is moonstruck'. Here the ugly face of metaphysics is presenting itself at our logical front door. Nor is the case a whit better under the falsifiability principle. Take 'this is white' again. This proposition is falsifiable by perception, and so is meaningful. But logic tells us that the negation of a proposition implies the negation of the conjunction of that proposition with any other: $\sim(p) \supset \sim(p.q.r. \ldots)$ Hence we cannot deny 'this is white' without committing ourselves to the appalling implication 'it is false that this is white, that the Absolute is moonstruck and that reality does not evolve'. Nor does even Ayer's formula, as we have seen, exclude these wanton intruders. Now all this is intolerable. We must put our foot firmly down. We must find some means of excluding such unwelcome visitors once for all.

The fact that implications of this kind could be seriously offered as difficulties, while the implication that no-one else in the world could be meaningfully judged to be conscious was scarcely accounted a difficulty at all, throws a revealing light on the positivist mentality. Largeness of philosophic vision was never a conspicuous element in its constitution. In Britain the positivist theses were rapidly worn down to relative innocuousness by the attrition of a sturdy common sense. In America they offered a harder surface. Perhaps the Teutonic professorial genius is less amenable to this kind of correction; in any case, on American soil it kept the admirable thoroughness and scholastic subtlety which are its virtues along with that immunity from infection by common sense which, in many minds, is its vice.

Stage VII: Expressibility in an Ideal Language.
39. The Viennese-American school thought it idle to continue the process of adjusting the criterion piecemeal to new statements that kept cropping up as meaningful. The Gordian knot should be cut, not laboriously untied. The sharp and gleaming instrument with which this was to be done was language—not the language of ordinary speech, which was full of vestiges of primitive metaphysics and confusion, but an ideal language specially designed to exclude all that was cloudy and illogical. This language was to have two kinds of component only. First there were the customary signs used by symbolic logic in the formulation of statements, signs that if read in English would be such as 'and', 'not', 'or', 'all', 'some', 'if-then'. Secondly, the vocabulary of the language, its subjects and predicates, would all be supplied by names referring to observable things, or observable characteristics of things. 'Observable' here means 'sensible'. Could one speak in such a language of composites like apples? Yes, but only if the object referred to had been defined in terms of simpler observation predicates, such as 'red', 'juicy', and 'round'. No words would be admitted except such as could pass the test of being primitives, that is, of referring to simple, undefinable characters, or else of being definable in terms of such primitives. Heidegger's profound pontification that 'nothing nothings', even Bradley's judgment that the Absolute does not evolve, could no longer worm their way into recognition through serving as parts of compound statements, for in the new language they could not be

formulated at all. Such words as 'nothing' and 'the Absolute' would be excluded by the rules of formation of the empiricist vocabulary, since they could not be defined in terms of observation predicates. The next criterion of significance, then, is translatability into this empiricist language. If a sentence in English admits of such translation, it is meaningful, and all the deductions from it allowed by the transformation rules of the new language will themselves be meaningful. If it resists translation, it may be good poetry or religion or metaphysics, but it *asserts* nothing at all.[1]

40. This is offered as a great advance over previous criteria. But we have somehow missed the potency of it. We cannot see where the advance has occurred. Of course if there were an empiricist language, all of whose terms, and those alone, were agreed upon as significant, translatability into the language would provide a useful test. But no such language exists. The first step, therefore, must be to construct it. In constructing it, we must admit only terms that are meaningful, and must of course decide on their meaningfulness without benefit of the language itself, for this is not yet constructed. But then every difficulty that has arisen earlier presents itself again. The general problem will now be whether a term qualifies for admission into the empiricist language. But that is merely the old problem of meaningfulness under a new name. The solution is purely verbal.

It may be said that this is less than just, since definite criteria have been offered for admission into the language. For factual terms the test is being an observation predicate; for logical terms, it is standard use in symbolic logic. Unfortunately neither test is of value. As for 'observation predicates', the phrase is either equivocal or begs the question; if it includes such unobservables as other people's thoughts, it is so equivocal as to be useless, while it begs the question if it excludes them as meaningless. As for the logical constants and quantifiers, they too are battlegrounds. To say, for example, of 'all' that it is to be admitted in the sense used in symbolic logic is to ignore the fact that it has no accepted sense in such logic, that Wittgenstein, Ramsey, and Russell—to name no others—have contradicted each other flatly as to what it should be taken to mean. The use of the translatability criterion must then be deferred till the prior criterion is settled of how the terms of this language are to be admitted; and toward that prior and essential settlement the theory contributes nothing.

[1] For statements of this view, see Hempel, *Revue Internationale de Philosophie*, January 1950, 59–62, and Carnap, 'Testability and Meaning', Part IV, *Philosophy of Science*, Vols. 3 and 4 (1936–37).

41. We have now completed our review of the main stages through which the verifiability theory has passed. The formulations have been so various that one cannot talk responsibly of *the* verifiability theory; one must specify one or other of its forms. Yet as we look back over the stages traversed, we seem able to detect in all of them a tendency toward one result. Through all the variations of the theory there seems to have been a pressure toward one end; when the variations have been out of line with it, as was Wittgenstein's solipsism and the requirement of *de facto* verifiability, they have been generally rejected by positivists. This common and implicit end seems to us to be the essence of the positivist claim. It is a two-sided conviction. On the one hand is the thesis, held unwaveringly, that what a statement means is what would assure us of its truth. On the other hand is the thesis, always present as a pendant, that the only experience that can so assure us regarding fact is sense experience. The view combines— to put it otherwise—the semantic intuition of Schlick with the meta-physical intuition of Hume, the intuition that a term means what would logically verify it, 'its mode of verification', with the intuition that whatever exists is sensible. These two theses are so intimately blended that they can hardly be dealt with separately. It is obvious, furthermore, that much we have said about particular forms of the theory might be said again about this joint thesis toward which all the forms converge. We shall try not to repeat. But this final version of the theory, which seems to us at once the most essential and the most plausible version, plainly calls for some further examination.

42. Since so much that is severe has been said about the theory, and more remains to be said, it may be grateful to pause for a moment and note that, whatever its degree of truth, the crusade on its behalf has had valuable effects. These seem to be chiefly two. The theory has contributed to a more vigilant self-criticism in thought and to a more determined endeavour after clarity of expression. To be sure, a price has been paid for both of these. In range of interest and wealth of reflective insights, some of the leading analysts seem pinched and poverty-stricken when compared with such speculative predecessors as Hegel, or even with lesser men like Edward Caird. Still, when Hegel talked about the notion, or Caird about self-consciousness, it was sometimes desperately hard to know what they meant. The fact that reading these great men has acquired a new and special difficulty is a testimony to the influence of the analysts. The difficulty is that many terms that we should once have taken in our stride now put hurdles in our way. What precisely is the 'cash-value'

of 'the notion' or of 'self-consciousness'? We have become aware as
never before of how hard it is in philosophy to talk sense; we have
become suspicious of any attempt to pass off emotive meaning as
cognitive; unction is a danger signal; our reading is apt to be punc-
tuated with silent and sometimes audible snorts and cavillings. And
if reading has become more difficult, so has writing, and in greater
measure. Many a philosopher can testify to the paralysing effect of
the analyst who now looks over his shoulder as he writes, demanding
that he be able to give an account of every term, and grunting in
contempt at his little rotundities and sonorities. That this should have
led to much crabbed writing is natural enough. But it should be
added that, even when crabbed, the writing is generally clear. What
readers are most familiar with are sights and sounds, pain and
pleasures, tables and chairs; and the kind of thought and writing that
implicitly tests itself by its nearness to these things is felt by most
men to be much clearer than writing that moves, with whatever
assurance, among abstractions. In this respect the line of British
empiricists running from Locke through Berkeley, Hume, and Mill,
to Professor Ayer, had a notable advantage over their rationalist
contemporaries. They had a theory of knowledge—granted—that
left too many things undreamed of in their philosophy. It must be
admitted that, for all that, their implicit theory of meaning exerted a
steady push toward clearness of style.

43. What now about the verifiability theory in the form we have
taken as the essential one?

Unhappily, there is a fatal confusion in it. Lovejoy has remarked
its presence in Carnap's writing,[1] and we took brief note of it at
Stage IV,[2] but it seems to have afflicted the whole movement from
Schlick forward. To put it in our own way, it is the confusion
between two different standards involved in the two theses that are
united in the criterion. One is a standard designed for terms, the
other for propositions. Terms have meaning when they are used to
refer to what is sensible. Propositions have meaning when they are
logically verifiable. And since verification is assumed always to occur,
if at all, through sense perception, it is further assumed that the two
requirements will coincide. But they do not. Much that is admitted
by the first requirement is excluded by the second. Consider the
proposition that a chair exists when unobserved. One cannot verify
this by observation. By the second part of the criterion it is therefore

[1] In *Philosophical Essays in Honor of E. A. Singer*, p. 8 ff.
[2] See above, Sections 29–30.

meaningless. But by the first part, the reference to the chair is still the reference to something in its nature sensible, and so is obviously meaningful. Carnap and others have been ruling out ancient issues in metaphysics on the ground that they could not be settled by empirical observation, and has implied that because they could not be thus settled, they were meaningless. But by the other part of the positivist standard, which made meaningfulness depend on whether the object was of such a nature as to be experienceable in sense, this conclusion was a *non sequitur*. Under that standard Carnap was ready to admit the reference to colours that no one had ever experienced or ever would, colours dependent on waves beyond the ends of our present spectrum, because such colours would, if they existed, be sensible. But unobserved tables and chairs are also in their nature sensible. The reference to them *is* then meaningful. Similarly with the sense data experienced by other people. One cannot verify in one's own perception the existence of such data. The suggestion that they exist is therefore meaningless, and we have returned to Ayer's curious theory that other people are our sense data. Yet nothing is more obvious than that sense data are in their nature sensible, and if so, the thought of them is intelligible after all. This two-edged sword has proved an extremely convenient weapon in the cut and thrust of the positivists' dialectic. When they wish to dismiss metaphysics, they use the verifiability edge of their Excalibur, and the foe falls ignominiously. When they are charged with abolishing from their world what is clearly thinkable, they have only to prick the prostrate foe with the other side of the blade and he leaps up again to a new life and respectability.

That the two requirements of verifiability and sensibility are different is even more easily seen in ideal cases. A philosopher has mooted the question whether his watch is really run by a leprechaun who becomes invisible the instant the watch is opened and who never has been, or will be, seen by anyone. Most positivists would scout the suggestion as nonsense because it is unverifiable. If by calling it nonsense they mean that there is no ground for calling it true, they are no doubt right. But their criterion requires that they mean more than that; it requires that the suggestion be unthinkable. And in this it is plainly wrong. At any rate I find no difficulty at all in imagining a tiny leprechaun wandering about among the wheels of my watch and perversely vanishing when I try to catch him at it. Take again a proposition that exercised some Cambridge wits in the thirties, that quadratic equations do not go to the Newmarket races. This no doubt is wildly at variance with the syntax of any ideal language, and is quite incapable of verification in sense. But as Dr Ewing has pointed out, it must be meaningful because it happens to be true.[1] Indeed the reason why it is silly to make such a remark is that it is so obviously true that none but idiots and philosophers would ever have occasion to use it. But an assertion that is true must have a meaning. If not, what is there to be true?

44. There is no need, however, to resort to extreme cases to show how meaning and verifiability fall apart. What is the positivist to make of modern physics? The physicist is constantly talking about protons, electrons, positrons, neutrons, mesons, and photons, none of which have ever been seen, and none of which, he assures us, ever will be seen, since the movement of any of them in isolation could never provide a sufficient stimulus for vision. Physicists talk about these invisible and intangible things with a confidence that is most curious if they are really talking about nothing. The operationalist, who is essentially the positivist in physics, says that what we mean by such terms is the operations by which we study their behaviour. The invisible entities *are* nothing but the pointer-readings, the trails in a cloud-chamber, and so on, which the physicist would offer as evidence of their existence if he were challenged. But when the physicist offers such evidence for them, he does not mean to *identify* the visible evidence with the invisible entities. Indeed the ordinary physicist would be contradicting himself in doing so. For in offering something as evidence, he is assuming that there is something else that it is evidence *for*. The pointer-readings, the wake in the cloud-chamber, verify what is meant, not in the sense that they *are* what is meant, but in the sense that they are effects of what is meant, which would not have occurred unless the hidden entities had existed to cause them, and from which the behaviour of these entities may be inferred. To be sure, there are able philosophers of science, like Herbert Dingle, who would resolve the sub-microscopic particles into concepts of our own, useful in ordering our experience and making predictions, but not really existent. Whether they exist or not is fortunately not our problem. Our problem is whether the ordinary scientist, in talking about such things, means only the empirical changes that he can perceive, or something more. It seems perfectly clear that he means more.

To the positivist this proved a continuing embarrassment. For science, and particularly physics, into which, according to Carnap, all the natural sciences in the end resolved themselves, was the object

[1] 'Meaninglessness', *Mind*, Vol. 46 (1937), 360.

of the positivists' chief veneration. Physics therefore should set a scrupulous example of avoiding all contact with metaphysics. Yet here was the science that was supposed to be the paragon of empiricist propriety sporting wantonly with Amaryllis in the shade. The spectacle seems to have induced in Carnap a divided mind. Protons and electrons had never been directly experienced and were apparently not experienceable, and hence should be unmentionable. Yet not only were they talked about with abandon; the assumption that they existed led to triumphant results in practice. So Carnap was driven to a position of uneasy compromise:

'If anyone wishes to be so rigorous as to banish such propositions from science, no conclusive objection to his doing so can be raised. Nevertheless it must be remembered that the customary method of the natural sciences, even of physics, does not regard such propositions as meaningless, but admits them as hypotheses. . . . We shall therefore *not* adopt this rigorous standpoint, but shall regard such propositions as meaningful (though not on that account necessarily true).'[1]

But the positivist can hardly have it both ways. If protons and electrons may be talked about, though never observable, the criterion must be overhauled. If not, positivism, instead of being the exponent and champion of physics, is saying that the science, from J. J. Thomson forward, has consisted very largely of mythology.

45. We come now to a difficulty that has dogged the verifiability criterion from the beginning and in all its forms. It makes a statement about what is, and what is not, meaningful. Is this itself meaningful? No statement is meaningful, it tells us, which cannot be verified in sense perception. Little by little the suspicion grew and was confirmed that such a criterion was doomed to die by self strangulation.

(*a*) In the first place, it laid down a universal negative, but it was clearly impossible to exhaust all statements and verify that no statement that failed to conform had meaning. Strictly, therefore, the statement of the criterion should itself be meaningless. Schlick was disposed to hold that a statement might be partly meaningful and partly not, and to say that that part of a statement in which reference was made to the sensible might be accepted and the rest rejected. But how could one verify *in sense* the statement that one's meaning contained no non-sensible component? Nor does it help to

[1] *Scheinprobleme der Philosophie*, 29, quoted by Lovejoy, *op. cit.*, 11.

throw the statement into affirmative form and say that all meaningful statements are empirically verifiable. The positivists of course believed this to be the case, but this also was a belief that was beyond establishing by experience. If the criterion was offered as a statement of fact applying to empirical statements generally, it must thus be rejected under its own requirement.

But if not an empirical statement, what was it? The fact that it was obviously meant to be general and was asserted with so much confidence suggested that it might be a priori. Perhaps it expressed an insight into the properties of meaning similar to that of geometers when they lay down a priori assertions about circles and triangles. This was tempting, but it was not accepted by the positivists because it would have conflicted with another and equally essential doctrine of the school, namely that all a priori statements are tautologies, to deny which would be self-contradictory. The assertion that sentences, so far as they signified at all, referred to what was sensory in nature, was plainly not a tautology, like the statement that a bachelor is an unmarried man; and it can be denied without any obvious self-contradiction. Furthermore, a genuine tautology is not likely to be attacked by citing contrary instances; if one wanted to refute the statement that all bachelors were unmarried men, one would hardly do so by looking round for exceptions; yet that is the commonest and most natural mode of attack on the verifiability view. The statement, then, must be synthetic, not analytic. And the positivists were clear that if it was synthetic, it could not be a priori, for they were convinced that there was no such thing as a synthetic a priori statement.

46. If the criterion of meaningfulness was, then, neither an empirical nor an a priori statement, what kind of statement could it possibly be? For these were the only types of statement recognized by the positivists. Might it not be a something other than any kind of statement? Might it not be a convention or recommendation, an injunction to accept some sentences as meaningful and not others, an admonition to cling to the empirical in the course of our thinking? It is to this interpretation of their criterion that most positivists who would still call themselves positivists appear to have been drawn. Will it serve? Unfortunately not. For (i) a recommendation is neither true nor false. But when the positivist says that statements about the Absolute lack meaning in the sense in which statements about red patches have it, he is plainly saying something that he believes to be true; and he believes that when metaphysicians deny it, they are making a mistake. (ii) Recommendations are supported by pointing to the advantages to be gained by following them. What is the advantage to be gained by avoiding unverifiable assertions? The main advantage, presumably, is that it facilitates our reaching true beliefs. How do we know that it does this? By seeing that unverifiable propositions could not give us truth. Why could they not? Because they are meaningless. But this is surely meant as a true statement about them, not some kind of exhortation. The utilitarian defence of the criterion thus depends on the prior assumption of its truth. (iii) Conventions are arbitrary, in the sense that we are at liberty to break them if we wish. But positivists do not regard the preference of science to metaphysics as a convention in this sense. To be sure, they have sometimes written as if it were. 'It is indeed open to anyone,' wrote Professor Ayer, 'to adopt a different criterion of meaning and so produce an alternative definition which may very well correspond to one of the ways in which the word "meaning" is commonly used.' 'Nevertheless,' he continued, 'I think that, unless it satisfied the principle of verification, it would not be capable of being understood in the sense in which either scientific hypotheses or common sense statements are habitually understood.'[1] In the light of this last sentence, it seems plain enough that the proposal about usage offered by positivists was not one that we were really at liberty to take or leave. They were informing us how 'scientific or common sense statements are habitually understood', and the alternative we were free to take was in truth the privilege of talking nonsense. (iv) The reading of their criterion as a convention only was quite inconsistent with the importance they commonly attached to their programme. It is of no great moment that the word 'meaningfulness' should be used in a certain way, if no issues of truth or falsity are raised by that usage. What aroused so much apprehension among the metaphysicians and theologians was not a mere proposal about language. They were excited about what was put forward as a 'revolution in philosophy', based on the conviction that the metaphysicians of the past, from Plato to McTaggart, had in fact been talking nonsense. If this was what the positivists meant, it was idle to insist that they were offering merely a recommendation about usage. On the other hand, if such a recommendation were really all they had to offer, the 'revolution' was a teapot affair.

47. (b) The new criterion was thus self-destructive. There was no status in the positivist theory of knowledge which it could consistently

[1] *Language, Truth and Logic*, 2nd ed., 16.

be accorded, since it resisted interpretation as empirical, as a priori, or as conventional. Nor was this the only obstacle that the criterion placed in its own path. It assumed that you could tell by looking into your own thought or intention what it was that you meant, and by such a scrutiny could separate the empirical sheep from the metaphysical goats. But what sort of scrutiny is this? What does an empirical sheep look like? The object referred to through such a meaning is clear enough; it is some experienceable sense datum or group of such data. But what of the mental content, the idea or judgment, by employing which we bring to light the object intended? What is that like? It is of course different from that object itself. To be sure, the positivists often talked as if it were not, as if the meaning entertained in the mind were identical with the object meant, as if the idea *were* the sense data that would verify it. But obviously in any statement about past and future this could not be true, since the reference occurred at one time and the observations, or observable facts, at another. The self-inspection by which the reference was brought to light must be different in both nature and object from the process of verifying that reference. Was it an empirical process at all?

The positivists' struggles over this are matter for tragi-comedy. Their general doctrine was that only those factual statements were to be admitted as meaningful that referred to the sort of fact apprehensible through sense, the 'here-blue' sort of facts reported in the atomic statements of Wittgenstein and the 'protocollsätze' of Carnap; to say that something existed, as Ayer put it, was equivalent to saying that certain sensations were obtainable.[1] But it is clear that you do not discover by *sensation* what your meanings are, for however sensible Napoleon or the polar ice may be, the thought of them is something that cannot be sensed at all.

48. The positivists were therefore driven to the most desperate expedients to deal with this process of meaning-inspection. They declined to use the term 'judgment', used by such logicians as Bradley and Bosanquet, since that carried an aura of the purely mental which seemed to them perilous. 'Proposition' tempted them, since it was used by such eminent exponents of their favoured extensional logic as Russell, but it too was regarded with suspicion, since it named what was unobservable. A proposition is not a sentence, but something expressed by a sentence; the same proposition might be expressed in a variety of sentences, couched in different languages,

[1] *Language, Truth and Logic,* 49.

but it was not itself identical with any of them. It was a non-sensible entity deeply tainted with metaphysics. Russell himself suggested that a proposition might be defined consistently with empiricism as a class of synonymous sentences. But it was hard to define 'synonymous' except by reference to a similar meaning, and that took the empiricist back to the sort of entity he was trying to avoid. Carnap suggested that a proposition could be distinguished from a sentence as that which was designated by sentences that were logically equivalent. But according to his variety of logic, two sentences, p and q, were logically equivalent to each other if it were self-contradictory to assert p and deny q. The two sentences, then, 'That figure is a circle' and 'That figure is the smallest figure that could be drawn with a perimeter of equal length', are logically equivalent. But they clearly do not express the same proposition. Worn down by the tension of having to talk about meanings which were not observable entities, unable to talk, without prickings of their puritanical empiricist consciences, about ideas or judgments or propositions, the positivists succumbed to talking about sentences. These at least could be seen if written and heard if said. Even so sensible a person as Miss Stebbing, no positivist herself, began to say that what the analyst was analysing was sentences;[1] and Carnap talked uninhibitedly of sentences as true and false, as deducible and implying, as consistent with each other or contradicting each other.

About all of this we can only say, as John Wisdom frankly did, that 'it is nonsense to talk of analysing sentences'.[2] A string of visible marks or audible sounds is not true or false, nor could it conceivably imply or contradict another such string. It may be replied that there is no claim that the sentence itself can do these things, but only the sentence as interpreted. But that too is inaccurate. For it is not the string of marks, even when interpreted, that implies or contradicts; it is something that these marks serve to express. A wholly different string of marks would serve the purpose equally well, and many cognitions in the form of recognition and perception take place without the use of sentences at all. Indeed the resort to sentences is in our minds a confession of bankruptcy. The logic of it is as follows: to analyse meaning, in the sense in which philosophers used the term, involved referring to the scientifically unobservable. All that was observable about the act or process of meaning was its sensible expression. Since, according to the criterion, 'meaning' must refer to the observable if it was to be significant, meaning must be equated

[1] *Mind*, 1933, 351.
[2] *Philosophy and Psychoanalysis*, 16.

with this expression. The conclusion was unavoidable if the premises were sound. Unhappily, to accept that conclusion was to escape from the frying-pan into the fire. Instead of taking the obvious course of recognizing that thought is not a sensible object at all, and therefore abandoning the premise which would confine significant reference to such objects, the positivists remorselessly drew their impossible conclusion and tried hard to conform to it. They did not want to talk about thought. Their attitude towards this process was curiously like that of Dr Watson a generation earlier, who reported that he had never found such a thing in his test-tubes. They were talking, they insisted, about sentences. Thus arose the dreary flood of sentences about sentences that has threatened to drown philosophy under its spreading inundation.

49. One way of preventing this result is to give up the demand that the experience required to verify a statement should be sense experience.[1] It may equally well be the experience of introspection. If the requirement is widened in this way, we are told, the determination of meaning is provided for. Such a widening is of course to be welcomed. But we have two hesitations about it. (i) The determination of meaning is not really a process of introspection in the sense of a Lockean 'idea of reflection', i.e. an inner perception, or awareness of a psychical process. It is not like the consciousness of having a headache or feeling tired. The attempt in a Socratic dialogue to capture what one means by 'justice' or 'courage' is a process of conceptual analysis very unlike what Titchener, for example, would have accepted as an introspective report. (ii) Hence if experience is to be so widened as to include such processes, it must go beyond anything that is naturally called perception or observation. And then what is the point, one wonders, of Wittgenstein's reduction of factual statements to atoms of the 'here-blue' pattern, of the emphasis on protocol statements, of Ayer's definition of other minds in terms of his own 'sense-contents', of the physicalism of Neurath, of Carnap's reduction of everything existent to that which has position in space, indeed of the constant insistence on empirical observation? The value of the test was supposed to lie in its eliminative power, which was certainly considerable so long as experience meant sense experience. If that is abandoned, on what principle is an 'experience' to be admitted? If Socrates's insight into what he means by justice is an experience, is Plotinus's 'experience' of the One an experience, or George Fox's of an inner light, or G. E. Moore's of a non-natural

[1] This course is taken by Professor Pap, *Elements of Analytic Philosophy*, 340.

goodness? If these are rejected, as they presumably would be, on the ground that no such objects can be experienced, it is purely sense experience that is being made the test, whatever the protestations to the contrary. On the other hand, if these are admitted as the sort of experiences they claim to be, positivism has become so latitudinarian as to stand for nothing distinctive.

50. (c) There is a third way in which the verifiability criterion of meaning cancelled itself. It could give no account of the process of verification. What do we mean by verifying a statement? We say today that on June 24th next we shall see an eclipse of the sun, and on that day we see it. But the process of verification does not consist of seeing merely. The least that is required for the process is the recognition that this is the experience I meant and that having it makes my prediction true. That is, I must grasp a peculiar kind of relation between my prediction and that which verifies it, in this case the relation of truth. What this relation is it is notoriously hard to say. Professor Tarski offered a 'semantic conception of truth' to the effect that 'I shall see X' is true if, and only if, it is the case that I shall see X. Yes, of course; no one would deny that. But what one wants to know is what sort of relation subsists between the judgment (it is mere confusion to talk about the sentence) that I shall see X and the actual seeing of X. Carnap adopted the expedient of identifying a true proposition with the fact of which it is true.[1] But that which is true is something present to me now, while the fact to which this refers, and of which it is true, has yet to come into existence. And what is to be done with false propositions, which are false because there is *no* fact answering to them? Carnap meets this by saying that though the proposition as a whole is not to be identified with any fact, its terms may be identified severally with the properties referred to. But this will not do either, for if the terms are conjoined in the proposition while not conjoined in the fact, the fact and the proposition must be different. The various positivist expedients to escape the plain conclusion that here we have a relation between a non-sensible reality and what is at times, though not always, a sensible one—the expedients of reducing judgments and propositions to sentences, of identifying proposition with fact, of denying that there is any problem in the nature of truth, etc.—all seem to me to fail, either through misconceiving the nature of that which is true, or through making inconceivable its relation to that which verifies it. It is the latter failure that we are here stressing. Between our

[1] *Meaning and Necessity*, 30.

present judgment and the observations that may verify it, which may be far removed from the judgment in space and time, there is a relation that is not verifiable by any sort of sense experience, but can be apprehended only by intelligence. To see that this which is before us is what we meant, and that the experience of it confirms what we meant, is to lay hold of a relation that is as essential in the positivist theory of knowledge as in any other, but which is unprovided for in its lexicon of permissible terms. According to the criterion, only those statements are to be admitted that could be verified by observation. But that leaves the phrase 'verified in observation' meaningless, for such verification, and the relation employed in verifying, can never themselves be observed. The positivist can never meaningfully say that any prediction is verified or any statement true.

51. There is a further difficulty that has so far resisted every positivist attempt to overcome it. What about hypothetical statements? It is important not to forget these, since the standard way, on positivist principles, of dealing with categorical statements about the absent is to turn them into hypotheticals; 'there is snow at the North Pole' becomes 'if I were to go to the North Pole and make the appropriate observations, I should experience something white, cold, etc.' Though we have argued that the translation does not exhaust what the original intends, there is no doubt that this hypothetical statement itself can be verified. But does that hold of hypotheticals generally? Suppose I say, 'If I went to the North Pole, I should see snow there', but do not go. How can I, or anyone else, verify what I should have seen under conditions that never were realized? One way to meet the difficulty is to translate the statement into 'All observers who go to the North Pole see snow there'; but these statements are not the same, for while the second or more general statement entails the first, the first does not entail the second. Indeed the verification of a contrary-to-fact conditional of this sort is a logical impossibility. For the statement is equivalent to 'If I were in a position to observe something, which I am not, I should observe X'; and one cannot maintain that something is observable, while in the same breath denying the conditions of observability to be fulfilled. Such conditional statements must, therefore, be meaningless. But this is absurd. The meaningfulness of a statement cannot depend in this way on what the speaker happens later to do. We cannot say that if he decides to go to the Pole, his statement has meaning, whereas if he fails to go, precisely the same statement must be set down as meaningless. Obviously the statement is equally meaningful whether he goes or not. Once again meaning and verifiability turn out to be different things.[1]

52. The mass of difficulties encountered in this search for a criterion of meaningfulness is bound to raise the question whether the search itself is well advised. I must confess to grave doubts whether it is. For one thing it is questionable in point of logic. If anyone proposes a test of meaningfulness, the natural way of appraising it is surely the way we have adopted, of adducing assorted propositions that we know to be meaningful and asking whether on the test proposed their meaningfulness would be recognized. But this implies that the test must itself be tested by propositions seen to be meaningful without it. The criterion must conform to a prior meaningfulness; the meaningfulness does not wait on endorsement by the criterion. And obviously the question whether the criterion itself is meaningful can hardly be decided by appeal to itself, for that would be circular; it must be settled by inspection. An objector might say that such inspection was possible only through the application of a criterion already implicitly present. This may be true, but any attempt to define that criterion before all types of case have been reviewed is dangerous, for the definition rests on case law; it must be derived from what is found meaningful in individual cases, and cannot be settled a priori.

In the fixing of a criterion of meaningfulness there is this further practical danger, which has been amply illustrated already, that it is likely to involve the exclusion of many genuine insights. It may be little more than the crystallization of parochial experience or of imperfect sympathies. The man who would bring everything to the test of sense experience feels that he is only formulating a requirement of clear thinking, whereas in assigning all the greater rationalists and mystics to the discard, he is more probably revealing the narrow walls within which he lives. Of course empiricism has no monopoly of such narrowness. There was a time when rationalism was in the ascendant and everything must be brought to the test of the 'clear and distinct perception' of the mathematician. The result was on the one hand an attempt to force all knowledge of fact into this rigid framework and on the other to degrade it into second-class knowledge. But the a priorists of recent years have been the empiricists; it

[1] Cf. I. Berlin, 'Verification', *Proc. of Arist. Soc.*, Vol. 39 (1938–39), 235 ff. On logical empiricist principles, 'an assertion such as "If a body moved at the velocity of light, its length would be zero, its mass infinite, and a clock attached to it would stand still" cannot possibly be true, since it fails to correspond to any situation in actual fact'. Marie C. Swabey, *Logic and Nature*, 108.

is they who have taken their stand at the passes of the Jordan and insisted on their shibboleth. We have agreed that this insistence has led to more clarity of speech. But it has furthered a lamentable contraction of philosophers' sympathies and interests. They have said little of importance for decades about problems of politics or aesthetics, for example, and the interest in metaphysics is only slowly making its way back into life and respectability. To continue saying that speculation in these fields is meaningless or a matter of words is to impose a bar to progress.

53. It is time we brought this long review to a close. In appearance it has been almost wholly negative. We have had marching before us a procession of theories; we have inspected each as it passed; and we have refused with monotonous regularity to grant them the credentials they sought. But our result is only in appearance negative. The truly negative attitudes are those we have been reviewing, those of critics who would deny to philosophy the right to pursue its ancient calling, critics who set down as pseudo-problems issues of concern to plain men and philosophers alike, and the answers to them as meaningless. To show such criticisms mistaken is not a merely negative undertaking. If successful, it might open the gates again to speculative reason. This is what we have attempted, however fumblingly, to do. If our strictures are well taken, the regions of speculation that the empiricist criteria of meaning sought to close are still open, though they must be entered more warily than before. There is no reason why we should not think and speak meaningfully of the self, of other minds, and, whether or not it exists, of a divine mind. We can freely think of non-sensible relations—of implication, of likeness and difference, of time, of causality; we can reflect upon whether causality involves implication and whether the world is therefore a necessary system. We can discuss responsibly the new world of science with its unsensed waves and particles, and its imperceptible laws. We can talk of numbers, finite and infinite, and of existing things that no one has ever perceived or even thought of. We need not dismiss freedom as a matter of words, or rule out immortality as unthinkable, and we may be able to follow Plato and Aquinas with some understanding as they speculate about creation. We can still debate the meaning of goodness and justice without fear that they will be ruled out as senseless because non-sensible. It is of course no part of our task to propose answers to these old problems, but merely to ask whether they are meaningful and therefore still worth pursuing. And to that question we think we have found the answer. They are.

CHAPTER VI

ANALYSIS AND A PRIORI KNOWLEDGE

1. Reason, in the sense of reasoning, is of course the main instrument of philosophy. The reasoning that has been offered has been commonly regarded as conclusive or demonstrative, and not of the merely probable kind that must serve in the natural sciences. 'All daffodils I have seen have been yellow, so the ones I have still to see will probably also be yellow'; refinements apart, the generalizations of natural science all rest on reasoning of this type, and none of them are certain, in the sense that we can see them to be necessarily true. But philosophers have sought certainty, and have commonly believed themselves to have an instrument that would provide it. This instrument is a priori thinking. The philosopher who may have discovered it, Pythagoras, was convinced that he had found the key to the nature of things, and its power seems to have left him intoxicated with wonder and delight. Nor was its use confined to an intellectual élite. Socrates was convinced that the faculty for it was present in all men, even in the untutored slave boy of the *Meno*, and that the education of this faculty was the supreme requisite not only for the philosopher, but also for the statesman. In documents that provided the first large-scale exhibition of it, the Platonic dialogues, Plato undertook to show how the new tool could be used both to direct conduct and to give insight into the permanent structure of the world.

2. Until the time of Aristotle no attempt was made to isolate the reasoning process, to put it under the lens and examine it systematically. Aristotle made up handsomely for this neglect. In what is perhaps the only passage in which he permits himself any praise of his own work, he says that while other sciences had been built up by slow accretion, he had succeeded in bringing logic into being whole. He believed that in the syllogism he had the true design of the instrument which Plato had been using with such impressive effect in the dialogues. His analysis seemed to make clear that we possess at least three distinguishable types of rational or necessary insight. Take the argument that since whatever has shape has size, and every particle of matter has shape, it has size also. (1) We can see that if the premises are true, the conclusion *must* be true. This kind of insight is present whenever, in the strict sense, we reason at all; reasoning *is* passage along such a line of necessity. (2) But of course one may draw the conclusion from such premises without being a logician, for the logician is the man who makes it his specialty to study the principles implicit in our reasonings, and to set them out distinctly. For example, there are thousands of arguments with the same form as the one just given. The logician isolates that form. In this case it turns out to be, 'If A is a B, and B is a C, then A is a C'. What guarantees *it*? Aristotle replied that it was simply self-evident or necessarily true. Here then is a second guise in which necessity appears; the principles of reasoning are themselves necessary truths. (3) But what about the major premise from which we started, 'Whatever has shape has size'? We cannot rely on the conclusion unless we can take this as true, but how do we know it is true? Aristotle held that here was a third place where necessity appeared. Sometimes we can see, either directly or with the help of such examples as geometers put on blackboards, that one character or property entails another, that shape, though a different property from size, carries size with it, not sometimes or usually, but always and of necessity.

3. As philosophy developed, forms of necessity were recognized that seemed to be different from any of these, such as those involved in Augustine's ontological argument, Descartes's 'I think, therefore I am', and the deductions in Hegel's logic, in which a fragment of a whole seems to necessitate other fragments and ultimately the whole itself. Many of the new forms were either mere mistakes or veiled forms of the original three. But we shall not concern ourselves with the question how many forms of necessity there are; we are concerned with the more fundamental question whether in our thought about the world there is any necessity at all. There can be no doubt what the main tradition in philosophy and theology has taught. It has followed the Greek conception outlined in our second chapter, that an extensive knowledge of the nature of things is open to us by necessary reasoning either from empirical fact or from statements that are self-evident. Aquinas depended on such reasoning in his proofs of the existence of God. Descartes believed that, starting with his 'cogito', he could deduce both the existence of the Creator and the structure of the created world. Spinoza believed that the world was a

single substance, and that, starting with the definition of this substance, one could deduce in geometrical fashion innumerable facts
about the nature of things. Leibniz had no less confidence in reason.
For him the world consisted, to be sure, not of one but of countless
substances or monads. But the history of each of these was self-
enclosed and logically determined in detail, so that if we grasped the
nature of Alexander, for example, we could in principle deduce the
occurrence of every battle he fought and every word he said. The
extent to which the great philosophers have relied on necessary
reasoning has varied greatly. Hume tried to dispense with it altogether. At the other extreme, McTaggart employed it so exclusively
that there were only two points in his entire system where he felt
called upon to rely on empirical fact. But then Hume's abjuring of
such reasoning meant scepticism about all that was not immediately
given. Few of the theologians and probably none of the philosophers
who have arrived at conclusions going beyond their own experience
have not at some time or other, and usually very often, appealed to
rational insight into the nature or structure of things. After all,
philosophy is an attempt to think logically about the world; and
unless the logic that governs our thinking answers to the way in
which the world is put together, why attempt by any effort of thought
to trace the lines of the world order?

4. Nevertheless our power to lay hold of necessary connections, so
constantly appealed to by philosophers, has proved a standing
puzzle for them. The difficulty has been a little like that raised for
the biologists by the apparent heredity of acquired characters. If
these really are inherited, there must be some mechanism by which
changes in the mature body can effect corresponding changes in the
sperm or ovum which determines the next generation; and if
biologists deny such inheritance, it is largely because of the difficulty
of seeing how this influence could possibly be exerted. Similarly of
our knowledge of necessity. We have the appropriate organs for
seeing colours, and hearing sounds, and feeling hards and softs; but
is there in addition a faculty of pure intellect, which, without evident
bodily organs, somehow lays hold of the network of chains connecting
these qualities? Before accepting such a view, perhaps it would be
best to examine the chains. There may be nothing necessary about
them, and if so, we shall be saved the trouble of accepting this
strange faculty. Philosophers who have attempted the examination
have unfortunately not agreed about the nature of these connections,
or therefore about the nature of a priori insight. If we dismiss such

quaint and half-serious views as Socrates's theory of reminiscence, which held that we acquired such insight in a former life, but neglected to explain how we came by it in that life, there are four positions of major importance about the nature of this insight.

5. (*a*) First, there is the traditional view of the rationalists. They held that it was a mere misreporting of fact to reduce the elements that composed experience to greens and reds, hots and colds, and other such data open to the senses. These were there, of course, but they were neither the only elements of experience nor the most important of them. There were also concepts or universals. Besides this given green, there was greenness, which all greens had in common, and colour, which all colours had in common, and quality, which all qualities had in common; and none of these universals were open to any of the senses. Besides the right-angled triangle on paper before me there is the right-angled triangle *as such*, of which this is only one of endless instances. And starting with the concept of a right-angled triangle, we can deduce a great many properties of it by purely demonstrative reasoning. These properties and the links that connect them with the triangle and with each other are not inventions of ours, but discoveries; men discovered them as truly as they discovered Antarctica or the Pleiades; they are realities in precisely the same sense as the triangle from which they are deduced. Most rationalists have been realists about necessary knowledge, even when they were idealists about what the world was made of. They believed that rational knowledge was a direct apprehension of the way in which the timeless universals that in some sense lay behind the changing order of things were necessarily linked together.

6. (*b*) The second theory, offered by Kant, turned the tables on the first. It was one of the most daring and dramatic ventures in the history of thought. Kant started from mathematics, which he regarded as typical of rational knowledge. If there was anything in the world he was certain of, it was the propositions of the multiplication table—for example, that seven and five are twelve; he was perfectly certain that even if he were transported to some remote planet, he would still find this true. How was such certainty to be explained? He thought, as we have earlier seen, that the most plausible way to account for it was to say that we impose the rational order upon things, not that they impose it upon us. Automatically and because of the constitution of our minds, we arrange what is given in sense in numerical order and geometrical pattern. The relations within these orders are necessary; Kant accepted that as fully as any rationalist; indeed he is often counted as a rationalist himself. But there is a deep difference between his view and that of the rationalism just referred to. For to say that necessity is imposed by our own mind is after all to commit oneself to scepticism. If all logic and mathematics, and as Kant went on to say, all our necessary reasoning about time, space, and causality, are only projections on a screen of the framework of our own mind, direct access to things as they are seems to be cut off. Between us and the real world a veil is interposed, and all our efforts to go behind it by refining our logic or enlarging our systems leave us still on the hither side of it. Reason in all its forms, whether those of space and time, or of the categories of the understanding, or the so-called 'ideas of pure reason', is a web of our own weaving, which instead of revealing reality to us, hides it from us impenetrably.

7. (c) The third account of necessary knowledge is that of traditional empiricism. It was worked out by a succession of clear-headed British thinkers from Locke through Hume and Mill to Spencer. It is the simplest of all the theories. It holds that the 'necessities' of our rational thinking are really habits. If every daffodil we see is yellow, we shall expect others to be yellow, and shall come in time to think that it belongs to the nature of daffodils to be yellow, so that a blue or purple daffodil would be a shock. Now take a habit of longer life and suppose that no exception ever occurs. We may have experienced fire every day of our lives, with never a case where the fire was not hot. After such a run of experiences, the suggestion of a fire that is not hot will seem an absurdity. Now extend the life of this habit through the history of the race. Suppose that a connection is presented many times a day, not merely to ourselves but to all our ancestors for thousands of generations, without a single exception in these untold millions of cases; what sort of connection will establish itself in our thought? A connection so firm, the empiricists answered, as to be unbreakable. A fire that is not hot will seem like a contradiction. The habit of regarding a straight line as the shortest line, or of two lines as unable to enclose a space, will have fixed itself so firmly that an exception will seem not only absurd but impossible.

Unfortunately this theory too entails scepticism, and of a more radical kind than Kant's. To be sure, Kant did not believe that the necessities in our thinking reflected any like necessities among things in themselves, but he at least accepted necessity as holding among our experiences of things. Even this, according to the British empiricists, is an illusion. Necessity, said Huxley, 'does not lie in the observed facts, and has no warranty that I can discover elsewhere. For my part I utterly repudiate and anathematise the intruder. Fact I know, and Law I know; but what is this Necessity save an empty shadow of my mind's own throwing?'[1] It is an empty shadow because what looks like necessity is only habit, and there is nothing logical or self-evident about that; what has become fixed by mere association might in theory become unfixed. If the very laws of logic might have been different from what they are, then what they tell us, and what reasoning in accordance with them tells us, about the nature of the world is unreliable. It *may* be that the habits we have acquired in our little corner of the universe are an index to its nature everywhere and always. But it would be sheer good luck if that were so. For all we know, the world may be littered with round squares, and pairs of lines enclosing spaces, and sevens and fives that make thirteen, and other such surprises. If we cannot enjoy them, Spencer tells us in effect, it is because we and our fathers and their fathers have eaten sour grapes and the children's teeth have been set on edge.[2]

8. (*d*) We come now to the fourth account, that of contemporary logical empiricism. This view has been presented so persuasively as to have gained wide acceptance even from philosophers outside the school. It is a compromise between the rationalism of the first two views and the empiricism of the third. It agrees with Plato and Kant that we lay hold of genuinely necessary connections. These are not mere masks for firm association, as Mill and Spencer held; a necessary proposition is not merely one that is very, very probable. So far the positivists are on the side of the rationalists. But having said this, they add that empiricism is right on the point of philosophic importance, namely whether an insight of this kind can tell us anything about the world. They answer that it cannot; knowledge of the actual world comes exclusively from perception. But if necessary propositions say nothing about fact, what do they say? Here comes the essence of the present-day empiricist's contention. Such statements are reports of our own procedure in thinking and speaking. They reveal relations not between things, but between our own ideas or meanings. They provide an explication or analysis of what we mean by certain words. Far from being revelations of the eternal and immutable structure of things, as rationalists have supposed, they are

---

[1] *Methods*, etc., 161.
[2] The difficulties in this theory have been canvassed in my *The Nature of Thought*, II, Chap. 28.

the extreme opposite of this; they are conventions of our speech and thought, and thus alterable by our own will.

Everyone will recognize this as an extremely important contention. When first announced, it was accorded a chilly reception by most philosophers, for in reversing so completely an ancient conviction, accepted by the majority of philosophers, it seemed irresponsible and queer. It no longer seems so. How plausible it is will appear more clearly if we distinguish its main theses and set them out a little more fully. There seem to me to be four of these, all closely interconnected, yet different in what they stress. They are (I) that necessary statements are reports of linguistic usage; (II) that they represent conventions; (III) that they are analytic; (IV) that they say nothing about fact. Let us first get clear what these mean.

9. (I) Take a few necessary statements at random. All bachelors are unmarried; a straight line is the shortest line between two points; a material thing cannot be in two places at once. Positivists would say that these are all reports of linguistic usage. In the first case this seems even obvious; when we say 'all bachelors are unmarried', we are surely not declaring an insight into the connection of two attributes in nature; indeed there are no two attributes involved, for being a bachelor and being unmarried are the same thing. That, in fact, is what we are saying. We are saying that we use the word 'bachelor' and the phrase 'unmarried man' with the same reference, that if we applied one of them to a person, we should never think of denying the other. The statement 'A straight line is the shortest line' seems at first somehow different. Are we not asserting something true and important about lines in space when we say this? The positivist does not think so; he holds that in making the statement, we are merely explicating our use of 'straight'. If we ever came across a line that was not the shortest line between the points it connected, should we call it straight? Clearly not, and this again is what we mean to say. We are reporting that, in our usage, 'straight' and 'shortest' go together, in the sense that wherever we use one of them we should be ready to use the other. The third proposition above would seem hardest of all to interpret in the linguistic way, but the positivist would say that it is in the same position as the others. 'A material thing cannot be in two places at once.' Is this a profound and universal insight into what being a material thing entails? Not at all. It simply makes clear one of the conditions under which we should be prepared to use the words 'material thing'. If we were confronted with something—a universal, for example—that could be in two places at once, we should not think of calling it this. 'The question, "What is the nature of a material thing?"' says Professor Ayer, 'is, like any other question of that form, a linguistic question, being a demand for a definition. And the propositions which are set forth in answer to it are linguistic propositions, even though they may be expressed in such a way that they may seem to be factual. They are propositions about the relationship of symbols, and not about the properties of the things which the symbols denote.'[1]

10. (II) If this is true, it follows that necessary statements reflect conventions. For about 'the relationship of symbols' there is certainly nothing fixed and unalterable; we could, if we chose, make the symbol 'bachelor' interchangeable with 'married man' rather than 'unmarried man'; we could elect to call straight whatever other people called curved; and we could, if we cared to, reserve the words 'material thing' for exclusive reference to universals, ghosts, or angels. ' "The question is," said Alice, "whether you *can* make words mean so many different things." "The question is," said Humpty Dumpty, "which is to be master—that's all." ' Words are our servants, and we can use them as we wish. Necessary statements 'simply record our determination to use words in a certain fashion. We cannot deny them without infringing the conventions which are presupposed by our very denial, and so falling into self-contradiction. And this is the sole ground of their necessity. . . . It is perfectly conceivable that we should have employed different linguistic conventions from those which we do actually employ.'[2] This freedom applies not only to such words as we have just considered, but to the expressions of logic itself; we can redefine the word 'implies', for example, so as to render all syllogistic reasoning invalid and to install new forms in its place. In *The Logical Syntax of Language*, Carnap wrote: 'the view will be maintained that we have in every respect complete liberty with regard to the forms of language; that both the forms of construction of sentences and the rules of transformation (the latter usually designated as "postulates" and "rules of inference") may be chosen quite arbitrarily.'[3] In reading these remarks, we might easily fail to note how revolutionary they are. There is nothing particularly disturbing in hearing that the use of words is arbitrary, and most people would accept with equanimity the news that our

---

[1] *Language, Truth and Logic*, 2nd ed., 64–65.
[2] Ayer, *ibid.*, 84.
[3] P. xv. '*In der Logik gibt es keine moral.*' German ed., 44.

syntax—our pattern of sentence structure—may also be changed at will. But if there is anything unalterable at will, it would seem to be the laws of logic. Still, these laws are necessary statements, and if the empiricist view of necessary statements is true, it must apply to them too. Messrs Carnap and Ayer leave us in no doubt that it does. The laws of logic are themselves rules of language, and like other such rules, are conventions. 'The principles of logic and mathematics are true universally simply because we never allow them to be anything else.'[1]

11. (III) Necessary statements, according to positivists, are analytic. They merely explicate what we mean, and therefore give us nothing new. They may, to be sure, report insights that are new to the learner. When Hobbes, at the age of forty, came across the demonstrations of Euclid for the first time, he was so astonished at the results that he declared them impossible, though of course he accepted them on closer study; and there is perhaps none of us so shrewd that, wondering how much 28×37 is, and seeing the figure 1036, we could say at once, 'that is what I meant'. A positivist is not disquieted by such facts. When he says that a necessary proposition gives us nothing new, he means nothing *logically* new, not psychologically new. The fact that Hobbes was surprised by Euclid's results or that we are not prepared for the number 1036 does not show that these results are not in some sense contained in the primitive propositions with which geometry and arithmetic start; all it shows is that the person surprised is not clever enough to see what is contained in his own concepts. But what is meant by this weasel word 'contain'? Empiricists commonly explain it in one or other of three ways. (1) Sometimes they follow Kant. According to Kant a proposition is analytic when the predicate concept is a part of the subject concept; when we say that bodies are extended, we are saying nothing new, because being extended is part of what we mean by 'body'; our predicate merely makes explicit and underlines an element in the subject idea. But positivists usually prefer another way of explaining the lack of novelty in necessary statements, since many such statements do not have the subject-predicate form at all, such as 'Full brothers of the same man are full brothers of each other'. Here they prefer to say (2) that the proposition is analytic because its truth follows from the meaning of the terms alone. One needs nothing but the notion of brotherhood between differing men to see that this relation is transitive, that if it holds between A and B,

---

[1] Ayer, *op. cit.*, 77.

I

and B and C, it holds also between A and C. (3) Sometimes, however, this reference to the empirical content of terms and what one may be able to see about their relation strikes the positivist as still too psychological, and he looks for a more purely formal test. The true warrant of an analytic proposition, he suggests, is the law of contradiction; the contradictory of such a proposition will always turn out to be self-contradictory. Thus to say that something is a body and not extended is at once to affirm its extension (as part of what body means) and to deny it; if one admits that A is a full brother of B, and B of C, and yet refuses to admit that A is the brother of C, one finds oneself committed to denying one or both of the premises.

12. (IV) Besides being linguistic, conventional, and analytic, necessary propositions are held to be non-factual; that is, they say nothing about nature, nothing about the realm of existent things and events. 'They none of them provide any information about any matter of fact. In other words, they are entirely devoid of factual content. And, it is for this reason that no experience can confute them.'[1] This last remark is important. It is true and startling that no experience could confute an a priori statement; but why? Kant had a way of accounting for it, but, for the positivists, this way consisted of burning down the house to get roast pig; the fact can surely be explained without making the whole of nature a construct of mind. If nothing experience can offer will ever confute us, they would say, it is because such statements are not about experience at all, or anything given in experience. In saying that seven plus five are twelve, we are not talking about things, but meanings; we are reporting that what we mean by 'seven plus five' is the same as what we mean by 'twelve'. If someone points out that seven lambs added to five lions do not necessarily make twelve, we see at once that this is no exception to what we meant, though it may take a moment to see why it is irrelevant; it is really a causal, not a numerical statement. The only relevant doubt would be whether someone might some day discover a collection that numbered seven plus five but was also not twelve; but this doubt itself would rest on a confusion. We should be confusing the question 'What is the actual number of the collection?' (which could be settled by counting again) with the quite different question whether what is meant by seven and five could be different from what is meant by twelve, and supposing that because the first is doubtful, the second may be doubtful too. But about the second, once clearly distinguished, there can be no doubt. We know that if

[1] Ayer, *op. cit.*, 79.

there are seven plus five, there *must* be twelve, for by the two terms we *mean* the same. No observations of things or events could affect this identity of meaning. That is why the statement is beyond confutation.

13. This account of a priori knowledge is ingenious, plausible, and extremely important. It is important because, if true, it effectively discredits the main instrument of speculative philosophy and theology, and also many of what were supposed to be their self-evident conclusions. We have seen that the main instrument of metaphysicians from Plato to McTaggart has been reason, conceived as revealing the nature of things. In the positivist conception of reason, the necessity of an insight is no guarantee that it applies to nature or reveals anything outside the confines of meaning. Again, many of the questions raised by philosophers have received answers that, once understood, were supposed to be seen as self-evident and necessary. 'What is matter?', as answered by Berkeley, 'what is mind?', as answered by Bosanquet, 'what is causality?', as answered by McTaggart, 'what is justice, or piety, or courage?', as answered by Plato—these and countless other insights have been offered as at once self-evidencing and as revelatory of the constitution of things. They were supposed to tell us not only what words mean, but what things are. If positivism is right about necessity, this is a mistaken pretension. And indeed it may be so. One of the worst dangers in philosophical and theological thinking, as in political thinking, is professional self-justification. That a new theory would find us with our occupation gone is no argument against it. A great many occupations obviously ought to go, since their ends and assumptions conflict with those of others, and both sets cannot be right. What the philosopher is called upon to do if his methods are questioned is not to fly incontinently to their defence, but to examine as objectively as he can the proposals offered in their place. This is what we shall try to do.

A word of assurance may be in order: this is not a threshing of last year's straw. Anyone who attempts to appraise a position held by analytic philosophers must be prepared for the comment, 'But that position has now been abandoned', a comment that is often justified, since philosophy in recent decades has been moving with inordinate speed. But the comment would here be inept. For the positivist view of a priori knowledge, unlike some other positivist theories, has been taken over by the majority of analytic philosophers; indeed it is regarded by many of them as hardly worth discussing for a reason the very opposite of that just noted, namely that it has been so conclusively established. Whether it has or has not we are about to inquire. But however the inquiry may turn out, it will not be an autopsy on a dogma that is dead.

14. I. The first of the positivist's contentions about necessary propositions is that they are in some sense statements about language. 'They call attention to linguistic usages, of which we might otherwise not be conscious . . .'; 'they simply record our determination to use words in a certain fashion'; 'although they give us no information about any empirical situation, they do enlighten us by illustrating the way in which we use certain symbols'. Even when they seem to answer factual questions like 'What is the nature of a material thing?', 'they are propositions about the relationship of symbols, and not about the properties of the things which the symbols denote'.[1]

Though statements of this kind are scattered through the literature of logical empiricism, they are ambiguous. Those just repeated certainly sound like statements about how words are in fact used. In one of them, however, a different suggestion enters. Necessary propositions 'simply record our determination to use words in a certain fashion'; is it the fact or the resolution that is here recorded? Positivists would now generally take the latter view. But since both views have been insisted upon, we shall do well to leave neither unexamined. Let us look first, then, at the view that necessary statements are records of actual usage. 'A straight line is the shortest line' tells us that the two adjectives are commonly applied to the same thing; 'blue is a colour' tells us that people do not use the first word in situations where they would refuse to use the second.

Now the most obvious criticism of this view is that it is inconsistent with some of the central teachings of positivism on this very head. Doctrine No. IV, as given above, is that necessary propositions say nothing about fact. The present thesis is that they do say something about fact; they report facts of actual linguistic usage. It is clear that both theses cannot be true. Doctrine No. III is that all necessary propositions are analytic. But it is clear that statements about how words, that is certain marks or sounds, are used by myself or others are not analytic in any sense of the term; they are one and all synthetic. Such contradictions are so obvious that one can only suppose that the dictum, 'necessary truths are statements about usage', is not intended to mean quite what it says.

[1] Ayer, *op. cit.*, 84, 79, 65.

15. Consider too that usage is always English usage, or French or Swahili or some other particular usage; there is no usage *überhaupt*. But when a person talks about the colour red, he is clearly not talking about the use of the English word 'red'. He would recognize that what he is referring to would be the same if he spoke German and said *rot*, or French and said *rouge*. And if he is not talking about words when he uses 'red', neither is he talking about sentences when he says 'red is a colour'. For sentences, like words, are English or French or German, and he is clearly not discussing those of a particular language only. What he means to say could be expressed equally well by '*rot ist eine Farbe*' or '*le rouge est une couleur*'. It is clear, then, that since he is not talking about the usages of any particular language or set of languages, he is not talking about usage at all, but about something that could be equally well referred to in any number of languages, namely the colour red and its characteristics.

The difficulties of supposing that necessary statements are statements about usage come out very clearly when one takes as illustrations the principles of logic. The law of contradiction will then be some such statement as that it is uncustomary in a given language to conjoin a certain subject with a certain predicate both by 'is' and 'is not'. This is a straightforward doctrine. But it has little in common with what logicians mean by the law of contradiction. Indeed

'a case might be made out that "formal" for the logician means just the opposite of what it means for Carnap. It means that the relations between propositions described in logic hold *irrespective* of the language in which the propositions are expressed. A proposition imples the negative of its contradictory in Chinese as in French, in Hindustani as in Arabic, in German as in English. Logic is formal precisely because it disregards linguistic factors in its concern for generality.'[1]

But there are difficulties more obvious still with the view that necessary statements record facts of usage. If my statement that red is a colour did record common usage, it could be refuted by discoveries about that usage. If I were working in a school for the blind, I might discover that, to those around me, 'red' meant a kind of sound; one recalls the case of the blind man who, when he achieved his sight, said that what red was most like in his former experience was the sound of a trumpet. But would the discovery that people around me attached a different meaning to 'red is a colour' affect

[1] H. Ruja, *Journal of Philosophy*, XXXIII, 396.

what I meant by it, or the truth of what I meant? Not in the least. One does not refute a statement about red by a statement about a mark or a noise; the second is simply irrelevant to the first. Again, suppose I were talking about usage and saying that people in fact used the mark or noise, 'red', to refer to a visual quality—perhaps of the sort one could see in yonder billiard ball. Would it make sense for someone to reply, 'Not so, for red is at one end of the spectrum'? The remark would be silly, for it does not bear on the same subject. The word 'red' and the colour red are utterly different things.

16. The reader may wonder why positivists have so often insisted on speaking of words or expressions rather than ideas or concepts, and sentences rather than judgments, statements, or propositions. One gathers that a word is a sound or a mark, and that a sentence is a succession of these, and yet that these successions of sounds or marks can be true or false, or entail or contradict each other. The chief reason for this odd usage seems to lie in the positivist theory of meaning. A word or a sentence is something whose existence you can verify; ideas, judgments, and propositions are not sensibly verifiable at all, and to talk about them is to introduce an unpleasant suggestion of metaphysics. But unfortunately a sentence must be in some particular language, such as English or Hittite; and it is perfectly plain that necessary propositions such as 'red is a colour' or 'two straight lines do not enclose a space', are not statements about English or Hittite sentences. How were the positivists to hold at once that necessary statements had to do with the use of language and also that they had a universality independent of any particular language?

Carnap hit upon what looked like a middle road. He suggested that this was a lowest common denominator of the grammars of all languages, an abstract quintessential syntax common to all tongues. Pure syntax, he explained, does not deal with this or that language; it concerns itself 'with the possible forms of sentences, without regard either to the designs of the words of which the sentences are composed, or to whether any of the sentences exist on paper somewhere in the world'.[1] For syntactical study, 'the meaning of the words is quite inessential to the purpose, and need not be known'. 'For instance, given an appropriate rule, it can be proved that the word series "Pirots karulize elatically" is a sentence, provided only that "Pirots" is known to be a substantive (in the plural), "karulize" a verb (in the third person plural), and "elatically" an adverb . . .'[2]

[1] *The Logical Syntax of Language*, 7.
[2] *Ibid.*, 2.

Syntax might then include a classification of the various kinds of symbol in general use, such as substantives, verbs, and adverbs, the rules for combining them into sentences, and the rules for transforming these sentences again into equivalent sentences.

This is a possible undertaking. But if the definitions and rules were arbitrary, the new syntax would provide nothing more than the code of a rather pointless game. If they were inductively arrived at, they would not conform to the rest of the positivist programme. For the rules of syntax would now be empirical generalizations whose reference would be to sensible fact. That such generalizations could not be warranted by any observations open to us is plain enough, but let that pass. Suppose they could be so warranted; what would they be about? They would be about the classification and combination into 'structures' or 'orders' of meaningless marks. Now if these structures are of the kind commonly called sensible, the sort of relations that consist of one squiggle being to the right of another on a page, they will certainly not suffice as the subject-matter of logic or syntax. Logic deals with such relations as subject and predicate, syntax with such relations as substantive and verb. These relations are not present among squiggles as such. Before we can deal with the syntax of 'pirots karulize', we must know, as Carnap agrees, that a 'pirot' stands for a substantive and 'karulize' stands for something that a substantive does. But then the words are *not* meaningless. Furthermore, the relations they hold to each other are relations they sustain only through the relations of what they stand for; we could not recognize that two marks were noun and verb to each other unless we went beyond them to the substantive they refer to and its behaviour. It is idle to deal with words except through their meanings. Indeed words without meanings are not strictly words at all. Now are these relations among the objects meant, in virtue of which syntax among words becomes possible, always *sensible* relations? 'Red is a colour.' Here the relation between the terms signified is that of a species to its genus. Is that grasped through any of the senses? Plainly not. It is grasped in a different manner, through what used to be called intelligence. Nevertheless it is a relation that holds in fact. Thus the positivist is caught on the horns of one of those dilemmas that seem fairly to hedge him round. If his linguistic propositions deal with sensible marks merely, words and sentences devoid of meaning, they are not even statements about syntax. If they deal with syntax proper, they have gone beyond the sensible to the structures symbolized, which, contrary to his main contentions, may be at once necessary, factual, and non-sensible.

17. Enough, then, of the view that a priori statements are statements about the syntax of any existing language, or of language generally. Positivists seem to have held this view only intermittently when, recognizing that a priori propositions may be true, and recalling their own insistence that what is true must be true of the empirically given, they looked round somewhat helplessly for anything else of which the truth of such propositions could be plausibly alleged. They would all now agree, I believe, that this is not very plausible, and would regard a priori statements rather as expressing resolutions, or injunctions. 'I think,' wrote Professor Ayer in 1936, 'that our view must be that what are called a priori propositions do not describe how words are actually used, but merely prescribe how words are to be used. They make no statement whose truth can be accepted or denied. They merely lay down a rule which can be followed or disobeyed.'[1]

Is this the true account of these statements? Surely not. (*a*) A priori statements, the positivists would agree, are necessary. Rules of usage, they would also agree, have no necessity whatever; 'we have in every respect complete liberty', wrote Carnap, 'with regard to the forms of language.' To hold at once that such propositions are necessary and also that they are arbitrary prescriptions about usage is thus self-contradictory. It may be replied that the necessity and the freedom fall in different steps, that 'red is a colour' is necessary, but only because we have already defined 'red' so as to make it entail colour, and that it is this prior process which is arbitrary. But this is untrue. If one starts with the quality commonly meant by 'red', its entailment of colour is as little arbitrary, in the sense of dependent on one's choice, as the presence or absence of Gibraltar. There is no possible manipulation of words that will affect it in the least.

(*b*) If a priori statements were really prescriptions about usage, then not only would they not be necessary; they would not even be true or false. Positivism has at times accepted this consequence. 'If we reject them,' Professor Ayer wrote, 'we are merely adopting another usage from that which they prescribe. It is in this sense only that they cannot conceivably be false.'[2] Let us try this out. The proposition we have just used, 'red is a colour', would no doubt be accepted as one of those propositions that 'cannot conceivably be false'. This inability to be false, says Mr Ayer, lies in the fact alone that if we deny it, we should be adopting another usage. Very well; let us deny it and say 'red is not a colour'. Why is this false? Is it

---

[1] *Analysis*, Vol. 4, 20.
[2] *Ibid.*

merely because words are being used in a new way? This may mean either of two things. It may mean that 'is not' in the new form is taken to mean the same as 'is' in the original; but then the new proposition is not new at all, nor would anyone call it false. Or the meaning may be that whereas before, whatever we called red we also called coloured, we have now decided that it shall not be so called. But it is obvious that as a mere decision or resolution about words, this is not false either; anybody may *call* a thing what he pleases. If his statement is false, it is not because of the words he uses, but because, whatever words he uses, the proposition asserted by means of them is in conflict with fact; in this case, the fact is that the character commonly called 'red' entails the character 'coloured', and the falsity consists in the disagreement of proposition and fact. What holds here holds generally. Never in any case does mere usage enter into the logic of the case at all.

(c) How irrelevant all this insistence on language is may be seen from one further consideration. A priori truths may be recognized not only without the assistance of language, but without any traceable reference to it. It is no doubt true that when thinking reaches any high level of abstractness or complication, language is necessary, perhaps in the form of ordinary speech, perhaps in that of an artificially contrived symbolism. But many of the 'insights' commonly recognized as a priori are so simple and fundamental as to be relatively free from ties to words. Even the dog that cuts a corner in chasing a rabbit must be in some sense perceiving a straight line as the shortest line to its quarry; and it would seem absurd to say that a savage, and still more one of ourselves, could not recognize red as a colour, or three as greater than two, or two straight lines as not enclosing a space, without formulating his recognition in words. To say then that such recognition *is* the adoption of, or acquiescence in, some rule about words must be untrue.

Nor is there any illicit importation of psychology in pointing this out, though the positivists have, to be sure, encouraged such importation. For they say that a priori propositions invariably have to do with people's psychology in the form of their resolutions and prescriptions about words, whereas we hold that they have to do with something impersonal, with lines and numbers, genus and species, in short, with the architecture of nature. Words are psychological aids to fixing thought on the patterns of this architecture; in this context they are nothing more. And when thought has once been fixed by their aid, it often can and does dispense with them. A student of Laplace has recorded that whenever, in reading the *Méchanique*

Celeste, he came to a statement beginning 'it is obvious that', he knew he was in for an intellectual struggle to fill out the steps in the master's elliptical expression. Very probably Laplace did not always know that the steps were there. Thought is quick, as Hobbes said, and sometimes it takes long leaps over verbal and other stepping stones. How can the statements in a deduction consist of prescriptions about words if, as one becomes proficient in such deductions, the words become less and less necessary?

Both the linguistic positions that we have just been considering, the theory that a priori statements are reports of actual usage and that they state prescriptions about usage, have been abandoned by many or most positivists, and, one gathers, for some at least of the reasons we have been considering. In the significant preface to the 1946 edition of *Language, Truth and Logic*, Mr Ayer wrote:

'Just as it is a mistake to identify a priori propositions with empirical propositions about language, so I now think that it is a mistake to say that they are themselves linguistic rules. For apart from the fact that they can properly be said to be true, which linguistic rules cannot, they are distinguished also by being necessary, whereas linguistic rules are arbitrary. At the same time, if they are necessary it is only because the relevant linguistic rules are presupposed.'[1]

This is not easy to interpret, since much that might seem to have been retracted is retracted again by the last clause. Mr Ayer would agree that 'red is a colour' is necessary, and hence that it cannot be a linguistic rule, since such rules are arbitrary. But he would hold it is necessary only because it presupposes or depends on a prior linguistic rule which itself is arbitrary. It is hard to conjecture what this prior rule is. If it is merely a dictionary statement about how 'red' and 'colour' are being used, the necessity does not depend on it in any way worth canvassing. If the rule is not taken in this sense, it will reduce, I suspect, to the original statement. Indeed there is no way of getting round the question: when I say that red is a colour, am I intending to say something about the way in which the words are used, or to say that being red entails being coloured? For myself I can only report that I seem to mean the latter.

18. II. Let us now turn from the first of the positivist theses about a priori statements, that they are reports or resolutions about language, to the second, that they are conventions. The transition is not a

[1] P. 17.

sharp one, since the conventions, as we have seen, are alleged to be themselves linguistic. But the point that must now concern us is not whether they are verbal but whether they are arbitrary. Positivists insisted that they were: 'the rules of language,' said Schlick, 'are in principle arbitrary';[1] the postulates and rules of logical inference, said Carnap, 'may be chosen quite arbitrarily';[2] 'it is perfectly conceivable,' said Ayer, 'that we should have employed different linguistic conventions from those we actually do employ'.[3] What are we to think of this thesis?

The most obvious comment to make on it is that, taken at face value, it is self-contradictory. To say that a proposition is necessary is to say that the state of things it asserts could not be otherwise, and hence that there are no possible alternatives to it. To say that it is conventional is to say that there *are* possible alternatives to it. Hence to hold that it is both necessary and conventional is to hold both that there are, and that there are not, alternatives to it. It is well to be aware of this at the outset, if only to bring home to ourselves how extreme a position positivists have taken. They shock us, and mean to shock us. They are intimating that the almost unanimous judgment of philosophers and plain men is in error about the very propositions about which they had supposed themselves most certain. They are maintaining that 7+5 need *not* make twelve, that red need *not* be a colour, that two lines *may* enclose a space, that the same proposition may be *both* true and false. For the ordinary mind, such statements seem absurd. But if necessary statements are really arbitrary conventions, it is open to us to choose their opposites as our conventions, and then all the above statements may hold. How is it that anyone can urge upon us paradoxes of such violence?

I suspect that what is at work is a confusion bred of that tiresome obsession with language which has done so much in our day towards making philosophy trivial. When positivists say that 'red is a colour' might be different, what precisely is it about this statement that they are asserting might be otherwise? It could be any one of three things. (*a*) The words. We could perfectly well use the symbol 'grey' for what is now called 'red', and 'odour' for what is now called 'colour'. We should then accept 'grey is an odour' without demur. (*b*) What is alleged to be alterable might be what is commonly called the 'proposition', i.e. the content that is entertained in, or by, the judging mind, and is either true or false. That something of this sort is

---

[1] Feigl and Sellars, *Readings in Philosophical Analysis*, 165.
[2] *Logical Syntax of Language*, xv.
[3] *Logic, Truth and Language*, 2nd ed., 84.

involved in judging is indicated by the fact that half a dozen persons, all speaking different languages, may by general admission be 'asserting the same proposition'. Many questions might be asked here, but for the moment it does not matter how they are answered if only it is admitted that what is true or false is something distinguishable from the words on the one hand and the fact referred to on the other. (c) There is this fact itself, the state of affairs in nature, of which the proposition is true or false, and which is commonly supposed to be what it is, whether anything is asserted about it or not.

Now when people say that necessary statements are conventions, they may well be arguing in cloudy fashion that because (a) is conventional, (b) and (c) are conventional too. That (a) the language, is conventional is plain enough. There is no reason why what we mean by 'red is a colour', should not be expressed by 'grey is an odour' or 'a slithy tove is a borogove'. But is (b) conventional? Can we conceive of what we call red as not being a colour, but something else instead? Is (c) conventional? Might some actual surface be red and yet not be coloured? That question, so far as answerable, has been met by what we have just said of (b). If a state of affairs is inconceivable, the option of saying it exists is not open to us, for what should we then be saying? Thus (a) is clearly conventional, while (b) and (c) are clearly not. One can only suppose that when positivists call necessary statements conventional they have been led by their preoccupation with language to fasten on sentences, and because they see that these might be different, have inferred that the propositions expressed, or the facts referred to, or both, might be different—an invalid inference to a false conclusion.

19. It is perhaps another way of making the same point to say that the positivist confuses real definitions with verbal ones. A verbal definition is a convention; every word in the Oxford dictionary might obviously have been defined otherwise if popular practice had so decreed. On the other hand, a real definition is an attempt to state, not the usage of a word, but the character of some object thought of. Now many a priori propositions are essentially real definitions, in that they are at least preliminary attempts to analyse the character of some presented or presentable object. If we are tired of 'red is a colour', let us look at an instance or two of another kind. Mr Ayer tells us that the proposition 'a material thing cannot be in two places at once' says nothing except about how we use the phrase 'material thing'.[1] Of the statement 'relations are not particulars but universals',

---

[1] *Logic, Truth and Language*, 2nd ed., 58.

he says that it 'is not a proposition about "things" at all, but simply about words. It records the fact that relation-symbols belong by definition to the class of symbols for characters, and not to the class of symbols for things.'[1] Again, 'if I say, "Nothing can be coloured in different ways at the same time with respect to the same part of itself," I am not saying anything about the properties of any actual thing . . . I am expressing an analytic proposition which records our determination to call a colour expanse which differs in quality from a neighbouring colour expanse a different part of a given thing'.[2] Since all these statements are about usage, and usage is conventional, the statements could be quite otherwise if I saw fit to make them so.

All this seems to me fantastic. Its artificiality becomes apparent at once if one asks *why* this particular convention should have been adopted. Why should we say that a given part of the surface of a thing cannot be green and red at the same time? Of course if all this question means is, Why is it that, perceiving that the same surface cannot be diversely coloured at once, we came to use one noise or mark to express this insight rather than another?, the question is a historical one, and in its answer we shall presumably find no necessity at all. But this is not what we should normally take the question to mean. It asks rather, Why is it that, assuming 'red' and 'green' to mean what they commonly do, we refuse to apply the names to the same surface at once? Mr Ayer seems to suggest that this too is a matter of convention, to which an alternative is possible. But this is not the case. Assuming 'red' and 'green' to mean what they ordinarily do, the convention became what it is because no alternative was possible or conceivable. People could not if they tried make what was *meant* by red and green belong to the same surface at once. If they did not *apply* the names jointly, it was because they saw that the qualities could not *belong* jointly. They conformed their language to the structure of things, not the structure of things to their language. Language is a partial map for the distinctions and connections that we find in experience. The positivists are telling us in effect that the only reason why the Rocky Mountains do not appear in the Great Lakes is that the map forbids them to.

20. The question why we should have adopted these conventions in thinking is a crucial one for the conventionalist in another way. Our own answer to it is simple enough: they are necessary; we cannot

---

[1] *Logic, Truth and Language*, 2nd ed., 58.
[2] *Ibid.*, 79.

think the opposite of them if we try; and our language expresses the perceived necessity. The conventionalist who holds that we can think their opposite must explain why in fact we never do. His explanation may be historical, as we have seen. But sooner or later it must go beyond that, since once we realize that there are alternatives open to us, we shall begin to choose among them deliberately. And if our choice is not to be governed by seen necessities, what *is* to govern it? 'What we must understand,' an able writer has told us, 'is that the choice between distinct systems of logic is not decided by logic. It may happen that one system is more suitable for this, the other for that purpose; or our decision may be guided by aesthetic preference; but neither has anything to do with any insight into the "truth" of a system.'[1] Normally, then, the choice of an intellectual convention must be made by reference to some end which its use would subserve.

But why is one such end to be preferred to another? The positivist, at least, has no answer, and insists that no answer can be given. People do in fact choose one end rather than another, but he holds they never do so for reasons, only for causes, that is, because they happen to like one thing more than another; indeed the statement that anything is *better* than anything else is, for him, not an assertion at all, but only an expression of feeling, which is neither reasonable nor unreasonable. Thus there is no rational ground for preferring any convention of thought or conduct to any other. Not only is there nothing in the nature of things to justify thinking, for example, that a material thing cannot be in different places at once; it is also meaningless for a person to say to another that it would be better for him to think so, since any such statement of value expresses the speaker's feeling solely. The suggestion that men would be better off if they obeyed the canons of logic or mathematics than if they chose to flout them is a suggestion strictly without meaning. Rationality in the logical sense is now to be justified only by rationality in the ethical sense, and rationality in the ethical sense does not exist. Looked at in this light, positivism appears as a curious reversion to something like the 'personal idealism' advocated early in the century by F. C. S. Schiller, who maintained that the laws of logic were postulates to be justified in practice, and that the only reason why a man should accept any logical or metaphysical belief was that it worked for him personally. This position did not widely commend itself when offered, and for reasons that seemed conclusive. They seem to me conclusive still.

[1] F. Waismann, *Proc. of the Arist. Soc.*, Vol. 46 (1945–6), 80.

21. When a priori statements are called conventional, the discussion comes round sooner or later to the character of logical laws. This is almost inevitable. For the validity of all reasoning rests on their soundness; and on the soundness of some of them, such as the laws of identity and contradiction, depends our power to make any meaningful statement whatever. They are the bottleneck of all thinking. If they are really only conventions, it is hard to see how any position but one of scepticism would be eligible in either philosophy or science. For in that case no conformity to them, however strict, would give any guarantee that our 'knowledge' was following the framework of the actual world. There would remain, for all we know, a great gulf between mind and the world order, between the sort of pattern that would satisfy our logical impulse and the pattern of existent nature. One of the anomalies of recent philosophy is the vacuum in which this issue is discussed; there seems often to be a complete unawareness that the prospects of every department of knowledge hang upon the way it is settled. The existence of alternative logics is treated as if it were an ingenious novelty whose interest was confined to the mathematical technician instead of being, what it is if it is a fact at all, the end of all hope of stable and rational knowledge. One must of course be grateful for any technical proficiency that is brought to its discussion. One must also be on one's guard against allowing an aversion to scepticism to affect one's appraisal of the evidence. But it would be idle to pretend that we are discussing this issue as if it were on a par with a proposal about the rules of chess, and we should never introduce it in this place if we thought it were. If the laws of logic are conventions merely, in the sense that alternative laws which deny them have an equal claim to validity, then there is not such a thing as a reliable proposition, either a priori or empirical, in the range of what was once called knowledge.

22. What is it that prompted the suspicion about logical laws? It seems more than anything else to have been the development, described in an earlier chapter, of alternative geometries. The axioms and demonstrations of Euclid had been taken by mathematicians and philosophers as paradigms of certain knowledge, models to which thought in all other fields should do its best to approximate. The discovery that there were alternatives to Euclid was so heavy a blow to rationalist philosophers that they took it badly; instead of observing and parrying it coolly, their tendency was to deny indignantly that it was possible and so not only to receive it in full force but to make themselves somewhat ridiculous in the process. This was quite unnecessary. Now that the discovery has been reflected on at leisure, there appears to be no reason either to deny that it is a discovery on the one hand, or to assert, on the other, that it offers any evidence for the possibility of alternative logics. The reason for saying this can be put very simply.

The point of attack on Euclid was, as we saw, the axiom of parallels, whose modern version is that, starting with a given line, you can draw through a point outside it only one line that is parallel. This, when considered, did not appear quite self-evident.[1] Nor was there any way of proving it from the other postulates of Euclid. There was nothing then, either in itself or in its context, to make it a necessary truth. Since it was not necessary, an alternative to it was conceivable. Suppose it is replaced, as Lobachewski replaced it, by the proposition that through the point in question one can draw an indefinite number of parallels. This proposition then can be conjoined with the other postulates to yield an alternative geometry. Or instead of this one may substitute, as Riemann did, the proposition that one can draw no parallels at all, and from this and the other postulates one can then derive still another system of geometry. It is idle to deny that such things can be done, for Lobachewski and Riemann did them. The question before us is what this shows. Does it show that there are alternatives to necessary propositions, in the sense that such propositions, and more specifically the laws of logic, are no more valid than other propositions we might substitute for them?

It has now been clearly recognized that it shows nothing of the kind. The 'axiom' of Euclid could be replaced precisely because it was *not* seen to be necessary. Nor is there any contradiction between any later proposition of Euclid and any proposition in either of the two systems nor any contradiction in either of these of the other. There is no inconsistency between saying, '*If* you start with premises *ab* you will get *xy*', and saying '*If* you start with *ac*, you will get *yz*'. Nor do the logical laws in accordance with which the deductions are made in the various systems differ in the slightest. All that has happened is that for a proposition that was less than certain another has been substituted and the consequences rigorously drawn. The inference that because this was possible, the laws of logic themselves could be responsibly denied is a plain *non sequitur*. To be sure, the new development did show something. It showed how easy it was to suppose a proposition to be self-evidently true when it was not. But in this there is nothing surprising except to the sort of person who supposes that if something is self-evident, it must be self-evident to

[1] See above, p. 115.

everybody under all conditions. The fact is, as every logician and mathematician knows, that the grasp of the self-evident may be an extremely difficult and treacherous business.

23. Unless I have much mistaken what is going on, somewhat similar comments would apply to recent attempts at alternative logics. These seem to proceed on one or other of three principles: (*a*) an omission of one or more of the usually recognized primitive concepts, (*b*) an addition to them, (*c*) a redefining of implication. (*a*) The intuitionist logic of Brouwer is an example of the first of these. It professes to have omitted the law of excluded middle and to have developed a consistent logic without it. This, if successfully done, would be a surprising and disquieting feat. But what was actually done appears to have been something different. It was, rather, to give the old name to a quite distinct law, namely, '*p* is either true or impossible' and then to develop a logic in which *this* principle was dispensed with. And there seems to be nothing in this that offers an alternative to the familiar logic, in the relevant sense of an alternative that denies it.[1]

(*b*) Similarly of attempts to develop many-valued logics by adding distinctions to the traditional logic. Dr Waismann has pointed out that in ordinary thought we do not always, or even very commonly, treat statements, in the manner of the standard two-valued logic, as simply true or false. We are more likely to think of them, for example, as true, nearly true, not quite false, and entirely false; and if we embodied these distinctions in our logic, we should have a system of four values rather than two. He suggests that negation is usually a matter of degree; we may say 'yellow is not quite the colour of what I saw yesterday', or 'the colour was not in the least yellow'; and he suggests that if these two gradations of denial were defined, we should have a new logic in which our present concept of negation was replaced by two. Now it is a useful service to point out how far short of the subtle distinctions of actual thought are all the systems of logic ever devised. We can only agree with Dr Waismann—and with Hegel—that the black-and-white distinctions of formal logic are quite inadequate to living thought. But why should one say, as Dr Waismann does, that in adopting a more differentiated logic one is adopting an alternative system which is incompatible with black-and-white logic? What he has actually done is to recognize a number of gradations *within* the older meaning of the word 'not'. We do not doubt that such gradations are there, and indeed as many more as he

---

[1] See the discussion by W. C. Kneale, *Proc. of the Arist. Soc.*, Supplementary Vol. 21 (1947), 127 ff.

cares to distinguish. But a refinement of the older logic is not an abandonment of it. It is still true that the colour I saw yesterday was either a determinate shade of yellow or not, even though the 'not' may cover a multitude of approximations, and even though I shall never know which was the shade I saw.

(c) Another way of constructing 'alternative logics' is to vary the definitions of implication. Suppose that p and q are two propositions, either of which can be true or false. When we combine them, there are four possibilities:

1. p true and q true
2. p false and q true
3. p true and q false
4. p false and q false

Now it is theoretically possible to define p's implying q in terms of any one of these combinations or in terms of selected groups of them. As is well known, *Principia Mathematica* holds p to imply q if there is present any one of the combinations 1, 2, or 4. Professor Lewis defines implication more strictly as the impossibility, not the mere falsity, of p's being true and q false. One might, again, define implication, as older logicians thought preferable, without reference to the truth or falsity of either proposition. And by adhering to one's definition whatever it is, one may build up a logical system that has never been thought of before. But what does all this prove? That a proposition previously found necessary is now seen to be merely conventional, and to have alternatives? Not at all. It only shows that, when we play games with symbols, we are free within limits to make our own rules. We say 'within limits' advisedly. For if our symbols are to stand for characters in the real world, we are plainly not wholly free. We have seen that if a stands for red and b for coloured, our manipulations are under constraint from the character of what they refer to. This is still true if our object is left unspecified. We cannot say that a is b and also that it is not b, for that is forbidden by the common nature of all things. We cannot say that a is a b, and b is a c, and then deny that a is a c, for while our meanings remain steady, we cannot think that. Indeed the development of alternative logics appeals at every step to a necessity not regarded as conventional. Such a logic says that *if* you start with such and such primitives and postulates, such and such consequences *follow*. It may be explained that they follow only in an arbitrary sense; *if* one defines 'follows' to mean 'is materially implied by', it follows that 'coal is black' follows from 'snow is white'. But the first 'follows' here is different from the second; it stands for the seen necessity that is a requirement of every system, not for a convention confined to one. Professor Williams puts the point vigorously; 'although we can invent artificial systems of logistic *ad infinitum*, whatever postulates, definitions, formative rules we lay down, with whatever language or metalanguage we operate, their consequences are what they are, irrespective of convention and convenience, by the one inescapable sort of necessity'.[1]

24. The truth is that no one, not even the positivist, has succeeded in living up to the theory that logic is convention merely. In the very assertion of the thesis, it is assumed that the position is false, for we are supposed to understand that the logic used in establishing the conventionality of logic is itself somehow exempt from the conventional character ascribed to other logics. For example, we are offered as true the statement that all logic is conventional, and expected to accept without question that the contradictory proposition, 'some logic is not conventional', is false. But if the law of contradiction is really only a convention with alternatives, why should we be expected so firmly to take this contradictory as false? If there really is an alternative to the law, *both* sides of a contradiction may be true, and to insist on either to the exclusion of the other is dogmatism. But in spite of their view that logic is conventional, positivists do not think it dogmatic to insist that if their view is true, its contradictory must be rejected. Such insistence is significant. For it implies that the logic of their own assertion is regarded as more than conventional.

Again, to say that logic is conventional, is to say, as we have seen, that whatever laws of logic we accept, including the law of contradiction, have alternatives. But for the positivist what kind of statement is this? Not an empirical statement, for he insists that no statements of logic are empirical. It must, then, be the only other kind of statement that he admits as an assertion at all, an analytic statement. But it cannot be this either. For an analytic statement is defined as one whose contradictory is self-contradictory, and this rules the present statement out. Let us be clear about this. The statement in question is the denial of the law of contradiction. If this is to be taken as an analytic statement, its contradictory, namely the law of contradiction itself, must be set down as a self contradiction. This is nonsense, as positivists would agree. But if so, their statement that logic is conventional is neither empirical nor analytic, and hence on their premises no statement at all. They would thus appear to be saying nothing.

[1] *Analysis*, Vol. 5 (September 1938), 93.

Even if a place is found for the denial of the law of contradiction, the denial will remain unthinkable. To deny the law means to say that it is false *rather than* true, that its being false excludes its being true. But this is the very thing that is supposedly denied. One cannot deny the law of contradiction without presupposing its validity in the act of denying it. If one says to oneself, 'I am not going to be trapped by this wretched logicocentric predicament, I am going to plant myself within the new convention I am advocating and make my statement from within it', one finds oneself defeated again. For then *what* is one asserting? In a realm where no proposition excludes its contradictory, nothing could be asserted as true rather than its opposite; assertion and negation would vanish. This seems to have been accepted even by the inventors of multiple logics. None of them appears ever to have proposed an alternative to the law of contradiction. Nor can one suppose this an accident. Since they are moved by the strongest desire to dispense with everything dispensable, the fact that they have all found the law indispensable suggests that if it is a convention, it is one of a curiously universal and coercive kind.

To us the source of this constraint seems clear. If it came from our own will, as conventions do, we could change it, whereas we cannot. If it came from experience, the law would be only probable, and positivists agree that it is more. To say with Kant that it comes from some uncontrollable region of our own minds compels us to say that though the contradictoriness of the real world may be unthinkable, it may nevertheless be true. Our own view of the source of constraint is presumably that of the 'plain man'. We accept the law and must accept it, because 'nature has said it'. If we hold that a thing cannot at once have a property and not have it, it is because we *see* that it cannot. The law of contradiction is at once the statement of a logical requirement and the statement of an ontological truth.

25. This view has been challenged in an interesting paper on 'Logic Without Ontology' by Professor Ernest Nagel. He holds that the law of contradiction amounts to a stipulation regarding terms. Since he puts the case clearly, it will be well to have it in his own words:

If someone were to maintain that a penny has a diameter of 11/16 of an inch and also a diameter of 12/16 of an inch, he would be told that the assertion is impossible, because even though the attributes are not 'the same', in predicating the former one implicitly excluded the latter. . . . In short, since the assertion in effect maintains 'the same attribute' to belong and also not to belong to the same object, it is absurd. But let us press the question why, if the penny has the first of these attributes, it cannot have the other. . . . The impossibility arises from the fact that we use the expressions 'length of 11/16 inches' and 'length of 12/16 inches' in such a way—in part because of the manner in which they may have been defined in relation to each other—that each formulates a different outcome of measurement. We may be sure that no penny will ever turn up with a diameter having both dimensions, because what it means for the diameter to have one of the attributes of dimension is specified in terms of the absence of the other attribute.[1]

We have met this kind of argument before. It is an application to logic of the theory that led Professor Ayer to say of the assertion that a surface could not be green and red at once that it 'records our determination to call a colour expanse which differs in quality from a neighbouring colour expanse a different part of a given thing'.[2] Professor Nagel says that the reason why the *physical penny* cannot have two different lengths at once lies in our use of the words; we have decided to call one length, as measured, 11/16 of an inch, and to refuse that name to any other measured length. And the reason why, if the penny has the first length, it cannot have another, is that we have defined the first length as meaning, in part, the absence of another. So to define it is to lay down a stipulation, a stipulation being presumably a rule that we may or may not decide to lay down. But *is* the definition of one length in such fashion as to exclude another a stipulation in this sense? To say so implies that we could make the length we now call 11/16 of an inch into something that would *not* exclude the length called 12/16 of an inch by some process of redefining words. And that is clearly not possible. If it were possible, the question would require an answer, Why do we not follow some other convention? According to Professor Nagel it is nothing in the nature of things that prevents our doing so; to say it was would be to assign to the laws of logic an ontological meaning, which is what he wants to avoid. But the attempt to avoid it only results in putting the cart before the horse. The two lengths are not incompatible because we call them so; we call them so because we see that they *are* so. Nature is not to be ordered by our own processes of definition.

Among those who have held that the laws of logic have significance for the nature of things is Leibniz, who thought they asserted structures present in all possible worlds. Professor Nagel considers

[1] *Naturalism and the Human Spirit*, 213–14.
[2] Above, p. 269.

this view, and concludes that Leibniz too was making into a constitutive principle what was only a stipulation. How was he to know that the law of contradiction holds of all possible worlds? Only by making conformity to logic the test of what is possible. And of course it is easy enough to show that all possible worlds conform to logic if all you mean by 'possible' is that they do conform to logic. But then you are really saying nothing except about your use of words; you are saying that you will not *call* anything possible unless it does so conform.

I cannot think Leibniz would be convinced. He would probably admit that by 'possible' he meant logically possible, and that his statement did in some sense guarantee in advance that it would never turn out false. He might admit that on the surface, therefore, it could be interpreted in the verbalist way; it could be read *either* as a report of how he proposed to use words *or* of an insight into the structure of things. There is no doubt, of course, that he intended the latter, though Mr Nagel thinks that if he had been clear about what he was doing, he would have intended the former. Looking not to his intention, but solely to the theory as stated, is there nothing to choose between these interpretations? I think there is, for one involves consequences which the other does not. If we choose the first and take logical principles, as Mr Nagel suggests, merely as stipulations about the combining of 'elements of discourse, constellations of signs of varying degrees of complexity', we should be able to rearrange these at will, since there is nothing in 'elements of discourse' by themselves that would resist our doing so. But if we try that upon the law of contradiction, we find that this is precisely what we cannot do. Nature will force its way back through any verbal decrees by which we try to alter the law, in the abstract or in application. We may call white 'non-white' and non-white 'white', and the mutual exclusion between the states of affairs referred to will continue to stare us in the face. We may resolve to use the same word for both, and to apply it impartially to the colours of snow and coal. Would the effect of such usage be to persuade us that a thing could be white and non-white at once? On the contrary it would merely force us to recognize how undiscriminating our language was and to import a distinction of terms that would answer more sensitively to the incompatibilities of fact.

26. But while Mr Nagel holds that logical laws are linguistic conventions, he declines to follow some other conventionalists in holding that they are arbitrary. Though not dictated by nature, they have the

relative coerciveness of necessary means to ends. They are prescribed for us in the sense that if we want the ends, we can gain them only through these means; they are optional in the sense that we can dispense with them if we wish to pursue other ends. Mr Nagel writes: 'the "justification" for a proposed set of regulative principles will not be arbitrary and can be given only in terms of the adequacy of the proposed changes as means or instruments for attaining the envisaged ends.'[1] Logic is an instrument in 'formulating and regulating the pursuit of human ideals' and 'the relative success of a system of logic in doing these things is the sole identifiable and objective basis for measuring its worth'.[2] What are these ideals or ends? One of them appears to be the systematization of knowledge; we read that the choice of regulative principles is to be grounded on 'the relatively greater adequacy of one of them as an instrument for achieving a certain systematization of knowledge.'[3] Another is precision; 'the laws of thought . . . indicate the direction in which the maximum desired precision may be obtained'. At the same time Mr Nagel seems to take as intelligible the question why we should seek to be precise, and answers it by saying that precision is a means to a further end: 'it must, nevertheless, be acknowledged that the ideal of precision in using language is not an arbitrary one. It is not arbitrary because communication and inquiry are directed to the achievement of certain objectives, and these objectives are best obtained when language is employed in a manner approximating as closely as possible the norms expressed by the laws of thought.'[4]

Let us follow one of the means-end threads that are here singled out. We are to choose conformity to the law of contradiction because this gives greater precision; we are to choose greater precision because it facilitates inquiry; we are to facilitate inquiry—why? Inquiry, we are assured, is 'directed to the achievement of certain objectives', but we are left vague as to what these are—which is a pity, since the validation of logic itself is made to depend on them. The nearest approach to an answer is suggested in the phrase, 'the systematization of knowledge'. Most philosophers would have answered that the characteristic aim of inquiry was simply to know, and perhaps Mr Nagel would agree. But let us not take liberties with his phrasing. He says that conformity to logic is indispensable if we are to *systematize* knowledge. The question then becomes, Why

[1] *Naturalism and the Human Spirit*, 228.
[2] *Ibid.*, 233.
[3] *Ibid.*, 228.
[4] *Ibid.*, 226.

should we want to systematize it in this particular way? All answers but one seem to me relatively trivial. We might say, to be sure, that we preferred knowledge which was self-consistent because it gave us more aesthetic satisfaction, or because it was practically more convenient. I am sure that Leibniz would not deny that consistent knowledge did serve these ends. But I think he would regard the suggestion that these are the main or characteristic reasons why we want to make knowledge logically consistent as merely eccentric. We want consistent knowledge, he would say, because we can see that that alone gives us *truth*, because that alone will tell us what the world is like.

27. Even here the verbalist will no doubt reply that all Leibniz is doing is announcing that he will not *call* anything 'true' or 'real' unless it conforms to logic. I will not press again the bed-of-Procrustes reply that this is making things follow words rather than words things, valid as that would be. I will only point out that in this dialectical seesaw the insight theory is bound to have the last word. For when the verbalist maintains that in outlawing the inconsistent he is only declaring a certain usage to be inconsistent with his own, what is the status of this latter inconsistency? Is this too something which one is at liberty to deny if one prefers another convention? I do not suppose that even the conventionalist thinks in this fashion. When he says that one linguistic convention is inconsistent with another, he is surely reporting a relation that he sees to be objectively valid, not his employment of a linguistic rule that he and others are free to reject in the interest of changed purposes. He sees directly the inconsistency of one rule with another and his judgment reports that insight. And if such insight is possible in one case, why not in others?

This pragmatic defence of a given logic on the ground that it is a means to an end we happen to prefer implies, of course, that we might have other ends to which other means would be more conducive. There is a fine air of tolerance about this. But the tolerance is illusory. We are told that if we choose a certain logic, it is because that logic conduces to successful inquiry. But what ends other than successful inquiry are open to us? None, it would seem, but unsuccessful inquiry, which no sane man would elect. It is true that Dewey and others have spoken at times as if logic were an instrument to ends that were not cognitive at all. But he could give plausibility to such a theory only by including the pursuit of such ends (confusedly, I think) within his conception of inquiry; and broad as he made that, he would never have suggested that it included the liberty to contradict oneself. And to suggest that a logic may be selected on grounds that have no connection with knowing whatever has no plausibility. Thus the present argument starts by making the law of contradiction, for example, a means to an end that we may reject if we please. Such rejection assumes that other alternatives are genuinely eligible. But there are none such for anyone we should recognize as sane.

Even in a narrowly logical regard, the argument for a conventionalist logic breaks down. We should adopt the law of contradiction, it says, because this conduces to successful inquiry. When is an inquiry successful? When it has introduced into a situation order, coherence and system. What do these things mean? A minimum for all of them is consistency. Thus the reason why we should think consistently is that if we do, we shall have achieved consistency. The argument is circular.

It is incoherent in another way. It says that the reason for our selecting a particular logic is its value in the 'systematization of knowledge'. But then logics are surely all systems and ways of systematizing knowledge. There must, then, be other ways, perhaps numberless other ways, in which this end of the systematization of knowledge could be effected. If so, the explanation of why we should choose our particular system is no explanation unless it is assumed that our kind of systematization is the only right end. And then the question is begged again.

Once more, the argument implies that the laws of thought, though necessary within the logic we prefer, may not be necessary within other systems. But if I am not mistaken, there are a number of logical principles besides the law of contradiction that keep turning up in all the 'alternative logics' and without which it would be impossible to construct a system at all. There is no reason to consider the denials of these principles to be equally available with themselves. To say that they are really expendable is to run beyond any evidence that even the most uninhibited of intellectual experimenters has adduced. There are some logical rules that we apparently cannot dispense with if we try.[1]

28. Our treatment of the conventionalist theory has been drearily negative. But to deny the denial of the power of reason to know the world may fairly claim to be constructive criticism. Bosanquet used to say that though Acts of Parliament could not make men good, they

[1] I have been aided in this criticism by an unpublished paper of Dr Charles Landesman.

could help by hindering the hindrances to the good life. The notion that all our insights into necessity are merely reports about how we use language has been one of the chief hindrances in our time to the free movement of thought. It has had an influence out of all proportion to its cogency. This result is natural enough. Just as students of ethics have often come to feel, in the light of Freud, that there is something disingenuous about all pretensions to high motive, and to think, a little reluctantly, that though subjectivists may be cynics, they are probably in the right, so students in the speculative field have seen so many travellers of 'the high priori road' squabbling with each other over what each claimed to be self-evident and in the end being passed ignominiously by and forgotten, that they are quite prepared for the account of the verbalist that these over-simple searchers were all attempting the impossible, were all fatuous victims of the treacheries of words.

There is a further reason for the spread of conventionalism. It has become associated in many minds with the development of mathematical logic and has thus acquired a certain aura of modernity and sophistication. Unfortunately, the services of mathematical logic to philosophy have proved far less than were hoped of it. Furthermore, skill in mathematical manipulation is no guarantee of insight into the meanings and structure of actual thought. Russell has left it on record that in his own logical researches it was his habit to disregard meaning altogether and confine himself to manipulating marks. A volume might be written about the misinterpretations of thinking wrought by the attempt to formalize it, to trim, distort, and compress it into quasi-mathematical moulds. This attempt perhaps reached its queer limit with the suggestion of Carnap that every statement in any science can be translated into a statement about language. But whatever may be the claims of the logic with which it has been associated, we have maintained that conventionalism itself has no claim to belief on the evidence. Though it is a spectre that has repeatedly arisen from the time of Hobbes to that of Wittgenstein to haunt thinkers preoccupied with language, the ghost has always been successfully laid by the process of merely looking at it steadily till one sees it for the unreal thing it is.

Once this wraith has been got rid of, we may return to a priori knowledge with renewed confidence. There is no reason why it should not be what reflective men for millenniums have taken it to be, and why our logic and arithmetic, our insights into temporal and causal necessity, our grasp of genus and species, of the mutual exclusiveness of things in space, of the necessitation of size by shape, of extension by colour, and much else, should not be taken as genuine knowledge of how the world is put together. No doubt the amount of such rational knowledge now owned by us is limited, and the analysts have served a useful purpose in putting a brake upon the tendencies of some philosophers to spin the universe out of their almost paranoiac heads. No doubt, too, it is easy to deceive ourselves as to when we have uncovered genuine necessity; the self-evidence that belongs to it when clearly apprehended may all too easily be simulated by mere strength of association, or even by that emotion of certitude which may be felt by the fanatic about anything whatever. But we do not discredit other functions because they are capable of abuse, nor judge them by taking them at their worst; and neither can we so discredit reason.

29. III. Unhappily the strictures of analytic philosophers on a priori statements are not yet exhausted. In addition to holding such statements to be linguistic and conventional, they hold them also to be analytic, that is, to be mere tautologies. The first two contentions we have found reason to think ill-founded. But even if anti-rationalist critics are mistaken in both these charges, their case will have been largely made out if they are right about the third. For the seeker after knowledge a tautology is a vain repetition; it gives truths of a kind, but certainly not of the kind he most wants. Whether a priori knowledge does in fact give only tautology is a difficult and technical question which we should gladly avoid. But no account of reason could pretend to adequacy that did not face it frankly and fully. Dr Ewing puts the point forcibly:

the question is one of the most important in the whole of philosophy. If there are no synthetic a priori judgments ... thought can never give us new truth but only the same truth as we had before but expressed in different words; all deductive inferences and self-evident propositions will be a matter of arbitrary verbal convention; there will be no philosophy beyond the ordering and clarification of propositions known, if known at all, in some other way; mathematics will be merely a game with symbols; there will be no relation of entailment or necessary connection in the objective world but merely a set of brute facts any of which might perfectly well exist without the others existing also.[1]

It goes perhaps without saying that most rationalists have believed

[1] *A Short Commentary on Kant's Critique of Pure Reason,* 20–21.

that a priori knowledge went beyond tautology. Plato and Aristotle, Augustine and St Thomas, Descartes and Spinoza, Hegel and Bradley, Royce and McTaggart, were confident that by the use of reason they could travel from point to point in the conceptual framework of the world, moving along lines of logical necessity to truths that were genuinely new. In this not unimpressive succession it was apparently Kant who first realized to the full the difficulties of this conviction; and since his treatment of the issue has dominated the discussion of later years, we shall do well to start with him.

30. On the surface, as so often with Kant, the matter is laid out with order and clarity. He proceeds to draw two distinctions, that between a priori and empirical knowledge, and that between analytic and synthetic knowledge. As for the first distinction: a priori knowledge is that which is necessary and universal, 'necessary' meaning such that we could see that it could not be otherwise, and 'universal' meaning the obvious consequence of this, that the knowledge has no exceptions. Such insight, Kant pointed out, could not be derived from sense, for no run of sense experiences, however long, could establish more than a probability. An example of it is '$7+5=12$'. On the other hand, empirical knowledge is that which *is* derived from sense experience, and refers to what is, or might be, presented in such experience. An example would be 'granite is hard'. As for the second distinction: an analytic proposition is one whose predicate only asserts something already contained in the subject concept. The proposition, 'matter is extended', for example, is analytic because occupying space, or being extended, is clearly part of what we mean by 'matter'. Finally, a synthetic proposition is one in which we do say more in the predicate than is contained in the subject concept, as in 'Jones has bought a new house'.

With these four types of knowledge before us, it is natural to ask whether each of the first two kinds of knowledge cannot be combined with each of the second two. If so, we shall have four more determinate types as follows:

1. A priori analytic knowledge
2. A priori synthetic knowledge
3. Empirical analytic knowledge
4. Empirical synthetic knowledge.

Do we actually possess knowledge of all four types? Kant had no doubt about the first, a priori analytic knowledge; his example was the one we have taken, 'all matter is extended', which is commonly thought to be a clear case. Of the second too, he thought we had clear cases, though this had been disputed. Any arithmetical equation such as '$7+5=12$' would provide an example, since, besides being necessary it had a predicate that is in some sense not contained in the subject. Regarding the third, empirical analytic knowledge, he was confused. He recognized that in such a statement as 'gold is yellow' the predicate sets out part of what we mean by 'gold', and that its relation to the other parts was purely empirical. The statement would therefore seem to qualify as an example. But Kant was disinclined to admit as analytic any statement whose predicate was not included *necessarily* in the subject, though in insisting on this he was going beyond his own definition of the analytic. The result was that the third class was left empty. All its ordinary occupants, such as 'gold is yellow', were transferred into the enormous fourth class, which included nearly all the assertions of natural science and common sense.

Though critics of Kant might jib at this lumping together of classes 3 and 4, they would regard it as at worst a venial sin. Kant well knew that it was upon the existence of class 2 that the fire would be concentrated, for to recognize that there was such a thing as a priori synthetic knowledge meant to concede that in advance of all experience of the connection one was asserting, one could gain fresh knowledge of the nature of things simply by sitting down and thinking. To empiricists it has seemed incredible that we should have such a faculty, and they have scrutinized Kant's account with sceptical and hostile eye. In their opinion there were two major blunders in Kant's account.

31. In the first place they say that he admitted irrelevant psychological considerations into his test of the analytic. We may suppose, he writes, that '$7+5$' on the one hand and '12' on the other stand for exactly the same concept, but 'if we look more closely, we find that the concept of the sum of 7 and 5 contains nothing save the union of the two numbers into one, and in this no thought is being taken as to what the single number may be which combines both.'[1] Here Kant seems to be arguing that because the thought of $7+5$ does not necessarily contain the thought of 12, the logical concept of $7+5$ does not contain the logical concept of 12, and that the proposition is therefore synthetic. This, say the critics, is deplorable confusion; it confuses psychological with logical containment. It is perfectly true that we can *think* of $7+5$ without thinking of 12, but that is

---

[1] *Critique of Pure Reason*, Introduction, Sec. 5 (Kemp Smith's trans.).

wholly beside the point. What Kant ought to have done was, excluding the vagaries of our personal thinking, to attend to the relation between the concepts as mathematically defined. And if he *had* fixed attention on these, he would have seen that '7+5' and '12' are absolutely equivalent terms; each may serve as the definition of the other; each may replace the other in any arithmetical process in which either appears. So Kant's example and his analysis of it give no reason whatever for supposing that synthetic a priori knowledge exists.

The criticis here pointed out, secondly, that there are large ranges of judgments to which Kant's distinction does not apply. Following Aristotle, he supposed that every judgment asserts a predicate of a subject, and because he did so, he thought that all judgments could be divided into those whose predicates were contained in the subject concept and those whose predicates were not. But modern logic has insisted that there are *relational* judgments which cannot be naturally analysed in the subject-predicate way at all, for example, 'A is equal to B'. This is no more a statement about A than about B, and even if it were treated as two distinct statements, asserting of each subject equality to the other, still this equality to the other is not an attribute characterizing either, but a relation uniting the two. To ask about such a statement whether its predicate is included or not included in the subject concept is thus to ask a pointless question, since it assumes that the statement is the ascription of a predicate to a subject, which it is not.

The critics would reject Kant's case for the synthetic a priori because it seems thus to rest on a distinction that is both drawn in psychological terms and is inapplicable to a large range of our judgments. Is the distinction therefore worthless? No, they would say; it may still be retained if the distinction is more precisely drawn. But once it is so drawn, we shall see 'that there are no other a priori judgments than the analytic, or rather, as we prefer to say today, that only tautological propositions are a priori'.[1] What is this new and more accurate basis of distinction? It is proposed in two chief forms.

32. (1) According to the first form, 'a proposition is analytic when its validity depends solely on the definitions of the symbols it contains, and synthetic when its validity is determined by the facts of experience'.[2] Does this give us the needed clarity? I fear not. Indeed I doubt if it is any improvement on Kant, since it begs the essential

---

[1] M. Schlick, in *Readings in Philosophical Analysis*, 280.
[2] A. J. Ayer, *Language, Truth and Logic*, 103.

question twice over. This appears when we attempt to apply it.

Suppose we ask whether 'red is a colour' is analytic. To find out, we are told, we should look to the definitions of the terms, and see whether its validity can be made out from them alone. Very well, we ask for the definition of 'red', and find that any attempt at logical definition must begin 'red is a colour which . . .'. And then it is obvious that the validity of 'red is a colour' does follow from its definition, for it is merely a partial repetition of this. Whence the statement would appear to be clearly analytic. Unfortunately the conclusion is worthless, for the problem is still there in full force within the definition. Though it is clear that red so possesses colour that any definition of it must stress the connection, the point of importance is what sort of connection this is. The mere fact that the connection follows from the definition shows nothing, for between the definiendum and the definiens there may be only an arbitrary relation. We may define a sergeant as a non-commissioned officer who wears three stripes on his arm, and then the statement 'a sergeant wears three stripes on his arm' will be an analytic statement, since its validity follows from the definition of its terms. But to define 'analytic' so loosely as to include under the same head the relation of a sergeant to his stripes and of red to colour is, as we have said, to beg the essential question. By failing to recognize that the characters within a definition may be connected in extremely different ways, it assimilates judgments whose elements are necessarily connected to those whose elements are connected arbitrarily. If all statements are to count as analytic whose validity follows from the definition of their terms, the cases that have commonly been thought the clearest instances of the synthetic a priori will be brought into the analytic camp by mere stipulation.

Having explained how we are to identify the analytic, the prescription goes on to say that a proposition is synthetic 'when its validity is determined by the facts of experience'. But if this is offered as a criterion of the synthetic, it begs the question more plainly than its predecessor. The contention of rationalist philosophers is that there are synthetic judgments that are a priori, that is, *not* determined by the facts of experience, but presented to intelligence as necessary. If synthetic judgments are *defined* as empirical, these philosophers are of course all mistaken. But they have not been shown to be mistaken. They have merely been ruled mistaken by so defining terms that they could not be right.

33. (2) A second way in which analytic philosophers have formulated their criterion is to say that a proposition is analytic when its validity follows from applying to it the law of contradiction, that is, when to deny it would be to contradict oneself, when its contradictory would be, or would entail, self-contradiction. But this again casts so wide a net as to include a great variety of judgments of the most different types. It would include at one end such an obvious tautology as 'all extended bodies are extended', since its contradictory, 'some extended bodies are not extended', of course contradicts itself. It would include at the other end even our proposition about sergeants, if only we agreed that part of what we meant by 'sergeant' was a man with three stripes on his arm, for we should be contradicting ourselves if we ever recognized a sergeant without these stripes. But clearly the important distinction then breaks out again among the propositions warranted by the law. The characteristics that may be included within a definition and whose denial would therefore lead to self-contradiction, may have no relation to each other at all except that of pieces packed into the same parcel, or, on the other hand, they may be connected so intimately that they cannot be dissociated. If the test of the analytic is to be the self-contradictoriness of the denial, these will be equally analytic. And that deprives the classification of any genuine interest.

Neither Kant's basis of distinction, then, nor either of the two new ones offered by the positivists is satisfactory; Kant was confused as to what his basis is, and the positivists gloss over vital distinctions. The problem therefore remains, but it remains of the first importance, though it has become so obscured under loose and conflicting usages that it might be well to dispense with 'analytic' and 'synthetic' altogether.

34. What exactly is the problem? It does not concern the existence of a priori knowledge, which is admitted on both sides. It concerns the existence among propositions admittedly a priori of a fundamental difference in kind. Positivists deny such a difference. They would herd all a priori propositions into the same pen, and brand them all as the explication of the meaning of words. And since the meanings attached to words are held to be arbitrary, every a priori assertion is held simply to unpack the meaning that our usage has packed into it; hence it says nothing about the world, but only something about what we mean. The rationalist believes, on the other hand, that among a priori propositions there *is* a fundamental difference. He admits that there are such propositions as the positivist describes. But he also says that there is another kind of a priori, which for knowledge is immensely more significant. If we call the positivist type the arbitrary a priori, we may call the other type the conceptual a priori. Those who accept it believe that a priori insight, instead of unpacking contents arbitrarily thrown together, reveals a genuine necessity in the contents thought about, an entailment of one characteristic by another. The issue over analytic and synthetic judgment is really the issue whether this conceptual a priori can be reduced to the arbitrary a priori. And this issue is essentially the same as that presented by the earlier contentions that the a priori is linguistic and conventional. In all three cases the positivist is battling against the same abhorrent admission that we can have rational insight into the nature of things. And in all these cases equally we believe that his argument rests on confusion: in the first case between language and what it means; in the second, between the conventional and the necessary, in the third, between containment and entailment. Remembering that the fundamental issue is still the same, let us look at it in the light of this last distinction.

35. The positivist holds that what is asserted in any a priori proposition is *contained in* the meaning of its terms. This, on the face of it, is a paradox. 'What is red all over is not green all over'; is *not being green* part of what one means by 'red'? If so, the meaning of red will also include not being the south pole, the Fifth Symphony, or Greek civilization. No doubt every pair of characters are related internally, if only by the relation of difference, so that they would not be what they are if this relation were removed, but this is not the same as saying that all these differences are *contained* in what we mean when we speak of red. What could have led the positivist to propose this doctrine? It may be that he is attempting to construe ordinary thought on a mathematical analogy. He knows that mathematical theorists construct the series of whole numbers by definition: $2 = 1 + 1$; $3 = 2 + 1$; $4 = 3 + 1$, and so on. Then when they say $4 = 3 + 1$, or indeed anything else in the arithmetic system, there is a sense in which they are only repeating definitions. He then infers by analogy that when one lays down any other necessary proposition, such as 'what is red all over is not green all over', the necessity is to be accounted for on the same lines, by the tautology involved.

Now it is true that one *can* think in this way. We can reflect that a four-legged animal with hoofs and mane, called a horse, is four-legged or an animal. But nobody wastes his time on such thinking in ordinary life. What actually happens is not that we grasp a whole of which we pointlessly proceed to hold up a fragment, but that, starting

K

with a fragment, we find ourselves able to supplement it with another fragment that we were not explicitly thinking of; and we move from one fragment to the other along the road of entailment. Silly as it is to say that part of what I *mean* by calling anything red is that it is not green or the south pole, it is only good sense to say that these things are *entailed* by what I mean. Similarly, when I call anything red I do not mean by its redness the same thing as its extension; but I can see, if I raise the question, that its being red entails its being extended. If we take meanings as employed in ordinary thought, instead of those of the mathematician when he is formally laying his cards upon the table, we find them invariably of this kind. If it is said that to consider meaning as actually used rather than meaning as formally defined is to inject psychology into logic, the answer is that the only logical issue of any interest cannot be solved unless actual thought is consulted. That issue is not whether, if 'red' is formally defined as including extension, 'x is red' entails 'x is extended'; of course it does. The question of interest is whether what we actually mean by 'being red' is at once distinguishable from what we mean by 'being extended' and also entails this. I think the answer is Yes. And if true at all, this is a pregnant Yes. It is significant for logic, since entailment is a logical relation. It is a statement in ontology, for it is an assertion about the nature of things. It belongs to epistemology, for it says that we have a priori knowledge of how characters are related. And it is of importance to psychology, since it implies that our thought does actually move at times along lines of necessity.

Is it still insisted that the point is put more accurately by saying that a thing's being red or coloured *contains*, rather than *entails*, its extension? If so, consider the following. (1) We have two books, exactly alike except that one is red and the other green. Everyone would agree that they may be described correctly as differing in colour. But if part of what we *mean* by 'colour' is extension, it would be equally correct to say that they *resemble* each other in colour. And this is absurd.[1] (2) I once heard of a librarian in a small library who conceived the remarkable plan of classifying his books according to colour; he put all the green books together, all the red ones together, and so on. Would it be sensible to say that when he put the red books together, part of his basis for doing so was their resemblance in

---

[1] It will not do to counter this argument by saying that 'resemble each other in colour' means 'resemble each other in being coloured' and that in this there is no absurdity. If being extended is part of what 'being coloured' means, the ways of being extended will also be ways of being coloured, and if two surfaces are square they will resemble each other not only in having colour, but in the kinds of colour they have. The absurdity thus remains.

occupying space, or in the forms, such as squareness, which this spatiality took? Surely not; for in that respect they resembled equally the green books that he put elsewhere. And yet we should have to say this if being extended is part of what being red means, as being wooden, for example, is part of what we mean by 'lumber'. (3) If extension is contained in colour as part of its meaning, it is at least natural to expect that when the first character varies, there will be some variation in the second. If being honourable is part of what we mean by being virtuous, one's virtue does not remain the same when one becomes dishonourable. No such variation is observable as between colour and extension. We should certainly be surprised if, when we said that a coloured balloon had expanded or contracted, we should be taken as saying that it had changed in colour. The two characters vary independently of each other.

36. It is difficult to apply the analytic theory to actual thought without the help of a quasi-Freudian view that by quite ordinary terms we mean a great many things which we had never suspected we meant, and which the most careful inspection of our meaning does not reveal. Mr Langford has pointed out that though none of us would have any difficulty in identifying a cube, most people do not know how many edges a cube has. Probably the simplest way for such a person to settle the matter would be to get a lump of sugar or something similar and count the edges; but 'the notion of having twelve edges can be no part of the notion of being a cube, since, if it were, he would not then know what it was the edges of which he was counting'.[1] Of course it is possible to define a cube in such manner as to include the having of twelve edges within the definition, but neither plain men nor mathematicians commonly do so. And whether they do or not, it would be perfectly possible, as Mr Langford shows, to define a cube without reference to this property, as, for example, 'a solid whose faces were squares, or a regular solid with eight vertices, or a regular solid with six faces'—all of which apply to cubes universally and exclusively. It is clear that, in thinking these notions, we do not need to know that the object thought of has twelve edges, nor does this property follow analytically, if that means by logical principles alone, from any of them. Yet if we start with an object defined for us in any of these ways, we can see that it *must* have this further property. We are proceeding by reasoning that is necessary and is therefore a priori, not empirical. The reasoning proceeds

[1] C. H. Langford, 'A Proof that Synthetic A Priori Propositions Exist', *Journal of Philosophy*, Vol. 46 (1949), 21.

from one character to another which is not included in the first; hence the reasoning is also synthetic. In sum, what we have here is a synthetic a priori inference.

There is no reason to suppose that this is a rare or exceptional case, and if it is a genuine case at all, geometry must swarm with similar ones. Let us take one further example, this time suggested by Professor Broad:

'Suppose, e.g., that four points A, B, C, and D are all at the same distance from a point X. Then it necessarily follows that the angle A B D is equal to the angle A C D. This consequence about the relations of the points cannot be called merely analytic; for it is certainly not a mere restatement or weakening of the statement that A, B, C, and D are all at the same distance from X. It might have been recognized by a person who had never suspected that there was a point X from which these four points were equidistant.'[1]

The reply may perhaps be made that what contains the conclusion is not the proposition about the points, but the axioms and postulates of Euclidean geometry generally. But in order of deduction it is closer to the deduced conclusion than they are, and if we find it hard to see how it can 'contain' the conclusion, it is still harder to see how they do.

Mr Langford thinks that some cases in which the necessary linkage seems more intimate still turn out to be synthetic on closer analysis. Perhaps most people would say that, whether extension is included or not in what they mean by being 'red', at least being coloured is so included; it seems impossible that a person should mean the first without at the same time and in the same act meaning the second. But Mr Langford maintains that if 'colour' means what it must to most people, the two meanings can be dissociated. Our idea of colour is built up step by step, like our idea of chair or man. Just as the child is told that this thing is a chair, and that other thing is a chair, and so on, till he attains in course of time the comprehensive meaning we all use, so he is told that red is a colour, and green and yellow are colours, till he has in the end an idea that answers to them all. Now if we think that the idea of red must *include* this general idea, we are mistaken, for it is possible to have the first without the second. Suppose a man born with vision so limited that he could see only one colour, red; everything not so coloured would have some shade of grey. Such a person could attach a meaning to 'red', but he could not possibly attach to 'coloured' the meaning it commonly bears, for he

[1] C. D. Broad, *The Mind and Its Place in Nature*, 568–9.

has never had the experience that makes this possible; and hence it is idle to say that this meaning is analytically contained in 'red'. Similarly, we can see that if anything is orange in colour, it is intermediate between red and yellow. Though the colours are of course presented empirically, the insight is more than empirical, for we can see that given the colours, this relation between them *must* hold. But if we say that this relation falls necessarily within the meaning of 'orange', we are met by a decisive objection: it is not at all inconceivable that a man's range of colours should be limited to orange and then while 'orange' would have a meaning for him, the relations to the adjoining colours, supposed to be lodged in its very essence, would remain a blank to him.[1]

37. Even in arithmetic it is better to say that definitions and postulates entail the propositions that follow from them than to say that they contain these. For in what intelligible sense could they be said to contain them? If the meaning is that one could not know the premises without in the same sense knowing the conclusions, it is clearly contrary to fact. If what is meant is that one could not deny the conclusions without denying the premises, that is true, but it does not commit one to the containment view, for it would hold equally on the entailment view. If it is meant that the conclusions logically follow from, or are implied by, the premises, the question still remains why these words should be construed as 'contained by'. If the meaning is that one who knows the premises knows the conclusions implicitly, in the sense of having a subconscious or unconscious grasp of them, it is quite unverifiable; and 'implicit' otherwise seems to mean no more than implied. Finally, if the meaning is that a sufficiently powerful mind, given the premises, would find nothing new in the system deduced from them, the present question is being begged. Mathematicians often say that a statement *means* all that it implies; and if they wish to use the word thus, they are of course at liberty to do so. It will then follow by definition that to grasp the meaning of the premises would be to grasp everything that logically followed from them. But if this mode of settlement is to be admitted, one can get an opposite result merely by defining meaning otherwise; and we may leave such manipulations to those who have an interest in them.

The issue here is not over how a word is to be used but over the nature of a relation that is constantly employed but imperfectly

[1] C. H. Langford, 'A Proof that Synthetic A Priori Propositions Exist,' *Journal of Philosophy*, Vol. 46 (1949), 23, 24.

understood, the relation of following. That the conclusions do follow from the premises is common ground. Positivists say that to follow from something is to be contained in it. We counter by asking that the sense of 'contain' be specified more precisely. When a person ordinarily says that something is 'part of' or 'contained in' what he means, he is saying that he knows it to be there, at least in the sense that if he were asked, he would be able to say it was there. It is agreed on all hands that most of the conclusions that might be drawn from our premises are *not* there in this sense. But no other plausible sense seems to be forthcoming.

An interesting attempt to meet the difficulty has been made by Professor Malcolm, who proposes to ask, not whether two statements 'mean the same', since this itself is decided by differing criteria, but whether they state the same fact. He thinks that in no case where *p* entails *q*, will *p* and *q* be found to state differing facts. 'We shall define the expression "different fact" in the following way: we shall say that A and B are different facts, if and only if either A is a further fact in addition to B, or B is a further fact in addition to A.'[1] Now I confess I should have thought that the only way to decide whether *q* did express a fact different from that of *p* was to ask whether they meant the same, and that we can see quite clearly that we are not expressing the same fact when we say '*X* is red' as when we say *X* is 'extended'. But Professor Malcolm apparently thinks that the ambiguities of this phrase can be avoided by asking whether the two propositions would be verified in the same way; if they would, they express the same fact, if not, not. But this test supports his conclusion, I think, only if taken in too broad a sense. It is true, no doubt, that one would verify the proposition '*X* is red' by 'the same perception' through which one might verify '*X* is extended'. But a perception of this kind is a complex affair, and one can certainly discriminate within it elements of which one would verify one statement and another another. And it seems to me clear that the element within it which verifies '*X* is red' is different from that which verifies '*X* is extended'. If so, the extension of *X*, would, by Mr Malcolm's own criterion, discriminatingly applied, be a 'further fact in addition to' its redness.

Kant, after all, seems to have been nearer right than his critics. He would admit that 12 followed from definitions of '7', '5', and 'plus'. But he would deny that everything meant by '12' need enter into our meaning when we thought of '7 + 5'. Perhaps his conclusion

---

[1] *Mind*, Vol. 49 (1940), 342, 'The Nature of Entailment'; see also *ibid.*, 189 ff, 'Are Necessary Propositions Really Verbal?'

will be admitted more readily when the cases taken are more complex. $6 = 19^3 + 371 - 7224$; $17 = \sqrt[5]{1419857}$. Kant would have the temerity to say that he could conceive the first term of each of these equations without conceiving the second. His critics would reply that this was a flagrant shift of issue; they were talking about logical containment; he was talking about psychological containment. To which Kant would rejoin that he was trying to make out what they meant by logical containment; it could not mean that the second term or proposition was merely identical with the first; $6 = 6$ is not the same proposition as $6 = 19^3 + 371 - 7224$, nor is this latter term a fragment within the logical definition of 6; nor can the two expressions always be substituted for each other, since in drawing up a list of primes, for example, one would furnish material and the other not. In fact there seemed to be no natural sense of containment except that the thought of 6 included the thought of 19^3, etc.; and to Kant that seemed plainly false, as it does to us. The retort so often made to Kant may be expected again, that this solves the problem in a purely psychological way, that what is synthetic to the beginner in arithmetic will now be analytic for the veteran, for whom the relation is familiar and obvious. But this misses the point. Entailment is not transmuted into identity merely through becoming obvious. And how is one to tell whether the object 6 includes something except by asking whether 6, as clearly conceived by us, includes it nor not? If to talk about 6 as known is to talk psychology, Kant was talking psychology. But then physicists and chemists and biologists are also talking psychology when they talk of their own objects as known to them. Is it suggested that they might better confine themselves to things as *not* known?[1]

38. The propositions we have been discussing, and all other a priori propositions, positivists would range alike under the broad heading of the analytic. The assertion by which they do so—All a priori propositions are analytic—is of course itself a proposition of importance, and we may well ask at this point where it falls in the positivist classification. It is not meant to be empirical, for then it would be probable only; one could never be certain that the next a priori

---

[1] 'I have never been able to discover the difference between the question "do you know what it would be like for p to be false?" and the question "can you *conceive* (or *imagine*) p to be false?" And if the questions are synonymous, then "empiricists" are covertly employing just that "psychologistic" criterion of necessary truth which they so emphatically repudiate.' Arthur Pap, *Semantics and Necessary Truth*. Professor Pap's book contains the most complete discussion I know of the problems touched upon in this chapter.

proposition one met would confirm it; and positivists say un-
hesitatingly that *all* such propositions are analytic. But if a proposition is not empirical, we are told, it must be a priori, and, if a
priori, either self-contradictory or analytic. Since there is no suggestion on either side that it is self-contradictory, it must be analytic.
But this term has borne different senses for positivists. For many,
perhaps most, an analytic proposition has been a report of how it is
proposed to use an expression. But if the above proposition is
analytic in this sense only, it is of no importance; it is a resolution
which says nothing true or false. But it is hard to believe that
positivists have intended anything so trivial, even when their own
doctrine required it. They have surely intended to say something
important about an important class of propositions. Sometimes, of
course, they say that by propositions they mean only sentences, but
then their assertion is clearly empirical, and by admission cannot be
known to be universally true. If they interpret propositions in a more
usual and plausible way, they are still in difficulties. For if the statement that all a priori propositions are analytic is arrived at neither
empirically nor by definition, just how is it arrived at? To say that
it is an explication of what is commonly meant by the a priori would
be untrue, since that is so widely denied. It looks very much as if the
positivist were trying to assure himself of this universal assertion by
the kind of insight he disowns. 'I strongly suspect,' writes C. D.
Broad, 'that some people accept the theory that there are no synthetic
a priori propositions because the epistemological principle that *no*
synthetic proposition could possibly be self-evident (which is
certainly a synthetic proposition) *does in fact* seem to them self-
evident.'[1]

39. In discussing a priori statements, we have spoken both of
concepts containing other concepts and of premises containing the
conclusion. This is quite justifiable, since those we have been
criticizing hold that both statement and inference, if a priori, are
tautologous in much the same sense; 'if p follows from q, the sense
of "p" is contained in that of "q".'[2] But it may be well to say a
separate word about their view of the repetitive character of inference.
They hold, for example, that nothing new ever emerges in the conclusion of a syllogism, because, like Mill, they read the premises in

---

[1] *Proc. of the Arist. Soc.*, Sup. Vol. 15 (1936), 116. Cf. Royce's remark, 'I am
very willing to hear people condemn the a priori; for I notice they do so on a priori
grounds.'

[2] Wittgenstein, *Tractatus*, 5.122.

extension, and say that you cannot know that all men are mortal without knowing that Socrates is, but that if you do know this, then your conclusion is already a part of your major premise, and a fraud if offered as anything novel. Now I do not think for a moment that Mill's analysis applies to universal propositions generally, but I can only say that his view of them seems far more plausible than that offered by the type of logic which positivism has followed. According to that logic, the model for interpreting 'whatever is red is extended' is $(x).\varphi x \supset \psi x$, which, interpreted for this case, means 'for all values of x, x is red implies that x is extended'. Now it seems to me obvious that in such a judgment, we are not thinking primarily about cases at all; we are thinking about characters; we are judging that the quality red is such as to entail extension; and it is only because we see this, that we are ready to commit ourselves to the secondary extensional judgment that all *cases* of the one will be cases of the other.

But apart from this, what are we to make of the '$\varphi x \supset \psi x$' formula? The symbol '$\supset$' means, of course, 'implies', and in this logic one proposition, p, is said to imply another, q, when $\sim(p.\sim q)$, that is, in all cases except where p is true and q false. Any proposition will imply another, for example, if they both happen to be true; sea-water is salty will imply that Chinese communists invaded Korea. Now to interpret the asserted relation between 'x is red' and 'x is extended' in this manner seems to me grotesque. The relation between them is one of seen necessity, and when this is watered down to the bare conjunction involved in saying that the first is never in fact true while the second is false, the essential insight is lost. Since it is entirely possible that this conjunction should hold while the relation asserted was absent, the form is inadequate to the content. One may argue, of course, that the form never leads us practically astray, since if there is necessity in the intension, the extension (the required correlations among truth-values) will always follow suit. This is true. But the business of analysis is to be accurate, not to put us off with something which, though inaccurate, works. And once this looseness is accepted, the inflexible, dead, formal shell comes to be regarded as all there is to the organism of living thought, and the nature of inference is misread. Put as your major 'for all values of x, "x is red" implies "x is extended"', and for your minor 'x is in fact red'; then the conclusion 'x is extended' will follow analytically, for your major has already said that the second is true wherever the first is; and the reasoning is a *petitio*. But no one thinks that way, and if he did, he would not properly be thinking at all. The nerve of our inference is:

being red *as such* entails being extended; and since x has the first character, it must have what this character entails. There is no tautology in such thinking. The tautology has been imposed from without by an insensitive and distorting logic.

One would think that positivists would acquire some distrust of this logic from the very ease with which it may be turned against their own position. They maintain that when we derive the implications of a proposition, we are unpacking what is 'contained' in it. But consider what, according to that logic, an analytic proposition must contain. By the definition of material implication, all analytic propositions, being necessary, and therefore true, will imply each other. But it is absurd to say that every conceivable analytic proposition contains in itself all other conceivable analytic propositions. As Mr Pap has reminded us, 'when I say "all bachelors are unmarried" I need not be thinking of the fact that 4 is the cube-root of 64.'[1] It may be replied that this is a return to the psychological meaning of 'contain'. But it is useless to protest against the psychological meaning unless some intelligible alternative can be supplied. Students of positivism are still waiting for any plausible explanation of how precisely statements about squares and cubes, colours and geometrical relations, are contained in the innocent-seeming remark that bachelors are unmarried.

40. IV. We can glance at only one more consequence of this doctrine that a priori statement and reasoning are proposals regarding usage, namely that they say nothing about the actual world. This is the fourth contention about a priori knowledge that we set out to examine. When I say that it is raining, I am saying something about the weather; when I say it is not raining, I am doing the same; but 'I know nothing about the weather', says Wittgenstein, 'when I know that it is raining or not raining.' Similarly, when I say that two straight lines cannot enclose a space, or that the same surface cannot be black and non-black, or that a line is divisible without limit, or that the difference in intensity between two pleasures is not itself a pleasure, I am not saying anything about the objects mentioned, but only illustrating my usage.

We must agree, I think, that these statements are not verifiable in the same way as affirmations of sense qualities; and if any philosophers have supposed they were, the positivists have done well in disillusioning them. But if the argument here is that because a proposition says nothing about sensible fact, it says nothing about

[1] A. Pap, *Elements of Analytic Philosophy*, 339.

fact at all, we have returned to the verification theory of meaning, for which, as we have seen, there is little to say, even when it begs the question less plainly than it does here. Indeed we saw that our experience of nature is shot through with relations of time, degree, causality, number, genus and species, resemblance, and so on, which, as Kant insisted, are as indispensable to our experience as sensation, but are not sensible themselves. Now many of these relations are, or involve, relations of entailment; for example, if a precedes b, and b precedes c, then a precedes c, whether the series is interpreted for time, causality, genus and species, or degree. Positivists tell us that in asserting such entailment we 'say nothing'. To be sure, they also commonly assume that such statements are true; and then they are in the curious position of saying that propositions that 'say nothing' are somehow true. *What* it is that is true if nothing is said is an intriguing speculation. In any case, one cannot have it both ways. If nothing is said, nothing is true; if something is true, then something must have been said.

41. I think that the latter course must be taken, that something *is* said in these propositions that is meant to hold of the actual world, and that direct inspection of our meaning confirms this reading. When Bradley, or anyone else, says that reality is consistent, he means something about the world; he is not merely making a declaration about his linguistic practice. We can only suppose that positivists at times make similar judgments. We have seen that when they call an a priori proposition conventional, they would take it as inseparable from their meaning that it is not other than conventional, that if what it says is true, this truth excludes its contradictory. But *this* exclusion they do not take as a convention merely, which one may abandon if one sees fit. They do not conceive that there is anything in the least arbitrary about the incompatibility between being a convention and not being such; on the contrary, they assume that in reporting it, they are reporting an arrangement that is fixed for them and not made by them. If anyone were to announce to them, as his own favourite convention, that statements might be conventions and yet not so, they would give him very short shrift. Yet if this *is* their meaning, their position is incoherent. They hold that the law of contradiction is not a statement about the nature of things at all, because such statements must be capable of empirical verification, and this is not. But unless the law does hold of the nature of things, the conventional character they ascribe to it will not exclude its own opposite; a convention may be no convention. The law therefore must be more than conventional. Their theory of convention is at war with their theory of meaning. One or the other must go.

The grounds on which it is denied that necessary statements tell us anything about fact are curious. Sometimes they take the form of including among statements of fact only those to which exception can be imagined or conceived. In a telling critical article on 'The Linguistic Theory of A Priori Propositions', Dr Ewing maintained that the statement 'You cannot take a shilling from a purse which contains only sixpence' was a necessary statement that also said something about reality.[1] A critic in *Analysis* replied that in thinking it said something about reality, he must be confusing it with some such statement as 'You cannot grind coffee beans with a book'. Each states that something is impossible, but the two impossibilities are entirely different. If you cannot grind coffee beans with a book, that is a merely factual 'impossibility', because it is conceivable that a fact should appear that would falsify it. But if you cannot take a shilling from a purse containing only sixpence, that is a logical impossibility, which states nothing about fact, since you can see that no fact *could* turn up that would falsify it.[2]

This is odd reasoning. Does the insight, which we are conceded to possess, that no fact *could* falsify the statement, disclose nothing about fact at all? To know that no exception to your generalization has ever occurred or ever will—is that knowing nothing about the course of nature? If you know that in *some* cases you could not draw a shilling out of a purse with only sixpence in it, that would be granted to be knowledge of fact. If you know that in *no* cases could you do it, that is not knowledge of fact. What is the reason for this apparently arbitrary distinction? So far as one can judge, it is only this, that to admit that necessary statements may state about fact would destroy the neat classification: necessary-linguistic on the one hand, contingent-empirical on the other. But when that classification is itself in question, to ground an argument for its validity on the assumption of its validity is without force. To be able to forecast with confidence that certain things will never happen because we see that they cannot happen is, if you will, a very strange power. But one cannot disprove its existence by saying that it is too strange for belief. One must ask oneself whether certain impossibilities, seen to hold in theory, are not also seen in the same insight to hold in fact. To this question it is hard to see how any answer but one can be given. In

[1] *Proc. of the Arist. Soc.*, Vol. 40, 207.
[2] Beryl Lake, 'Necessary and Contingent Statements', *Analysis*, April 1952, 115 ff.

the logic in vogue among positivists, the universal proposition is a pure hypothetical; it does not state or imply that any of its terms exist; it says only '*if* A, then B'. On the other hand the particular proposition is read as a statement about existent cases or instances. One could raise questions about this mode of interpretation, but let us accept it and see where it leads in the issue before us. A priori statements, being universal, are to be regarded as pure if-thens. But suppose we deny one of them—the proposition, for example, that all lines are either straight or curved; this gives us the contradictory, 'some lines are neither straight nor curved'. This is, of course, a particular proposition, and it is interpreted as referring to particular cases which contravene the general rule; the denial of $(x).\varphi x$ is $\exists x. \sim(\varphi x)$. It would be admitted, I take it, to apply to existence and to be false in fact. But it is hard to believe that in asserting a proposition, you are saying nothing true of fact if, when you deny it, you are saying something false of fact. If the first statement says nothing about actual lines, how could the denial of it say anything about them either? If it did, it would be talking about different things, and thus would not contradict the first. But if it is admitted to refer to existence and to deny a predicate of the same things (or some of them) of which the first affirms it, then the universal too must be admitted to refer to existence.

42. It is sometimes said that 'rules of inference, like the rules of grammar, chess, etiquette and military funerals, are performance-rules', about which the question whether they are true or not is in-appropriate. This position has been inherited from Wittgenstein and the positivists by many later analytic philosophers. Mr Ryle, for example, writes: 'The world neither observes nor flaunts the rules of inference any more than it flouts the rules of bridge, prosody or viticulture. The stars in their courses do not commit or avoid fallacies any more than they revoke or follow suit.'[1] Now it is clear that the laws of logic *are* performance rules; they are rules for thinking. But surely thinking differs from such performances as 'bridge, prosody and viticulture' in one significant respect, namely that its aim is to find out what is true. And if it is to succeed in finding this out, it must adjust itself to its object; if its object is really square, it cannot judge it to be round, or round and square at once. Now if we lay down certain rules of thinking rather than others, it is not, as in bridge, because they offer the most promising among many alternative ways of constructing an amusing game, but because we *must* think so if we are to think truly. Of course if we do not want to know what is

[1] G. Ryle, *Proc. of the Arist. Soc.*, Sup. Vol. 20 (1946), 22, 23.

true, there is no reason whatever why we should submit to the logical straitjacket; logic does not say that we cannot or should not contradict ourelves to our heart's content. What it does say is that we cannot contradict ourselves and *also* think truly, since two contradictories cannot both be true. When it says that, it is of course proposing a rule of performance. But why this rule rather than others? Because, as we saw long ago, the aim of this kind of performance is to know the nature of things, and this nature requires us, if we would know it, to think consistently. The laws of logic are mandatory for thinking precisely because they are, first, laws of ontology. Bradley saw more clearly in these matters than some of his successors. 'In thought the standard, you may say, amounts merely to "act so"; but then "act so" means "think so", and "think so" means "it is". . . . Thinking is the attempt to satisfy a special impulse, and the attempt implies an assumption about reality. You may avoid the assumption so far as you decline to think, but, if you sit down to the game, there is only one way of playing. In order to think at all, you must subject yourself to a standard . . . and while you doubt this you accept it, and obey while you rebel.'[1]

The more we reflect on it, the more we shall be puzzled how a priori statements can be true at all if they are not true of the actual world. When one says that whatever is red is extended, one ordinarily supposes oneself to be talking about all possible red things, including all the red things that have existed, do exist, or will exist. To hold that one is saying nothing about the existent at all is so very odd as to suggest that the doctrine arose, not from an examination of what in fact we mean, but from some antecedent commitment as to what we must, or ought to mean. Indeed we have seen that this is the truth of the matter, that the doctrine springs from the prior conviction that a statement about the existent must be a statement about what is sensory, and that this in turn seems to rest upon an antiquated metaphysic alleging all that exists to be sensory. We shall do no further burrowing in these sandy foundations.

43. But it may be well to look at another reason that has moved people to deny a priori propositions to be true of the actual world. These propositions, it is said, are universal; the terms they connect are as-suches; but all that exists is particular, and hence such statements cannot be true of it. 'What is red is extended' means '*if* anything is red, *then* it is extended', and this neither says nor implies that there is, has been, or will be, any red thing in the world.

[1] *Appearance and Reality* (2nd ed.), 152–3.

The argument is unsound. It is true that a priori statements deal with as-suches, but these as-suches may exist and be given. When I look at this specific shade of red, I am seeing what is at once given (since it is no construct or inference), existent (since it occupies space and time), and universal (since this shade could appear in other instances). If, in looking at it, I judge that whatever has this shade is extended, I mean to make the statement about this instance and all like it. There is no reason to doubt the occurrence of Aristotle's 'intuitive induction', by which one apprehends, in and through the individual case, the necessary connection of attributes. Through seeing that *this* surface cannot be at once red and green all over, one achieves the insight that this holds of surfaces as such; through seeing that *this* pair of straight lines cannot enclose a space one grasps the truth about all such pairs. In the fact that a priori assertions deal with as-suches or universals, there is nothing whatever to prevent our asserting that they hold, and are meant to hold, of individual cases. Indeed the attempt to draw a line between the universal and the existent is fundamentally wrong-headed, for unless universals were present in individual cases, it would be meaningless to call them cases at all. But if necessary propositions may thus be meant and seen to hold of individual cases, they may clearly be true of the existent.

The fact is that the most general of them, namely logical laws, far from being true of no existents, are true of all of them. This point, already made against the conventionalists, must be made again here. It is a delusion to suppose that because such laws say nothing particular, nothing about this rather than that, they say nothing at all. No doubt as one climbs the tree of Porphyry to higher and higher abstractions, eliminating what differs among objects and retaining only what they have in common, one gets less and less of specific content. But does it follow that when concepts are reached that apply to everything alike, they must be without content altogether? Surely not. Nor if they were, would they deserve the name, for as Kant pointed out, a concept that is wholly empty, a thought that is not a thought of anything, is something less than a thought. It is much the same with relations. One may peel off from an object relation after relation in the hope of finding something that is free of all relations. But one is always baffled, for in the centre of the onion there is something still standing in the relations of identity and difference; these are conditions both of its being, and of its being conceivable. And it is absurd to say that a relation becomes nothing through being necessary and universal; 'formal logic,' as Morris Cohen contended, 'is not empty of all content, but is rather the most general branch of ontology, dealing with all possible beings.'[1] Or as Leibniz put it, 'possibility, impossibility, and necessity (for the necessity of one thing is the impossibility of its contrary) are none of them chimeras of our own making, since all we do is to recognize them in spite of ourselves and in a constant manner'.[2] The time-worn jest is here in point to the effect that the scientist goes on knowing more and more about less and less till he knows everything about nothing, while the philosopher goes on knowing less and less about more and more till he knows nothing about everything. The positivist takes the view seriously that the philosopher's knowledge about everything is really a knowledge of nothing, and hence no knowledge at all. We must grant that logic tells us little about the world. But that little is vital, since it has to do with relations essential to the being and nature of all that is.

Suppose, however, that the positivist is right about the truth of a priori propositions, right, that is, in saying that while they are not true of the actual world, they are somehow true nevertheless. Of what realm or region *are* they true? If they are statements about what we actually mean by our words, they are obviously statements of fact, though how the positivist is to find room for meanings among his observable facts is a difficult point. If, again, they are statements about pure concepts and their linkages, about an order of Platonic ideas, subsistent but not existent, they introduce a kind of non-sensible entity that the positivist wants above all things to avoid. Nor do they apply to possibilities alone as opposed to the actual; the statement that these two straight lines can intersect only once is not confined to merely possible lines. But if a priori statements are true neither of the existent nor of the subsistent, neither of the actual nor the merely possible, of what realm or region are they true? One is baffled to think what. No doubt it was with such considerations in mind that some positivists denied that these assertions were propositions at all, and held them to be arbitrary rules of syntax. But that theory, as we also saw, ends in shipwreck upon the hard fact that to this particular type of 'convention' there is no thinkable alternative.

44. Let us bring this protracted discussion to a close by briefly taking our bearings. Philosophers and theologians from Pythagoras forward have assumed that by reflective thought one could gain knowledge about the nature and structure of the world. They placed their trust in reason. Their logic set out the principles of reason as

[1] *Journal of Philosophy*, Vol. 33 (1936), 690.
[2] Letter to Foucher.

exhibited in what they took to be certain knowledge. They sought by reason to justify or amend their faith. The most influential moral philosophers from Socrates on were convinced that moral insights, so far as valid, were rational insights, and most of the political philosophers from Plato on have thought that if laws and rights were to be defended, it must be in the last resort on the grounds of a common reason. Speculative philosophy, because it was conceived as the most thorough embodiment of that reason, held the position of highest honour among cognitive disciplines. In the last half-century the estate of this philosophy has fallen precipitately. The chief discrediting agent on the technical side has been logical empiricism, which was developed in the first quarter of the century in Vienna, and spread in the second to Britain and America. The chief weapons of this school were a doctrine of meaning and a doctrine of necessity. The first would confine meaningful thought to assertions of what might be verified in perception. In the last chapter we examined this doctrine in all its principal forms and found that none was plausible. The second doctrine undertook to show that all a priori thinking, every statement or inference which exhibits necessity, is a report of our own meanings merely, and therefore without significance about the world. The doctrine had four chief aspects: it maintained that a priori assertions were (*a*) statements about linguistic usage, (*b*) conventions, (*c*) tautologies, and (*d*) uninformative about the actual world. In the present chapter we have examined these positions, and found each in turn to disintegrate under inspection.

It would be both untrue and ungrateful to say that the movement of logical positivism has left the practice of philosophy where it was. We owe a debt to the determined insurgents who insisted that if philosophy was to be queen of the sciences she must earn her keep, and not indulge in superior airs while maintaining in her own conduct a slackness and irresponsibility which would be permitted in no other science. If positivism over-reached itself when it demanded not only that all thought should have a cash value, but that the cash should be in its own clipped currency of sensation, and even descended to the abject nonsense of 'physicalism', it at least forced philosophers and theologians to inspect their meanings more sharply; and it showed that many of these meanings were cloudy and muddled, to say the least. If it was at times brash and juvenile in its assumption that the world's great age began anew with Volume I of *Erkenntnis*, it also raised a quite legitimate suspicion about that mass of 'intuited certainties' from which metaphysicians of the past have so freely drawn the mortar and even the foundations of their edifices. In showing that Kant and Mill were both mistaken about those geo-metrical axioms which seemed most transparently clear and simple, it showed that we are on treacherous ground everywhere in claiming certainty for our insights. Positivism has left the philosopher a sadder and not improbably a wiser man.

But if the question is not of the stimulus that positivism has offered to better practice, but of its validity as a body of doctrine, the verdict must be different. Not one of its main tenets will hold water. There is none that has not suffered damaging admissions and patchings from the school itself; each indeed has spawned so many sub-doctrines in the course of its self-amendment as to embarrass the work of criticism. Each principle, as we approached it, proved to be hydra-headed.

The attempt of positivism to discredit the claims of reason as an instrument of knowing the world seems to me to have failed. Reason may perhaps be discredited in other ways, but we may say with some confidence that it is not to be discredited in this way. For all positivists have said to the contrary, we can still think meaningfully of God, freedom, and immortality, grasp necessary connections in the nature of things, achieve by rational thinking new knowledge about the world, and discuss intelligibly and hopefully the issues that have given interest to the speculative life—the problems of body and spirit, of space, time and causality, of self and an external world, of the nature of knowledge and truth, of matter, life, mind, and God. These great issues are of course more exciting than the somewhat dreary one we have chosen, namely whether they can profitably be discussed at all. But it is almost idle to canvass such issues, however important, in an atmosphere heavy with suspicion of the only instrument that can deal with them, and our melancholy office has been to attack, not the problems, but the suspicion that has made dealing with them so difficult. Along the road we have still to travel we may meet more ancient and inveterate suspicions than this of positivism. We shall meet none, I think, more acute, more com-petent, or technically more formidable.

Unfortunately we are still far from the end of our road. Con-currently with the later phases of positivism there has grown up a set of linguistic philosophies that have developed a fresh line of attack on rationalistic constructions. None of them are avowedly positivistic; they are as a rule eager to dissociate themselves from positivism. Yet they have been so deeply influenced by it that their position is hardly intelligible without reference to it; and one conspicuous figure, Wittgenstein, was at different stages of his career a leader in both camps. Among the linguistic philosophers there is a persisting distaste for speculative philosophy and a renewed disavowal of rational insight into the nature of things. The views of these linguistic philosophers are harder to deal with than those of positivism for they are more tentative, amorphous, and unsystematized. But their influence in recent times has been immense, and no discussion of the difficulties presented to the rationalist by analytic philosophy would be complete without a consideration of their views. We turn then in the next two chapters to some types of linguistic philosophy.

CHAPTER VII

LINGUISTIC PHILOSOPHY—
SOME EARLIER FORMS

1. By the beginning of the second world war it had become clear to the more critical positivists that the kind of analysis they had first proposed would not serve. They had sought the ultimate meaning of every statement about the world in atomic facts of the form 'this is blue' or 'this is bluer than that'. The progress of this sort of analysis was clogged and eventually brought to a halt by a mounting mass of difficulties. Had the analysts ever arrived at a single agreed-upon atomic fact? No, it was admitted that they had not. Did they have a clear idea of what they were looking for in such a fact? They did seem to be clear about one side of it, the attribute or relation involved; but the subject to which this was ascribed was left a mysterious and faceless something of which, in itself, nothing could be said. Furthermore, many kinds of meaningful statement stubbornly resisted analysis. Some of them did so merely because they were vague, like statements about the behaviour of nations; if one tried to reduce these to a set of precise sensory comments about the behaviour of Smith, Jones, and Brown, the lack of equivalence was manifest. More important were the statements that had a perfectly definite meaning and still resisted analysis. 'There are a dozen chickens in the yard'; what were the sensible facts that answered to that 'dozen'? Could I point to any sensible fact as what is meant by 'John is thinking of Jane' or even by 'I am thinking of Jane'? How many atomic facts should we need to verify with certainty 'this is an apple'? An infinite number, the positivists admitted. Are we not, then, indulging in a bout of metaphysics if we are rash enough to say anything about an apple? So it would seem. And our metaphysics becomes even wilder if we venture on a remark about the table in the living room when no one is there. Of course we believe that the table is there, but if our statement must refer to observable facts, and we have specified that they shall be unobservable, our statement ought to mean nothing. And what of the verifiability principle itself? It was the alpha and omega of the positivists; it was what sustained the demand for analysis, and supplied it a direction and a test. But when the principle was applied to itself, it collapsed, and not with a whimper, either, but with a portentous bang. It was plainly not an inductive generalization, nor could it be called *a priori*; and if it was the only other thing that it could apparently be, an arbitrary rule of practice, why should it be binding on anyone who preferred some other rule?

2. The positivist kind of analysis had broken down. Did this call for a return to uninhibited metaphysics? Those who had followed with sympathy the positivist adventure were not ready for such a retreat. To be sure, there were far more things in the world than were dreamed of in this philosophy, but that did not imply that the doors of the metaphysical menagerie were to be flung wide and the landscape dotted again with the unearthly monsters that lurked in it. Was there not some kind of analysis that would preserve the gains so hardly won by the positivists, without going to their unbridled extremes? Perhaps the trouble was that their analysis had been too simple and naïve. After all, it allowed for only three kinds of statement: a tautology, an assertion about atomic facts, and the expression of an emotion. Would these three pigeon-holes really hold all that people tried to say? Many analysts doubted it. Frank Ramsey had suggested long before that a general proposition expressed none of these things, but rather a rule adopted to guide belief in particular cases. Willard Quine and Morton White protested that they were unable to find the sharp line drawn by positivists between the analytic and the synthetic. The younger moralists at Oxford were soon pointing out that moral statements expressed an indefinite number of things besides emotions, for example commendations, exhortations, and commands. How was this wealth of expressible content, which burst the seams of positivist theory, to get justice done to it? The answer that gradually emerged was this: do not assume in advance that what you mean will fall into any preconceived categories at all. Do not prejudge what you mean by assumptions as to what the world must be like. Let each statement speak for itself; it may have its own kind of meaning, and that kind of meaning its own logic. The key to these varieties of meaning is language. Only through the nuances of language can we explore the manifold content of idea, impulse, and feeling that human beings can express. We should no longer say 'Look for the meaning', for that suggests an object that may not be there. The new rule, and the right one, is '*Look for the use*'.

The main emphasis in British philosophy after the second war thus shifted to linguistic analysis. But this analysis, like that which preceded it, took many forms. It is hard to give these a historical order, for most of them developed concurrently, and to try to exhaust them would be idle, since a new one would probably present itself while one's remarks were in the press. All that I shall attempt in what follows is to indicate a few high points in the growth of linguistic analysis, following a historical order where it is discernible and accompanying the narrative with an occasional hiss or cheer.

3. The analytic sects have had their church fathers. The patriarch of the verifiability theory was Schlick. The father of logical atomism was Russell. The patron saint of analytic a priorism was Wittgenstein. By many he has been regarded as the founder also of the newer linguistic analysis. But that honour, if honour it is, should go rather to G. E. Moore. Moore was never a positivist; he rejected the positivist position in all the chief areas of knowledge—necessity, fact, and value. There were few philosophers of the pre-Wittgenstein era that the younger analysts greatly respected, but they made an exception of Moore. He always took his own line; he disagreed with them on cardinal points; yet they acclaimed him, to his embarrassment at times, as a leader. Why was this? Partly because he shared with them a distrust of metaphysics: partly because of an intellectual integrity so sturdy that even iconoclasts had to respect it; partly because of an exactitude and subtlety in argument that they could only envy; partly because of a common distaste for rhetoric and unction and a common preference for simple language and homely example; partly because of Moore's almost reverential generosity to Wittgenstein, who was to succeed him at Cambridge; lastly, and not least, because he gave to 'the philosophers of ordinary language' the suggestion that started them on their way. He suggested that common sense and its language supplied to philosophy both its main problems and a touchstone by which its speculative claims might be checked. 'It has been Professor Moore,' writes a contemporary analyst, 'who has made philosophers see how easy it is to slip into nonsense by even apparently trivial deviations from standard English. . . .'[1] 'Moore's great historical role,' writes another, 'consists in the fact that he has been perhaps the first philosopher to sense that any philosophical statement which violates ordinary language is false, and consistently to defend ordinary language against its philosophical violators.'[2]

[1] A. G. N. Flew, in *Logic and Language*, 1st Series, 9.
[2] N. Malcolm, in *The Philosophy of G. E. Moore*, ed. by P. A. Schlipp, 368.

4. Moore's influence was due more to his example than to his precepts, more to his strenuously self-critical effort to think clearly than to any assured results of that thinking or to any theory of his own about what he was doing. Indeed, though he was engaged in analysis most of his life, he professed not to know clearly what he meant by the term.[1] Regarding one point in his practice, however, he was clear and firm: he was not dealing primarily with words. One never finds him talking, in the mannner of the later positivists, about philosophy as the analysis of *sentences*. 'When I have talked of analysing anything, *what* I have talked of analysing has always been an idea or concept or proposition, and *not* a verbal expression. . . .'[2] A sentence was for him a string of sounds or marks on paper; the proposition they expressed could be expressed equally well by a string of marks or sounds in some other language; and such strings were of no special interest to the philosopher. The analysis of a sentence, he said, would consist of resolving it into its constituent words and letters, and he felt that a grown man and a philosopher could find more profitable things to do. It was the thought expressed through language, and this alone, that interested Moore, and if he attended as closely as he did to words, it was because he thought that differences in expression were the most useful keys with which to unlock the subtle and manifold differences in meaning. He found concentrated in common usage the result of an immense amount of experience and intellectual experiment. If a philosopher took liberties with that usage, he must, in justification, accept a heavy burden of proof.

5. For the analyst, Moore's most important essay was 'A Defence of Common Sense', published in 1925. In this essay he offered a long list of propositions for which eminent philosophers had argued, and went on to the arresting conclusion that he could see all of them, without argument, to be false. Philosophers had held that no material things existed unperceived, indeed that there were no material things at all; they had held that space and time were unreal; they had maintained that, though there were some things that one could perhaps know for certain, such as 'I now have a headache' or '$2+2=4$', the commonest assumptions of common sense fall beyond the range of such certainty; one does not really *know*, for example, that there are other minds besides one's own, or that one's memories of the past are not all illusions imposed by some gigantic hoodwinker.

---

[1] N. Malcolm, in *The Philosophy of G. E. Moore*, ed. by P. A. Schlipp, 666.
[2] *Ibid.*, 661.

Moore thought such doubts absurd. It was impossible even to hold them consistently. The philosopher who doubted that material things existed ought of course to be in doubt whether there were tables and chairs, and whether he had any hands or feet, but he gave little evidence of being so. Moore titillated the British Academy some years later by refuting all such philosophers merely through holding up one of his hands, and saying 'This is a material object, so at least one material object must exist.' Philosophers like Bradley would in all seriousness write down sentences denying the reality of space and time, when unless there were paper spread out to write them on and time to do the writing, the sentences could never have been formed. The philosopher who insisted that his memory or his belief in other minds might be illusions would have no doubt that his wife had asked him to get some groceries on his way home; and if someone were to tell him he had no right to believe either that his wife had given him the injunction or that he had a wife at all, he would not think much of the jest.

6. Were all these philosophers hypocrites? That seemed hardly the right judgment. Moore thought that their state of mind could be better understood if we supposed them to have overlooked a pair of important distinctions. One was the distinction between a proposition and the analysis of that proposition. We might be perfectly certain, for example, that material things existed while genuinely uncertain how the concept 'material thing' should be analysed. The doubts of the philosopher must apply to the analysis of the proposition, not to its truth, since to doubt its truth would be merely silly. If the philosopher insists on being silly, the only reply that he deserves, and indeed the only valid reply, is a return to common sense, to the plain knowledge, beyond the reach of metaphysical cavil, that tables and chairs and other persons do in fact exist. This does not take away the philosopher's business. There is still plenty of work for him to do in analysing common sense notions; the concepts of mind and self and life and matter and cause present tremendous problems. But henceforth the analysis should proceed within bounds appointed by common sense. If a philosopher comes up, as Berkeley did, with an analysis of matter that makes him say there is no such thing, common sense can tell him he is wrong; and if behaviourists inform us that there are no minds, we do not need to examine their argument to discover whether it is sound or not; we know it is unsound before they state it. Common sense thus provides a touchstone for speculation.

7. The other distinction that helps us to understand the state of mind of these philosophers is the distinction between ordinary and extra-ordinary uses of language. Moore was convinced that such words as 'time', 'space', 'material thing', 'mind', and 'know', possessed a common or standard meaning that could be called *the* meaning, and that many of the paradoxes exploited by philosophers were essentially plays on words, which scored their startling effects by substituting some freakish new sense for the standard meaning without due warning of the change. Thus when Bradley declared that time was 'unreal', he evidently did not mean that it was unreal in the standard sense in which dreams and hobgoblins are unreal, for he was ready to admit that his writing a sentence did in fact take time, and that this was anything but a dream. If he meant to deny what plain men meant, his high-sounding declaration was absurd; if he did not, he was using the word 'unreal' in a strange sense of his own, and gaining his effect through people's supposing he used it in the ordinary sense. So with the other metaphysical paradoxes. Some philosophers have impressed and astonished us by asserting that the earth did not exist before we were born.

'They seem to think that the question "Do you believe that the earth has existed for many years past" is not a plain question, such as should be met either by a plain "Yes" or "No", or by a plain "I can't make up my mind", but is the sort of question that can be properly met by: "It all depends on what you mean by 'the earth' and 'exists' and 'years'; if you mean so and so, and so and so, and so and so, then I do; but if you mean so and so, and so and so, and so and so, or so and so, and so and so, and so and so, then I don't, or at least I think it is extremely doubtful." It seems to me that such a view is as profoundly mistaken as any view can be. Such an expression as "The earth has existed for many years past" is the very type of an unambiguous expression, the meaning of which we all understand.'[1]

We can of course saddle ordinary words with new senses if we will, and ride off on them to cheap and easy victories over common sense. But they will be verbal victories only. For where the new conclusions conflict with common sense statements carrying their standard meanings, common sense is clearly right.

This was a challenging doctrine, which lost none of its effectiveness in Moore's vigorous and even vehement statement of it. He had an unequalled gift for exploding pretentious obscurity in language that

[1] *Contemporary British Philosophy* II, 198.

was as simple as it was exact, and for many years he was the *enfant terrible* of British philosophers. His influence on them was salutary. Though they could no longer write with the old freedom while Moore was looking over their shoulders, that meant that they were more vigilant in self-criticism. Granting, however, that Moore's example was admirable, the question remains whether we can justifiably appeal, as he proposed, from philosophy to common sense and common usage. I do not think we can, and for the following reasons.

8. (1) For many words of philosophic importance there is no single standard use, but a variety of uses, all equally standard; and if the philosopher were to employ all of them, his language, far from being clear and unambiguous, would be an intolerably blunt and blundering instrument. Take such key words as 'know' and 'certain' and 'doubt'. They are ordinarily used for many kinds of apprehension and many degrees of assurance. We say we know or are certain or have no doubt that we now have a headache, that $2+2=4$, that there is a table in the next room, that Waterloo happened in 1815, that Boisé is the capital of Idaho, that lying is wrong, that God exists, and that the sun will rise tomorrow. But the philosopher who admitted that people were certain of all these things, in the plain man's sense of *knowing for certain* that they were true, would be speaking most uncritically, for if certainty has anything to do with clearness and strength of evidence, these beliefs differ enormously in their certainty. Adherence to common usage in such cases would be so undiscriminating as to make philosophic discussion all but impossible.

9. (2) Common usage at crucial points is excessively vague. Professor Barnes has pointed out that if he were to ask Moore whether he knew the meaning of 'This is a good big inkstand', Moore would no doubt reply that this all depended on what you meant by 'knowing the meaning'; if you meant understanding the meaning, the answer was Yes; if you meant knowing the correct analysis of the meaning, the answer was No. But this was just the sort of reply that Moore was deprecating.[1] To be sure, it was a legitimate kind of reply, but it made painfully apparent the inadequacy of the common language approach, since it admitted that the phrase 'know the meaning of' had itself no standard meaning on which the philosopher could rely. Within the vague limits that it laid down, the philosopher had to frame more definite meanings of his own before he could give a

[1] W. H. F. Barnes, *The Philosophical Predicament*, 36.

satisfactory answer. This would have been needless if common usage gave any clear guidance.

10. (3) Because of this vagueness of meaning, common sense was quite capable of giving inconsistent answers to the same philosophic question. What is the plain man's view, for example, on the question of freedom? If you asked him whether he had free choice at this moment to lift his hand or not to lift it, he would presumably say Yes. If you then asked him whether he agreed with the scientist that all events are governed by law, he would presumably say Yes again. But if he is right that every event follows from some other in accordance with law, he cannot also be right that his choosing to lift his hand, which is plainly an event, does not itself follow in accordance with law. On the problem of freedom, common sense thus plants itself on both sides of the fence. It would no doubt be found to do so on many other important issues.

11. (4) This brings us to the main difficulty with Moore's proposal. It makes common sense an arbiter in fields outside its competence; it offers the answers of common sense as adequate answers to questions that common sense has never thought of raising and would be unable to deal with if it had. Take the question whether material things exist. Moore says, Of course they do, since common sense says they do. But Moore also says (most helpfully) that if we are to get a clear answer to any question, we must know precisely what it is that we are asking. Now common sense has never raised the question at all about the existence of a material world. How could it, therefore, give the exact and guarded answer needed by the philosopher? Moore would reply that the plain man understands the meaning of what he is saying and can see it to be true, even though he cannot give the correct analysis of it. But what this implies is that one can see what one is saying to be true—indeed Moore says 'wholly true'— without knowing just what it is that one is saying. How strange this doctrine is may be seen from Moore's own practice. He devoted vast pains and patience to reflecting on what we mean when, looking at an inkstand or a match-box, we say that this is a material thing. After a characteristically minute consideration, he concluded that there were three and only three possible answers to this question. We might mean that the sense datum directly perceived was part of the surface of the material thing; we might mean that, though not part of the surface, it was in some sense an appearance or manifestation of this; or we might give the phenomenalist answer of Mill about 'permanent possibilities of sensation'. Moore admitted that to each of these answers there were 'very grave objections'; he professed himself unable to choose between them, and went so far as to say that 'no philosopher has hitherto suggested an answer which comes anywhere near to being certainly true.'[1] Now is it not odd to say that the plain man can be perfectly sure of his answer when the meaning of that answer, as correctly stated, breaks up into a set of alternatives none of which he has ever heard of, and all of which remain uncertain under the most thorough examination? What Moore is suggesting is that beliefs entertained at one level, that of unreflecting assent, should be accepted as answering questions raised at a very different level, that of reflective criticism. If true to his programme, would he not have to accept Dr Johnson's answer to Berkeley, which consisted of kicking a stone and saying it was obvious that matter existed? This was common sense, but surely it takes more than that to refute Berkeley. Johnson presumably meant, in part, that stones were hard when no one touched them; Berkeley explicitly denied this, but he denied it at a level of reflection on which Johnson had not begun to move; and if we take the doctor's dogmatism as refuting in advance all that reflection can say to the contrary, we throttle philosophy at its birth.[2]

12. Moore's appeal from philosophy to common sense was not, then, very convincing. Some of his followers thought that with a relatively slight change they could make it so. According to Professor Malcolm, all that was needed was a greater stress on the importance of language; Moore had not made sufficiently clear that what philosophers were doing when they differed with common sense was merely proposing a different usage. Some students of his writing did indeed take this as his main contention. They thought of him as not only the father but also an active member of the school of ordinary usage. Moore never accepted this role. He noted with astonishment the conclusion of one of his followers 'that when, for instance, I tried to show that Time is not unreal, all that I was doing was to recommend that we should not use certain expressions in a different way from that in which we do!' and he added, 'If this is all I was doing, I was certainly making a huge mistake, for I certainly did not think it was all. And I do not think so now.'[3] He believed, it is true, that philosophers would be

[1] *Cont. Brit. Phil.* II, 219.

[2] 'In a philosophical court the place for common sense is in the dock, or on occasion the witness-box, never the bench.' G. R. G. Mure, *Retreat from Truth*, 153.

[3] *The Philosophy of G. E. Moore*, 675.

saved much futility and confusion if they had more respect for ordinary language. But, for him, what proved the paradoxes of the philosophers to be mistaken was the conflict between these paradoxes and the *insights* of common sense, not the divergence between the *language* in which they were formulated and the *language* of common sense. It was here that his more linguistically minded followers thought he had made his mistake. What he ought to have held, they said, was that when the philosophers departed from common sense, all they were really doing was misusing words, and in order to refute them all that was needed was to point this out.

This position was developed by Professor Malcolm. 'The philosophizing of most of the more important philosophers,' he said, 'has consisted in their more or less subtly repudiating ordinary language.'[1] They are recommending new usages for old and important words. Of course this is not what they think they are doing; they suppose themselves to be offering new and profound insights into the nature of things. But here they are suffering from an illusion which has become a chronic disease. How has the strange malady come about?

It has come about through carelessness in the use of words, through the extension of legitimate usages to the point where they become illegitimate without noticing what has been going on. Mr Malcolm takes in illustration a statement of Bertrand Russell's. Russell noted that when we perceive anything, our percept of it arises as a result of a causal chain starting in the external world and ending with an event in our brain. He held that our percept *was* this event in our brain, and was thus led to the startling generalization that all one ever sees when one looks at anything is a part of one's own brain. This is not, perhaps, a very convincing conclusion, but that is not here in point; the point is what becomes of this conclusion, linguistically interpreted, and how it is then refuted. What Russell is saying, in effect, is that all perception is deception; we do not see what we think we see, but something radically different. Now when he holds that we are thus deceived, is he saying that we are deceived in the same sense as when we are deceived about a bent spoon or a mirage? Clearly not, Mr Malcolm says. For when we are deceived about the spoon or the mirage, the error is an exception to the general soundness of our perceptions, and one that can be set right by the appeal to further perception; but what Russell is here saying is that we are *always* deceived, and thus that our deception is not of the sort that further observation could correct. When he says that perception always deceives us, what kind of statement is he making?

[1] *The Philosophy of G. E. Moore*, 365.

It looks like an empirical statement, and Russell apparently so took it. But an empirical statement is one that *can* be checked by perception, one whose truth entails that the perceived world will be different at some point from what it would otherwise be. And in Russell's perceived world there is nothing distinctive whatever that corresponds with this generalization of his, or that could serve to verify it. In spite of saying that all his perceptions were of his own brain, he would report seeing postmen and post-boxes just as the rest of us would, and would scoff at the suggestion that he was being deceived. But if he is not making an empirical statement, is he making an a priori one? No, not that either; for his assertion is clearly not a necessary one, whose denial would be self-contradictory. But if it is neither a priori nor empirical, what can it be? Russell's disagreement with the plain man was not about facts; it was really 'about what *language* shall be used to describe those facts. Russell was saying that it is really *a more correct way of speaking* to say that you see a part of your brain, than to say that you see the postman.'[1] And the way to meet an assertion about language is clearly by another assertion about language. All we need to do to refute Russell's apparently philosophical statement is to show that his use of language is not the correct use. And this is easy. No one but a bemused philosopher would dream of saying, as he looked at a table, that he was seeing his own brain.

13. Mr Malcolm soon abandoned this theory, at least in part. It is to his credit that he did. What is wrong with it? (1) For one thing, it too plainly misconstrues the intentions of philosophers. Most of them would repudiate as emphatically as Moore did the suggestion that in offering their paradoxes they were merely proposing a new usage as the correct one. Russell was not saying that when one looked at a table, the sentence 'I see a state of my brain' was correct usage, while 'I see a table' was not. He knew quite well that what determines correctness of usage is the generality of actual use. H. W. Fowler has pointed out that the word 'asset' is a 'false form'; coming from the French *assez*, it should have *ts* on the end, corresponding to the French *z*; it is a corrupt substitute for 'assets', which is itself singular in meaning. This is an interesting observation. But if everyone does use asset in the singular and assets in the plural (a point I leave undetermined), it is idle to argue that such usage is incorrect; to appeal to etymology against established practice is pedantry, as indeed Fowler would agree. The charge that Russell is arguing for 'I see my own brain' as correct usage is equivalent to saying that he holds this

[1] *The Philosophy of G. E. Moore*, 350.

to be the established usage. No sane man would say such a thing.

14. (2) Again, there is no good reason for denying that Russell's proposition is an empirical one. Though it is a generalization about *all* percepts, asserting them all to be causal products, it is quite capable of being argued for in the same manner as other hypotheses. Assume it to be true, Russell would say, and you can explain far more readily the facts of illusion, colour-blindness, and many other perceptual anomalies. So the desperate argument, 'Neither a priori nor empirical, therefore a statement about language,' starts from a false premise. Furthermore, if we are right about its conclusion, the argument is so clearly contradictory that we cannot believe for a moment that Russell would be taken in by it; a statement about general usage is obviously itself an empirical statement.

15. (3) Once more, there is no reason either for Russell or for ourselves to take common usage, with all its freight of traditional meaning, as sacrosanct. People say that the sun rises and sets; astronomers know that it does not; but why, as Berkeley asked, should reflective men not think with the learned while speaking with the vulgar? To tie the thinker to the meaning and truth of ordinary speech would impose on him an appalling conservatism, in which common sense is set up as an inquisitorial board with powers of excommunication against every future Berkeley and Russell. This is all the more absurd from the fact that if it had been adopted earlier, what we know as common sense would itself have been banned; for our present common sense is impregnated with speculative conclusions; even its statements about tables and chairs show an implicit epistemological realism. It is surely wide of the mark to say that philosophers of the acumen of Berkeley and Russell are engaged in a game of word catching. They were not talking about the usage of words; they were pointing out that plain men, even when their usage was impeccable, could be mistaken, and were indeed fundamentally mistaken, about the nature of things.

16. To all such criticisms Mr Malcolm's type of linguism had its reply. This was that there were certain conditions under which common sense, when using the language correctly, *could* not be mistaken. What were these conditions? They were that the expression employed should have (1) a descriptive and (2) an underivative use. (1) An expression has a descriptive use when there are objects or situations to which it actually applies. The expression 'round square' has no descriptive use because it applies to nothing. The word 'ghost' has a descriptive use because there are situations to which it does apply; many people have reported experiences of which the only natural account is, 'I saw a ghost'. But such cases make it clear that adherence to ordinary language is no proof against error. So Mr Malcolm added a second condition. (2) Such expressions must also be underivative. 'It is important to note,' he says, 'that people can learn the meaning of the word "ghost" without actually seeing any ghosts. That is, the meaning of the word "ghost" can be explained to them in terms of the meanings of words which they already know.'[1] But there are some terms that cannot be so explained; they refer to situations that must be known at first hand if they are to be known at all, expressions such as 'earlier', 'behind', 'material things', 'it is possible that', 'it is certain that'. And when such expressions are used with their ordinary meanings, it is impossible that they should be mistaken. 'Whenever a philosophical paradox asserts, therefore, with regard to such an expression, that always when that expression is used the use of it produces a false statement, then to prove that the expression is an *ordinary* expression is completely to refute the paradox.'[2] 'It is not possible for an ordinary form of speech to be improper. That is to say, ordinary language is correct language.'[3]

Linguism is here guarding itself carefully; Mr Malcolm writes with an elaborate and patient meticulousness which to the casual reader is somewhat intimidating. He deserves a better cause, for this one is surely hopeless.

17. First, there is the fundamental and disastrous confusion between the truth of a proposition and the propriety of the words that express it. Note Mr Malcolm's conclusion above: 'it is not possible for an ordinary form of speech to be improper. That is to say, ordinary language is correct language.'[4] If that means what any writer on English usage would mean by it, it is true enough, as we have seen, but quite without philosophic interest. It is perfectly plain, however, that Mr Malcolm does think he is saying something of philosophic importance. And there is only one thing that this could be. It is that ordinary language is not only correct in the sense of *proper* but correct in the sense of *true*, that its being correct is *equivalent* to its being true. This is further implied in his contention that all one needs to

---

[1] *The Philosophy of G. E. Moore*, 360.
[2] *Ibid.*, 361.
[3] *Ibid.*, 362.
[4] *Ibid.*, 362.

refute a philosophical paradox, i.e. to show it untrue, is to show that it is a misuse of language. Now these two things, the truth of a proposition and the propriety of the words expressing it, are about as different as two things could be. Try interchanging their predicates, and you find that you cannot do it. The *truth* of a proposition is never proper or improper though its enunciation may be; and no mere *expression* is ever true. Truth is commonly taken to be the accordance of a proposition with fact; propriety is the conformity of a usage with established practice. To confound them is to darken counsel. Under an appearance of scrupulous exactitude it hides a muddle, and a peculiarly unfortunate muddle; for it tends to reduce to triviality the whole enterprise of speculative thought.

18. To this the language-philosopher may reply that there is no real confusion of truth with propriety, that is, no identification of the two, but only the new insight, to which earlier philosophers have been blind, that the two things are intimately connected, that one never finds a descriptive and underivative expression which in its ordinary use involves us in falsity. But this too is demonstrably untrue. We often use terms in Mr Malcolm's own list in such a way as to involve us in untruths. Take the expression 'it is certain that'. Can anyone soberly say that whenever we use these words in the ordinary way, they express knowledge that is beyond doubt or amendment? The religious man declares his 'certainty' that God exists; we all in ordinary speech call it a 'certainty' that the sun will rise tomorrow; the mother is 'certain' that her son is a good boy, though the jury has just, with equal 'certainty', found him guilty of murder; we are 'certain' that we passed Jones on the street yesterday, 'certain' that it would be best to write him a note of greeting, 'certain' that he will be appreciative if we do. In all these cases common usage would raise no protest at what we said. But surely in all of them we may be mistaken. Or consider 'it is possible' and 'it is probable', two more of the expressions that, as ordinarily used, are supposed to be safe against error. The ordinary man says that miracles are possible; Hume held them to be highly improbable; Spinoza held them to be impossible. Are we to say that there is no problem whether, for example, the 'miracle' of Fatima is possible, more or less probable, or impossible, because ordinary men, in contemplating it, would use the word 'possible' rather than the others? And even if we were to grant this, what if usage shifted? What if most men came in time to refer to miracles as impossible? Would that prove that Spinoza, though wrong when he announced his doctrine, since it then went

L

against ordinary usage, is now right, since people have come round to his use of words? It is hard to see, in the light of such cases, how common usage can preserve its inerrancy; for whatever base one takes it turns out to be mistaken. If the older base is accepted, from which Spinoza was condemned, then the newer usage is mistaken. If the newer base is accepted, then the usage of the past must have been mistaken. In either case, common usage is a false guide.

This kind of linguism clearly would not do. The plain man, adhering to ordinary usage about certainty and possibility and the greenness of grass, may be wrong. The philosopher who departs from ordinary usage in all these and many more respects may be right. Conformity to common usage seems, so far, to have nothing to do with truth.

19. Nevertheless the conviction that philosophy is tied up with language in some peculiar way persisted. It came out in another form in A. J. Ayer's *Logic, Truth and Language*. Ayer did not take as his touchstone common sense, as Moore did, or common usage, as Malcolm did; and yet, as his title indicated, he made linguistic considerations of the first importance for philosophy. 'For the philosopher, as an analyst, is not directly concerned with the physical properties of things. He is concerned only with the way in which we speak about them.'[1] 'We may speak loosely of him as analysing facts, or notions, or even things. But we must make it clear that these are simply ways of saying that he is concerned with the definition of the corresponding words.'[2] To define words—that, though he may not have realized it, is the true business of the philosopher.

To understand what Ayer meant by this strange-sounding doctrine, one must recall the positivist background from which he spoke. Positivists held that there were only two kinds of statement that were capable of truth or falsity. One was the statement of fact, which referred to, and must be tested by, sense experience; the other was necessary or priori, but purchased necessity at the price of tautology; it said nothing about fact. Philosophical statements will presumably belong to one or other of these classes. Did they belong to the first, the group of empirical statements? No, because the province of fact is already covered by the natural sciences, and every empirical statement will be found to belong to one or other of them; hence the philosopher who makes such statements is merely a scientist in disguise. Are philosophical statements then of the second class?, are

[1] *Logic, Truth and Language*, ², 57.
[2] *Ibid.*, 59.

they all tautologies? This too seems false, for when philosophers have talked about matter and mind, life and God, they obviously meant to say something important about the world. Philosophical statements, then, would seem to belong to neither class, and hence not to be statements at all. And Professor Ayer was more than willing to accept this conclusion about metaphysics, which he considered meaningless. But not all philosophical statements were metaphysical, and for those that were not he thought some office could be found. He described them as definitions.

But what kind of definitions? If definition here meant what it did for traditional logic, the statements of philosophy could be filed in a pigeon-hole which was ready and waiting, that of tautologies, for definition by genus and differentia is a mere analysis of meaning. If definition is what Webster practises, the philosopher becomes a lexicographer. If definition is an arbitrary 'by "X" I propose to mean "Y" ', it may be interesting to the proposer, but is of no importance to anyone else. If it means the finding of synonyms, philosophy will be in a bad way, for some of its key terms have no synonyms at all; indeed an eminent authority has suggested that there are only two exact synonyms in the language, namely 'gorse' and 'furze', which would leave the philosopher's outlook somewhat bleak. To take the work of philosophy as definition in any of these senses was highly implausible, and Ayer in fact rejected them all.

He really meant something technical. The definitions to which philosophy was to be reduced were 'definitions in use'. And what are these? 'We define a symbol *in use*,' said Ayer, '. . . by snowing how the sentences in which it significantly occurs can be translated into equivalent sentences, which contain neither the *definiendum* itself, nor any of its synonyms.'[1] Why should this special kind of definition have been hit upon? And why should positivists have wanted to make of it the main work of philosophy? The answer to both questions is that it enabled them to eliminate a large range of entities which philosophers had believed in, but which, as unverifiable in sense, were really fictions. How did it do this? Here the positivists fell back on two theories of Bertrand Russell, from whom, indeed, the phrase 'definitions in use' had come. These were his theory of 'definite descriptions' and his theory of 'logical constructions'. In order to understand what Ayer's linguistic proposal meant in practice, we must see what these theories are.

20. We have already noted that in his early days Russell was a logical

[1] *Logic, Truth and Language,* ², 60.

atomist, and that according to the atomists, every true empirical statement could be resolved into one or more statements of atomic fact such as 'this — cold' or 'that — blue'. These atomic statements were supposed to reflect in their structure the facts they asserted, for each word corresponded to a component of the fact. And the atomists dreamed of an ideal language in which every component had one name, and every word its component. With such a language we might still go wrong through attaching a predicate where it did not belong, but at least we could be sure that in using words we were not talking about mere nothings. Unfortunately that is something that our actual language, with its extremely loose correspondence to fact, not only permits us, but constantly tempts us, to do.

I say 'this is blue'; and here I am safe enough, for I can hardly be mistaken that there really is something that presents itself to me as blue. Again, when I name someone with whom I am acquainted, and say for example 'George is stout', I may be sure that someone answering to this name exists, or has existed. But if I go an inch beyond this I am in danger. Suppose I say something about the horse Bellerophon rode or about the Loch Ness monster; I seem to be referring to individuals, but no such individuals have existed. It may be protested that this is the sort of confusion made by children, not by philosophers. Russell would reply that the classes are not mutually exclusive, and that even philosophers who were incapable of confusion so gross were quite capable of it in subtler forms. They say to themselves, 'the Loch Ness monster has never been seen by anybody'. This they take as a true statement, but what is it true *of*? If, when they refer to the monster, they are referring to nothing whatever, how can this mere nothing have properties or exclude them? To affirm or deny is to do so of some subject. We can see this even in such an extreme case as 'the square circle does not exist'. *What* is it that we are here alleging not to exist? Nothing at all? But we are surely not trying to assert the non-existence of nothing. On the other hand, if we are making an assertion about something, then of what? Presumably of the square circle. But in that case the square circle must have some sort of being, if only to render the statement that it does not exist intelligible. And the pressure of language enforces what logic seems to require. We speak of 'the all-wise and omnipotent being', of 'the proposition that men are mortal', of 'the idea of justice', of 'the unknowable', of 'the triangle' or 'the ego' or 'the unconscious', and because we use the words as grammatical subjects and attach predicates to them, we tend to take them as standing for things or substances in their own right.

21. Now this, said Russell, is a gross error. The value of the theory of descriptions is that it shows how the error comes about and where it lies. It comes about through accepting grammatical form as a key to logical form. To take a familiar example of Russell's own, we suppose that because 'the author of Waverley was Scotch' resembles grammatically 'Scott was lame', it resembles this also in logical structure. The error lies in supposing that 'the author of Waverley' is, like 'Scott', a name that refers to an object, whereas, says Russell, ' "the author of Waverley" means nothing';[1] there is no individual or object that it refers to. The proof is that the statement can be re-written in such a way that this phrase, with its supposed reference to an individual, is eliminated entirely without any loss of meaning. The best way to bring to light what the statement really asserts is to ask what would serve to deny it. There are three obvious ways of denying it: you could say that *Waverley* was never written at all; you could say that, since it was written by more persons than one, it is false to suggest that only one person wrote it; or you could say that, though one person wrote it, he was not Scotch. The assertion means to cut off all these possibilities, and it is thus an omnibus statement with three parts:

(1) At least one person wrote Waverley;

(2) At most one person wrote Waverley;

(3) Whoever wrote Waverley was Scotch.

In none of these statements is there the sort of reference we find in a name; no individual is singled out; what we are really talking about is attributes or universals; we are saying that the attributes of having written Waverley and being Scotch were united in one person only, who remains undesignated. This expression of our original sentence is itself an example of 'definition in use'. We have defined the phrase 'the author of Waverley' without employing the *definiendum* or any synonym of it, and yet in such a way as to bring out the significance it bears in its context. Russell held that every 'the'-phrase could be dealt with in like fashion, with the result of a wholesale exposure of metaphysical impostors. From now on it was needless to assume that the square circle of Meinong or the transcendental bed of Plato or the triangle discussed by Euclid had any existence or subsistence. Such phrases as 'the absolute' and 'the Trinity', even 'the south pole' and 'the heart of a maid', could no longer be presumed to refer to anything.

[1] *Principia Mathematica*,[2] I, 67. For other statements of the theory by Russell, cf. *Introduction to Mathematical Philosophy*, Ch. 16; 'On Denoting', *Mind*, 1905, 479–93; and for statements of it by others, L. S. Stebbing, *Modern Introduction to Logic*,[2] 144–158; G. E. Moore, 'Russell's Theory of Descriptions' in P. A. Schilpp, ed., *The Philosophy of Bertrand Russell*.

They were mere claims that certain attributes were somewhere or other realized. The assumption, implicit in the 'the', that they are in fact realized may be true, or it may not.

22. It is obvious why Mr Ayer and the positivists, intent on doing away with metaphysics, should have appropriated Russell's theory of descriptions. It is even more obvious why they welcomed his theory of logical constructions. This provided another form of the definition in use which was peculiarly potent in exorcizing fictions. Russell seems to have discovered its efficacy first in mathematics, and his collaborator Whitehead gave a useful illustration of it in his method of extensive abstraction. A point was formerly regarded as a limit, having no magnitude, of a line or of a series of converging volumes such as one sees in Chinese boxes. But this leaves it doubtful whether there are such things as points. Whitehead hit upon the expedient of so defining a point that there was no doubt of its existence; he took it as the series of volumes themselves, continued as far as one wished, and found that this series had all the required properties of the old hypothetical point.

Russell showed that a like method could be applied to irrationals, cardinal numbers, and even classes. He then went on to apply it to things. What does the term 'thing' mean when applied to so-called material things and when the meaning is carefully analysed? A physicist would say 'a mass of protons, electrons, etc.' The traditional philosopher would say 'a material substance in which sensible qualities inhere'. Such answers seemed to Russell too speculative; they involved inferences to entities of which we were not certain, if indeed they meant anything at all. He accordingly proposed the rule, 'Wherever possible, logical constructions are to be substituted for inferred entities.'[1] This substitution is effected when a sentence referring to a questionable inferred entity is replaced by an acceptable equivalent whose reference is confined to what is empirical and indubitable. The reference to my desk as a metaphysical substance or even as a collection of sub-microscopic entities lies at the end of a dubious inference. Substitute for it the reference to my desk as a class of sensory data resembling each other from moment to moment and occupying a stable place in my own experienced space and that of others, and you have something relatively certain. In accordance with his preference for logical constructions, Russell therefore defined a material thing as the class of its appearances. The notion of material substance had evaporated.

[1] *Mysticism and Logic*, 155.

23. Mr Ayer and his positivist colleagues accepted the new method with enthusiasm and went to lengths in applying it which Russell himself would not have sanctioned. Ayer saw that if we were to eliminate inferred entities beyond the reach of our acquaintance, then not only material substances but also other minds, if these meant private centres of experience, must go; it will not do to talk of your thoughts and feelings if they are really inaccessible to me; 'you' will either mean nothing or the term will be defined by a logical construction referring to a class of my own sense-data, a class held together by continuities and resemblances of form, colour, and motion. Reference to bodily and mental substances alike may thus be eliminated. And since the metaphysical side of philosophy has been engaged with such inferred entities—with changeless Platonic ideas and Aristotelian potentialities, with the material substance of Descartes and Locke and the mental substance of Berkeley, with unknowable transcendental things and egos, with Bradleyan absolutes that unaccountably invade the world of change from their eternal Elysian fields, with Heidegger's irrepressible 'nothing' and its habit of 'nothinging' in our faces—these fauna and flora of a legendary world may now be left in peace. Of course the theological world of gods and demons will go into retirement with them. As for immortality, if that means the persistence of minds after their bodies have ceased to be, it may now be very simply disposed of, for the belief is a contradiction in terms. But all this does not mean that the occupation of philosophy is quite gone. For there is more to philosophy than metaphysics. Its more grandiose metaphysical adventures have usually been accompanied by a humbler work, namely analysis, and that remains. This remaining part of philosophy, which will from now on form the whole of it, will concern itself with language. It will try to provide definitions, and chiefly definitions in use, of the more important words of scientific and common discourse.

24. What are we to say of this programme? Certainly with much of it we can sympathize. It makes short work of some things in philosophy that might well be defunct, of obscurities passing as profundities and pomposities nourished on little but the wish to believe. Nor can we fairly regard it as negative merely. It is a kind of Puritanism in philosophy, an austere speculative asceticism; and its stern self-exactions—its requirement of rigour of statement, its demand for clarity, and its insistence on fidelity to fact—seem, to me at least, admirable. But of course the question is whether it is true.

25. Our first interest for the moment must be in the contention that what we have here is a linguistic programme. Ayer, like Carnap, insisted on this. The true business of philosophy is to define words. The theories of description and logical construction are theories, not about things, but about the language in which we talk about things. Ayer writes: 'we may regard any philosophical "theory" such as Russell's "theory of definite descriptions", as a revelation of part of the structure of a given language';[1] and 'when we refer to an object as a logical construction out of certain sense-contents, we are not saying that it is actually constructed out of those sense-contents, or that the sense-contents are in any way parts of it, but are merely expressing, in a convenient, if somewhat misleading, fashion, the syntactical fact that all sentences referring to it are translatable into sentences referring to them.'[2] To many readers such statements were an invitation to close the book. Assuming that it was a book on philosophy, they opened it to get some light on the nature of the world they lived in, on matter and mind for example, not to read about the syntax of sentences. Why this reiterated insistence that what the philosopher is doing is what most readers could only regard as comparatively trivial? It could hardly spring from a deliberate desire on the part of positivist philosophers to write themselves down. Probably it sprang, in part at least, from the realization that if they talked directly about matter and mind, rather than about our talk about matter and mind, they could be accused, with some reason, of talking metaphysics, a charge that would be hard to bear.

26. Did they succeed in escaping metaphysics? Let us look further at those definitions in use that were now to constitute the philosophic staple, and first at the theory of descriptions. This professes to be a theory about the translatability of certain sentences. But to me at least it seems to turn, both in motive and in application, on metaphysical beliefs. It bids us, for example, translate 'the Loch Ness monster is a sea-serpent' into three other sentences in which 'the Loch Ness monster' is not used. Why do this? Because the original sentence is misleading. Why misleading? Because it leads us to suppose that 'the Loch Ness monster' is a name instead of a description. What is the harm in that? The harm is in leading us to suppose that something exists which does not exist; 'the Loch Ness monster', 'the square circle', 'the proposition that', 'the class of', lead us to think these are particular existents, of which these are the names. Is it

---

[1] *Language, Truth and Logic*[2], 62.
[2] *Op. cit.*, 123; and cf. 63–64, 140–141.

suggested, then, that there are, or may be, no such things? If the analyst does say that, he is talking, not about language, but about what does and does not exist. If he does not mean that, his term 'misleading' has no sense. A term in such a case misleads because the belief it induces does not correspond to fact; but to see that it does not correspond to fact, you must see something about that fact itself. The need for the theory of descriptions sprang from a felt discrepancy between the structure of language and the actual nature of things, and the need of removing the tension.

It may be replied that though the need sprang out of a felt tension involving fact, the remedy proposed was purely linguistic. The theory of descriptions was accepted, by the positivists at least, as a theory about the translatability of sentences; what it says is that all 'the-sentences' are translatable into other sentences of the form given. But what does 'translatable' mean? If it means that people do actually use the sentence and its translation with the same sense, it is no doubt a statement about language, to be tested by empirical methods. Certainly Russell did not so intend it. But if it is not a statement of what people do, it is presumably a statement of what they ought to do—at least the philosophers among them; they should translate 'the-sentences' in the manner suggested. Why should they? Because then the grammatical form of what they say will reflect more accurately its logical form. Why adhere to this logical form? Because it is this and no other that corresponds to the form of the fact. The test whether sentence A should be translated into sentence B is whether B's logical form is closer than A's to that of the fact which both alike are trying to express. When the theory says that 'the-sentences' should be translated in this way, it is because of the conviction that the fact intended by such a sentence is of one form rather than another, that it is a connection of universals rather than the inherence of a character in a particular. The theory is indeed linguistic in the sense of saying that one pattern of words is preferable to another in expressing this form. But it is preferable because the form of the *fact* requires it.

27. The same holds of logical constructions. We have found Mr Ayer insisting that this too is a linguistic theory; when he calls a table or a self a logical construction he is not saying anything so metaphysical as that it is composed of sense-contents; he is only expressing 'the syntactical fact that all sentences referring to it are translatable into sentences referring to them'. Why this circumambulation of Robin Hood's barn? Sentence A is translatable into sentence B if what A means or intends is the same as what B does. If two sentences, one about a table and the other about certain sense contents, are called inter-translatable, it is natural to assume that it is because the things we are talking about are the same, in this case the table and certain sense-contents. Mr Ayer declined to say this. Why? Partly, perhaps, because of the metaphysical sound of it, but probably in part also because Professor Wisdom, in his articles on logical constructions, had shown that there were difficulties in identifications of this kind. When we say 'England fears France', for example, we are clearly referring to Englishmen, but what we mean seems not to be exhausted by the words or deeds of any particular Englishmen. One would have thought the right conclusion from this, however, is that 'England fears France' is *not* translatable into a set of statements about particulars, since there is something in the meaning of the first not covered by that of the second.

Mr Ayer takes a more puzzling course. He says both that 'when we refer to an object as a logical construction out of certain sense-contents, we are not saying that it is actually constructed out of those sense-contents, or that the sense-contents are in any way parts of it' and at the same time that any sentence referring to the object *is* translatable into one referring to the sense-contents. Now, as already remarked, to assert that A is translatable by B is to assert that, though verbally different, they say the same thing. If the sense contents *are* not the table, or even parts of it, then it is idle to say that a sentence about the one translates a sentence about the other, for they mean, and are admitted to mean, different things. On the other hand, if the one *can* be translated into the other, it must be because what they mean is the same, and then the table *is* the sense contents. Nor could it help matters to say that though the subjects referred to are one, what is said about them differs; for that leaves the translatability equally mysterious.

The theory of logical constructions professes to be a linguistic theory, a theory about the translatability of certain sentences. If this translatability is a linguistic matter merely, it asserts that, given a certain fact or event, it may be referred to with equal correctness by a form of words A or another form B. That is undoubtedly a statement about language, but to the philosopher it is of no interest. Since it is clearly supposed to interest the philosopher, it must go beyond this. When it says that sentences are inter-translatable, it must be saying that they are so because what they mean is the same. And to say that what they mean is the same in the case of table and sense-content sentences is to talk what used to be called metaphysics.

28. That it does involve us in metaphysics might indeed have been guessed from the prospectus of the new philosophy. Philosophy was now to consist chiefly or wholly of definitions in use; and a definition in use showed that, given a sentence in which appeared the term to be defined—'the table', 'material object', 'myself'—an equivalent sentence could be framed in which this term and its synonyms were eliminated. This, as we have noted, was an unusual kind of definition, though its popularity with positivists was not hard to explain; it provided them a telling weapon for dealing with metaphysicians. When the metaphysician spoke about selves or material objects, you could call him to account by asking what he meant, and as he groped about, you could offer him a definition in use which pretty clearly said all he was trying to say, but said it without any reference to his metaphysical excrescences.

Unfortunately, your task is not as easy as that. If your concern is really with language, you will nowhere come to grips with the metaphysician; you do not refute him by talking about words; you merely change the subject. If the definition in use is to get any purchase on him, it must propose a more convincing analysis of the object meant, and this is precisely what, in spite of disavowals, it attempts to do. The metaphysician talks about himself, for example, as the same yesterday and today, wonders what sort of being he is, and comes up with some such answer as Berkeley's, or Kant's, or McTaggart's. How are you to clear his mind of such superstitions? Certainly not by embarking on linguistic discourse and pointing out that the word 'self' is used by him, or most people, or all people, in a certain way, and might be used in such and such others. You proceed by giving him a new analysis of the object meant. Granting that by 'self' he means something sufficiently definite to make discussion possible, you try to show that this self could consist of sense-contents while still in a plausible sense enduring through time, distinguishing him from other people, and so on. If he finds that this way of conceiving the object covers the ground and is at the same time simpler than his old way, he will, if a reasonable man, accept it. If he does so, it will be because your definition in use promises not merely a definition of the word 'self', but a truer conception of the thing. You have won him over by a bit of metaphysics, the kind of metaphysics in this instance with which Hume dealt with Berkeley, and which both these philosophers would have denied with spirit to be a mere exercise in linguistics.[1]

---

[1] It should be added in fairness to Russell that it was his positivist interpreters, not he, who insisted on the linguistic reading of his theory of constructions. He was

29. We have seen that Russell was led to his theory of descriptions by considering the misleading form of such statements as 'the Loch Ness monster is a sea-serpent', that he would regard this as misleading because the subject phrase is so easily taken as a proper name, and this as dangerous because it leads so naturally to the belief that there is in fact a Loch Ness monster. That it does mislead in this way is a psychological observation which is no doubt true. But this is not the whole story. Behind it in the background of Russell's thought lay a theory about proper names which implied a further theory about meaning, a theory so dubious as to deprive the theory of descriptions of much of its force. Let us try to explain.

In the days of his logical atomism, Russell held that all true factual statements could be resolved into atomic statements in which the subject term was 'this'. That to which the 'this' referred was given in sense; any significant use of the word guaranteed the existence of what it referred to. It was a 'logically proper name', in the sense that it had no connotation; it referred to no characters of any kind; its use was purely and simply to denote. Any word or phrase that went beyond such pure denotation was not logically proper, since it then characterized or described. 'Socrates', for example, and 'Man o' War' and 'Constantinople', though commonly called proper names, were not purely proper because descriptive elements clustered round them and were inevitably involved in their use; when we say 'Socrates' we think of a certain appearance or of an eminent Greek philosopher, and these are characterizations. But if this is true, what becomes of subject-predicate statements? It is precisely statements with grammatical subjects of this kind—'Socrates is mortal', for instance—that have traditionally offered the stock examples of them. If these are not to be subject-predicate statements on the ground that their subjects characterize rather than denote, where are such statements to be found? Presumably only in 'this is blue' and the like. But then, as we saw long ago, even this statement is in difficulty. For if it refers to a particular which is nothing rather than anything else, it is a relapse into that peculiar mysticism which we found so implausible in Wittgenstein; and if it refers to some *what*, then instead of giving us a true subject, namely that which, though the bearer of characters is no character itself, it only gives us a further character. In either case the subject-predicate statement, as a distinctive and significant

quite ready, at least on occasion, to read it in what we have called a metaphysical sense. E.g. 'The real man too, I believe, however the police may swear to his identity, is really a series of momentary men each different one from the other, and bound together not by a numerical identity, but by continuity and certain intrinsic causal laws.' *Mysticism and Logic*, 129.

assertion, has gone by the board. This is a very odd result. Russell, to be sure, had waged a vigorous polemic against the view that all judgment was of the subject-predicate type, but he certainly did not intend to abolish it altogether.

30. How did this strange result come about? Partly at least as follows. In considering the proper name, Russell identified the meaning with the referent or the *denotatum*; the meaning of 'this' was the particular before me; the meaning of 'Socrates', so far as it could be considered a proper name at all, was the actual historical Socrates. But if 'meaning' is to be taken in this sense, then where there is no existent thing or event for the subject to refer to, that subject will be meaningless; 'the Loch Ness monster is a sea-serpent', for example, will say nothing. And what is more curious still, it will mean nothing even if there is such a monster. For 'the Loch Ness monster' is, after all, not a name, but a description, and descriptions mean nothing, since there is nothing in the realm of existents that they single out and denote. Thus Russell in *Principia Mathematica* could say flatly, ' "the author of Waverley" means nothing'.[1] In reacting from Meinong's view that even if Scott had never lived, the phrase would still refer to some queer kind of existent, he went to the opposite extreme of saying that all such phrases were meaningless.

But if they *were* meaningless, how could they be used with such effect in ordinary discourse? How is it that when I say 'the Loch Ness monster is a sea-serpent', people have no trouble in understanding me, whether there are such monsters or not, and whether or not they believe in them? Russell was much puzzled by this, but some readers, including myself, have been puzzled as to why he found in it so portentous a problem. I confess that I have never been able to see that this problem was of exceptional difficulty or importance. Russell plainly thought it was, and from our present position, we can perhaps see a little more clearly why he did. He seems to have been proceeding on several questionable assumptions. These were (1) that a proper name is purely denotative, (2) that meaning should be conceived in terms of such denotation, and (3) that since descriptions lacked this, they were meaningless. These assumptions are untrue. (1) It is untrue to say that a proper name is purely denotative, for the least descriptive and most purely proper name one can find, like 'this' or 'that', makes use of characters and relations to help locate its reference; indeed pointing itself does so. And if even names as

---

[1] 2nd ed., I, 67. And cf. the remark in *Mind*, XIV, 481, that the expression 'a man' by itself is 'wholly destitute of meaning'.

'proper' as these are in part descriptive, then, (2) meaning is always more than denotation; it has an indispensable non-denotative part, which is more generally identifiable as present than denotation itself. It follows (3) that descriptions which do not denote at all, in the sense of referring to anything actual, are still meaningful. Hence the problem with which Russell started, how descriptions can signify when in fact they signify nothing, loses its paradox. Non-referential meaning is a perfectly good and extremely common kind of meaning, which an expression may still possess when standing alone, and apart from its use in specific contexts. Russell's difficulty arose because he was trying to assimilate this general meaning to referential meaning and found that it resisted such treatment.[1]

We may put it in another way. All terms mean with the aid of characters or relations; we refer to things through *whats*. But the reference to the point in the real world that bears the characters may have various degrees of definiteness. In 'this is red', as actually used, it is most definite of all. In 'the man with a red head is the mayor' it is less definite; there may be more than one such man. In 'the horse is a quadruped', a type of statement that seems to have been overlooked when the theory of descriptions was framed, the reference, if to existents at all, is more widely dispersed. In 'the Loch Ness monster is a sea-serpent', the characters thought of would be used by some people to refer to a supposed existent, and by some not. In 'the sun-god drives his chariot across the sky', they would probably be used by no one as referring to any individual, though I follow the philosophical logicians in thinking that the reference to a real world has not evaporated even here. What this series indicates is that descriptive expressions are used to achieve every degree of definiteness in referring, and that the degree of definiteness turns on the context. Russell's problem seems to have sprung from the conviction that a the-phrase could have definite meaning only if it had a definite reference in the fashion of a logically proper name. As soon as one sees that descriptive meaning has nothing essentially to do with such reference, though it *may* be used to facilitate it, the special problem vanishes.

31. The other principal method of providing definitions in use was that of logical constructions, and we have seen that this method in its real intent was not a new method of translating sentences so much as a new way of conceiving things. It was intimately connected on one

---

[1] P. F. Strawson has criticized the theory pointedly in his article 'On Referring' in *Mind*, 1950, reprinted in A. Flew (ed.), *Essays in Conceptual Analysis*.

side with Russell's view that we could understand terms only if they referred to objects with which we were acquainted, and on the other side with the positivists' verification theory of meaning. In the hands of both parties the new method had a wide range of application. In accordance with the principle that constructions were to be preferred to inferences, all objects of philosophic, scientific, or common-sense thought into whose conception inference entered were so far as possible to be reconceived in such manner as to press the inference out.

Now inference in fact enters into our conceptions of everything. We see shapes and colours, and say that we 'see' a post-box, a flag-pole, a spaniel or a policeman. Strictly speaking, no one *sees* any of these things. The recognition that something before us serves the function of a post-box or a flag-pole, or belongs to the genus spaniel or policeman, is not an act of sensing, and is best regarded, I think, as an elementary form of inference.[1] If this is so, Mill's remark that the drawing of inferences is the main business of life is fairly near the truth, for in every waking hour we are engaged in it, and our very lives depend on doing it successfully.

Still, for both Russell and the positivists, inference might be, and often was, a leap in the dark. It landed metaphysicians in mental and material substances, mythical first causes and absolutes, and a vast Platonic trellis of universals which somehow supported, from beyond time, the visible veil of nature. There is no objection to such inference if it is really necessary or really explains. If it is superfluous and explains nothing, it is offensive to both the logical and the aesthetic sense, and should be got rid of. That it is in fact superfluous the theory of constructions enables us to see.

We have no space to review the many ingenious ways in which the method was applied in psychology and the physical sciences.[2] Two of the best known applications were Russell's definition of a material thing as the class of its appearances and Ayer's definition of other minds in terms of the sense-data through which one apprehends their bodies. The first was subjected to so full an examination in Lovejoy's *Revolt Against Dualism* as to render any further scrutiny needless; the second has been briefly adverted to in our review of positivist theories of meaning. Both theories seem to have been later abandoned by their proponents.[3] But it may be worth while to

---

[1] The point is discussed in my *The Nature of Thought*, I, Chap. 2.

[2] Morris Weitz enumerates more than twenty applications of it by Russell alone; *The Philosophy of Russell*, 108.

[3] Though in the second edition of *Language, Truth and Logic*, Ayer said of his theory only that 'it has an air of paradox which prevents one from being wholly confident that it is true'. 20.

mention a few general considerations that obstructed the proposed new course for philosophy.

32. (1) One was the realization that a material thing could not be exhausted by observable data, however much they were added to.[1] Let one try to 'construct' the clock on the mantel out of one's own sense-data, or even of one's own plus other people's, and one soon realizes that however many are accumulated, they will never overtake the concrete thing. The thing has innumerable facets and attributes which we should recognize at once as belonging to it if presented to us, but which our attempt at construction with the materials at hand is bound to miss. The thing and our construction inevitably fall apart.

(2) Such constructions can be arrived at only by means of the inferences they were supposed to enable us to avoid. My logical construction of the clock is not confined to my own small group of sense data; it includes a great many sensibilia not experienced by anyone at all. But how do we know that those aspects of the clock which we *should* see if we were standing in the corner are really there to see? We do not in fact know it at all; it is merely the conclusion of a highly probable inference. Yet these sensibilia are obviously included in what we mean by the thing. The constructionist is thus in a dilemma. If he equates the thing with his own fragmentary sense data, the equation does gross violence to our actual meaning; if he includes a mass of unknown others, he makes the construction depend on inference, which was precisely the process supposed to be excluded.

(3) To apply the method in physics is to turn one's back on modern developments in the field. For whatever the physicist means by the electrons, protons, and neutrons that he talks about, he does not mean a set of observable sense-data (or sensibilia). Russell later admitted this with characteristic candour. 'There are some,' he wrote, 'who would deny that physics need say anything about what cannot be observed; at times I have been one of them. But I have become persuaded that such an interpretation of physics is at best an intellectual game, and that an honest acceptance of physics demands recognition of unobserved occurrences.'[2]

(4) In a world where things are constructions out of sense-data, it is impossible to apply causal laws in the normal scientific way. For

---

[1] Cf. R. B. Braithwaite, 'Propositions about Material Objects', *Aristotelian Soc. Proceedings*, Vol. 38.

[2] Schilpp (ed.), *The Philosophy of Russell*, 701.

example, what causes an eclipse of the sun? Are we to say that light-rays coming from the sun are blocked by an intervening mass of sensibilia? Indeed, what causes us to have sense-data at all? If one accepts the causal theory of perception (and it is hard to avoid), one never senses a physical object at all, but only the effects it produces in experience. The cause of these effects is in the nature of the case beyond direct apprehension, however extended, and therefore is to be reached, if at all, only through causal inference.

(5) Logical constructions fail to provide us the essential bridges not only to much of the physical world, but to the social and historical world as well. Other people's sensations, thoughts, and desires are obviously not data of ours, though the inference by which we assure ourselves of them are practically irresistible. We explain people's actions, not by causal laws connecting earlier with later sense-data of our own, but by reference to thoughts, desires, and emotions that can never come within our own experience; and if hypothese are to be warranted by their success in enabling us to make predictions and adjustments, no hypotheses are better justified. Furthermore, as far as history is an account, which it chiefly is, not of natural events, but of action, in the sense of motived behaviour, this vast region too must be a realm of inference rather than construction. The method of constructions consistently applied, would shrink the universe to a small and dull island.

33. It is time to sum up with regard to this phase of linguistic philosophy. Mr Ayer proposed as the chief business of philosophy the framing of a peculiar kind of definitions, namely definitions in use. The most important illustrations of these were to be found in the theories of descriptions and logical constructions proposed by Russell. Neither of these, we found, was in truth a linguistic theory. And when we inquired what they said of a non-linguistic kind, we found that the first, when its assumptions were corrected, had little left to say, and that the second offered us a metaphysic in conflict with science and common sense. The defence might be suggested that since such conflict is inevitable, it provides no ground of objection to any metaphysic. I cannot agree. Common sense is itself a metaphysic which holds the ground, and any philosophy that flouts it must accept the burden of proof. As for science, Russell himself has reminded us that 'to set up a philosophy against physics is rash; philosophers who have done so have always ended in disaster'.[1] The great strength of this type of analytic philosophy was supposed to lie

[1] *The Philosophy of Russell*, 700.

in bringing philosophy into line with science and providing it a
scientific basis. If it ends by making meaningless the judgments of
both the natural and social sciences, its *raison d'être* is gone.

Mr Ayer came to agree, in time, that philosophy had a wider
province than defining terms. In the second edition of his book,
appearing ten years after the first, philosophy was 'very largely a
matter of exhibiting the inter-relationship of different types of
propositions'. The definition in use of 'material thing' was conceded
to be impracticable, but one could still show 'how statements about
material things are related to observation-statements'.[1] Now what has
been said about the view that philosophy consists in defining words is
largely applicable anew to the view that it consists in statements
about statements, and we shall not repeat this. What should be noted,
however, is that there appears here another conception of the task
of philosophy. It is suggested that ordinary language may hide the
difference between statements of different type and that the business
of philosophy is to display their logical grammar and show how the
types are related. Moore had pointed out that when we say 'tame
tigers growl' and 'tame tigers exist', we are making statements
grammatically similar but logically quite unlike, and Ayer agrees
that to say this is 'philosophically illuminating', though it has nothing
to do with definitions. It is illuminating because it reveals differences
of logical type and requires reflection on how they are related. The
task of adjusting language to these newly perceived differences of
type was undertaken by the 'ordinary language philosophers' of
Oxford in the forties and fifties. To their work we turn in the chapter
that follows.

---

[1] *Language, Truth and Logic*, ², 23–24.

CHAPTER VIII

LINGUISTIC PHILOSOPHY—SOME
LATER FORMS

1. The form of linguistic philosophy to which we now turn is often described as 'ordinary language philosophy' and associated with the Oxford of the forties and fifties. The nature and ground of its appeal to language has been widely misunderstood, and the impulse that led to it came rather from Moore and the later Wittgenstein than from any teaching indigenous to Oxford. This new way of philosophizing is hard to describe or to assess. For one thing, its exponents deny that they form a school at all, and have avoided the sort of manifesto or platform by which some groups of American philosophers have clarified a joint programme and eased the task of critics. The new method has been applied in different ways by writers working independently and in fields remote from each other, and the attempt to find a common core of method or conclusion in what Ryle and Austin have said about knowing, Strawson and Warnock about logic, Pears and Paul about metaphysics, Weldon about politics, Hart about law, and Hare, Toulmin, Urmson, Hampshire, and Nowell-Smith about ethics—to name but a few well-known members of the group—would seem an unpromising enterprise. It is complicated still further by the notorious reluctance of these philosophers to talk about what they are doing in general terms; if they are asked what philosophy means for them, they are apt to say, 'it is the sort of thing I am doing now' and return to their work.

A further difficulty for any observer attempting to get their philosophy in focus is that it never stays still. It is in continuous motion, whose phases melt into their successors like the scenes of a colour-organ. Most of its literature lies not in books—one member has remarked that the day of books in philosophy is over—but in *fliegende Blätter*, articles in the professional journals, which sometimes, as in *Analysis*, are short even for articles. This has made possible a rapid cross-fire of proposal and counter-proposal, of commentary and epi-commentary, in which the conclusions become more esoteric with each exchange. Few extended applications of the new method have been offered, Ryle's *Concept of Mind* being a notable exception.

2. In spite of their demurrers and differences, however, these philosophers clearly belong to a single movement. They are united in both likes and dislikes. As for their dislikes, they jointly deprecate the grandiose in philosophy—all-embracing metaphysical systems, moral philosophies sweetened with unction, the pretentious and pedantic language with which speculators of the past have too often tried to dignify foggy thought. To anyone whose expectations had been set by the Oxford of a generation earlier, the Oxford of Caird and Bradley, the new philosophy was in a low key, and its almost ostentatiously casual language about 'doing philosophy' as studying 'the jobs' of 'a lot of words' was not always prepossessing.

Along with these philosophers' distaste for the high-flown goes a distaste for the expression of their views in the terms of formal logic. We have seen that the analysts of the Vienna circle were chiefly mathematicians or theoretical physicists, who hailed *Principia Mathematica* as providing the rudiments of an ideal language, and here the American analysts followed their lead. Very few of the Oxford analysts came into philosophy from either mathematics or the natural sciences. Though they have sought to do their duty by symbolic logic, they do not, for the most part, think easily in its terms. What is more significant, where they have mastered it sufficiently to examine its claims, they have been unimpressed. We have already noted the rejection by their most accomplished logician, Mr Strawson, of Russell's theory of descriptions as distorting the current use of 'the'; and most of the other Oxford philosophers would generalize this criticism in the sense of holding that symbolic logic is too blunt an instrument for dissecting out the nuances in the actual use of language.[1]

We said that these philosophers are united also in their admirations. For one thing, they are Aristotelians rather than Platonists; their interest is in analysis rather than synthesis; not in the study or construction of systems, but in the piecemeal solving of particular puzzles. Again, they show a common loyalty to what is surely one of the most attractive sides of the English philosophical tradition, its concern for intelligibility, clarity, and simplicity in thinking and writing. Hobbes, Locke, Berkeley, Hume, Bentham and Mill were all in their different ways exemplars of these qualities, and the Oxford

---

[1] See, e.g., G. J. Warnock's criticism of Quine's classing under one formula expressions whose 'logical behaviour' is different; 'Metaphysics in Logic', *Proc. of the Arist. Soc.*, Vol. 51.

philosophers, when accused of stirring up a revolution in philosophy, like to reply that they are really returning to an old tradition that had been temporarily abandoned under alien influences. And their sympathy with the older tradition extends to its empiricism. To be sure, there is not a professing positivist to be found among them. But though they protest, too loudly some think, against identification with positivism, they have been much influenced by all three of its main positions—the verification theory of meaning, the analytic theory of the a priori, and the emotivist theory of value; and many of them would accept all of these positions with amendments that, to the outsider, seem of minor importance. A further emphasis shared with the positivists is the stress on the contemporary as opposed to the historical. No one can go through the Oxonian philosophical mill without a considerable acquaintance with the history of philosophy, and it is therefore the more surprising that one can read hundreds of pages of these philosophers' writings and come on very few references to the historic figures of philosophy. This does not indicate ignorance; Austin, for example, was a distinguished Aristotelian scholar. But it does suggest that for this group the history of philosophy is a subordinate interest, and that their pre-occupation is with fresh work in analysis.

To the outside world, by far the most arresting and novel of the common interests of these philosophers lies in the place they give to language, and we must now try to get clear what this is. They are said to champion the study of language in its ordinary use. What is meant by 'use', and what by 'ordinary'?

3. First as to 'use'. To study the use of a word is not, of course, to study its usefulness or utility. More surprisingly, to study the use of English words is not merely to study English use; Professor Ryle says that when Hume was discussing the use of 'cause', he was equally discussing the use of its German synonym '*Ursache*'; though the words are different, the use is the same.[1] The philologist would fasten on their differences of form, sound, and origin. But these are of no interest to the philosopher. What concerns him is that in his sense of 'use', a German discussion of the use of *Ursache* would cover the same ground as an English discussion of 'cause'.

A further distinction of some subtlety is now called for. The use of a word is not its usage. You know its use when you know how to use it; you know its usage when you know how in fact it is used. A use is a way or technique of doing something; a usage is the 'more or less

[1] 'Ordinary Language', *Philosophical Review*, LXII (April 1953), 171.

widely prevailing practice' of doing this.[1] The distinction is hard to hold firmly because the first step towards the mastery of use may be the noting of usage, and we cannot survey a usage without reference to the use whose prevalence we are surveying. But Ryle insists that the two are distinct. One can know how to use a boomerang without knowing how in fact it is used by Australian aborigines and American schoolboys. One can know the use of 'cause' or 'person' without knowing the mass of information that philologists provide for us under these heads in the Oxford English Dictionary. 'Job-analysis is not mass observation.'[2]

The use of a word or expression means, then, the kind of work it does, our mode of employing it or operating with it. But this too is vague. Is the child making use of words when he constructs them out of blocks, or contemplates them at the bottom of his alphabet soup, or tears pages of them out of the dictionary? No. What kind of use, then, is contemplated? Strawson, in his article on referring, would confine the 'use' of expressions to their mentioning or referring to something, and of sentences to their making true or false assertions. Ryle prefers not to speak of the use of sentences at all, since such use could hardly be correct or incorrect, but rather of words and expressions. This latter use, however, would go far beyond mentioning or referring; it would cover, for example, describing, commanding, asking, and exclaiming. Since this sense seems more representative, we shall follow it here.

Now what is meant by *ordinary* use? Not ordinary as opposed to technical, for technical words too have their ordinary uses, for example 'quantifier' in logic or 'enzyme' in biology. An ordinary use may be possessed equally by colloquial and technical words, by poetical, professional and slang words. 'Ordinary' means *stock* or *standard*. The word 'enzyme' has a standard use among biologists, however many other uses it may be put to; such common words as 'know', 'cause', and 'ought', are put to a far larger number of uses, but these are chiefly variations on a still commoner standard use. Thus a philosopher who commits himself to studying the ordinary use of words need not confine himself to the kind of talk that goes on in the streets or at tea-parties. When Berkeley discussed infinitesimals, he was obviously not examining the use of a common or colloquial word; 'he was examining the regular or standard use of a relatively esoteric word. We are not contradicting ourselves if we say that he was examining the ordinary use of an unordinary

[1] 'Ordinary Language', *Philosophical Review*, LXII (April 1953), 175.
[2] *Ibid.*, 178.

expression.'[1] What the philosopher studies is ordinary use in this enlarged though carefully specified sense.

4. If we are clear now as to the meaning of 'ordinary use', we must ask next what makes this so interesting to the 'ordinary language philosophers'. The answer they give is strikingly different from that of Moore. Moore thought that if we took the statements of common sense about tables and chairs, time and space, with their ordinary meaning, we had statements which, in their truth and certainty, provided touchstones for philosophy. Ryle holds, on the contrary, that ordinary language produces confusions that are the prime source of philosophical perplexity. Not that it produces these in the plain man himself. When he says 'Satan does not exist' or 'the arrow flew through the centre of the bush', he is not in the least confused, nor is he using words in a questionable way. He is talking on a pre-philosophical level on which neither the questions nor the answers of the philosopher have yet appeared, nor therefore the muddle philosophers fall into. The difficulty arises when the philosopher does arrive on the scene. He begins to analyse what the plain man is saying. He distinguishes subject from predicate, and tries to classify what they refer to under appropriate headings. In this classification he has been guided ever since Aristotle, and to a far larger extent than he knows, by distinctions of grammar and by analogies implicit in verbal usage. He assumes, for example, that a proper name designates a substance and that predicates assert attributes or relations. So when he comes to the statement 'Satan does not exist', he assumes that Satan names a substance and 'exist' names an attribute, and then there flies open the Pandora's box of troubles on which the theory of descriptions was designed to shut the lid. Satan does *not* designate anything that exists; existence is *not* a predicate; the misleading suggestions of ordinary speech must be discarded before we can come near what the statement means. Similarly with the innocent-looking remark, 'the arrow flew through the centre of the bush'. This sounds like 'the arrow flew through the curtain' or 'over the target', and since curtain and target are things, it is assumed that 'the centre' names a thing; and then disaster hovers again. For a centre is not a thing, not anything that can have characters at all, but a relational character belonging to something else.[2]

Such words as 'Satan', 'exists', 'centre', Ryle called 'systematically

---

[1] 'Ordinary Language', *Philosophical Review*, LXII (April 1953), 170.
[2] G. Ryle, 'Systematically Misleading Expressions', in A. Flew (ed.), *Logic and Language*, 1st series.

misleading'. Why 'systematically'? Because all words of their type would similarly mislead—words like 'Pegasus' or 'Mr Pickwick', words like 'real' or 'actual', words like 'top' or 'boundary'. Then as to 'misleading': can any account be given of the *sort* of confusion that arises when we are thus misled by grammar? Ryle thought that an answer to this question would be most important philosophically. As early as 1931, he was suggesting that the following of false scents provided by ordinary language was the prime cause of the philosopher's disorientation, and that the business of philosophy was 'to cure this disease'.[1] Ordinary speech deceives by its form regarding the structure of the fact it asserts. 'And we can often succeed in stating this fact in a new form of words which does exhibit what the other failed to exhibit. And I am for the present inclined to believe that this is what philosophical analysis is, and that this is the sole and whole function of philosophy.'[2] To reveal the sort of confusion into which we are led by language is thus to reveal at once the nature of philosophic problems and how to go about it to solve them.

5. Very well; what sort of confusion is it that language imposes upon unsuspecting philosophers? Ryle's answer, given in a series of later essays, is 'the category mistake',[3] that is, the attempt to make one category do the work of another. But now what is a category? Ryle uses the term in a somewhat difficult sense of his own. In arriving at this sense, he draws on his two most distinguished predecessors in this field, while differing from both. For Aristotle a category was one of the ultimate forms of being. If you asked what a table was, the first answer might be 'an article of furniture'; if you asked what that was, the answer might be 'a material thing'; if you asked again what that was, the answer might be 'a substance'; if you asked what substance was, there was no answer; you had reached the end of the road. Substance is an ultimate form of being in the sense that it is like no other and has no genus but being itself. Or what is Wednesday? It is a day. What is a day? It is a stretch of time. What is time? Here again you are at the end of the road. Time is a unique and ultimate form of being, as you see when you try to define it; you can define it only by itself; if you say, for example, that it is the form of being whose parts exist successively, the 'successively' means in *time*. Now

---

[1] G. Ryle, 'Systematically Misleading Expressions,' in A. Flew (ed.), *Logic and Language*, 1st series, 35.

[2] *Ibid.*, 36.

[3] Most helpfully perhaps in 'Categories' (1938), reprinted in Flew, *Logic and Language*, 2nd series; an inaugural lecture on *Philosophical Arguments* (1945); and the Tarner Lectures on *Dilemmas* (1953).

to confuse any of these ultimate forms of being with another, to say for example that a place or a stretch of time is a thing, was for Aristotle to commit a category mistake. Ryle agrees that this attempt to distinguish ultimate heads of classification and to keep them distinct in the work of philosophizing was of first importance. But he thinks that Aristotle was too casual about it. Categories in his sense do exist, but there are far more than the ten he recognized; and they are related in far more complex ways. He accepted only those whose names could stand as terms, that is, as subject or predicate, in simple propositions; and since in such propositions the terms could be interchanged and were coupled in only one way, his categories were too much like dominoes that could be shuffled about at will. His common sense might make its protests, but so far as his logic was concerned, 'Saturday is in bed' and 'the equator is late' would be perfectly good propositions.

Kant's table of categories is as riddled with defects as Aristotle's. But in one respect his treatment shows a great advance. Categories are not confined to terms; they are extended to include the relations between them; indeed all four of the types he expressly recognizes—quantity, quality, relation, modality—are said to belong to judgments and to characterize, not terms, but the relations between terms or propositions. Aristotle compared terms and found general similarities among them; Kant compared propositions and found further similarities among these; and he began to see that the two types of category were not independent of each other, that terms do not live in isolation, but that their character appoints the relationships in which they can and cannot stand. 'Kant sees that there is a galaxy of sorts of coupling and that these determine or are determined by the sorts of factors that can be coupled. Aristotle's is an "alphabetic" theory of factors and a simple "juxtaposition" theory of their combinations; Kant's is a "syntactical" theory about the combinations of factors. . . .'[1]

6. In his own treatment of categories, Ryle proceeds two steps further along the line of march that runs from Aristotle through Kant. First, instead of Aristotle's ten categories and Kant's twelve, he holds that there are an indefinite number, and secondly, he holds that terms appoint their relations with a complexity and firmness that Kant himself scarcely guessed at.

The need for extending the list of categories is implicit in Ryle's mode of selecting them. Aristotle confined his classification to terms. Ryle holds that statements may have many things in common besides

[1] G. Ryle, 'Categories', in Flew (ed.), *Logic and Language*, 2nd series, 74.

terms, and that these may have an equal right to the name of categories; even 'syncategorematic' words like 'a' or 'not' may indicate categories. Instead of studying terms, therefore, Ryle studies 'sentence factors', and a sentence-factor is 'any partial expression which can enter into sentences otherwise dissimilar.'[1] 'Thus in the sentence "I am the man who wrote this paper", "I", "the man who", "who wrote this paper", "wrote this paper" are all sentence-factors.'[2] Each of these expressions belongs to a distinguishable type that could have an indefinite number of instances; 'I', for example, might be replaced by 'Smith' or 'Socrates'. These sentence-factors, or rather what they signify, which Ryle sometimes calls 'proposition-factors', are his substitutes for the older categories. How does he tell when they are really different? By trying them out in the same sentence. You want to know whether Socrates is a sentence-factor of the same type as Saturday, the South Pole, or Santayana. You start with a meaningful sentence such as 'Socrates is in bed', and instead of 'Socrates' you try the candidates in turn. You find that when Saturday or the South Pole is substituted, the statement is absurd, and when Santayana is substituted, it makes sense again. The first two sentence-factors are thus of distinct types from 'Socrates', while the third, by the present test at least, is the same. There are as many different types of sentence-factors as there are types that, in possible sentences, would reveal collisions with some other.

This brings us to the second respect in which Ryle revises the doctrine of categories. He conceives them as inter-related in a great variety of ways. It is not merely that a given type within a proposition will admit certain companions and exclude others; it will cast its long shadow over all the implications of the proposition. Implication in both Aristotelian and mathematical logic turns on the form of the proposition, and Ryle may be thought to be denying this and saying that implication turns also on matter. I think he would prefer to say that much that was formerly considered matter must now be regarded as form. The logical form of a proposition depends on the types of factor that make it up, so that if any one of these types is changed, the form of the proposition is altered and its logical behaviour—its range of implications, compatibilities and hostilities—will also change throughout. In the statement 'Socrates is in bed', change the words 'in bed' to 'wise' and all its liaisons will likewise change. Are these changes to be called logical? In a strictly formal logic, No. In Ryle's logic, Yes. For logical behaviour depends on logical form,

[1] G. Ryle, 'Categories', in Flew (ed.), *Logic and Language*, 2nd series, 68.
[2] *Ibid.*

and logical form is as various as the relations between types.

7. How is all this supposed to help us philosophically? It helps us, Ryle would reply, by clearing our minds as to what philosophic puzzles are like and how in principle they are to be dealt with. It is precisely a confusion between types or categories in the sense just discussed that gives rise to philosophical problems generally. Because a sentence-factor looks so much like one of another type, we use it in the same way, only to find it fighting with our other sentence-factors, and then we have a philosophic puzzle on our hands. To take some examples from Mr Flew,[1] we say 'it goes on to infinity', supposing this to be like 'it goes on to London', and then we have on our hands the problem of the infinite. We say 'this is past', which sounds like 'this is red', so we suppose that the past has the sort of being that red does; and then are puzzled as to how the past can be and not be. We say 'nobody came', and suppose we are making the same sort of remark as 'somebody came'; and then are puzzled how that which is nobody and nothing can manage to do things.

Such confusion, says Ryle, is the beginning of philosophy; its end and special business is to clear up the confusion. It does this by making us aware that we really are mixing categories. In simple cases like those above, it shows us that two sentence-factors that look alike are of extremely different types, and when this is pointed out to us, we can often see it at once. But sometimes mere pointing is not enough, and philosophical argument is called for. Ryle devoted his inaugural lecture to the question whether there is any characteristic type of such argument.[2] He believed he had found it in the *reductio ad absurdum*. This proceeds by assuming a proposition to be of the form its expression suggests, and then working the assumption out till it ends in contradiction. For example, someone says that time began in 4004 B.C., and assumes that he is saying the same sort of thing as 'the rain began at four o'clock'. To expose the error you point out that if time, like the rain, began at a certain moment, it began at a certain moment *in* time, that is, at *this* moment rather than at the moment before or after. And a moment in time *means* one that came after a preceding moment and before a subsequent one, whereas 'time began' suggests a moment that came after nothing. And that is absurd because 'moment' is being used in contradictory ways.

8. We must now attempt some appraisal of this view of the problems

---

[1] *Logic and Language*, 1st series, 7.
[2] *Philosophical Arguments*, 1945.

and function of the philosopher. The view is striking, sophisticated and largely original,[1] and it seems to me the most cogent statement of philosophic policy that has emerged from contemporary Oxford. Furthermore, the theory does not remain in the air; in two able books, *The Concept of Mind* and *Dilemmas*, its author has shown us how he means it to be applied. To dismiss it as concerned merely with words is plainly unjust. Some of its positions seem, to me at least, true and important. There can be no doubt that many persons have been led into intellectual puzzles by specious linguistic resemblances. Categories are clearly of prime importance; and in insisting that there is an indefinite number of them and that they are not related like 'hard, round shot', but are interlinked in an elaborate fretwork, Ryle has set his face away from the atomism of the earlier positivists.

Probably the question that arises most often, as one reads his account, is whether it covers the ground, that is, whether it applies to philosophic problems generally. That the person who says 'time began' is confusing time with a thing or event in time is certainly plausible. But as we meet, one by one, the other problems of the philosophic family, do we find a continuing family resemblance to this category-confusion? A complete review is of course impracticable; so let us take a few random samples.

The speculative problems that are of most universal interest are perhaps those of ethics. A young man has enough savings for a car or a year at the university; which should he take? If he is of a reflective turn, he may well go on and ask, What things are most worth having, and how can one judge between them?, which are of course ancient ethical questions. Do such questions arise from a confusion of categories? Some ordinary language philosophers would protest that this is an idle inquiry, since ethical questions are not in the relevant sense questions at all. To say that the enlightenment gained from a year of study would be more worth having than the pleasure gained from the car is not to assert anything, but only to express a feeling or an attitude of one's own. This is of course a possible ethical position, but I do not think it is possible consistently with respect for ordinary language. Whether he is correct or not in doing so, the plain man

[1] Some would say it comes straight from the later Wittgenstein. It was outlined, however, as early as 1931. I have chosen Ryle rather than Wittgenstein because I seem to be able to understand him. I have not dealt with the *Philosophical Investigations* because any critic of that work must face the facts (*a*) that its most admiring exponents do not agree on its interpretation, (*b*) that no matter how effective one's criticism, it will be dismissed as having failed to catch the profounder meanings of the prophet.

certainly does not mean, when he calls something good or right or a duty, to express merely his own feeling or attitude toward it, and I think that the ordinary language philosopher who says he is has already abandoned ordinary language as his guide. If he does take such language as his guide, and recognizes ethical problems as genuine ones, he will not find much plausibility in saying they arise from confusing categories. The problem what things are most worth having surely springs not from conflicting categories but from conflicting desires, the desires of the young man, for example, both for education and for pleasure. The suggestion that his problem arises out of his attempt at some point to combine incongruous sentence or proposition factors seems to bear no relation to fact.

Next to the problems of morals, those of religion are perhaps the commonest and most urgent. Does God exist? Now if anyone were to suggest that this question arises in human experience because the order of subject and predicate in the sentence 'God exists' is the reverse of the logical order, and that men's religious problems were thus a by-product of their bad grammar, the appropriate answer would be a laugh, in which I can only think that Ryle would join. Religious problems have far longer roots than this, of which the one stressed by Freud—the need for security in a world we did not make and cannot control—is surely a principal one. Still it may be said that however religious problems may have arisen, the religious beliefs that were taken to solve them are type-confusions and are seen to be no solutions when this is recognized. People think of God, perhaps, in terms of Professor Wisdom's allegory, as a world-gardener, and suppose that when they call him invisible and intangible they are using words of the same type as 'immense' or 'inert', whereas if they were to try these words with the word 'mountain', they would see that the types were different. With this they would presumably recognize that the beliefs were confusions, and be prepared to see them dissolve. Strangely enough, however, such beliefs have a way of persisting stubbornly, even after this difference of type is seen with all clearness. Nor is this due merely to the fact that they rest on so broad a base of desire. The fact is that the belief in God, whether warranted or not, is neither a meaningless belief nor involves of necessity any sort of type confusion. There is no mixing of categories in my believing that there is a consciousness more or less like my own expressing itself through your words and acts, or that my dog is fond of me, or that lobsters feel pain, or even that a 'mighty being is awake' and manifesting itself in nature and history. How would you verify such a belief? it may be asked. The question is irrelevant. If it implies that because the statement purports to refer to what cannot be sensed it is therefore meaningless, the question presupposes a theory of meaning that we long ago saw to be discredited. The suggestion of Fechner and Paulsen that the galaxies of stars may subtend a world-consciousness very much as the galaxies of atoms in our brains subtend our personal consciousness may quite well be a fantasy merely. But it is not confused or contradictory or meaningless; and if this consciousness is alleged to have a scale of values like our own, one can argue for and against it on grounds that have been familiar since Job. So of most other religious dogmas. Most of them may be false. What I fail to see is that they spring from a confusion of categories or would disappear if this were dispelled.

I am convinced that we should be met by the same conclusion monotonously if we made the round of philosophic problems. Take for a mere mention that of surviving death. The belief that personality does survive, that it can remember and desire, though without a brain, and see and hear without eyes or ears, is a belief with much to be said against it, and something—as the psychical researchers have made clear—to be said for it. To dismiss it, as Mr Ayer once did, as self-contradictory because consciousness, being bodily behaviour, obviously could not outlast it, is itself a category mistake. Survival is perfectly conceivable, and how probable or improbable it is forms a legitimate and fascinating problem, in which there is no need of type confusion at any stage.

What about the problems of the theory of knowledge? The question whether $7+5=12$ is analytic or synthetic is one of some standing in respect of both years and popularity. Does it involve a confusion of types, the removal of which would dissolve it? No doubt confusion exists, or opinions would not differ, and the confusion concerns the sense, if any, in which $7+5$ 'contains' 12. But it would be odd to call this a confusion of type or category, unless indeed all confusions are to be so described. What about metaphysical problems, causality for instance? Professor Braithwaite thinks that on the whole Hume was right in regarding causal statements as statements of uniform sequence; Dr Ewing thinks Hume was wrong, that in some cases we can see that the character of the cause entails that of the effect, and that this entailment is a contributing factor in the occurrence of the effect. A type difference between *is* and *must* is involved here. But the problem is not removed when they are clearly distinguished. It then becomes for the first time definite; what we want to know is whether both of these two quite different components are present, or only one.

9. We apparently have to conclude that most philosophic problems do not spring from type-confusion and are not solved by its removal. It would be going too far to say that no problems arise thus, for Ryle has shown unquestionably that some of them do. But here arises a second doubt about this theory. Some of the problems that have been accepted as clear cases of it look more doubtful as one inspects them closely. The statements 'Satan does not exist' and 'the king of France is bald' have sometimes been offered as the clearest of cases of how language has misled philosophers. Not that they mislead the plain man, it is carefully added, but only minds bent on generalizing about the status of subjects and predicates. Philosophers are misled by the grammar of such sentences, according to Russell and Ryle, because it is supposed that what they are about is something named by the subject and that this something must therefore exist; and furthermore that the predicate signifies an attribute ascribed to this. They are then committed to holding that Satan and the king of France are actual beings of some kind, and that existence is an attribute asserted or denied of them, whereas the ostensible predicate should be the subject, and the subject the predicate. So much has been made of these blunders that one assumes them to have been epidemic among philosophers. But just who are these philosophers? Meinong perhaps, who thought that Satan did have, in some sense, a being of his own; perhaps St Anselm and his followers, who argued in an obscure way that to think of certain predicates was equivalent to asserting their existence. But who else? It is often assumed that the philosophers of a more metaphysical day at Oxford, such as Bradley and Bosanquet, were peculiarly easy victims of such confusion. Hence a quotation or two may be in order. This is Bradley, writing seventy-five years ago:

'In existential judgment . . . the apparent is not the actual subject. Let us take such a denial as "Chimaeras are non-existent". "Chimaeras" is here ostensibly the subject, but is really the predicate. It is the quality of harbouring chimaeras which is denied of the nature of things.'[1]

And here is Bosanquet, two years later:

'We cannot accept the relations of the parts of speech as we find them in a sentence, for a final determination of subject and predicate . . .

[1] *Principles of Logic*, I, 120 (2nd ed.).

there is no presumption at all in favour of identifying the logical subject . . . with the grammatical subject.'[1]

It is not, perhaps, surprising that those who were given these passages to read in their youth should have been puzzled by the acclaim accorded to the theory of descriptions.

It may be said that these men were exceptions who had been alerted to the dangers of language, whereas most philosophers had not. Professor Ryle remarks that 'partly through accepting the grammatical *prima facies* of such expressions, philosophers have believed devoutly in the existence of "ideas", "conceptions", and "thoughts" or "judgments" as their predecessors did (from similar causes) in that of substantial forms. . . .'[2] He knows his Plato well, and he would strengthen his case if he showed that it was indeed confusions incident to Greek grammar that produced the belief in substantial forms. That Plato had at least considered how treacherous language might be in this matter is clear from long drawn out discussion in the *Sophist* of τὸ μὴ 'ὸν, ending with the conclusion that this referred to the fact of difference rather than to a substantial non-being. As to the four words just noted by Professor Ryle as especially deceptive, three—'conception', 'idea' and 'judgment'—have been pointed out by Professor Passmore to be words not originating in common usage at all, but coined by philosophers.

' "Conceptions" (in the form of "conceptus") was coined by a Latin commentator on Aristotle; and the Bishop of Worcester rebuked Locke for introducing that upstart technicality, the word "idea", into a book which professed to use "common words and expressions". The word "idea" is now part of common idiom, these facts suggest, only because the theory of ideas has gradually seeped down into everyday thinking: the theory originates the idiom, not the idiom the theory.'[3]

If philosophers have in fact been as generally deceived by grammar as is alleged, it could be shown only by historical study. This study has not, so far, been made.

One consideration suggests, however, that philosophers might survive such an inquisition fairly well. If they have really been so

[1] *Knowledge and Reality*, 181.
[2] *Logic and Language*, 1st series, 29.
[3] 'Reflections on *Logic and Language*', Australasian Journal of Philosophy, December 1932, 161.

much swayed by grammar, if they are really inclined to take as substances whatever the subjects of their sentences denote, why have they not done this more widely still? The subjects of their sentences do not name only persons and things; they include abstractions, and abstractions from abstractions. Philosophers, like other people, say 'scarlet is lighter than crimson'. They say 'the difference between scarlet and crimson is less than that between blue and green'. They say 'the difference between these two differences is less than that between colour and sound'. These statements all ostensibly ascribe properties to something that owns them. Grammatically minded philosophers should therefore have felt a strong temptation to regard these subjects as naming substances that exist in their own right. They have not in fact done so. And if, turning to self-examination, one asks oneself whether, having talked about two things as different, and then had occasion to remark about the difference between them, one's use of the word 'difference' as subject sets up a tendency to regard it as a self-subsistent thing, one can only say No. It is not news to us that language sits loose to fact. Normal eyes are not so easily blinded as this to the chasm between a relation and a thing.

10. The thesis, however, that most people have found arresting in the language philosophers is not that philosophy has been thrown off the trail by language, but that the consideration of language forms its main business. 'It is then salutary to keep on reminding ourselves and one another,' says Professor Ryle, 'that what we are after is accounts of how certain words work. . . .'[1] And what does the working of a word mean? Not how it is actually used, not how it might be used to secure various effects, but its working in the special sense of its 'informal logic'; 'we are interested in the informal logic of the employment of expressions, the nature of the logical howlers that people do or might commit if they strung their words together in certain ways. . . .'[2] Now how does one tell when words are strung together in objectionable ways? If someone says 'Saturday is in bed' or 'Socrates is 9', I can see that he is linking words absurdly, but how do I see it? By considering whether the facts could be what his words suggest they are. The moment I do consider that, I see that Saturday, a stretch of time, is not the sort of thing that could lie in bed, and that Socrates, as a human being, could not also be a number. The reason why the words should not be strung together thus, and the

---

[1] *Philosophical Review*, LXII (1953), 185.
[2] *Ibid.*, 186.

M

only conceivable interest for the philosopher in ordering them in one way rather than another, is that the things and qualities referred to are related in a certain way. If philosophers note, for example, that Hobbes was talking absurdly when, anticipating Dr Watson, he said '*ratio* now is but *oratio*', that is because they see, or think they see, that the two things he was trying to identify are as different as any two things in the world; to see this is to see that Hobbes's kind of metaphysic cannot be true. When they say that his way of stringing words together was a bad way, they are saying either that or nothing. The point is worth insisting on. According to the new way of thinking, when we study Hobbes we are studying whether his manner of stringing words together was legitimate or not. It is admitted that the way to decide this is to see whether his language involves 'logical howlers' or not. Now the only way to decide whether it is a howler to say 'thinking is speaking' is to get clear whether thinking *is* speaking. If this is in truth the way to decide, then philosophy will remain what men have commonly thought it to be, a reflective exploration of the nature of things. If the way to decide is to appeal to linguistic considerations, to accepted usage or literary propriety or grammatical rule, then philosophy has become trivial. I see no third alternative.[1]

Are these mere platitudes? They seem so to me. Occasional remarks of Professor Ryle's suggest that he too would find them so. He points out that the test whether sentence-factors will go together is whether the proposition-factors they refer to will go together; and these latter factors are those of things, not of speech. That seems to imply that his interest in words and expressions is secondary to, and an instrument of, his interest in fact. But we are no sooner assured on this point than we are thrown off balance again by such statements as this: 'To say that a given proposition-factor is of a certain category or type, is to say that its expression could complete certain sentence-frames without absurdity.'[2] Surely this is getting things backward; it suggests that to recognize the category to which a thing belongs is to see something about sentences. Or take this: 'it is, on the whole, prudent to talk logic in the semantic idiom and to formulate our theories and inquiries in such a way as to advertise all the time that we are considering whether such and such expressions may or may not be coupled in such and such ways with other expressions.'[3]

---

[1] Cf. the effective criticism by the Warden of Merton: G. R. G. Mure, *Retreat from Truth*, 143 ff.

[2] *Logic and Language*, 2nd series, 70.

[3] *Ibid.*, 76.

Oxford philosophers know, of course, of the storms of dismayed protest that have rolled across the hinterlands in response to such teaching, but they have not, one gathers, been greatly moved. Why is this? If a view of their task so much at odds with that of most philosophers of past and present is thus firmly adhered to, there must be important reasons.

11. In Professor Ryle's writing on these matters, I seem to have found several reasons. (1) The first is that if one were to talk directly about fact rather than about one's talk about fact, one would be setting philosophy up as a science or a rival to science, that is, as a distinct way of achieving knowledge about the actual world. And this is not its business. Its business is rather 'the resolution of type-puzzles about the logical powers of ideas'.[1] And for this latter business, assertions about fact are irrelevant; Ryle indeed denies that facts have 'any evidential force in the resolution of philosophical problems'.[2] This is very disconcerting. We had learned earlier that what made language 'systematically misleading' was that its 'syntactical form' was 'improper to the fact recorded',[3] and that the reason for recasting it was to make it conform to fact better. For example, it is because we know that there is not, or may not be, any such person as Satan, that we should avoid language suggesting there is. But if facts are to have no evidential force for us in this effort at recasting our language, it is hard to see why any form of sentence should be thought better or worse than any other. Recasting will have lost its purpose. Our compass will be gone. To put it more generally, if philosophy, out of the conviction that the kingdom of fact belongs to science, declines to enter that realm, reserving for itself only the humbler task of discussing the propriety of our language, it will soon find even this province lost. 'Propriety', if it here means anything, can only mean propriety to fact, and a philosophy without convictions about fact can have no very helpful views about language either.

12. (2) A second reason for the insistence on language is closely connected with the first, and might indeed be taken as answering our objection to the first. Professor Ryle would not accept the dilemma that if philosophy declines to discuss facts, it must discuss words merely. He proposes that it should move along a middle lane between

[1] *Philosophical Arguments*, 11.
[2] *Ibid.*, 5.
[3] *Logic and Language*, 1st series, 14.

them, a lane of *reductio ad absurdum* argument; it will concern itself neither, like the sciences, with things and events, nor, like philology, with usage, but with the logical behaviour of words. And this is a study of the relations between the types or categories to which the words, or rather the proposition-factors denoted by them, belong. Such a study, as we have seen, is hardly logic in the traditional sense, for it would multiply the logical forms of statements indefinitely though making them depend on the relations and types of their components. But it would still be logical in the sense that it would deal with the necessary and non-factual. Types can be seen to involve each other, to repel each other, or to be neutral to each other, without reference to fact at all.

Now is this true? In a sense it clearly is. One can see that 'Socrates is 9' expresses an absurdity without knowing whether Socrates ever existed; what one sees is the incongruity between being a man and a number. But does it follow that we can avoid absurdity in our language without commitments as to the nature of things? I think we can see through the present instance that we cannot, and why we cannot. There are two steps in grasping the type-conflict involved here. First, we must see to what types the terms belong. We must know that the Greek thinker with a sharp mind and a blunt nose—if that were what 'Socrates' meant to us—falls in the class of men; and we must know that 9 is a number. To know these things is in some sense to know facts, though admittedly a somewhat out-of-the-way kind of facts. Secondly, to see that the two categories cannot characterize one thing is also to see something about the nature of things. That whatever is a man is not and cannot be a number, is no very novel or thrilling insight; granted; but I do not know how to deny that it is a fact, and indeed a fundamental one. In short, to say that Socrates is 9 is absurd because he could not *be* 9. The very meaning of 'absurd' here is 'conflicts with obvious fact'.

Persons who take positivism seriously may say that if relations between categories are logical relations, and logical relations are necessary relations, then to apprehend them will not give us knowledge of fact, since of course no knowledge of necessity is ever a knowledge of the nature of things. Now we have examined this strange dogma long ago, and found no good ground for holding it, even when logic is conceived in the most formal terms. The dogma is even less plausible when all possible relations between proposition-factors are included in 'logical behaviour'. To see that 'Jones's pleasure weighs eight pounds' is an absurdity will now be an insight into the 'logic' of the word 'pleasure'. But then this 'logic' is what it is because pleasure excludes what it does; and this excludes what it does because of what it is; pleasure is such by nature that it cannot have weight. To talk 'logic' in this sense is to talk about the relations between certain general characters of things and persons. Older logicians sometimes thought that because the law of contradiction said nothing of anything in particular, it said nothing of anything at all. This does not follow. One does not cease to talk about the world of things and persons merely because what one says applies to many of them, or to all of them.

13. (3) In Professor Ryle's writing I find what looks like a further reason for his preference for talking about words. Suppose one starts with the conviction that the business of philosophy is to expose howlers or absurdities; where are such things to be found? Professor Ryle thinks they are to be found only in expressions; hence his concentration on them. This clearly calls for argument, and he does not fail to supply it. If absurdities occur elsewhere than in expressions, then where? Not in nature certainly, for we shall find no embodiments of category-conflicts walking about in the flesh. Shall we find them, then, in the domain of propositions? No again, though the argument here becomes subtle. Suppose you start with a proposition, and by working out its implications, show that it involves an absurdity. 'But if the consequences of a proposition are absurd,' says Professor Ryle, 'that proposition is absurd, and then there can be no such proposition. It is absurd to say that there are absurd propositions. . . . The solution is that expressions and only expressions can be absurd.'[1] It might be supposed, indeed, that a capacious lurking-place for confusions, howlers, and absurdities could be found in our thoughts. In another context Professor Ryle considers this too and dismisses it in a passage that should be set out more fully:

'if it is suggested that the non-philosophical author of an expression . . . does know but only knows dimly or foggily or confusedly what his expression means, but that the philosopher at the end of his exploration knows clearly, distinctly and definitely what it means, a two-fold answer seems inevitable. First, that if a speaker only knows confusedly what his expression means, then he is in that respect and to that extent just gabbling. And it is not the role—nor the achievement—of the philosopher to provide a medicine against that form of flux. And next, the philosopher is not *ex officio* concerned with ravings and ramblings: he studies expressions for what they mean

[1] *Philosophical Arguments*, 12.

when intelligently and intelligibly employed, and not as noises emitted by this idiot or that parrot.' Ryle concludes 'that if an expression can be understood, then it is already known in that understanding what the expression means. So that there is no darkness present and no illumination required or possible.'[1]

If the confusions and absurdities which it is the philosopher's business to expose occur, then, neither in nature, propositions, nor thought, there would seem to be only one domain left for them, and that is the domain of expression.

This is a complex case, in which there are at least five distinct theses of interest to us: (i) philosophy is primarily the exposure of absurdities, (ii) absurdities do not occur in nature, (iii) nor in propositions, (iv) nor in thoughts, but (v) in expressions. It will serve clearness if we say at once that we accept the second of these theses (there are no absurdities in nature) but not the others.

14. (i) Professor Ryle concluded his influential essay on 'Systematically Misleading Expressions' by saying candidly that he 'would rather allot to philosophy a sublimer task than the detection of the sources in linguistic idioms of recurrent misconstructions and absurd theories', but that the sort of analysis which led to this was its main function, and—he was 'inclined to believe'—its 'sole and whole function';[2] and we found him arguing later in similar vein that the *reductio ad absurdum* is an argument 'proper and even proprietary to philosophy'.[3] Now this seems a needlessly thin and self-abnegating role for the philosopher. He has conceived himself in the past—and one can only think with justice—as something more than an exposer of absurdities, wherever they may lie. He has thought of himself from Greek times forward as a lover of truth, as a seeker of new truth; he has raised large questions about the nature and extent of knowledge, about causality and its relation to freedom, about goods and rights and duties. In trying to answer such questions, he would have said that he was looking for light, trying to understand what sort of creature he was and what to do with his life. He was not just trying to avoid absurd locutions. One may say, of course, that to avoid absurdities is itself to get light, in the sense that to remove a confusion is to see more clearly. This is true; indeed we have just been insisting on it. But it is misleading if taken as the whole or the main truth about

---

[1] *Logic and Language*, 1st series, 12.
[2] *Ibid.*, 36.
[3] *Philosophical Arguments*, 6.

philosophy. For it suggests that the world of fact is presented to the philosopher from without, presumably by common sense or science, for his passive acceptance, and that his business is simply to adjust his language better to these facts. No doubt the philosophers of the past would have accepted this linguistic commission as part of their business, but it would have been a relatively small part. For they thought of themselves as widening the domain of known fact itself, not by duplicating the work of the scientist but by supplementing it, by composing its conclusions, for example, into some large and consistent view. Regarding any of the men whom common consent would nominate as great philosophers—such as Aquinas, or Spinoza, or even so ardent a student of language as Locke—would it be correct to say that the detection in linguistic idioms of misconstructions and absurdities was what they thought they were about? Clearly not. Is it what they were really doing? No, again. Is it what they ought to have been doing? To say this would be to ask of them something they would have regarded as impossible, because destructive of their main interest. They would have seen the point readily enough of avoiding misconstructions as a means to a fuller knowledge of things, but if told to limit their interest in such knowledge to the avoidance of misconstructions, they would have become as unruly as a healthy patient in a straitjacket. There is something like a category difference between achieving truth and avoiding error. There is, if possible, a still larger psychological difference.

15. (ii) Professor Ryle says that absurdities, in the sense of conflicts of categories, do not occur in nature. We agree, and are tempted to leave the matter so. But while accepting it, we can only wonder how Professor Ryle can do so. For it is a universal and necessary statement, made about the nature of things—not a statement about what language is permissible, but a statement about how the world is constructed. It reports how nature is articulated; it tells us that it is put together in accordance with a certain pattern of categories, to which no exception will be found. Statements of this kind far exceed the role of a philosophy assigned to the exposure of linguistic confusions. They are excursions into metaphysics.

16. (iii) Professor Ryle says that there are no absurdities among propositions. If you start from a certain proposition, and deduce an absurdity from it, then the proposition from which you started must be absurd, and an absurd proposition is no proposition. What is meant here by 'absurd'? Not of course the comic and unexpected.

Nor does it mean merely what is false; to disprove propositions by deducing falsities from them is standard scientific procedure, though there is no suggestion that the propositions therefore say nothing. For Professor Ryle an absurd proposition is much more than a false proposition. It is one that reveals a collision of types or categories, and which is therefore incoherent and meaningless, like 'cube-roots are succulent'. Such statements, he maintains, are not propositions because they assert nothing, and 'propositions' that require them as 'consequences' must likewise be no propositions.

Now this view itself has a curious consequence. It implies that in their characteristic work philosophers do not in the ordinary sense argue or reason at all. Their office, it will be recalled, is to point out that certain linguistic idioms are absurd or lead to absurdities. What does 'lead to' mean? What it is naturally taken to mean is *imply* or *entail*, since that which is led to is 'consequences'. But if neither the 'proposition' from which one starts nor the 'consequence' to which it leads says anything, then there can be no logical relation between them; what is meaningless can entail nothing and be entailed by nothing. Hence the *reductio ad absurdum*, which was to be the staple of philosophical argument, is not an argument, a bit of reasoning, at all. And the upshot of Professor Ryle's discussion of 'philosophical arguments' would appear to be that there are no such things.

Though this conclusion is certainly surprising, Professor Ryle would probably agree with it if it were put less provocatively. 'Philosophical arguments are not inductions,' he holds, because inductions assert matters of fact, and philosophical arguments do not. 'On the other hand philosophical arguments are not demonstrations of the Euclidean type. . . .'[1] But if neither inductive nor deductive, what are they? The answer given is that they belong to a peculiar type, which may be described, perhaps, as arguments from non-analogy. With an approved proposition in mind, you go on un-thinkingly to take what looks like a similar proposition as saying the same sort of thing; then you see that this makes nonsense, and this seeing is the essence of philosophical argument. You start with the model, 'the rain began at three o'clock'; then in talking about time you use the same model and say that time began at a certain moment; then you feel that there is something wrong, and suddenly see that this case is not like the model and makes nonsense. Or you begin with the model of pyramids lasting a tremendously long time; then you hear it said that numbers are timeless; you suppose this to mean that numbers too last a very long time, and then you are forced into

[1] *Philosophical Arguments*, 5.

distinctions. Professor Ryle does not say that this process will now be the whole of philosophy, only that it will have the 'primacy' in philosophy and is 'proprietary' to it. Still, it is the only kind of argument he recognizes in an essay expressly devoted to the topic.

17. Two comments suggest themselves. First—to repeat—this is not in the ordinary sense a process of reasoning at all. You feel that 'rain began' and 'time began' are somehow not alike; you then suddenly see that time is not an event *in* time, and is different in kind. The perception of a difference is hardly reasoning. Nor can the reasoning lie in developing the idea of a beginning of time into its logically absurd consequences, for Ryle denies that there is any implication here for thought to follow. To talk about philosophical reasoning and argument looks like a misuse of two useful words.

From our point of view, however, even if not from Professor Ryle's, this is a venial sin. More important is a second comment, namely that such an account of philosophical thought is inadequate, inadequate both as a description of the past and as a programme for the future. It is needless to argue that the hundreds of deductive trains of reasoning to be found in the rationalist philosophers from Descartes to McTaggart could not be forced into the pattern proposed; Professor Ryle would no doubt admit this and be undisturbed. He would say that these men were exceeding their briefs as philosophers. And this amounts to a proposal of policy to the effect that philosophy should so limit itself in the future. Whether there are any good reasons for this is the question we are discussing. So far we have found none. Here we may content ourselves with saying that whoever proposes so severe a curb on the philosopher's activities, a curb that would exclude all inductive and deductive argument, is assuming a large burden of proof. Philosophers have offered many arguments, both inductive and deductive, that do not clearly fall in the domain of any established science and have been commonly thought to be meaningful and even illuminating. Such thinking would be put out of bounds by the new test. Since we owe light to these philosophers, since indeed part of the light we owe to Ryle shines through infractions of his own ordinance, we can hardly be content with this ostracism.

18. (iv) Thesis (4) states that the absurdities which the philosopher is to expose do not occur in thought, thesis (5) that they do occur in language. We shall take the latter point first, and then the former, arguing that they reverse the truth, that absurdities never occur in language, and that they occur exclusively in thought.

Take a simple case of a 'systematically misleading expression', such as 'the equator encircles the earth'. This is misleading because we are apt to interpet it on the analogy of 'a hoop encircled the barrel', or 'a fence encircled the park', and to think of a band or ribbon running round the earth. Of course there is no such band; there is only an invisible line. To ascribe to this line the properties of a band or ribbon is to ascribe to something of one type properties that belong only to things of an extremely different type, and this is absurd. Where does the absurdity lie? Not of course in the earth or the equator; and, according to Ryle, neither in propositions nor thoughts about them, but in something that can be contrasted with both, namely, expressions. And what is an expression? Something composed of words. And a word is what? In its commonest acceptation, a set of written or printed marks, an uttered sound or series of sounds, or in the case of 'words spoken under our breath', a set of muscular movements. Now there is no absurdity in these, any more than in other marks, noises, or muscle-contractions. Is it meant, then, not that the words or expressions are absurd, but that their use is absurd. Certainly not if 'use' has the ordinary meaning appearing in 'I used these words, but might as well have used others instead.' My use of these words is an event, and no event can be absurd in the required sense. If you regard their use as an act on my part, it is still not absurd, even though it may be an unfortunate, or ill-advised, or immoral act. Nor would it have been absurd if I had said 'hocus-pocus is abracadabra', for the mere choice of a set of words to express what one means is not a type-confusion. Neither in the words nor in their use is there, so far, any room for absurdity.

19. Let us try again. It is sometimes said that what is true or false, what is absurd or consistent or relevant, is not words, nor the strings of these called expressions or sentences; it is, rather, these words or strings *as interpreted*, as meaning this or that, as used to make an assertion. Thus when we say 'the equator encircles the earth', what is absurd is the expression *as meaning* that a band or ribbon encircles the earth. The expression-as-meaning-this is then called a statement, and one says that what is true or false or absurd is not the sentence or the use of the sentence in any of the above senses, but this complex of words *and* meaning.

Unfortunately this confounds confusion. The sequence of thought appears to be this: first you say that what may be absurd is the sentence; then you see that a sentence by itself, on a page or a phonograph, could not possibly be absurd; then you discern that there must be something else in your judgment to be absurd; but remembering your loyalty to the sentence, you try to save its face and your own by saying, 'Well, anyhow, if it is not the words, it is the-words-and-this-other-factor lumped together.' It will not do. If a Frenchman, a German, and an Englishman, all speaking at once, make what we should call the same remark about the weather, is what is true the French words as used by the first, the German ones as used by the second, and the English ones as used by the third? To anyone who suggested that, we should surely say, 'Why drag in the words at all?' If the three men meant to say the same thing, the varying noises they made in saying it are of no interest, for it is this common meaning alone that is true, false, or absurd. The words of course are practically useful, if you will essential, to their expressing and communicating what they meant. But there is a world of difference between saying that words are instrumentally or causally essential to the making of an assertion and saying that they belong to the assertion itself, in the sense of what could be true or absurd. To say that they do belong there is itself absurd as involving a plain confusion of categories. It is like saying that if Picasso had to use brushes to paint a certain picture, the brushes are beautiful or absurd because the picture is.

20. I conclude that expressions neither are nor can be absurd. The discussion of words and their uses is either irrelevant in philosophy, or should take at most an ancillary part. I do not mean that such discussion is unhelpful. I agree that we are often misled by words in the ways Ryle has described, and that it is therefore a counsel of prudence that the philosopher should be on his guard about them. I agree that when our thought becomes abstract or complex, words or other symbols are indispensable; it is as if we were at home only in the concrete and needed a concrete tag or label if we were to get or hold the abstraction before us. This has led some philosophers, indeed, to say that we think only in words. Wittgenstein says, 'You learned the *concept* pain when you learned language'.[1] This is surely wrong. One can think in the simpler ways without words. One can recognize someone as present in the room, or as having entered it or left it, without mumbling to oneself 'Jones is here', or is 'coming' or 'going'. But—to return to our agreement—I should agree with the linguistic school, further, that much can be learned about what philosophers have meant through studying the usages of their time and place; consider Descartes's 'eminent causes', Locke's 'enthusiasm',

---

[1] *Philosophical Investigations*, Sec. 384.

and Hegel's *aufheben*. I agree, once more, that philosophy has often started, as the Platonic dialogues so frequently did, from a discussion of what some word means—'justice', or 'temperance', or 'courage'. But the discussion of what the word meant gave only the springboard for the philosophic discussion. Common use and common sense grow hesitant after the first few exchanges, and ultimately break down; and from then on the discussion is less and less about what words mean, and more and more about what things are. It will be clear from all these admissions—and the list could be made much longer—how important I think the consideration of words is. But I come back to my contention: the discussion of words in philosophy is prefatory and preparatory only. How expressions are used is not a philosophical problem. How they ought to be used *is* a philosophical problem, but not primarily one about words at all, but about the character and relations of the objects talked about.

21. One can, to be sure, always speak about an inquiry into objects as if it were an inquiry about words. One can say that when Hume was trying to get clear how the movements of the famous billiard balls were related, he was studying the use of the word 'cause'. At the end of his inquiry he had a different notion of this relation from the one he started with, and presumably used the word in a modified sense. So one may say, if one wishes, that what he was concerned with was use of the word. One can also imagine the snort with which that sensible man would have greeted such an account of his enterprise. He would surely have said that the cart had got before the horse and was pulling it perversely about. For what he was trying to achieve was an understanding of the relation that linked the two balls, or the hammer and nail. In the course of his endeavour he had to use the common word for that relation, and indeed to consider continually how best to express and convey his meaning. But his controlling interest was in achieving an insight into the nature of this relation, not in the verbal machinery by which he expressed his meaning about it; and the meaning appointed the words, not the words the meaning. A parallel may help us. If we had come upon Hume in the Advocates' Library writing his *History* and had asked him what he was doing, he might have replied with perfect truth, 'I am using my quill pen'. But we should certainly have been puzzled if he had, and have suspected that he was snubbing us or putting us off. For this was obviously not 'what he was doing' in the relevant sense, which was presumably writing a history, but an insignificant detail of it. I am similarly puzzled as to why people say such queer things as that

Hume, in analysing 'causality', was studying the use of a word. This is not exactly untrue. It merely throws things out of focus and proportion. One suspects, as the astronomers did about Neptune, that when philosophers say these things there is some powerful force in the background pulling them out of their normal orbit. There is not much doubt as to the identity of this force. It is pretty clearly Wittgenstein, with his uncanny genius for making molehills out of mountains.

22. (v) But if it is not in sentences nor even in statements that category-mistakes are found, where is it? I have suggested that it is in *thought*. An illustration may help us again. You see someone walking ahead of you with the coat and hat and peculiar gait of your friend John. Can this be he? you look again; yes, there is no doubt about it; that is John. You run after him and tap him on the shoulder; he turns round; and you are confronted by a total stranger. You have obviously made a mistake. To say that what is mistaken is certain words you have used, or a statement you may have made, is out of the question, for you may have made no use of either. To say that it is the mental act or event of taking the man for John, also fails to make sense, for an event, as we have seen, cannot be erroneous. What is in error is surely 'the objective component of the judgment', as Broad might call it, namely, what is expressed by a that-clause in such a sentence as 'I thought that it was John'.

We commonly call this a proposition. It is evidently not what Ryle means by a proposition, for he stipulates that this should be incapable of category-mistakes. But it is a proposition nevertheless, if that means the content or objective component of a judgment. It is an element in our thought; we naturally say 'I had the idea that . . .' It might indeed be asked what is meant by a thought or idea. There are passages in Ryle's writings that are apparently designed to answer this question. He suggests that a thought or idea *is* simply what we should commonly call its expression, that it consists in the use of certain words pronounced covertly or under one's breath. With all respect, I cannot take this seriously. To do so would be to believe that one of the clearest-headed of philosophers, in the course of a determined search for category-mistakes, should have perpetrated the worst such mistake that is open to human faculty. And if Professor Ryle did at times allow himself this way of speaking, he has made amends for it with admirable inconsistency.[1] Of course if thought is

[1] Cf. 'Ryle on the Intellect' by C. A. Campbell, *Philosophical Quarterly*, III (April 1953), 115 ff. Professor Campbell has laid his finger very precisely on the

to be identified with linguistic reactions, it could not be true or false, since it would then consist of movements, and no movements, however subtle or complicated, could be true or false. What we are looking for is that which a mind expresses through such movements. And I suggest that it is both natural and accurate to say that what is thus expressed is a thought, idea, or belief. It is not something fixed and changeless, as Platonic ideas were supposed to be, for it comes into being, dies away, and perhaps gives place to its opposite; it is not out there in nature independently of my mind, for as Ryle points out, nature does not harbour mistakes; it is private to my own mind. What could this be but my thought?[1]

Category-mistakes, like other mistakes, seem to me to occur exclusively in this region of thought or belief. Though the equator cannot be at once a line and a band or ribbon, we may confusedly take it to be both. Not that we can do so if we think clearly; but it would be odd to say that we are not thinking at all unless the thinking is perfectly clear. Our thought varies from heights of clearness to the most abject confusion. One wonders indeed whether there are any confusions beyond the powers of the more remarkable forms of stupidity. Numberless people have felt sure that they have discovered perpetual motion, squared the circle, and exposed the muddles of Einstein; in Hyde Park one day I found a particularly interesting speaker who proclaimed that he was the Deity, adding 'Before the world was, I am'. He was by no means necessarily a charlatan.

23. Professor Ryle seems to question all this—to hold that an expression is either understood or not, and that there is hence no room for a confused or imperfect understanding. He writes: 'if an expression can be understood, then it is already known in that understanding what the expression means. So that there is no darkness present and no illumination required or possible.' On the other hand, 'if a speaker knows only confusedly what his expression means, then he is in that respect and to that extent just gabbling'.[2] This takes undue liberties with ordinary usage. It would class as gabbling much if not most of what everyone would commonly call thinking. How

difficulties of this form of behaviourism. If one is going to accept behaviourism, it is better to accept it in the old-fashioned fundamentalist form, which is that of Dr Watson. Both the Oxonian and the later American attempts to revise the doctrine into credibility end, I think, by giving away the case.
[1] Cf. Frege: 'A thought is something immaterial, and everything material and perceptible is excluded from this sphere of that for which the question of truth arises.' 'The Thought: A Logical Inquiry', *Mind*, July, 1956, 292.
[2] *Logic and Language*, 1st series, 12.

many scientists or philosophers, to say nothing of plain men, are perfectly clear in their meanings? Of how many of them could it be said that 'there is no darkness present and no illumination required or possible'? Is any man who falls below so exalted a level 'just gabbling'? I should have thought that the roomy purgatory which on this theory does not exist is precisely where most of us fall, that our thoughts on science, on religion, on politics, indeed—if we are pressed—on tables and chairs, are neither mere gabbling nor so clear that further illumination is impossible. Our thought on all these matters is likely to be vague, confused, or even downright contradictory. Nothing is easier than to contradict oneself in all sincerity if the two sides of the contradiction are not forced into glaring juxtaposition. It is possible for a very clear-headed biologist on Saturday to scout the possibility of a dead body's being re-animated and to say without misgiving on Sunday 'I believe in the resurrection of the body'. The kind of reflection described in the past as philosophy has had as a principal aim the removal of these confusions and incoherencies from one's belief, sometimes described as a penetration through appearances to reality. This aim, I think, was sound.

24. Here we come round again to the fundamental difference between the standard view of philosophy and the linguistic view. On the standard view, philosophizing is an attempt to gain fuller and clearer knowledge by reflecting on the nature of things; on the linguistic view at what seems to me its best, it is still an attempt to gain such knowledge, but now by ridding one's language of absurdities. The chief criticism we have offered is that the only way to detect these absurdities is to consider the nature of the objects thought of. Professor Ryle often writes as if he believed this too; he insists that we should mould our expressions into closer conformity to fact, and that, by ridding our talk of absurd statements, we should try to see more clearly the logical geography of the world. In taking this view, he seems to me to be a metaphysician, self-hobbled, as older metaphysicians were not, by a linguistic ball and chain. The phrase 'the logical behaviour of words' looks like the compromise of a mind drawn in two ways at once, committed to discussing verbal uses, and yet really interested in them only as reflecting better or worse *den logischen Aufbau der Welt*. Because of this latter interest, his work seems to me to have philosophic interest and importance. He never wraps himself, as Carnap sometimes does, in a cocoon of words from which there is no escaping into the world; words are his pointers to a

knowledge of those categories and relations which older philosophers have thought of as the bony framework of the world.[1]

25. Unfortunately among his co-admirers of Wittgenstein, this interest seems often at the vanishing point. Wittgenstein had little interest in, or knowledge of, philosophic systems, and small capacity for systematic exposition; his gift was for the sharp handling of minute and isolated questions; and those questions he preferred latterly to approach through considering the uses of words. It became clear to him that the popular idea of words as names for something denoted—the 'Fido'—Fido notion of their office—was grossly inadequate, for they performed all sorts of functions besides this, and many of these had nothing to do with knowing or asserting. They might express emotions, or entreaties, or commands, or hopes, or wishes, and have no meaning at all in the sense of naming or referring to an object. In reflecting, then, on our own processes of thought, there was not only the well-marked danger of confusing one cognitive meaning with another, but also the less clearly advertised danger of supposing ourselves to be asserting something when we had no cognitive meaning in mind. Hence Wittgenstein's warning of later years, 'Don't look for the meaning, look for the use'. 'Use' covered all kinds of meaning.

Now the term 'use' has tended to confound itself with 'usage'. We have seen that Ryle tried to keep the two distinct: to know the use of an expression, he said, is to know how to use it, to be able to apply it appropriately, to be master of the technique of employing it; on the other hand, to know its usage is to know how it is used in fact. This distinction in practice became quickly blurred. How do you know when you have mastered the technique, or when you are using an expression appropriately? The easiest answer is an appeal to usage: if you are using the expression in the stock or standard way, you are using it correctly; otherwise not. And then if the question arises what 'knowing' means, or 'right' or truth' or 'good', you can settle the matter by studying actual usage.

This not unnatural development was furthered by a somewhat

---

[1] Cf. Russell: 'The treatment of words by the Logical Positivists has in it, to my mind, an element of superstition. They seem to think that we can know all about words without knowing anything about "facts". The logical tendency of this theory is towards a Platonic idealism: The Real World will be that of words, while the world of sense will be condemned as illusory. . . . All this is implicit in the insistence upon the formal as opposed to the material mode of speech. We must not say "There was a man called 'Socrates' ", but " 'Socrates' is a name".' *Proc. Aristotelian Soc.*, 38 (1937–38), 12.

more complicated consideration. When Ryle first reported his conversion to linguistic philosophy in 1931, there was no idolatry of ordinary language in his attitude. On the contrary, ordinary language was the wellspring of philosophic error, not indeed as used by the plain man, whose limited purposes it served well enough, but as used by the philosopher, who was reduced by its grammatical caprices into taking them as revelations of the nature of things. It was the business of the philosopher to develop an immunity to these seductions, and to see that his discourse was ordered, not in accordance with these caprices, but in accordance with logical form. At first this meant for Ryle what it did for Russell and the early Wittgenstein, namely making grammatical form reflect the structure of fact. But with the decay of logical atomism, this became an impractical ideal. As we have seen in our earlier study, the ultimate and simple facts with which every empirical statement was supposed to accord dissolved in an impenetrable mist. Yet logical form was obviously different from grammatical form, and more important. It still remained the business of philosophers to make their discourse accord with it. Ryle dealt with the difficulty boldly. He reconceived logical form. It was not now a relation whose supreme example was the connective in 'this-blue', but a vast set of relations holding between categories, themselves now reconceived as 'proposition-factors', identical in all propositions of the same structure. And philosophy became a process of uncovering these relations by trial and error, eliminating those that on experiment proved absurd, until a complete new logical geography was achieved. A geography of what? Clearly of the actual world. But that, as we have seen, is metaphysics. Younger analysts felt the danger and shied away. They had been brought up to think metaphysics an engulfing Slough of Despond, 'where armies whole had sunk'. That swamp at least they were going to avoid.

26. But the problem remained how, if they were to avoid antiquated talk about 'knowing the real world', they were to separate the wheat from the chaff in their winnowing of expressions. Wittgenstein had said, 'Bring your language into conformity with fact', but then Wittgenstein had never been able to produce an example of fact and had lost interest in trying. 'Bring your language into conformity with the true geography of the categories,' said Ryle, but there was an almost Hegelian ring about this that grated on tender ears. Why not say, if you were determined to go to such lengths, 'Bring your thought into conformity with the nature of things'? Then we should know where we were. The philosophical clock would have been turned back a half-century or so, and the great revolution would have been fought through for nothing.

There was one resort left, a resort which the younger analysts noted with pleasure that Ryle himself not infrequently took. They could accept as the test of appropriateness standard usage itself. They could say that if you penetrated behind the irregularities of ordinary speech you would find a meaning which was itself proof against confusion and sufficient to rectify all irregularities. Ordinary usage, sensitively discriminated and faithfully followed, was as good a test as we could hope for. No less an authority than Wittgenstein was reported to have said, 'Philosophy must not in any way, however slight, interfere with the ordinary use of language; in the end, philosophy can only describe it.' This sounded strangely like Moore as interpreted by Malcolm. Indeed Antony Flew in introducing the first series of essays on *Logic and Language* thanks 'that apostle of common-sense and linguistic propriety, Professor G. E. Moore. For it has been Professor Moore who has made philosophers see how easy it is to slip into nonsense by even apparently trivial deviations from standard English . . .'; and in introducing the second series he asks, 'how else could one investigate the concept of knowledge than by studying the various correct uses of the word "know"?'[1] 'Philosophical questions,' wrote Dr Macdonald, 'are not factual but verbal'; 'philosophical problems can be solved by understanding how language is ordinarily used, how certain uses of it have provoked these problems and how it has been misused in many alleged solutions'.[2] Such language became common among writers known to be careful in weighing their words. 'Knowing *what a thing is*,' said Professor Austin, 'is, to an important extent, knowing what the name for it, and the right name for it, is.'[3] Mr Strawson remarks in passing that he takes 'the philosophical problem of truth' to be the same as that of 'the actual use of the word "true" '.[4] 'There would be no need for philosophy,' writes Mr Urmson, 'if language were not inadequate.'[5] Professor Hart writes, summing up on the transformation in philosophy: 'Not only has much changed in philosophy in the intervening thirty years [since 1919], but the most important of the changes has been the replacement of the traditional philosophical conception of language as simply the vehicle in or by which an internal non-symbolic

[1] *Logic and Language*, 1st series, 8–9, 2nd series, 4.
[2] *Ibid.*, 1st series, 80, 100.
[3] *Ibid.*, 2nd series, 129; italics in original.
[4] *Analysis*, June 1949, 83.
[5] *Philosophical Analysis*, 50.

activity of thought about or knowledge of objects is expressed or communicated, by a conception of language as logically inseparable from what is meant by "knowledge" and "object".[1] And Professor Findlay has made it delightfully clear that the new gospel is for him a full-blooded affair, not one of dry leaves only: 'to me, at least, the question "What shall I say to speak well?" is as solemn and important as the old question: "What shall I do to be saved?" '[2]

27. It will not do to dismiss such writers as mere word-catchers. They are among the most acute philosophers of our time. We have already conceded to them much, and we may concede more. Let anyone who has investigated the nature of matter or mind or substance, reflect for a moment on the way he goes about it. Suppose he is reflecting on substance. His first move may well be to ask himself what the word 'substance' means. He gropes about for a synonym of it, but finds none that is satisfactory, and reflects perhaps that even if he found one, it would hardly help, since he wants an analysis of what is meant, not an equivalent word merely. Very well, how analyse the meaning? The classical way is to run over instances where the word is applied, as various as possible, and then to look for something common to them in virtue of which it is applied. Lead is a substance, and stone, and wood, and water, and even fog. What about dreams, ghosts, and shadows? No; at best they are dubious; it is safer to leave them out. The inquirer looks over the successful candidates. He notes that they are all more or less heavy; perhaps it is having weight that makes something a substance. But if a ball of lead were out in space at equal distances from planets of equal mass, it would still of course be a substance, but would it have any weight? He doubts, and tries again. He notes that all his 'substances' occupy space; they are spread out or extended. Substance, then, is extension. But this will not quite do either, since there seems to be something in lead, stone, etc. over and above extension—something that *has* the extension. He starts looking for this something. Sometimes he seems to find it; often he fails. But his method remains the same. If a suggestion fits, he accepts it, at least so far. If it fails to fit—that is, if there are things it does not cover that would be called substance, and things it includes that would not be so called, he abandons it and tries again.

Note that his lodestar throughout is *what he means by the word*. However hard it may be to bring what he means to light, he assumes that he has a meaning, and in a sense that he already knows it. He

---

[1] *Proc. of the Arist. Soc.*, Supplementary Vol. 23 (1949), 71.
[2] *Proc. of the Arist. Soc.*, Vol. 50 (1949–50), 46.

does not, to be sure, know it explicitly, for then there would be nothing to look for. But unless he knew it implicitly, he would have no check on his search, no way of knowing whether the suggestions that cropped up matched with what he actually meant. What he actually means, then, is what he is hunting for. His successive proposals are approximations to this, experiments in making the implicit explicit. Through all the lower-lying strata of meaning through which he may delve, the controlling end and purpose of his inquiry, is fixed by the meaning of the word. The moment he can be assured of having uncovered this, the search will be over. Is it not clear, then, that to describe the search as an inquiry into the *nature* of substance is a misnomer? What he is really doing is inquiring into the usage of the word.

28. I have put the case for this sort of analysis as plausibly as I can. I shall now try to say why I do not accept it.

(1) I do not accept it, in the first place, because through its employment of 'meaning', 'use', and 'usage', it begs the main question. It assumes that the jewel I am in search of is somehow already in my possession, so that all I need to do is to compare it with the brummagem that successively offers itself to see how bogus this is. But unhappily the jewel is not there. My antecedent meaning cannot itself supply the answer I am looking for; it only fixes the direction of my search and tells me in a rough way what to expect. I am not already mysteriously *enceinte* with the object of my search, needing only Socrates to bring it to birth. What I normally want to know is the character or structure of fact in some area demarcated by my meaning, and I test my successive suggestions only by constant glances from these to the fact and back again. At the beginning I know only that I apply the term 'substance' without hesitation to some objects rather than to others. I assume that I do so in virtue of a common structure of character. This I try to bring to light. But it is the analysis of the *objects called substances* that must bring this to light; I cannot spin it , like a spider, out of my own vitals. My meaning can do much for me in holding me to the line and giving me warning twinges when I take wrong turnings. It cannot supply the answer to my question. Only the facts can do that.

In our search the word is a question mark. So to consider it sets in a clearer light the sort of guidance that meaning can exercise. A question may have every degree of definiteness. As Moore used to say, it is of the utmost importance in philosophy to know what question you are asking, and when you succeed in making this definite, you are often half way toward an answer. But he never said that defining the question was all there was to answering it. If you do not fully know what a term means, specifying such meaning as it has for you may take you to a point where the answer falls in your lap, but that is a very different thing from conjuring it up from within. 'I look up,' said Emerson, 'and put myself in the attitude of reception, but from some alien energy the visions come.' If the question is what is the sum of a column of figures, or what will complete a crossword puzzle, it would be absurd to say that you know the answer, even implicitly; what you know is certain rules of the game which are definite enough to enable you to see, when the answer suggests itself, that it fits them. If you are trying to make clear the meaning of 'horse', you can no doubt produce from your own resources all that is needed for practical purposes, but not if your interest runs beyond the acquired meaning of 'horse' to what a horse is. It may take the scrutiny of an expert zoologist, studying the facts long and carefully, to discover the answer to that question. The fullest analysis of what you mean may fall short of a knowledge of the object meant.

29. (2) This shows, again, why ordinary usage is a particularly inadequate guide for philosophical thinking. Practical men refine their meanings as much as they need to for practical purposes, and in general no more. A jockey has of course no trouble in identifying horses; he may 'know' them intimately and handle them with the greatest expertness without the faintest notion that a horse is of the genus *equus* and the species *caballus*. But since he has never raised the question of the nature of the horse, that is, of its place in the animal kingdom, it would never occur to a zoologist to ask him for light about it. So also a theologian who was debating whether one person could unite three substances or a metaphysician debating Bradley's question about the 'it' that owns the qualities of a lump of sugar would get small help from him or his usage. Plain men, that is, all men outside of a classroom, speak of 'it' as having these qualities; but ask them what precisely they mean by this 'it', and they are bankrupt. They have never raised that point, or had any occasion to; and there is nothing in their experience or past reflection or present thought that could settle it for them. If John Stuart Mill were to discuss it with them, they would probably accept his theory as fitting their meaning nicely; but if Locke had reached them first with his opposite theory, they would have accepted that with equal readiness. It is true that a contemporary positivist would settle the question against Locke and in favour of Mill by an appeal to meaning. But he is not appealing to anything that plain men would have reported independently as their meaning. He is appealing to what a philosopher's meaning would be if regulated in strict accordance with the verifiability theory, which is something very different. Broad and McTaggart, in turn, would reject the positivist view by insisting on the presence in the lump of sugar of an 'it' that is not a quality but may possess qualities nevertheless. Which of all these views is true? The decision between them turns on points of extreme subtlety in metaphysics and the theory of meaning. To say that these issues could be settled by inspecting ordinary usage is to use 'ordinary usage' in a most unordinary way. The plain man would be bewildered by the linguistic legerdemain which produced all these sleek rabbits from his unassuming hat.

The philosopher who settles speculative issues by appeal to ordinary usage is really enabled to do so by endowing it with ranges of meaning not its own. If he really adhered to his programme, if he accepted as ordinary meaning only what is indubitably there, the philosophic enterprise would seem a tame affair, even to him. Professor Baier has remarked that 'all Englishmen, except the incapacitated, morons and very young children, do know the language. Hence we all know the ordinary use of words'.[1] If the philosopher is to confine his flights to meanings known to everyone but the 'incapacitated, morons and very young children', he will not get far off the ground. The political philosopher will have his wings particularly closely clipped. One of the most devoted of the language philosophers, Professor Flew, admits that if we restricted ourselves to the 'logic of our language', 'we should find ourselves committed to excluding almost everything that had previously been called political philosophy: for only the most heroic and extreme measures of reinterpretation could fit Hobbes, Locke, Rousseau and Burke to this mould'.[2] Many moralists would now be inclined to echo Sidgwick's comment on 'the fragmentariness and superficiality of treatment to which mere analysis of the common usage of ethical terms is always liable to lead'.[3] Russell has argued that what thus applies to political philosophy and ethics applies to linguistic philosophy itself, with stultifying effects. According to this philosophy, we should proceed through studying the use of words, of which perhaps the most essential word of all is the word 'word'. Very well, what is a word? Russell goes into the matter and sums up: 'we cannot define the word

[1] *Proc. of the Arist. Soc.*, LII (1951–52), 50.
[2] *Logic and Language*, 2nd series, 7.
[3] *History of Ethics*, 64.

"word" without (*a*) a logical theory of classes, and (*b*) a psychological understanding of intention. These are difficult matters. I conclude that common sense, whether correct or incorrect in the use of words, does not know in the least what words are.'[1] If this is true, and the case for it is strong, linguistic philosophy itself is one of the casualties of the appeal to ordinary usage.

30. (3) There seems to be a radical unclearness as to what 'ordinary usage' means. We have seen the difficulty Ryle had in drawing a satisfactory line between use and usage. Leaving that aside, let us remind ourselves that for him there is no objection to the sentence 'the equator encircles the earth' as good use and good usage. At the same time such a sentence is considered a snare and delusion to the philosopher until he discovers its logical grammar. How is he to do this? If we answer, 'By appeal to ordinary usage', we are back where we started, since ordinary usage gives unequivocal sanction to the very form to be corrected. The appeal then must be to some meaning carried by this deceptive sentence, a meaning capable of reflecting itself back and exposing the corruptness of the grammatical form. But we had been told that the reason why plain men were not deceived by it was that they had never raised the philosophic questions that would call for such correction. We are now told that their meaning carries in itself all that is required for answering these questions. But in that case, why did they express themselves so badly in the first place, and why, with all the materials at their disposal for correcting themselves, have they never done so? They somehow have the answers that the philosophers have been seeking, yet they continue to use the language of deception. There is something wrong here. If the plain man does have secrets that would solve the philosopher's problems, must he not be alive to the distinctions which raise and solve these problems? And if he is so alive, then he is not a plain man at all, but something like a super-philosopher in disguise. On the other hand, if he really is a plain man, with nothing beyond ordinary meaning at his command, then to set him up as the supreme court in disputes of philosophical experts seems capricious and irresponsible.

When linguistic philosophers try to make clear the form that this pregnant meaning takes in our minds, they say very puzzling things. Mr Strawson says, for example, that 'the meaning of an expression is not the set of things or the single thing it may correctly be used to refer to: the meaning is the set of rules, habits, conventions for its use in referring.'[1] Whether this is supposed to give the ordinary usage of 'meaning' I do not know. But if I am asked whether the meaning of 'magnanimity', for instance, is a set of rules, habits and conventions of speech on the part of myself and other people, I can only shake my head. This looks like another case, so frequent among these philosophers, of putting the cart before the horse. My thought of magnanimity is the thought of a special trait of character. With this trait in mind, I shall see that it belongs to some people like Lincoln, and not to others, like Hitler, and I shall ascribe it accordingly. When I have so applied the term for a time, I may notice that in my series of applications certain rules or habits of application are discernible. But what I mean by 'magnanimity' is no habit of mine. The nature of what is meant, namely a certain generosity of temper, appoints my habits in ascribing it; the habits do not appoint or constitute the meaning. Nor is the meaning in the sense of my thought or idea a habit. One wonders how, on Mr Strawson's terms, the word could ever have been used for the first time. No habits, rules, or conventions for its use then existed. Nevertheless it was in fact used, and perhaps more vividly and clearly than it was later, when habit had made the use more automatic. I am not suggesting, of course, that the true 'meaning of meaning' lies on the surface for anyone to see. Though in a sense this is perfectly familiar, it is extraordinarily difficult to catch and analyse. What is needed for that analysis, however, is not a general resolution of meanings into word-habits, but a more sensitive psychology and metaphysic.

31. (4) Ordinary usage is full of ambiguities. Philosophers have often speculated, for example, on the nature of law. For them the problem will now be, What is the correct usage of the word 'law'? Very well, what is it? People speak with equal propriety of the law of contradiction, Boyle's law, and the law of libel. In which of these do we find the stock or standard use? The answer is, in all of them, and no doubt in others too; there is no one use that can be called *the* standard or ordinary one. Philosophy, then, will be committed to one or other of two tasks. It may study all the ordinary uses, however many of them there are, and however trivial some of them may be; and then it will become a promiscuous and largely pointless enterprise. Or it may concentrate on some uses and ignore others. But if it does so concentrate, on what principle will it do so? Mere usage will not help here. It will concentrate, one hopes, on those meanings that are important for natural science, for example, or for logic, and if further choice

---

[1] *Essays in Conceptual Analysis*, ed. by A. Flew, 32.

is necessary, on that meaning whose understanding would contribute most to understanding the world. And to raise such questions seriously is to return to philosophy as it has been practised in the past.

32. (5) The appeal to ordinary language confuses correctness with truth. This is a comparison we thought we detected long ago in Professor Malcolm's view,[1] but there is probably no form of linguistic philosophy that has escaped it. Nor is it hard to see why. The linguistic philosopher does not want to be a lexicographer in the sense that Webster was, or in the sense that Fowler was. He has plaintively insisted that he has no interest in listing usages or giving advice to would-be authors. Nevertheless, he thinks it all-important to single out the standard use of an expression, to study it, and to adhere to it in his professional practice. Why? Not because he is moved by a secret passion for the ideal of the Society for Pure English, but because he has persuaded himself that correct usage has something to do with his business as a philosopher. That business is to discover truth. And one can account for his interest in correct usage only by supposing him convinced that if he uses expressions with correctness he will be using them with truth, or at least that if he uses them incorrectly, he will be using them with untruth. There is no good ground for this. Even if every expression used in the standard way did give us truth, which it does not, truth would still not *be* correctness. To use an expression correctly, or with propriety, is to use it in accord with prevailing practice or with philological authority. To use it with truth is to express through it a judgment that accords with fact. There may indeed be some tendency for the first to coincide with the second. But if the linguistic philosophers are counting on such coincidence they are depending on a miracle. If they are assuming an identity between them, they are depending on a confusion. And the importance they attach to language is inexplicable unless they are depending on one or the other.

33. (6) Ordinary usage may mislead, distort and deceive. Care is needed here, for many linguistic analysts would admit this in a sense; 'Satan is a fiction' is ordinary usage, but the unsuspecting philosopher may be seriously misled by its language. It is best therefore to consider only cases in which ordinary usage is logically unexceptionable. But even here there is an obvious danger that the philosopher will be led up the garden path, this time by the linguists.

[1] See above, p. 320.

For they are all too likely to test linguistic form by logical form, and logical form by fact. Good usage, then, will always lead us into conformity with fact, since if it does not, it is not good usage. But this is futile. If there is to be any point in the insistence on good usage, such usage must be determinable independently of its truth. Is it the case, then, that expressions which are indisputably warranted as sound ordinary usage lead us securely in the philosophical way we should go?

Philosophy would be greatly simplified if they did. But instances to the contrary are so many and varied that it is hard to know where to begin or end. So we shall plunge in at random. There is no doubt, presumably, that 'I see a table' is sound common sense expressed in unimpeachable ordinary usage. We suppose ourselves to see the surface of an independently existing physical thing. But to say this seriously, as Russell has pointed out, is to deny physics.[1] For if what physics says is true, there is always a spatial and temporal interval between our percept, or at least its cortical condition, and the physical table; what we immediately see is not the thing in nature, made up, the physicist tells us, of billions of 'wavicles', which sends out light rays to our eyes. The best of usage thus states an untruth. Such use is at equal odds with astronomy. 'I see a star flaring up.' We take the star to be flaring up when we see it, but the event may have happened years ago. Again, impeccable use or usage states what is false. 'The sun is ascending to the zenith'; 'the sun is sinking'. There is no reason to doubt that in making such remarks, plain men have meant what they said. It was precisely because they did that they received such a shock when Copernicus showed that the fact was otherwise, that what was revolving was not the sun round the earth but the earth round its axis. Common sense, expressed through common and unexceptionable usage, was wrong.

Or consider the odd things to which ordinary usage commits us in regard to colours. Professor Linton has pointed out that there are tribes that use the same word for blue and green.[2] In accordance with sound tribal usage, they would presumably describe the colour of the grass and the colour of the sky in the same way. It might be thought that they saw no difference, and hence that the description would, for them at least, be true. But Linton adds that by actual tests they could distinguish shades as accurately as Europeans do with their far richer colour vocabulary. Thus in following standard usage and describing

---

[1] *Philosophy of Russell* (ed. by Schilpp), 704–5. I do not think this point is invalidated by Chap. VII ('Perception') in Ryle's *Dilemmas*.

[2] *The Study of Man*, 52–3; I owe notice of the passage to Professor John Irving.

grass and sky in the same way, they are belying facts that their senses make undeniable.[1] Again, both we and they would say that grass is green and the sky blue, whether anyone at the time is looking at it or not; and if we happen to be asked at night what the colour of our piano is, we do not hesitate, because it is in the dark, to say that it is mahogany red. Most philosophers would consider both these statements untrue in the sense that was presumably meant, and would certainly think it absurd to take them as true merely because they were ordinary usage. Even when ordinary usage is filtered and refined to its purity by linguistic philosophers, it not seldom yields something incredible. Mr Paul, in a much-read essay, asks 'what is meant by saying of *someone else* that he is seeing a sense-datum of a certain sort'. He answers that it is 'his behaving in certain ways in certain situations . . .' and likewise that 'his being colour-blind is his behaving in certain ways'.[2] I cannot convince myself that this *is* what we mean. But if it is, it is surely wrong, for neither my own seeing of a sense-datum, nor someone else's seeing of one, *consists in* behaving in certain ways.

34. We have been considering cases in which adherence to ordinary usage gives untruth as determined by other standards; let us now consider some cases in which it leads to untruth even by its own standards. Where such usage is as vague and ambiguous as we have seen it to be, one would expect some of its alternative meanings to collide with each other. And they do. In Professor Austin's acute essay on the language in which we discuss our knowledge of other minds, we learn that the word 'know' is used correctly in all of the following cases: 'I know the election is today; I read it in *The Times*';[3] 'I know your feelings on the matter'; 'he knows his own mind';[4] 'he knows the town well'; 'he has known much suffering'; 'my old vanity, how well I know it!'[5] 'I know because X told me that he knew.'[6] Indeed 'we are often right to say we *know* even in cases where we turn out subsequently to have been mistaken. . . .'[7] On the other

---

[1] Since I wrote the words above, Professor H. D. Lewis has pointed out to me that the same peculiarity occurs in Welsh. 'We do have a word for "green", derived from Latin, namely "gwyrdd". But we use "glas" very extensively for blue and green. I would never say "gwellt gwyrdd" for green grass, but "gwellt glas". I would likewise say "awyr las" for blue sky: "las" is a mutated form of "glas".'

[2] *Logic and Language*, 1st series, 115.

[3] *Logic and Language*, 2nd series, 128.

[4] *Ibid.*, 140.

[5] *Ibid.*, 141.

[6] *Ibid.*, 144.

[7] *Ibid.*, 142.

hand, Professor Austin argues, and I think convincingly, that even within that citadel of certainty supposed to be offered by sense statements, it is often inappropriate to say we know; 'I *don't* know it's mauve, that it definitely looks to me now mauve.'[1] No doubt the legitimate uses of the word 'know' could be extended almost indefinitely. But if the word is used, and used correctly, to cover so many different kinds of insight and assurance, if the court of usage would justify us in saying we know that which in fact is false while also, surely, at other times disallowing this, if it permits us to say we know what we read in a newspaper while demurring if we say we know what something now looks like to us, if 'know' may be used in situations where it would be equally correct to use 'believe', or 'infer', or 'think probable', or 'can't bear to disbelieve', or many another phrase, then it is hopeless to extract from mere usage any clear or consistent guidance. 'How else,' inquires Professor Flew, 'could one investigate the concept of knowledge than by studying the various correct uses of the word "know"?' It seems to me that Professor Austin has supplied, or at least suggested, the answer. The word 'know' is apparently applied on no consistent principles whatever. Austin admits that 'it may be unwise to chivvy language beyond the coarser nuances.'[2] It is to be doubted whether language follows even the 'coarser nuances' with anything like consistency.

35. The linguistic philosophers would rather philosophize in their own manner than talk about philosophy, and their programme cannot be fully appreciated without following them into their discussions of the language we use about time and induction and universals and fact and truth. It would be interesting to do this if there were space for it, which there is not. But I cannot think our main conclusions about this way of philosophizing would be greatly affected by such a review. We should find many fine hairs split into still finer hairs. We should find a virtuosity in ferreting out verbal distinctions, particularly in such masters of the craft as Austin, which would fill any unprejudiced reader with admiring astonishment. We should find many curious details in our use of such words as 'if' and 'can' and 'seems' and 'ought' lit up sharply by flashes of light. And yet at the end we should feel strangely unilluminated. Such a prodigal expenditure of power, acuteness and ink, adding up to— what? Disappointingly little in view of the powers that went into it.

The reason is not far to seek. Words give the philosopher no

---

[1] *Logic and Language*, 2nd series, 138.
[2] *Ibid.*, 138.

compass. The interest in usage is centrifugal and dispersive, and unless guided by something other than itself, dissipates itself among minutiae, some idle, some important; and mere usage cannot tell it which is which. When philosophers in the past asked themselves What is the nature of knowledge? instead of What are the uses of the verb 'know'?, they usually did so with a conviction, having nothing to do with language, that some types of knowledge, or some claims to it, were of central importance—the insight of the mathematician, the scientific grasp of natural law, the claim of the mystic or the religious authoritarian. These types or claims were then fastened upon for special examination. The inquiries of the linguistic philosophers have, to be sure, thrown light on these claims. But if so, it is because a way of philosophizing different from their own, disruptive of their own, has not been wholly abandoned. A genuine philosopher can draw nourishment even from what W. E. Hocking has called 'this new method of milking stones'. 'If', 'can', 'know', 'true', are after all key words, and one is bound to derive profit from their study. So our complaint is not that these studies are profitless, but that the profit is so meagre in proportion to the price. There are grains of wheat, many of them indeed, and of high quality, among the chaff. But why should one have to hunt for them in these bushels and bushels and bushels of words about words?

CHAPTER IX

UNIVERSALS

1. The dominant meaning of reason, as it is considered in this book, is the power and function of grasping necessary connections. That such connections exist there is no doubt. None of the empiricist theories we have discussed, however sceptical, denies this; the old empiricism of Mill, which reduced necessity to association, is now dead. The present issue among philosophers is not whether necessity exists, but how much of the world is subject to its sway. Does it link only the components of our own arbitrary definitions, as the more extreme of the positivists maintain, so that the only necessity in the world will occur in such tautologies as 'all bachelors are unmarried'? Or does it link genuinely diverse characters presented in our experience, such as colours, sounds, shapes, and sizes, and if so, how generally? Or does it extend still further to the things and events that are presumed to exist in nature, whether we experience them or not? Or, lastly, does it include the whole universe in its domain, as the Hegelians think, so that to a reason fully developed the world would be a system in which every thing and event was caught in one vast web of necessity? This is the problem that any philosophic defence of reason must ultimately face, and we must now indicate our line of answer to it.

2. It is clear from what has just been said that there will be a reciprocal influence between one's conception of the world and one's notion of the work and importance of reason. If one believes, as logical atomists do, that the world is a heap of particulars, none of them necessarily connected with any other, reason will have a humble office, for it will have nothing to do but study definitions and what they imply, and will have lost all interest in those speculative flights which attracted philosophers in the past. On the other hand, if one holds the world to be an intelligible system, one is bound to take reason, which is our means of knowing that system, as all-important both for philosophy and presumably also for practical life. The lines of influence move in the opposite direction too: one's conception of reason will affect one's view of the world. If reason, as Mill held, is nothing but a grasp of particulars which happen to have been presented often together, then a world that is rational in Spinoza's sense, for example, will be unthinkable. At the other extreme, a person for whom reason is the grasp of natural necessity will certainly reject any pluralism that takes the world as a litter of loose ends.

In gauging the importance of reason, then, where is one to begin? With a conception of the real, or with an analysis of reason at work? I do not think one can begin with either to the exclusion of the other. We have seen that there can be no logic without ontology; if a necessary judgment is a judgment at all, it must be true or false; but this means that it must be true or false *of* something; and where could this something fall except in the real world? To study reason at work *is* to study the structure of the world of which its statements are true, and which it reveals. On the other hand to begin with an announcement that the world is a necessary system, of which reason is the progressive revelation, would in these days leave one with no hearers. Most philosophers regard the proofs that the world is such a system as inconclusive at best, and so do I. Perhaps the most magnificent attempt at such proof ever made is to be found in the two *Logics* of Hegel; but it requires no very sharp eye to see that many of the deductions in this elaborate chain of reasoning are dubious, to say the least.

3. My own way of estimating the importance of reason proceeds neither from analysis nor from ontology to the exclusion of the other, but from both together. What I mean is this. Though one cannot without some absurdity say that anyone has ever *proved* the world to be a necessary system, one can still postulate it and then examine how far the actual exercise of reason goes toward justifying the postulate. There is no leap beyond the evidence here, no proceeding under metaphysical illusions. The study will be an empirical one in that best sense of empirical that is ready to admit necessities as well as contingencies so far as they actually appear in experience.

4. But why make a postulate at all? Why not study the work of reason in a scientific and descriptive way without compromising clarity by vague talk about the ultimate nature of things? The answer, briefly, is that thinking is not a process like the rolling of a ball or the working of a motor, which can be explained by descriptive law. It is a teleological activity that can be construed only in the light of its end, and that end is the understanding of the nature of things. It is essential that we be clear what this means.

Thinking is not the working of a machine but the pursuit of an end. The notion that it is the working of a machine and therefore describable by scientific law explains much of the sterility in psychological accounts of thought since the time of Ward and James. I am not referring merely to 'clever-silly' theories like behaviourism, which was founded on the refusal to see the difference between a nerve current and a pain, but to all theories that attempted to account for the course of thought by association or 'conditioning'. The crucial fact to be explained is that the suggestions which come to the thinker in the attempt to solve his problem are so largely governed by relevance to his end, and that such relevance may override association and conditioning. Relevance is not a descriptive relation at all, and no purely natural science is disposed to admit it as a determining factor of anything. Yet the course of thinking is inexplicable without it, and the more so as it rises in its level of competence. The *Gestalt* psychologists, Dewey, and Freud, are exceptions to the general psychological dreariness, both in their recognition of teleology and in the many helpful things they have had to say about the process of thinking. But the light thrown on the process by *Gestalt* was dimmed by an undeveloped notion of 'requiredness'. Dewey's account of thinking, recognizing that the process is governed by ends, is marred by a virtual refusal to grant it any end of its own and by his demoting it in consequence to the position of a servant of practice. Freud, holding a rather similar view, explains with much revealing detail why thought goes off the rails, but is unable to explain the fact, which is the all-important one, that it manages at times to stay on them.

5. Do we have any account of our own of this remarkable fact? Yes. In outline it is as follows.[1] There is in human nature a distinct drive to know, a distinguishable theoretical impulse or urge to understand. It is at work at every level of cognition, from the simplest impersonal judgment, like 'it is hot', to the most comprehensive mathematical or metaphysical system. But like other fundamental drives, the moral, for example, and the aesthetic, what it is seeking—what will ultimately satisfy it—is far from apparent at its lower levels and is defined only gradually in the course of a long advance. But that advance is not simply a matter of blind trial and error. Its direction is set by its end, which works as an immanent ideal within the process

[1] The case is developed in fuller detail in my *The Nature of Thought*.

of thought. The pressure exerted by this ideal increases as intelligence rises in the scale. In the childhood of the race, and again of each man, thought adheres fairly closely to the laws of passive conditioning. To these laws the psychologists who would assimilate all thinking to the reaction-patterns of the rat suggest that it is subjected permanently. This is contrary to plain fact. As thought matures and realizes in fuller measure the end it is seeking, that end lays its movement under increasingly firm constraint. The practised composer, to take an analogy, knows that if he would develop his theme in accordance with the aesthetic standard at work in his mind, he must eliminate those last five bars that intruded themselves yesterday, for that way lies dissonance and disaster. The practised logician, or the logical genius with little practice or none, sees that from given premises there is only way of developing the argument that would satisfy his logical sense. The higher our altitude on the long ascent of intelligence, the better is our position to discern what lies at the summit. To be sure we never see this clearly. In no human activity do we ever fully know what we are about. We are aware of the end, or we could do nothing but wander aimlessly. We never see it clearly, so we are condemned to much groping.

6. When we 'sit down in a cool hour' and ask ourselves what, to our present vision, lies ahead of us, what sort of apprehension would bring our theoretic impulse finally to rest, we are not simply at a loss. We can at least compare better understandings with worse, plot the curve of our advance, and infer what would be involved in a still better understanding than any we have achieved. If someone asks us why a galaxy of distant stars should be at its place in the sky, we may honestly have to say we have no idea; we rummage vainly about for the bare beginnings of an explanation. If someone asks us for an explanation of cancer, we are almost as helpless, but not quite. We know that cancer is an abnormal proliferation of certain tissue cells, and that there must be a reason for it somewhere among the chemical processes of the body, though we have no notion where. If someone asks us to explain malaria, we can do rather better. We know that it is due to the action of one-celled organisms of a particular type introduced into the bloodstream through the proboscis of the anopheles mosquito. That gives us a comfortable feeling that we understand at least pretty largely, even though we should be helpless to make the explanation exact by saying how many protozoa produced what intensity of the disease. When in any case we are able thus to specify quantities, we feel that we are another stage forward. Why

N

does a baseball, if tossed from the top of the Washington monument, drop to the earth, describing at an increasing speed the arc it does? Here our grasp is more precise. Given the mass of the earth and the ball, we can predict the path almost exactly, and the rate of movement at each instant. We have the law of the inverse squares; we know the acceleration per foot; we know how the acceleration is slightly retarded by the density of the air. But suppose someone then asks us why the law of inverse squares itself should hold (or the law with its slight Einsteinian correction). Here at present science is bankrupt. There are those who say it always will be, since the question is really meaningless. I do not agree. We have a perfectly good right to ask why matter should behave in one way rather than another; indeed we know what sort of insight would clear it up for us, whether achievable or not. It would be the insight that the constitution of matter, or some character within it, *necessitated* such behaviour. To try to go beyond *that* point, indeed, would be merely absurd, for when we have arrived at necessity, the question Why? is no longer in order; the final answer has been given; the theoretical impulse has, on this point, come to rest. If someone wants to know why any angle in a semicircle should be a right angle, and you show him that this follows necessarily from theorems he admits, he cannot, if he sees this, ask Why? again. He could ask this with perfect propriety about the law of gravitation, because we do not as yet see its necessity; he could not do so here because he already has the only conceivable answer. When one sees that A *must be* B, the reiterated question Why? shows only that one did not see after all.

7. There is one sense, however, in which further understanding is possible. Absurd as it is to ask why A should be B if one sees that A's nature necessitates this, one is certainly making progress if one sees that this truth does not stand alone, but belongs to a wider system with which it must stand or fall. Many truths of geometry, for example, may be seen to be *both* necessary in themselves[1] and necessitated by others. The explanation of a property is always regarded as more complete if the necessity with which it inheres in its subject is shown itself to inhere in a larger system. The certification of the proposition about semicircles is more complete if we can say about it, 'either accept this or abandon geometry generally'; of '$7+5=12$' if we can say 'either this, or all arithmetic goes'; of the law of contradiction, 'either this or nothing'. The ideal of understanding demands more than isolated bits of necessity. We can quite

[1] Subject to what will be said later about internal relations.

intelligibly ask even why $7+5=12$ if this is a question whether the proposition is warranted only by itself or also by a context which requires it and which it in turn requires. The theoretical impulse could come to rest only in a system in which the question Why? could at no point be raised again, either about the possession by a subject of a property or relation, or about the connection between the fact of this possession and other such facts. With the achievement of such a system, understanding, which is explanation on its inner side, would have proceeded as far as it could. In practice, of course, we never come near this goal, and indeed are generally content to fail, provided only that our explanation goes far enough to serve our immediate needs. If we can demonstrate a theorem from any other that we know to be true, we shall probably be well content. If our hypothesis about the cause of a disease can adduce in its support a fair constancy in a statistical table, we shall feel that our triumph is complete.

Reason has been sometimes identified, as it was by the Stoics, with reason in nature, an objective and static framework, a web or pattern of necessity holding all things in its meshes. This is an important conception. But the person who takes it seriously needs to be clear whether it is for him a fact or an ideal. If he regards it as a fact, he should be aware of the extreme difficulty of establishing it as such. But in knowledge, as in morals, an ideal may be valid and compelling whether realized in fact or not; and the notion of a system at once exhaustive in its extent and completely articulated in content seems to have been present in the minds of all the great speculative rationalists as the appropriate end of reason. In this conviction I concur. But here reason is being used in a different sense, as a human power or function. Such powers or functions are normally brought into play by impulses, i.e. felt 'urges' towards their exercise; and it makes little difference which of the three terms—power, function, impulse—we use about reason, since they refer to aspects of a single conative drive. Like other and less fundamental drives, the drive towards understanding was at work in human nature for millenniums before it reached any express idea of the end that would satisfy it. Its office has been a continual half-conscious pressure to arrange the materials of experience in a more intelligible order. I have argued in another volume[1] that it exercises a similar pressure toward rationality of conduct, its material in this case being impulses rather than concepts. Our present concern, however, is with its specially cognitive office of ordering experience in terms of necessity. Reason

[1] *Reason and Goodness.*

as conceived in this book is a drive toward intelligibility under the guidance of the implicit ideal of system.

8. But why one kind of system rather than others? For clearly the kinds are many. Objects in space form a system. Events in time form a simple system through their connection in temporal order. The parts of a picture or a statue are intimately related in a little system of their own. All the events in the universe may well be connected, directly or indirectly, in a single system of causation; they have been taken to be related also as means to a single end. There is no doubt that the sort of understanding we immediately want is often in terms of these other systems. When we ask, for example, why a disease occurred, what we want is clearly a causal explanation; when we ask how the Venus de Milo's arms might best be restored, we want an arrangement that will satisfy our sense of beauty; when we ask why Lee ordered Pickett's charge at Gettysburg, what we want is an explanation through means and end. Granting, then, that seeing things in these other orders does give light, why do we not study them all equally instead of concentrating on logical system?

The answer is that the light they give is of a different kind, or else that, if of the same kind, it is of lower illumination. How the Venus's arms should be placed is an aesthetic, not a logical, problem. To enter fully into the values that governed Lee, is again more than an intellectual enterprise. To be sure, the grasp of how his orders led to certain results is an intellectual act, but then it resolves itself into a grasp of causation; and we have seen that causal apprehension, satisfying as it is so far as it goes, is not full understanding. Much the same must be said of explanation in spatial and temporal terms. To know the positions of the planets around the sun is a step toward understanding the solar system, but only a step. So far as they can be regarded as points in a geometrical system, their relations pass over into those of geometrical necessity; so far as they are regarded as things or events, the explanation will again be causal, with the attendant strength and weakness of such explanation. So of time. How far the temporal order is a necessary one may be disputed. But it is at least necessary to the extent that if A precedes B, and B, C, then A *must* precede C. Still, if one asks why any concrete temporal event occurred when it did, the explanation reverts to causality. To sum up: explanation in other orders seems to be either not intellectual at all in the strict sense of the term, or else to be an undeveloped form of explanation through necessity.

9. We have next to note that such explanation proceeds at every level through 'as-suches', abstract characters. Intelligence is never content to work with events or individuals, and if it were, it would get no light from them that it could use in other cases. What it is always looking for is connections of content, the more precise the better. Suppose a savage drops a stone on his toe, and is hurt. What has caused the pain is the stone, but if the only connection he could seize is the one between this particular stone and his pain, the experience would give him no reason to avoid dropping bowls, axes and logs on his unfortunate toe. He does in fact find in it a reason for avoiding these things; and if so, it is because he can abstract from the stone as a whole and connect his pain with one character within it to the exclusion of others; it was not in virtue of its roughness or coldness or colour that the falling stone caused his pain, but in virtue of its weight. Because he can abstract in this way, he can see that he should avoid dropping *anything* heavy upon his toe; he connects *heaviness as such* in these objects with the prospect of this sort of pain. Or a child is playing with a set of balls and blocks. Some of them will roll and others not. He soon discovers that whether a thing will roll depends not on its size or colour or weight, but on its roundness. Not of course that he formulates this in a proposition; that may come very much later or not at all; but it is soon clear, from his behaviour when given a ball and a cube, that he has come to expect of the one what he does not expect of the other, and that he has grasped the connection between roundness and rolling.

We may suppose that in practice people first deal with individual things and only later proceed to characters and their connections. But even when their interest is most exclusively practical and they are manipulating things on the most primitive level, they are able to do so only through grasping the connection of characters. If a stone-age savage wanted to make an axe-head, he would sharpen it at one end, see that the stone thickened gradually, and keep its weight and size within narrow limits. In doing each of these things, he would be applying causal laws which he must have apprehended at least implicitly. Such laws do not connect particular events. A statement of causal law says that something of the *kind* X will be followed by something of the *kind* Y. In a curious way reason is our escape from time; it can apparently deal with time only in its timeless aspects. A connection between the characters of two events is not a temporal relation, any more than the connections in the multiplication table, though the succession of events in time takes place in strict accordance with it. The assumption of rational inquiry is that the world, or

at least the sector of it that we are concerned with, has a fixed, discoverable structure, indeed that change itself has a structure that is
not carried away down the river but provides its banks and direction.

10. Rationalists are often accused of inventing fables about the
primitive mind and making it more 'intellectual' than it is. And of
course it would be a fable to say that the use of abstract connections
involves the power to think them explicitly. Perhaps the most
remarkable achievement of the century in psychology has lain in
showing how great is the range of purpose and intelligence below the
threshold of explicit thought. Even on these lower levels, however,
action follows lines of connection between characters. 'Knowing
how' may be genuine knowledge, even in the absence of 'knowledge
that', as Professor Ryle has reminded us. Piaget, who spent many
years in observing and experimenting with young children, thinks
that the only way to account for his results is to deny that pure or
undirected groping occurs. In the initial impulse to suck there is a
predisposition to connect the nipple at the lips with a certain kind of
response, and to link together the corresponding experiences.[1]
Claparède would go farther. He finds in every conditioned reflex a
link that he frankly calls 'implication'. The dog conditioned to
expect a meal upon perceiving a certain sound or colour does not
wait for a repetition before he begins to make a linkage. 'Implication
is a process indispensable to our needs of adjustment. *Without it, we
should not know how to profit from experience.*' 'Implication is the
principle at once of generalization and of induction . . . it sends its
roots deep into the motor bases of our being. We may say that life
itself implies implication.'[2]

Claparède is right, I think, in holding that necessary relations
function at very low levels. There is a danger, however, in putting
the case in this unqualified way. If, as he admits, later experience
may disconfirm and destroy linkages described as implications, they
could hardly have been necessary, nor therefore in the full sense
implications, at all. What happens was perhaps better put by
Bosanquet when he said that 'the spirit of necessity' is awakening in
the lowest of perceptual judgments. Minds at the human level never
take it as accident or bare conjunction that fire is hot or water wet.
To be sure, they do not clearly see, even now, how such associations
go beyond this, and to say definitely that they do would beg the

---

[1] *The Origin of Intelligence in the Child*, 30 ff, 395 ff.
[2] 'La Genèse de l'Hypothèse', *Archives de Psychologie*, Tome XXIV (1934),
104–5. Italics in original.

question. What these associations do is to supply the suggestive instances in some of which implication will eventually be found. These connections of character, which provide the raw material for reason, are plainly beginning to form themselves even at the sub-human level. Bradley illustrates the point vividly:

'When today I reach the place where yesterday my dog either chased a cat or fought with an antagonist, the perception as we say "calls up" the ideas, and he runs eagerly forward. His experience, we will suppose, was of a white cat or a black retriever with a large brass collar. . . . Today it is a black cat that is found in the place, but with an ordinary dog that will make no difference. The whiteness of the image is quite irrelevant. Or again, if today another dog be perceived, if only that dog be not glaringly different, an ordinary dog will certainly attack him, and the less intelligent he is the more catholic is his action.'[1]

11. Bradley does not hesitate to say that the dog is using universals. If universals mean identities or resemblances between earlier and present experience, there is no doubt that he does use them. Professor Price has made the use of universals in this broad sense 'the fundamental intellectual process' and given it the name of 'recognition.'[2] He points out that it begins far earlier than the use of words, and indeed that any use of words presupposes it. The point is currently important. There are philosophers of our day who discuss the problem of universals as if it were simply a problem of how words are used, or should be used, of whether abstract nouns, for example, are to be classified as proper names. But the problem is not one of how words are used, or might or should be used, for it has nothing essentially to do with words at all. 'You learned the *concept* pain when you learned language,' says Wittgenstein.[3] That is to exalt words absurdly. The use of universals both antedates the use of words and is presupposed by it; one could not use the word 'cat' in one's recognition of cats unless one already recognized the mark or sound 'cat' as itself an instance of the word.[4] If, in order to recognize this instance, one had to have a further word for it, then to recognize this further word one would need a still further word, and so would have to go through an infinite series of words before one recognized

[1] *Principles of Logic*, I, 36 (2nd ed.)
[2] *Thinking and Experience*, 34.
[3] *Philosophical Investigations*, Sec. 384.
[4] Price, *op. cit.*, 38.

anything. This process is plainly needless. If so, it is because the recognition of something as the same or similar is so far from being a verbal matter that it can occur in both the race and the infant before language arises.

12. The semantic way is not the only way of dismissing the problem of universals. Some philosophers say that if you refer to an entity, you can make clear what you mean only by noting the observations that would be called for if you were to verify the existence of what you refer to, and by observations they usually mean sense perceptions. Very well; what sense perceptions would verify the existence of the non-sensible common property called 'justice' or 'colour'? Obviously none. Hence to refer to such entities is meaningless. But this is a *petitio* in more than one way. If some people maintain that they can intuit non-sensible common properties, you do not refute them by proposing an empirical test of meaning, for the question at issue is whether, in view of the intuitions alleged, such a test is acceptable. Nor is it even clear that universals must be non-sensible, as the critic is assuming. The specific shade of white on the page before me is certainly sensed; but it can also presumably be given in other contexts. If so, it is a universal, and there are some universals at least that can be presented in sense experience. Thus one does not get rid of the problem of universals either by talking semantics or proposing exclusionist theories of meaning. For in both, the problem arises again before one has finished stating one's case.

13. We cannot evade this problem of universals, much as we should like to. 'The problem of universals, rightly posed, is still fundamental and urgent; for to understand universals is to begin to understand thinking.'[1] Reason, we have suggested, involves the grasp of a necessary relation between characters, and these characters are not particulars, but qualities, or complexes of them, that might occur elsewhere; and hence they are universals. For what we mean by a universal is a quality or relation or complex of these that may be identical in diverse contexts. The existence of such universals has been commonly taken by rationalist philosophers as the condition of every form of knowing from the simplest perception to the most abstract inference. To perceive a tree as a tree, they would say, is to grasp it as an instance of a universal that is presented also in other trees. To judge from its light grey bark that it is a beech is to grasp a connection between universals. To infer from its dry and shrivelled

[1] R. I. Aaron, *The Theory of Universals*, vii.

leaves that it has not more than five years to live is to pass from one universal to a connected universal. To know the law of gravitation is not to know millions of different laws, one for each snowflake or drop of rain, but the same law as it manifests itself in many instances. In short, without universals, there would be no identities, and without identities there would be no persons, no things, no recognition or prediction, no use of words, no kind of reasoning, not even the simplest form of knowing.

14. Yet in these days the existence of universals is widely denied. It may be well to put at once the position about them that will be maintained in what follows. It lacks the simplicity of either a sweeping acceptance of universals or a sweeping rejection of them. I accept the existence of specific universals and deny the existence of qualitative and generic universals. By a generic universal, I mean one whose instances are individual things or persons, for example, man, horse, or stone. By a qualitative universal I mean one whose instances are qualities or characters of one kind, for example, colour, sound, or shape. By a specific universal I mean a quality or character that is incapable of sub-division into kinds, for example, this shade of red or this degree of loudness in a sound. Let us begin with universals of the third type, which I hold to exist.

15. Suppose you lay two red stamps on the table before you. Does it make sense to say that they have the same colour, or more precisely, that there are any two spots on them that have the same colour? Common sense would say with equal readiness that the two have the same colour or were exactly alike in colour; so not much is to be learned from it. If one is more critically minded, one may hesitate and call for clarification: 'Are you asking the question of fact whether these stamps do have the same colour in the sense that no eye, however sharp, could detect a difference between them? Or are you asking the question of theory, whether the two stamps *could* have precisely the same shade?' The answer is, the second only; the first question is irrelevant. Of course it is perfectly possible that someone with keener sight should see a difference where we see none. But the interesting question is not this, but the one of principle: *could* the two stamps, or any two spots on them, have literally the same shade? If they could, universals exist. For what makes a character universal is not the *fact* of repetition; a red shade that appears for the first time in the world does not have to wait for a second instance to become a universal; it is one now, because it *could* occur in other contexts, whether it does or not. The question, then, is not whether the shade of red in the two stamps is in fact and verifiably the same, but whether it might be the same.

The answer is, I think, that it might perfectly well be the same. Indeed I very much doubt whether it makes sense to deny this. Perhaps the case may be made clear as follows: start with the two stamps, lying there on the table before you. Perform on them an experiment in thought by way of removing one by one the qualities and relations that make them different. They differ in place; very well; abstract from that difference and attend to what remains. They differ slightly in shape, since their edges are torn somewhat differently; so write off shape and narrow the focus again. You can note some difference in every respect but one; when you come to the colour, no difference whatever is discernible. Now to say under these circumstances that what you have left is two differing shades seems unintelligible. It is not an empirical statement, for there is no claim that a difference is, or can be, seen. The contention may, indeed, be a mere confusion. When it is said that the shades are two not one, perhaps what is meant is not that there is a qualitative difference, but merely that the shade appears in two different patches, and that you do not get rid of this twoness by recognizing the shade as the same. But no one, surely, is suggesting that you do. It may be said, again, that when the shade is called the same, what must be meant is not that the same shade is at two different places, but only that instances of it are. But are these instances of the same shade or not? If they are not, the point is irrelevant. If they are, then what makes them instances of the same shade must be the presence of that shade in each, and we are back where we were before. It looks very much as if the person who denies identity here is trying to maintain a difference where there is no distinction; he must admit that by diverting one's attention from the respects in which there is a difference, one comes eventually to a respect, namely colour, in which no difference is discernible; and yet he insists that even here we have two somethings, not one. What can be the ground of this insistence?

Ultimately it is this, that identity *means* resemblance. Even when you have two patches of colour in which the shades are indiscernible, the truth about them, we are told, is not that they are the same shade, but two shades exactly alike. But if there is no difference between them, we are moved to ask, what ground have you for calling them two? If, as you admit, there is no qualitative difference, does not that mean that there is qualitative identity? How can you both admit that the qualities do not differ and yet deny that they are the same? This looks like sheer self-contradiction.

16. It may be useful to remind ourselves that this question was asked by Leibniz, and that he answered it, as we do, by affirming the identity of indiscernibles. He applied his doctrine, to be sure, to substances rather than particulars, but the issue is essentially the same. No two substances, he held, resembled each other completely; if they did, they would be one, not two; they could not differ in number alone.[1] If two things differed numerically, that difference must be based on some difference of character or content, and if there is no such difference, it is absurd to call them two. This view was accepted by Bradley; 'what must be rejected everywhere is the idea of a similarity which does not imply sameness'.[2] McTaggart accepted it also under the name of 'the dissimilarity of the diverse', and added: 'the view that diversity requires a dissimilarity not dependent on itself is the view which has, I believe, been adopted by the majority of philosophers'.[3] Russell has wavered on the issue, holding strongly to universals in his *Problems of Philosophy*, and returning to them in his *Inquiry into Meaning and Truth*,[4] yet always hesitating to say that classes were more than groups of similar particulars. Ayer writes: 'In spite of all that can be urged against it, I am still inclined to hold that the principle of the identity of indiscernibles is necessarily true.'[5] This view has been vigorously contested. It was rejected by the British empiricists, as one would expect. Many logicians of later times have questioned it. C. S. Peirce called it 'all nonsense'.[6] Wittgenstein dismissed it in an oracular sentence or two: 'Russell's definition of " $=$ " won't do; because according to it one cannot say that two objects have all their properties in common. (Even if this proposition is never true, it is nevertheless significant.)'[7] More important, C. D. Broad has offered a reasoned criticism of the view;[8] Messrs Quine and Goodman have tried to show that a logic can be constructed without resort to universals;[9] and Max Black has undertaken to adduce an ideal case where there

[1] What he held, in his own words, was 'qu'il n'est pas vrai que deux substances se ressemblent entierement, et soyent differentes *solo numero*'. *Die philosophischen Schriften* (Gerhardt), IV, 433.
[2] *Principles of Logic* (2nd ed.), I, 297.
[3] *The Nature of Existence*, I, 97.
[4] P. 343, ff.
[5] *Philosophical Essays*, 35.
[6] *Collected Papers*, 4.311.
[7] *Tractatus Logico—Philosophicus*, 5.5302.
[8] *Examination of McTaggart's Philosophy*, I, 171–177.
[9] *Journal of Symbolic Logic*, Vol. 12, December 1947.

is complete resemblance between the numerically different.

17. Now for two things to differ numerically only is to be sheerly different, that is, for one to be different from the other while not differing from it in any character or relation except that of being other than it. Otherness, in such a case, would not depend on dis-similarity, but could still exist when the characters of the two things were even in theory indistinguishable. I must confess that to me this makes no sense. It is an attempt to maintain a difference where there is not even a possible ground of distinction. If A is to be other than B, there must be some element of content, some attribute or relation possessed by one which is not possessed by the other; if there is none, on what ground could it be called other? We do not first note two things to be two, and then note, perhaps with surprise, that they are at some point dissimilar; it is because they observably differ in some respect—in quality, in location, in time—that we call them two. We never ascribe twoness or otherness in the absence of any perceived distinction at all. If, looking at a lamp-post, I say 'Both lamp-posts are green,' you may well answer, 'I see only one lamp-post; where is the other?', and if I insist that there are two, though oddly enough they do not differ in colour, size, shape, or location, you would begin to harbour suspicions about my health of mind. For otherness is based on dissimilarity, not dissimilarity on a logically prior otherness.

18. If it is conceivable that things should be other while being in no wise dissimilar in either attribute or relation, it should be possible to give an example. Here Professor Black undertakes to help us. Let us conceive of a universe, he suggests, that consists of nothing but two spheres, each a mile in diameter, and with their centres two miles apart. Every attribute and relation possessed by the one would then be possessed by the other also, but they would still be two. One's impulse is to say, 'Oh but they would plainly be dissimilar in *some* respect, if only that one would be the left and the other to the right, or one above and the other below. But that violates the conditions, since these relations could only exist from the point of view of an observer outside both, and that is excluded by hypothesis. Nor could you call one of them 'A' and the other 'B', and so differentiate by mark or name, for that means selecting one rather than the other to start with, and to start thus would be impossible, since there is absolutely no ground on which either could be distinguished from the other. Take any attribute of either that you wish to—being spherical, being a mile in diameter, being two miles from the other sphere, having any one of the thousand properties that spheres are heir to—and you will find that the other has this property equally. The two are dissimilar in no way whatever. Nevertheless, they are two. Two things may therefore be other while yet exactly alike.

Now I think we can see on reflection that even this specially devised example begs the question it is supposed to settle. When Mr Black says that *each* of the spheres has similar characteristics, that the one has all the properties and relations of the other, what does he mean by 'each', and what by 'the one' and 'the other'? Are these phrases translatable into 'this one' and 'that one', sphere No. 1 and sphere No. 2? No, because he is maintaining that if the characters are indistinguishable, there can be no ground on which we could call either of them 'this' rather than 'that', 'No. 1' rather than 'No. 2'. Now we who hold that twoness is based on dissimilarity are maintaining that where you have nothing on which you could base a 'this' and 'that', you cannot have two things; and hence to begin by saying in effect, 'Take a world consisting of two things that do not even differ as this and that', is asking us to do what we are maintaining we cannot do. The directions sound as if they could be fulfilled, but with no 'this' and 'that' they cannot be.

Is the example really intelligible? How can you speak of 'each' of a pair or a series when you expressly remove the possibility, in either practice or theory, of discriminating one member from another? It is true that we often use 'each' without specifying what distinguishes one from another in a set; we speak of each of the beads on a string or of each man in the crowd. But in such thought there is always the presumption of a ground on which each *could* be distinguished if necessary: the third bead from the end can be marked off from the fourth; the man with the brown hat can be singled out from those around him. Numbers themselves are always assumed in application to mark more than numerical differences. We never say, 'I saw a dozen on my walk today'; we say 'a dozen men, or cars, or accidents', and when we speak of a dozen cars, for example, we assume the possibility of counting. And to count is to distinguish a first from a second, or a second from a third, by some observable difference which makes it another case. As Jevons says, 'The symbols $1+1+1$ are thus the empty marks asserting the existence of discrimination'. 'Abstract number, then, is *the empty form of difference;* the abstract number *three* asserts the existence of marks without specifying their kind.'[1] In the absence of anything recognizably different to count, number would have no meaning.

[1] W. Stanley Jevons, *The Principles of Science*, 159, 158.

You cannot legitimately say 'each', then, unless you can also say 'this' and 'that'. Suppose this is conceded. 'This' and 'that' must then be applicable in some way to the two spheres. Now these terms in actual use are never purely denotative, but always have descriptive meaning. This apple as opposed to that means, for example, the one in my hand as opposed to the one on the mantelpiece. As applied to the spheres, 'this' may mean the one in which I am standing, and 'that' the one two miles away in a certain direction. Then the character in virtue of which one is called 'this' will not attach to the other, and the character in virtue of which the other is called 'that' will not attach to the first. Otherness will depend on the possibility of distinguishing this from that, and the possibility of so distinguishing them on that of detecting diverse characters or relations.

19. There is one way in which the person arguing for the identity of indiscernibles could make the case easy for himself. He could say, as regards any two objects, however similar, that each of the pair will inevitably have two relations that will not be shared by the other: A will be identical with itself and different from B; B will be identical with itself and different from A. And it may be thought that this is a better way to establish the principle than to look round for other differences, for these formal differences are involved in the very notion of diversity. True enough; but for that very reason they are useless to us. Since they are part of what is meant by calling things different, to argue that two things, however similar, must be different in these senses, is merely to say that different things must be different, or two things must be two. What must be shown, therefore, if the principle is to have importance, is that for things to be different there must be something distinguishing them other than mere difference itself or anything that is analytically involved in this notion. And one way of seeing this is to see that these merely formal differences never divide anything from anything else. If any two things are different, the identities that separate them are not identities in the abstract, but the identity of A with itself and B with itself; unless there is this difference of content, the two self-identities themselves would lapse into one. Indeed the very statement of a formal difference by the use of differing symbols gives the case away, for it suggests what is the truth, that if things really differ, they always differ more than formally. A *purely* formal difference is unthinkable.

We embarked on this discussion to remove the main objection to our view that there are specific universals. That objection was that where two things had a quality—a shade of colour, for instance—that would normally be called the same, it was not literally the same; there were really two shades precisely similar. And that precise similarity was possible in the absence of identity was attested by a specially contrived example. We have remained unconvinced. If there is no qualitative difference in shade, for example, it is sheer self-contradiction to talk about two shades; what is two is not the shade, but the instances of the shade, which do obviously differ in place. Universals seem unavoidable, if by these are meant identical specific characters, appearing at different points in space and time.

20. Are these universals of common occurrence? They are very common indeed. In fact, there is no fully specific quality we ever experience that is not a universal of this kind. Every sound or odour or taste that anyone experiences, every sensation of hot or cold, every ache and pain, has a quality that in principle could be repeated and hence is a universal. These are sensible qualities. We must say the same of some non-sensible characters, such as numbers. It is difficult to believe that when we speak of three matches and three clothespins, we mean something different in each case by 'three'; the objects numbered may be different, but it would seem strange to say that their number is not the same, but two different numbers that are very much alike. Likewise of spatial qualities as immediately apprehended. The shape of this particular spoon may be reproduced in no other, but it surely might be. If so, it is a universal.

21. This reasoning seems to be conducting us precipitately toward a conclusion of metaphysical moment, namely that our immediate experience is of *nothing but* specific universals. That is indeed the conclusion I think we must draw. After all, why not?

The answer will probably be: 'you have given the reason yourself. You spoke just now of "this particular spoon". But surely what makes the spoon the particular spoon it is is not a set of universals, for these are repeatable, either singly or as a group. It cannot be resolved away into its characters. So even if we admit that its qualities and relations are universal, it does not follow that the "it" which has them is universal, or that we do not in some fashion know it. This raises a very large question that cannot be properly dealt with in passing. But we may perhaps pause upon it long enough to make our position clear.

When you perceive a spoon, are you apprehending, over and above the specific universals of colour, shape, and so on, a particular something to which they belong? Many philosophers say yes. If you then ask them what this is like, they answer, not unnaturally, that this is an improper question, since what they are talking about is not a 'what' of any kind; it is not a content or quality or set of qualities, but a faceless indescribable 'it', with no character of its own. Now we can only doubt whether this stands for any clear idea at all. Why should anyone believe in it?

22. For one thing, people often think that they make contact with it in sensation, and grow more sure of this as the sensation grows more vivid. They would think it somewhat absurd to say that they were making contact only with universals. There is very little force in this consideration. What one feels in a sensation of hot is the quality called 'hot'; what one feels as the hotness intensifies is increasing hotness, not an indescribable 'it' possessing this quality. The same is true of hardness, brightness, or pain. And there is no more reason for denying universality to a vivid quality like extreme hotness or pain than to a less vivid or intense one. Both are repeatable, and equally so.

Secondly, people who hold to this 'it' may be arguing from a bad analogy. A hammer does a great many different things like driving tacks, pulling nails, and breaking crockery, yet it is the same hammer that does them all. So a spoon has many properties, such as smoothness, coldness, hardness, but the same spoon owns them all; so *this* spoon must be different from any of these properties. But the analogy breaks down. For the hammer that has the various uses is not a qualityless ghost; it has a familiar size, weight, and shape, while the spoon that underlies its properties is supposed to lack character altogether. One cannot argue that because the first of these is plausible, so is the second. The two 'its' involved have no resemblance.

Thirdly, it is held that in any *instance* of a universal, there must be more than the universal itself. But one would like to know what more. One senses a certain shade of red in a stamp; is it suggested that what one is sensing is not the shade itself, but something else called an instance of it? Surely unless the shade is itself there in the instance, what is before one is not an instance of it; and if one examines this instance for something other than the universal, something that serves to instantiate it, one finds nothing.

Fourthly, it is replied that one does find something quite definite. What particularizes or instantiates is relations in space and time. The red I see in the stamp is located to the left of certain things and to the right of others, and it is presented at this one moment rather than a moment before or after. But these relations of right and left, before and after—what are we to say about them? Are they universal or particular? Universal, obviously, since they are relations that may be present in innumerable contexts. The very relations, then, that are supposed to particularize turn out to be universals. And how can the addition of universals make anything particular? The conclusion that we live in a world of universals remains untouched.

23. This may be questioned. If we take a limited set of spatial or temporal relations, we are indeed left with what might in theory appear in another context, and is therefore universal; it is conceivable, for example, that not only the red shade one sees, but the shape of the patch and its spatial relations to everything else in the room might have a replica elsewhere in the universe. But extend the range of these relations, and the conclusion, it is said, will be otherwise. If one were to take the relations of this patch to *everything* else in space, then one would have what, as unrepeatable, would be particular, not universal. Now I must confess that I do not see why. If spatial relations are universal, you do not make them particular merely by taking more of them. The space of direct apprehension is not self-evidently unique. There is no reason in principle why there should not be two spaces, both infinite in extent and one the duplicate of the other, just as there is dream space and waking space. And though time in its greater abstractness is always harder to deal with than space, there seems again no reason in principle why there should not be more than one time series.

The critic may reply: 'Even so, you cannot deny the unique and particular altogether. Suppose you take the relations of this patch, not to the things immediately around it, and not even merely to everything else in its spatio-temporal world, but to all things and events in all actual and possible spaces, times, and other frames of reference. Then would you not have the unique?' Yes, you would. You would have arrived at the universe as a whole, and that is unique by definition. And if all the critic means when he says these are particulars is that the universe is unique, we may agree with him. But it is most unlikely that he will be content with that. He is presumably insisting that behind or below or otherwise involved in the specific red that we are now seeing is some characterless existent that sustains it. Such an existent we cannot find. Things for us *are* sets of qualities in relation.

24. On our view the work of reason is to lay bare the connections between universals. But here a further difficulty arises. The universals between which connections are most commonly discovered do not seem to be of this type. 'Ethiopians have black and curly hair'; but 'Ethiopian' does not seem to point to any specific universal, such as a determinate shape of face or body, but has a much more general reference. 'Black' and 'curly' do not mean the precise shade of blackness or degree of curliness to be found on any one Ethiopian head, but covers many shades and degrees, which would all equally pass muster as fulfilling the specifications. Again, 'Man is mortal', enunciates a biological law that has so far had no exceptions. What are the terms it connects? Not manhood as exemplified in one man only and the specific form of death that overtook him. The statement seems to affirm a connection between manness or humanity generally and death as such. Now do any such terms exist in nature?

I do not think they do. If they did they would provide examples of qualitative and generic universals, and I have suggested that neither of these exists outside our thought. Nevertheless, the fact that science has assumed for centuries that they do is bound to make us pause. An assumption that has led to so much success can hardly be without ground. Let us look at these universals more closely.

25. 'Ethiopians' hair is black.' That states a connection between 'universals', of which black names one; and black is what we have called a 'qualitative universal'. Now any shade between jet black and greyish black would be accepted as a case of what was meant. If the universal is to be a single character, it must presumably be what these shades have in common. What is this? The curious thing is that we are unable, even when we stop and think about it, to give a satisfactory answer. A specific shade of black could quite well appear, as we have seen, on two different African heads, but if these heads have different shades, to extract an identical blackness appearing in both of them seems beyond us. If, in attempting to arrive at what is common, we leave out what is special to one shade, we find we have left out the whole colour; we cannot draw a line within this shade between what is general and what is special. We are defeated in the same way by the curliness. The curls in A's hair are tight and kinky; those in B's hair are long and loose; what is the pattern common to these two? One may say 'the general shape or design'. But is there such a thing in nature as a *general* shape? If a shape is anywhere to exist, can we not see that it must be this or that specific shape, not shape in general? Indeed do we even known what we mean when we speak of a general shape? If we do, we should be able to produce an

example of it; but if we attempt to do so, what emerges is always one or other specific shape. Shapes exist, and as many of them as you please. But shape as such, mere shapeness, no.

26. We have been speaking about qualitative universals—universals whose instances or species are characters. The same difficulty meets us with generic universals, whose instances are individuals. We are obviously saying something true and important when we say that man is mortal, but if we try to point out precisely the terms that our judgment connects, we find them slipping in tantalizing fashion through our hands. It is not in virtue of everything about the individual man Jones that he dies; his height and complexion, for example, would seem to have nothing to do with it; what is connected with his mortality is his being a man, and it is this character, therefore, that we must abstract and connect with our predicate. But when we attempt to make the abstraction, what do we get? Nothing but a miserable wisp, so tenuous as to leave many in doubt whether they have caught anything at all. Aristotle would say firmly that what we get is the pair of combined abstractions, rationality and animality. But what precisely are they like? Rationality and animality take extremely different forms in different individuals. Animality is owned in common, for example, by Aristotle himself and an amoeba, and rationality is an essence common to Aristotle and everyone else who can talk or read. If we try to abstract and hold clearly in mind the identical components in these ranges of individuals, we are defeated. The defeat is as decisive as it was when we sought for the common element in a range of 'black' shades.

27. Yet the conclusion that there are no such universals seems disastrous. It appears to be belied not only by every scientific generalization, but by every prediction made by common sense, every proverb reporting the consequences of prudence or vice, even our everyday recognitions of tables and chairs. How but by the use of the universal 'chair' could we perceive this chair as *a* chair? And if 'chair' has no general meaning, how could we apply it so confidently to all sorts of different chairs? Indeed the characteristic work of intelligence, as we have ourselves insisted, is to link characters or as-suches. If no as-suches can be found except the specific universal, then it would appear that by far the greater number of our general statements will have to be discarded as meaningless.

This conclusion is, of course, intolerable. Indeed if it is true, it must itself be meaningless, for it is a generalization of the type in question. We must either abandon reason as leading us for the most part up blind alleys or reach some view of the qualitative and generic universal that will make sense. The plausible alternatives are not many, and with a question before us of such theoretical importance, it will repay us to examine them briefly.

28. First there is the Platonic view, which, as traditionally held, teaches that the universal of a class, the 'intension' or common properties connoted by the class name, can not only be clearly conceived in abstraction from its embodiments, but has an existence of its own before and after embodiment. This view is more plausible in some fields than in others. The terms and relations of the multiplication table are timeless in the sense that it is meaningless to speak of their beginning or ending; and some mathematicians (e.g. G. H. Hardy) and philosophers (e.g. W. P. Montague) have held that mathematics supplies knowledge of the permanent structure of the world. If specific universals exist and have necessary connections, as we hold they do, this may well be true. But the Platonic view goes beyond this and insists that qualitative and generic universals also have timeless being. And this is harder to accept. Apart from the difficulty of conceiving such universals clearly, there is the objection that it is bad economy to introduce what is superfluous, and these reified class intensions do seem to be superfluous. One begins to be uneasy when in the tenth book of the Republic Plato talks about the unseen and eternal bed, or quintessential bedness, by participation in which any bed becomes a bed. Is it true that we cannot have our bed at any lower metaphysical cost than this? Aristotle did not think so, and most philosophers would now agree. Besides, beds may be classified in many ways—as artifacts, as articles of furniture, as things of utility or beauty or ugliness; hence each bed—and everything else —will embody a host of universals. Are *all* of these equally objective and timeless? It is logically possible, but the suspicion grows that one is overpopulating the universe. Furthermore, if these universals are really timeless, how did they come to be entangled with transient and sensible things? And once they are entangled, how are you to single them out within the perceived thing, putting what is invisible and eternal on one side and what is sensibly grasped on the other? To these questions neither Plato nor his followers gave satisfactory answers.

29. The second or Aristotelian view is probably the one that has been most commonly held. It is the view of traditional formal logic. Without committing itself to *universalia ante rem*, it still holds to *universalia in rebus*; beds 'laid up in heaven' are gratuitous, but still there is an identical bedness in all beds, an identical humanity in Smith, Jones, and Brown. This is, of course, a concept or abstraction, and therefore non-sensible; both it and its relations are apprehended by intelligence. It may have innumerable degrees of abstractness, and in any given thing there are numberless layers of universals. A man, for example, obviously embodies being, which is the highest and thinnest of all abstractions; but in descending order he embodies also the universals of material-being, animate-material-being, sentient-animate-material-being, and rational-sentient-animate-material-being; he is, as it were, a transcendental layer-cake of the most ingenious confection. All these universals indubitably exist in him, and when we make generalizations about him, it is these abstract characters, selected from a certain level, that we assert to be connected with others. Untutored minds may have some trouble in grasping these universals, particularly those on the higher rungs of the long ladder of abstraction. But their difficulty is psychological only. The practised logician or scientist, who is the connoisseur in these matters, apprehends them with perfect distinctness.

This view was implicitly taken over from formal logic by traditional science, and it must be admitted to have worked well. The prime difficulty, which we have already suggested, is simply that it is hard to verify the existence of these universals. If we try to distil from the colours of the spectrum an identical colour or colouredness appearing in all of them, but neither red nor blue nor any other colour; if we try to abstract from the amoeba and Aristotle a solid granule of animality, present without modification at every level of the animal scale, we cannot do it. We do think somehow of colour; we do succeed in making generalizations about animals. But this colourless wraith of colour, this bodiless and featureless animality, which combines height that is no height in particular, girth that is merely girth in general, complexion that is neither light nor dark, and habitat and time that defy location, seems to be fabricated of thin air. The difficulty is not merely, as often alleged, that of forming a composite *image* of qualities that cancel each other out, an image in which white and black, fat and thin, are somehow combined. Granting such an image to be impossible, many have thought that the concept could do what the image could not. The difficulty, however, is more serious. One cannot isolate even conceptually an invariant character where the instances vary so widely. The test is to try it and see for oneself.

30. There is a further difficulty. Not only is it hard to extract an identical genus from such different species; one cannot even be sure of the species from which one is supposed to extract it. According to the theory, blue is blue, and remains identical through all the changing hues of blue. But where does blue end as it passes through violet and purple towards red on the one side, and through peacock blue toward green on the other? If the concept of blue is definite, there should be no doubt where it is present and where not, but there is doubt on both sides. Indeed, one could quite well start with some intermediate quality like purple and include under one's new genus a set of qualities that had previously been assigned to blue and red. Thus qualitative universals, if they exist at all, will be so blurred as to melt away into each other.

So, unfortunately, will generic universals. The theory of such universals was first offered at a time when the species of living things were regarded as fixed, so that man was marked off from other species by a definite essence peculiar to him. Aristotelian logic received an unexpected blow from the theory of biological evolution. For it now became evident that to find *the* essence of a certain organism was not only practically difficult but theoretically impossible, in the sense that any precise boundary dividing it from forms above and below it could only be arbitrary. Was *pithecanthropus erectus* a man or not? If the indistinctness lay in our knowledge merely, there was some hope of removing it. Unhappily, it lay in nature itself. The sharp boundaries required by Aristotelian concepts were not there.

31. In view of these troubles with the universal, what view of them was now to be accepted? The natural next move was to conceptualism. One approaches this with pleasant anticipations from its having been advocated by that eminently sensible head, John Locke. Locke held roundly that both Platonic and Aristotelian universals were fictions. 'All things that exist are only particulars';[1] 'general and universal belong not to the real existence of things; but are the inventions and creatures of the understanding made by it for its own use, and concern only signs, whether words or ideas.'[2] How, then, does the illusion that there are universals arise? It arises out of the projection into things of our own abstract ideas. And why do we 'invent' such ideas? Because they are extremely convenient tools. It is in theory possible that everything we experience should have its own name, but that would call for a supply of proper names running

[1] *Essay Concerning Human Understanding*, III, iii, 6.
[2] *Ibid.*, III, iii, 11.

into the millions. What happens is that when a new object is very like something we know already, we call it by the same name, 'man' for example, and this name comes to be associated with the thought of the qualities common to these objects. With its help, we can think, if we wish, of the set of qualities in which all men are alike. We can then, by dropping out some, go on to think of the qualities in which all animals are alike, attaching the name 'animal' to this thinner group. But the unity or identity of such classes lies in the idea itself, not in the nature of men or of animals. Each man, as we experience him, is a bundle of particular qualities; there is nothing in him over and above these qualities, in the way of manness or humanity, in which he is identical with other men. Thus the only 'universal' involved is the idea, which we devise for our convenience and whose locus is our own mind.

32. Now this theory, as it is stated, is inconsistent with itself. It says first that things possess nothing in common and then that we form abstract ideas by fixing our attention on what they have in common.[1] But if they really have nothing in common, how could we fix attention on it? Presumably what Locke means is that they are similar, and that we fix attention on the points in which they resemble each other. Will the theory serve as thus amended?

Not quite. (1) It was offered as a theory of universals generally; but we have seen reason to believe that specific universals are genuine identities, not merely sets of similar characters. Locke seems, indeed, to admit this when he talks of 'the same colour being observed today in chalk or snow, which the mind yesterday received from milk'.[2] But this 'same' is inconsistent with his general theory that there are no universals among things. If he is to carry that theory through consistently he must hold that not even such a specific universal as this shade of whiteness is ever the same in two cases. And we have found this an unplausible view.

(2) Even with regard to qualitative and generic universals, the theory is imperfectly worked out. Locke assumes that, though there are no Aristotelian universals, thought acts as if there were. We have found him saying that we abstract 'common' properties. Is this surrender to the universal to be averted by substituting 'similar' for 'the same'? The case certainly calls for argument. In saying that

---

[1] In forming the idea of man I 'leave out of the complex idea of Peter and James, Mary and Jane, that which is peculiar to each, and retain only what is common to them all.' III, iii, 7.

[2] *Ibid.*, II, xi, 9.

Socrates and Plato are alike, we ordinarily assume that they are alike in some respect, namely in being men. This *respect* in which they are alike seems to be common property. In the very attempt to make clear what we mean by calling them alike, we seem to be carried back to the universal we sought to avoid. It is obvious that some account must be given of the relation between being similar and being the same. Locke never gave it. He was content to say that from merely similar particulars the mind could glean the concept of an identity which was not there. And of course if it was not among the events of nature, it was also not among the events of one's own mind. No two thoughts of 'the same thing', held by different persons or successively by the same person, ever had anything in common. Nor did we ever use the same word. 'Man', as used a second time, was just another particular, which had nothing whatever in common with the first.

33. Is it possible to accept frankly this pulverization of things and to work out a theory, as Locke did not, in which universals, both in things and in thought, are consistently denied? This attempt has been made by the nominalist, whom we shall therefore consider next. There have been few representatives in history of thoroughgoing nominalism. Cratylus, who protested that he could never step into the same river twice, and Thomas Hobbes in his more extreme statements have been taken as examples. Hobbes writes that there is 'nothing in the world universal but names; for the things named are every one of them individual and singular'.[1] But even Hobbes falls short of pure nominalism in two respects. For first, if you asked him why one name is given to various objects, he would reply, 'one universal name is imposed on many things for their similitude in some quality';[2] secondly, in speaking in this way of 'one universal name', he seems to be admitting that some things at least, i.e. names themselves, may be the same in various instances; and if some, why not others? An absolutely pure nominalist would presumably make neither concession. He would hold that if 'the same name' is given to two things, it is on the ground of nothing whatever in the things themselves in the way of either identity or similitude, and that between the two uses of 'the same name' there is again no real identity or likeness.

Now this is an impossible position. It is a denial that there are such things as recurrent features in our experience at all, and it is perfectly plain that in some sense there are. Why do we use the word 'book'

[1] *Leviathan*, Ch. IV.
[2] *Ibid.*

rather than 'hippopotamus' of the object now before us? The only sensible explanation is that we recognize this object as being 'the same sort of thing' as other things we have called books; if this is not the reason, then no one should be surprised if we call it a hippopotamus or George Washington, and our calling it a book is an inexplicable coincidence. Nor, if we do call it a book, are we using a word that is in any sense the same as we have used before. For whether we take a word as a noise or a mark, there is no resemblance between any earlier use and this one. Such a theory cannot even be stated consistently. For in speaking of this use and that, we are obviously choosing the word 'use' on the ground of something identical or similar in the two cases.

34. The four theories we have now considered—the Platonic, the Aristotelian, the Lockean, and the nominalistic—represent a swing of the pendulum from the far right to the far left. Neither of the extreme positions is plausible. The truth must lie somewhere between them. As regards specific universals, we have agreed already with the second or Aristotelian view. The specific shade of white before me, or the threeness of these matches, could surely be the same in diverse instances. Regarding qualitative and generic universals, on the other hand, Locke's case is very persuasive. If we use the same name for a series of colours, or a series of men, it is not, he says, because of an identity between them, but because of a 'similitude' only. Is it possible to settle this old problem of universals eclectically? May we combine an identity theory for specific universals with a resemblance theory for qualitative and generic universals? I think we may. Since the identity of specific universals has already been argued, it remains only to show that the other two types can be dealt with on the ground of resemblance.

35. What does a resemblance theory mean? It means, in the first instance, that resemblance may be ultimate, and is not resoluble in all cases into partial identity. Is this true? The issue was debated many years ago by F. H. Bradley and William James in a series of exchanges in which Bradley was incisive, clever, and scornful, and James was modest, bumbling and (I think) right.[1] Bradley argued

---

[1] James states his position in his *Principles of Psychology*, I, 490–4, 532–3. These followed an exchange of five articles in *Mind*, 1893, as follows: Bradley, 83–88; James, 208–10; Bradley, 366–9; James 509–10; Bradley, 510. For Bradley see also his *Principles of Logic*, I, 286–8 (2nd ed.). Bradley's three articles have been reprinted in his *Collected Essays*, I, Ch. 15, 16, 17. In summarizing the discussion I have reorganized it in the interest of clearness.

that when any two things or characters are similar, their similarity will be found on analysis to be based on partial identity; there will be a core in both that is the same, though this identical nature will be attended in the two cases by other and differing features which serve to distinguish them. If two coins are alike, that is in virtue of their being in some respect not merely alike but identical—identical, for example, in shape, weight, value, or use, though differing otherwise. To assert resemblance is thus to assert identity in difference.

James dissented, and in effect on three grounds. The first was that in some cases the identity alleged could not be found, even after diligent search. We may plausibly say, to be sure, that when one line is longer than another, they are identical in having length, and differ in that one has more of this than the other. 'But is blue yellow *plus* something? If so, *plus* what?'[1] The series of colours is not made of an identical something called colour, of which one amount makes blue and another amount yellow; nor can one single out an unchanging component which is combined with something else to make now one colour, now the other. Similarly of such series as hot-cold, sounds, and roughnesses. What we actually find in such cases is a series of apparently simple qualities resembling each other in a way not further analysable.

Secondly, James adopted from Stumpf the argument that identity would lead to a vicious infinite regress. Take a scale of tones a, b, c, etc. and assume that what makes them all tones is a common element X. Then the series will really be Xa^1, Xb^1, Xc^1, etc. What makes the succession a series does not lie, then, in the X, since this is the same throughout, but in the accompanying a^1, b^1, c^1, etc. But if these are to form a series, they must do so in virtue of a further identity X^1, which remains the same throughout. This means that the series is to be represented by X^1a^2, X^1b^2, X^1c^2, etc. It will not, however, be in virtue of X^1, that they form this series, but in virtue of the a^2, b^2, and c^2 that accompany this X^1. But if these really form a series, it must be in virtue of an X^2, the same in all of them. It is obvious that we have here an infinite regress which must be completed before the series can be formed; and such completion is impossible.[2]

Thirdly, the identity theory led to another incredible series. The resemblance of any two objects would involve an unending set of chinese boxes, one inside the other. Suppose you have two billiard balls, a and b. This likeness must be based on a common nature m, in which they are identical. But then m will resemble the common

[1] *Principles of Psychology*, I, 493.
[2] James, *ibid.*, I, 533, note.

nature, *n*, of any two apples, in respect *o* and will resemble the common nature *p* of any two boulders in respect *z*; and *o*, *z*, etc. will all somehow be within *m*. Any resemblance then between any two objects will commit you to an indefinite series of encapsulated identities, abstractions within an abstraction. James thought it absurd to say that we could not even call two billiard balls alike without committing ourselves to such a nest of wire-drawn *abstracta*. 'I say,' he concluded, 'that there must be *some* things whose resemblance is *not* based on such discernible and abstractable identity.'[1] Blue and yellow were classed together not because of a common colour that could be isolated and set over against their differences, but because of an ultimate unanalysable relation of resemblance.

36. Bradley was a better logician than James, and my own sympathies in reading this controversy were initially on his side. But I must own that I cannot get his 'identity-in-difference' clear, and suspect that it stands for an imperfect analysis. To James's first argument, that the alleged identity between similar things is often not discernible, he answered that this was true, but that the identity must be there none the less. 'You cannot, e.g., point out what general colour is; but, on this ground, to deny that particular colours have for your perception anything in common appears not reasonable. . . . And to tell me that these characters in and for my mind do not exist, because I cannot make them explicit and distinct, appears quite arbitrary.'[2] But it is arbitrary only if one can offer some proof that what one 'cannot make explicit and distinct' must still be there. Such proof is not forthcoming. Bradley's analysis of resemblance as 'an impression based upon experienced partial identity' he apparently takes as self-evident, in spite of his admission that the identity so often eludes us. The alternative view that resemblance is a relation which can stand on its own feet he denounces as 'nonsense unwarranted either in psychology or logic',[3] and speaks of 'that insane mythology which Resemblance begets'.[4] But so far as I can see, he offers no evidence that would justify such violent language; he does not show that resemblance *must* be analysed through identity; he does not show that ultimate resemblance is nonsense.

37. To James's second argument, Bradley's reply is various. The

[1] *Mind*, II (1893), 509.
[2] *Ibid.*, 84.
[3] *Ibid.*, 510.
[4] *Ibid.*, 368.

argument was, it will be recalled, that if, in a series, you distinguish an identical element, the differences will themselves form a series requiring another common element, and so on without end. Bradley replies, first, that James is supposing the identity to be separable from the differences in the sense that it can exist apart from them. But James neither said nor implied this; he was talking about the logically distinguishable, not the physically separable, as he speedily made plain. Secondly, Bradley insists that, whatever the difficulties, we cannot even think of a series with a direction, such as shades that get lighter or notes that get higher, without thinking of it as more or less of something common. 'How can we speak with any meaning of "more" and "less", if it is to be a "more" and a "less" of *nothing*?'[1] Later logicians would not find this question hard to answer. We can think of a series of darker and lighter shades, not as one that embodies more of an identical whiteness, but one whose members increasingly resemble pure white, taken as an end term. Indeed this notion is easier to grasp than that of a whiteness that remains somehow identical as it changes from the colour of smoke to that of snow. Thirdly, Bradley replied that on his view one could not, even in thought, separate the identity from the differences. 'Identity and difference on this view are inseparable aspects of one complex whole. They are not even "discernible", if this means that you can separate them in idea, and so treat one as remaining itself when the other is excluded.'[2] James's answer was that this sort of reciprocity was not involved in either the plain man's idea of identity or the logician's. If we say that between resembling coins or colours there is some 'point of identity', we mean some positive character that could at least in principle be singled out and clearly conceived, not something so tenuous as to disappear altogether if some coin or colour were removed. Bradley's identity, says James, 'is only one aspect of an integral whole on which you may lay stress for a moment, but if you abstract it, or put it ideally in a box by itself, you make it self-inconsistent, or reduce it to nothing. But an "identity" thus conceived is so different a thing from the stark self-sameness which "identity" denotes in logic, that it seems unfortunate to describe it by the same name.'[3]

38. To James's third argument, that on the identity theory every resemblance between concrete things would call for an identity that

[1] *Mind*, II (1893), 84.
[2] *Ibid.*, 366.
[3] *Ibid.*, 509.

'encapsulated' within itself an unending series of further and more abstract identities, Bradley replied by saying, first, that the problem of the series did not arise for him, since none of these 'encapsulated' entities could on his theory be recognized. What this meant, however, as we shall shortly see, is not that they were absent, but that, although present, they could not be clearly distinguished, an answer that may well give rise to suspicion. Secondly, Bradley replied that if these encapsulated entities were supposed to be increasingly abstract, the series would have an end. You can trace an identity in all colours, and a more abstract identity in all qualities, but when you come to being itself, which for Bradley is the same as experience, it is idle to try to go further. 'Experience or being is the last term in my regress and is where I stop.'[1] Unfortunately, an infinite series is involved even so. The resembling things in the world are without number; each of these resemblances is based on an identity; and each identity resembles, and is therefore partially identical with, every other. Each identity thus encloses an infinite series of others.

39. Bradley regarded his theory of identity as essential to his logic and metaphysic and complained that 'to deny the principle of identity is to destroy the world'. We should try to be clear about a principle for which so much is claimed. In holding that identity underlay resemblance, Bradley was not accepting the abstract universal; he held that from a series of colours or of men you could not isolate an abstract colour or humanity and think it clearly by itself; and here we agree. What he insisted on was an 'identity-in-difference', a whiteness-in-differing-shades, in which the whiteness was meaningless apart from the shades, and the shades apart from the whiteness; they formed a kind of organic whole in which thought, if it would deal with either, must deal with both. Here again in a sense he was right. Whenever we grasp something *as* an identity, it must be an identity in difference, for that is what identity means. If there is to be an identity between things, there must be at least two of them to have the feature in common; and 'two' means two of a kind, even if of a very abstract kind. But I am not clear that this amounts to more than the formal requirement that in affirming anything to be X, we must at the same time deny that it is anything other than X; X is what it is by thus excluding whatever differs from it. In this sense, everything is, and must be, an identity in difference. But it is not this formal contrast that logicians have had in mind when they spoke of the identity in the class of men that can be set over against the various men. They

[1] *Mind*, II (1893), 367.

meant a specifiable common content. Bradley admits that this is sometimes undiscernible, and yet insists that something identical is there. What is this something? Something that may be attended to, even though it cannot be specified; something so bound up with the differences as to be unthinkable without them; a pole of 'an integral whole' that must therefore be thought as a unity. Now I suspect that this is an incomplete analysis. Two poles that imply each other must have some character of their own as a condition of implying anything. Bradley's identity, when one tries to pin it down, seems to vanish into a set of relations to its differences. But if it has no positive character of its own, how could it be related? And if it does have such a character, why should we not be able to single it out? 'I will say at once', he writes, 'that in the full sense of the term intelligible I do not think the union of these aspects of the world is intelligible.'[1] Before accepting an analysis admitted to be unintelligible, it is perhaps well to try another.

40. On the theory we propose, two things may resemble each other on different grounds. They may be partially identical, in the sense of owning a specific universal in common; the balls over a pawn shop are like the angles of a triangle in the sense that there are three of each; and the three in these two cases is not two threes that are very much alike; it is an identical three. But two things may also resemble each other when there is no such isolable identity, for example, two tastes or two sensations of hot and cold; and here resemblance is enough. On such a theory, a class may be constituted either by the possession of a common character, like the class of all trios or quartets; or it may be constituted by resemblance within specified limits to certain objects taken as standard. 'Red' will mean what resembles the red of this stamp I am pointing at, or—more precisely —whatever resembles either the red of this stamp or the red of this ink not less than they resemble each other. Does this make classes into arbitrary creations existing in our own minds only? Yes and no. It does in one unimportant sense, namely that the objects selected as standard depend on our choice. But it does not do so in the only important sense. Classes are not subjective or arbitrary if that means that they do not exist in nature. That this three is the same as that three and one red like another are facts about the nature of things which are and remain what they are regardless of our thoughts about them.

41. Against this resemblance theory two objections have been made

[1] *Mind*, II (1893), 368.

which have often been thought decisive. It is objected, first, that the theory must accept at least one universal of the type it purports to reject, the universal of resemblance itself. For consider: you set out to replace identity by likeness. Whenever you find colours or men that are alike, you call the relation that links them resemblance. But when you say *the* relation, you are obviously thinking of one relation, the same in all cases. But if it is the same in all cases, it is obviously a universal. Even in rejecting abstract universals, therefore, you are accepting at least one of them, and if one such exists, then there can be no objection to them in principle, and you may as well admit others. To Russell this argument seemed conclusive. It is not quite easy to see why. Resemblance offers no special or exceptional difficulty. Perhaps it is more complicated to say that resemblances resemble each other than to say they are all the same, but there is no incoherence in it, and indeed it seems closer to verifiable fact. For suppose you say that two colours, orange and yellow, resemble each other, and then that two generals, Belisarius and Marlborough, resemble each other. Is the resemblance between the first pair literally identical with that between the second? There would seem to be no more reason for saying so than for saying that between the terms of the pairs themselves there is a nuclear granule of identity. Nor is there any reason why resemblances, like qualities, should not be placed in an order of increasing resemblance, with the identity of the specific universal as the limit of the series.

42. It has been argued, secondly, that the resemblance theory assumes universals in another way. If A resembles B, it must resemble it in a certain *respect*. Two billiard balls resemble each other in respect to shape; two apples in respect to taste or size; two generals in tactical skill; two states in their form of government. Now these 'respects'—so the argument goes—are always characters owned in common by the objects compared. But that is just what being a universal means. Once more, then, the resemblance theory pre-supposes the theory of universals. But the argument is less conclusive than it seems. For one thing, as already said, the respect in which two objects resemble each other may resist all attempts to specify it. You may be quite sure that two patches resemble each other in colour or two wines in taste, while quite unable to bring to clear light the colouredness in all colours that makes them colours, or the common character in all tastes. Secondly, the assumption that a 'respect' *must* be dealt with as an abstract universal appears to be untrue. The account of it given by the resemblance theory, though a little more complicated, is quite straightforward. It would say that wine A resembles wine B in that both have qualities belonging to a series the members of which resemble a specific taste defined ostensively. It may be objected that to speak of this as a taste is clearly to classify it as a taste and thus again to subsume it under an abstract universal. This does not follow. It again assumes that classes can be constituted in one way only, by the possession of an identity. And a class may quite well be formed by similarity to something given.[1]

43. Our discussion has been concerned with universals as they exist in things, not primarily with our thoughts of them. And our conclusion is that while specific universals such as the number three or this specific red do exist in things, qualitative and generic universals such as the supposed redness common to all reds, or the humanity common to all men, do not. These cloudy and elusive entities, so indefinite as to arouse grave doubts as to their conceivability, have no place in nature. This or that colour exists, but not a colour that is neither red, nor blue, nor any other; this or that man or philosopher exists, but not manness or philosopherness. It may be insisted, nevertheless, that we do use such universals, that we coin words for them and apparently refer to them continually. Is there any doubt that 'the triangle' as used by the geometer, or 'colour' as used by the artist, or 'the genus *canis*' as used by the biologist, is a genuinely

---

[1] The claims of identity *versus* resemblance have been much canvassed by recent writers. H. H. Price discusses them in his British Academy lecture, *Thinking and Representation* (1946) 31 ff, and concludes that the resemblance theory must fall back on the theory of universals to make itself intelligible. Seven years later, in his *Thinking and Experience*, Chap. I, he holds that it need not do so, but is an alternative though more complex theory, covering intelligibly the same ground. Russell, in his *Inquiry into Meaning and Truth* (1940), 343–7, was much more hesitant about universals than he was in *Problems of Philosophy* (1912), 150 ff, but was still inclined to accept them on the ground that resemblance itself is a universal. The issue is further explored by R. I. Aaron in *The Theory of Universals* (1952), Chap. XI, and by A. D. Woozley in *The Theory of Knowledge* (1949), Chap. IV. All these discussions are admirably clear and helpful. Perhaps I may be permitted a complaint about the tendency, now fashionable, to deal with the problem as if it were an issue about language. In Professor Woozley's excellent chapter we read, for example: 'The fundamental difference between the Resemblance theory and the Realist theories is that, while for the latter general words are proper names, for the former they are not' (92–3). But (1) the issue is not primarily one of how words are to be classified, but of how the resemblance of characters is to be understood; (2) it is misleading to suggest that, for one who believes in universals, the term 'red' stands for 'one thing' as the proper name 'Westminster Cathedral' does; (3) the contrast between general words and proper names can be helpful here only if we have settled already what we should mean by them, and this in turn can be settled only by asking, for example, whether there are any identities among things to refer to, or only resemblances.

meaningful term? If such terms refer to nothing in nature, must not nine-tenths of our general thinking be put down as delusion?

Scientific thinking does, of course, use such terms constantly, and to call them meaningless would set us hopelessly at odds with science. And that would be merely foolish, for it is far more certain that science makes sense than that any theory of universals is the right one. But then in expelling the abstract universal from nature, we are in no way disparaging science. We are only denying a theory by which scientific generalization has in the past been interpreted, and, we should hold, misinterpreted. Scientific statements are commonly generalizations; and generalizations are statements about classes. So long as class statements are retained as fully meaningful, no man of science will worry. And we do, of course, retain them. Classes need not be based upon identity, and are not destroyed with its removal. A class based upon similarity to a given character is as good a class as any other, and as truly existent in nature. Indeed we have seen that the attempt to apply the Aristotelian view in biology ends in precisely the sort of 'arbitrariness' which that theory charges upon the resemblance view. The classes of living things, constituted as they are by numberless resemblances, and shading into each other on all sides, answer in fact to the resemblance theory more nearly than to its rival.

44. The question may be asked whether the mathematical logic which has so largely superseded the Aristotelian logic has not itself settled the issue over universals. Russell and Whitehead in *Principia Mathematica* thought they could dispense with classes, and it has often been supposed that they were dispensing with universals also. And it is true that they would interpret the proposition 'All sounds that have pitch have loudness' not as saying that having pitch entails having loudness, but in accordance with their extensional formula for universal propositions, $(x).\varphi x \supset \psi x$ 'for all sounds, if a sound has pitch it also has loudness'. But this has not dispensed with classes. To be sure, in the new statement the old class name, 'sounds that have pitch', has disappeared, but it has disappeared in name only. For the symbol φx means any sound characterized by the function φ of having pitch, and that is surely a class.[1] We have dispensed neither with the class of sounds having pitch nor with the function or universal assumed to tie its members together; nor have we dispensed with the predicate class. Our main achievement has been to distort

[1] 'every propositional function determines an appropriate class.' Russell, *Introduction to Mathematical Philosophy*, 185.

O

what we originally meant to say, namely that having pitch entails having loudness. Mathematical logic does not solve the problem of universals, and its exponents are in deep disagreement about what to do with them. *Principia Mathematica*, as Professor Aaron remarks 'leaves the problem of universals very much where it finds it'.[1]

45. Granting now that there are classes, and these are of more than one type, what sort of idea do we have in mind when we think of a class? The traditional theory answered this question simply and confidently: You form a class concept through abstracting the common properties and thinking of them in some sort of isolation. The higher you mount in the scale of generality, the more abstract your concept becomes: man, animal, organism, substance, being, represent successive levels, to which there correspond increasingly abstract ideas. Unfortunately, this theory will not do. In Joseph's words, it confuses 'little that is definite' with 'a definite little'. We must admit, however, that it is no easy matter to describe what does occur in one's mind when one thinks a general idea. Since our interest is not primarily psychological, a few remarks will have to serve.[2]

(1) The concept itself is neither an image nor a word, though one or the other is usually present. The act of meaning or referring is plainly different from either. When we think of planets, it is a great help to have the word 'planet' at our disposal, or, failing the word, a visual image, and we may be unable to achieve the thought without such help. But unless the word or image is used to mean with, unless it serves our thought as a pointer to what lies beyond it, we have not employed a concept. To say that the concept *is* simply the word, or a physical response of some kind, is plainly untrue.

(2) If some writers have nevertheless said this, it is because the attempt to describe the act of meaning or referring has proved strangely baffling. One feels a sense of direction, or 'intention', as the phenomenologists say, in one's thought, and is ready to accept or dismiss proposed examples instantly as what one did or did not mean, and yet the way in which one means them is curiously elusive and indescribable. Some of the difficulty springs from the fact that the having of a general idea is in fact the having of a disposition as opposed to the entertaining of an explicit content, and a mere readiness to recognize something does not lend itself to introspection. Nor can we get any help from other people. We cannot observe what

[1] *The Theory of Universals*, 227.
[2] A further discussion will be found in my *The Nature of Thought*, Bk. II.

is going on in their minds when they use concepts as we observe how
they slur or articulate their words; so we test what they think by what
they do. We are content to say that if a person says 'planet' when we
point to a planet in the sky, if he uses the word in the same contexts
as we do, and if he defines it in what we accept as equivalent symbols,
he has a meaning in mind that is like our own. Some philosophers of
the day hold that we are ascribing nothing more than this to other
persons when we say they are thinking of something. All that is
necessary to refute this view is to point out that these things might
conceivably be done by a very complex automaton which had no
trace of consciousness. If we knew that what was behaving in this
way was really only a machine, then however complex and 'appropriate' its behaviour might be, we should not say that it was thinking,
any more than that it was happy or miserable. To use a word is to
mean with it, and if we try to substitute for meaning any other kind
of use, we end in disastrous confusion.

46. (3) Our concepts of specific universals are normally precise;
those of qualitative and generic universals are vague. This follows
from the differing character of their objects. It follows, too, from
their mode of formation. The successive instances of a given red or
of the number three are, in respect to these characters, precisely the
same. On the other hand, the colours and the animals that we meet
with vary greatly, and the words 'colour' and 'animal' hence come to
be associated with widely differing objects. Some philosophers, for
example T. H. Huxley, have thought that a general idea was a
composite image imposed upon the mind by a succession of similar
things, the sort of blurred picture that is printed by a succession of
exposures on a photographic plate. This image had a relatively vivid
part where the characters duplicated each other, and indistinct parts
where they tended to cancel each other out. This account will hardly
do, since a concept is not an image at all. But it is helpful nevertheless,
in a way in which the traditional notion is not. That notion was that a
concept is a clear-cut thought of clear-cut abstractions, of man for
example as an animal that was rational and two legged. If an unfortunate man turned up who was an idiot or whose legs had been
amputated, the old concept had to hide its face in embarrassment, for
here was a being who lacked the essence of man and yet was a man
undeniably. The resemblance theory is in no such difficulties. If the
class of man is constituted, not by the presence of a clear-cut essence,
but by a set of resemblances, the resemblance may still be dominant
when some character is wholly lacking. Thus Huxley and his

empiricist friends were in a sense nearer right than the logicians. Our concepts of this kind of universal are the product of experience, and have the indeterminacy one would expect of ideas that are the deposit of countless differing percepts. Such concepts are general impressions. They lack definiteness because their objects do. Taken as attempts at the apprehension of sharply demarcated abstract universals, they are failures. Taken as referring to sets of resemblances with indeterminate limits, they do very well.

47. One final illustration to make as clear as may be the three kinds of concepts answering to the three kinds of universal. We see an apple before us. Its shade of red is a specific universal which may be conceived with complete precision both while we are looking at it and after we have turned our heads away. The concept of redness, as covering other shades of red—what we have called the qualitative universal—is not the thought of an identical redness present in these shades, but the thought of a range of similars, united by their resemblances to a given or imagined shade. The concept of apple is more complex. In the apple before us, many differing qualities, each a specific universal, are combined; it is red, round, and sweet, each in a definite degree; it has a definite shape, size, and weight. The thought of *this* apple is the thought of this set of qualities in the relations in which they exist to each other and to the things around them. The thought of apple-as-such is not the concept of appleness, the generic universal, for this type of universal has disappeared. It is the thought of the class of apples. This class is loosely constituted. It is the class of patterned sets of qualities resembling the set before us, or more commonly, resembling any one of a group of sets that we should be willing to take as standard. The degree of resemblance required for each quality is indeterminate. For each of them there will be limits, varying from person to person. We should all be willing, for example, to accept as apples things with tastes that varied from sweet to sour; but confronted with an 'apple' that tasted like an orange or a red pepper, we should very probably rebel. Similarly with the range of shapes, sizes, weights, and colours. The generic universal is not a set of sharp *abstracta*, one for each of these ranges. It is itself a range of patterns in which these ranges of qualities are variously combined. The concept of it is therefore bound to be indeterminate. But the indeterminacy is solely in our thought. There is no vagueness in nature.

48. The work of reason has been traditionally conceived as a finding and following of the connections between universals. And since nature was supposed to be replete with abstract universals, reason had its task laid out for it. Necessary connections awaited it on every side. Being a man entailed dying; gall-lessness was obscurely but necessarily linked to longevity; virtue could be seen by a sharp eye to be its own adequate reward; hope springs eternal in the human breast because it is human. Man and nature were shot through with such threads of necessary connection, and it was the office of reason to trace their luminous course through the fabric of the world. Now we hold that this tradition was sound, and that this *is* the right work for reason. Unhappily, neither the terms nor their linkages are what this tradition took them to be. The terms we have just been examining. We have seen that most of them do not exist, and that the concepts of them were so vague that no clear lines of connection could possibly be traced. The linkages we are about to study are not between such entities, or rather nonentities, but between the only universals that clearly exist, namely specific universals. It must not be supposed that this limits us to studying the link, for example, between this specific sound and this specific feeling, for necessary connections may join complexes of characters as surely as they join the characters singly. Hence the relatively loose thinking represented by such general-izations as the above may be in large measure true and enlightening. It may point to, and approximate, the truth even when it fails to see it distinctly. Still, it is the more distinct apprehension that we want. To the work of reason in achieving this, its work of dissecting out the nerves of necessity that run through the body of nature, we shall turn in the next chapter.

CHAPTER X

NECESSITIES IN NATURE

1. We have held that the prime office of reason was the discovery of necessary connections. The tendency of recent thought has been to restrict this office by confining necessity within increasingly narrow limits. It is insisted, first, in the spirit of Hume, that necessity never links existents, but only our own meanings. It is then added that not all meanings admit of such linkage, but only those that can stand as terms in propositions, simple or compound. Next propositions themselves are scrutinized, and many that were thought to be necessary are excluded; only analytic propositions are admitted to the inner fold. Finally, many even of these are questioned, on the ground that they contain empirical elements. 'All bachelors are unmarried' is analytic, of course, but the content of its terms is drawn from experience, and, strictly speaking, empirical contents are never linked by necessity. So we are left in the end with such luminous assertions as '*a* is *a*', or '*a* is not non-*a*', or $p \supset \cdot p \vee q$ as the most characteristic achievements of reason.

In the minds of many philosophers there is a rising revolt against all this. They feel that the retreat of reason has gone too far, that it is time to call a halt and to start reclaiming territory needlessly surrendered. This retreat seems to them to evince a strange failure of nerve. Philosophy has suffered from a creeping palsy of suspicion that reason, its chief weapon, is not much more than a toy, of use only in playing 'language games' or arranging symbols in arbitrary patterns.

It is possible, to be sure, that the philosophers from Plato downwards who have relied upon reason to provide knowledge of the nature and structure of the world were uniformly mistaken. A sceptical inquiry into their procedure must at all times be welcomed, and indeed the findings of recent years have shown that with regard to both the terms and the connections of our so-called rational knowledge, earlier philosophies were unduly complacent. They floated a paper currency of terms only part of which could be redeemed in coin, and they often indulged lavishly in a priori argumentation without any clear view of its true nature and limits. It is therefore conceivable that their whole speculative enterprise was an uncritical dream. Contemporary analytic philosophers have alleged that it was, and have brought particularly severe charges against the traditional employment of reason. Necessary knowledge, they insist, is not knowledge in the strict sense at all. The connections it reveals, if not always purely formal, are at any rate conventional, and provide us merely with the rules of our linguistic practice. Of nature it tells us nothing. And even if it did, what it said would be tautologous, containing only what a clear enough eye could see in that which was already before us.

We have examined these contentions in our discussion of a priori knowledge, finding in them some truth, but not a little also that was superficial and confused. We found no good ground whatever for regarding necessity as arbitrary or conventional or linguistic, nor again as analytic merely. And if these charges fail, there is no good ground, either, for saying that necessary judgments can tell us nothing of nature.

Let us suppose now that reason is acquitted of these charges. How much light on nature may be hoped for from its exercise? Have we any intimations that nature is governed by necessity, either as a whole or in any considerable part? Even if necessity does hold among existent characters and things, it may hold in so small an area that the fullest success we could hope for would bring little illumination. Our best course would seem to be to make an inventory of such necessities as we have already in possession, and then to raise the further question how far we may legitimately hope that such knowledge may be extended. Our first question, then, must be, How large a capital of necessary knowledge do we now have?

2. (1) First, we have logical law. The assumption that at least the law of contradiction holds of the real world was the basis of a famous 'metaphysical essay' by Bradley. 'To think is to judge, and to judge is to criticize, and to criticize is to use a criterion of reality . . . in rejecting the inconsistent as appearance, we are applying a positive knowledge of the ultimate nature of things. Ultimate reality is such that it does not contradict itself; here is an absolute criterion. And it is proved absolute by the fact that, either in endeavouring to deny it, or even in attempting to doubt it, we tacitly assume its validity.'[1] Nearly three-quarters of a century have passed since Bradley wrote these words, and philosophy has taken directions that he could not

[1] *Appearance and Reality*, 120.

have foreseen. Has it effectively belied these words of his? I do not think so. The chief developments that might have affected it are the appearance of a linguistic theory of a priori statements, of a conventionalism that would justify logical rules pragmatically as means to desired ends, and of 'alternative systems' of logic. We have inquired into these developments, and have found nothing to render it plausible that such logical laws as $\sim(p.\sim p)$ apply exclusively to thought or language rather than to things. The issue here is so important that we must briefly return to it.

Professor Popper has pointed out that there are 'three main views on the nature of logic'.[1] It is worth seeing that on all of these views logical laws must be interpreted as asserting about the world. The three are (A) that such laws are laws of thought which either (a) describe how we actually think, or (b) tell us how we ought to think; (B) that they report about the constitution of all actual and possible objects; (C) that they are rules for the use of words and sentences.

3. When theory (Aa) says that these laws describe how we actually think, it is pointing out that in a sense we always think logically, that we cannot violate a law of logic if we try. We can say both that Caesar did, and that he did not ride a three-toed horse, but in a sense we cannot *think* both. But in *what* sense? Is it in the sense that we cannot *believe* both, or that we cannot *see* or *understand* how both could be true, or that we can see that both *cannot* be true? Not the first, certainly, because we often do in fact accept contradictory beliefs. The second sense, that we cannot in fact see both sides to be true, is undoubtedly correct, but it does not content us as a final answer, for we are at once moved to ask the further question, *Why* can we not see both sides to be true? Is it because of the limitations of our own thought or because we can see of the real that it *could not* be self-contradictory? The view that logic gives us laws of thought only would take the first line. It would presumably say that though we cannot conceive how Caesar could both ride and not ride a three-toed horse, he might in fact have done so. But if this latter statement has any meaning for us, then we *are* conceiving of his both doing and not doing it, which is precisely what was declared inconceivable, and we have contradicted ourselves. The statement that the laws of logic are laws of thought only, and not of things, cannot be coherently stated.

The second form of the first theory (Ab), to the effect that these laws are normative and tell us how we ought to think, seems more

[1] In a symposium on 'Why are the Calculuses of Logic and Arithmetic Applicable to Reality?', *Proc. of the Arist. Soc.*, Sup. Vol. 20 (1946), 48.

promising. In saying that we ought to think in accordance with them, it assumes that we can also break them. And in a sense we plainly can; most of us have surprising gifts for believing contradictory things. But granting that we can do this, why should we seek to avoid it? The answer seems clear enough. It is because if we do not think in accordance with logical law, we shall not think in accordance with fact. The 'ought' is a hypothetical imperative; it tells us that we must avoid thinking illogically if we want to think truly. And this implies that the reality of which our thought is true is itself governed by logic. If contradictory assertions cannot both be true, it is because the reality of which they are asserted does not admit contradictory characteristics.

4. Leaping next to the third view (C), that logical laws are linguistic rules, we may content ourselves with adding a consideration or two to the many that have been mentioned earlier.[1]

If a logical law is a rule of usage, we may always legitimately ask why this rule has been adopted rather than some alternative. Suppose, for example, we adopt *ponendo ponens* as a rule, that is, we decide so to regulate our thought and speech that when we have asserted sentence S^1 and the further sentence 'S^1 implies S^2', we should go on to assert S^2. How should we justify this procedure? Those who take the linguistic line do not generally hold this rule to be purely arbitrary, and to do so would certainly not be plausible. They ordinarily fall back on a statement of the calculus of propositions, namely $(p.(p \supset q)) \supset q$, and show by the truth-table method that this is necessary because a tautology. But to say that it is a tautology means that the *truth* of q is among the assertions already made by $(p.(p \supset q))$. The rule of language is adopted because of a set of relations holding among the *truth*-values of propositions expressed by that language. It may be said that a relation among truth-values, for example that p and $\sim p$ are not both true, is itself a rule of language. But (1) the linguistic logicians never so interpret it. They would think it absurd to accept $(p.\sim p)$ as a rule of procedure, though if $\sim(p.\sim p)$ is only such a rule, we should be at liberty to do so. (2) If it is only such a rule, we may again legitimately ask how to justify it. Why should we shrink from saying that p and its contradictory, that this crow is black and that it is not black, are both true? To which the simple and sufficient answer is: Because the crow itself cannot have incompatible attributes, and we see that it cannot.

We shall indicate one more way in which the rule theory negates

[1] Above, 271 ff.

itself, a difficulty that Arthur Pap takes as 'perhaps the most decisive objection against the theory that the laws of logic are not propositions, but rules of symbolism. Briefly, the objection is that whatever rules one may have initially stipulated, and however arbitrary such stipulations may be, one will thereafter have to *find out* what these rules entail, and the statement that such and such is entailed by the rules could hardly be characterized as itself a rule.'[1] Take as an example *ponendo ponens* again. It is not now asserted to be true; it simply reports part of what we propose to mean by deducing one proposition from another. We apply it to the axioms of some system, and in the course of so applying it we make a new discovery. In such a case 'it will be perfectly proper to say . . . "now I *know* that this is a theorem in the system, i.e. that this formula is entailed by the axioms". But that formula F_1 entails formula F_2 . . . is itself a logical truth, and it would be simply nonsense to characterize it as a *rule*.'[2] Suppose, to take a rough parallel, that I make it a rule to get up with the sun. The adoption of this rule entails that I shall never see what the world looks like just before dawn. But that my adoption of it does entail this is not itself a proposal or rule of procedure. It is a true proposition apprehended by a cognitive act. Sooner or later the logician who starts with logical rules is bound to develop their implications, and when he does so, he is moving over into the sphere of logical truths. And if a 'truth' is not true of reality, what else is it true of?

5. We are left with position (B), namely that logical law tells us something about the actual structure of things. This has been the view of all the rationalist philosophers, and it has been defended in recent times by Bertrand Russell in Britain,[3] by Morris Cohen in America,[4] and by Ferdinand Gonseth in Europe.[5] The view has been brushed aside in a sentence by Wittgenstein on the ground that while 'it is raining' gives us information about fact, 'it is either raining or not raining' gives us none.[6] And obviously enough it gives us none if the only things counting as information are ruled beforehand to be items verifiable in sense. But we have found no ground for this dogma. And the fact that a logical law applies necessarily and to everything does not show that it says nothing. Nor does the fact of

---

[1] *Semantics and Necessary Truth*, 184.
[2] *Ibid.*
[3] *Problems of Philosophy*, Ch. VII–VIII.
[4] *Reason and Nature*, 202–205; *Preface to Logic*, 53–56.
[5] *Qu'est-ce que la Logique?* Chap. 7–9 (1937).
[6] *Tractatus*, 4.461.

its being empirically irrefutable. To say this would commit one to saying also that nothing a logician or mathematician said was true, for how could it be true without saying anything? And we have found no plausible alternative to the position that such laws are true. That the desk I am writing on is either a desk or not may be admitted to be a most unhelpful truth and one in which nobody but a philosopher would take the slightest interest. Does it say something true, however? Try to deny it and see. Does it say something about this particular desk? Yes, and this is not controverted by pointing out that what it says holds equally of all desks, clouds, and lamp-posts. We must repeat that a statement does not say nothing simply because it applies to everything.

6. (2) In apprehending logical law, then, we know something about the nature of things. Do we have other rational insights of the kind? In descending order of abstractness the next step is to arithmetic. The multiplication table has generally been taken as offering prime examples of propositions which are at once necessary and true, and there is no good reason to deny this. Their applicability to nature, however, is a curiously treacherous matter and has often been misunderstood. Mill thought that it was guaranteed by our having found them to hold with unbroken regularity among experienced things. If this is true, they are not really necessities apprehended by reason, but connections that have so impressed themselves on our minds as to have induced fixed habits of expectation. Laws thus empirically arrived at should be capable of empirical confirmation or disproof. But the evident truth is that we never seriously resort to either. Would it occur to us that a bank teller, because he counts money all day long, knows with more certainty than the rest of us that 5 and 5=10? And can we think of an instance in which any sort of perceptual experience would make us doubt the truth of this proposition? Someone may, indeed, put 5 drops and 5 more drops of water into a dry pitcher and challenge us to get 10 out; he may put 5 rabbits and 5 more in a hutch and find 20 when he comes back; and he may then say triumphantly that in the first case 5 and 5 make less than 10, and in the second case more. Should we be ready, in the light of such cases, to say that, after all, 5 and 5 sometimes fail to make 10? Obviously not. We are far more certain that they do than we are of the validity of any alleged exceptions. We can usually see by a moment's reflection that these are not exceptions at all. The multiplication table says nothing about what will *causally* ensue if we put drops in a pitcher or rabbits in a hutch; it leaves out everything that characterizes any of its units as opposed to any other, and interests itself only in units as units, that is as entities regarded simply as distinguishable. It says: Take any set of 5 units, of which, for the present purpose, we know nothing except that they are distinct, add to them in thought 5 other such units, and you *must* have 10. If one sees this *must*, one will not be shaken by suggestions that in this or that queer instance an exception has turned up. One will merely start hunting for the fallacy that led anyone to suppose he had found such an exception.

7. Now does this fact that in arithmetic the appeal to empirical confirmation is needless show that arithmetic is not true of the empirical order? I do not see that it does. The assertion seems to rest on two confusions. (*a*) The first is the now familiar confusion of supposing that because a statement says nothing about this rather than that, it says nothing at all. What arithmetic says is that so far as things are regarded merely as classes of units, certain necessary relations will be found among these classes. Now things *can* be so regarded. One may abstract in a set of ten clothespins from everything about them—everything that they have in common and everything that differentiates them—except that here are ten somethings distinguishable from each other. We know that to this group of ten *X*'s all the properties applying to the number ten will also apply. We know, further, that all actual and possible groups, because their members are distinguishable somethings, will have arithmetical properties, and that every thing and quality will be a member of many such groups. Thus our knowledge of the multiplication table supplies us, so far as it goes, with knowledge of the world. As Whitehead says, 'the first noticeable fact about arithmetic is that it applies to everything, to tastes and sounds, to apples and angels, to the ideas of the mind and to the bones of the body'.[1]

(*b*) A second source of the error that arithmetic tells us nothing of the real is a confusion about form and content. It is supposed that form would still be significant if there were nothing it could apply to, and that when we talk logic or mathematics, we are saying something not only without reference to this or that thing, but without reference to any possible content. This is not true. In a world that lacked distinguishable things, numbers would be meaningless, like 'up' with no 'down', or 'out' with no 'in'. Number means number *of* something. Where there is nothing numerable, there is no number. Not that the numerable things need be of any specified type; numerical state-

[1] *An Introduction to Mathematics,* 2.

ments do not have to wait for what is called 'interpretation' in order to become meaningful. They are of the highly abstract but important kind that says something about all that is.

8. There is something very odd in having to defend the view that mathematical statements give us light about the world at a time when natural science is scoring its greatest triumphs with the aid of mathematics. There is also something paradoxical in having to defend it against the very philosophers—the logical empiricists—who think that science gives us our only reliable knowledge. These philosophers draw the sharpest possible line between the necessary statements of mathematics, which are alleged to say nothing about nature, and these statements as 'interpreted', which are then taken as empirical generalizations to be tested by sense experience. Starting from this sharp division, they naturally find it a problem how the propositions of the multiplication table can be true of empirical things. Professor Hempel writes: 'the propositions of mathematics are devoid of all factual content; they convey no information whatever on any empirical subject matter'. This he says as a logical empiricist. But he immediately adds, as a physical scientist, 'This result seems to be irreconcilable with the fact that after all mathematics has proved to be eminently applicable to empirical subject matter, and that indeed the greater part of present-day scientific knowledge has been reached only through continual reliance on and application of the propositions of mathematics'.[1] His way out of the impasse is a simple one. It is to distinguish within a proposition of applied mathematics a part that is purely formal, which is admitted to be necessary, and another part that is empirical and without necessity. While agreeing that $5+5=10$, he would, if I follow him, deny that '5 apples and 5 apples are 10 apples' is a necessary statement on the grounds (a) that whether the formal concepts do apply, whether the groups before us do number 5, 5, and 10 respectively, is an empirical matter, in which we might be mistaken, and (b) that anything said about *apples*, which are known only empirically, is likewise fallible and subject to empirical check. Now this doctrine seems to imply that we can never be sure that any mathematical 'truth' (whatever that now means) has any applications anywhere, since any possible example would be open to both these objections. But the doctrine implies more: it implies that instead of being 'eminently applicable', as Mr Hempel suggests,

---

[1] 'On the Nature of Mathematical Truth', Feigl and Sellars, *Readings in Philosophical Analysis*, 234. See his equally good article that follows on 'Geometry and Empirical Science'.

mathematics never will or can apply anywhere. For to say that it applies is to say just such things as that 5 and 5 apples make 10 apples; and so far as this proposition is mathematical, it has nothing to do with apples, while so far as it concerns apples, it is not mathematics. It would thus appear that the real tendency of positivist doctrine is not to exalt exact science but to depreciate it by making 'the queen of the sciences' sterile of any knowledge of the world.

9. Our own way out of the impasse is to deny both (*a*) and (*b*) in their unqualified forms. (*a*) It is true that we determine the number of an aggregate by counting, and that our result may be mistaken. But (i) the likelihood of such error is often negligible. If we can never be sure that we have five apples before us rather than four or six, there is little or nothing of which we can be sure. (ii) Even if we err in counting, there is a curious fact about such error. Though we may be mistaken as to the particular number of things we are trying to count, we cannot be mistaken in our report that there are countable things, or, therefore, that things exist to which number applies. If we mistake six things for five things, we have at least found a numerable aggregate of distinct things in the world, and if there is a numerable aggregate, arithmetic applies to it. The objection might be offered that it is theoretically possible to think one has found a plurality where no plurality exists. I do not think this even theoretically possible. For if the plurality counted is an illusion, at least the plurality in the acts of distinction in which the counting consists can hardly be an illusion. Furthermore, to deny plurality is to say that this is true rather than that; this admits *two* distinguishable entities; and with the number two, carrying all other numbers in its train, arithmetic steals back into the picture.

(*b*) In the proposition '5 apples+5 apples=10 apples', is it true that the mathematical part says nothing about apples, and that so far as anything is said about apples, it is empirical merely? The division seems to me too sharp. The logical and the empirical are more intimately united than this. We may grant that whether what is before us is an apple, whether it is red or round or hard, must be determined empirically, and that arithmetic has nothing to do with apples or reds as such. But we must remember also that the simplest recognition of an apple is logically complex. It is not only the identification of this apple as opposed to other apples, or of apples as opposed to other kinds of thing, but of what is more abstract still, a something distinct from something else. And such abstract *distincta* are precisely what arithmetic deals with. In counting five apples, even if every identification is mistaken, it remains true that we have arrived at five somethings-or-other which in this abstraction constitute numerical units. Is our achievement of such units an empirical or an intellectual affair? Such either-ors are hardly in place here. It is both. The successive objects of our sensation would no doubt be called empirical, and perhaps also the successive strokes of our attention; but each of these objects and acts has implicit in it that character of a *distinction* which makes it amenable to arithmetical handling; and the explicit apprehension of this character, or of the number of the instances in the case before us, is presumably an intellectual act. Reason and sense work so closely together here that to mark off their contributions sharply is impracticable. They work in interdependence.

10. (3) We have seen that logic and arithmetic supply us with their own highly abstract truth about things and classes. Can we say the same of geometry? There are three different questions here, corresponding to the three levels of abstractness on which geometry may be pursued. Pure geometry starts from primitive terms and propositions so abstract that the ordinary connotations of 'point', 'straight line', and 'surface' are not involved, and there may be nothing to indicate that one is dealing with spatial relations at all. Such geometry does not advance beyond the kind of knowledge we have been discussing. Secondly, Euclidean and non-Euclidean geometries do go beyond this and deal with space, but each with its own kind of space, defined by its special postulates, and with no assumption that its space is that of the actual world. Euclid's space, for example, is that in which, if one starts with a straight line, one can draw through a point outside that line only one parallel line; Lobatschevsky's space is one in which a variety of such parallels can be drawn; and Riemann's is one in which none can be drawn. Each system is valid, and each tells us, therefore, what would be true in a space constructed according to its postulates. But none of them, as developed by modern geometers, offers itself as an account of relations in physical space. Thirdly, at a lower level of abstraction than either of these types, stands physical geometry. It is this that particularly interests the philosopher, since what it seeks is a geometrical knowledge of nature. Is there really any such thing? Does it make sense to speak of a *rational* knowledge of actual spatial relations?

That we do possess such knowledge was for many centuries taken for granted; Euclid had supplied it and Newton's physics assumed that he had. But a very simple reflection is enough to call the assumption in question. The points, lines, and planes of which Euclid was speaking were not empirical things at all. A geometrical point, for example, was supposed to be without parts and without magnitude, and it is obvious that what has no size would be invisible; we can see nothing smaller than a dot. Further, a line is supposed to be a continuous series of points; but if a point is really without size, you cannot produce something that does have size by putting a great many points side by side; indeed they have no sides. Thus the lines of the geometer are as far removed from chalk lines on a blackboard as his points are from dots. Again geometrical surfaces are made up of an infinite number of lines drawn side by side, and geometrical solids of an infinite series of stratified surfaces; but neither sort of entity has ever been felt or seen. If it is such remote and fictional things as these that geometry deals with, what reason have we to say that it tells us anything about nature at all? The logical positivist would say quite simply that it tells us nothing, and that our knowledge of actual space is purely empirical. But in view of the confident and successful use of geometrical theorems in the building of bridges, the construction of tennis courts, and the guidance of rockets, this is a paradox. 'It is surely not insignificant to ask whether there may be constructed with ruler and compass a circle equal in area to a given square.'[1] Does the geometrical demonstration that this is impossible tell us nothing about what we may expect in actual experience?

11. At least two suggestions have been made in recent years that help us to bridge the gap between the ideal figures of geometry and the actual ones of experience. One comes from C. D. Broad.[2] Broad points out that empirical series may be of different kinds: we can see of some of them a priori that they have no limits, and of others that they have. If we take a series of increasing hotnesses, for example, we can see that there is nothing in the series to require a halt at any point; when we had reached the hotness of boiling water, we could go on to that of a furnace, and from there to the heat of the sun, and so on apparently without limit. On the other hand, suppose we take first a very jagged line, like that of the edge of a cross-cut saw, and then a less jagged one like the edge of a carpenter's saw, and proceed to decrease the jaggedness at each step; is this series without limit? No; we can see a priori that there is a limit to it; when we have reached zero jaggedness, we have a straight line, beyond which the continuation of the series is logically impossible. Now if this sug-

[1] M. R. Cohen, *Preface to Logic*, 54.
[2] *Examination of McTaggart's Philosophy*, I, 42–45.

gestion is correct, we have a priori knowledge about empirical fact, in the sense that of some empirical series we can see a priori that they have a certain kind of limit. Even if no line that we ever see is perfectly straight, we can still say of a given line that it belongs to an imaginable series whose limit would be a line of a certain kind, and we can talk of that line with the aid of any member of the series. Similarly of the arc of the moon or a rocket or a rainbow in relation to the perfect geometrical circle. Actual figures may always fall short of geometrical ones, and still be related to them necessarily. Such a theory, instead of having Platonic figures 'laid up in heaven', builds an intelligible bridge to them from the figures of actual space.

12. Another pregnant suggestion was made by Whitehead in his 'principle of extensive abstraction'. He proposed to regard a point, or a line, or a surface, not as the limit of a series, but as the series itself. This is a welcome suggestion to those who are averse to Euclidean points and Platonic figures. Suppose one holds, for example, that the Euclidean point, something with position but no parts or magnitude, is unreal and inconceivable; is geometry therefore to be bereft of meaning? Not at all, says Whitehead. For even if there is no such thing as this shadowy point, we can still conceive the series of volumes that would ordinarily be said to converge upon it. We can conceive of a series of Chinese boxes one inside the other, or a series of concentric spheres growing smaller and smaller. Whitehead's discovery was that for geometrical purposes, the series of these concentric volumes had all the properties traditionally assigned to points while at the same time requiring us to deal only with finite and verifiable magnitudes, and that lines, surfaces, and other mathematical entities could be dealt with in the same way.

It might be objected that volumes are different in kind from points, and that one is not solving the problem of their relation by substituting the one for the other. There are two answers. First, in mathematics a thing is defined by its properties, and if, for all purposes of the science, the properties of the converging series of volumes are the same as those of the original points, the two concepts are interchangeable. Secondly, even if one sticks to points, the new notion can be made to approximate to the old within any desired degree. One of the functions of a pair of points, for example, is to determine the connection between them which we call a straight line. If we substitute basketballs for these points, the line that connects them, being an imaginary cable as thick as the balls themselves, will hardly be accepted as a line at all. But substitute billiard balls for the basketballs, marbles for the billiard balls, and birdshot for the marbles, and the terms will come closer and closer to defining your notion of a line; and the series provides for making the line as gossamer as you please. The older geometry would have it that the line talked about is the line of zero thickness forming the limit of this series. Whitehead held that for all purposes of the physical geometer this line could be dismissed as an airy nothing in favour of the series of converging volumes, and geometry would retain all its validity. We can conceive of any actual dot or ball as enclosed in such a series, and base on the latter our geometrical deductions. We shall thus have a genuinely geometrical knowledge of the physical world.[1]

13. Broad's suggestion differs from Whitehead's; one, as I understand it, would still have physical geometry deal with the limit of an empirical series, the other with the series itself. But they agree that such geometry is more than a compound of tautology and sensory report. It supplies us with necessary knowledge about actual things. This answers to an old conviction of common sense, which has found a persistent and at times a passionate expression in both speculative rationalism and physical science. 'God forever geometrizes,' said the Plato recorded by Plutarch. 'Nature's great book,' said Galileo, 'is written in mathematical language.' 'What a deep conviction of the rationality of the universe,' Einstein exclaimed, 'and what a yearning to understand, were it but a feeble reflection of the mind revealed in this world, Kepler and Newton must have had to enable them to spend years of solitary labour in disentangling the principles of celestial mechanics!'[2] This attitude has largely remained in the new scientific era that Einstein ushered in. It may be that Sir James Jeans was going beyond his scientific brief, as Professor Stebbing alleged, when he said that 'the universe can best be pictured, although still very imperfectly and inadequately, as consisting of pure thought, the thought of what, for want of a wider word, we must describe as a mathematical thinker'.[3] But he was not exceeding his knowledge as an astronomer when he said that 'nature seems very conversant with the rules of pure mathematics'.[4] It has sometimes been thought that quantum mechanics is inconsistent with such a view. An event of

---

[1] Whitehead's explanation of extensive abstraction is given in *The Concept of Nature*, Ch. IV, and *The Principles of Natural Knowledge*, Pt. III. There is a brief and clear account of it also in Broad's *Scientific Thought*, 38–52.

[2] *The World As I See It*, 27.

[3] *The Mysterious Universe*, 2nd ed., 124. For Miss Stebbing's criticism, which is perhaps unduly severe, see her *Philosophy and the Physicists*, Ch. II.

[4] *Op. cit.*, 113.

such dimensions that we can perceive it is composed of minute and invisible events of whose behaviour singly nothing is known; we must study their behaviour in masses or great aggregates, and when we do so, we find that the laws governing it express probabilities only. But then probability itself, if quantitative, must be formulated in mathematical terms, and laws do not become less open to such formulation when they become statistical.

Working scientists like Jeans, Eddington, and Einstein are sometimes charged by persons not conspicuously qualified to do so with mere romancing when they talk about the mathematical framework of the universe. And it must be admitted that actual masses, velocities, and distances have no place among the terms of pure mathematics. 'By "pure mathematics" is meant those departments of mathematics which are creations of pure thought, of reason operating solely within her own sphere, as contrasted with "applied mathematics" which reasons about the external world, after first taking some supposed property of the external world as its raw material.'[1] To let the mathematical x stand for any actual mass or velocity always involves a venture in the dark which may come to nothing. On the other hand, it may strike a spark or a flash which suddenly illuminates the structure of things. Suppose you have two x's possessed respectively of properties M^1 and M^2 and of a mutual and quantitative relation R. And suppose you form the hypothesis that there is a second relation between them, G, which varies with the quantity $M^1 \times M^2$ and inversely with the quantity R^2. Suppose that with this precise but barren formula in mind, you introduce substitutions. You let the two x's be the earth and the moon, let M^1 and M^2 stand respectively for their masses, assumed to be concentrated at their centres, let R be the distance between these centres, and G stand for gravitational force. Then suppose that, based on these substitutions, you make a dozen or a hundred predictions as to the course the moon will follow, and find with the closest observable accuracy that it does follow that course. Next suppose that for the variables of the formula you go on to substitute other masses at random—including tides and apples, the sun and the planets—and find that their behaviour answers to the predictions required by your formula. When such things have been successfully done, is it visionary to say, as Newton did, that one has found a mathematical framework in nature? We suggest that he was amply entitled to say so. But what if some bodies, or even all bodies, are found to diverge slightly from the formula? Would not this be enough to destroy the notion of a mathematical order in nature? No,

[1] Jeans, *op. cit.*, 113–114.

not at all, if the divergences are themselves found capable of form-ulation and prediction. The predictions based on inserting into our formulas gross masses and crudely measured distances are perhaps never quite precise; but 'although there is always a remainder, we can still maintain the ideal of mathematical analysis, always looking in the deviations of our theories for those mathematical threads of identity which bind new laws and new fields of experience to our problem'.[1]

14. (4) Further chains of necessary connections in which all existing things are bound are those of *serial order*. Some types of order, such as those of ordinal numbers and of points on a line, may be fairly thought to belong among the arithmetical and geometrical relations already considered, but the orders of degree, of temporal succession, and of the series that lead to the infinitely large and infinitely small may well have separate mention.

When an order is called 'serial', it is usually assumed to have a direction, so that A is not related to B as B is to A. But where these relations are the same—in technical usage 'symmetrical'—the type of order remains unchanged, however the terms are re-disposed. The order of equality is an example. Necessity enters into this order in the sense that things equal to the same thing are necessarily all equal to each other. Of course the equality must be in the same respect. A is equal to B in height or weight or speed, and B to C in the same respect; hence in that respect A and C are equal. Are such insights purely formal, or can we see them to hold of actual things? Where the respect in which things are declared equal is numerical, we can often reason thus with a certainty that it would be merely captious to question. If the graces equal the muses in number, and the muses equal the team that the New York Yankees now have on the field, then it must be conceded, however surprising, that in one respect the Yankees equal the graces. Where the respect in which equality is ascribed is height, weight, or speed, the principle of the inference is still certain, but whether the conclusion is true will depend on the material truth of the premises, and this in turn on the exactitude of our measurements. Exact equality in any respect would be identity in that respect, as we have argued earlier, and there is no reason to deny that such identities occur in nature. But even where they do, the best we can assert in fact will as a rule be similarity.

The term 'order', however, is usually reserved for series in which one cannot move indifferently forward or backward. Such series are

[1] M. R. Cohen, *Reason and Nature*, 204.

asymmetrical; if A precedes B, B cannot also precede A; they are often transitive also, in the sense, for example, that if A precedes B, and B, C, then A precedes C. Now the beads of our particular experiences are strung on a large number of such serial threads, each of them constituting lines of necessary relation. As Kant pointed out, every quality we ever sense is on the same scale of intensity with every other of the same kind; everything that is hot or hard, sweet or sour, bright or loud, sharp or heavy, rough or large, is related, and necessarily related, to all other things possessing a quality falling under the same 'determinable'. 'When one term does, by virtue of one and the same point in it, stand in a relation of degree with two or more other terms, then these others are also related in degree.'[1] Of anything that is visible we may say a priori not merely that it is identical with or similar to everything else that is visible in respect to having brightness, but also that if it differs in brightness from B in the same way as B differs from C, then it differs itself in the same way from C. Such a priori knowledge of serial order does not apply to intensities only. It applies to length of lines and acuteness of angles, to sizes, masses, and velocities; and it is the basis of every variety of *a fortiori* argument. Perhaps its most obvious application is to times, for we are arguing constantly that if A comes before B, it will also precede anything contemporary with or subsequent to B. Sometimes we intertwine several strands of serial reasoning together. If General Wolfe died in 1759, Macaulay in 1859, and G. E. Moore in 1959, if Moore was a better philosopher than Macaulay and Macaulay than Wolfe, and if Wolfe was a better soldier than Macaulay and Macaulay than Moore, then there died, two centuries after another, a man who was a worse soldier but a better philosopher.

15. It has already been pointed out that empirical series may be seen a priori to have certain properties, for example, the property of having a certain kind of limit. It seems also to be the case that some can be seen to be endless, and this raises at once the question of external and internal infinities. An external infinity is one determined by the extension of a series beyond given limits, an internal infinity one determined by the continued division of a whole into smaller parts. Consider, for example, the extension of the series of moments in time, either into the past or into the future. Is there any reason for saying that the series had a beginning or will have an end? Apparently not. There is nothing in the constitution of the series that calls for a first or last term, and to halt the progression at any moment, no

[1] Bradley, *Principles of Logic*, I, 266.

matter how far away, is arbitrary. Indeed a beginning or end of the temporal series seems strictly unthinkable. If one carries one's thought back to a certain moment selected as the first, one places this moment within the temporal series by contrasting it not only with the moments that follow it but also implicitly with the moments that precede it. One cannot think of a moment preceded by eternity or by nothing at all, not even empty time. And there is a like difficulty for anyone who would bring the series to an end.

What of internal infinities? Are we to say of any segment of the temporal series that it may be divided endlessly? Again this seems to be a necessity in the very nature of time. When an hour is divided into minutes, and a minute into seconds, and a second into shorter components, we soon reach a point where our power to distinguish still shorter durations ceases, but there is no reason to suppose that such durations do not exist merely because we cannot perceive them; in principle any duration, however short, may be divided and subdivided without end.

16. (5) Differing attributes and even categories may be so connected that we can see that whatever has one must also have another. Shape and size are different attributes, but if a thing has shape it must have size also. Colour is not the same attribute as extension, but if we know that something is coloured, we need not wait till we inspect it to assure ourselves that it covers some extent in space. If we know that a sound has some pitch, is it a matter of probability only that it will also have some degree of loudness? Clearly not. We can see that, different as they are, the first character could not occur without the other. Once more, according to Aristotle and others who have drawn up lists of categories, qualities are ultimately different from relations. But could qualities exist without relations? Obviously qualities in the plural could not, since they would be connected at least by the relation of difference. Could a *single* quality exist in a world where there were no relations at all? It could not exist in time, for if it did, an earlier phase of it would be related to a later phase. Nor could it exist in space, since if it occupied space, its parts would be spatially related, and if it existed somehow at a point, the point would have to be somewhere, and this 'somewhere' again implies relations. Even in a world in which space and time were done away— if such a world can be conceived—a single scent, for example, could be what it was only by being different from other possible qualities; in short, to be at all is to be this rather than that, and the rather-than-that is an inseparable adjunct of being this.

Not only can we see at times that if something has a certain character, it must also have another; we can often see that if something is of a certain kind, it *cannot* belong to certain other kinds. There is necessary exclusion as well as necessary accompaniment. Joseph proposed as a necessary judgment, 'Thought is not laryngeal motion'. I agree, and can only suppose that if behaviourists do not, there is radical confusion on one side or on the other. Husserl offered 'A judgment cannot be coloured'. Descartes suggested, 'Unity is not a quantity'. Other similar insights are 'Number is not the thing that is counted', and 'The difference between two degrees of quality is not itself a quality'. These are all exclusions, and apparently necessary ones, that cross categorial lines.

17. (6) There are similar relations of necessity that link, both positively and negatively, the determinates of the same determinable. Consider the inter-relation of colours. There have been many attempts in recent years to show that statements of colour relation are merely empirical. No doubt the statements that this patch of grass is green and that patch of sky is blue are, so far as present insight goes, empirical purely. Is this also true of the statement that in the table of colour affinities, orange is between red and yellow, or the statement that it is nearer to yellow than to blue? Is it true of the statement that purple is more closely related to blue and red than it is to green? No answers I have seen have effectively challenged what seems to be the position of common sense on these points. If one asked the ordinary man, who had just remarked that a given orange shade fell between given shades of red and yellow whether it would also fall between them in other instances where the shades were the same, he would think the question a silly one; of course they would, for if the relation is really between the colours, it must hold wherever the colours are the same. As Isaiah Berlin puts it, 'invited to conceive of a world in which the shades we call pink, red, black, occurred in some order other than that presented in ours, we must say that we cannot do so: not because of a failure of imagination, but because it is inconceivable: the invitation is itself nonsensical'.[1]

Thus determinates of the same determinable may be necessarily linked with each other. There is also a negative linkage: they exclude each other necessarily when asserted of the same subject. A surface that is pure red cannot, at the same time and to the same observer, be pure green. It has been alleged that this is an analytic statement, that it says only that the two colours are different, which is already involved

[1] *Proc. of the Arist. Soc.*, Supplementary Vol. 16 (1937), 77.

in their being two. But the statement clearly goes beyond this. A colour and a shape are different, but they can belong at once to the same surface; what our statement tells us is not merely that the colours are different, but that in the same subject they are exclusive of each other. Again, being exclusive of green, though it is entailed by being red, is hardly part of what we *mean* by being red, nor not-being-red part of what we mean by being green. Nor is there any *formal* contradiction in saying that what is red is also green, any more than in saying that what is red is also square. The *must* arises from the content; it is in virtue of the special character of being red, in distinction for example from being square, that the red excludes the green. What we have is a particular kind of incompatibility, based not on the form of the propositions but on the nature of the predicates.

18. (7) There has been a stubborn tradition in western philosophy that necessity is to be found also in the sphere of values. This has been challenged of late years by an ethical theory which holds that judgments of good or evil, right or wrong, are not judgments at all, but imperatives or expressions of feeling. If we say that Plato's wisdom was good and the suffering of Bruno's martyrdom evil, we are, to be sure, implying matters of fact, namely that Plato was wise and Bruno a martyr; but the value words in our statements assert nothing whatever; they are not even *reports* of our own attitudes; they are rather exclamations expressive of these, like 'ouch!' or 'cheers!'. If this is true, all statements of value would seem to be removed from the sphere of necessity at one stroke. Necessity links characters or the propositions that ascribe them; but values are not characters, nor are value statements propositions. And the attempt to prove or refute a feeling by reason is inept, as if, when you said 'cheers!', I said, 'Nay not so, and on the following grounds'.

I do not think that this attempt to reduce value statements to expressions of attitude has succeeded.[1] To say that when we call Plato's wisdom good or suffering evil we mean nothing that held of these things at the time they existed, but are expressing only our present feelings about them, remains very unconvincing. However hard it may be to bring to light and define what we mean here by 'good' and 'evil', we do mean something by them, and something that does not come and go with our fluctuating attention. If such words refer to characters in the object, are these characters linked to fact and to each other by relations of necessity? I do not myself know how to deny it. The judgment that intense suffering as such is evil—

---

[1] For one statement of the case, see my *Reason and Goodness*, Ch. VIII and IX.

intrinsically as opposed to instrumentally evil—is not a merely empirical one like 'grass is green' or 'snow is white'. We know that grass is often in fact not green, and that snow could conceivably be other than white. But that a given pain should be bad as felt by one man, and that a pain of precisely the same kind and intensity as felt by another should be good—this I think we can see to be inconsistent and absurd. Again, when we say that Plato's wisdom is intrinsically good, our ultimate meaning, I am inclined to hold, is that such wisdom fulfils and satisfies human nature;[1] and the perception that, given the desires and capacities of our nature, such wisdom would partially fulfil these seems to me more than a merely contingent insight. Still again, the perception that one value, for example that of clear understanding, is intrinsically better than another, for example that of ignorance or confusion, may be a necessary one. I say *may* be, for claims to necessary insight in ethics may be as mistaken as they sometimes are in mathematics. But if the fact that they are sometimes mistaken in mathematics does not imply that they are always so, neither should it in ethics.

19. Necessity appears also at other points in ethical thinking. To say that I *can* do something is not the same as to say that I *ought* to do it, and clearly does not entail this: but if I ought to do it, it does follow, and follow necessarily, that I can do it. Once more, if Jones, a land-lord, has a right to the payment of rent by his tenant, Smith, Jones's right is not the same fact, or at least not the same aspect of the same fact, as Smith's duty to pay; but it does entail or necessitate this duty. Many moralists have sought to find in ordinary rules of truth-telling, promise-keeping, etc., statements that were necessarily true. The attempt has usually foundered on the consideration that what is necessary must be also universal, and that there are no rules of this intermediate level that seem to hold without exception. It was shown, however, by that most judicial of moralists, Sidgwick, that the claim to necessary ethical principles could be made good at a higher level of generality. He pointed to certain propositions in ethics which were genuine axioms in the older sense of that term, principles which, though undemonstrable, were necessary and exceptionless. There were at least three of these—the axioms of prudence, benevolence, and equity.[2] 'It does on reflection strike us as self-evident,' says Rashdall in summarizing them, 'that I ought to promote my own good on the whole (where no one else's good is affected), that I ought

---

[1] Cf. *Reason and Goodness*, Chap. XI-XIII.
[2] Sigwick, *The Methods of Ethics*, Bk. III, Ch. 13, Sec. 3.

to regard a larger good for society in general as of more intrinsic value than a smaller good, and that one man's good is (other things being equal) of as much intrinsic value as any other man's'.[1] These principles may be so stated as to be tautologies merely, but as actually used in moral reflection Sidgwick did not consider them so. I agree.

If what we have said about value judgments is true, ethical reflection is shot through with rational insight. The inference that a certain action will produce consequences of a certain kind is indeed based upon experience and may have no seen necessity about it. But the insights that a certain consequence would be good, that it would be better than a certain alternative consequence, and that the good to be produced should be distributed in certain ways—all these are, or may be, genuine apprehensions of necessity. And if they are, the pursuit of morality is a rational pursuit. The good life, as the three great Greeks maintained, is the life of reason, not in the sense that it consists of thinking merely, though Aristotle at times suggested this, but in the sense that the judgments most essential for the guidance of life are rational judgments, open only to minds that can grasp necessities in the field of value.

20. This chapter began with a reminder of the current revolt against reason as a means of knowing nature. It is alleged that so far as reason deals with necessities, it is confined to the conventions of our own minds and can tell us nothing of necessities in the world of things and events. We have reviewed seven fields of experience in which the knowledge of necessity seems clearly present, not as a convention but as a discovery, not as a relation among meanings only but as linking the attributes of things and persons. The notion that the world is a gigantic ragbag of loose ends, in which nothing is connected intelligibly with anything else, will not stand even a cursory examination. The world as we know it is shot through and through with lines of necessity, and there is every reason to believe that if we knew it better, we should see those lines to be more numerous and far-ramified than at present they seem. Even now we must take the world as a consistent whole; it is at least governed by the law of non-contradiction; thought must start with that, not as a rule of usage merely, but as governing the structure of things. We saw that numerical and geometrical thinking, rightly interpreted, also applies to the existent. We found, again, that qualities come to us in serial orders such that in a given order all the members are necessarily connected with each other. We found that there are bridges of

---

[1] *The Theory of Good and Evil*, I, 90–91.

necessity from one quality to others of different kinds, that there are necessities linking the determinates of a determinable, that necessities seem to abound even in our thought about value.

No claim for exhaustiveness is made for this review, and no doubt many other types of necessity could be brought to light. But fragmentary as it is, the list makes a massive demurrer against the claim that reason reveals no necessities in nature. The resolute rationalist would of course go much further. He would point out that these, after all, are only scattered threads of necessity tying abstractions together, and that they are bound to raise two further questions about the range of necessity in the world. First, does necessity link universals only, or does it also link things and events? Again, does it supply the warp of nature without its woof; does it link some items and not others; or is its network all-involving? The first question raises the issue whether the main link between events, causation, is itself a necessary relation. The second asks whether the cosmos itself may, with any ground, be regarded as an intelligible whole. We shall say what we can about these issues successively in the two remaining chapters.

CHAPTER XI

NECESSITY IN CAUSATION

1. Causation is only one strand in the network of relations that holds things together, and any one of these relations might in theory be singled out by the philosopher for special attention. Most of them have in fact been passed over as of minor importance. But a few of them have held a continued fascination for both the scientific and the speculative mind. Among this select few causation is perhaps the most conspicuous member. Why is this? There are several reasons.

(1) It is a relation, as Hume pointed out, to which we have to appeal if we are to take one step beyond the given into the world of physical things, or to past or future. If we perceive a voice as a wife's or a friend's, or assume that the postman has left the mail in the hall, or expect the floor to hold us up when we walk, we are depending on causal relations. If there were no such relations, we should have no reason for believing that there were any physical things or that anything would behave in one way rather than another. Causation is the lifeline connecting us with the world.

(2) It is also our instrument of *control*. Our intellectual interest, as Dewey has emphasized, tends to follow our practical needs, and science to enlist in the service of technology. A grasp of the causes of things will give us command over them if anything can. As long as the causes of malaria and yellow fever were unknown, we were helpless about them; once their causes were brought to light, we could see what must be done to eradicate them. If such other plagues of mankind as cancer, juvenile delinquency and senile decay are to be eliminated, the first step is to master their causes.

(3) But science does not aim merely at control; its primary aim is at *understanding*. It considers that the understanding of a thing or event has been achieved when the laws that govern it have been formulated. Not all these laws, indeed, are causal laws. The laws of motion, the laws that all mammals are vertebrates, the law that all ruminating animals have cloven hooves, the law that light travels at a certain speed, are not statements of causal connection. Nevertheless, causal laws are the staple of science. They are laws that would

have first mention as examples of scientific explanation, for they carry with them the strongest sense of understanding. When we ask the question Why? about any event—a disease, a tidal wave, a war, a motor 'accident'—what we are asking for is an explanation in terms of its causes. In natural science that is what explanation normally means.

(4) If the mastery of causal laws gives control and understanding, it is because such laws are more than devices of our own. They belong to nature; they are part of the network, the set of objective ties, that bind events together. The scientist's traditional assumption has been that nothing happens by accident, that whether he knows the cause of an event or not, it is there to be found and is the condition of the event's occurrence. Indeed every event seems to be implicated with every other. Not only does each event have a precursor in a line that stretches backward without beginning and forward without end, but these lines of causation intercross. My use of a pen at this moment would seem to have no causal connection with someone's eating his lunch at the same moment in Los Angeles. And this is no doubt true if one means a connection in a straight temporal line. But there are indirect causal lines. After all, it is not fancy but highly probable fact that the occurrence of either event depends on another celebrated event that happened at Marathon some twenty-five centuries earlier, so that each of the present events is connected through a common cause with the other. The universe itself may be regarded as one gigantic congeries of events linked directly or indirectly by a network of causal laws. And since the strands that form this network belong to the nature of things no less than the items linked, philosophers have often felt that to understand them fully would be to grasp the necessary order of the universe.

2. The philosophy of science that has been most popular in recent years denies that there is any such order. A causal law is a statement that an event of the kind A is regularly followed by an event of the kind B. That is the end of the matter; the question *why* B should follow is an idle question; it asks for what cannot be given because it is not there. Here Russell and Wittgenstein returned to Hume. According to Hume, 'we may define a cause to be an object followed by another, and where all the objects similar to the first are followed by objects similar to the second'.[1] We know that a billiard ball, when struck by another, does in fact roll away; a child knows, after sticking

[1] *Inquiry Concerning Human Understanding*, Sec. VII, Pt. 2.

its finger in a candle flame, that the flame does in fact burn; that is all we know in either case and, in principle, all we shall ever know.

This doctrine, when first announced, was a shock to both common sense and philosophy, and rumblings of discontent continue in both quarters. There was no objection to holding that causality did involve regular sequence; the objection from both parties was that the regular-sequence view left out something that was plainly there and was of prime importance. The missing element, however, was not the same for the two parties. What common sense thought had been left out was the element of constraint or compulsion. When one billiard ball struck another, it surely gave it a push; it compelled it to move by exerting force on it. For ordinary thought, this is surely the essential element in the case, and to ignore it seemed perverse. On the other hand, what philosophers particularly objected to was the exclusion of necessity. They had been in the habit of thinking that one could *reason* from effect to cause, that the two were so related that, given the first, one could with sufficient acumen *deduce* the second. Aquinas thought that, given the existence of the world, he could deduce its Creator; Spinoza that, given the existence of a pebble, he could deduce an absolute substance; Locke that, given his percept of a sphere, he could deduce a physical thing that caused it and was like it. If such reasoning was illicit, much that had passed as sound metaphysics would have to be discarded. Plain men and philosophers were thus united in feeling that a causality from which force and necessity were omitted was a mere shell of itself.

3. The genius of Hume is apparent in the persuasive clearness with which he met these objections. Never perhaps, except by Berkeley, has a major metaphysical upset been effected with arguments so simple. In causation, rightly seen, he held, there is no trace of either compulsion or necessity, and without these all that is left is regular sequence. To the contention that the cause exercises force or compulsion he replied that this supposed force is really our own experience wrongly projected into things. It is true that when we push a table we feel sensations of strain and resistance, but the billiard ball that strikes another has no such sensations. It is true that when, after repeatedly seeing a ball roll away upon being struck, we next see a ball rolling toward another, there is a felt tendency to expect the second to roll away. To that extent there exists in our minds a gentle feeling of constraint. It is natural and easy to project this constraint, belonging only to our habit of thought, into the action of the outward cause. But the projection is plainly illicit. Does it follow that when a

hammer strikes a nail or a bolt of lightning splits an oak, we speak uncritically in ascribing to the cause any exercise of force? Yes, Hume would reply, the inference is not to be escaped. The only force we know is a kind of sensation. There is no such sensation in the hammer that strikes the nail or the bolt that splits the oak. To place it there is a regression to animism.

4. As for the element of necessity in causation, Hume dismisses it in a similar though slightly more complicated way. He bases his argument on the assumption that ideas are copies of sensations, and that if we claim to have a certain idea, we must be prepared to point to the sensation or sensations from which it is derived. Now rationalists had said that when the flame produced the burn, or one ball made another roll, there was a logical *must* in the situation; the effect *had* to happen; we could see that once the cause occurred, the result *could* not have been otherwise.

Hume's reply was threefold. (1) If it is true that we have this idea of necessity, we must be able to point to the sensation that gave rise to it. Now a logical relation of this kind is not the sort of thing that could be seen or heard or smelt or otherwise sensed at all. Hence, never having sensed it, we have no copy of it in the way of an idea. We only delude ourselves if we think we have. (2) Hume undertook to confirm this view by means of a rapid survey. There were three types of situation in which causality appeared, and he sought to show that necessity was to be found in none of them. (*a*) Cause and effect might both be physical, as when the rolling of one ball made another roll. We have seen already how he handled this. What we are experiencing is the fact of sequence, not the necessity of it; the necessity ascribed only reflects the firmness of our habit of expectation. (*b*) Cause and effect may both be mental; the thought of Theodore Roosevelt 'suggests by association' the thought of Franklin Roosevelt. But in such association of ideas, which is no doubt a fact, is there any logical necessity? If we think of the first Roosevelt, *must* we go on to think of the second? Obviously not, and of course we often do not in fact. (*c*) A physical event may cause a mental one, or a mental a physical one. (i) A flame, to take our former example, may cause a burning sensation. Now we have no doubt that flames have been followed by burning sensations, or that they will continue to be. But do we see that they *must* produce them, in the same transparent way in which we can see that the diameter of a circle must cut it in equal halves? Clearly not. The question why?, asked about this latter statement, would be pointless, since we have already reached the necessity which the question why? is asking. But between the action of the flame on the finger and the feeling of a burning sensation there is a long series of intermediate steps about any one of which, let alone the series as a whole, we could perfectly well ask why. And if we did, we should not get a glimmering of an answer. Why a change in the skin on our fingertips should be followed by the mental event called pain lies in total darkness. (ii) Nor do we seem to be better off as to the action of mind on body. We will to lift our hand and the hand comes up, and it may be thought captious to make a mystery of it. But after all, familiarity is not intelligibility. Hume pointed out that if the volition was to make our arm move, it must somehow affect the motion of the atoms in our heads, and that there was no profounder mystery in the world than how it did this; we are as ignorant of the process as we should be if our wish were to move mountains or enable beggars to ride.

(3) Hume offered a third argument which he thought clinched the case completely. This was a *reductio ad absurdum* designed to show that the cause-effect relation could not possibly contain the ground-consequent or implying relation. Take any case of logical implication, for example that in which being the diameter of a given circle implies that it cuts the circle in half. If you know that the 'halves' of the circle before you are not equal, you know that the line cannot be a diameter; in logical jargon, $(p \supset q . \sim q) \supset \sim p$; to deny the consequent and still affirm the antecedent is held to be self-contradiction. Now is there any self-contradiction in saying that the effect in a causal sequence might not have occurred, while the cause occurred nevertheless? None whatever. There is no contradiction in supposing that I make the same volition that has always caused my arm to rise, and that nothing happens. If this were self-contradictory, it would be strictly inconceivable, whereas it is perfectly easy to conceive; indeed it is what actually occurs when the man with paralysis wills to lift his arm. Can the effect equally be conceived without the cause? Undoubtedly, Hume would reply. It is entirely conceivable that the second billiard ball should roll away by itself, or should suddenly secede from the universe, or start talking Hebrew. To say that this is improbable is to miss the point. What is alleged is that it is logically impossible, and this it clearly is not, since such an impossibility could not be conceived, and this quite obviously can.

For Hume and his many followers, such considerations were decisive. It seemed clear to them that causation had no necessity about it. The linkage that it supplies between events is not intelligible in the sense that entailment is intelligible; that two events should accompany each other is just as little necessary as the chance that two dice should both fall with a six up. The man who argued that because one die showed a six the next must do so too would be regarded as absurd; and he would really be arguing with equal absurdity if he held that because one event happens any other event *must* happen. Nor does the fact that, so far as we know, events of this kind have always gone together make any difference in principle. The fact that snow has always been white does not make it more intelligible *why* it is white, or less thinkable that it should be black or purple. Regularities we can admit. But there is no ground whatever for converting these regularities into necessities. All that we can sensibly mean by saying that A causes B is that whenever there occurs an event of the kind A—defined as precisely as possible—it is followed by an event of the kind B—defined with similar care. And this is what is meant by the 'uniform-sequence' view.

What are we to say of this defence? It evidently depends on three propositions: first, that all our ideas come from sense; second, that we never apprehend necessity as having a part in causation; third, that cause and effect may be dissociated without contradiction. I may as well say at once that no one of these arguments, as stated, seems to me convincing.

5. (1) No doubt Hume is right that a relation of necessity cannot be touched, seen, or tasted, indeed is not a sense content of any kind. But the conclusion that we never find it in our experience of nature does not follow unless in conjunction with the further premise that our experience of nature is wholly sense experience. And to say that is to beg the question. For the contention of the non-Humians is that they do in fact apprehend (if not by sense, then by some other appropriate faculty such as reason or intelligence) necessary connections between certain sensibly presented qualities. It is no sufficient answer to this to say that experience is confined to sense qualities. Whether it is so confined is precisely the point at issue.

The question, then, is whether we do find in experience nonsensible necessities. And it seems plain enough that we do. Here are six or eight of them chosen at random: that this scarlet patch is more like this crimson patch than like that azure patch; that this surface cannot at once be blue and red; that this pink shade is a colour; that the space between the ends of this ruler can be divided without limit; that any two leaves on that tree and any other two make four; that these two lines do not enclose a space; that if this triangle has equal sides it has equal angles; that this sweet taste is different from that

P

sour one. This last example is extremely simple, and if admitted, it will carry necessity right through our perceptual world. And does it not have to be admitted? What we mean by 'sweet' is not the same as not being sour, but if any taste is sweet it excludes sourness, not in fact merely, but necessarily. The world of perceptual experience is honeycombed with necessary involvements and exclusions. Hume's suggestion that since ideas come from experience, they must all come from sense experience turns on a pre-judgment of what experience is like.

6. (2) It will be convenient to look next at the third argument. This is that if causality involves necessity, then a denial of the consequent would, as in hypothetical reasoning, commit us to denying the antecedent, whereas in this case it does not. We can perfectly well imagine the second billiard ball's not rolling while supposing the first to behave normally, or the failure of our arm to rise, though we make the customary volition. If the cause entailed the effect, we should see that, given the antecedent, the consequent *had* to happen; to say this and also to admit that sometimes it does not happen should be merely to contradict oneself. Yet no such contradiction is involved.

Now note, to begin with, that the argument is stated, following Hume, in terms of imagination. We can *imagine* the first ball's rolling without the second doing so; we can *imagine* resolving to lift an arm and the arm's not rising. But the question whether, given a set of conditions, something might have happened other than what did happen is not to be settled by asking whether we can imagine it to have happened. It is likely enough that we can, but that proves nothing beyond the liveliness of our imagination. I can imagine myself stealing off to a work-room in the cellar and emerging with a perpetual motion machine; I can imagine myself spending an evening over figures and diagrams and showing the world next morning that at last the circle has been squared. But the ability to imagine such events does not show that they are in fact possible. This depends on whether they are consistent with certain conditions, consistent in the second instance with the postulates of geometry and in the first instance with the laws of mechanics. It may be said that the laws of mechanics at least are themselves empirical only, so there would be no inconsistency in supposing them suspended. But whether they are or not is hardly a point to be settled by appeal to the imagination. If a scientist maintained that there was something in the nature of matter that rendered Newton's three laws of motion necessary, we could not refute him by imagining a ball to cease rolling when there is no obstruction or to turn suddenly into a cow and leap over the moon.[1]

7. Whether causality involves necessity can be tested only by a case in which the cause and the effect are conceived clearly and distinctly and one then asks oneself whether the first conception entails the second. A causal law, whether stating a uniform sequence or an entailment, is always a statement that something of the *kind* A causes something of the *kind* B, and a kind is something conceived rather than imagined, as is also the linkage of kinds. Now just as the disproof that such linkage is necessary is not to be found in imagination, so also it is not to be found in actual cases. At first we seem to have such a case in the paralysed man who wills to lift his arm without result. If the cause entails the effect, it is argued, we should be able to see that the arm *must* rise, but since it does not, we have here a clear case in which the cause does not necessitate the effect. But the example proves nothing. For if the arm does not rise, then even in the uniform-sequence view, what we have is not a case of cause and effect at all; the failure of the 'effect' to follow shows that the sequence is not uniform, and therefore not causal. Indeed the uniform-sequence theory cannot hope to disprove the entailment theory by instances in which cause and effect are disjoined, for if they are thus disjoined, they are *ipso facto* not cause and effect.

If the entailment theory is to be disproved, then, it must be not through an imagined or actual disjoining of cause and effect, but through a conceived disjoining. The critic must produce a case in which two events are admitted to be causally related and in which we have a clear and complete apprehension of the connected terms; and we must then be able to see that no necessity connects them. In the abstract, this test may seem easy to apply. Unfortunately it is very hard to apply, for the reason that the full and clear grasp of either cause or effect is itself so difficult to achieve. The critic produces a sample in which cause and effect, though never disjoined in fact, seem divorceable in theory, only to find, when challenged, that the true cause or effect or both have not yet been arrived at. It is not improbable, indeed, that one ground for doubt whether A is really the cause is the inability to see any reason why it should produce B. At any rate, as long as there remains an interval not bridged by any

---

[1] Speaking strictly, we must admit that the logically impossible is unimaginable as well as inconceivable. If Flatland or a square equal in area to a given circle is not logically possible, one cannot imagine it in full detail. I am using 'imagination' here in its looser popular sense.

visible necessity, the reflective mind continues to look further. Perhaps the commonest of these intervals are those presented, on the one hand, by space and time, and on the other, by the increasing complexity of the cause as we study it.

8. Consider how we reject an antecedent as the cause until it achieves approximate identity with the effect. A man gets malaria, and we say that he has been bitten by an anopheles mosquito. Of course there is nothing in such a bite, so far as we can see, to make malaria necessary. But then are we quite clear that the bite *is* the cause? It clearly happens at times without an ensuing malaria. The disease must be caused by something nearer to it in time and space. This would seem to be the pouring into the bloodstream, by means of the bite, of a mass of parasites called *plasmodia*. But we cannot stop here either. The mere presence of the parasites in the bloodstream is not the cause; they may be present while their host shows no sign of the disease. They must not only be present; they must attack the red blood corpuscles in the stream. But even this is not the proximate cause, for there is still a temporal interval between it and the appearance of the recognized forms of the disease. Following the attacks of the parasites, the blood corpuscles are systematically drained of their haemoglobin. Is this, then, the cause? It is natural enough to say so, but we might still intelligibly ask, Could not this happen and the disease still not happen? So we again move nearer to the effect. Since haemoglobin is the means by which oxygen is conveyed to the tissues, its disappearance means that these tissues are starved and cannot function. Here at last we have reached a condition which cannot occur without the occurrence of the disease. But then this condition *is* the disease; this starvation of bodily tissues is the essential constitutive factor in it. As long as the series of changes presents us merely with state A followed unintelligibly by a different state B, we continue to hunt for a cause that will somehow bridge the gap in both necessity and time.

9. Consider again how, with reflection, we broaden the scope of the cause. We begin by taking it as the efficient or precipitating cause, that is, the one change occurring immediately before the effect and in proximity with it. What caused the gun to go off was pulling the trigger; what caused the window to break was the impact of the stone; what caused malaria was the bite of the mosquito, or some other event known to physicians that preceded the disease more closely. But if the cause of an event includes that without which the event would not have happened, it includes much besides the efficient cause. 'The real cause of the phenomenon,' as Mill recognized, 'is the assemblage of all its conditions.'[1] A man's contracting malaria has many conditions that no one would think worth mentioning, but are as essential to what happened as anything that an expert would point out. If the patient had no air to breathe, if gravitation did not hold him to the earth, if the sun did not provide him with a certain amount of warmth, if any one of dozens of co-operating organs in his body were not functioning in its normal way, if his prevailing cast of mind were more sanguine or melancholic, the course of his disease would not be precisely what it is. Each one of these is what is called a necessary condition of the disease's occurring as it did. When all of them are put together, they form the sufficient condition. And it is the sufficient condition that is here meant by the cause.

It will now perhaps be apparent why it is so difficult to show that causality does not involve necessity, even if it does not in fact. The critic would have to ascertain and clearly conceive the sufficient cause on the one hand and the total proximate effect on the other, and he would have to show that though these two were never in fact dissociated from each other, there were no reasons why they should not be, since there was no necessity lurking within this uniformity or behind it. This is an impossible undertaking. It would require one to prove a negative by exhausting in thought the nature of the cause and the effect, and we have just seen two reasons why this is impracticable. We never reach the proximate cause of anything, since between any alleged cause and effect an intermediate state exists, and since the cause as the sum of the conditions is too complex to be exhausted. Hume's argument, then, to show that causation excludes necessity carries little conviction. That argument was that whereas in a case of genuine necessity the denial of the consequent committed us by clear necessity to denying the antecedent, in a case of cause and effect we could always deny the effect and see that there was *no* necessity constraining us to deny the cause. But any such negative insight would require a knowledge of the terms and their sequence that we do not in fact possess.

10. (3) It is possible that our knowledge, while unable to support a sweeping negative, might still suffice to show positive traces of a necessary connection. Hume's remaining argument is aimed at this possibility and attempts to explain all such traces away. They are really projections upon the object of a habit or tendency in our own

---

[1] *System of Logic*, Bk. III, Ch. 5, Sec. 3.

mind, which has no necessity about it. This projection theory has so often been effectively dealt with that I do not propose to linger over it.[1] I shall follow another line that has seldom been taken. Critics of Hume have often held that he was wrong about the projection, but right about what was projected, since there was really no necessity to project. I think the reverse is the truth, that in the sequence of our ideas a genuine necessity can often be found, and that it is legitimate to surmise something like it in the sequence of physical events.

11. Consider a case of inference in which one arrives at a new conclusion following logically from the premises. The emergence of the conclusion in our thought is of course an event with causes and conditions, which are as little exhaustible as those of a physical event. But there is a striking feature in such a sequence: we can see that the logical relation connecting premise with conclusion is also one of the conditions that govern the temporal succession; it had a part in the emergence of the conclusion as a psychical event. Take a very simple case. A person is presented with an arc of regular curvature and asked to complete it. He completes it into a circle; why? He could have drawn a hundred other lines, but he may not even feel tempted to do so, and may go straight to his result. If asked to explain why he chose this line rather than others, he will probably say that he had no alternative, that if he were to continue the curve he started with, he could do so in only one way. On the logical point he is clearly right; the curve he started with did appoint its continuation in the sense that if its curvature were to be maintained, it could be extended in one way only. But it may be held that this necessary relation between the two segments of the curve had nothing whatever to do with the emergence in his mind of the pattern of its completion. Such a denial seems to me at odds with introspectable fact. The natural thing to say is that he completed the curve as he did because the character of the given curve *required* it. And this 'because' is not a merely logical because. It conditioned the factual sequence itself. The logical nexus had something to do with channeling the thought in one direction rather than another. This supplies the most natural and enlightening answer to the question why the line was continued as it was.

It may be objected that this is not a typical inference, since the conclusion is only implicit in the act of extending the line, and that an example of explicit and full blown inference would be more

---

[1] For an older criticism, see T. H. Green's *Works*, Vol. I, 270 ff. For a more recent criticism, see C. J. Ducasse, *Nature, Mind and Death*, Ch. 7.

helpful. Very well, let us take such an example.[1] One is presented with two straight lines crossing each other at any angle. Are the opposite angles, say A and B in the figure below, equal, or are they not? They may look equal, but are they really so? One begins to

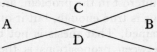

reflect. The line on which A and C are angles is a straight line, and therefore A and C add up to 180 degrees. The other line, on which C and B are angles, is also straight, and therefore C and B add up to 180 degrees. A equals 180 degrees minus C. B also equals 180 degrees minus C. That means that they must be equal. The equality of the angles has emerged as a new and necessary insight from the data before us.

Now the steps in this reasoning are a succession of judgments occurring in time. Each asserts a proposition and the logical relations that link these propositions with the conclusions are valid timelessly. Does it make sense to say that timeless relations holding between the propositions asserted in a succession of judgments actually affect the course of that succession? Each person must decide this for himself. Let him suppose himself to be trying to answer the problem set, and to have the succession of simple insights we have described. He comes to see that angles A and B are less than 180 degrees by exactly the same amount, namely by the size of the angle C. It leaps into his mind that if that is true, then A and B themselves are equal. Why the leap to this particular conclusion? Present-day Humians tell us that the logical relation between the last step and the next to the last had nothing whatever to do with that last step's being taken; if the question Why? is a request for necessity, we are as much in the dark as to why the thinker took it as if he had made a judgment about the Spanish Armada or the rising cost of butter. What seems to me odd about this view is its firm refusal to decide the matter empirically; no one would say this kind of thing who took his cue from the observed facts of his own thinking rather than from an antecedent theory. When, having reached the final step, he asks himself why he took it, the only natural answer is that he took it because the preceding step led to it logically.

Why has this answer been so strenuously denied? Perhaps because it is seen as the thin edge of a rationalist wedge. At any rate it will be well to set out and briefly consider the main objections.

[1] It has been suggested by Max Wertheimer; cf. his *Productive Thinking*, 79 ff.

12. (1) First it is objected that the explanation is insufficient. Even if logical necessity does link the propositions asserted and even if this necessity somehow works, the emergence of the conclusion is surely conditioned by much else—for example the thinker's state of freshness or fatigue, his interest in the problem, and the normal functioning of his brain. This is true enough, but it quite mistakes the thesis that is being maintained. That thesis is not the absurd one that an abstract relation between propositions is the *sufficient* cause for a concrete event. It is the comparatively modest one that this relation is a *necessary* condition, which means that, except for this relation, that precise event would not have happened as it did.

The same objection is sometimes put in another way by saying that causation is being confused with causal law. An actual event is a concrete occurrence whose attributes and relations are inexhaustible, and its cause must be as concrete as itself; a causal law is a connection between attributes abstracted from these concrete wholes. To suppose that when one has stated an abstract law governing the occurrence of malaria, one has explained the actual event, is an illusion, for the obvious reason that there are so many features in the concrete event that the law leaves out. True enough again. But we shall not get very far if we reject every partial explanation on the ground that it does not explain wholly. The scientist thinks that he has gone some way towards explaining an event when he can bring it under a law that states a mere conjunction; we have certainly gone farther if we can see in that law a filament of necessity; but even here the event as a concrete whole is not explained. This we grant. But what follows? That we should accept nothing because we cannot have all? To see a necessary link between partial features is surely an insight worth achieving. It does explain so far as it goes.

13. (2) It has been objected that causality links events, and that a timeless relation is no event. When we say that A causes B, we normally mean by A some event that precedes B; any component of that cause will also be something that precedes B; and we are changing the meaning of 'cause' if we include in it timeless relations. There is some pith in this semantic comment. It may be that both the plain man and the scientist most commonly mean by 'cause' the efficient cause, the only conspicuous *change* occurring in the temporal and spatial neighbourhood of the effect. And of course if we begin by so defining 'cause', necessity will be excluded by stipulation. But such stipulation, as Mill pointed out, is highly arbitrary. It sacrifices to the dramatic what reflection shows to be essential. The stroke of the cue makes the billiard ball roll as it does; but neither would it roll in this way if the table were not level, or the air were not of a certain density, or gravitation were not exerting its normal pull. It is perfectly legitimate to use the word 'cause' in its philosophically more interesting sense of the sum of the conditions given which the effect will occur; and in the absence of any of which it will not occur. And if we do use the word in this sense, then the necessities linking the objects of our thought cannot be omitted. Granted that they do not provide the same *kind* of condition as antecedent events, or the presence of permanent bodies like the earth and the sun, still if they are *conditiones sine quibus non*, they belong as truly among the essential conditions as efficient causes themselves.

14. (3) It has been objected that what channels the inferential movement is not the logical relation itself, but our grasp or apprehension of that relation. If Socrates is a man and all men are mortal, then Socrates must be mortal; it is not because the premises entail this last proposition that we go on to assert it, but because we *see* that they entail it. This objection, sensible enough at first glance, is seen at a second glance to be worthless. We are trying to explain why a certain conclusion should present itself, and we are offered an explanation which assumes that the conclusion has presented itself already. To see that p implies q, we must clearly have q in mind as well as p. And when the question before us is how q came to appear there, it is no help to say it appeared there because it had already made its appearance. The explanation is circular.

15. (4) A cognate objection has been offered by Professor Hempel, who thinks the ascription of a causal role to logical relations 'an inherently obscure idea'. 'Surely Mr Blanshard must be using a metaphor—and I think a misleading one—when he speaks of an abstract, non-temporal ideal as getting hold of an artist and moulding his work, or of a timeless relation serving as the condition of a temporal passage.' We must look for the determinants of a man's line of thought to agencies within himself. What moves him to follow a logical line is not the logical connections in the subject matter, but a 'certain disposition, namely that of acting in accordance with the standard'.[1] Now in turning from necessities to dispositions are we really moving from obscurity into light? I doubt it. 'Disposition' may mean various things. (*a*) In our case of the intersecting lines, to say that I have a disposition to think of the angles A and B as equal may

[1] *Determinism and Freedom*, ed. by Sidney Hook, 162.

mean that in point of fact I always, or usually, think this thought after I have taken the preceding steps. No doubt I do, but the question still remains, Why? It is not enough to offer in explanation the fact to be explained. (*b*) To explain through a disposition may mean that as a result of repetition I have acquired a *habit* of passing to the final thought upon completion of the earlier steps. The disposition at work will then be of the same type as leads me, after saying 'do, re, mi' to go on with 'fa'. This sort of explanation was once accepted by associationists, even for a priori thinking, and it amounts to a denial that such thinking takes place at all. It has been dealt with so often that we do not feel called upon to traverse the ground again.[1] And it would be particularly needless to do so here, since Professor Hempel rejects this antiquated empiricism as emphatically as any rationalist would. (*c*) A disposition may mean a capacity. The disposition to infer the equality of the angles from the preceding propositions would be the power to make the inference, once the figure is presented and the problem set. Unfortunately this does not help either. The fact that one *can* do something does not help to explain why one does it, and is equally consistent with one's not doing it. The question is: Granted that a man has the requisite intelligence, why is it that when he is set a geometrical problem he may never have faced before, he comes up with one special and valid answer rather than any one of a thousand others? If he does it, we know of course that he can do it, that he has the requisite intelligence to do it. But our question remains unanswered. We want to know what guided that intelligence down the particular track it took. And how could we answer more faithfully to fact than by saying that his intelligence was responding to, and following, certain necessities in its subject-matter. He did not fabricate these himself. He may attend or not attend, but he cannot make them otherwise by any act of will; they are in some sense there to be apprehended and adhered to. His intelligence, that is, his capacity for apprehending them, is indeed a condition of his thinking as he does, but this intelligence would have no direction if cut off from the structures that form its objects.

(*d*) The only other relevant sense of 'disposition' I can think of is drawn from *Gestalt* psychology. Experimenters of this school have shown that our interest in certain regular figures like circles and squares is not due to association merely, but is in a sense inborn. When presented a field of dots or stars distributed at random, we tend to find in them these simple patterns, and if given fragments of

---

[1] One need only refer to the names of Green, Bradley, and Cook Wilson. I have tried to set out the argument in some detail in *The Nature of Thought*, II, Chap. 28.

the patterns we tend to complete them into these regular wholes. Now the 'disposition' to do such things is again ambiguous. If it means a native or unacquired interest in some figures rather than others, it has no obvious bearing on our problem. If it means a tendency to complete fragments into certain types of whole because of this natural interest, it looks as if it might have a bearing. But we must distinguish once again. To complete a fragment into a pattern because one likes or prefers that pattern is not reasoning, nor is it very plausible to say that our reasoning in logic and mathematics reduces to a large-scale indulgence of instinctive pattern-preferences. If this were true, it would be a puzzle why such reasoning should give us knowledge, and why one should not cultivate opposite preferences if one wished. But it is clear that not all Gestaltist dispositions are of this kind. In genuine reasoning, necessity is not the plaything of non-rational preferences; there is a genuine 'requiredness' in the object of thought, and inference is under the constraint of this requiredness. Wertheimer has described many cases in which the thinker is really doing what he would naturally say he was doing, namely following the argument where it leads. If such guidance of the steps of inference is to be included in the work of dispositions, we should agree with Mr Hempel in using them as the chief element in our explanation. But, so conceived, they are not alternatives to necessity. They include it; indeed without it they are as blind as moles.

16. (5) Several critics of the necessity view have offered an argument which has been very clearly stated by Professor Pap:

'. . . if implications have such causative force—directing the movement of thought the way a river bed directs the flow of water—they must have it whether the thinker sees them or not. Yet it is notorious that we may think of a set of premises and not see what follows from them or draw the wrong conclusion from them.'[1]

One can only think that this criticism has been made under a misapprehension, since it invites so obvious a reply. This misapprehension we have met already in the first criticism above, and we must try again to scotch it. If the necessity linking premise and conclusion were offered as the *sufficient* condition of the conclusion's appearance, then the failure of that appearance, or the occurrence of

[1] Arthur Pap in *Determinism and Freedom*, ed. by S. Hook, 204. Cf. *ibid.*, 169 (Mr Hook), 162 (Mr Hempel), and E. Nagel, *Sovereign Reason*, 287–8.

some other judgment instead, would of course refute the theory decisively. And for all I know, this theory may have been urged by someone; I can only plead not guilty myself. To make necessity the sufficient condition of a train of thought is to make the thinker a disembodied intellectual machine controlled by the drive-wheels of logic. No such monster has ever existed. If Archimedes at a triumphant moment cried, 'Eureka', it may have been in part because he had had a good night or a large draught of the Syracusan equivalent of coffee. If these were necessary conditions for the achieving of his insight, the famous cry would not have been heard without them, even though all the data for the solution were there. But what does this prove? Only that other conditions besides the necessities in his subject-matter were needed if his thought were to function effectively. This no one would deny. It has no tendency to show that when he did reach the solution, its entailment by the data before him had nothing to do with his reaching it. In short, the criticism assumes that if necessity plays any part in inference it must play the whole part; and there is no good ground for this whatever.

What if the thinker draws the wrong conclusion? The answer is the same. There are other factors at work besides the necessity in the subject-matter, and when inference goes astray, these are in control. There is nothing in this inconsistent with saying that necessity sometimes *is* in control. To draw a wrong conclusion is, strictly speaking, not to reason wrongly, but not to reason at all; it is to engage in a process that simulates reasoning while following the track of association or prejudice—an unhappily common experience. 'Man thinks not always', as Locke said, even when he seems to be doing so. But the fact that some idea-sequences are irrational does not show that all of them are. It merely attests that, as human beings, we are still brokenly and imperfectly rational.

This criticism becomes more important if interpreted in another way, which most critics of the theory seem to have missed. In a world in which causality involves necessity, how could errors and inconsequences occur at all? Suppose that someone makes an untrue judgment. This judgment is an event; as such, it has been caused; and on our theory the event follows by necessity from preceding events. The false judgment, then, is as genuinely necessary as the true. If John says that p is true, and James says that it is false, both judgments are necessary, and both are necessitated by the nature of things. Both, therefore, must be true. And this is self-contradiction.

I do not think it is. The appearance of contradiction lies in the confusion of a necessary proposition with a necessary judgment, the necessitation of a proposition with that of a psychical event. In the first case, interpreted in our way, two propositions, a premise and a conclusion, are linked by implication, and because of this linkage, when the first presents itself in the mind of the thinker it facilitates his passage to the second. The necessary nexus does, to be sure, link the two judgments as psychical events, but solely through linking their cognitive objects. If the inference is really determined by the implication thus linking its objects, it will be valid, and if its premises are true, its conclusion must be true. Now turn to the other case, in which a false judgment has been made. It is possible that this too has arisen through valid inference, this time from a false premise. But either in the judgment or in the premise we shall find ourselves with something whose appearance must be explained on different principles from that of the conclusion just described, namely a judgment that is not a *conclusion* at all. It is not a judgment that has arisen under constraint from any cognitive necessity, but one whose chief roots lie in the psycho-physical organism and may well be involved with a tangled mass of likes, antipathies, and desires. So far as a man judges falsely, we say that he is not under the influence of reason, or that his thought is determined not by reasons but by causes. This puts the matter helpfully. What should be added, on our theory, is that these causes are not in principle unintelligible. If we knew enough, we could see that, given James's heredity, his past experience, his thyroid deficiency, and so on, the cropping up of that stupid suggestion in his mind was necessary. It is thus correct to say that John's true judgment and James's false judgment are both necessitated. There is no contradiction in saying so because the necessitation in the two cases operates from different bases, one of which does not require the truth of the consequent. The necessitation in the first case operates from presumably true premises to produce a conclusion through valid inference. In the second case it operates, not from premises, but from 'non-rational' factors, perhaps deeply buried from knowledge in the body and mind of the agent, to produce what we call an 'irrational' belief. Though the judgments are contradictory, our account of their origins is not.

17. (6) The most popular argument against the necessity view is, as one might expect, that it confuses implication with inference.[1] Of course the two are profoundly different. Implication is a timeless relation connecting propositions. Inference is a temporal, psychological

[1] It is offered, for example, by Ernest Nagel, *Sovereign Reason*, 288–9, by Durant Drake, *Invitation to Philosophy*, 372, and by many others.

passage from one judgment to another. Implication is objective, in the sense that it holds whether we recognize it or not. Inference is subjective, in the sense that it is a process in our own mind. The items linked by implication are not, in the ordinary sense, existents; the propositions of Euclid, for example, are neither things nor events. On the other hand, the items linked by inference, commonly called judgments, are actual mental occurrents. No one will accuse us, so far, of confusing the two kinds of connection. What is it exactly that provokes the charge? It is our contention that implication, though different from inference, may serve as a causal component within it. We hold that the necessity linking propositions together does sometimes account causally for the inference's taking one path rather than another, and that the explanation of the temporal passage is therefore not complete unless this timeless relation is introduced. There is no evident confusion here, though some confusion does seem to be discernible in the minds of critics. They offer examples of a proposition's presenting itself without being followed by an implied sequel, of the consequent's appearing with no antecedent announcing it, and of both presenting themselves successively without any inferential passage; and they say that these things could not possibly be if implication ever really participated in inference. We freely admit that all these things take place, and add merely that the admission leaves our theory intact. To elaborate this after all that has been said would only bore the reader. The charge of confusion between implication and inference itself rests on a confusion as to the identity of the culprit.

18. (7) One final point before leaving this debate. When I briefly stated the necessity view in my book on *The Nature of Thought*, I added that unless this view were true, 'no conclusions are ever arrived at *because* the evidence requires them', and that this was inconsistent with an assumption we always make in arguing with men supposed to be reasonable. We set before them the evidence that has constrained us to accept a proposition and assume that it will, or at least may, move them to a like acceptance. Professor Nagel agrees with me as to the importance of this kind of reasonableness, but thinks it possible to hold to it without going to the extreme of assigning necessity an actual part in the causal process.

'A man who first notes a premise A, and then perceives that A logically implies B, *is* moved by reasons when he accepts B on the evidence of the premise—even if the causal sequence, the thought of

A, the perception of the connection between *A* and *B*, the assertion of *B*, is a logically contingent one. Such a thinker might not assert *B* did he not *perceive* the connection between *A* and *B*; and his *perception* of this connection is doubtless one of the factors which causally determine his thought and acceptance of *B*. But is there any reason for maintaining that if the connection between this factor and the effect attributed to it is a logically contingent one, its manifest operation is illusory?'[1]

Let us see what the theory here suggested involves. A man is engaged in a process of reasoning; starting with a belief that A is true, he sees that A entails B, and therefore accepts B; then that B entails C, and therefore accepts C; then that C entails D; and therefore accepts D. Mr Nagel's theory of the process appears to be this: thought leaps in a contingent way from point to point in its advance, but once it has reached a new point, it can look back and see that between its present position and the point just left there is a necessary connection. As a result of seeing this connection, it accepts the new proposition; then uses it as the base for another contingent leap which will be similarly seen to be justified on arrival and review. There are two comments to be made.

(*a*) When, by a process in which necessity has played no part, the thought of A has given rise to the thought of B, the thinker sees that A entails B, and because of this insight, we are told, he accepts B; 'his *perception* of this connection is doubtless one of the factors which causally determine his thought and acceptance of B'. This can hardly be correct. It cannot be the perception of the connection that 'determines his *thought*' of B; for he cannot perceive a connection between A and B without having the thought of B already; we have paid our respects earlier to this circular explanation. Leaving this aside, however, we read that it is the grasp of this connection which determines his *acceptance* of B. Now his acceptance of B is a psychological act, and the presentation of a timeless logical connection is said to have 'determined' this act. This concedes in principle the main point that is being demurred to, namely that a timeless necessity can determine a psychological event. It may be replied that what determined the acceptance was not the necessity apprehended but the apprehension of it. This might mean (i) that when a thought works causally, it is the bare contentless act of apprehension that works, and hence that it makes no difference what the thought is about. I do not think this is plausible or that Mr Nagel would so

[1] *Sovereign Reason*, 290.

regard it. If what works in the mind is the apprehension of necessity, then the necessity apprehended must be one element of what works. Without this element the mere apprehension would neither be what it is nor work as it does. Or what might be meant is (ii) that if the content or object is taken into account, it must be the ostensible object only; it need not be real necessity that is present, but only what appears to us as necessity. This too will not bear examination. It would mean that when we accept, for example, $2+2$ as equalling 4, we never do so because $2+2$ are really equal to 4, but only because they seem to be so. Such a theory would indeed imply that we never grasp necessity at all—the necessity that really links concepts and propositions. It is never this necessity that moves our acceptance or works in our minds, but some surrogate of it confined to the psychological order. This theory would lead to a profound sort of scepticism which I cannot think that Mr Nagel would care to embrace. But if he is to avoid it, I see no alternative to the admission that non-temporal necessities contribute to the causing of temporal events.

(b) Still, all he would have admitted, even so, is that a seen necessity contributes to our *acceptance* of B. He has not admitted that the necessity linking A with B has contributed to B's following A in our thought. He would hold, I take it, that if we are asked to continue the sequence 2, 4, 8, 16, in accord with the rule of this series, and we answer with '32', the logical necessity of 32 as the next step in the series had nothing to do with our leap to the thought of that number; the leap is wholly contingent. *After* we have reached the number by this contingent leap, we can see that it really is next in the series and can accept it as such. Then, using it as a new basis, and seeking to go on, we manage to say '64', though again we must say that it is as strictly unintelligible how we got there as if we had said '1776' or 'the Queen of Sheba'. To explain in terms of habit would not render the connection intelligible, even if such an explanation were generally available in these cases, which it is not. What is Mr Nagel's own explanation of the inferential movement? He hints that in such a sequence the thinker is really carried along 'by the happy working of his own body', and he is content to think that in this 'happy working' there is nothing but contingency. One can only envy him the ownership of so co-operative a body. It continues in accommodating fashion, though always by pure contingency, to throw up suggestions which when examined are found to be connected necessarily with premises just entertained, but since there are no necessities at work in the body, the fact that one judgment follows on another logically as well as temporally must be set down as happy accident. In spite of his modest avowals, I cannot believe that Mr Nagel's thinking is composed of such a chapter of accidents; it seems to me more firmly directed than that. How one would *prove* to him that he is not the beneficiary of so large a bounty of mere fortune I do not know. All one can do is to urge him to examine his thought at first hand and to report what he actually sees, not what he ought to see on the assumptions of a naturalistic metaphysic.

19. We have dealt at such length with necessity in inference because this is the region in which we can most clearly see it at work in causation. Not that we are wholly in the dark as to why causation moves as it does in other regions of the mind; I do not think it is utterly unintelligible, for example, why a person should fear death, or why he should grieve at the loss of a friend. But we must surely admit Hume's contention that through the larger part of the known world—he would say all of it—the nature of the causal process is at present impenetrable to us. We do not know why a volition moves a muscle, or why a burn hurts, or why a nail sinks at the blow of a hammer. Is it reasonable to believe that there is necessity in such behaviour, in spite of our failure to detect it? I think it is, and shall try to state the chief grounds for thinking so.

20. (1) The first is that, hard as it may be to accept the necessity thesis, it is still harder to accept the alternative. Scientists sometimes say that uniformity is all they need or want. Perhaps it is; their interest is in the discovery of laws, not in the explanation of why laws should be what they are. Nevertheless uniformity cannot by itself be the whole story, for if it were, there would not be even that. Let us suppose for a moment that between two events, A and B, there is no sort of constraint or inner connection, no reason why B should follow rather than anything else. If this were true, B's regular attendance upon A would be a miracle. With no ground for its appearance in the nature of anything preceding it, B's occurrence along with A would be a matter of chance, and if we made any calculations about it, they would have to be based on the theory of chance. This theory is clear enough in simple cases. Suppose we throw a die and get a 3. We then ask what the chances are that we shall get a 3 on the next throw. They are 1 in 6. What are the chances that we shall get two successive 3's? They are 1 in 36. The probability that we should get any of the numbers on the die n times in succession is $\dfrac{1}{6n}$, and it is obvious that this fraction dwindles with enormous speed as one goes on. In an

Q

actual game with dice where it was important to get 3's, how long should we be willing to assume that nothing but chance was involved if an opponent continued to get them? Suppose he got 3's three times in succession. The odds against that are 215 to 1, and we should regard him as remarkably lucky. Suppose he got five 3's running; the odds against that are 7775 to 1, and we should certainly grow suspicious. A few more such successes, and we should be confident that either he or the dice or both were in need of rigorous inspection.

Now suppose that one billiard ball hits another which rolls away, and suppose there is no link whatever between these events but chance conjunction. If that were true, the likelihood that the second ball would behave in that way again when struck by the first will have to be calculated, if at all, by the theory of chances. It is true that since the ball could behave not in one of six ways only but in any one of an unlimited number of ways, the chances are not definitely calculable; but we can see that the odds against a single repetition would be enormous, and the odds against this repetition continuing would be enormous beyond conception. Yet it is just this constant repetition that we actually find. It continues not merely for a few cases, or a few hundred ones, but so far as we can see, through an inexhaustible series of cases. To suggest that this constant accompaniment is a matter of chance is to abuse the meaning of the word. If it were a matter of chance in the strict sense, the lawfulness we find in nature would simply not be there. Something more is clearly at work.

21. (2) If asked what this is, we can only say that it is some kind of necessity. Here we shall probably meet the question, 'How can you insist that necessity is present and also admit that you cannot see it? When you say that the diameter bisects a circle or that what has shape has size, you can say that necessity is present because you do see it; you are laying hold of what is self-evident. When you say that the causal connection is necessary, one assumes that you can point to something that is similarly self-evident. But you have just admitted that causal connections throughout the physical and psycho-physical realm are entirely opaque to us.'

We have granted, it is true, that we cannot generally see why the effect follows the cause. But that is not the same as to say that we wholly lack a priori insight into causation. I am inclined to follow Professor Broad in holding that we do have such insight. He thinks we know a priori several propositions that apply to the causation of changes generally.[1] (*a*) 'Every change has a cause.' It is perhaps not self-evident that the mere continuance of a process requires a special explanation—the continued resting of a ball, for example; but if anyone were to suggest to us that at some point the ball began to move, or increased the speed of its movement without any cause at all, we should say he must certainly be mistaken. (*b*) The second proposition goes on to say something about the natures of A and B, though what it says remains highly abstract. It says that 'the cause of any *change* contains a change as a factor. This seems to me as evident,' Broad adds, 'as any proposition that I have ever met with.' A change cannot come from nothing at all; *ex nihilo nihil fit*. Nor could it come from a state that remained unchanged through time, for then there would be nothing to account for its appearance at one time rather than another. We are convinced that there must be something to account for this, and that it can only be another change. Thirdly (*c*) 'if a change issues from a moment *t*, then all changes which are factors in its cause are changes which enter into *t*'. 'I think,' says Broad, 'that this proposition is the accurate expression of the common dictum that a cause must precede its effect and be continuous with it in time.'[2] (*d*) To these propositions I would add another, namely that the cause and the effect are linked through their characters, that it is in virtue of A's being a change of the character *a* that it produces B with the character *b*. This does not exclude the possibility of alternative causes of B. It does imply that if there are such causes, it is something in the nature of each of the alternate causes in virtue of which the effect is produced.

I am inclined to think that these are all a priori insights into causality. If they are, it is untrue to say that the causal relation is wholly opaque and impenetrable to us. Even if we do not know why a particular change produced another, we do have necessary knowledge about the causation of changes generally.

22. (3) Can we say anything more about the nature of this necessary knowledge? Here again we may start from Broad. 'It may be noticed,' he writes, 'that in English we have the three sentences, "Nothing has

[1] *Examination of McTaggart's Philosophy*, I, 232–235. In *The Philosophy of C. D. Broad* (ed. by P. A. Schilpp), 741–744, he offers a further analysis of some of these propositions.

[2] *Examination*, I, 233. Broad adds a fourth proposition about causality that seems to him self-evident: 'A given change in a given process issuing from a given moment cannot have more than one total cause.' But upon further analysis of this proposition in *The Philosophy of Broad*, 744, he writes that it seems not impossible that a change should have several co-existing total causes. I doubt therefore whether he would wish to hold to his original proposition.

Q*

φ and lacks ψ", "Nothing can have φ and lack ψ", and "Nothing could have had φ and lacked ψ". The first expresses a Universal of Fact, the second a Universal of Law, and the third an Absolute Necessity.'[1] The universal of fact, 'nothing has φ and lacks ψ', would be exemplified, I suppose, by the observation made by Darwin that tom-cats that are white and blue-eyed are also deaf. The universal of law, 'nothing can have φ and lack ψ', Broad illustrates by 'anything that had inertial mass would have gravitational mass'. Absolute necessity he illustrates by the proposition, 'anything that had shape would have extension'. To which of these types does a causal statement belong?

Suppose I decide to lift my arm, and the arm moves; here we should say that the decision caused the movement. Regarding this sort of sequence Broad says, 'I *know* that *this* change would not have issued from that moment unless *that* decision had entered into that moment.' If it is objected that my body might have been electrically stimulated to such behaviour, the statement may be amended by the addition 'if the other conditions were as I believed them to be'. Two points about this case should be noted, for when put together they make it clear why causality is such a puzzle to philosophers. On the one hand, the way mind acts on body is as mysterious as anything in our experience. On the other hand, if one can say, as Broad does, and perhaps most people would, 'I *know* that *this* change would not have issued from that moment unless *that* decision had entered into that moment', then one is claiming a very different kind of knowledge from that of a 'universal of fact'. To say of a tom-cat simply on the ground of its not being deaf, 'I *know* that it is not white and blue-eyed', would seem presumptuous, since between these characters we see no linkage except that they have in certain cases been found together. To say that I know that my arm would not have moved as it did if I had not decided to move it is certainly to claim more than that such events have regularly accompanied each other; it is to claim that the decision was a *necessary* condition of the movement. What sort of necessity belongs to such a condition?

Broad suggests only two types of necessity in terms of which it could be understood, the 'universal of law' and 'absolute necessity'. The universal of law he illustrates, as we have seen, by the connection between inertial mass and gravitational mass. What distinguishes this necessity from absolute necessity is that it is contingent in the following sense: though, given the structure of the actual world, a thing could not have the one kind of mass without having the other, still there *might have been* a world in which the one appeared without

[1] *Examination of McTaggart's Philosophy*, I, 243.

the other, whereas if the characters were connected by absolute necessity, there *could not have been* a world in which a thing had the one character (e.g. shape) without the other (e.g. extension).

Now it seems to me that the notion of contingent necessity is a half-way house in which we cannot rest. To be sure, it is a notion continually used in scientific and other explanation; to explain a fact, we bring it under a law; to explain the law, we show that it follows necessarily from a more general law, and the more general the better. But the necessity here lies merely in the linkage between the propositions, not in the propositions themselves; if the more general law is true, the less general follows, but there is no implication that the general law is itself a necessary truth, nor therefore that the derived truth is. Such explanation is of course valid, but it leaves the question of chief interest unanswered. Suppose we have traced our derivative laws back to ultimate laws; we explain the fall of a particular raindrop in the end by appeal to the law of gravitation. These ultimate laws will state principles on which the universe is constructed. To say that they are themselves contingently necessary would be meaningless, since there is nothing further on which they could be contingent. Of the three types of universal statement with which Broad provides us, then, only two are available; these ultimate principles must be either universals of fact, presumed to be mere conjunctions, or absolute necessities.

23. Confronted with this choice, we hold them to be absolute necessities. We cannot show them to be so by simple appeal to self-evidence. But there is other evidence available. Let us look again at the fourth of our a priori causal propositions. This was that if A produces B, it was in virtue of a linkage between the characters *a* and *b*. Now what could be meant by saying that A produces B *in virtue of* its character unless the character of A *determined* what was to emerge?

'If two plants, whose nature is really the same, can determine the growth of totally different seeds, how can we call either the seed *of* that plant at all? Grant that a seed may sometimes be produced by a plant of its own kind, and sometimes by a plant of another kind, without any difference of circumstances, and merely because causes do not act uniformly, and you have really granted that anything may produce anything; flint and steel may produce seed instead of a spark, and oil raise the waves or quench a conflagration. But to say that anything may produce anything is to empty the word "produce" of all its meaning. For the causal relation is a necessary relation, such that if you have one thing you *must* have another. To add that it does not matter what that other is, destroys the force of the *must*.'[1]

The point here is a simple one. To say that A produces B in virtue of its special nature *is* to assert necessity. If it is in virtue of a certain character in A and not of something else that B comes into being, then if B was not there, A was not there, and could not have been there. If it was in virtue of being belladonna that something dilated the pupil yesterday, then you know that if, under circumstances otherwise the same, something does not dilate the pupil today, it *cannot* be belladonna; to say that it might be would be to deny that belladonna *as such* acts in a certain way, which is what our causal statement meant. We should be saying that though it was of the nature of belladonna to dilate the pupil, nevertheless, since it sometimes fails to do so, it is *not* of its nature to do so. That is mere incoherence.

Joseph goes so far as to hold that to deny necessity in causation is to deny the law of identity itself. 'To assert a causal connection between *a* and *x* implies that *a* acts as it does because it is what it is; because, in fact, it is *a*. So long therefore as it is *a*, it must act thus; nd to assert that it may act otherwise on a subsequent occasion is to assert that what is *a* is something else than the *a* which it is declared to be.'[2] Now this is obviously true if the causal properties of a thing are introduced into its nature by definition. We often conceive things in terms of such properties. 'Glass is brittle, fusible, transparent, hard; gold is malleable, soluble in *aqua regia*, of a certain specific gravity, etc. Matter is impenetrable, mobile, etc. A man is wise, benevolent, quick-tempered, etc.'[3] These may all be taken as causal properties. If gold did not dissolve on being placed in *aqua regia* we should not call it gold because its so behaving is taken as a defining property of gold. But as Professor Stebbing pointed out, we do not commonly include in the nature of a thing all its causal properties.[4] A billiard ball has the causal property of being able to initiate motion in another billiard ball if it strikes it with a certain velocity, but this causal property, Miss Stebbing would say, forms no part of the nature of the ball as we ordinarily think of it. In this she seems to me right. She then goes on to argue that, for all we can see, it is a

---

[1] H. W. B. Joseph, *Introduction to Logic*, 2nd ed., 407.
[2] *Ibid.*, 408.
[3] G. F. Stout, *Studies in Philosophy and Psychology*, 305.
[4] *A Modern Introduction to Logic*, 285 ff.

completely external relation, that is, that the ball could still be precisely what it is if it did not have this property. Here I think she is mistaken. To include a causal property in the definition of a term is not the only way of arguing for its internality. Even if a thing *is* not its behaviour, still if we say that it behaves in this way in virtue of having this nature, that it is *such as* to behave in this way, then we are saying, I suggest, that it *could not* lack the causal property while possessing this nature. The roundness of the ball is a constitutive, not a behavioural property, but if it is in virtue of its roundness that the ball rolls, then a ball that was unable to roll would not be a ball.

24. I do not think that any of the three arguments we have offered, or all of them together, *prove* that the link between a particular cause and a particular effect involves necessity. It is just conceivable that the regularities in the world, though infinitely improbable on the theory of chances, are what Montague calls 'an outrageous run of luck'. It is conceivable that while we have some self-evident knowledge of causality generally, there remain enclaves of contingency in the occurrence of particular events. It seems barely possible that we are suffering from a deep and distorting illusion in thinking that A's acting as it does follows from its being what it is. We should be adducing more impressive evidence—granted—if we could show in a particular case of hammer and nail that the cause entails the effect, as we can show that being a triangle entails having angles equal to 180 degrees. This we cannot do. But 'C may perfectly well entail E without our being able to see that it does so, and we may have general grounds for assuming the presence of a logical necessity which we cannot grasp ourselves, or at least see that this assumption is really presupposed in all our scientific reasoning'.[1] It is the part of reasonableness to accept a conclusion, even when indemonstrable, if it makes sense of things and no alternative does.

---

[1] A. C. Ewing, *Idealism*, 167. For another defence of the view that 'natural laws are principles of necessitation', see W. Kneale, *Probability and Induction*, 70 ff.

CHAPTER XII

SOME INTIMATIONS OF COSMIC NECESSITY

1. We have found that nature is shot through with filaments of necessity. We have seen reason to believe that there is such a filament in the causal connection, whether at present we can dissect it out or not. These considerations suggest a final question: How much does the network of necessity include? Does it provide merely the formal framework of nature, within whose limits particular things are free to indulge in wanton liaisons and little explosions of waywardness, or is their particular nature and behaviour also involved in the network? That the universe is not a mere heap of things and events thrown together in hit-or-miss fashion, that it contains at the lowest estimate many extensive sub-systems, we have argued in some detail. But is it a single system? Granted that some things are related through a necessity linking their qualities, and that some events are related through the necessity implicit in causation, is there any good ground for holding that *all* things and events are inter-related necessarily?

2. Yes, there is impressive ground. Look first at the cosmic implications of causality. We commonly think of causality as linking one event with one other, as a string may link two beads. But on reflection we must go beyond that. (*a*) For one thing, the string is infinitely long with a infinite number of beads on it. A Yorkshireman shoots a gun at a bird and if the bird falls, he says that his shooting caused it. But between the fall of the bird and the pull on the trigger there is a line of intermediate causes, and behind the pull is another long line extending into an interminable past. (*b*) Any actual event is complex, and thus is the focus of a 'pencil of forces' coming in from many directions. The movement of the bullet is determined by the wind as well as by the charge in the gun, and that too has its line of causes. The wind that caused the deflection was caused perhaps by the low atmospheric pressure over the North Sea, which was connected in turn with a hurricane that a week before had crossed Siberia. (*c*)

Causal lines issuing from the same event may diverge to widely scattered events. A sportsman is shooting a gun in Yorkshire; a poet is writing a lyric in Bloomsbury; these events are different and seemingly unrelated. Both men however had ancestors who came over with the Conqueror, and it is safe to say that except for the Conqueror's action, neither would be where he is or doing what he is, if indeed he existed at all. (*d*) The two events are therefore causally connected, even though not connected directly. It would be strange to say that the sportsman's shooting in Yorkshire caused the poet's writing in Bloomsbury or vice versa. Nevertheless if one had not happened, neither probably would the other. Cancel the act of shooting, and you are committed to cancelling with it the sequence of causes that led up to it, including the action of the Conqueror, and if the Conqueror had not so acted, the sequence of causes leading to the poet's penning his lyric would likewise have to be cancelled. (*e*) Is it reasonable to hold that *all* events are thus bound up with each other causally? This is sometimes denied. We hear it said that events in the sun cannot be causally connected with simultaneous events on the earth, since even gravitation does not exceed the speed of light, and light takes some eight minutes to cover the distance. But this case does not differ in principle from the previous one. The two sets of events are connected, and connected causally, though in a round-about way. Events on the sun eight minutes ago are the common source of events on both sun and earth, and because they are connected through this intermediary, neither group of events could have failed to happen without consequences for the other. But of course indirect causal relations are always based on direct ones. The law of gravitation is a causal law by which every particle in the universe is linked directly with an infinite number of others. Sir James Jeans remarked that 'every body pulls every other towards it, no matter how distant it may be. Newton's apple not only exerted its pull on the earth, but every star in the sky, and the motion of every star was affected by its fall. We cannot move a finger without disturbing all the stars.'[1] It was an astronomer who wrote this, not a speculative philosopher. As Russell says, 'the world of physics is intended to be a causally interconnected world, and must be such if it is not to be a groundless fairy tale, since our inferences depend upon causal laws'.[2]

3. Russell appears to think that causal inferences may be valid, even though there is no necessity in them. In the world he has in mind,

[1] *The Stars in Their Courses*, 74.
[2] *The Analysis of Matter*, 325.

everything is connected with everything else by law, though the law is not itself necessary. We go with him about the interconnection, but go beyond him about necessity. The law of gravitation, precisely stated, would be a necessary law. It is worth meditating for a moment on what this implies. We do not understand how a wave motion, striking our retina, could induce a sensation of light, and nothing could seem more indifferent to us than minute changes occurring at some remote time on the surface of a distant star, yet we have reason to believe that a complete explanation of our present sensation as we look at the sky would involve both our own body and the star in one tissue of necessity. The sun is of obvious concern to us, since if it should cease to exist, human life on this planet would also cease to exist a few minutes later. But if we look at the Andromeda nebula, which can be just seen with the naked eye, our experience cannot be fully explained without taking into account what happened eighty-five hundred centuries ago in a place about four quadrillion, eight hundred trillion miles away. What happened there was in turn conditioned by the nebula's being there, which was itself conditioned by other events unimaginably distant in space and time. Thus the appearance of a pinpoint of light in one's visual field engages much of the known and unknown universe, and if we take into account the way in which lines of causation intercross, it is hard to escape the conclusion that every event in the universe is involved, directly or indirectly, in this one minute occurrence. In view of what physics tells us about the range of gravitational action, the burden of proof would seem to rest on anyone who denied this. Now if causality is a necessary relation, and necessity is in principle intelligible, the system that links all events together is an intelligible system. The argument is as simple as that.

Nevertheless there are many to whom the argument will seem unconvincing. Their objection will probably rest on one or other of two grounds. They may hold that in view of developments in quantum mechanics, we can no longer say that the law of causality applies to all changes in nature. The objection is an important one, and if examined adequately, would take us on a long excursion to the frontiers of physics. It raises an issue on which theoretical physicists are still locked in debate. Few persons—and certainly not the writer —are qualified to serve as umpire in this debate. But one may perhaps say that to a layman the arguments and the names (including such as Planck, Einstein, and Russell) supporting the unrestricted reigns of causality are at least as impressive as those on the other side; and it is more prudent to leave the brief in their hands. The other objection will probably be that causality, though universal, is not necessary, and that if necessity is claimed, it must be presented in visible and self-evident form. Regarding this we have said what we could in the last chapter. But we fully agree that the best attestation of necessity is self-evidence, and we shall rely on it where we can. Are there any arguments of a self-evident kind for saying that necessity links all things together?

4. We are confronted here with the tortured issue of internal versus external relations. If one is to show that everything is related necessarily to everything else, one must show that it is related *internally* to everything else. A given term is internally related to another if in the absence of the relation it could not be what it is. A term is externally related to another if the relation could equally be present or absent while the term was precisely the same. On this issue the obvious possibilities are three: (1) that everything is related externally to everything else, (2) that everything is related internally to everything else, (3) that neither of these extreme positions holds, but that some things are related internally, and some externally, to certain other things. It is clearly this last that is the position of common sense. To plain men, that is, to all of us when not philosophizing, it would seem absurd to say that the table is related internally to the book that lies on it, for the book could surely be absent while the table remained what it is. It seems almost equally absurd to say that everything is related only externally to everything else. Shakespeare had the relation of authorship to a set of plays; are we to say that if he had never set his hand to them and had followed the plough instead, he would have been precisely the mind that he was? That certainly calls for argument. The truth of the matter would seem to lie somewhere in the middle: some relations are internal, some external.

5. One suggestive way of formulating this dispute is to say that it concerns what is to be included in the 'nature' of a term. If we were asked what the nature of the table is, we should probably answer by trying to say what it is *essentially*, what makes it a table as distinct from anything else; e.g. it is a table in virtue of its being an article of furniture consisting of a flat top supported on legs or a central pillar and used to place things on. So conceived, the nature of the table is a character abstracted from the concrete thing and held before the mind as its essence. And it is plain that we can think of this essence without any reference to what may be on the table; so far as we can see, the essence could be present equally whether there was a book on the table or not. The only way to make a relation to the book essential, it would appear, is to *identify* the nature of the table with all its qualities and relations. It will then be part of the nature of the table to have a book on it, to stand ten feet from the door, and to have been polished yesterday by Bridget. In the absence of any one of these relations, it would plainly not have the nature it does have, since that nature now includes them all, and of course an infinite number of other relations as well. To say that it would be what it is without any one of these would be simply self-contradictory. The table is thus internally related not only to the book but to everything else in the universe.

This looks more like a sleight-of-hand performance than a sober argument. Of course we can get the conclusion if we wish by packing all these peripheral relations into the thing's nature, but it seems merely arbitrary to do so. Furthermore, it really leaves the problem on our hands. Instead of asking how the nature of a term is related to other things, we shall now ask how the multitudinous items included in its nature are related to each other. And the answer to this question will be the same as before. The qualities we had formerly elected to the position of core qualities will still be wholly independent of the qualities that accompany them. We crowd all of a thing's relations into its nature only to find that this nature itself is falling apart.

6. The Shakespeare case seems different. We cannot define the nature of Shakespeare in the same sharp way as we can the nature of a table. We may say indeed that he is a man or a rational animal, but since he can be either of these without writing plays, his greatest powers will not be included in his nature, which is absurd. Indeed it seems as artificial in this case to seek the nature of the person in some segregated cluster of characters as it was natural to do so in the case of the table. Shakespeare's rational animality is not a hard core of qualities to which his relations to his own creations are externally affixed; his nature *is* that which expresses itself through his creations, and could neither be nor be conceived without them. Shakespeare without Othello, Lear, Macbeth and Hamlet would be all too much like Hamlet without the prince.

The task of singling out in something an abstract and essential 'nature' is thus far harder in some cases than in others. In a bit of inanimate matter like a stone, any group of qualities that we may mark out as the essence would appear to be related externally to the others; if we put its shape in the essence, that seems indifferent to its size; if we make the primary qualities as a whole essential, nothing seems to follow regarding the secondary qualities; any shape or size may be combined with any colour, odour, or felt temperature. On the other hand, as one goes up the organic scale, the problem of finding an essence that is indifferent to its associates gets harder and harder. An organism is a whole in a sense in which a stone is not, and the organism called Shakespeare (or Smith or Jones) is an enormously complex psycho-physical whole whose parts are related intimately. A stone, we say, would have exactly the same shape and size if it had a different colour. Is it obvious that Shakespeare (or Smith or Jones) would be rational or affectionate or irascible in exactly the same sense and degree if he lacked a sense of humour or were deaf or black or had a club foot? If these things are externally related to his nature, that nature would be the same with them as without them. And who would venture to say that? Anything we could plausibly specify as his nature would be necessarily modified by such relations.

7. It may be complained that 'necessity' is not being used here as current logicians use it. This may be true, but the usage is not inadvertent. We deplored long ago the logical convention that would confine necessity to the uninteresting sort of relation linking subject and predicate in 'all bachelors are unmarried'. In our view necessity links any thing or predicate or relation with any other if we can truly say that one could not *be* without the other. If shape could not be without size, or colour without extension; if orange could not be what it is without its relations to red and yellow, or a man's sense of humour be what it is without his intelligence, then necessity in our sense is present; and with all respect to logical convention it is a most important sense. Unfortunately it may be harder to see than mere tautology, and we cannot bring it to light with equal clearness in all cases where we are confident of its presence. When we are dealing with circles and triangles, which are in a sense constructs of our own, freed by stipulation from irrelevancies, we can isolate the terms and relations and see them plainly. When we apprehend that a man's sense of humour would be different if his intelligence were lower, or that his religious faith is conditioned by his sense of insecurity, it is much harder to give precision to our terms; but I suggest that we are still in the presence of necessity. It is sometimes difficult, as in this instance, to say whether we are grasping a logical connection between two meanings or a causal connection between two states, though if it turned out to be causal, that would not of course disprove its necessity. In any event, there is in our view something parochial and crippling about defining necessity as tautology and then dismissing all other

R

connections that experience may present to us as being equally mere conjunctions.

8. Let us return to the question what is involved in the nature of a term. We have seen that in dealing with an inanimate thing like a stone or a table, it is at least *prima facie* possible to mark off a few properties as essential to the thing and hold that these are related externally both to other things and to the other properties of the same thing. We have seen that as one goes up the biological scale this division becomes more difficult, that an organism, and still more obviously a mind, is not the sort of term in which a nature thus marked out will be related to its associates in the same external way. This gives rise to a question. Is this difference in interdependence an ultimate difference, or does it spring from our defect of knowledge? Is it possible that with more insight we should have to level down, that the characters of organic wholes would be seen to have as little necessary connection as those of sticks and stones? Or is it possible that we should level up, that even the characters of a physical thing, which appear to ordinary sight so indifferent to each other, should turn out to be necessarily conjoined?

Professor Ernest Nagel is clear that there is no hope for this latter view. He holds that the very attempt to mark out the characters forming the nature of an individual must be arbitrary; in an individual, 'it is quite clear that just what characters are included and just where the boundaries of an individual are drawn, depend on decisions as to the use of language. These decisions, though motivated by considerations of practical utility, are *logically arbitrary*.'[1] And he goes on to hold that with any group of characters thus taken as constituting a thing's nature, many of its other characters can be seen to be conjoined only externally. I find it difficult to accept either of these views without amendment.

9. As Mr Nagel points out, 'it is frequently said that the nature of a given individual (e.g. Socrates) is to be a man'. But suppose someone, contemplating Socrates, said that his nature was to be snub-nosed. Mr Nagel takes it as 'quite clear that just what characters are included in an individual' is 'logically arbitrary'; there are no reasons except those of 'practical utility' for identifying the nature of Socrates with his humanity rather than his snub-nosedness. But surely this is difficult doctrine. No doubt some disciple of Henry Moore, looking at Socrates's singular countenance with a sculptor's eye, might be

---

[1] *Sovereign Reason*, 275; italics in original.

taken by the line of the nose and classify the object before him as essentially a snub-nosed entity. But to say that all such ways of regarding Socrates's nature are equally sound or unsound because all alike are arbitrary is in effect to say that Socrates has no nature at all except as reflected in the convenience of observers. And this we cannot accept. Granting the notorious difficulty of isolating what is essential in an individual, we need not therefore accept the view that any candidate for this office is as good as any other. Socrates was a moral and philosophical genius; he was also snub-nosed; and we are so rash as to say that the first description records what was more essential to his nature than the second. Mr Nagel recognizes that from some characters 'the systematic organization and logical derivation of a large number of other traits' is possible, but appears to think this is of no help in finding what is essential, on the ground that 'we bring into systematic order only a *selected* group of traits and actions'.[1] He is thus criticizing *any* selection as arbitrary, no matter how massive and well organized the entailed group of characters may be. The moral and philosophical genius of Socrates will therefore be as arbitrary a candidate for his nature, as little revelatory of what he really was, as the fact that he was snub-nosed. This seems to me merely odd. Certainly our common assumption is that some features of his nature are more central than others. How determine their centrality? Is there any better way than by ideally removing them and seeing what would follow? Remove the moral and philosophical genius of Socrates, and the Socrates that the world has known goes with it; alter his nasal profile and less goes with it. I am not arguing that such an alteration would make no difference to Socrates, still less to Cleopatra. I am advancing the not very reckless thesis that his moral and philosophical genius was more essential in Socrates's nature than the curve at the end of his nose.

10. Suppose this is admitted. Suppose we have found a character or group of characters that gives more adequately than others the nature of the individual. Mr Nagel would say that, even so, there remains between this 'nature' and most of the other qualities owned by the individual a purely external connection. 'For example, if to be a metal is taken to be the nature of a concrete thing, this nature *may* entail the fact that the thing is malleable; but this nature will not, by itself, determine the specific degree of malleability exhibited by the thing, nor will it determine the specific shapes the thing may

[1] *Sovereign Reason*, 274.

assume at various times.'[1] In one sense this is obviously true. Yet many philosophers have in fact thought it false. What are we to think?

In the sense Mr Nagel probably gives to the contention, I think it must be accepted. If one knows about a lump of matter only that it is metallic, one cannot infer from this its degree of malleability or its shape. Mr Nagel says that its being metallic '*may* entail the fact that the thing is malleable' in some degree or other, but by this he presumably means only that one may include malleability in the definition of 'metal' if one wishes. But even if one does so define the term, he would rightly say it still does not follow from a thing's being metallic that it has malleability in this particular degree. Why not? Because—we should answer—one is then arguing from the more abstract to the more concrete, and entailments do not hold in this direction. You cannot deduce from the fact that something is an organism that it is a man, or from its being a man that it is an Athenian, though you can go from being an Athenian to being a man, and from this to being an organism. Why this difficulty in the downward passage? The traditional answer is that it is a matter of intensional inclusion; the most concrete term includes the others, which grow thinner as you go up. But there is more to it than that. A generic concept like man or organism is always vague or indefinite, and we cannot get definite rabbits out of indefinite hats. Though there is no vagueness in nature, our thought of man or metal as such is incorrigibly vague; there is therefore nothing in nature that precisely corresponds to it. If we try to abstract a set of definite characters identical throughout the class, we find ourselves defeated. We have already pointed this out in discussing the generic universal, and need not repeat the argument. As regards the term 'metal', it is instructive to note in passing the struggle of the Oxford English Dictionary to arrive at some definite meaning, even for the chemical elements called metals; 'of these some possess all the properties, such as high specific gravity and density, fusibility, malleability, etc., formerly viewed as characteristic of a metal, while others possess hardly any of them, the metallic lustre being perhaps the most constant'. These properties again are all vague, and name nothing in nature. There is no lustre as such, identical in all lustres, from which a specific lustre could be derived. From a vague and thin abstraction nothing but a vague and thin abstraction follows.

11. It is not true, however, that from the form in which a general

[1] *Sovereign Reason*, 276.

term is realized in a particular case nothing follows. Merely from the fact that a patch is coloured, one cannot see, to be sure, how its colour is related to other colours. But from a specific embodiment of colour in this patch—and there is no such thing as colour not so embodied—specific facts do follow: if the shade is orange it *must* fall between red and yellow; if purple, between red and blue. Similarly, though no fully determinate consequences follow from metal as such, they do undoubtedly follow from the definite form taken by the metallic character in this particular case. What the form is we do not clearly know; our knowledge of it is still too general. But if the term is capable of being given a determinate meaning at all, we should no doubt find that what constitutes this lump a metal is some perfectly determinate arrangement of elements within its atoms. And once the term is given this definite meaning, *is* it incredible that the degree of malleability should be entailed by it, and with sufficient knowledge might be seen to be thus entailed? That this would follow causally I suppose there is no reasonable doubt, and we have argued that if it follows causally, it must be presumed to follow necessarily. The same must be said of the object's assuming a particular shape. Its having this shape is not a mere brute inexplicable fact. The other facts from which this follows will not, to be sure, be facts of its own nature only. Its ultimate elements are engaged in manifold interactions, by way of attraction and repulsion, with things around it, and these almost certainly determine its shape down to the last detail. This particular shape, like this degree of malleability, is not externally related to its other characters; they are bound up with these causally and therefore, we have held, necessarily.

We set out a few pages back to distinguish the truth and falsity in the statement that the characters of an individual are only externally related to each other. We saw that if a character were a generic universal, such as being human or being a metal, the individual's specific characters did not follow from it. What exists is completely specific; generic universals are not thus specific; and from the indefinite the definite does not follow. If, however, we take the completely specific characters in whose form alone our generalities may be said to exist, there is no good reason to suppose that they are related only externally. Reduce an individual in thought to a set of abstractions such as density, irregular shape, colour, size, and temperature, and it seems like a ragbag whose contents are thrown together at random. Specify these abstractions till we have what answers to them in nature, and there is nothing random or accidental left.

12. This enables us to answer more explicitly a question touched on a moment ago. If the characters of an individual are related necessarily, then it could not be what it is if *any* of them were removed. Now it is clear enough that Socrates without his intellect would not be the man he was. But on our theory, we may be told, Socrates without his snub nose would equally not be the man he was; and this surely goes too far. An oak that has lost a leaf will have to be denied to be the same oak. Cromwell without his wart would not be Cromwell. And is not this really absurd? The answer turns on the word 'equally'. The nose, the leaf, and the wart are not accidents, to be sure; there is something in the individual's nature—we may not know what—that appointed just these details. But there is nothing in our position to commit us to the view that the absence of the snub nose would entail an *equal* change in the individual with an absence of intellect, or the absence of a leaf with that of a trunk, or that of a wart with that of a head or a heart. We do hold, of course, that the absence of any such detail would have repercussions on the individual's nature, indeed that it would have far wider repercussions still, but we do not hold, nor is there any reason why we should, that these repercussions would be as massive as if, for example, space and time were to cease to be. Every character counts, but not all characters count equally.

13. Reflection has gone through a number of stages about individuals. Primitive thought often attributes to inanimate things something like wills of their own; the sea is angry, the twisted tree is sinister and malevolent. When animism disappeared, a doctrine of substance still lingered, perhaps as a vestigial trace of it. Aristotle was sure that there must be matter to receive the forms imposed on it, even though this matter eluded all attempts to catch and define it; and Locke clung to a material substance against the express requirements of his theory of knowledge. Hume dismissed these figments, and conceived the individual simply as a cluster of related qualities, none of them essential and all of them conjoined with each other externally. But this also would not do, for reasons we have considered; in an individual like Socrates, some characters are clearly more essential than others, and some obviously entail others. Nevertheless in one important point we agree with Hume; a thing *is* a set of characters which exists in time and space. Those characters are never exhaustible, nor do we ever fully grasp their structure. Still, with the structure they have, they give the nature of the thing; they are what exists when we say the thing exists, and in this sense the thing *is* its nature. This will surprise no one who has read our discussion of universals. But to some critics it seems a strange doctrine. If I return here to Mr Nagel, it is because he has done me the honour of examining at length a study I once made of internal relations. He thinks the view just advanced 'disastrous'. It will be instructive to consider his reasons briefly.

14. He states three of them. 'In the first place, the nature of a thing, like the thing itself, would be something that is in principle indefinable and could not therefore be made the basis for bringing into systematic order any of the characters which the thing displays.'[1] The answer is: It is true that the nature of the thing would be indefinable, as anything must be which includes an inexhaustible set of characters. But would this deprive us of any basis for bringing the characters of the thing into order? I do not see why. It does not remove our power to distinguish within the nature of a thing essential from less essential characters or to show that from the more essential ones a great many others follow. Indeed in this respect we are in a better position than our critic, to whom any attempt to state what is essential to an individual is arbitrary, and any attempt except by tautology to develop what this entails is bound to fail.

15. 'In the second place, every statement which mentions the nature of an individual would express no more than a trivial analytical proposition.'[2] It is true that if a character B is part of what I mean when I speak of an individual A, then the statement that A (say a cube) is B (say twelve-edged) will be analytic and trivial. And a mind of super-intelligence who could see at a glance all the properties implied by being a cube would perhaps include those properties in his meaning and thus speak analytically and trivially when he ascribed them to it. But is anything like this true of our own thinking? We must always conceive an individual in terms of some of its properties only, and the thinking by means of which we proceed to its further properties is neither automatic nor analytic nor trivial. To see what is implied in being a cube may cost us a sustained and arduous effort, and indeed it never wholly succeeds. When we do succeed in capturing an implication, it does not come to us as contained in what we started with, as merely part of what we meant; even our thinking in geometry is not in this sense analytic.[3] Nor therefore is it trivial. Indeed it would not be trivial even for an ideal intelligence in the

[1] *Sovereign Reason*, 276.
[2] *Ibid.*
[3] Cf. above, p. 291.

sense that the passage from property to property would travel merely in a circle, for entailment is not inclusion. The contention, therefore, that to identify a thing with its nature would make all our statements about it analytic and trivial is quite without ground.

16. Mr Nagel writes that 'in the third place, since discursive thought would be inherently inadequate to the task of discovering the natures of things, the goal of understanding the natures of things could not be a pertinent ideal for human reason'.[1] One wonders just why not? What is meant by this inadequacy of discursive thinking? If it means that we shall in all probability never understand the nature of things fully, no matter how hard we try, it is true, but scarcely relevant. We shall never be morally perfect; we shall never write a perfect poem or even a perfect letter; but we do not therefore say that perfection is not a 'pertinent ideal' to aim at. Perhaps what is meant, however, is that for one who believes in internal relations the terms themselves change their characters when seen in wider contexts, and hence that the characters they bear at any given level of understanding would in the end call for revision. Even so, however, it is only through discursive thought, only through carrying the attempt at understanding to its greatest possible completeness, that the further goal could be attained. Rationalists have differed about the character of the insight that would belong to a final understanding. Some have held, as Descartes did, that it would be a grasp of the ultimate interconnection of terms which even in that final context would remain what they now are. Others have held, with Spinoza and Bradley, that it would be a *scientia intuitiva* in which terms as we now know them would disappear in a higher immediacy. But whether the goal is the one or the other, the route to it is the same, namely hard discursive thinking. Only through singling out the characters of things and following the filaments of necessity that link them into an intelligible network is there any hope of either kind of understanding. If our road to B lies through A, and A is the furthest visible point on that road, then it is toward A that we must bend our course.

One further comment: those who think it disastrous to identify a thing with its nature may well consider what the alternative is. Are they suggesting that beneath the properties of a thing there is some substratum in which these properties inhere? If so, what sort of entity is this? Presumably not the Aristotelian matter or the Lockean substance or the Kantian thing in itself. As philosophic sophistication has advanced, the notion of the 'it' in which qualities inhere has

[1] *Op. cit.*, 276.

become more and more attenuated until in the highly self-critical philosophies of McTaggart and Broad it has all but dissolved into thin air; the very question *what* it may be is regarded as not pertinent.[1] I am sceptical of all these views of substance. To me a thing *is* a set of characters in relation, and ultimately in necessary relation. There may be 'dark unfathomed caves' in things that would reveal this notion to be superficial. But whoever thinks so should give us some suggestion of how and where we should look for them in the topography of the thing.

17. In denying that the properties of a thing or individual are externally related to each other, we are not suggesting, of course, that it is a self-enclosed or independent system. The lines that demarcate a thing—a snowball, a cloud, a stick—from other things are commonly drawn because certain qualities conspicuously accompany each other or contribute to a joint purpose, not because these qualities are seen to entail each other.[2] An organism or a mind is a whole whose parts are more obviously interdependent than those of a cloud, but no thing or individual stands by itself; it is what it is in consequence of lines of determination—causal, logical, or both—running out into an illimitable universe. In our chapter on necessities in nature, we examined the character of some of these lines. Everything that has a number of parts or attributes, for example, is related numerically to every other such object. All things occupying space are related to each other by the laws of that geometry, Euclidean or non-Euclidean, which governs the space of physics; and since all such things have shape, each has innumerable properties of its own entailed again by geometrical necessity. Every event is related to every other in time, and these relations are necessary in the sense that if A precedes B, it must precede all that is contemporary with B or successive to it. Every thing is related necessarily to every other through scales of intensity or degree, whether of weight, density, brightness, loudness or speed, so that if its particular degree were altered, its relations to all other things on the scale would be altered, and a change in these relations would entail a change in its own nature. Anything that has being at all can have it only in virtue of being this rather than that, of having some specific nature, and through this nature it involves itself with a variety of entangling orders. In our present ignorance we must depend chiefly on these orders and on causality to show the

[1] I have offered some criticism of their ideas of substance in *The Philosophy of C. D. Broad*, ed. by P. A. Schilpp, 237 ff.
[2] Cf. *The Nature of Thought*, I, Ch. 3.

interdependence of things. We cannot show it in detail, and the work of knowing would be over if we could. Is there any way other than the laborious following of specific threads of connection to show the interdependence of things?

18. One surprisingly simple argument has been offered by such rationalists as Hegel and McTaggart to show that everything is directly and logically dependent on everything else.[1] Take any two things, say a plane circle on the earth and a plane triangle on Mars. Nothing would seem to be more independent of each other. But they are obviously related in two common ways. They are related by likeness in respect of being plane figures, and they are related by difference, since they have differing shapes. Now each one of these relations is internal and necessary, for if either of them were altered, the terms could not remain the same. Consider the relation of difference only. A differs from B in nature because a circle is different from a triangle. Suppose this difference removed; then A could not be what it is, for a circle that did not differ from a triangle could not be circle. An internal relation *means* one that could not be absent while the term remains the same. The relation between the circle on the earth and the triangle on Mars is therefore an internal relation.

To some philosophers this train of thought is suspect. When so simple an argument is offered as establishing so unlikely a conclusion there must be some hocus-pocus about it. The conclusion, if generalized, is nothing less than that everything in the universe is connected necessarily with everything else. This is not a very enlightening conclusion, to be sure, since, applying to everything equally, it tells us nothing distinctive about anything. But we saw long ago that logical statements are not the less true because they apply universally. And the above argument, so far as it goes, seems conclusive.

19. Professor Nagel, however, has challenged it, and since he speaks with a special competence in logic, it will be interesting to consider his demurrers to it. The first seems to me so little plausible that I may well have misunderstood it. It is that if one distinguishes a thing from its nature, as one apparently ought to do, the conclusion will not follow. 'Undoubtedly, given that B is triangular in shape, A could not be circular unless A differed in shape from B. But to say that A would fail to have the shape it does in fact have, did it not differ in

---

[1] Hegel, *Science of Logic*, I, 138 (Johnston and Struthers' trans.); J. M. E. McTaggart, *Commentary on Hegel's Logic*, 29–30; *The Nature of Existence*, I, 29–30, 87.

shape from B, is *prima facie* not equivalent to saying that A's *nature* would be affected were A not different in shape from B. However . . . it is this *latter* claim that must be made good if the relation of *difference* is to be established as internal to A.'[1] Let me put in my own way what this argument seems to mean. We are looking at a round patch A. The shape of this patch differs from that of a triangular patch B. The *shape* of A could not be what it is unless it differed from the *shape* of B; this is admitted. But it does not follow that the patch A could not still be what it is without differing in shape from B. For its shape may not be part of its nature at all. We can show that A is internally related to B only if we make the assumption that the roundness of the round patch *is* part of its nature, and this has not been proved.

Now we must admit that in talking about A's difference from B, we were making the rash assumption that a round patch is round and that being round is part of its nature. If this is illegitimate, I do not know how we can say that anything is like or unlike anything else, for their likeness or difference must always be in respect to some characteristic, and we shall be open to the charge of begging the question if we assign to the nature of either term any characteristic at all. We have argued above that there is no good ground for so wholesale a scepticism. And if we are ever justified in saying that a character belongs to the nature of something, we surely are in the case of the roundness of a round patch. Note that it is quite unnecessary to the argument to include in this nature the relations of the roundness to anything else; roundness may be defined and conceived without any reference to triangularity. Nevertheless it is internally related to triangularity by a relation of difference whose disappearance would cancel it utterly.

20. A second criticism runs as follows: even if roundness and triangularity are admitted to the natures of A and B respectively, the argument that A and B themselves are necessarily related does not follow. For the facts that A is round and B triangular are themselves contingent facts. 'If, then, the relational property of being different from B is alleged to be internal to A, it is internal to it only relative to the contingent facts that A is circular and B is triangular.'[2] Thus if the line of necessity runs as follows, A-circle-triangle-B, it fails, for both the first step and the last are contingent, not necessary. Now what is meant by saying that A's being circular or B's being triangular

[1] *Sovereign Reason*, 278.
[2] *Ibid.*, 279.

is a 'contingent fact'? Presumably this, that the subject could be what it is without having the character in question. And what is the subject in our assertion that A is circular? We commonly say it is the patch. When we say, then, that the patch is circular, are we stating a contingent truth or a necessary one? Unfortunately the statement is still vague, and without further analysis no answer is possible.

The statement would be analysed by present-day philosophers in different ways. One way is that of the analysts who have followed the earlier Russell and Wittgenstein. They would say that the patch is not the ultimate subject, for it is itself a complex the facts of which can only be expressed in a set of further statements such as 'that is red', 'this is bright', and so on. Every empirical statement can be analysed into one or more atomic statements in which the subject is not a quality but something denoted by 'this' or 'that', and in which a quality is ascribed to this subject (or a relation to two such subjects). Now if this is really what we are saying, the question whether our statement is necessary or not cannot arise. For necessity can only link contents, and the denoted subject is not a content but a wholly indescribable *it*. We examined this view long ago, finding reason to doubt whether it made sense, and whether a wholly characterless something could even be pointed at. We recommended the proponent of the view to follow the later Russell and abandon it.

If he does abandon it, he will no doubt turn to an analysis that gives the subject a content as well as the predicate. When we say 'that patch is round', we shall be saying that along with the other characters, such as red and bright, which form the nature of the patch, there is the quality round. Not of course that we are asserting redness and brightness to be round, or roundness to be red or bright. The subject will be the patch, taken as a composite of qualities in relation, and we shall be saying that among them is that of being round. Assuming this statement to be true, does it state a contingent truth or a necessary one?

Here again we must make a distinction. Is the connection that is asserted a connection between abstractions or a connection between facts? If it is the former, if it is merely a statement that an X that is red may also be round, then it is apparently a contingent statement. There is nothing in redness as such, so far as we can see, that necessitates roundness; an X that had it might equally have had some other shape. And if one takes universals at random—loudness, three-sidedness, sweetness, a weight of ten pounds, kindness, the speed of light—it is hard to see any path by which one could pass from one to another. I do not wish flatly to deny that there is any such path, but I have no idea what it might be.

21. But then I do not think that when we say 'that (red) patch is round', we are stating a connection between pure abstractions. We are stating a connection between facts. We are saying that in a concrete individual the fact of being red at time t accompanies the fact of being round at that time. And I do not think this connection *is* contingent. We do not see the necessity; granted; what cannot be granted is that with fuller knowledge this accompaniment would turn out to be contingent merely. The argument by now is familiar. If it is a *fact* that a thing at time t is round, that is no accident; it is determined, as we have seen, in accordance with laws governing the position and movement of its ultimate components and those of adjoining things. If it is also red, this again is no accident, for there are laws, largely known already, governing the appearance of the sense-datum red. The question, then, whether the truth of 'this (red) patch is round' is necessary or not will depend on whether the atomic or sub-atomic structure that conditions the thing's being round has a necessary or only an accidental connection with that which conditions its being red. Now one may be sure that a competent physicist would not set this down as mere inexplicable togetherness, even if he could not yet see what closer connection there was. Of course we shall be told here once more that what we are showing is only a causal connection, not a logical or necessary one. And if causality is indeed nothing but conjunction, the point is well taken. But we have found ourselves unable to believe this. What is caused, we hold, is necessitated. And if this is true, then the facts that this thing is round and that thing triangular are not contingent facts. They are necessarily what they are.

22. A further argument has been offered to show that the circle on earth and the triangle on Mars are only externally related. 'Suppose that the individual figure B were to be destroyed so that A, though retaining its circular shape, would no longer be different from B—for the simple reason that there no longer would be the figure B from which it could differ . . . A remains the thing it is in spite of the fact that one of its relations is altered.'[1] But surely the *logical* relation between the natures of A and B is neither removed nor altered by the physical destruction of B. Even if B has ceased to exist, it is still true of the circular object A that its nature differs from that of the triangular

[1] *Sovereign Reason*, 279.

object B, whose annals may have been brief and have ended long ago. And that relation is internal in the sense that it could not be removed without a change in the nature of A.

What has changed is not the relation of difference between the natures of A and B, but the relation of contemporaneity between A and B, regarded as events. B first has the relation of being contemporaneous with A and then loses it. And the relation of contemporaneity between two events does not have the same obviously internal character as the relation of difference in nature. On the ground of that relation alone we cannot pass from the occurrence of a certain kind of event on the earth to the occurrence of a certain kind of event in Mars; so far as we now see, the latter event could occur or not occur without making the slightest difference to the event on the earth. But that is not the whole story. We know that if an object or event B ceases to be contemporaneous with another, more than a relation of time is involved; causality also is at work. And then the path of the argument is clear. We have seen that between events remote in space and time there are causal relations, direct and indirect, in whose absence there is no reason to believe that the events would have occurred as they did. The ceasing to be of the triangular object in Mars has infinitely long causal roots that are entwined beyond reasonable doubt with those that determined the existence of the circular object on earth. To say therefore that the one event is connected only externally with the other, if that means that the second might not have taken place while leaving the first the same, has no good ground. To be sure we revert again here to causality. But provided causal law is accepted as universal, the conclusion just stated would still hold without assuming that causation is necessary.

We conclude from this review that the argument of the rationalists to the effect that all things are connected through the relation of difference, that this is in truth a necessary relation, and hence that all things are connected necessarily, is a valid argument. Its conclusion is highly abstract, and if the argument is to establish what is hoped of it, it must fall back at more than one point on a relation, namely causality, whose necessity is often questioned. It is impressive, even so. And if put together with the earlier argument that the qualities of the individual are internally related, it provides an intimation at least of cosmic necessity.

23. It is no part of the present enterprise, which has already continued too long, to discuss the implications for feeling or for practice

of the belief that the world is a necessary system. To say this is to say in a sense that the world is rational, and many persons have found in this belief a source of ethical and religious reassurance. They have taken the term rational in a much broader sense than the one given to it in this discussion. For them the assertion that the world is rational is roughly equivalent to 'God's in His heaven, all's right with the world'. Must not what is rational be right? Must not a rational world be one in which seeming wrongs and injustices are rectified? Two things must be said in comment.

First, between the rational as the logically necessary and the rational as the morally right, there is an abyss of difference. To show that the things and events of the world are necessarily interconnected is not to show that any of these things, or all of them taken together, are what they should be. To establish that, we should have to show that they are good, and this is a different matter, to be made out, if at all, on very different grounds. Necessity applies everywhere and to everything, while in our own view goodness applies only to the experiences of sentient beings. To say of the fall of a star or of the tenth proposition of Euclid that it is necessary is not to say that it is good; what indeed could anyone mean by calling such things good? The *experience* of the observer as he looks at the star may be good, or of the geometer as he follows the proof, but that is not the same thing.

24. Secondly, to pass from 'everything is rational', in the sense of necessity, to 'everything is rational', in the sense of right, is to stultify one's moral perception. No one doubts that the wholesale destruction of life in the course of evolution, or the appearance of the Black Death, or of the influenza of 1918, was necessitated at least in the sense of being causally determined. A contemporary writer has reminded us that 'wild beasts destroy 3,000 persons every year in India, and 20,000 die of snake bite. There are 700 million sufferers from malaria in the world. Forty per cent of the children born in central China perish from cold or famine before they are a year old.'[1] Given the circumstances, these facts too are no doubt necessary. But to call them rational in the sense of good or right or justified is to confuse one's values hopelessly. To be sure there have been philosophers who have held that if the misery of the mouse, tormented to death by the necessary play of the cat, were seen in its complete context of relations, it would be not bad but good. The argument, innocent enough in purpose, ends in callowness and moral anarchy.

[1] MacNeile Dixon, *The Human Situation*, 79–80. One hopes that the figures have already changed.

For if intense and gratuitous pain is not bad, as natural insight testifies, but good, then why should we not inflict it at will? and if such perception as we have is so feeble as to see white as black, why trust it about anything? The questions whether something is necessitated and whether it is good are utterly different questions.

25. So too are the questions whether an act is necessitated and whether it is right. It would be absurd to raise the vast problem of moral freedom for casual settlement in a paragraph, but if a writer holds to a universe of necessity, readers have a right to know whether he finds room for morality in such a world. I shall confine myself to two remarks.

First, that necessity in the form at least of causality does govern human action is essential, I suggest, if we are to make sense of moral judgments. If an act B was not caused by A the agent, then it is meaningless to say that A did the act, and it is unreasonable to hold him in any sense responsible for it. One cannot even hold him responsible in the sense that one may justly punish him in the interest of reform or deterrence, for such punishment assumes that very determination of future acts which it is questioning about present ones. It may be replied that though the choice to do action B rather than C was caused by A in the sense that it issued necessarily out of his nature, his nature at the moment of choice was itself undetermined. That such a view would be disastrous to one's own brand of psychology is not perhaps important, since psychology has so many brands; but such a view would make *any* scientific psychology impossible. If the selves out of which actions emerge are not causally conditioned, if states of the self may suddenly appear which are connected by no laws at all with the past interests or habits, the character or education, of the agent, then human behaviour becomes not only inexplicable in principle, but, so far, impossible to influence by discipline or instruction. This may indeed be the case, but it seems to me increasingly improbable as our knowledge of human nature grows.

26. Secondly, the objection commonly felt to including human nature itself within the domain of necessity is largely based on a misunderstanding. It is assumed that causality is all of one type and that this type is the sort exemplified in the pulling about of puppets in a Punch-and-Judy show. Any self-respecting person would be humiliated at the discovery that his conclusions and moral choices were the product of nothing but mechanical clockwork. But there are levels of causality; and there is no reason whatever to suppose that conclusions and moral choices are mechanically determined. In the last chapter we studied a case in point. When a thinker follows a line of implication, the course of his thought is conditioned by the necessity in his subject matter, but far from being humiliated when he realizes this, he finds in it a ground of pride. For a rational being to act under the influence of seen necessity is to place himself at the farthest possible extreme from the behaviour of the puppet. For a moral agent to choose that good which in the light of reflection approves itself as intrinsically greatest is to exercise the only freedom worth having. In such cases the line of determination runs through the agent's own intelligence. To think at its best is to find oneself carried down the current of necessity. To choose most responsibly is to see alternative goods with full clearness and to find the greatest of them tipping the beam. This, in a way, is to be determined. But there is nothing mechanical about it. For it is what the rational man means by freedom.

BOOKS MENTIONED IN THE TEXT

Aaron, R. I. *The Theory of Universals*. Oxford: Clarendon Press, 1952.

Abbott, E. *Hellenica*. London: Rivingtons, 1880.

Adams, G. P. et al. *California Publications in Philosophy*, Vol. 21 (1939). Berkeley: Univ. of California Press.

Aristotle, *Metaphysics*, ed. by W. D. Ross. London: Oxford Univ. Press, 1942.

Arnold, Matthew. *Poems, 1840–1867*. London: Oxford Univ. Press, 1909.

Asquith, Herbert. *Moments of Memory*. London: Hutchinson, 1937.

Ayer, A. J. *Logic, Truth and Language*. 2nd ed. London: Victor Gollancz, 1946.

—— *Philosophical Essays*. London: Macmillan, 1954.

Barnes, W. H. F. *The Philosophical Predicament*. London: A. and C. Black, 1950.

Berkeley, G. *Works*, ed. by Fraser. Oxford: Clarendon Press, 1901.

Bevan, Edwyn. *Hellenism and Christianity*. London: Allen & Unwin, 1921.

Blanshard, B. *The Nature of Thought*. London: Allen & Unwin, 1939.

—— *Reason and Goodness*. London: Allen & Unwin, 1961.

Bosanquet, B. *Knowledge and Reality*. London: Swan Sonnenschein, 1885.

—— *The Philosophical Theory of the State*. 4th ed. London: Macmillan, 1923.

—— *The Principle of Individuality and Value*. London: Macmillan, 1912.

Bradley, F. H. *Collected Essays*. 2 vols. Oxford: Clarendon Press, 1935.

—— *Principles of Logic*. 2nd ed. London: Oxford Univ. Press, 1922.

Broad, C. D. *Examination of McTaggart's Philosophy*. 3 vols. Cambridge: Univ. Press, 1933.

—— *The Mind and Its Place in Nature*. London: Kegan Paul, 1925.

—— *The Philosophy of C. D. Broad*. ed. by P. A. Schilpp. Evanston: Northwestern Univ., 1960.

—— *Scientific Thought*. London: Kegan Paul, 1923.

Carnap, R. *The Logical Syntax of Language*. London: Kegan Paul, 1937.

—— *Meaning and Necessity*, 2nd ed. Chicago: Univ. of Chicago Press, 1956.

—— *Philosophy and Logical Syntax*. London: Kegan Paul, 1935.

Clarke, F. P. and Nahm, M. C., editors. *Philosophical Essays in Honour of E. A. Singer*. Philadelphia: Univ. of Pennsylvania Press, 1942.

Cohen, M. R. *Preface to Logic*. New York: Holt, 1944.

—— *Reason and Nature*. New York: Harcourt, Brace, 1931.

Dewey, J. *Reconstruction in Philosophy*. New York: Henry Holt, 1920.

Dixon, Macneile. *The Human Situation*. London: Edward Arnold, 1937.

Drake, D. *Invitation to Philosophy*. Boston: Houghton Mifflin, 1933.

Ducasse, C. J. *Nature, Mind and Death*. La Salle, Ill.: Open Court, 1951.

Einstein, A. *The World as I See It*. New York: Covici, Friede, 1934.

Eliot, T. S. *Notes Towards the Definition of Culture*. London: Faber & Faber, 1948.

Ewing, A. C. *Idealism*. London: Methuen, 1943.

—— *Reason and Intuition*. Hertz Lecture. Proc. of British Academy, 1941.

—— *A Short Commentary on Kant's Critique of Pure Reason*. London: Methuen, 1938.

Feigl, H. and Sellars, W. S. *Readings in Philosophical Analysis*. New York: Appleton-Century-Crofts, 1949.

Flew, A. G. N., ed. *Essays in Conceptual Analysis*. London: Macmillan, 1956.

—— ed. *Logic and Language*. 1st series, 1951; 2nd series, 1953. Oxford: Basil Blackwell.

Frank, Philipp. *Modern Science and Its Philosophy*. Cambridge: Harvard Univ. Press, 1949.

Frazer, J. G. *The Golden Bough*. 12 vols. London: Macmillan, 1890–1915.

Freud, S. *Civilization, War and Death*. ed. by J. Rickman, 2nd ed. London: Hogarth Press, 1953.

Gonseth, F. *Qu'est-ce la logique?* Paris: Hermann & Cie, 1937.

Goodman, Nelson. *The Structure of Appearance*. Cambridge: Harvard Univ. Press, 1951.

Green, T. H. *Principles of Political Obligation*. New Imp. London: Longmans Green, 1913.

Green, T. H. *Works*, 3 vols. London: Longmans Green, 1885.

Hampshire, S. *Spinoza*. London: Penguin, 1951.

Hegel, G. W. F. *Science of Logic*, 2 vols., tr. by Johnston and Struthers. London: Allen & Unwin, 1929.

Hobbes, Thomas. *Leviathan*, ed. of 1651 reprinted. Oxford: Clarendon Press, 1909.

Hobhouse, L. T. *The Metaphysical Theory of the State*. London: Allen & Unwin, 1918.

—— *Morals in Evolution*. London: Chapman and Hall, 1906.

—— *The Rational Good*. London: Allen & Unwin, 1921.

Hook, S., ed. *Determinism and Freedom*. New York: N.Y. Univ. Press, 1958.

Horkheimer, Max. *The Eclipse of Reason*. New York: Oxford Univ. Press, 1947.

Hume, David. *Enquiry Concerning Human Understanding*, and *Enquiry Concerning the Principles of Morals*, ed. by Green and Grose. London: Longmans Green, 1889.

—— *Treatise of Human Nature*, ed. by Selby-Bigge. Oxford: Clarendon Press, 1896.

Huxley, T. H. *Methods and Results*. London: Macmillan, 1893.

Inge, W. R. *The Fall of the Idols*. London: Putnam, 1940.

James, W. *Principles of Psychology*, 2 vols. New York: Holt, 1910; London: Macmillan.

Jeans, J. *The Mysterious Universe*. New York: Macmillan, 1932.

—— *The Stars in Their Courses*. Cambridge: Univ. Press, 1931.

Jevons, W. S. *Principles of Science*. London: Macmillan, 1874.

Joachim, H. H. *A Study of the Ethics of Spinoza*. London: Oxford Univ. Press, 1901.

Johnson, W. E. *Logic*, 3 vols. Cambridge: The Univ. Press, 1921–24.

Joseph, W. H. B. *Introduction to Logic*, 2nd ed. Oxford: Clarendon Press, 1916.

Kant, I. *Critique of Pure Reason*, tr. by Meiklejohn. London: Bell, 1910.

—— *Critique of Pure Reason*, tr. by N. Kemp Smith. London: Macmillan, 1929.

Kneale, W. *Probability and Induction*. Oxford: Clarendon Press, 1949.

Krikorian, Y., ed. *Naturalism and the Human Spirit*. New York: Columbia Univ. Press, 1944.

Krutch, Joseph Wood. *The Modern Temper*. New York: Harcourt Brace, 1929.

Kuhn, Helmut. *Encounter with Nothingness*. Hinsdale, Ill.: Henry Regnery, 1949.

Laski, H. J. *Communism*. New York: Holt, 1927; London: Butterworth.

Leibniz, G. W. *Philosophische Schriften*, ed. by C. J. Gerhardt. Berlin: Weidmann, 1875–90.

Linton, Ralph. *The Study of Man*. New York: Appleton-Century, 1936.

Livingstone, R. W., ed. *The Legacy of Greece*. Oxford: Clarendon Press, 1921.

Locke, J. *Essay Concerning Human Understanding*. First pub. London, 1690. Many ed.

Lovejoy, A. O. *The Revolt Against Dualism*. La Salle, Ill.: Open Court, 1930.

Lowrie, Walter. *Kierkegaard*. London, New York: Oxford Univ. Press, 1938.

Lucas, F. L. *Style*. London: Cassell, 1935.

Mach, Ernst. *Die Analyse der Empfindungen*. Jena: G. Fischer, 1900.

McTaggart, J. M. E. *Commentary on Hegel's Logic*. Cambridge: Univ. Press, 1910.

—— *The Nature of Existence*, 2 vols. Cambridge: Univ. Press, 1921.

—— *Studies in Hegelian Dialectic*. Cambridge: Univ. Press, 1922.

Mannheim, Karl. *Ideology and Utopia*. London: Kegan Paul, 1936.

Maritain, J. *The Dream of Descartes*. New York: Philosophical Library, 1944; London: Editions Poetry, 1946.

Mill, J. S. *System of Logic*, 2 vols. London: Parker, 1843.

Minto, W. *Logic*. New York: Scribner, 1893.

Montague, C. E. *A Writer's Notes on His Trade*. London: Chatto and Windus, Pelican, 1949.

Moore, G. E. *Philosophical Studies*. London: Kegan Paul, 1922.

—— *The Philosophy of G. E. Moore*, ed. by P. A. Schilpp. Northwestern Univ., 1942.

Morgan, J. H. *John, Viscount Morley*. London: John Murray, 1924.

Muirhead, J. H., ed. *Contemporary British Philosophy*, 2 vols. London: Allen & Unwin, 1924.

Murray, Gilbert. *Then and Now*. Romanes Lecture. Oxford: Clarendon Press, 1935.

Nagel, E. *Sovereign Reason*. Glencoe, Ill.: Free Press, 1954.

Pap, Arthur. *Elements of Analytic Philosophy*. New York: Macmillan, 1949.

—— *Semantics and Necessary Truth*. New Haven: Yale Univ. Press, 1958.

Pater, Walter. *Marius the Epicurean*. New York: Boni and Liveright, Modern Library.

Peirce, C. S. *Chance, Love and Logic*, ed. by M. R. Cohen. New York: Harcourt Brace, 1923.

—— *Collected Papers*, ed. by C. Hartshorne and P. Weiss. Cambridge: Harvard Univ. Press, 1931–58; Oxford Univ. Press.

Piaget, Jean. *The Origins of Intelligence in Children*, tr. by Margaret Cook. New York: International Universities Press, 1952; London: Routledge, 1953.

Plato. *Dialogues*, tr. by Jowett. Oxford: Clarendon Press.

Popper, Karl. *Logik der Forschung*. Wien: J. Springer, 1935.

Price, H. H. *Thinking and Experience*. London: Hutchinson, 1953.

Ramsey, F. P. *Foundations of Mathematics*. London: Kegan Paul, 1931.

Rashdall, H. *The Theory of Good and Evil*, 2 vols. Oxford: Univ. Press, 1907.

Robinson, James Harvey. *The Mind in the Making*. New York: Harper, 1921.

Robinson, Richard. *Definition*. Oxford: Clarendon Press, 1950.

Runes, D. D., ed. *Twentieth Century Philosophy*. New York: Philosophical Library, 1943.

Russell, Bertrand. *The Analysis of Matter*. London: Allen & Unwin, 1955.

—— *History of Western Philosophy*. London: Allen & Unwin, 1946.

—— *Human Knowledge: its Scope and Limits*. London: Allen & Unwin, 1948.

—— *Inquiry into Meaning and Truth*. London: Allen & Unwin, 1940.

—— *Introduction to Mathematical Philosophy*. London: Allen & Unwin, 1919.

—— *Mysticism and Logic*. London: Allen & Unwin, 1929.

—— *Our Knowledge of the External World*. London: Allen & Unwin, 1922.

—— *The Philosophy of Bertrand Russell*, ed. by P. A. Schilpp. Evanston: Northwestern Univ., 1944.

—— *The Problems of Philosophy*. London: Williams and Norgate, 1912.

—— *Unpopular Essays*. London: Allen & Unwin, 1950.

Russell, B. and Whitehead, A. N. *Principia Mathematica*, 3 vols. Cambridge: Univ. Press, 1910–13.

Ryle, Gilbert. *The Concept of Mind*. London: Hutchinson, 1949.

—— *Dilemmas*. Cambridge: Univ. Press, 1954.

—— *Philosophical Arguments*. Oxford: Clarendon Press, 1945.

Sabine, G. H. *Democracy and Preconceived Ideas*. Columbus, O.: Shepard Foundation, Ohio State Univ., 1945.

Santayana, George. *Winds of Doctrine*. New York: Scribner; London: Dent, 1913.

—— *Works*. Triton ed. 15 vols. New York: Scribner, 1936–40.

—— *The Philosophy of George Santayana*, ed. by P. Schilpp. Evanston: Northwestern Univ., 1940.

Schlick, Moritz. *Gesammelte Aufsätze*, 1926–1936. Wien: Gerold & Co., 1938.

Sidgwick, Henry. *History of Ethics*. London: Macmillan, 1886.

—— *The Methods of Ethics*, 2nd ed. London: Macmillan, 1877.

Spinoza, Benedict. *Works*, tr. by Elwes. London: Bell, 1912.

Stebbing, L. S. *A Modern Introduction to Logic*. London: Methuen, 1930.

—— *Philosophy and the Physicists*. London: Methuen & Co., 1937.

Stout, G. F. *Studies in Philosophy and Psychology*. London: Macmillan, 1930.

Strawson, P. F. *Introduction to Logical Theory*. London: Methuen, 1952.

Sumner, W. G. *Folkways*. Boston: Ginn and Co., 1907.

Swabey, M. C. *Logic and Nature*, 2 vol. ed. New York: New York Univ. Press, 1955.

Urmson, J. O. *Philosophical Analysis*. Oxford: Clarendon Press, 1956.

Von Mises, Ludwig. *Socialism*. New York: Macmillan; London: Cape, 1936.

Wallas, Graham. *The Art of Thought*. London: J. Cope, 1926.

Weinberg, J. R. *An Examination of Logical Positivism*. London: Kegan Paul, 1936.

Wertheimer, M. *Productive Thinking*. New York: Harper, 1945.

Westermarck, Edward. *Origin and Development of the Moral Ideas*, 2 vols. London: Macmillan, 1906.

Whitehead, A. N. *Concept of Nature*. Cambridge: Univ. Press, 1920.

—— *Principles of Natural Knowledge*. Ibid., 1919.

—— *The Function of Reason*. Princeton: Princeton Univ. Press, 1929.

—— *Process and Reality*. Cambridge: Univ. Press, 1929.

Whittaker, Thomas. *Reason*. Cambridge: Univ. Press, 1934.

Wisdom, John. *Philosophy and Psychoanalysis*. Oxford: Basil Blackwell, 1953.

Wittgenstein, L. *Philosophical Investigations*, tr. by G. E. M. Anscombe. Oxford: Basil Blackwell, 1953.

—— *Tractatus Logico-Philosophicus*. London: Kegan Paul, 1922.

Woozley, A. D. *The Theory of Knowledge*. London: Hutchinson, 1949.

Wright, H. *Cambridge University Studies*, ed. by H. Wright. London: Nicholson & Watson, 1933.

INDEX

Aaron, R. I., 392, 416, 418

Adams, G. P., 26, 48

Alternative logics, 271, 273

Analytic philosophers, common traits, 93; conception of philosophy, 96

Analytic statements, for Leibniz, 79; for the logical empiricist, 257, 283ff; Kant's treatment of, 284; criticism of Kant, 285; positivist criteria for, 286; analytic *vs* synthetic, 288ff

Animal mind, 50–51

Antisthenes, 51

A priori knowledge, 113; its place in philosophy, 250; rationalist view of, 252; Kantian view of, 252; Mill's view of, 253; logical empiricists' view of, 254ff; importance of the latter, 259; a priori knowledge of causation, 466

Aquinas, 446

Archimedes, 460

Aristotle, 50, 52, 57, 59, 63, 67, 172, 249, 303, 482

Arithmetic, applicable to reality, 428

Arnold, M., 45

Atomic facts, 131ff, 142, 170ff, 181

Atomic propositions, 170

Atomism, logical, 127ff; conception of analysis, 127; on atomic facts, 131; on particulars, 132; on logic, 134; on logic and fact, 140; appraisal of, 145ff

Augustine, 96

Austin, J. L., 153, 339, 341, 370, 380

Ayer, A. J., 25, 124; on judgments of the past, 207; on other minds, 210, 335; on survival, 223, 350; on realism, 225; on conclusive verifiability, 227; on weak verifiability, 229; on necessary statements as linguistic, 256, 257, 264, 277; as conventional, 267, 268; on analytic statements, 286; on the work of philosophy as definition, 322ff, 337

Babbitt, I., 46

Baier, K., 374

Barnes, W. H. F., 93, 208, 314

Behaviourism, 210ff

Berkeley, G., 92

Berlin, I., 230, 247, 439

Bevan, E., 55

Black, M., 395

Bohr, N., 108

Bolyai, F., 115

Bosanquet, B., 29, 42, 45, 62, 90, 145, 351, 390

Bradley, F. H., 38, 90, 96, 145, 168, 233, 302, 313, 331, 391, 395, 423, 437, 438, 484; on identity, 409ff

Braithwaite, R. B., 146, 155, 183, 226, 336, 350

Brandes, G., 54

Broad, C. D., 94, 296, 374, 395, 432, 467, 485

Brouwer, L. E. J., 273

Browne, Sir T., 74, 97

Brownell, W. C., 46

Burnet, J., 54

Caird, E., 235

Campbell, C. A., 365

Carnap, R., 106, 170, 204, 213ff, 226, 234, 243, 245, 256, 262, 267, 282

Categories, for Aristotle, 344; for Kant, 345; for Ryle, 345; category mistakes, 344; these not primarily linguistic, 361; categories and logical form, 369

Causation, importance of the relation, 444; Hume on, 101, 445ff; his dismissal of necessity from, 447; reply to Hume, 449ff; causation in inference, 454ff; uniformity and necessity, 465; causal laws necessary, 465ff; as linking all events, 473

Certainty, 60

Chamberlain, A., 42

Church, A., 231

Claparède, 390

Classes, 414, 417; concepts of, 418, 420

Clemenceau, G., 42

Clement, W. C., 179

Cohen, M. R., 28, 47, 303, 426, 432, 436

Coherence, 91

Common sense, Moore's defence of, 311

Communism, 43

Concepts, 418

Conklin, E. G., 38

Consciousness, 211ff, 224

Containment, and entailment, 257, 289ff, 293

Contradiction, law of, 79, 261, 276ff

Conventions, necessary propositions as, 117, 256, 266ff; laws of logic as 271ff, 299; dangers of this theory, 281

Correctness and truth, 320, 377

de Burgh, W. G., 64
Definition, real and conventional, 268; in use, 323; philosophically important, 371
Descartes, 69–73, 250, 439, 484
Descriptions, theory of, 323ff; its implicit metaphysic, 328ff; anticipated by earlier logicians, 351
Determinables, necessity within, 178, 439
Dewey, J., 31, 39, 52, 280
Dialectic, in Hegel, 88
Dickinson, G. L., 46
Dingle, H., 238
Dispositions, 457
Dixon, M., 27, 491
Ducasse, C. J., 454

Eddington, A. S., 219
Einstein, A., 116, 191, 434
Eliot, T. S., 46
Emerson, R. W., 373
Entailment, 158, 169, 289ff
Essence and accident, 475ff
Evil, 81
Ewing, A. C., 28, 230, 238, 283, 300, 350, 471
Existentialism, 34; theological, 36
Explanation, levels of, 385; kinds of, 388
Extensional logic, 138, 297
Extensive abstraction, 326, 433

Feigl, H., 25, 210
Findlay, J. N., 371
Flew, A. G. N., 310, 347, 370, 374, 380
Form, 55ff; as essence, 56; as end, 58; as law, 60; as system, 65; in logic, 160
Formal logic, 160, 164
Fowler, H. W., 318, 377
Frank, P., 106, 119
Frazer, J. G., 39
Freedom and necessity, 78, 492
Freeman, E., 12
Frege, G., 366
Freud, S., 37

Galileo, 434
Geometry, non-Euclidean, 115, 271, 431; informative of reality, 431ff
Gonseth, F., 426
Goodman, N., 179, 393
Greeks, love of reason, 54
Green, T. H., 42, 454, 458

Hampshire, S., 74, 339
Hardy, G. H., 404
Hare, R. M., 339

Harris, E. E., 147, 204
Hart, H. L. A., 339, 370
Hegel, G. W. F., 273; his conception of reason, 86; his clay feet, 107; his logic, 168, 250; on the notion, 235; on internal relations, 486
Heidegger, M., 35, 233, 327
Heisenberg, W., 109
Hempel, C. G., 206, 215, 216, 229, 231, 234, 429, 457, 459
Hendel, C. W., 12
Hobbes, T., 266, 354, 408
Hobhouse, L. T., 25, 28, 40
Hocking, W. E., 381
Holden, R., 46
Hook, S., 459
Horkheimer, M., 28
Housman, A. E.
Hume, D., 92; his current revival, 100; on God, 101; on necessity, 102; on values, 102; debt to him of positivism, 103; his atomism, 180, 364, 482; his theory of causation 101, 445ff; criticism of theory, 449
Husserl, E., 439
Huxley, T. H., 254, 419

Idealism, 28
Identity, James and Bradley on, 409ff
Identity of indiscernibles, 395ff
Implication, 158, 274, 297; and inference, 461
Individuation, principle of, 400
Inference, as tautologous, 296; rules of, 301; for Claparède, 390; necessity in, 454
Inge, W. R., 45
Instrumentalism, 31, 52
Internal relations, 475
Irving, J., 378

James, W., 59, 90; on resemblance, 409ff
Jaspers, K., 49
Jeans, J., 434, 473
Jevons, W. S., 397
Joachim, H. H., 77
Johnson, W. E., 168, 178
Joseph, H. W. B., 184, 418, 439, 469–70

Kant, on reason, 82; on a priori knowledge, 114; criticism of positivists, 115; on analytic and synthetic statements, 284; criticism of his distinction, 285; its essential soundness, 294

Kelvin, Lord, 108
Kierkegaard, S., 49
Kneale, M., 215
Kneale, W., 273, 471
'Know', ambiguity of, 379
Krutch, J. W., 39
Kuhn, H., 35

Lake, B., 300
Landesman, C., 281
Langford, C. H., 92, 291
Language, ideal, 136–40, 233
Laplace, 160, 266
Laski, H. J., 44
Law, 60ff; ambiguity of the word, 376
Lawrence, D. H., 47
Leibniz, on reason, 78; on logic and reality, 277, 304; on identity of indiscernibles, 395
Lewis, C. I., 224, 274
Lewis, H. D., 12, 379
Linguistic interpretation of necessary statements, 233, 260ff
Linguistic philosophy, 33; Moore as forerunner, 310ff; Malcolm's revision of Moore, 316ff; Ayer on definition in philosophy, 322ff; implicit metaphysics, 328; 'ordinary language philosophers', 339; linguistic confusion as root of philosophy, 343; this view criticized, 347; verbalism, 353; reasons for insistence on language, 355ff; sentences not true, false, or absurd, 361–5; Russell on, 368; concessions to, 371; criticism of, 372
Linton, R., 378
Lobachevski, 115, 272
Loch Ness monster, 324, 328, 332, 333, 334
Locke, J., 52, 91, 172, 446, 460, 482; on universals, 406
Logic, as conventional, 222, 271, 276, 301; as a means to ends, 279; as assertion of reality, 423ff
Logical constructions, 326; their implicit metaphysic, 329; criticism of theory, 336
Lotze, R. H., 168
Lovejoy, A. O., 236
Lowrie, W., 49
Lucas, F. L., 28

Macdonald, M., 370
McDougall, W., 37
Mach, E., on matter, 109; on mind, 111

McTaggart, J. M. E., 50, 89, 94, 374, 395, 485, 486
Malcolm, N., 294, 310, 370; on ordinary language, 316; criticism of his view, 318ff
Mannheim, K., 41
Maritain, J., 70
Material implication, 158
Mathematical logic, 134ff, 155ff; on the syllogism, 162; on incompatibility, 165; on possibility, 166; its inadequacy to actual inference, 167; among later analysts, 340; use of classes, 417
Mathematics, 55, 60, 64, 70, 76, 79; as identical with logic, 119; as an ideal language, 134; as applicable to real world, 427ff
Meaning, 189–248; Socrates's search for, 191; Peirce on the test of clarity, 192; Wittgenstein on the limits of, 197ff; verifiability by self, 205; by me in principle, 208; by anyone in principle, 221; falsifiability, 228; weak verifiability, 229; expressibility in ideal language, 233; two components of verifiability theory, 235; their conflict, 236; difficulty over the sub-microscopic, 238; the theory self-destructive, 239ff; the search for a test dubious, 247; as a lodestone in philosophy, 372
Michelet, J., 32
Mill, J. S., 92, 173, 453
Minto, W., 54
Mises, L. von, 44, 53
Montague, C. E., 46
Montague, W. P., 404, 471
Moore, G. E., 34, 93, 146, 171, 370, 373; as an analyst, 310; defence of common sense, 311; criticism of this defence, 314ff; not a linguistic analyst, 316
More, P. E., 46
Morley, J., 42
Motives to philosophizing, 95
Mure, G. R. G., 310, 354
Murray, G., 44, 47

Nagel, E., on logic without ontology, 276ff; on necessity in inference, 459, 461, 462; on the nature of a term, 478, 483; on difference as an external relation, 486
Naturalism, 30
Nature of a term, 475ff

Necessary truths, for Leibniz, 78; for Aristotle, 249; necessary statements as linguistic, 255, 260ff; as conventional, 256, 266ff; as analytic, 257, 283ff; as non-factual, 258, 298ff

Necessity, in atomic facts, 176; between such facts, 181; in generalizations, 186; in natural orders, Ch. X; in serial orders, 436; as crossing categories, 438; as linking determinates, 439; in ethics, 440; in causation, Ch. XI; Hume's denial of, 445; reply to Hume, 449; in inference, 454–64; vs chance, 465; contingent vs absolute, 468; in causal law, 465ff; among attributes of a thing, 475ff; does not entail goodness, 491; and freedom, 492

Nelson, E. J., 166

Nettleship, R. L., 64, 69

Neurath, O., 213, 220

Niebuhr, R., 37

Nietzsche, F., 49

Nominalism, 408

Nowell-Smith, P. H., 339

Number, as the form of difference, 397, 428

Ogden and Richards, 189

Orders, of degree, 178; serial, 436

Ordinary usage, its vagueness, 314; its inadequacy for philosophy, 318ff; 'ordinary language philosophers', 339; use vs usage, 341–2; as a court of appeal, 370; deficiencies, 372ff

Pap, A., 93, 244, 295, 298, 426, 459

Particulars, 132; atomists' embarrassment over, 171ff; resolution into universals, 401

Passmore, J., 352

Past, judgment of, 206

Pater, W., 45

Paul, G. A., 339, 379

Pears, D., 339

Peirce, C. S., 192; criticism of, 194; on universals, 395

Philosophy, positivist conception of, 122; as the logic of science, 143

Physicalism, 210; its incoherence, 215ff

Piaget, J., 390

Pictures, propositions as, 141; criticism of the theory, 146ff, 174

Plato, 51, 53, 57, 56–69, 95, 404, 434

Poincaré, H., his conventionalism, 117; his criticism of Kant, 118

Popper, K., 227, 228; on the nature of logic, 424

Positivism, 32; its main theses, 99; its roots in Hume, 100ff; the Vienna Circle, 105; reaction to speculative philosophy, 106; debt to Mach, 109ff; attitude toward rationalism, 113; toward Kant, 114ff; influence of Poincaré, 117; of Russell, 119; of Wittgenstein, 120ff; implications for philosophy, 125; its atomism, 127ff; its theories of meaning, 189ff; its theories of the a priori, 249ff; its service to philosophy, 305; breakdown of its analysis, 308

Pragmatism, 31

Price, H. H., 131, 391, 416

Principia Mathematica, 119, 134, 155ff, 164, 167, 274, 340, 417

Proper names, 173, 332–4

Propositional functions, 184

Propositional signs, 142, 151

Proposition-factors, 346

Propositions, 243

Psychology, 37

Pythagoras, 55

Quine, W. V., 309, 340, 393

Ramsey, F. P., 170, 171, 176, 185, 186

Rashdall, H., 441

Rationalism, of Plato, 60ff; of Descartes, 69; of Spinoza, 73; of Leibniz, 78; of Kant, 82; of Hegel, 86; of British idealists, 90; the positivist criticism of, 113; does not imply moral perfection, 491

Realism, 30; its difficulty for positivists, 224

Reason, meaning, 25; revolt against by naturalism, 30; by pragmatism, 31; by positivism, 32; by linguistic philosophy, 33; by existentialists, 34; by theologians, 36; by psychologists, 37; by sociologists, 39; by political theorists, 42; by artists, 45; in animals and man, 50; Greek view of, 54–69; Descartes's view of, 70; Spinoza's view of, 78; Kant's view of, 82; Hegel's view of, 86; British idealist's view of, 90; for the logical atomist, 145; as a priori insight, 249; survives positivist criticism, 306; and ontology, 382; as structure and as function, 387; recent restriction of, 422; grasp of necessities in nature, 423ff; in ethics, 440

Reichenbach, H., 204
Relativism, 41
Resemblance, 409ff; universals and, 414ff
Riemann, G. F. B., 116, 272
Robinson, J. H., 39
Robinson, R., 58
Royce, J., 296
Russell, B., 30, 47, 58, 58, 128, 131, 169, 220, 282, 331, 426; on logic and mathematics, 119, 122, 155; on atomic facts, 131, 170; on particulars, 132, 171, 172, 176, 488; on mathematics, 134; on an ideal language, 139; on logical atomism, 140, 310; on Wittgenstein, 147; on inference, 164; on proper names, 173, 333; on propositional functions, 184; on general facts, 185; on seeing one's own brain, 317; theory of descriptions, 323; of logical constructions, 326; on physics, 336, 337, 473; on linguistic philosophy, 368, 374, 378; on universals, 395, 415, 416
Rutherford, E. 108
Ryle, G., 30, 52, 146, 190, 208, 301, 339, 340, 378, 390; on ordinary use, 341; on systematically misleading expressions, 343; on categories, 344; on category mistakes, 347; criticism, 347ff; language and fact, 354ff; language and absurdity, 357ff

Sabine, G. H., 43
Santayana, G., 30, 47, 48
Schiller, F. C. S., 270
Schlick, M., 105, 123, 178, 191, 204, 209, 210, 221ff, 227, 267, 286, 310
Self-evidence, 272, 283
Sellars, W., 93
Sentence-factors, 346
Sentences, 243, 262
Serial order, 436
Sheffer, H. M., 137
Sherman, S., 46
Sidgwick, H., 374, 441
Sigwart, C., 168
Silone, I., 43
Socrates, 57, 191
Spencer, H., 254
Spinoza, 73–8, 96, 113, 446, 484
Stebbing, L. S., 243, 434, 470
Stout, G. F., 470
Stevenson, C. L., 124
Strawson, P. F., 137, 334, 339, 340, 342, 370, 375

Stumpf, C., 410
Substance, for the positivist, 109, 130, 172; the attempt to define, 371, 373; what owns qualities?, 400, 484
Sufficient reason, law of, 80
Sumner, W. G., 39
Swabey, M. C., 247
Synthetic necessities, 86, 288ff
System, Platonic idea of, 65; world as causal system, 472; as intelligible system, 475ff
Systematically misleading expressions, 343, 358, 362

Tarski, A., 245
Tautology, 122, 162; in inference, 296
Taylor, A. E., 211
Theology, 36; for Leibniz, 81; for Kant, 85; for Hume, 101
Thomson, J. J., 239
Thought, its constraint by necessity, 384; its rational end, 386
Titchener, E. B., 154
Toulmin, S., 339
Translatability, 329, 330
Truth-functional logic, 138
Truth tables, 136

Ulysses, 53
Uniform sequence view of causality, 449
Uniqueness, 401
Unity of science, 111, 213
Universal propositions, 185ff, 227, 303
Universals, as existents, 303; use by animal mind, 391; not dependent on words, 391; definition of, 392; fundamental to thought, 392; specific universals, 393, 399, 420; qualitative, 393, 402ff, 409, 419, 420; generic, 393, 403ff, 409, 419, 420; Platonic view of, 404; view of formal logic, 405; view of Locke, 406; of nominalism, 408; resemblance theory of, 409; concepts of, 418
Unwin, Sir S., 12
Urmson, J. O., 140, 146, 130, 186, 339, 370
Use, 341; ordinary, 342, 368; standard, 370

Value statements, 124
Verifiability theory of meaning, as held by Wittgenstein, 194ff; verifiability by self, 205; by me in principle, 208; by anyone in principle, 221; falsifiability, 228; weak verifiability, 229; expressibility in ideal language, 233;

excludes realism, 224; conflicts with science, 226, 236; essential form of the theory, 235; its utility, 235; its ambiguity, 236; its self-condemning character, 239

Vienna Circle, 105; its reaction to German philosophy, 106; its debt to Mach, 109; its views on the unity of science, 111; its attitude toward metaphysics, 112; toward rationalism, 113; towards Kant, 114; its debt to Poincaré, 117

Waismann, F., 270, 273
Warnock, G. J., 339, 340
Watson, J. B., 30, 244
Weinberg, J. R., 203
Weitz, M., 335
Weldon, T. D., 339
Wertheimer, M., 455, 459
Westermarck, E., 39, 40
White, M., 309
Whitehead, A. N., 27, 53, 69, 155, 326, 428, 433

Wholeness, 90
Williams, D., 275
Wisdom, J., 132, 146, 149, 150, 170, 243, 330, 349
Wittgenstein, L., 106; on factual statements, 120; on logical statements, 121, 140; on the office of philosophy, 122; on objects, 131; on picturing, 141; incoherence of the picture theory, 147ff, 174; on philosophy and science, 143; his atomism, 145; his character, 146; on proof as tautology, 162; on atomic propositions, 170; on particulars, 172; on necessity within fact, 176; on contingency among facts, 180ff; on general statements, 185; on solipsism, 194; its absurdities, 200ff; on inference, 296; logical statements non-factual, 298, 426; place in analytic movement, 310; on pain, 363; his lack of perspective, 365; on ordinary use, 370
Woozley, A. D., 416
Words, difficulty of defining, 374